The art of English: everyday creativity

Edited by Janet Maybin and Joan Swann

Published by Palgrave Macmillan in association with The Open University

The Open University, Walton Hall, Milton Keynes MK7 6AA United Kingdom

PALGRAVE MACMILLAN, Houndmills, Basingstoke, Hampshire TG21 6XS and
175 Fifth Avenue, New York, N. Y. 10010
Companies and respresentatives throughout the world

PALGRAVE MACMILLAN is the global academic imprint of Palgrave Macmillan division
of St. Martin's Press, LLC and of Palgrave Macmillan Ltd. Macmillan® is a registered
trademark in the United States, United Kingdom and other countries. Palgrave is a
registered trademark in the European Union and other countries.

Edited and designed by The Open University.

Typeset in India by Alden Prepress Services, Chennai.

Printed and bound in the United Kingdom by CPI, Glasgow.

This book forms part of an Open University course E301 *The art of English*. Details of
this and other Open University courses can be obtained from the Student Registration
and Enquiry Service, The Open University, PO Box 197, Milton Keynes, MK7 6BJ,
United Kingdom: tel. + 44 (0)870 333 4340, email general-enquiries@open.ac.uk

http://www.open.ac.uk

A catalogue record for this book is available from the British Library.

A catalog record for this book is available from the Library of Congress.

ISBN-13: 978-1-4039-8559-0

ISBN-10: 1-4039-8559-6

1.1

Book editors

Originally trained as a social anthropologist, **Janet Maybin** is a senior lecturer in Language and Communication at the Open University. She has written extensively for Open University courses on language, literacy and learning and also researches and writes on children and adults' informal language and literacy practices. She co-edited *Using English: from Conversation to Canon,* (Routledge, 1996) and *Language, Literacy and Education: A Reader* (Trentham, 2002). She is currently completing a book on 'Children's voices: talk, language and identity' (Palgrave, forthcoming).

Joan Swann teaches at the Open University, where she has many years' experience producing distance-learning multimedia materials on linguistics and English language studies. She is currently Director of the Centre for Language and Communications. Her research interests include language and gender and other areas of sociolinguistics. Recent books include *Introducing Sociolinguistics* (Edinburgh University Press, 2000, with Rajend Mesthrie, Ana Deumert and William Leap); *Children's Cultural Worlds* (John Wiley, 2003, co-edited with Mary Jane Kehily) and *A Dictionary of Sociolinguistics* (Edinburgh University Press, 2004, with Ana Deumert, Rajend Mesthrie and Theresa Lillis).

Other original contributors

Paul Baker is a lecturer in the Department of English Language and Linguistics at Lancaster University. His research interests include language and gender/sexuality, corpus linguistics and critical discourse analysis. He carried out his doctoral thesis on Polari, which produced a book: *Polari: The Lost Language of Gay Men*, (Routledge, 2002). His most recent book is *Public Discourses of Gay Men* (Routledge, 2005).

Mary Bock is an Honorary Research Assistant in the English Department at the University of Cape Town, where she has taught for many years in English literature and language. Her research interests are in fictional and non-fictional narrative and discourse analysis. She is currently working with Kay McCormick on narratives from the South African Truth and Reconciliation Commission.

Lynne Cameron is Professor of Applied Linguistics in the School of Education, University of Leeds. Her research interests include metaphor in talk and the development of English as an additional language in UK schools. She co-edited *Researching and Applying Metaphor* with Graham Low (Cambridge University Press, 1999). The research monograph, *Metaphor in Educational Discourse* was published in 2003 by Continuum. She has also written on the teaching of English as a foreign language at primary level: *Teaching Languages to Young Learners* (Cambridge University Press, 2001).

A one-time English teacher, **Daniel Chandler** is coordinator for Media and Communication Studies at the University of Wales, Aberystwyth, where he set up the Media and Communication Studies website (www.aber.ac.uk/media) in the early days of the Web. He specialises in visual semiotics, notably in relation to issues of gender. His papers on online identities grew out of his earlier research into the construction of identity in writing. His most recent book is *Semiotics: The Basics* (Routledge, 2001).

Guy Cook is Professor of Language and Education at the Open University. His research interests include discourse analysis, stylistics, language ritual and play, English language and literature teaching, and the language of the media. His most recent books are *Language Play, Language Learning* (Oxford University Press, 2000), *The Discourse of Advertising* (2nd edition, Routledge, 2001), *Applied Linguistics* (Oxford University Press, 2003) and *Genetically Modfied Language* (Routledge, 2004).

Penelope Eckert is Professor of Linguistics at Stanford University. Her research examines the relation between linguistic variation and social identity. Focusing on adolescents and preadolescents, she has done extensive ethnographic sociolinguistic work in and around schools. She is author of the high school ethnography *Jocks and Burnouts*, as well as *Linguistic Variation as Social Practice*, a sociolinguistic study based on that ethnography, and co-author (with Sally McConnell-Ginet) of *Language and Gender* (Cambridge University Press, 2003).

Julia Gillen, the author of *The Language of Children* (Routledge, 2003), is a Lecturer at the Open University. Her work has appeared in journals such as *Language and Education* and the *Journal of Early Childhood Literacy*, as well as in edited books including the *Handbook of Early Childhood Literacy* (Sage, 2003) and *Popular Culture, New Media and Digital Literacy in Early Childhood* (Routledge Falmer, 2005). Her teaching and research span English language studies, education and communication.

Angela Goddard has worked across all phases of education promoting the study of English language, and is currently Head of Programme for English Language and Linguistics at York St John, a College of the University of Leeds. She edits the Routledge Intertext series, for which she wrote *The Language of Advertising* (2nd edn, 2002) and co-authored (with L. Mean-Patterson) *Language and Gender* (2000). Her current research interests are in new forms of electronic text, both in how they work and in how they are represented within public discourses.

Anthea Fraser Gupta is Senior Lecturer in Modern English Language in the School of English at the University of Leeds. She came to Leeds from the National University of Singapore, where she was in the Department of English Language and Literature from 1975 to 1996. Her main research area is in English as a world language in general, and Singapore English in particular.

Sharon Inkelas teaches in the Department of Linguistics at the University of California, Berkeley. Her research interests centre on phonology, morphology, and their interface; in recent years her research has extended to first language acquisition as well. Her most recent book is *Reduplication: Doubling in Morphology* (Cambridge University Press, 2005), co-authored with Cheryl Zoll.

Margaretta Jolly teaches in the School of English at the University of Exeter, where she is lecturer in Twentieth Century Literature and Culture. Her research interests include life writing, cultures of gender and sexuality, and she specialises in the study of letters as a literary and social practice. She is the editor of *The Encyclopedia of Life Writing* (Fitzroy Dearborn, 2001) and *Dear Laughing Motorbyke: Letters from Women Welders of the Second World War* (Scarlet, 1997).

Nancy Macdonald is a director of a qualitative research company in London. Prior to this she completed her PhD about graffiti subculture at Brunel University. Publications include *The Graffiti Subculture: Youth, Masculinity and Identity in London and New York* (Palgrave/Macmillan, 2001) and 'Making a World of Difference: The Personal Benefits of Subcultural Membership' in K. Gelder (ed.) (2005) *The Subcultures Reader*, vol 2., Routledge.

Susan McRae has recently completed a PhD on language and gender in the workplace, and is currently teaching at Kingston University.

Sarah North is a lecturer in applied language studies at the Open University. Her background is in English language teaching and teacher training, and she has experience of working with teachers in a range of different countries. Her main research interests are academic literacy, and the role of new technologies in supporting the development of language and literacy skills. Her research in computer-mediated communication has also led to an interest in the use of humour within chat environments.

Uta Papen is Lecturer in Literacy Studies at the Department of Linguistics and Modern English Language. She is particularly interested in social and cultural aspects of literacy and in the comparative study of adult literacy education in developing and industrialised countries. Currently, she is working on a research project that examines the relationship between literacy and health. Current publications include 'Literacy and development: What works for whom?', *International Journal for Educational Development*, 25 (2005) and *Adult literacy as social practice - more than skills*, Routledge (July 2005).

Ben Rampton is Professor of Applied & Sociolinguistics at King's College London. He does ethnography and discourse analysis, and his interests cover urban multilingualism, ethnicity, class, youth and education. He was the author of *Crossing: Language & Ethnicity among Adolescents* (Longman 1995), a co-author of Researching Language: Issues of Power and Method (Routledge 1992), and has just completed a book *Language in Late Modernity: Interaction in an Urban School*. He co-edits *Working Papers in Urban Language and Literacy* (www.kcl.ac.uk/education/wpull.html).

Michael Toolan is in the English Department of the University of Birmingham, where he convenes the MA in Literary Linguistics, and teaches literary stylistics, narrative analysis, and language and the law. His current research projects include one applying corpus linguistics to the study of narrative progression and another on teenagers' personal narratives, identity, and life prospects.

Karin Tusting is a researcher at the Literacy Research Centre, Lancaster University. Her interests are in the detailed study of social practices using qualitative methods, including ethnography and discourse analysis, with a focus on the role of language in learning in communities. Recent publications include *Beyond Communities of Practice: Language, Power and Social Context,* co-edited with David Barton (Cambridge University Press, 2005).

David Vincent is Professor of Social History and Pro Vice-Chancellor at the Open University, and visiting fellow of Kellogg College, Oxford. His research interests cover the history of working-class autobiography, literacy, and secrecy and privacy. Recent publications include *The Culture of Secrecy: Britain 1832–1998* (Oxford University Press, 1998) and *The Rise of Mass Literacy. Reading and Writing in Modern Europe* (Polity Press, 2000).

Rupert Wegerif, Reader in the School of Education at Southampton University, has published over thirty journal articles about technology and dialogue in education. His most recent book, *Thinking and Learning with ICT,* (Routledge, 2004, co-authored with Lyn Dawes) takes a dialogic approach to the use of computers in classrooms; he is currently under contract with Springer to write a book called *Dialogic, Education and Computers.*

Anita Wilson is an ethnographer. She has a particular interest in the way that people in prison seek to maintain social rather than institutional identities and the relevance of language – written, spoken and visual – to these endeavours. She currently holds a Research Fellowship at Lancaster University in the Lancaster Literacy Research Centre. One of her most recent publications is 'Four Days and a Breakfast – Time, Space and Literacy/ies in the Prison Community' in *Space Matters: Assertions of Space in Literacy Practice and Research*, eds K. Leander and M. Sheehy (Peter Lang, 2003).

Contents

Introduction

In this book, we suggest that the kinds of language creativity and artistry found in art and literature can also be found in the communication practices of everyday life. Focusing particularly on the social, cultural and critical dimensions of creativity, the book brings together theory and insights from poetics, stylistics, sociolinguistics, New Literacy Studies and social history. It also makes its own distinctive contribution to the topic in exploring and developing a more sociocultural approach to understanding how language creativity works in a range of different contexts, from everyday conversation and internet chat to letter writing in prison, home-made advertisements in Namibia and Valentine cards in nineteenth-century Britain.

We see language creativity as including both textual artistry and also the ways in which people use language creatively to construct identity and manage relationships with others. This takes us into an exploration of the social, cultural and critical dynamic of everyday creativity in language, its role within social practices and its relationship to changing social, economic and technological conditions. Recurring themes are the use of literary-like language and performance in everyday contexts and the ways in which different forms of creativity are valued. Examples of research are drawn from textual analysis, corpus linguistics, interactional linguistics, ethnography and critical discourse analysis.

Chapter 1 introduces current arguments about the prevalence and significance of creativity in everyday talk and examines these in relation to poetic features in spoken language. It looks at different forms of verbal art, especially different types of word play and metaphor, and discusses the idea of a cline between 'everyday' and 'literary' language. It sets out a distinction that has been made between 'inherency', 'sociocultural' and 'cognitive' models of literariness.

Chapter 2 looks at the formal structure of conversational narratives, and also considers analytical approaches more concerned with social interaction and wider socio-historical and cultural influences. Like poetic language, conversational storytelling is seen as an essentially creative activity that serves important interactional and cultural functions.

Chapter 3 draws on a 'dramaturgical' model of interaction to look at the performances people routinely put on in their everyday conversations, and at how they use aspects of speaking style to construct and project particular identities. The chapter examines young people's performance of subcultural identities, 'language crossing' and contemporary ideas about language and identity that have come out of recent research on gender and sexuality.

Chapter 4 extends themes from Chapters 1–3 in an examination of word play, narrative and performance in children's language practices. Taking the view that creativity is evident from the earliest (pre-verbal) stages of development, it looks at how language play is involved in developing ideas, helping with problem-solving, maintaining relations between speakers and allowing children to explore identities and cultural values.

Chapter 5 examines creativity in email, online chat, conferencing and text messaging. It considers how technologies affect social behaviour and may stimulate or stifle linguistic creativity. Focusing on the way that users adapt to new technologies, it questions the role of novelty in language creativity and examines the prevalence of playfulness, self-dramatisation and intertextuality in online environments.

Chapter 6 focuses on creativity and identity in diary keeping (including web diaries), personal letter writing, graffiti and web homepages. The chapter argues that their creativity is interactional, contributing to the construction and performance of individual and group identity. It also examines how texts may be perceived, valued and transformed in unexpected ways.

Chapter 7 challenges the association of creativity with individual and original inspiration and argues that it should be seen as essentially collaborative and emergent from social practice. The authors draw on examples from a variety of cultural settings to examine how people use literacy creatively in relation to the opportunities and constraints of different contexts.

Chapter 8 focuses on nineteenth-century Britain, at the turning point when it was becoming a literate society. It examines the role of contemporary creative texts (chapbooks, broadsides, valentines and Christmas cards, working class autobiography) and the possibilities for creative writing within the lives of ordinary people.

Chapter 9 draws together the different approaches introduced in earlier chapters, and reviews textual and contextualised approaches to investigating language creativity. It then discusses work by a number of key theorists, picking up and further exploring ideas about voice and dialogue, reported speech and the performance of the self.

Each chapter is structured in the form of teaching text divided into sections, followed by three or four associated **readings**. The **activities** provide guidance on the readings or tasks to stimulate further understanding of the topic.

    Boxed text contains illustrative material or definitions.

    Key terms are set in bold type at the point where they are explained; they also appear in bold in the index for easy location in the text.

    Marginal notes are used for brief explanations, cross-references and editorial notes on the readings.

The section containing **colour illustrations** is located between Sections 6.4 and 6.5. These illustrations are referred to in the text as 'Colour Figures'.

The art of the everyday

Joan Swann

1.1 Introduction

> The pious fable and the dirty story
> Share in the total literary glory.
>
> (W. H. Auden, *Letter to Lord Byron*)

In this chapter, I look at an argument that has become influential within English language studies, and that seeks to challenge the distinctiveness of literature and literary language. The argument runs that certain kinds of linguistic creativity traditionally associated with poetry and other forms of literature – including play with the sounds and structures of language, repetition, metaphor, rhyme and rhythm – are a feature of ordinary, everyday conversation, and that there is a connection between such everyday creativity, or verbal art, and literature itself. Literary language has traditionally been thought of as distinctly 'non-ordinary', a highly valued form of language where words and phrases are carefully chosen for their artistic effect and responded to aesthetically by listeners and readers. The argument here, by contrast, is that rather than seeing literature as distinct from ordinary language, one can see the seeds of 'literariness' in much more mundane linguistic activity. From this stance, some authors prefer to see literariness in terms of a 'cline', or a matter of degree – that particular texts may be more, or less, literary. The chapter is based on readings and examples that address aspects of this argument. What forms does everyday verbal art take, for instance? How is it used in interaction with others? Why should people spend time 'playing' with language in this way rather than getting on with more serious business? In exploring these ideas I shall focus mainly on spoken interaction and on aspects of language that may be considered **poetic**, in that they have often been associated with poetry as a literary form. Later chapters cover a wide range of spoken and written genres.

As well as developing ideas about creativity, or verbal art, the readings and examples in the chapter represent different approaches to the study of everyday spoken language. I shall review these approaches at the end of the chapter.

1.2 The nature of verbal art

'Artful' language

Allow about
20 minutes

The examples in the box below illustrate some types of everyday language use that have been seen as 'artful', or creative. Do you agree with this evaluation? If so, how do you think they achieve this effect (i.e. what makes them 'artful')? Can you think of similar examples from interactions you have taken part in?

Everyday verbal art

1   A and B are sitting by some trees in a park:

   A: (feeling bark) These are plane trees, aren't they?
   B: No, they're quite patterned (wincing look)

   (Personal example)

2   After a picnic, a family is feeding leftovers to pigeons; they throw a few scraps to a slightly scruffy small pigeon:

   A: He might look scruffy but he's seen off that one over there.
   B: Obviously a thug amongst pigeons.
   C: Al Capigeon.
   D: The godfeather.

   (Personal example)

3   A woman is talking about a man who works in her office:

   And he knows Spanish,
   and he knows French,
   and he knows English,
   and he knows German
   and HE is a GENtleman.

   (Tannen, 1989, p. 48)

4   Darrel explains how his father persuaded him to study engineering at university, despite his uncertainty about his subject choice:

   DARREL: he said 'you might want to think about engineering as a major because you're just pretty flexible when you get out'. now I don't think he was actually twisting my arm,

   ELLEN: right.

   DARREL: but I was – I was just like a leaf in the wind at that point. so I majored in engineering

   (Adapted from Norrick, 2000/01, p. 251)

5   A family is eating a meal outside, facing a building with a door high in the wall that leads to its loft, to allow access for storage. The door is divided into four sections. Someone remarks: 'It's a four-door store door.' Instantly others begin to extend the phrase: 'If there was a battle here it would be called the four-door store door war'; 'If someone kept going on and on about the battle they'd be the four-door store door war bore' ... etc. The game runs sporadically through the meal accompanied by despairing cries of 'Oh no, not again!' before it finally peters out.

(Personal example)

6   A bilingual (Hindi/English) joke:

'What did the peas in the pod say to each other?
Mutter, mutter.' (Hindi *maTar* = 'peas')

(Amritavalli and Upendran, 1990)

Comment

Example 1 is a **pun**, a form of word play which relies on ambiguity in word meaning. Puns often use **homophones**, or near homophones (words with the same or similar sounds but different meanings, in this case *plane* and *plain*). Puns occur in everyday conversation, advertising catch phrases, newspaper headlines, etc. They were famously defined by Samuel Johnson as 'the lowest form of humour' – and the example above is accompanied by a bit of nonverbal self-deprecation. They are also, however, a feature of literature, and may be used for serious as well as humorous purposes: see the Shakespearean example on page 7.

Example 2, like example 1, relies for its effect on similarity in form between words – here, between *Al Capigeon* and *godfeather* and gangster names. In this case, however, the terms are made up: they are novel creations produced during a conversation. The example also illustrates how artful language may be developed between speakers – it's unlikely *godfeather* would have occurred without *Al Capigeon*.

Example 3 involves **repetition**, a common feature of conversation. In this case, the speaker repeats a set of words, a grammatical structure and probably also an intonation pattern that contributes to a sense of rhythm; the utterance takes the form of a list, foregrounding the knowledge of the man referred to. The list culminates in a 'concluding' utterance, the impact of which is enhanced by its break with the established grammatical pattern. It may not strike you as particularly poetic, but Deborah Tannen, who cites the example, notes that repetition is a frequently used poetic device. Repetition may operate on several linguistic levels: words and phrases, grammatical structures and rhythm, and speech sounds as in the case of rhyming words.

The focus of interest in example 4 is a type of **figurative** or **metaphorical** language: Darrel compares himself to *a leaf in the wind*, something that may be blown this way and that, a phrase that encapsulates his uncertainty and changeability. Metaphor is strongly associated with poetry and other forms of literature, but it also occurs frequently in everyday language. Everyday metaphors tend not to be particularly novel (as in the *leaf in the wind* example), but their very pervasiveness has led researchers to argue that our understanding of events may more properly be thought of as metaphorical, rather than literal; I shall return to this argument in Section 1.4.

Example 5 involves playing with **rhyme**, along with the formation of distinctly bizarre phrases and unlikely explanations of these. Unlike the other examples, it is a collaboratively produced game that runs across several speaking turns and involves all participants in the interaction. There may also be a competitive element to it, as each person tries to produce a longer or more incongruous phrase. Participants focus overtly on one another's language use and also provide mock evaluations of this: *Oh no …*. While this is a spontaneous and one-off event, different forms of competitive language games are widespread across cultures and often become ritualised, with elaborate sets of rules.

Example 6, like example 1, is a pun, but in this case is based on similarity of sound between words in two different languages; to understand the pun, listeners have to know both Hindi and English. Unlike the other examples, it is not spontaneous – it is cited as a well-known joke, and adopts a recognised joke format. In everyday conversation it would probably be signalled as a small-scale **performance** – I shall return to jokes as performance in Section 1.5. Amritavalli and Upendran (1990) comment that bilingual puns are common in India, both in conversations between children and between adults. As in monolingual contexts, they are also created by professional writers, such as those used in adverts and newspaper headlines.

In the extracts above, language is being used for routine, everyday purposes: to carry out the business of everyday interaction, conveying information from one person to another, getting on with others, engaging in disputes, etc. But in each case language also seems to draw attention to itself. Some **formal** aspect of language – such as sound, rhythm, grammar, meaning – is highlighted and this makes the utterance stand out: it may sound clever or amusing, for instance. Where we have evidence of listeners' reactions we can also see that such forms of language may provoke a response (e.g. evaluation of the rhymes in example 5). Within linguistics and other areas of language study there is a growing interest in such forms of everyday linguistic creativity (e.g. Carter, 2004; Cook, 2000; Crystal, 1998; Norrick, 2000/01; Tannen, 1989). These writers would argue that such ways of using language are pervasive – that verbal art is a routine phenomenon.

A Shakespearean pun

Shakespeare made frequent use of puns in his plays, often with a complex range of associations as in the following example from *Hamlet*. Hamlet has just met his father's ghost and learned that he was murdered by his brother, who has since married the queen, Hamlet's mother. The ghost departs with the words 'Remember me.'

> HAMLET: ... Remember thee?
> Ay, thou poor ghost, while memory holds a seat
> In this distracted globe.

(Act 1, Sc. 5, line 97)

Globe has three potential meanings here: 'my troubled mind' (which Hamlet may emphasise by gesturing to his head); 'this mad world' (where my beloved mother can marry my father's murderer); and 'this Globe Theatre' (where the play was performed, reminding distracted members of the audience to pay attention).

(My thanks to Maria Thomas for this example.)

It is generally accepted that certain forms of language, particularly those found in literature, are highly creative. However, the argument here is that there isn't a clear-cut distinction between 'literary' language and more everyday forms: creativity is not restricted to literary texts but is a common aspect of our interactions with others. A further argument is that artful language is functional, or purposeful: it is used to a range of effects in interactions. It may, for instance, create a friendly atmosphere, but equally it may be competitive, or perhaps used as a put-down. Some writers advance a much larger argument, that verbal art, like other forms of art or creativity, is an essential property of humankind; that there are evolutionary benefits to be gained from this, and also cognitive benefits for individuals.

I shall return to this latter argument in Section 1.3 below. For the moment, however, Reading A provides a more extended treatment of some of the points referred to in this section.

ACTIVITY 2   'Common language' and creativity (Reading A)

Please now work through Reading A: Extracts from 'Common language: corpus, creativity and cognition', by Ronald Carter.

- What kinds of evidence does Carter draw on in his discussion?

- What are the main points he makes about everyday creativity in language?

- How well do the points Carter makes apply to your own examples of everyday creativity (if you came up with any in Activity 1)?

Comment

Carter's evidence of verbal creativity is derived from a **corpus** of spoken English, collected in Britain and totalling almost 5 million words: this provides a relatively large sample of naturally occurring spoken language use. The sample includes a range of speech genres, with an emphasis on ' "common" informal discourse'. Although Carter doesn't attempt to quantify the amount of creativity in this sample, he does suggest it is substantial: it 'leaps out at researchers from almost every transcript of the data'. His claims about the prevalence of creativity more generally assume that the corpus is representative of contemporary informal discourse, at least in Britain. Different patterns might emerge in more formal settings or in different cultural contexts.

Discourse

Discourse is a rather slippery term, used with different meanings by different researchers. It is used here fairly straightforwardly in the sense of 'language use'. We shall indicate where it takes on other meanings in later chapters.

Carter identifies different forms of creativity: he refers to 'punning and playing', 'morphological inventiveness', 'echoing and converging'. He makes a broader distinction between what he terms 'pattern-reforming' and 'pattern-reinforcing' choices. Pattern-reforming examples include puns, invented words or expressions: usages which, in various ways, play with and transform words and phrases. Pattern-reinforcing examples include repetition or echoing a previous utterance, i.e. without deviating from expected linguistic patterns.

All of Carter's examples have to do with the formal properties of language, in other words, with particular linguistic structures.

Carter also argues that such forms of creativity serve particular interactional functions: they are often humorous; they serve in part to bring people together; they seem to be associated with informal, symmetrical social relations. Pattern-reforming choices involve a risk – they may not work, they may be embarrassing. But speakers also stand to gain if they are successful – e.g. they may achieve an 'enhanced regard'.

The prevalence of such uses of language suggests to Carter that some definitions of literary language (those that see this as exceptional or 'deviant') need to be revised.

A C T I V I T Y 3   **Creativity at large**

Allow about
15 minutes

How convincing do you find Carter's arguments about the prevalence of verbal creativity?

Comment

I find much of Carter's argument persuasive. His use of evidence from a relatively large, systematically collected corpus of spoken English lends credibility to his argument that artful language is pervasive in everyday talk. As mentioned earlier, however, this is a British corpus and the data come from certain types of context (e.g. mainly informal talk in non-institutional settings). Although it's clear that interactions between women and men are included, Carter gives no information about the gender balance in his sample, nor about other social factors such as class and ethnicity. It's not possible, therefore, to consider social, cultural and contextual factors that might affect the types of creativity people engage in and their interactional effects, and this would limit the generalisability of Carter's claims.

In terms of the examples Carter cites, I find it easier to see creativity in 'pattern-reforming' than in 'pattern-reinforcing' behaviour. Some types of repetition or echoing involve a degree of linguistic creativity – in the case of example 3 in Activity 1, the repetition of words, grammatical structures and rhythm for emphatic effect. But this seems to apply less to Carter's example 8. If the notion of creativity is extended to such routine and unremarked-upon forms of language, does this dilute the concept to the extent to which it is no longer useful? In response to my reservations, Carter has pointed to the danger of Euro- or Anglocentrism:

> It all depends on how creativity is valued. Contemporary culture in Britain is a culture which prefers and values creative language which is on display, language which draws overt attention to itself or to the individual user. But in other cultures and in other times what is valued is language that parallels what exists already, which seeks patterns that are the same rather than innovative, that creates and reinforces harmony and convergence, with perhaps less attention for the individual and more for the group or collective.

> (Carter, personal communication)

What counts as creativity clearly remains open to debate!

Another way of looking at this would be to suggest that everyday language sets the conditions for literary language. Repetition, for instance, is a fundamental characteristic of everyday language. Deborah Tannen (1989) goes so far as to suggest that this comes from a basic human drive to imitate

The argument that everyday language use provides the 'raw material' for literary language has been further developed in relation to metaphor, and I return to it in Section 1.4.

and repeat. Repetition may have certain interactional effects – e.g. bringing people together and signalling their mutual involvement – but in most cases it would not seem particularly creative. It may, however, be drawn upon more creatively and exploited to particular effect, in poetry and other literary uses of language.

Discussing the relationship between everyday linguistic creativity and literary language begs the question of what literary language actually is. Carter (1999) distinguishes three main models of literariness which underpin definitions: two established models which he refers to as an **inherency** model and a **sociocultural** model; and a more recent **cognitive** model.

An inherency model would see creativity or literariness as residing in certain formal properties of language: literary language is regarded as distinct from more 'practical' uses of language in that language itself is highlighted. One of the best-known exponents of this position, Roman Jakobson (1960, p. 356), referred to the **poetic function** of language, where there is a 'focus on the message for its own sake'. This property of language may also be termed **self-referential** – where language is referring partly to itself and not simply to entities in the external world that are the object of discussion. While the poetic function is evident in many examples of language use, Jakobson argued it was the dominant, determining function of verbal art.

A sociocultural model of literary language would, as the term suggests, see literariness as socially and culturally determined: for instance, drawing attention to the fact that conceptions of literature vary historically and culturally. The literary theorist Terry Eagleton (1983/1996) adopts a strong version of this position, arguing that there is nothing distinctive about literary language: any text can be seen as literature if it is defined as such by institutions or if people read it as such. Anthropological studies of literary performances in different cultural contexts also tend to take a sociocultural perspective on literariness. Many studies focus on **performance** in its conventional literary or theatrical sense, to include public displays of artistic activity that are responded to aesthetically by an audience, such as storytelling, song, dance or drama. However, the concept is frequently extended to more everyday activity in recognition of the fact that there are parallels between 'everyday' and 'literary' performance:

> ... this notion of performance can also describe what is often found in the most ordinary of encounters, when social actors exhibit a particular attention to and skills in the delivery of a message. To subscribe to and focus on this other notion of performance is more than the recognition of the fact that in speaking there is always an aesthetic dimension, understood as an attention to the form of what is being said. It also means to stress the fact that speaking itself always implies an exposure to the judgement, reaction and collaboration of an audience, which interprets, assesses, approves, sanctions, expands upon what is being said.

(Duranti, 1997, p. 16)

Cognitive models relate literary language to mental processes. Deborah Tannen's suggestion that linguistic repetition derives from a basic human drive to repeat is a kind of cognitive argument. Guy Cook (1994, p. 4) argues further that literary texts have an effect on the mind, helping us think in new ways and 'refreshing and changing our mental representations of the world'. Such benefits are not, however, restricted to established literature: Cook (2000) has similar things to say about everyday creativity or play with language. Similarly, Raymond Gibbs (1994) argues that human language and human understanding are often metaphorical, and that literary metaphor builds on and extends everyday metaphorical concepts.

Carter sees some value in both 'inherency' and 'sociocultural' models. In the case of his own examples verbal art is identified formally, and in this sense is close to an inherency model. However, Carter's examples are also responded to by an audience: in fact, one way of finding examples of verbal art in his corpus is to search for instances of laughter. This focus on what people respond to as artful (which may, of course, differ in different contexts) is consistent with a socio-cultural model. 'Cognitive' models, for Carter, are beneficial in that they help to explain the prevalence of creativity in everyday language. Carter's main argument is that literariness is best seen as a **cline**, or more accurately, a series of clines: whatever aspect of literariness is under consideration, it is appropriate to see texts as more, or less, literary rather than in terms of an opposition between literary and non-literary language. At the end of the chapter, I shall ask you to consider the value of seeing literariness in terms of a cline.

A literary cline?

The term **cline** has a similar meaning to *continuum*. It refers to relations along a particular dimension that are a matter of degree rather than having discrete cut-off points. The notion of a literary cline therefore suggests that literariness is a matter of degree.

You may have wondered about the range of terms used to refer to creative language use. Alongside **creativity**, terms such as **language play** or **verbal play**, **verbal art**, **literary language** and **poetic language** are used by different authors, sometimes with slightly different emphases but often to refer to the same phenomena: see the box below. In this chapter I shall use 'verbal art' as a general, umbrella term and other terms in relation to authors who prefer these terms, or when more specific meanings are intended.

'Artful' words

Literary language/literariness: 'literary language' may refer to a particular language or language variety used in literature (this may mark a stage in the development of a language, as in the establishment of the East Midland variety of English as a national literary norm by the sixteenth century [Leith, 1997, p.111]). It also refers to a type of language – a style or mode of expression associated with literary genres such as poetry, narrative fiction or drama. 'Literariness' refers to the quality of literature/literary language. When used in referring to language in more everyday contexts these terms tend to emphasise continuity with literature, e.g. Carter's argument about a cline of literariness.

Poetic language/poetics tends to emphasise formal properties of language, e.g. sound patterns, rhythm, figures of speech such as metaphor. The poetic function of language is said to be one of 'foregrounding', in which such forms of language draw attention to themselves. This is associated particularly with the ideas of 'formalist' scholars such as Roman Jakobson (1960). Sociolinguists such as Dell Hymes (1981, 2003) have been interested in cultural differences in poetic language – the term **ethnopoetics** is sometimes found for this area of study. When used of everyday language, 'poetic', like 'literary', tends to emphasise continuity with literature.

Language/verbal play, as the term suggests, emphasises the playful element in language and is often used in referring to popular forms such as rhymes, riddles, verbal duelling, as well as **word play**: puns, etc. (see David Crystal [1998] and Guy Cook [2000]). Cook discusses language play in relation to other forms of play (amongst adults as well as children) and also draws a contrast between 'playful' and more obviously 'useful' types of language. His intention is to emphasise the essential value of play (you will get a sense of his argument in Reading B). Cook attempts to bring some 'high culture' forms of language (literature, some types of religious language) within the remit of language play.

Creativity: in some areas of linguistics, 'creativity' refers to a speaker/listener's ability to produce or understand a (potentially) infinite number of sentences they have not previously encountered. This is a basic assumption of Noam Chomsky's transformational-generative grammar (e.g. Chomsky, 1965). In this book, however, creativity is used in a sense more akin to literary creativity, to refer to the way people use literary-like features even in everyday discourse. Creativity may suggest speakers or writers are doing something novel, as in Carter's 'pattern-reforming' examples; but Carter also uses the term to include 'pattern-reinforcing' examples such as repetition, which are not necessarily novel.

> **Verbal art**: while 'art' may suggest high culture, this is perhaps the most general term; it tends not to have the 'frivolous' connotations of 'language play' but may encompass forms of language regarded as playful as well as those regarded as more serious. It may suggest a comparison between verbal art (creativity, etc.) and art more generally. Henry Widdowson (2002) argues that literature is responded to as an art form, 'an aesthetic representation of some kind'. (Widdowson also includes jokes, doggerel, etc. as instances of verbal art.) Because of this association it may, more readily than other terms, stretch beyond the purely linguistic to include performance elements in spoken language or visual aspects of a written text.

1.3 Why verbal art?

If verbal art is so prevalent in everyday language, one obvious question is why this should be the case. Why should people spend time playing with language rather than getting on with more serious aspects of communication? In Reading A, Carter pointed to some interactional functions of artful language (it brings people together; successful word play may benefit the speaker). This discussion is extended in Reading B, where Guy Cook considers some potentially wider benefits of what he sees as a universal human activity.

A C T I V I T Y   4   Why play with language? (Reading B)

Please now work through Reading B by Guy Cook. Note that Cook uses the term 'language play' for similar phenomena to those discussed by Carter under the heading of 'creativity'. What benefits does Cook see in language play, and how persuasive do you find his arguments?

Comment

Cook focuses on two aspects of play: playing with the structures of language, and invoking fictional worlds. He argues that linguistic play and/or fiction are manifested in a variety of different activities: children's rhymes and games, adults' informal and private play with language, but also more public activity, such as adverts and other media language, and serious – even profound – examples such as Martin Luther King's speech. While these seem disparate, Cook argues that they are underpinned by similar functions. Like Carter, he refers to local 'immediate' functions of play: play binds people together and contributes to a sense of group identity; it also, necessarily, excludes others (implicitly and sometimes explicitly, as in the case of children's taunts). These are important social functions, but Cook argues that, on their own, they are not adequate explanations for the prevalence of play, and the fact that people, across languages and cultures, take pleasure in playing with language.

Cook's wider, and perhaps more challenging, argument is that playing with the structures of language introduces a random element into language use: the words we choose are constrained by form as much as by meaning (e.g. in choosing a word that rhymes the sound of that word becomes as important as its meaning). This random element produces new connections, and can change the way we view things. Similarly, escaping into alternative or fictional worlds allows people to envisage alternative realities. People are therefore enabled to 'break out of established patterns of thought' and 'think creatively and flexibly'. While literature is often felt to give readers new, or enhanced, insights and understandings, Cook's argument would suggest that there is at least the potential for this in more everyday uses of language. The mental adaptability associated with literary or artful activity is, according to Cook, beneficial to individuals but has also benefited humankind as a species.

I find this latter argument of Cook's powerful, although such a broad argument must necessarily rely on (informed) speculation. A related point made with respect to literary texts is that they are 'schema refreshing', they have 'a particular effect on the mind, refreshing and changing our mental representations of the world' (Cook, 1994, p. 4). This position has been challenged by some commentators who argue that literary texts have a range of different effects: for instance, a poem may call up familiar associations, pleasurably reinforcing a reader's existing representations of the world; and the same literary text may have different effects on different readers (Jeffries, 2001; Semino, 1997). Jeffries' and Semino's arguments could also be made about the effects of language play in more everyday contexts. They would not deny that literary, or playful, language can enable people to break out of established patterns of thought, but they would suggest that it will not always have this effect.

The notion of schema refreshment in literature is discussed more fully in the companion volume, **Goodman and O'Halloran (2006)**

If you are interested in Cook's arguments, they are developed more fully in his book *Language Play, Language Learning* (Cook, 2000). I now turn to another set of arguments about literary language – or literary-like language – and cognition. These concern the relationship between metaphor and the human mind.

1.4 Metaphor and cognition

In this section I'd like to focus on an argument that **metaphor**, rather than simply being a literary or poetic device, is an inherent property of language and the human mind, so that the 'fundamental roots of language are figurative' (Carter, 2004, p. 70). These ideas are associated with pioneering work carried out by George Lakoff, Mark Johnson and Mark Turner. In their now classic text *Metaphors We Live By*, Lakoff and Johnson (1980) are

interested in metaphor as a way of understanding the world: they argue that
we habitually understand one thing in terms of another. Language, and our
metaphorical use of language, is a window on this process: the way we use
language provides insights into how we perceive and think. Lakoff and
Johnson (1980, p. 4) argue that metaphorical understandings are not (usually)
idiosyncratic or 'one-off', but are organised systematically . In contemporary
western contexts, for instance, *arguments* are frequently seen in terms of *war*:
they may be *attacked* or *defended*, *won* or *lost*, a criticism may be *right on
target*. Lakoff and Johnson suggest that there is a **conceptual metaphor** – a
metaphorical way of thinking about argument – that underlies these
expressions. This is conventionally written in small capitals: ARGUMENT IS WAR.

Arguments may also be seen in terms of *buildings*, as may *theories*: thus
one can *build*, *construct* or *demolish* an argument/theory. A theory may have
solid foundations, or it may need to be *shored up*, or *buttressed* (p. 46). *Time*
is often seen in terms of *money*: it may be *spent*, used *profitably*, or *wasted*;
one may *invest* time in something, or have to *budget* one's time (p. 8). It is
also sometimes a moving object: time *passes*, or *flies* (pp. 42ff). In terms of
conceptual metaphors these would be written as: ARGUMENTS/THEORIES ARE
BUILDINGS; TIME IS MONEY; TIME IS A MOVING OBJECT.

Lakoff and Johnson suggest, furthermore, that it is possible to establish
links between different metaphorical systems: thus, *up* is generally positive
and *down* negative in the case of conceptual metaphors such as:

> HAPPY IS UP, SAD IS DOWN: 'I'm feeling *up*', '*boosting* one's spirits', that
> gives me a *lift*; 'I'm *down/low*', 'my spirits *sank*', etc.

> HEALTH AND LIFE ARE UP, SICKNESS AND DEATH ARE DOWN: '*peak* of
> health', 'in *top* shape'; '*fall* ill', '*declining* health', '*sinking* fast'.

> HAVING CONTROL/FORCE IS UP, BEING SUBJECT TO CONTROL/FORCE IS
> DOWN: '*on top of* the situation', 'a *superior* position', 'the *height* of
> someone's power'; '*under* someone's control', '*fall* from power', '*low
> down*' (in a hierarchy).

(Adapted from Lakoff and Johnson, 1980, p. 15)

It is important to emphasise that, for Lakoff and Johnson, metaphor is not
simply a way of talking or writing about something: metaphorical systems
are associated with cultural preoccupations and with the ways members of
specific cultures perceive and understand phenomena and act upon the
world. They ask their readers to imagine a culture in which *argument* was
conceived of as a *dance*. In such a case:

> ... people would view arguments differently, experience them differently,
> carry them out differently, and talk about them differently. But *we*
> [i.e. people who share the ARGUMENT IS WAR convention] would probably
> not view them as arguing at all: they would simply be doing something
> different.

(ibid., p. 5)

Similarly, TIME IS MONEY is a contemporary western conception of time, related to contemporary cultural activity.

ACTIVITY 5   Ups and downs

Allow about
15 minutes

It may be worth pausing here to consider how Lakoff and Johnson's arguments correspond to your own intuitions. To take the example of 'up' and 'down' words, do you think these are generally positive and negative respectively? Can you think of any counter-examples?

Comment

I can think of several further positive *ups* and negative *downs*: *things are looking up, riding high*, the words *high* and *low* as modifiers (*high ranking, low esteem*); *under the weather, beneath contempt.*

Also, though, I have a few counter-examples: *screwed up, things are a bit up in the air*; *downing a pint* (positive or negative?), *depth of understanding, get down* (in dancing – also *get on up*, of course), *getting the low down* on something.

Despite these counter-examples it does seem to me that it is easier to think of 'up' words as positive and 'down' words as negative in English, though it's also worth bearing in mind that the associations of *ups* and *downs* also depend on the context in which phrases occur.

Lakoff and Johnson's work influenced later research on language and cognition (e.g. Gibbs, 1994; papers in Gibbs and Steen, 1999), as well as studies of metaphor that look more closely at how it is actually used in everyday discourse. Reading C provides an example of such a discoursal approach.

ACTIVITY 6   Everyday metaphor (Reading C)

Please now work through Reading C, 'Metaphor in everyday language', by Lynne Cameron. Cameron discusses 'the cognitive shift in metaphor studies': how the idea of conceptual metaphor has led researchers to broaden the idea of what counts as metaphor in language use. As you read, try to identify the main points Cameron makes about this broadening of the notion of metaphor, and her points about how metaphor is actually used by speakers. Cameron also discusses 'the limits of metaphor', and certain criticisms of cognitive metaphor theory. I shall return to these issues below.

Comment

For Cameron, the 'cognitive shift' extends considerably what may be seen as metaphor in actual uses of language. Metaphors do not need to involve novel connections, or even to be recognised as metaphorical by language users. The term is also extended to a wider range of figurative language, such as similes and allegories (traditional distinctions between figures of speech become less important – at a cognitive level, these are similar).

Cameron relates the characteristics of metaphorical language to the 'affordances' of particular languages. **Affordance** refers here to what English (or any language) makes available to its users by virtue of its structure: some forms are possible, or easier, others less so. The idea of affordances recurs in later chapters in relation to different aspects of language use – e.g. in Chapter 5 we consider the affordances of particular media.

Cameron distinguishes between 'deliberate' and 'conventionalised' metaphor, and identifies uses of both categories in educational and medical talk. Important points for me are that Cameron focuses on the use of metaphor by particular speakers, in particular contexts (there may be differences between speakers/ contexts). She argues also that metaphor has a range of interactional functions: she emphasises the importance of an affective dimension, with metaphor used to mitigate a threat or create a climate of support.

There remains the question of the relationship between 'everyday' and 'literary' metaphor, which Cameron refers to briefly at the end of the reading in connection with the work of Lakoff and Turner. In *More than Cool Reason*, Lakoff and Turner (1989) argue that poetic metaphor builds on and extends everyday metaphor, and also that our understanding of poetic metaphor depends upon its relationship to everyday metaphorical systems. They give the example of a poem by Emily Dickinson, 'Because I could not stop for death'. The poem begins:

> Because I could not stop for Death—
> He kindly stopped for me—
> The Carriage held but just Ourselves—
> and Immortality.

> (Cited in Lakoff and Turner, 1989, p. 4)

Lakoff and Turner relate this to a way of thinking and talking about death that is common in many cultural contexts: the notion of death as departure (underpinned by the conceptual metaphor, DEATH IS DEPARTURE) that is heard in English in phrases such as 'he's *gone/passed away/no longer with us*', 'dearly *departed*', someone '*slipping away*', or being '*brought back* from the dead'. They suggest that Dickinson's own extended metaphor with Death as a coachman driving a carriage derives from this more everyday metaphorical system. In subsequent stanzas Dickinson incorporates and extends other everyday metaphors such as the notion of life as a journey. Lakoff and Turner comment:

> Dickinson extended and composed these metaphors in novel ways. But, though she created the poem, she did not create the basic metaphors on which the poem is based. They were already there for her, widespread throughout Western culture, in the everyday thought of the least literate of people as well as in the greatest poetry in her traditions.

(Lakoff and Turner, 1989, p. 8)

Everyday metaphor therefore sets the conditions for poetic metaphor – it provides the potential for poetic metaphor but also sets limits on its use and understanding. This can be related to an idea I mentioned in Section 1.2, that repetition is a fundamental everyday feature that may be exploited in more literary uses of language.

Lakoff and Turner make their argument about metaphor in relation to an established poet, but it could also apply to the use of more poetic metaphors in conversation (such as the 'leaf in the wind' example in Activity 1). Lakoff and Turner distinguish Dickinson's use of metaphor in terms of its relative novelty, and Cameron notes that everyday talk does not make much use of novel metaphors. It does, however, make some: this takes us back to Carter's notion of a cline of literariness, rather than a binary distinction between literary and non-literary language.

Metaphor and cultural knowledge

Different sets of metaphors are found in different cultural contexts. Lakoff and Turner cite examples of Sanskrit love poetry, which depend for their understanding on the cultural knowledge that illicit sexual activity often took place in the tall reeds that grew along river banks – e.g.:

> There where the reeds are tall
> is the best place to cross the river
> she told the traveller
> with her eye upon him.

(*The Peacock's Egg*, p. 155; cited Lakoff and Turner, 1989, p. 60)

Clines based on readily identifiable features, however, such as the degree of metaphorical language or the novelty of metaphorical connections, do not necessarily explain our sense of the quality of literary or artful language. An illustration of this can be found in the highly (wildly) metaphorical uses of language cited in the 'Block that metaphor!' column that used to run in the US paper the *New Yorker*.

Block that metaphor!

(Mobile, Ala.) – In the dwindling twilight of a storm tossed Thursday, Charlie Graddick grabbed the burnished levers of political demagoguery to whip up a hometown crowd and breathe life into a bid for governor that has seen more switchbacks than a snaky mountain road. (Oct. 27, 1986, p. 115)

(Montgomery, Ala.) – The mayor has a heart as big as the Sahara for protecting 'his' police officers, and that is commendable. Unfortunately, he also often strips his gears by failing to engage the clutch when shifting what emanates from his brain to his mouth. The bullets he fires too often land in his own feet. (Nov. 16, 1987, p. 146)

(Cited in Gibbs, 1994, pp. 3–4)

ACTIVITY 7   The 'fundamental' nature of metaphorical language

Allow about
20 minutes

This section contains some rather challenging ideas, and it may be a good idea to review these now. I suggest you look back over the section and Reading C, including Cameron's consideration of the limits of metaphor and criticisms of cognitive metaphor theory. How convincing do you find the arguments that 'the fundamental roots of language are figurative'?

Comment

The main arguments seem quite convincing to me – that metaphor is prevalent in everyday language; that it is functional (i.e. used to specific effects in an interaction); and that poetic metaphor builds on everyday metaphorical understandings. The idea of underlying conceptual metaphors is more difficult. Cameron pointed out that it is problematical to infer conceptual metaphors on the basis of individual metaphors in discourse. And the idea of conceptual metaphors is a highly abstract one: this does not mean (and indeed it would be unlikely) that people consciously appeal to underlying conceptual metaphors in using and responding to metaphor in the cut and thrust of everyday interactions.

There is some psycholinguistic (experimental) evidence that speakers have tacit intuitions about their metaphorical understanding of certain concepts – the box below provides illustrations of the kinds of experiments that have provided this evidence. But it is harder to demonstrate *whether* and *how* metaphorical thought affects speakers' processing of words and expressions as they actually interact with others. (If you are interested in these issues, see Gibbs, 1994; and, for a shorter review, Gibbs, 1999.)

Cameron notes that the 'cognitive shift' in the study of metaphor has considerably extended what counts as metaphor. Her own study takes account of 'conventionalised' as well as 'deliberate' metaphor. In discussing the limits of metaphor, however, she concedes that there is a danger of over-extending the notion of metaphor. It's also important to note that metaphorical connections will differ in different cultural contexts. Depending on your own cultural and linguistic background you may or may not share the metaphorical understandings discussed in this section and the reading by Cameron.

Finally, I pointed out that the prevalence of metaphor need not correspond to our sense of the quality of a text!

Experimental evidence for conceptual metaphors

Raymond Gibbs has carried out several experiments designed to tap into people's metaphorical understanding of words and phrases. One set of experiments relates to common idioms, often thought of as 'dead' metaphors. Gibbs (1992) investigated peoples' understanding of idioms such as *crack the whip* (to be in control), *spill the beans* (reveal a secret) and *blow your stack* (get very angry), assumed to be metaphorical in origin, but to have lost their metaphoricity over time. Gibbs hypothesised that, on the contrary, speakers make sense of such idioms because they are underpinned by conceptual metaphors. *Blow your stack*, for instance (and related idioms such as *flip your lid*) are associated with two conceptual metaphors: MIND IS A CONTAINER, and ANGER IS A HEATED FLUID IN A CONTAINER. These affect speakers' understandings of the idioms. For example, 'our understanding that too much heated fluid can cause a sealed container to explode is mapped onto the target domain of anger such that we conceptualise the "explosion" of someone's anger as being performed unintentionally and with great intensity' (Gibbs, 1992, p. 486). Gibbs' experiments tested this hypothesis.

In one experiment participants were asked to describe their understanding of how fluid would escape from a sealed container under certain conditions (e.g. when the container was heated); in a follow-up experiment, a different set of participants indicated their understanding of idioms such as *Sally blew her stack*, as well as the more literal *Sally got very angry*. Gibbs found that participants' understandings of anger idioms such as *blow your stack* showed some similarity with the earlier understandings of how fluid escapes from a sealed container: participants tended to agree quite strongly that the anger was due to being under pressure, that it was unintentional and that it happened in a forceful manner. They agreed less with these points in the case of the literal *get very angry*. Evidence from these and several related experiments suggested to Gibbs that idioms such as *blow your stack* differ from their literal paraphrases, and that their meaning is partially motivated by metaphorical schemes of thought, or conceptual metaphors. Such conceptual metaphors would also underpin related expressions such as *His pent-up anger welled up inside of him*; *My anger kept building up inside me*; *She got all steamed up*; and *I'm fuming* (Gibbs, 1992, p. 504).

1.5 Art in interaction

Previous sections have suggested that, while everyday verbal art may be considered in terms of its relationship to literature and its cognitive, or even evolutionary benefits, specific instances also have a local, interactional function (e.g. they may create a common bond, or competition between participants, or perhaps do both simultaneously). In this section I shall look more closely at the interactional functions of artful language: I shall consider how the language people use, and the ways in which it is used in conversation, depend on the setting, relationships between participants, their interactional goals, etc. Such aspects of context provide both the potential for and constraints on verbal creativity. There is no separate reading for this section, but I shall draw on research on conversational joking to illustrate these points.

A distinction is often made (e.g. Boxer and Cortes-Conde, 1997; Norrick, 2001) between conversational joking and joke telling. Joke telling may be regarded as a performance, set off from the surrounding conversation by some sort of preface or performance marker ('I heard this joke the other day ...'; 'Did you hear that one about ...', etc.); jokes adopt certain recognised formats, including a punch line; and they are subject to explicit evaluation – as in the example below.

Joke telling

LARRY:	What's the – did – didn't you tell the one about the – the guy in the bar who who suddenly uh – starts hearing these very nice things said about him?
CLAIRE:	I don't know.
LARRY:	Who told me that?
CLAIRE:	What were the nice things?
LARRY:	Guy's standing at the bar. And he – and this *voice* says, 'Gee, you're such a *great* looking guy.' And he looks around and there's nobody there. Turns back around and he hears the same voice say, 'Y'know I just think you're a really good person.'

[*Several listeners giggle*]

> Y'know he keeps looking around, he can't see anybody talking. And it keeps happening and he finally says to the bartender, he says, 'What's – what's going on here, I keep hearing all these – and I look up –' And the bartender says, 'It's the peanuts, they're complimentary.'

[*General laughter*]

CLAIRE: Now that's [*laughing*] that's cute.

(Norrick, 2001, pp. 1355–6)

Conversational joking involves spontaneous humour within the give and take of conversation rather than telling a joke with a recognised format, though a joking comment may still be explicitly evaluated and in that sense constitute a small-scale performance. Examples 1, 2 and 5 in Activity 1 above are instances of conversational joking.

The box below contains examples of joking in the workplace from research carried out in New Zealand by Janet Holmes and various colleagues. The research forms part of a larger study of workplace language. The workplace might seem to be a context in which there would be limited scope for humour, and in this particular study Holmes and her co-researcher Meredith Marra did find conversational joking was less frequent here than in more informal interactions between friends. Humour did occur, however, and was used with a range of interactional functions. Holmes and Marra make a broad distinction between 'reinforcing humour' (which reinforces or maintains existing relationships); and 'subversive humour' (which subverts existing relationships – in this case challenging power relationships).

Workplace humour

Reinforcing humour

Example 1: reinforcing solidarity (i.e. friendly, collegial) relationships

CONTEXT   Project team members at the start of a meeting.

SANDY: we should start in the traditional way and have Neville tell us a story about his weekend.

[*General laughter*]

Neville obliges with an amusing anecdote, reinforcing and further developing collegiality and friendliness within this team.

Example 2: reinforcing power relationships

CONTEXT   Project team members are discussing a long report they have been sent.

DUDLEY: have you read it?

BARRY: I have

DUDLEY: have you already?

BARRY: [*laughs*]

DUDLEY: you don't have enough work to do Barry.

[*Barry and group laugh*]

Dudley is higher in the organisational hierarchy than Barry. Dudley's humorous comment implies that more senior people have too much work to have time for reading such long reports, and could also be interpreted as hinting that Barry's workload may need increasing.

Subversive humour

Example 3: challenging power relations between individuals

CONTEXT   Project team member [Sandy] (acting as chair of this meeting) calls his manager, Clara, to order.

SANDY: can we get back to business

CLARA: [*laughs*] sorry sorry.

[*General laughter*]

Sandy is here taking the opportunity to reprimand a superior. He criticises Clara for digressing, a fault she often pulls him up on in meetings when she is in the chair, which is the usual scenario.

Example 4: challenging institutional values

CONTEXT   The team members discuss a proposal to record incoming telephone calls. Peg uses Troy's question on the logistics of recording for a cynical retort.

TROY: how far do you get before you know it's a personal call

PEG: [*laughs*] right at the end

[*General laughter*]

The organisation has proposed recording incoming telephone calls in the section, purportedly in order to monitor the business aspects of these calls. These group members are sceptical about the organisation's assurance that they shall not listen to personal calls.

(Adapted from Holmes and Marra (2002a), pp. 70–3)

ACTIVITY 8   Joking at work

Allow
10–15 minutes

In the examples of workplace humour above, do you agree that these serve either to reinforce relationships (Examples 1 and 2) or subvert these (Examples 3 and 4)? Do you find the examples funny? To what extent do you feel you know what is going on?

Comment

Responses to this activity are likely to vary. In my own case, it does seem to me that the examples serve the functions attributed to them by Holmes and Marra, but in making this judgement I'm going by the information provided by the researchers beneath each transcript as much as by the interactions themselves. I did smile at Example 4 – I can appreciate this as a quick cynical retort, and it's something I could imagine happening in my own workplace. The other examples didn't seem particularly funny to me, but I can understand that they were funny to others who were there and who laughed at the remarks. I feel I know something of what is going on – I also work in an office and attend similar meetings. But my understanding is still limited. I don't know anything about these particular meetings or about the speakers involved, relations between them, and their shared previous experiences. All of these seem to be important to an understanding of the joking.

As researchers, Holmes and Marra clearly have a more informed understanding of their data. They collected information on participants, workplaces and particular meetings and draw on this to interpret interactions. For instance they know, in relation to Example 3, that Clara often criticises Sandy for digression and that Sandy is turning the tables here. Holmes and Marra note that their study has an **ethnographic** component in that it takes into account contextual information and seeks to include participants' understandings of events.

Ethnography

Ethnography is an attempt to study systematically the beliefs and practices – or more generally the culture – of a community or social group. It is associated with a particular methodological approach: groups are studied in their natural settings; categories used to interpret activities tend to emerge during the study rather than being fixed at the outset; researchers try to obtain an 'insider' perspective so that activities are understood from the standpoint of group members; data may come from a range of sources, but generally involve close observation of activities; the approach is broadly qualitative. The term *ethnography of speaking* (subsequently and often interchangeably *ethnography of communication*) was coined by Dell Hymes in 1962 to refer to the ethnographic study of the ways of speaking evident in a speech community. Language is viewed here as a cultural activity that needs to be studied in context rather than as a more abstract decontextualised system: for a more recent overview of methods and approaches see Saville-Troike (2003). *Linguistic ethnography* is also found for approaches to the study of language use that draw on ethnographic methods and procedures.

(Adapted from Swann et al., 2004)

Studies such as those carried out by Carter, Cook and Cameron identify certain **forms** of language associated with creativity and also look at how these **function**, or how they are used within an interaction. Holmes and Marra, by contrast, are not concerned with linguistic form. They identify humorous episodes not formally but functionally – in terms of participants' perceptions of humour – whether an episode seems designed to be humorous and how it is responded to.

Holmes and Marra suggest that humour is used differently by different types of participants in meetings: it may be used by a person in authority to reinforce existing power relations or by someone in a subordinate position to challenge or subvert these. Humour may of course have several other functions, some of which are examined in other studies (e.g. Holmes, 2000; Holmes and Marra, 2002b). It may also be **multifunctional**. Example 3, for instance, is interpreted as the subversion by Sandy of Clara's authority; Sandy's comment would also, however, affect others in the meeting, in this case perhaps creating common ground.

ACTIVITY 9   Artful joking?

Allow about 10 minutes

Do you think the examples of joking from Holmes and Marra count as artful language? If so, in what ways?

Comment

These examples are unlike the poetic forms of language examined earlier in this chapter: there is no play with language forms, no punning, rhyming or other poetic repetition, no obvious figures of speech. There is, however, some manipulation of discourse, or language use. People may say something unexpected, playfully reproduce the kind of remark associated with another speaker, say something ironically, or potentially ironically. These may, I think, be seen as creative practices. The speakers are also engaging in what I earlier termed a small-scale performance: saying something for effect, and invoking a response from an audience.

Holmes and Marra's study seems to me to be consistent with a sociocultural approach to verbal art. Perceptions of humour are likely to differ in different contexts – what seems humorous to one group of people, in one workplace, may not be humorous to others and indeed may not be fully understood by them. The use of humour, and understanding of humour, is likely to differ between cultural groups: a study by Holmes and Hay (1997), for instance, suggests humour may not always cross ethnic boundaries in New Zealand (see below). Accepting participants' understandings of humour (or, strictly, analysts' interpretations of these) is likely to give culturally and contextually diverse examples of what counts as humour – or verbal art, more generally: in this case humour, or art, is whatever people conceive of as humorous, or artful.

Maori and Pakeha humour

'Pakeha' refers to New Zealanders of European descent.

Holmes and Hay (1997) discuss potential differences in the use of humour by Maori and Pakeha speakers in New Zealand. They found, for instance, that the use of humour to mark boundaries between Maori and Pakeha people was much more common amongst Maori speakers. They attribute this to the minority status of Maori people, which would arguably make them more aware of cultural distinctions and inequalities. Maori speakers also referred to Pakeha speakers' inability to understand Maori humour, as in the example below:

Two young Maori friends in conversation

A: cause the other thing you've ever found like you talk to a Pakeha and you trying to tell a joke and they don't get it

B: yeah

A: but when you talk to a Maori they do

B: and they get it yeah [yeah

A: [yeah

(Adapted from Holmes and Hay, 1997, p. 127)

1.6 Conclusion

This chapter has explored various aspects of the argument that 'artful' language is pervasive and purposeful: rather than seeing literature as a distinct way of using language we can find literary-like or artful language in a range of more everyday contexts. Literary language may also build on and extend more widespread features of language, such as metaphor. It is therefore more appropriate to talk about a continuity between literature in its conventional sense and more everyday uses of language.

In addressing these issues, the chapter has looked at different approaches to the study of creativity in (mainly spoken) language, reflected in the interests of the authors of readings and other research cited, and the different types of evidence they draw on. Guy Cook's reading (Reading B) drew on evidence from a range of sources to support his arguments about the universality and potential benefits of language play. Other studies are accounts of empirical research on language use and draw on this for their evidence. They also exemplify different ways of studying language use. In Reading A, Ronald Carter drew on evidence from a large computerised corpus of spoken language. This allows him to claim his data are reasonably representative of contemporary spoken interaction in Britain, and to make general claims about the forms taken by creative or artful language (his distinction between 'pattern-reforming' and 'pattern-reinforcing' examples, for instance). This focus on linguistic form can be seen as a **textual** approach to the study of language, i.e. the analysis is concerned with the formal properties of a spoken and transcribed text. Carter is also interested in the social functions of art in specific contexts (in how it brings people together, for instance), and in this respect his study has a **contextual** element – it is concerned with how language is used in context. With such a large corpus, however, contextual information is necessarily rather limited.

In Reading C, Lynne Cameron drew partly on her own study of language use in schools. In the larger study from which her examples are taken, she is able to focus closely on how metaphor is used in this specific context – i.e. the use of metaphor in teaching and learning in the classroom. Janet Holmes' research, which I referred to in Section 1.5, again focuses on a particular type of context: workplace talk. Her study contains an ethnographic component, looking more closely at the context of language use and attempting to take into account participants' own understandings in their interactions. She focuses on differences between speakers in terms of the power conferred by their institutional position. She is also able to say something about individual speakers – Clara frequently criticises Sandy for digressing, Callum is renowned for being pedantic – and this affects her interpretation of the talk. Holmes' study is therefore more strongly contextual than other research considered in this chapter.

These approaches to the study of creativity in language partly map on to Carter's distinction between different models, or conceptions of literature. A textual approach would map on to Carter's 'inherency' model, where what distinguishes literature are the formal properties of literary texts. A contextual approach would be more consistent with Carter's 'sociocultural' model, with its emphasis on social, cultural and contextual variability in what counts as literature. Carter's third, 'cognitive' model is somewhat different, as it relates to mental processes rather than to the properties of texts or how language is used. However, research on language use (whether textual or more contextualised) may derive from or provide evidence for cognitive processes. Cook, for example, makes inferences about the cognitive benefits of language play on the basis of its prevalence in language use. And the way Cameron identifies metaphor in discourse is based on ideas about conceptual metaphors.

In combination, the readings and examples discussed in the chapter support the argument that there is continuity between everyday creativity and literature with respect to all three of Carter's models, and this has sometimes been seen as a set of clines, where texts are more, or less, literary along different dimensions.

ACTIVITY 10   Literary clines?

Allow
5–10 minutes

Taking into account the evidence discussed in this chapter, how valuable do you find the notion of clines of literariness?

Comment

I find the evidence from the readings and examples persuasive, with respect to the argument that there are literary-like elements in everyday texts, that these are not uncommon and that they challenge the distinctiveness of literature. In principle, the notion of clines could apply to all three of Carter's models of literariness: to the prevalence of poetic features such as metaphor and word play, the cognitive benefits that might be associated with literary texts, how far texts are responded to as literary by listeners and readers. Texts could be seen as more or less literary along all these dimensions. It would be important therefore to emphasise the plurality of clines, running along different dimensions of literariness.

The issue of quality in literary texts is explored further in the companion volume, **Goodman and O'Halloran (2006)**.

The idea of clines in itself, however, does seem problematical in suggesting there are gradations, or degrees, of literariness in texts; a difficulty here lies in how to measure this. In terms of linguistic forms it would seem unreasonable, for instance, simply to total the number of 'poetic' features used in a particular text. Even within an 'inherency' model, whether a text is conceived of as literary is unlikely to derive simply from the presence of more or fewer literary features. The notion of a cline, or set of clines, may suggest a level of precision in the identification of literariness that cannot be attained in practice.

This chapter has examined literariness or artfulness mainly in relation to poetic forms of language. The chapters that follow focus on other types of verbal art, extending considerably the discussion of the forms this takes and how it works in everyday contexts.

READING A: Extracts from 'Common language: corpus, creativity and cognition'

Ronald Carter

Introduction: writing and literary language?

This article explores the extent to which examples of everyday spoken discourse display literary properties. [...] Studies of literary discourse and of the continuities between literary and non-literary discourse have for the most part focused on written language or on representations of spoken discourse in fictional or dramatic dialogues or on a range of individual sentence-level speech acts, reinforcing questionable connections between literature, literacy and the written language by assuming that spoken language is no more than a less patterned version of written language. [...]

Interest in spoken discourse has been re-awoken recently by the large collections of naturally occurring spoken data which have become increasingly available, such as the BNC (British National Corpus) and the spoken sections of the COBUILD corpus at the University of Birmingham. The data on which this article is based come from the CANCODE corpus assembled in the Department of English Studies at the University of Nottingham.

CANCODE data

Punning and playing

CANCODE stands for Cambridge and Nottingham Corpus of Discourse in English and is a multi-million-word corpus of spoken English. The CANCODE corpus is based in the Department of English Studies at the University of Nottingham. The working corpus from which examples can be drawn will soon total five million words, although the main aim is to construct a qualitative corpus and not simply a large quantitative corpus. In other words, data are carefully collected with reference to a range of different speech genres, with an emphasis on 'common' informal discourse collected mainly in non-institutional settings.[1] Although the emphasis in work on the corpus is on lexico-grammatical description, with the aim of producing a new pedagogical grammar of English, what cannot be ignored (indeed, it leaps out at researchers from almost every transcript of the data) is the inherent creativity of significant proportions of common language use.

Here are some representative samples from the corpus:

Example 1. (members of a family in Cardiff [1993] are preparing food for a party)

A: Now I think you'd better start the rice

B: Yeah ... what you got there

[4 secs]

A: Will it all fit in the one

B: No you'll have to do two separate ones

C: Right ... what next

[17 secs]

C: Foreign body in there

B: It's the raisins

C: Oh is it oh it's rice with raisins is it

B: no no no it's not supposed to be [laughs] erm

C: There must be raisin for it being in there?

Example 2. (members of a family are telling ghost stories over dinner in Canterbury, 1993. This story refers back to an earlier newspaper story involving a man having a premonition of death on the ship *Hood*. Speaker A begins by describing how the members of the crew were all lined up prior to being selected for the *Hood* and for an anticipated escape:)

A: Oh yes, I mean they were all eager to get on it they were really looking forward to being the chosen ones [B: Mm] and he was one of the ones who was called up [B: yeah] and he was getting ready to go and the chief petty officer came back and said, oh no it's a mistake

C: We've got one extra

A: Dymock, Dymock, er you're not needed [B: Mm] and er he was a bit disappointed and he went back, carried on with what he was doing and the boat sailed out and was torpedoed and

C: by a German ship [B: Oh yes]

D: Everyone, everyone died

C: Anyway, all hands lost but legs saved [All: laugh]

B: Well, sailors were always getting legless, weren't they, anyway [All: laugh]

A: Finding their sea legs

B: Yeah

'Metonymy' is a type of figurative language, like metaphor. Whereas metaphor links two domains of meaning (e.g. *She's a real squirrel*, where a person is compared to an animal), metonymy links entities whose meanings are related (e.g. *the Crown* for the British monarchy, or, in this case, *hands* for people [sailors]).

The creativity of speakers and listeners in Examples 1 and 2 here produces the most basic and widespread forms of verbal play. The comic identification in example 1 of the word *foreign body* with a raisin and puns on the word, *raisin/reason* and in example 2 *hand* and again in example 2 puns on the word *leg* in the fixed expression *find your sea legs* and the word *legless* (meaning unable to stand up or 'find your legs' as a result of being drunk) are the hinges of punning and ambiguity on which the discourses turn. We should also notice in example 2 a creative play with the metonymy (*hands*)

A 'meronym' is a term for something that is part of a whole: e.g. *cuff* and *collar* would be meronyms of *shirt*. In this case the point is that hands and legs are related to each other in that they are both parts of the body.

in [meronymic] pattern with *legs*. Similar creative play can be illustrated by examples 3–5 which follow. In these contexts the verbal play is with larger units or 'chunks' of language:

Example 3. (two friends in London [1996] are discussing a third friend's stormy marriage and the fact that, as a result of continuing infidelity, relations between the couple are 'frozen' and they are barely talking:)

A: ... he's at it again but he really wants you know just to sit down

B: like they just talk about how they both feel

A: out of the frying pan into the deep freeze this time

Example 4. (two colleagues in Leicester [1995], who are social workers, are discussing a third colleague who has a tendency to become too involved in individual cases:)

A: I don't know but she seems to have picked up all kinds of lame ducks and traumas along the way.

B: That that's her vocation.

A: Perhaps it is. She should have been a counsellor.

B: Yeah but the trouble with her is she puts all her socialist carts before the horses.

Example 5. (two students in Bristol [1995] are talking about the landlord of a mutual friend:)

A: Yes, he must have a bob or two

B: Whatever he does he makes money out of it just like that

A: Bob's your uncle

B: He's quite a lot of money erm tied up in property and things. He's got a finger in all kinds of pies and houses and stuff. A couple in Bristol, one in Cleveland I think.

These examples show speakers playfully and creatively extending metaphors of 'hot' and 'cold' (core figurations in the expression and evaluation of human feeling) alongside a creative extension of a fixed saying ('out of the frying pan into the fire') (example 3). Examples 4 and 5 show idioms being displaced into new patterns. For example,

She puts all her socialist carts before the horses

(Don't put the cart before the horse)

He's got a finger in all kinds of pies and houses and stuff

(He's got a finger in every pie)

And example 5 also contains the intriguing possibility of subliminal phonological/phonaesthetic echoing across speaking turns of the word *bob* in the fixed expression 'bob or two' and the idiom 'Bob's your uncle'.

'Morphology' refers to word structure. 'Morphological inventiveness' here means playing with the structure of words to form new words.

Morphological inventiveness: new words for old

The above examples (3–5) illustrate how speakers can create new meanings by means of reformulation of what have been conventionally described in linguistics as immutably fixed chunks of language. Also prevalent in CANCODE data are instances where speakers invent new words from existing words, 'morphological creativity' in Carter and McCarthy (1995b).

Here are two examples in the 'invented' words *heart drawers* and *crawly*:

Example 6. (a group of students in Nottingham [1996] are discussing items for a jumble sale:)

A: I mean stuff like this is what we need because it's quite quite an easy thing to design and it that looks really pretty. So what's that?

B: Yeah. It's got a lovely heart as well.

C: Heart drawer

A: Heart drawers

(all laugh)

C: Heart drawers

A: Somebody's knickers. And how much was that? Seventy five?

C: Seventy five pence ...

Example 7

A: I've done the letter

B: Right

C: But it's a bit bloody abrupt. It's quite sort of

B: Ah

D: You can sort of

B: No that's fine

A: That's fine?

C: That's fine

B: Are you sure?

C: Yeah. You don't want to feel crawly do you?

A: No it's not crawly is it. It's all right if I want this information isn't it?

C: Yeah

Echoing and converging

In parallel with the morphological creativity in example 7, there is also another phenomenon at work. Speakers regularly pattern each other's words, producing parallel structures in the form of lexical and syntactic echoes. For example, the repetition of:

That's fine;
sort of;
crawly;
yeah.

In the following extract from CANCODE data, the situation and speakers are the same as in example 1 (members of a family preparing food in a kitchen in Cardiff [1993]). In this sample there are no overt markers of verbal play or morphological or other kinds of 'inventiveness'. But there are patterns similar to those noted in example 7:

Example 8

A: How long does it take?

B: Erm

C: Oh that'll make a noise

B: Takes about thirty five minutes yeah that'll that that'll destroy your tape

A: Thirty five minutes

B: Yeah

C: Yeah

A: I thought the microwave did everything in about two minutes

C: You may as well turn it off now then

A: Yeah you can do it on the cooker for thir, in thirty five minutes

B: Then if you have to watch it ... you just ignore it

A: Mm

D: You don't have to wash the saucepan either do you?

B: You don't have to wash the saucepan after [laughs] [C:mm] you don't have to erm drain the water off either

A: I didn't know that microwaves ran that long

B: Yeah you don't have to erm drain the water off
     either cos er

A: I'll switch it off when you turn that on

This multi-party sequence of exchanges contains several examples of the seemingly random topic switching and overlapping, interruptions, unanswered questions, hesitations and false starts which characterise informal conversations. On the surface there is much divergence, disconnection and incoherence. Beneath the surface there is, however, much convergence and coherence marked in a distinctive range of pattern-reinforcing linguistic features, especially repetition. For example, the speakers use each other's words, employ parallel syntactic forms and generally pattern question and answer replies in such a way as to confirm that there are high degrees of affective connections and convergence. For example, the recycling and echoing of the following words and structures:

> *take*
> *thirty five minutes;*
> *do/did;*
> *yeah;*
> *drain the water off;*
> *you don't have to wash/drain;*
> *off/on.*

See also Tannen (1989) for related explorations.

Pattern-reforming and pattern-reinforcing

Patterns are always potentially present in language and language users always have options whether or not and what kind of patterns to create. CANCODE research suggests two main motivating choices: *pattern-reforming choices* and *pattern-reinforcing choices*. In the case of reforming choices speakers play more directly and overtly with language. They draw attention to the patterns by re-forming and re-shaping them. In extreme versions of reforming there is a more radical position created by the 'reform'. Co-conversationalists are prompted to pleasure and laughter, to more evaluative and affective viewpoints and to a more innovative re-shaping of our ways of seeing. Speakers who reform patterns can sometimes do so by radically displacing or deviating from expected linguistic patterns.

In the case of pattern-reinforcing choices, the patterns which are developed are less overt and work primarily to create an affective convergence and a commonality of viewpoint. The patterns may not draw attention to themselves in the same way as pattern-reforming choices; and it is also more likely that rules for existing linguistic structures will be conformed to rather than departed from. It is not, of course, suggested that these patterns operate discretely, for both pattern-reforming and pattern-reinforcing can be and often are combined.

Summary

Nottingham CANCODE research is revealing a number of characteristic features of such spoken discourse: first, that common, everyday language is far from being either everyday or common (on the contrary, it is pervasively 'poetic'); second, that verbal play with language is often undertaken for humorous purposes, serving in part to bring people closer together (these kinds of data can be easily found in multi-million-word corpora by running

A concordance identifies all instances of a particular word in a corpus and displays a list of each occurrence of the word in its immediate linguistic context (the word might be shown, for instance, with the five words that occur before and after it). This is usually used to let researchers see how a word is used in context, and what other words it is associated with. In the case of [laughs], a concordance would let researchers see where laughter occurred across all the conversations in the corpus.

concordances for the word [laughs]); third, that this kind of linguistic creativity and inventiveness is almost always contextually embedded insofar as it depends to a measurable degree on the social relations which obtain between participants (relations between people in the above data are informal and participants are on a mainly equal social and psychological footing); fourth, that creativity involves not only more overt attention-drawing *pattern-reforming forms* but also more covert *pattern-reinforcing forms*, the latter especially across speaking turns; fifth, that it is a *frequent*, not exceptional, feature of everyday language use and that it is also a *common* practice to share pleasure and convergence in and through language.

Since such language use is discoursally frequent, some of the definitions of literary language (for example, that it is 'deviant' discourse) may need to be revised. [...].

Bhaya et al. (1988), Toolan (1996) and Carter (1997) explore the extent to which the existence of creative and inventive language involves risks for the creator. The risks mainly involve failures of uptake, the embarrassment of unsuccessful performances and lapsed 'presentationality'. Puns and extended or newly minted metaphors, in particular, involve acts of language use which are relatively self-conscious and there are risks involved in the undertaking. On the other hand, the risks can bring communicative rewards. Pleasure can be conferred, convergence created and the presenter can in certain contexts achieve an enhanced regard or what Boxer and Cortes-Conde (1997) term 'identity display'. [...]

Example 9. (two friends – primary school teachers in Nottingham [1996] – are discussing arrangements for changing classes:)

A: So if Monday was clear which we need to check with

B: I teach Lenton on Monday

A: Right

B: If they're not going on a trip or anything like that

A: Well they won't go on a trip for sure

B: So they should be here

A: So it could be Monday if the test's on Tuesday. Right.

B: And that wouldn't upset any apple carts would it? No?

Example 10. (three Art College students who share a house in Carmarthen, Wales are having tea and chatting informally among themselves [1994]:)

A: I like Sunday nights for some reason, I don't know why

B: [laughs] cos you come home

A: I come home

B: You come home to us

C: And pig out

B: Yeah yeah

B: It's an earring, it's an earring

A: Oh lovely, oh lovely

B: It's fallen apart a bit but

A: It's quite a nice one actually, I like that, I bet, is that supposed to be straight?

B: Yeah

C: Oh I think it looks better like that

B: And there was another bit as well, another dangly bit

A: What, attached to

B: The top bit

A: That one

B: Yeah ... so it was even

A: Mobile earrings

C: Well, that looks better like that, it looks like that

These data illustrate the greater risks which attach to pattern-reforming choices as in example 9 speaker B introduces an idiom ('upset apple carts') which risks being seen as (in)appropriately inventive, affective and lightening amid the information transfer; and in example 10 the imagistic creativity produced by comparing earrings to a mobile may also not receive the desired uptake, though the informality and social symmetry of the context reduce attendant risks. And alongside such pattern-reforming runs an extensive set of pattern-reinforcing echoes and repetitions (especially in example 10) which on another level create a mutuality and commonality conducive to the verbal play. [...]

Notes

1   For further discussion of corpus design, see Carter and McCarthy [1995a]; McCarthy and Carter [1995]; McCarthy [1998].) All CANCODE data collected are the property of Cambridge University Press, which has funded the project. Plans are already laid to extend the corpus to include a wider variety of international Englishes produced in different discourse communities and to compare non-British spoken Englishes with the kinds of British English data reported on in this article.

References

BEX, A.R. (1996) *Variety in Written English: Texts in Society, Society in Texts*, London, Routledge.

BHAYA, R., CARTER, R.A. and TOOLAN, M. (1988) 'Clines of metaphoricity and situated risk taking', *Journal of Literary Semantics*, **17**(2), pp. 81–93.

BOXER, D. and CORTES-CONDE, F. (1997) 'From bonding to biting: conversational joking and identity display', *Journal of Pragmatics*, **27,** pp. 275–94.

CARTER, R.A. (1997) *Investigating English Discourse: Language, Literacy, Literature*, London, Routledge.

CARTER, R.A. and McCARTHY, M. (1995a) 'Grammar and the spoken language', *Applied Linguistics*, **16**(2), pp. 141–58.

CARTER, R.A. and McCARTHY, M. (1995b) 'Discourse and creativity: bridging the gap between language and literature', in G. COOK and B. SEIDLHOFER (eds) *Principle and Practice in Applied Linguistics*, Oxford, Oxford University Press.

McCARTHY, M. (1998) *Spoken Language and Applied Linguistics*, Cambridge, Cambridge University Press.

McCARTHY, M. and CARTER, R. (1995) 'Spoken grammar: what is it and how do we teach it?', *ELT Journal*, **49**(3), pp. 207–18.

TANNEN, D. (1989) *Talking Voices: Repetition, Dialogue and Imagery in Conversational Discourse*, Cambridge, Cambridge University Press.

TOOLAN, M. (1996) *Total Speech: An Integrational Approach to Language*, Durham, NC, Duke University Press.

Source: CARTER, R. (1999) *Language and Literature*, 8(3), pp. 195–216, © Sage Publications, www.sagepub.co.uk

READING B: Why play with language?

Guy Cook

There's a bison down by the lake

Through language, humans share knowledge across generations and communities on a scale no other species can approach. It would be easy to regard this as the most important use of language, and even as the reason why our hunter-gatherer ancestors thousands of years ago first started to talk. The psychologist Robin Dunbar has characterised such a notion of language origin as the 'There's a bison down by the lake' view[1] (p. 79). The idea is that if one prehistoric hunter could say this to another, then they could go after the bison together, and stand a better chance of catching it.

There is still plenty of information-oriented language use around today, even if the environment, the medium, and the information is different from that of this hypothetical hunt. Scrolling down my emails, I find that a good number are mainly concerned with sending me necessary facts. One, for example, tells me where to go for a talk I am giving.

Dear Guy

The talk will take place at the main site (2-3 minute walk from the department). The room is B034. It's down the stairs in the basement. You can always ask at reception in the main entrance. The talk will start at 6.

Kind regards

Though framed with brief social niceties (*Dear Guy, Kind regards*...), it is essentially still about finding a bison. And it is not only such necessary but ephemeral information which language can communicate. Through lectures, libraries and electronic resources, we can access more durable information: humanity's accumulated knowledge of the social and natural world.

Children's language play

This interpretation of language, however, does not fit all its uses. Little children, for example, can seem oblivious to its capacity to bring them real-world facts. Their favourite language uses (whether invented by themselves or by adults) tend rather to be about unreal and improbable events: witches and wizards, animals that talk. And many pre-school rhymes just do not make much sense at all:

Diddle diddle dumpling my son John
Went to bed with his trousers on

It could be argued that pre-school children are still at the stage of acquiring language, and that once that is past, this trivial nursery nonsense will have served its purpose, and can be discarded.

Yet this is not what seems to happen. Though children are bombarded with useful information at school, they refer to it as 'work' and are impatient to get back to 'play'. In the 'playground', they produce language of their own ('children's lore'), often parodying the more serious factual discourse of the classroom, or revelling in things they are scolded for saying elsewhere. So listening in upon playtime in a primary school, it is not excited discussions of arithmetic or science that you will hear, but rather such things as:

Julius Caesar, the Roman geezer,
Squashed his wife with a lemon squeezer.[2]

and:

Ladies and gentlemen
Take my advice
Pull down your pants
And slide on the ice.[3]

Back home their preferences are similar. They hurry to put any homework aside and to re-enter the fictional worlds of computer games, TV and video, and bed-time stories.

The features of language play

This playful children's language has a number of typical features.

Firstly, it is characterised by repetition and patterning at all linguistic levels, making exact wording very important. Thus, sound patterns repeat as rhymes and rhythms. Grammatical structures repeat with only minimal lexical changes. Episodes repeat in stories with only slight variation. Whole instances are repeated verbatim. As all parents know, children say the same rhymes, sing the same songs, read the same stories, watch the same videos, tell the same jokes, again and again and again.

Secondly, a good deal of it refers to fictional worlds. It may be a story about pirates and treasure, playing at pretending to be someone else, or a game in which children take on new relationships (one person is 'it' or 'on' and must chase the others until they are caught).

Thirdly, it performs two opposite social functions. It bonds those who use it together, and in doing so, it necessarily implicitly excludes others. In some cases, this excluding function can become explicit and aggressive, reminding us that children's play is not always friendly. Taunting rhymes exclude another child from the group or draw attention to some unpopular attribute:

> *Inky pinky, pen and inky*
> *I smell a dirty stinky*[4]

Adult language play in private

How does such children's language play square with the notion of language as serving primarily to communicate information? It could be dismissed as a temporary stage – *childly*[5] when used by children, *childish* if it persists, apparently atypically, into adulthood. Yet though adults think of their own behaviour as much more serious than children's, language play by no means disappears with maturity, though it is less evident. Adults are more reluctant and embarrassed to disclose certain uses of language – necessarily so, as it is this very secrecy which makes them intimate.

In Britain, an interesting glimpse into such forbidden territory is provided by the strange annual phenomenon of Valentine's Day messages in newspapers and magazines, in which lovers parade anonymously their way of talking to each other. For example:

> *Weedy wiggy woo woo*
> *Wiglet will always love you*

and:

> *Chucky bum*
> *I love your tum*
> *And now you're slimmer*
> *The sex will simmer.*

Such messages reflect a tendency for adult expressions of affection to reactivate the language of infancy (as in the use of terms like *baby* for lover). They are full of alliterative pet names with diminutive endings (like *wiglet*), nonsense words (*woo woo*), taboo topics (*sex will simmer*), and private meanings (*chucky bum*). In general, they are driven more by rhyme and rhythm than by meaning, while the meanings which do emerge are, like those in children's rude rhymes, rather risqué. Embarrassed as someone might feel if these particular examples were their own, many people nevertheless probably would use such 'silly' language to express affection privately to partners, friends and family.

So adults share with children a penchant for playfully patterned language. They are also, like children, inordinately fond of fiction – a curious fact which has been largely ignored in both psychology and sociology. Successive advances in communication technology – print, film, radio, sound recording, television, the internet – have been used as much to communicate fiction as fact. Novels are the largest category of books; the bulk of TV programmes are dramas (soap operas being the most popular); pop songs are the highest profile sound recordings; documentary films are a rarity; and the so-called 'information revolution' of the internet is in fact largely used for games, chat rooms and fantasies. Though the content of all these technologies is in one sense very public, their recreational use remains a private or family affair. When the day's practical business (catching bison or giving lectures) is over, we experience books, television or the internet as though in one-to-one interaction. Even the crowded cinema, because of the darkened auditorium, creates this sense of privacy.

All of these activities moreover, just like children's playground rhymes, reflect and create a sense of group identity. We define ourselves partly by the books, television programmes and internet sites which we do (or do not) like. And when establishing or maintaining relationships, we make frequent reference to this shared experience and knowledge.

Adult language play in public

It is not only in private and recreational uses of language however, that adult language continues to manifest the characteristics of child language play. Some of the most public, powerful and widely distributed uses of language display the same traits. A striking example is advertisements. As in rhymes and stories, it is the form of the message, just as much as the meaning, which is crucial. Distinctive voices or letter shapes, rhythm, puns and memorable phrases are integral to the effect of the whole. Many adverts are also fictional vignettes.

A recent British television chocolate-bar ad displayed all of these characteristics. A young couple are shown sitting side by side on a beach. The woman is unwrapping a Mars Bar. The man edges tentatively closer as though shy about a first kiss. Then he suddenly leans forward and bites off the end of the Mars Bar. Up come the punning words (written in the product's distinctive calligraphy):

Love Bite

and then the product's latest slogan:

Mars. Pleasure you can't measure

Such uses of rhythm and rhyme are almost as old as advertising itself. An earlier product slogan was:

A Mars a day
Helps you work, rest and play.

And the very name 'Mars Bar' has internal rhyme.

Advertising is by no means the only adult genre with a predilection for word-play of this kind. Songs, jokes, comedy, football chants, graffiti, and tabloid journalism all show similar uses. In addition, everyday conversation is characterised by playful and creative uses of language, and repeated phrases and words [see Reading A by Ronald Carter].

Competition and aggression

All of these genres can on occasion take very competitive forms, suggesting that as with children, adult language 'play' can also become aggressive. One well-documented instance is known as verbal duelling. In this, participants – usually males – rapidly exchange insults referring to taboo topics and fantastical situations. A simple example[6] is the following exchange between two youths using African American English:

A: *Your momma drink pee.*
B: *Your father eat shit.*

The riposte exploits language patterning, reproducing the grammar and rhythm of the first insult, though with different lexis. Verbal duelling has been extensively documented in a range of social contexts. Recently, it has become well-known in contests between rappers such as the following example in which Terra, from a club in California, takes to the stage in order to dispatch another rapper who has refused to stop and pass on the microphone:[7]

What happened to your apology?
It's time for a little sermontology
That's hypocrisy
You jump to the microphone
But you ain't knocking me
You stepping up to poetry
Yeah, you know it's me
Yeah it's Terra

> *Terror – whatever you want to call me*
> *In any section*
> *I'm not battling you*
> *I'm looking for something bigger*
> *you need to be trudging*
> *In some other corner of the globe*
> *Some other corner of this episode*

Sociolinguistic studies of verbal duelling have tended to concentrate upon traditional societies as well as underprivileged social groups in modern urban society (such as the African American youths above). Yet the phenomenon is equally prevalent among the privileged and powerful, and elements of it are evident in prestigious institutionalised encounters such as those between academics, barristers, or politicians. One famous instance, for example, is Prime Minister's question time in the British House of Commons where witty repartee and name calling are as much a part of the event as reasoned argument.

Play elements in serious genres

This last point brings us to a crucial observation about genres of language use. Radical differences in the status of participants and situations can blind us to similarities of both form and function. Though it is easy enough to see some similarity between rude words in the playground and the language of verbal duelling (explaining the latter perhaps as a childish throwback), children's language play does not so readily associate with the most highly valued discourses such as those of political rhetoric, poetry and prayer. Yet the same characteristics predominate. Martin Luther King's 1963 speech provides an example:

> *I have a dream that one day this nation will rise up and live out the true meaning of its creed: 'We hold these truths to be self-evident: that all men are created equal.'*

> *I have a dream that one day on the red hills of Georgia the sons of former slaves and the sons of former slave owners will be able to sit down together at a table of brotherhood.*

> *I have a dream that one day even the state of Mississippi, a state sweltering with the heat of injustice and oppression, will be transformed into an oasis of freedom and justice.*

> *I have a dream that my four children shall one day live in a nation where they will not be judged by the color of their skin but by the content of their character.*

> *I have a dream today!*

Poetic in character, and drawing upon the evangelical rhetorical traditions of Southern Bible-belt Christianity, it lends itself to powerful declamation. It has a repeated grammatical structure, a vivid description of an alternative reality, and a focus upon exclusion and inclusion: unifying the listeners in their struggle, seeking to end division in society at large. Significantly, it is one of the best known and most highly valued pieces of English ever produced.

Nature and explanations

So we have a strange phenomenon: a wide range of genres which display markedly uniform characteristics, yet whose similarity is obscured by the fact that they embrace apparent opposites:

child/adult   friendly/aggressive

private/public   intimate/powerful

ephemeral/durable trivial/profound

Many of them are also universal. Though my examples have been contemporary and in English, comparable uses of language can be found in many times, cultures and languages.

Creative thinking

Why should this be? All of the language uses we have looked at so far – from playground rhymes to political rhetoric – can be seen as contributing to group formation and definition. In this, they and similar genres seem to create and contribute to conformity. Mass activities such as public worship, parades, football matches, pop concerts, and political rallies all use language – in chants, anthems and choral repetition – to this effect, and help to create a uniform world view among those participating. Such an interpretation can contribute to a narrowly utilitarian view of the use and origin of language, as follows. Humans have always survived by collaboratively manipulating the environment in complex ways, and to do this they not only need to exchange information ('there's a bison down by the lake') but also to organise themselves into large and coordinated groups, which then compete with others. Yet even if partly true, this need not be the only explanation – nor does it do justice to all but the simplest of examples. Even if such language uses do serve this purpose, this does not explain everything about them. Why can patterned language and fictional realities create such pleasure, and, in some instances, such a sense of profundity? Why do we feel that some instances broaden our horizons, and help us to break away from established values and ideas?

Poems and songs in particular (two genres which share all of the characteristics we have identified) have the capacity to do these things. Why? One possible reason is that their partial surrender to chance coincidences in the language system may help us to think creatively and to break out of established patterns of thought, and rebel against conformist ideas. Consider for example how ideas and associations develop in a stanza from the song *Subterranean homesick blues* by Bob Dylan:

> *Ah get born, keep warm*
> *Short pants, romance, learn to dance*
> *Get dressed, get blessed*
> *Try to be a success*
> *Please her, please him, buy gifts*
> *Don't steal, don't lift*
> *Twenty years of schoolin'*
> *And they put you on the day shift*
> *Look out kid*
> *They keep it all hid*
> *Better jump down a manhole*
> *Light yourself a candle*
> *Don't wear sandals*
> *Try to avoid the scandals*
> *Don't wanna be a bum*
> *You better chew gum*
> *The pump don't work*
> *'Cause the vandals took the handles*

(Dylan, 1965)

Though Dylan's satirical view of an unfolding life history makes sense, he uses a rhyme scheme which is so intense that it sometimes allows only one syllable between rhymes ('Short p*ants*, rom*ance*, learn to d*ance*'). In such highly patterned poetic and playful uses of language, words cannot be chosen primarily to convey meaning (as they are when we say some banal fact about bison or room locations), but are partly determined by the coincidences of linguistic form. Though this seems to be placing an unnecessary extra obstacle in the way of communication, it is one which we humans seem to enjoy creating. We also admire and enjoy the skills of those who overcome it. (Hence the great popularity of Bob Dylan and other skilful manipulators of words.)

Perhaps one reason for the popularity of such language use is that, by surrendering to chance coincidences of form and meaning, or listening to others do so, we allow our minds to range more freely, thinking creatively through a process which yields new associations and new ideas. Thus, constrained rhythmic patterned language, which can in some circumstances be the instrument of conformity (for example, in parades, ceremonies and rallies), can also, in poetic and playful discourse, be liberating. We may feel that a song or poem brings with it new ways of seeing the world. Another reason may be that manipulations of form focus our attention away from what is being said and towards language itself, helping us to develop our linguistic skills. We become more aware of the complexities, surprises and mysteries which the language seems to contain within itself, and to experience it as an immense resource.

Conclusion

Yet paradoxically, this surrender of control *to* language also demands a greater degree of control *over* language. Evolutionary psychologists[8] would say that we admire the achievements of poets, singers, punsters, jokers, duellers, orators – and other wordsmiths – because successful play with language demonstrates mastery of an essential human faculty. Through play, animals develop and hone the skills which they need to survive, and in this, we humans are not so different from other species. Kittens stalk and pounce, antelopes jump and run, because that is what they need to do well. In a similar way, we play with language, both as children and adults, because it is an attribute on which our survival and success depends, whether as individuals or as a species.

And we need language for many purposes: not only as an instrument for locating a bison (or similar information), but also for pleasure and relaxation, to create group identity, to express affection and aggression, and to think creatively and flexibly, developing new ways of seeing both the world and – reflexively – language itself.

Notes

1   Dunbar, R. (1996) *Grooming, Gossip and the Evolution of Language*, London and Boston, Faber and Faber.

2   Quoted in Opie, I. and Opie, P. (1959) *The Lore and Language of School Children*, Oxford, Oxford University Press, p. 20.

3   ibid., p. 97.

4   ibid., p. 48.

5   For explanation of this term see Sealey, A. (2000) *Childly Language*, London, Longman.

6   Sherzer, J. (1992) 'Verbal play' in W. Bright (ed.) *International Encyclopedia of Linguistics*, New York/Oxford, Oxford University Press, p. 221.

7   Cited in Morgan, M. (2002) *Language, Discourse and Power in African American Culture*, Cambridge, Cambridge University Press, p. 112.

8   Carroll, J. (1995) *Evolution and Literary Theory*, Columbia, University of Missouri Press.

Source: commissioned for this volume.

READING C: Metaphor in everyday language

Lynne Cameron

Metaphor is a matter of both language and thought. Philosophers and literary scholars have traditionally focused on the linguistic, with metaphors being novel and lively 'figures of speech'. Metaphors were identified within phrases and sentences through some clear disjunction or tension between their two parts, the Topic (the subject of the metaphor, what it is about) and the Vehicle (a word or phrase used to refer to the Topic but which is somehow incongruent or untrue). In *the ship ploughs the waves,* for instance, the Topic would be 'moving through the waves' and the Vehicle *ploughs.* Clearly, the ship is not literally ploughing, and so the Vehicle term creates a disjunction with the rest of the clause. The disjunction is resolved through an active process of interaction between the two ideas, giving us a new image of some kind of slow but determined and powerful movement through a heavy substance.

> Italics are used for examples from language use in the body of the text, with the Vehicle underlined.

The publication of *Metaphors We Live By* (Lakoff and Johnson, 1980) shifted attention to the cognitive work of metaphor, backgrounding metaphors in language as just traces of cognitive activity. Rather than being simply a figure of speech, metaphor is seen as a 'figure of thought', with the key unit being 'conceptual metaphors', metaphorical mappings between two conceptual domains that have become embedded in our thought and language. Lakoff and Johnson supported their claims with now familiar examples of conceptual metaphors such as LOVE IS A JOURNEY or ARGUMENT IS WAR. A conceptual metaphor appears in language through a range of linguistic expressions: *we are at a crossroads in our relationship; partners in a marriage travel on together.* Conceptual metaphors include many of the basic ways we have of seeing and physically interacting with the world. Take for example the conceptual metaphor MORE IS UP. This has physical and concrete origins, in that a taller pile of food or money contains more. When the conceptual metaphor is filtered through into language, it produces linguistic expressions such as *career ladder, rising prices, high costs, upper age ranges.* The Vehicle terms in these linguistic metaphors (*ladder, rising,* etc.) would earlier have been seen as 'dead' metaphors or not metaphorical at all. Because they can be linked to the underlying conceptual metaphor of MORE IS UP, they are now classed as metaphor. Language is full of such expressions, used every day and usually without speakers noticing their metaphoricity.

> Small capitals are conventionally used to indicate a conceptual metaphor.

The cognitive shift in metaphor studies has thus, by changing the parameters of 'metaphor', increased the number of 'metaphors' we see in everyday language use, including 'dead' metaphors (*rising prices*) as well as more novel, 'active' metaphors such as *The ship ploughs the waves.* Furthermore, metaphors are no longer restricted to word or phrase level; from a cognitive perspective, a whole allegorical story can also be seen as metaphorical thought in action. The extension of the meanings of prepositions, such as the use of *over* in *I'm over that relationship* or *on* as in *on Tuesday*, also counts as metaphorical. The precise linguistic form with which the domains are brought together is also less important, so that the traditional distinction between metaphor and simile (marked by the absence or presence of the word *like* or equivalent) becomes redundant. Some similes can also be seen as metaphorical.

Metaphor in language use

In post-cognitive times, when working with metaphor as it is actually used in discourse, the researcher faces new issues around the nature and identification of metaphor. Linguistic metaphor is language with the *potential* for metaphorical processing, arising from an underlying domain difference, and we no longer need evidence of an imaginative leap between disjunctive domains. Metaphor can be identified without evidence that users intended or invoked metaphorical processing.

The form that linguistic metaphors take will depend on the affordances offered by the vocabulary and grammar of a particular language. Users of English appear to make particular use of:

Delexicalised verbs are verbs such as go (as in go back to) and put, make, get, etc., used with limited lexical meaning.

- delexicalised verbs and prepositions, often in combination, for conventionalised metaphors, e.g. *now go back to your memory (= think about it again)*
- the use of nouns in formulations such as 'the xxx of xxx', for strong, deliberate metaphors, e.g. *the blanket of gases; the overall picture of the age*
- the condensation of comparisons into modifier + noun metaphors, e.g. *trees like little lollipops → lollipop trees*.

Once we take a broader perspective, we find that everyday talk does not make much use of novel metaphors. This is not surprising, since the communicative pressures of talk do not allow time to compose new and vivid metaphors. Instead, users make deliberate use of metaphors that they draw from a common stock available to members of the speech community. In the following extract from my own research into metaphor in educational discourse, a teacher uses deliberate metaphors as she tries to explain to ten- and eleven-year-old boys how to position their feet in a dancing lesson:

Extract 1   Teacher explains a dancing position to pupils

1   boys (.)
    can you try and have your feet in what's called (.)
    first position (.)
    where your heels are just touching (1.0)
5   and your knees are straight (3.0)
    and your toes are a little bit out (.)
    but not that much (2.0)
    about at five to one (.)
    not like this (.) [stands with feet wide apart]

10   it looks funny (.) <u>like Charlie Chaplin</u>
        [pupils laugh]

(Cameron, 2003, p. 135)

Transcription conventions:

Brackets show pauses.

(.) indicates a micro-pause.

Longer pauses are shown to the nearest second, e.g. (2.0) indicates
a two-second pause.

Two deliberate metaphors (lines 8 and 10) are used to emphasise the position.
The first uses the shape made by the hands of a clock, and the second offers a
contrasting metaphor in the characteristic shape of Charlie Chaplin's feet.

   Most metaphors in talk (around 90% in my dataset), however, do not seem to
be deliberately used, but rather occur because they are conventionalised and 'just
the way to say it'. In Extract 2, the teacher uses several conventionalised
metaphors in the course of explaining how igneous rocks are formed:

Extract 2   Igneous rocks

1   right (.) let's <u>go back</u> (.) <u>to</u> these rocks (1.0)
       fire formed (2.0)
       I think you probably all know (.) how (.)
       igneous rocks <u>come</u> to be formed (2.0)
5   you should know this (1.0)
       you love watching this on the telly (.)
       and if one starts <u>working</u> again (.)
       it's very exciting (.)
       and it's <u>on</u> the news for days (.)

(Cameron, 2003, p. 103)

Here the underlined Vehicle terms are very frequent lexical items and their
metaphorical use is so common that users probably do not notice them
as metaphors.

   Metaphor conventionalisation is always relative to a specific discourse
community – what may be conventionalised for one socio-cultural group may
be unfamiliar to another. Children and other novices in a group will need to
learn the metaphors as they grow into group membership. These group
metaphors may be technical, as with computer terms *windows, menus,* and
mouse, or they may function more as shared shorthand, as with *lollipop trees*
that seemed to become an abbreviated way to describe simplistic pictures of
trees as circles on top of sticks in the talk of a group of children and their
teacher (Cameron, 2003, p. 117).

Extracts 1 and 2 also show some of the characteristic features of metaphor in classroom talk:

- Deliberate metaphors are usually used to summarise preceding talk, rather than to introduce a new idea (as in Extract 1, *five to one* summarises the position already explained non-metaphorically and non-verbally).

- Conventionalised and deliberate metaphors, and mixtures of the two, often occur in clusters or bursts (Corts and Pollio, 1999). It is as if using one metaphor prompts the use of others. There are probably several forces that contribute to this phenomenon, including repetition as a normal feature of talk (McCarthy, 1988) and mental activation of connected words and ideas.

- Personifying or animating metaphors are very common in talk to children and in explanations of scientific ideas to both adults and children e.g. *a volcano starts working; the creep of evolution* (Cameron and Low, 2004).

Why people use metaphor

Metaphor appears to draw on a basic human cognitive capacity for noticing similarities between disparate entities, and on an affective capacity for enjoying playing with language and ideas.[1] A metaphor is a kind of package which compactly brings together two concepts and their properties, entities, relations, connotations and evaluations. As we interpret this bringing together through our personal experience and knowledge of the Vehicle domain, we can gain new insights or adopt particular perspectives on the Topic of the metaphor.

Deliberate use of metaphor is thus a communicative tool or strategy that we might expect to find in use wherever participants in interaction have communication problems to solve. In the classroom talk, such problems were often concerned with the need to talk about and explain unfamiliar ideas. Similarly, Extract 3 shows data from a doctor's surgery, in which metaphor is used as the doctor explains his proposed treatment to a patient with a urinary infection.[2]

Extract 3   Doctor explains the treatment to the patient

1   actually what's required is a behavioural approach
      to try and tackle that problem
      and re .. re-calibrate those messages in a way
      so that actually your brain re-acclimatises to only passing
5   only getting the message pass urine
      when the pressure volume is significant
      so it actually is quite an uncomfortable process to go through
      we call it bladder drill

The doctor uses metaphor, such as _drill_ and _messages_, to mediate medical jargon for the patient. I found widespread use of this 'sub-technical metaphor' in the classroom, where teachers, like doctors, need to explain technical ideas to non-experts.

Children may also use metaphor to help express ideas that they don't know the words for, e.g. _a fire engine in my tummy_ for a stomach ache (Winner, 1988, p. 90).

In addition to helping to express ideas, metaphor often has an affective role, concerned with emotions and relations between people. It is my contention that this is more important in discourse than is commonly realised. For instance, metaphor appears to be an important tool for creating 'insider' language of groups – not just medical metaphors and other professional discourses, but also in more peripheral groups in society, such as the slang used by prisoners e.g. _doing porridge_ (Cooper, 1986). In this role it seems that metaphor answers a human need for intimacy and social inclusion.

The affective role of metaphor is also evident in Extract 1 above, where the teacher faces the problem of telling pupils they are doing something wrong. This is potentially threatening both to face and to motivation, and in many such situations, metaphor seems to be used to help mitigate the threat, often by bringing humour into the interaction, as with the Charlie Chaplin example. An affective impact is sometimes created by the cumulative use of conventionalised and deliberate metaphor. In the classroom, repeated choices of metaphor Vehicles, together with other language features, created an affective climate of support and warmth between teacher and pupils. We see this in Extract 4, as the teacher opens a lesson:

Extract 4   Agenda management

1   now what I'm going to do (.) this afternoon (1.0)
     because I can't think of any other way to do it (1.0)
     is to <u>give</u> you <u>a little bit</u> of information (2.0)
     <u>on</u> which we can <u>build</u> (.) our understanding (1.0) of (.) rocks (4.0)
     …. .
5   so there are really two <u>things</u> we're going to <u>look at</u> (2.0) this half term

(Cameron, 2003, p. 127)

Notice how the potential challenges of learning and studying are reduced to _giving_ and _looking at_, and how knowledge becomes just _a little bit_ of _information_. Such metaphorically used lexis combines with the repeated use of plural pronouns _we, our_ (lines 4, 5), with adjectives like _little_ (line 3), and with humour, throughout the data. The overall impact is one of support and reduction of challenge and possible demands on pupils.

The limits of metaphor

The example of *give information* raises the question of where metaphor stops. Is there a non-metaphorical way of talking about this concept? Indeed, Lakoff and Turner raised the possibility that all or most of our language in use may involve metaphor (Lakoff and Turner, 1989, p. 119), and if we also include metaphorical extensions conventionalised at some point in history (an etymological perspective) this possibility becomes even more probable. Non-metaphorical conceptualisations are restricted to direct physical experience of the world. In the case of *give information*, there is no non-metaphorical conceptualisation available. The concept of *information* is metaphorically structured; through metaphor it is made concrete, divided into *bits* which can then be *given* or *exchanged* or *passed*. It is precisely this reliance on metaphor to talk about concepts such as information that is stressed by cognitive metaphor theory.

A category of metaphor so broad that it includes nearly everything would actually be of very little use in theory development or empirical investigation. The extent of metaphor remains an empirical issue to be investigated. An important current development in the field involves separating metaphor more rigorously from other examples of figurative language such as metonymy (Barcelona, 2003; Dirven and Pörings, 2002).

As explained in Reading A, metonymy involves replacing a word or expression by another that is semantically related to it, or where there is a logical relationship between the two terms.

Criticisms of cognitive metaphor theory

The examples of metaphor in language use demonstrate the power of cognitive explanations. However, examination of metaphor at work in discourse also raises some fundamental questions for cognitive metaphor theory.

Lakoff and Johnson's work leaves unexplained the connection between individual minds and conceptual metaphors evidenced in the language system. Their claims are generalised across a discourse community, and there is much still to be uncovered about how children develop metaphors of their communities as they grow up.

The role of culture in the development of conceptual metaphor has also largely been ignored by cognitive metaphor theory (Gibbs, 1999). While some metaphors may be universal because of shared physical characteristics, it seems likely that different cultures and languages may also produce different conceptual metaphors.

In using ideas from cognitive metaphor theory in the analysis of metaphor in discourse, we face the methodological problem of labelling conceptual metaphors (Cameron, 2003; Semino et al., 2004). Any set of connected linguistic metaphors can be given a label that looks like a conceptual metaphor, merely by encoding it in the form A IS B. However, there may be several Vehicle domains which fit the lexical evidence. The teacher in my data praised children's behaviour with:

you all <u>deserve a medal</u>.

This metaphorical phrase could equally well be described as arising from CLASSROOM ACTIVITY IS A COMPETITION or from CLASSROOM ACTIVITY IS WAR. It is important to note that these are *not* conceptual metaphors, which would require further evidence of linguistic metaphors that could be related to the same conceptual metaphor; rather, they are descriptors constructed by the analyst, or 'metaphoric conceptualisations' (Gibbs, 2002).

Prosaic and poetic use of metaphor

Finally, we come to the question of how poetic, creative use of metaphor relates to our prosaic, everyday uses. Lakoff and Turner suggest that:

> Poetic thought uses the mechanisms of everyday thought, but it extends them, elaborates them, and combines them in ways that go beyond the ordinary.

> (Lakoff and Turner, 1989, p. 67)

The developing field of cognitive poetics sets out to examine how this is done and to uncover writers' distinctive and unique conceptualisations of the world (Freeman, 2003). However, the cognitive focus may once again downplay the affective impact that metaphor can have when instantiated in language. When skill with conceptual 'mechanisms' is combined with skill in the use of the lexical and grammatical resources of the language, both the affective and cognitive potential of metaphor can be exploited to move, shock or de-familiarise readers.

Notes

1   This claim is reinforced by the problems that metaphorical use of language presents to autistic and socio-pragmatically disordered children (Frith, 1990; Hampshire, 1996).

2   The author would like to thank Celia Roberts of Kings College, London, and Director of the 'Patients with Limited English and Doctors in General Practice' (PLEDGE) project, who kindly provided the data in this extract.

References

BARCELONA, A. (ed.) (2003) *Metaphor and Metonymy at the Crossroads*, Berlin, Mouton de Gruyter.

BROOKE-ROSE, C. (1958) *A Grammar of Metaphor*, London, Secker and Warburg.

CAMERON, L. (1999) 'Identifying and describing metaphor in spoken discourse data', in L. CAMERON and G. LOW (eds) *Researching and Applying Metaphor*, Cambridge, Cambridge University Press.

CAMERON, L. (2003) *Metaphor in Educational Discourse*, London, Continuum.

CAMERON, L. and LOW, G. (2004) 'Figurative variation in episodes of educational talk and text', *European Journal of English Studies* **8**(3), pp. 355–73.

COOPER, D. (1986) *Metaphor*, Oxford, Blackwell.

CORTS, D. and POLLIO, H. (1999) 'Spontaneous production of figurative language and gesture in college lectures', *Metaphor and Symbol,* **14**(1), pp. 81–100.

DIRVEN, R. and PÖRINGS, R. (eds) (2002) *Metaphor and Metonymy in Comparison and Contrast*, Berlin, Mouton de Gruyter.

DREW, P. and HOLT, E. (1988) 'Complainable matters: The use of idiomatic expressions in making complaints', *Social Problems,* **35**(4), pp. 398–417.

FREEMAN, M. (2003) 'Poetry and the scope of metaphor: Toward a cognitive theory', in A. BARCELONA (ed.) *Metaphor and Metonymy at the Crossroads*, Berlin, Mouton de Gruyter.

FRITH, U. (1990) *Autism*, Oxford, Blackwell.

GIBBS, R.W. (1999) 'Taking metaphor out of our heads and putting it into the cultural world', in R.W. GIBBS and G. STEEN (eds) *Metaphor in Cognitive Linguistics*, Amsterdam, John Benjamins.

GIBBS, R.W. (2002) 'Psycholinguistic comments on metaphor identification', *Language and Literature,* **11**(1), pp. 78–84.

HAMPSHIRE, A. (1996) 'The development of sociolinguistic strategies: Implications for children with speech and language impairments', *Current Issues in Language and Society,* **3**(1), pp. 91–4.

LAKOFF, G. and JOHNSON, M. (1980) *Metaphors We Live by*, Chicago, University of Chicago Press.

LAKOFF, G. and TURNER, M. (1989) *More than Cool Reason: A Field Guide to Poetic Metaphor*, Chicago, IL, University of Chicago Press.

McCARTHY, M. (1988) 'Some vocabulary patterns in conversation', in R. CARTER and M. McCARTHY (eds) *Vocabulary and Language Teaching*, London, Longman.

SEMINO, E., HEYWOOD, J. and SHORT, M. (2004) 'Methodological problems in the analysis of metaphors in a corpus of conversations about cancer', Journal of Pragmatics **36**(7), pp. 1271–94.

WINNER, E. (1988) *The Point of Words: Children's Understanding of Metaphor and Irony*, Cambridge, MA, Harvard Press.

Source: commissioned for this volume.

Telling stories

Michael Toolan

2.1 Introduction

One of my favourite examples of the power and ubiquity of narrative or story is a fragment written by the postmodern American writer, Leonard Michaels. The fragment purports to be a telephone conversation between a mother and her grown-up son. The son says 'Guess what happened', and the mother replies 'Oh my God'. And that is all we are given; end of text. But from it we can project a whole story; as indeed the mother seems to have done. She does so because the son's utterance invokes the essence of a story and storytelling: something important has happened and he is going to tell her about it.

Narrative or **story** (I shall use the two terms as equivalent and interchangeable) is a 'core' structuring form, found in major literary genres, such as novels and short stories, folk tales, fairy tales and epics, as well as in other art forms, both verbal and non-verbal, such as pictures and film, ballet and mime, etc. It is also, however, pervasive and routine in our interactions with others. Stories large and small appear all the time in conversation, like vegetables popping to the surface in a boiling soup. They are also frequent in a multiplicity of other language activities, from formal speeches to science textbooks to job interviews to medical appointments. While often associated with literary activity, storytelling is in fact a core way of structuring, representing, and making sense of the countless things we do.

We use narratives to capture and encapsulate two connected scenes or situations: (a) a state, and (b) a significant change of that state. In any narrative there are always *implicit* at least two connected scenes, even if the earlier scene has to be inferred or reconstructed from the depiction of the later one. A slightly fuller characterisation of narrative might be:

> A narrative is an account of a sequence of events that are perceived to be non-randomly connected, typically involving one or more humans or other sentient participants, these being the experiencing individuals at the centre of events; there is always a point to narratives – we human addressees can learn something from the experiences of others.

In conversational storytelling, most commonly we tell stories about ourselves, those close to us, those we value for one reason or another, and those whose experiences we find instructive. We use stories to entertain each other, to explain ourselves to others and to ourselves, to distance ourselves from some people (usually physically absent) and to get closer to others (in a spirit of rapport, solidarity, and friendship). Thus storytelling is directly connected to our making and remaking of our identity and our relationships.

Rarely are conversational stories the bare and objective facts about some connected events. They are often highly constructed, with 'artful' uses of language – clever phrasing, word play, irony and exaggeration – and a certain degree of performance. They are also fashioned and arranged, selecting (emphasising or downplaying) certain events and representing these from a particular or partial perspective. In all these ways, everyday storytelling can be seen as a creative activity.

In this chapter I shall look at a range of spoken narratives, with a focus on their creative potential. Some of these have been elicited from informants, but most occur more routinely in interaction with others. I shall look first at the formal properties of narratives, or how they are conventionally structured. I shall then consider interactional functions of narratives – and particularly how they are drawn on to construct particular types of identity and relations between people. Finally, I shall consider how narratives represent our experiences, and how they are embedded in particular cultural understandings.

2.2 How spoken narratives work

The most natural and commonest narratives are those we produce orally (or in Sign), without need of any technology, about ourselves and our associates, in the course of everyday conversation. When a participant in a conversation tells a story, they take or claim more time, and talk at greater length, than is usual in the symmetrical back-and-forth of casual talk. The telling may not be uninterrupted monologue – there may well be 'backchanneling' (brief reactive comments from addressees, such as *yeah, really?, right, um hmm, hmm, wow* ....) and questions seeking elaboration or clarification from co-conversationalists *(where was this?, so did you have to pay?)*. But all parties seem to be aware that one speaker is 'holding the floor'.

When it comes to describing the structure of spoken narratives, it is worth emphasising plurality: that in reality a range of related structures, rather than one inflexible template, needs to be recognised. But in what follows I shall present and treat the structure proposed by the sociolinguist William Labov as capturing much that is typical of a 'fully verbalised' oral narrative of personal experience, since several of the variant structures can be seen as abridged or compressed alternatives to it.

When Labov sought to elicit interesting stories from alienated African American young men in the 1960s, he was canny enough to realise that asking them, individually, whether there had ever been an occasion on which they feared for their life was a good way of spiking their interest and getting them talking. Below is one of the typical 'fight narratives' he collected, in the black vernacular style of south-central Harlem, told by a young man called 'Boot'.

Boot's story

Note: the terms to the left of the narrative are explained further below.

Orientation	1	It was on a Sunday
		and we didn't have nothin' to do after I – after we came from church
		Then we ain't had nothin' to do.
Complicating action		So I say, 'Calvin, let's go get our – out our dirty clothes on and play in the dirt.'
	5	And so Calvin say, 'Let's have a rock – a rock war.'
		And I say, 'All right.'
		So Calvin had a rock.
Orientation		And we as – you know, here go a wall
		and a far away here go a wall.
Complicating action (lines 10–24)	10	Calvin th'ew a rock.
		I was lookin' and – uh –
		And Calvin th'ew a rock
		It oh – it almost hit me.
		And so I looked down to get another rock;
	15	Say 'Ssh!'
		An' it pass me.
		I say, 'Calvin, I'm bust your head for that!'
		Calvin stuck his head out.
		I th'ew the rock
	20	An' the rock went up,
		I mean – went up –
		came down
		an' say [slap!]
		an' smacked him in the head
Resolution	25	an' his head busted.

(Adapted from Labov, 1972, pp. 355–6)

The first thing Labov emphasises is that conversational personal narratives tend to report actions or events strictly in the order in which the events occurred. In Boot's story there is no departure from this principle – we are literally given a blow-by-blow account. This constraint on the telling-sequence is also a powerful resource, because it means that only material in the discourse that contributes to the unrolling of events is fully 'narrative' material, reporting the most basic action sequence. By the same token all material that does not unequivocally advance the story can be understood to be performing other supporting functions. For Labov the crucial supporting functions are scene setting and evaluation. Thus, near the opening of the story, Boot tells us about the siting of two walls ('here go a wall and a far away here go a wall'). Clearly, this background information does not report on events or actions but rather is of value for setting the scene; Labov calls this 'orientation'. And near the end of the story we are told about the sound of the rock hitting Calvin's head ('say [slap!]'); again this is not an event, and especially not an event that precedes the next narrative clause telling us the rock 'smacked him in the head'. The 'say [slap!]' clause is an evaluative dramatisation of that following narrative clause, a kind of commentary on the event. In fact, four distinct lines separate Boot throwing the rock and the rock smacking Calvin in the head, and all four contribute to the evaluative 'slow-motion' postponement of the outcome.

One of Labov's key claims is that oral narratives of personal experience can have up to six basic parts:

1 **Abstract**: What, in a nutshell, is this story about?
2 **Orientation**: Who was involved, when and where was this, what *had* happened or *was* happen*ing* (in the way of ongoing background)?
3 **Complicating action**: What new thing happened and then what happened after this (recurring)?
4 **Evaluation**: So what? How or why is this interesting?
5 **Resolution**: So what was the final thing that happened?
6 **Coda**: How does this story 'connect' with the speaker, or all of us, here and now?

Not all of the above six elements appear in every conversational narrative, and many narratives do without one or more element without being in any way incomplete. In fact there is some evidence that the question of whether or not all six elements appear, and the degree or extent of each of these elements, varies in different situations and different cultures. Still, it's a useful structure to begin making comparisons with, and thinking about what is most central to stories.

In the stories Labov analysed, the one obligatory element is the complicating action (a report of something having happened). Least required, and frequently absent, are the two, usually smaller, sections that top and tail stories, the abstract (often a pre-story 'trailer' of what is to come) and the coda (a conversational 'bridge' back to the present conversational situation of the teller and addressee, or a summing-up of the 'moral', of what the incident taught the teller).

Five of the six elements tend to appear in narratives in the sequence given above. While the sixth, evaluation, tends to be most noticeable at the 'high point', before a story reaches its resolution, it can in fact emerge anywhere in the course of a story, or be spread throughout it. This reflects just how crucial an ingredient evaluation is. Despite the 'So what? How or why is this interesting?' questions above, there is no one specific question that evaluation addresses. Instead, it is a rich array of turns of phrase, verbal and non-verbal elaborations, which can be thought of as added to the barest form of a narrative, and used by the teller to add to the interest of the story – to make the story seem all the more worth telling and hearing. As noted above, evaluative material is often particularly clustered around the 'hinge' or climactic point of the action, just before – and in effect delaying – the resolving action or event. Evaluation is also, crucially, all the ways in which the teller's personal stake in a story is conveyed.

In Boot's story, as shown above, the first three lines are orientation (also often called 'setting'), telling us who is in this story, and roughly when and where and even why (*nothin' to do*) it happened. Orientation may tell you what was happening in a general way, but once a story turns to what *specifically* happened then you have entered the complicating action section. So the complicating action section begins with Boot's dialogue with Calvin in lines 4–7. There is then a brief further two lines of new orientation, about two walls, and then the complicating action resumes with Calvin throwing a rock (*stone* in British English). The rest of the telling is of complicating action, except the final line, which if it really was 'what finally happened', is the resolution. As for evaluation or evaluative material, this occurs in lines where some dramatising of or departure from factual reporting takes place, for instance: when Boot says a rock *almost hit me* (it didn't; but just think: it might have), when he 'performs' the sound of the rock whizzing past his head, *Say 'Ssh!'*, and when he tells us more about the rock he threw: *I mean – went up – ... an' say [slap!]*. All of these additions to the complicating action contribute to the interest of the story.

ACTIVITY 1   **Analysing narrative: Alison's story**

Allow
10–15 minutes

Below is another narrative, an account of a car crash told by a woman named Alison. Look at the first 39 lines (down to 'it was completely...'), which arguably contain a first full narrative. Try to identify those parts of the narrative which seem to be the orientation, complicating action and resolution components. The narrative also contains elements of evaluation, which I shall return to below.

Alison's story

1   OK erm my boyfriend and I were in a car we were travelling er to, erm, from Manchester to visit my parents in Yorkshire because they were there on holiday in a cottage. Erm we set off quite early in the morning and er it'd been raining and we were ... we'd made a really

5   good journey even though it'd been raining there wasn't that much traffic erm we then got along the country lanes because in Yorkshire there're quite a few of those, and we were probably about four miles erm from the cottage, and er we were coming along and er and we came over the brow of the hill, we weren't

10   going fast. Ben slowed down and erm and the brakes weren't working they kinda didn't respond and so we were kinda coming over this hill and er and sort of gradually starting to skid and (y'know) the rain hadn't helped either that had definitely made the brakes start to lock and as we came over the brow of the hill it was

15   then that we realised it went a sharp <u>left</u> so we were like [laughing intonation] coming over this hill not too fast but fast enough for it to be amazingly scary erm and he pressed the brakes again and we started to skid and I'll never forget the unbelievable screech as as we started to like move towards the right of the road and there was

20   a massive sort of erm err stone wall that we were heading towards and I've [laughing intonation] never been so scared in my life, I have no idea how he managed to control the car erm cos the way it's completely foul but er we ended up mounting this huge sort of verge that led up towards the towards the wall erm and I the wall

25   must have been like I don't know a couple of centimetres away from the car door and er we sort of mounted it and we were pretty tipped and I remember thinking then we're gonna turn over we are <u>gonna</u> turn over there's just no way that we're gonna come through this an' erm but it'd all happened so quickly and [cough] the next

30   thing I know with oh the massive <u>thud</u> as we went over something on the verge and came back down off the verge again there was steam pouring out of the bonnet and he managed to pull us over right to the left hand side steam billowing you've never seen two people get out of a car faster, we just pegged [laughing intonation]

35   it out of the car thinking well we don't y'know don't know if it's going to explode or whatever so, got out of the car and and er and oh my heart was racing and I mean thank goodness there was no cars coming in the opposite direction there was no pedestrians it was completely ... but then about a couple of minutes later a

40   woman came in the opposite direction, pulled over, stopped, asked if we need any help erm and er and she said well y'know I can take you to the nearest village or whatever erm or I can take you to your <u>parents</u> because we were literally like four miles away we were so close and em <u>yeah</u> so she waited while I phoned the AA y'know

45   I was absolutely hysterical erm and erm and we looked back over
      at what had happened and we later found out that the other side
      of the wall was a massive waterfall and if we'd gone through it we
      would have been quite certainly <u>dead</u> [nervous laugh] erm because
      it was it's like a beautiful landmark in Yorkshire and we nearly like
50   plonked a <u>car</u> right in it so erm yeah.

Note: Underlining here denotes emphasis or stress in the teller's delivery.

Comment

There is abundant orientation material in Alison's opening lines (lines 1–9): we are told who the main two participants are, where they are (in a car, in Yorkshire), what they are doing in general terms (travelling, visiting her parents), when the events happened (early morning). As Alison gets more involved in the telling of her story, she gets more orientationally specific and location is given more precisely (*we were probably about four miles erm from the cottage*, lines 7–8). Crucial new orientation is added later in the narrative where needed (e.g. *there was a massive sort of erm err stone wall that we were heading towards*, lines 19–20).

Complicating action, the sense of a 'new' action that breaks out of the less interesting routine of 'what we were doing', begins in earnest at about the point when Alison says *we came over the brow of the hill* (line 9). But deciding where the complicating action begins depends in part on our own narrative 'antennae', our own sense of when 'complications' begin to set in. Note that *we came over the brow of the hill* is not the first past tense action clause in the text (there is *we set off* in line 3, for example), but it is the first narrative clause that I interpret as introducing a disturbance of the ongoing routine. Similarly, there may be a degree of judgement and potential variation as to where a listener decides that the complicating actions have concluded and the resolution, 'what finally happened', is being told. Here, the resolution is from lines 34–5 *we just pegged it out of the car* (*pegged it* meaning 'ran'), later repeated (*got out of the car*).
So, in summary, the components of the narrative are:

Abstract: missing (I shall return to this below).
Orientation: mainly in the first eight lines.
Complicating action: begins with *we came over the brow of the hill … Ben slowed down.*
Resolution: *We just pegged [laughing intonation] it out of the car … got out of the car.*

I mentioned earlier that evaluation is different from the categories we have looked at so far in that it is spread throughout the story. Labov identified several different types of evaluation. Sometimes a narrator stands outside the flow of the narrative to give an evaluation (e.g. *and this is really sad*, or *I couldn't stop laughing*). Labov terms this 'external evaluation'. But, following Labov, analysts have paid much more attention to the kinds of evaluation that he calls internal (they are 'internal' in being fully inside the story, in fact usually inside the sentences that report the narrative actions). 'Internal evaluation' covers all kinds of highlighting and texturing devices, which can be thought of as *added* to the bare telling of the narrative clauses.

Labov distinguished different types of internal evaluation, of which perhaps the most obvious are 'intensifiers'. As the name suggests, these serve to intensify or emphasise aspects of the story. They include 'paralinguistic' features such as loudness, tone of voice, lengthening vowels (e.g. a speaker saying *He talked soooo slowly*); repetition; modifiers such as *quite heavy* or *really fast*. Other types of evaluation include 'modal' expressions that indicate degrees of uncertainty – e.g. *He wanted to kiss her* (but *did* he?), *Perhaps she had left it in the café* (but *had* she?); and statements of reason or cause – e.g. *I sat down in the nearest chair, because I couldn't move another step*.

ACTIVITY 2 Evaluation in Alison's story

Allow about
10 minutes

In Alison's story, can you identify examples of external and internal evaluation? In the case of internal evaluation, I suggest you focus on intensifiers.

Comment

There are several examples of external evaluation, for instance in lines 21–22: *I've [laughing intonation] never been so scared in my life, I have no idea how he managed to control the car...* Notice that Alison has switched out of the past tense of telling, to the present tense, to record what even today she thinks about Ben's controlling the car.

In terms of internal evaluation, there is a great deal of repetition that emphasises important points in the narrative action, intensifies the feeling of danger, etc. Particularly striking are the several times we are told about the car coming over the brow of the hill, of how they weren't going fast, and how the brakes failed to work. Soon after there is a similar repetitive telling about the wall they are sliding towards, and Alison's fear that *we're gonna turn over*. Later there is 'steam pouring', 'steam billowing' and several other examples.

Expressions such as *amazingly scary, the unbelievable screech, massive (stone wall), huge (verge)* also function as intensifiers.

Evident in the spoken version, though not in the transcript above, were paralinguistic features such as stress or emphasis. You had to have been at Alison's telling to experience it fully; but there were rich differences, alongside the repetition, in the way Alison said *we're gonna turn over we are gonna turn over*; there was panicked emphasis on the turning over, first time around, and very different emphasis on the certainty of this happening, in the repetition.

Conversational stories may begin with an abstract – for example, 'I finally got rid of Rusty Bernstein' (from a personal narrative about selling a very old Austin Maestro car). So why is there no abstract in Alison's story? The explanation is quite simple (and quite similar to Boot's situation, in the earlier story). Alison produced this story in class, in response to my enquiry whether any of the students present had recently been involved in a life-threatening experience. So her story was invited, or elicited, and in effect I had provided an abstract, parts of which were implicit rather than explicit: 'OK everybody, please pay attention, because Alison is going to tell us about something that happened to her, when she feared for her life'. It's worth emphasising that I didn't use the word *story* when asking the students to tell about a life-threatening incident; I asked Alison to tell what happened, and this emerged in story form. The story format is something we seem unconsciously but unerringly to opt for, when producing all kinds of extended answers, responses, explanations – even descriptions.

While there is no abstract, there may well be a coda, if we take into account the final part of Alison's account (line 39 *but then about a couple of minutes later* to the end). We saw earlier that *we just pegged it ...* was the Resolution of the first 39-line story, and that if Alison had stopped talking at that point there would be nothing further to note. But here Alison continues by telling us about the arrival of a woman motorist. Since we have found a number of narrative parts in the passage up to line 39, it is reasonable to treat this subsequent section as a second linked narrative with its own complicating action and some of the other elements too (its own resolution would be *she waited while I phoned the AA*). In the last few lines of this second narrative we get what amounts to a coda, more for the first story than the second: *if we'd gone through [the wall] we would have been quite certainly dead... we nearly like plonked a car right in it* [this beautiful Yorkshire landmark].

All these observations about the proficiency with which Alison structures her story and weaves evaluation into it are a way of acknowledging the art and design of everyday storytelling and everyday conversation. Art and creativity are not always demonstrated by originality of phrasing; sometimes the art lies in recycling a phrase familiar to us from a different genre or context. Consider Alison's phrase *we set off quite early in the morning*. In how many other oral stories and folktales has that phrase been used! As a result it may come to us (depending on our cultural background) laden with connotations (of expedition or adventure, sense of purpose, the fresh start, etc.). This creative calling up of other stories – along with the inventive reformulations, repetitions, selection of 'intensifying' words and expressions and the rhythmic drive of the long 'sentence' of complicating action – is part of the artful use of language in narrative.

2.3 Functions of conversational stories: art, affiliation, and identity

Despite our detailed scrutiny of structures and forms in Alison's story, some questions that are often very important to story addressees have yet to be asked, to do with why a story is told, and what multiple effects it and its telling may have on both the teller and the addressees. These questions warrant multiple answers.

We cannot ignore the fact that you will have derived some kind of impression of Alison, some mental picture of her. Her gender is declared, but what of her age, nationality, appearance, voice quality, her general temperament, her mood at the specific time at which she tells her narrative, her lifestyle? What sorts of things in the text prompt you to say she probably has some characteristics and not others? Can you *prove* she is not 80 years old, or Brazilian, or hearing impaired?

Tellers *may* disclose their mood fairly explicitly, and they may explicitly *tell* an addressee, during their story, what they regard as important to their **identity**. But there will often be *implicit* indications of identity and mood, which are best teased out by contemplating a contrastive identity for the teller with a contrastive wording of the story. For example, a man who begins his narrative with 'I was doing the weekly shopping with my teenage kids' is arguably implying and performing his identity as a middle-aged parent (and perhaps that of 'responsible parent' too!). If you postulate some contrastive identities for the speaker (elderly male, or male aged 20), the given wording is at best implausible. But judgements of what is plausible do very much depend on the analyst having insider knowledge of the culture to which the narrative belongs.

Somewhat related to questions of identity are ones about the general purposes behind the telling of a narrative. This is a larger issue than identifying the specific coda of a story, which is the moral or relevance of the story just told to the conversation now being resumed. This is a matter of the underlying picture of the teller, their co-participants in the narrative, and their listeners, that a narrative conveys or implies. It is the background representation of the teller and their world that is projected.

I think that in the 'car crash' story Alison does a lot of verbal work, to tell herself and her audience of fellow students (plus one tutor) that she is female, heterosexual, middle-class but not 'posh' (posh people don't say *pegged it*), 'ordinary', vulnerable, more lucky than unlucky (as we might all like to be), ordinary enough to be scared, terrified, in a car crash – but spirited enough to be able to be lighthearted about it afterwards. Her storytelling in part says: 'this is the kind of person I believe I am and, if you like some of these qualities then we may be kin'. It also undoubtedly says to the tutor: 'I know how to tell a danger of death story and thereby perform well in the seminar'.

And the very fact that Alison felt the incident was worth telling hints that she does feel she has been slightly changed by it: that she is a little bit more aware than beforehand that bad things can happen to you 'out of the blue' in ways that cannot be avoided, that disasters can threaten you in ways where it is luck or fate, as much as your wits and skill, that determines how much damage you suffer. Arguably, too, this narrative attests to a small but real change, or wished-for change, in Alison's identity, into someone a little more aware that disaster can be just a bend in the road away and a little more cherishing of the good health and youth that (her story implies) she currently enjoys.

Whenever we meet a narrative in the course of a conversation, then, we may spend as much effort inspecting and interpreting the teller as we do in examining their tale: we may notice their voice, their gaze, their gestures, how they move their body, and how all this becomes a kind of running commentary, intertwined with the running commentary provided by all the evaluative material in the language of the narrative. But the running commentary is as much on themselves, on what kind of person they are, as it is on the story they are relating. This is in parallel with what we meet in literary narratives, such as novels and short stories. The act and way of telling can prompt us to pay as much attention to the character or identity of the narrator as to the story itself. Often, though not always, it seems crucial to ask not just whether the narrator is reliable or not (a standard literary critical suspicion), but whether they are male or female, of one nationality or cultural background rather than another, optimist or cynic, and so on.

In the foregoing I have touched on clues to or signs of self-presentation and identity construction that can be teased out of any narrative occasion, the better to understand not merely the teller or the story participants, but the addressee as well. Scholars from many disciplines (but perhaps especially psychology and education) have offered accounts of the place of narratives in our sense of our selves and our identities. As one example of a study of the role of narratives in social interaction, the first reading looks at stories told about familiar events, in family settings, where those stories are clearly not being told for the first time.

ACTIVITY 3   Twice-told tales (Reading A)

Please now turn to Reading A, Extracts from 'Twice-told tales: collaborative narration of familiar stories' by Neal Norrick. In this reading, Norrick discusses the narration of 'old' stories, familiar to most if not all those present. On the face of it, this may seem an odd practice: why recount something that people already know? Norrick shows how such stories may get told for purposes of very 'local' identity construction: to build rapport, and to show shared values. Norrick's discussion of the stories emphasises the subtle, moment-by-moment, negotiation that may go on.

As you read, think about the form of the stories analysed by Norrick. Take the first story, 'Tipsy', as an example: how does this differ from Boot's and Alison's stories?

Turning to the functions of the stories, how does Norrick suggest they build rapport and shared values?

Comment

Unlike Boot's and Alison's stories, the 'Tipsy' story is not a single extended speaking turn. It is woven into the fabric of a family conversation. There is something like an initial orientation (*her and Vance were just great together ... they were really good*), and an account of a series of actions (going to the hairdresser, having a drink, walking out tipsy), but Norrick comments that the narrative does not conform strictly to Labov's model, illustrated in Boot's and Alison's stories:

- The actions do not always occur in temporal order (after Jean's *You walk out of there you're half tipsy*, Annie's *You were under the dryers* jumps back and adds detail to the wine drinking, and the drinking and walking out tipsy actions are then recycled).

- Nor does this narrative contain simple past tense clauses (as in Alison's *We came over the brow of a hill, Ben slowed down*, etc.). Because it is concerned with familiar and repeated actions, it uses forms such as the *two of us would go, he'd be pouring wine, we used to go there*.

- Particularly striking is the fact that this is not a solo telling. While Jean is the main narrator, Annie is a 'co-teller' and it is the point she sees in the story (following the hairdresser around) that is eventually agreed.

On the functions of the stories, Norrick sees the act of co-narration, with joint recollection of shared experiences, as building rapport and shared group identity. This occurs also in the second pair of stories, in which two daughters-in-law (one quite new) are building rapport – are performing a degree of identification – with their in-laws; and *vice versa*. All involved do this indirectly, by the way they tell and receive the familiar, previously told, previously heard, stories that they share.

It does not follow that all in-family re-tellings of the familiar are rapport-building in the way Norrick suggests. In the case of Norrick's 'Darned dish towels' and 'Rubber wallets' stories, we need to ask whether it is the act of re-telling a story, in front of a borderline insider/outsider (here, the daughter-in-law, Sherry), that fosters rapport and 'membership'; or whether it is actually the response to such a story, including the response to its content (e.g. by the marginal member hearing the story with approval, and following it with a story of their own with parallel content) that affirms rapport. You might also think about whether you can imagine situations of family interaction where old narratives are re-told in which the teller may not care about building rapport and common ground, or may even appear to be actively asserting differences. It may be unsurprising that the bleakest of these scenarios (e.g. where couples or siblings 'rake over' old grievances by re-telling old stories against each other in front of embarrassed outsiders) are less often recorded by analysts and paraded in published sociolinguistic research. But there are plenty of intermediate cases between such entrenchedly hostile re-tellings and the highly face-attentive cooperative re-tellings Norrick analyses. Conversations involving teasing, flirting, embarrassing, or praising, to name just a few, may also draw on re-telling of familiar stories with goals that are a complex mixture of rapport and distancing, identification and acknowledgement of difference. What does seem to unite all such re-tellings is a focus on interpersonal relations, affect or affiliation, and just how each participant's self or identity 'stands' in comparison with that of other participants.

ACTIVITY 4 Zelda's story

Allow
5–10 minutes

Below is another story about a mother-in-law/daughter-in-law relationship, collected from the mother-in-law (Zelda), and taken from Deborah Schiffrin's 1996 article 'Narrative as self-portrait: Sociolinguistic constructions of identity'. Like Norrick, Schiffrin (1996, p. 167) believes our narrative texts provide 'a resource for the display of self and identity'. As you read through Zelda's story, try to decide what it is really about, and how this relates to Zelda's sense of identity.

Zelda's story

1	DEBBY:	What does your uh daughter-in-law call you?
2	ZELDA:	Well, that's a sore [spot.
	DEBBY:	[hhhh
3	ZELDA:	My <u>older</u> daughter-in-law does call me Mom. =
	DEBBY:	Uh huh.
4	Zelda:	= My <u>younger</u> daughter-in-law right now is up to nothing.
5		She ⌈ had said-
	DEBBY:	⌊ Oh
6	ZELDA:	We had quite a discussion about it.
7		We did bring it out in the open.
8		She said that um ... that she – just – right now, she's: – it'll take her time.
9		Now they're marrie:d, it's gonna be uh ... I think eh ... five years, =
	DEBBY:	Uhm hmm.
10	ZELDA:	= that they'll be married.

11		And she said that eh it was very hard t's: – call someone else Mom beside her mother.
12		So I had said to her, 'That's okay!'
13		I said, 'If you – if you can't say Mom, just call me by my [first name!
	DEBBY:	[Umhm
14	ZELDA:	So, we had quite a discussion about it.
15		It was a little heated ⌐ at one time. =
	DEBBY:	Yeh
16	ZELDA:	She said, 'All right,' she'll call me Zelda.
17		But she still can't bring herself to say Zelda,
18		so she calls me nothing!

(Adapted from Schiffrin, 1996, p. 181)

Comment

It is possible that wherever identity and self are constructed through personal narrative, words and ideas that have to do with being the same or different ('like me/us/you/them' or 'not like me/us/you/them') will be at least implicit if not explicit. One moment in the story where Zelda talks about things being the same or different comes when she reports that her older daughter-in-law calls her *Mom* while her younger one calls her nothing. That daughter-in-law is reported explaining that she finds it hard to call Zelda by the same name she calls her biological mother, *Mom*. Zelda then indicates that for the younger woman to first-name her would be better, would be 'closer' to or more like the preferred *Mom*, than nothing. Finally, what the daughter-in-law *says* she'll do (call her *Zelda*) remains different from what she actually does so far.

Identity is rooted nowhere more deeply than in how we prefer to be named. This isn't a matter of 'one name for all occasions' of course, but will obviously depend on who the namer is, and will also vary from context to context. But everyone likes to think they know how they themselves should be named (to third parties) and directly addressed, including Zelda. So the daughter-in-law's reluctance can be doubly threatening: it challenges either Zelda's knowledge or her preference. To name is to characterise and to propose an identity: the daughter-in-law saying *Mom* proposes 'As a first priority in our relative identities, you are my Mom and I am your daughter'; while Zelda, suggesting to her other daughter-in-law that she use Zelda's first name, proposes 'Primarily, our relative identities are such that I name you just as your close friends (but not your children) name you and I expect you to first-name me in return: we are, or are like, close friends'; avoiding any name, on the other hand, amounts to saying 'I am currently not resolved on affirming that you are my mother or that you are my close friend ... our relative identities, for me, are still uncertain'. Schiffrin suggests that the daughter-in-law's resistance over naming is 'the threat posed by someone who has already become an "insider" ... but refuses [in naming behaviour] to act like one' (Schiffrin, 1996, p. 181). Furthermore, in calling her mother-in-law by no name, the daughter creates what Schiffrin calls 'a symbolic vacuum' (1996, p. 190). Can you think of other personal narratives where a teller reports a protagonist's behaviour in such a way that the behaviour can be regarded as 'troublesome', because it creates or implies a naming problem or naming 'gap'?

2.4 Stories as representations of experience

I mentioned earlier (Section 2.1) that narratives were not simply factual accounts of events, but that they were highly constructed, and that in this sense they could be seen as creative. Section 2.2 showed some of this construction at work, in the way narrators organise their stories and also use evaluation to indicate the point of the story – why it was worth telling. Section 2.3 showed how narratives can make and remake aspects of identity – again, a creative practice. In all these ways, narratives can be seen as representations of experience; in telling stories narrators necessarily represent themselves, others, and the events they narrate, in certain ways. This is more obviously the case in narrative fiction, where writers weave a story, construct a plot and people it with characters. But in conversational stories too narrators have to select certain events and portray people and events in certain ways. This is not to suggest that conversational narratives are fictions or fabrications, but that they always and necessarily present certain versions of events.

Evaluation, in Labov's sense of the term, is an important part of this process: both internal evaluation (i.e. evaluation woven into the core narrative clauses) and external evaluation (where the narrator steps outside the flow of the narrative to give an evaluation). A further type of evaluation that I have not mentioned so far is 'embedded evaluation'. This occurs where a sentiment is expressed by a character in the narrative, as when a character is directly quoted (e.g. *She said 'Come over here!'*). **Speech representation** plays an important part in literary narration, where dialogue allows readers to infer something about the characters and their perspectives on events. Something similar occurs when people's speech is quoted in conversational narratives.

ACTIVITY 5   **Direct speech in narratives**

Allow
10–15 minutes

Look back at some of the narratives you've already studied in this chapter. What use do they make of direct speech? How does it seem to contribute towards evaluation in the story?

Comment

Several narratives contain elements of reported speech. Boot, for instance, when Calvin scores a near miss with his rock, doesn't just say he wanted to bust Calvin's head: he cites himself calling out at the time: 'Calvin, I'm bust your head for that!' There is no direct speech in Alison's story, but she does report her thoughts: 'we're gonna turn over we are <u>gonna</u> turn over'. I mentioned the different ways these repeated words were uttered, conveying first Alison's panic and then her certainty the car would overturn. Zelda reports herself telling her daughter-in-law: 'If you – if you can't say Mom, just call me by my first name!' Jean, in Reading A, quotes her hairdresser: 'Want some wine girls?', and Sherry quotes Elizabeth: 'Did you see a really good price Mom?' Protagonists in the story are not simply talked about, they are also animated and given a voice. This is evaluative in that it adds to the interest and the 'point' of the story. In citing his own speech, Boot conveys his anger, and perhaps his bravado. Jean conveys her hairdresser's conviviality directly, in what she reports as his own words. Elizabeth, cited by Sherry, points up her mother's thriftiness.

The next reading extends our discussion of narrative as representation. Mary Bock has studied narratives given as testimony to the South African Truth and Reconciliation Commission (TRC), set up in 1995 to help people come to terms with the violence and human rights abuses that had taken place under apartheid. The commission investigated these abuses, provided support to survivors of them and heard applications for amnesty. In such a context it might seem that truth would be paramount, but Bock notes that the commission was required to hear the perspectives of both victims and perpetrators of abuse and recognised it would be unlikely to arrive at 'a single, uncontested version of events'.

ACTIVITY 6   Telling truths (Reading B)

In Reading B, Mary Bock examines just one of the tragic episodes that the TRC investigated. She presents and discusses the testimony of two key witnesses (a journalist, Chris Bateman and a police officer, Thapelo Mbelo) to the killing of seven activists in the township of Guguletu in March 1986.

As you read, consider how the two narratives differ, and how Bock relates these differences to the differing perspectives of the two witnesses. How does each man represent the events of March 3rd, and how do they represent themselves as narrators?

Consider also Bock's approach to the analysis: how does she draw on the different frameworks of Labov and of Gee? How convincing do you find her analysis?

Comment

These are clearly very different narratives, told by a journalist reporting on the killings and a police officer who was directly involved and shot one of the men. Bock notes that Bateman brought an 'outsider' perspective as a journalist. There is an 'overarching' narrative – Bateman's search for a story – as well as the narratives he reports from others, which give details of the killings. Internal and external evaluation in Bateman's story show how he viewed the evidence he was given (the use of *in fact* to contrast expected and actual police behaviour, stepping outside the narrative to comment on the similarity of the accounts). On the basis of her analysis, Bock suggests Bateman represents himself as a reliable observer, 'striving for accuracy appropriate to the formal nature of the hearing and his reputation as a journalist'. Mbelo has an insider perspective as a participant in the events, but Bock also comments on his ambivalent position – involved at the time but (at least ten years on and in this context) displaying some sympathy for the activists. Mbelo draws out a contrast between black and white police officers, distancing himself from the white officers and representing himself as obeying orders.

Bock draws on Labov's narrative structure, but follows Gee in dividing the narratives into stanzas. She uses Labov's notion of evaluation in identifying narrators' perspectives, alongside Gee's notion of themes ('thematic echoes') that run through the narratives. I found the analysis convincing, and Bock's way of transcribing and representing the narratives useful – in the case of Bateman's narrative, grouping the transcription into stanzas highlights the structure of the overarching narrative as well as the existence of internal 'mini-narratives' that can be analysed in their own terms. Note, however, that this is clearly an interpretative overlay rather than something unquestionably embedded in the teller's talk. Such framings are an inescapable part of transcription; a transcript without stanzas would be a different framing, not the absence of any.

Bock's reading shows how the commission proceeded by allowing witnesses to tell their narratives freely, without interruption or challenge. The rationale seems to have been that in the contentious circumstances, in which every account could be expected to be denied and re-told by those it implicated and where society-wide revenge on all those directly or indirectly implicated in apartheid-era crimes was felt to be neither feasible nor desirable, a positive outcome could be achieved simply by the state-underwritten hearing of victims' narratives. Narrative is a powerful mechanism for grieving over past tragedies, and the TRC used narration in enterprising but not uncontroversial ways to help people to grieve, acknowledge, and bring closure. At the same time, the truth and the reconciliation facilitated by the commission were partial rather than full in the specific sense that, whatever truth was exposed, it lacked the accompanying force of legal sanction (including prosecution, and possible redress or punishment through a criminal justice system).

In a more general sense, the point made at the beginning of this section about narratives as variant representations should remind us that 'closure', like the truth, the facts, always turns out to be local and temporary rather than absolute: every story can be re-opened, with the facts amended or seen and interpreted differently, creating a different and more truthful and satisfying account. But most of those involved seemed to recognise that expecting more from a commission would be to expect the impossible. Public narratives can be very effective for achieving some kind of 'release' from past injustices and enduring bitternesses. They rehearse what happened, what people experienced, but do so within clearly defined frames: these include the narrative frame itself and the frame of the commission's structured meetings, even the physical setting of the commission's hearings. The events and injustices become framed material from which, over time, victims and perpetrators can detach themselves and move on.

2.5 Stories, mind and culture

The idea of stories as representations of experience suggests that stories can be not simply tales of people and events *found* by the teller, but representations of people and events *made* by the teller. We see the world in large degree by means of the narratives we make and find and share – especially those which in one way or another we *assent* to. Chapter 1 discussed the ideas of certain cognitive linguists who have emphasised that there are deep, basic conceptual metaphors in our languages that 'we live by', in that they give sense-making shape to much of the way we talk about love, emotions, death, and so on. This is perhaps most true where we think of life as a state. Whenever we think of life as a process, as something sure to change, with possibilities of both advance and setback, then attention to the narratives we live by becomes even more salient.

Numerous scholars in many humanistic disciplines have shown how conversational narratives have a variety of articulating, socialising, diagnostic, disciplinary, and pleasurable functions (examples include Goffman, 1981; Tannen, 1988; Bruner, 1991; Wolfson, 1982; Polanyi, 1985; Mischler, 1999; Hall, 1992; Harré, 1998). Philosophers and scientists too, especially those with any interests in cognition and consciousness, seem increasingly to acknowledge the centrality of storytelling to what we refer to as mind, intelligence, and self-understanding (e.g. Damasio, 2000; Schank, 1995; Dennett, 1991). In the final reading of this chapter, extracted from Rukmini Bhaya Nair's book *Narrative Gravity: Conversation, Cognition, Culture*, the idea that humans tell stories as naturally and instinctively as beavers build dams or spiders webs is explored in some of its richness. Like the cognitive

These points clearly chime with the discussion in Chapter 1 of metaphor, and the reading from Guy Cook on the centrality of language play.

scientist Daniel Dennett (whom she invokes and responds to) Bhaya Nair is keenly aware of how *foundational* storytelling is to being human. My own view is that storytelling or narrativising may be the key species-distinctive thing we do, the chief means by which we adapt and change, over the course of our own lifetime and as a species across the millennia. Here Bhaya Nair underlines the universal centrality of storytelling to mind, intelligence and self-understanding, suggesting that our mental model of stories must include rules of inferencing to make full cultural sense of the narratives we encounter.

In Reading C, Bhaya Nair shows that two types of inferencing are involved if an addressee is to 'get' a story (or joke, or tall tale, or riddle) fully, as a cultural insider. There are general and basic principles of inferencing such as those proposed by the philosopher Paul Grice as underlying our interpretations of conversation (see the box below on **conversational implicature**). But we additionally draw on rich networks of cultural assumptions – **impliculture**, as Bhaya Nair dubs it – without which we wouldn't see the point, get the joke or feel the resonance of very many of our everyday stories.

Conversational implicature

Since the 1970s a few simple but powerful ideas proposed by the philosopher Paul Grice (1975) have been widely acknowledged as identifying some essential features of conversation. Firstly, conversationalists seem predisposed to cooperate, to make their response to another's contribution appropriate and helpful: Grice termed this the 'cooperative principle'. Speakers do this by attending to four 'maxims', *provided all other things permit this* – an important caveat. These are known as the maxims of Quality ('be truthful'), Quantity ('be adequately informative': say neither too much nor too little), Relation ('be relevant'), and Manner ('be brief and orderly'). The 'all other things permitting' qualification is important, because in many conversational situations we may want to depart from the bald, brief reply – as perhaps when a friend asks us what we think of their expensive and, to us, hideous new outfit.

Metaphorical remarks, irony, understatement, white lies, patently oblique or tangential replies all seem to disregard Grice's cooperative conversational maxims. However, they are better seen not as disregard for the maxims but as creative exploitations of them: the addressee knows that the speaker knows that they aren't conforming to the Quantity (or Relation, etc.) maxim straightforwardly, and the addressee can then figure out what the speaker means, by being indirect in that way. For instance, if A says to B 'Do you want to see that new film?' and B responds 'Mike's in London this evening', the response does not seem relevant – it flouts the 'Relation' maxim' – but it's likely that A will be able to draw on knowledge of B's circumstances to understand the response, say that Mike is B's partner who would normally look after their children but can't that evening. So, not *directly* observing one or more of the conversational maxims itself triggers some inferencing by the addressee. Grice called such maxim-based inferences 'conversational implicatures'.

ACTIVITY 7   The short, short story and the tall, tall tale (Reading C)

Now read the abridged extract from Rukmini Bhaya Nair's book *Narrative Gravity*, entitled *Implicature and impliculture in the short, short story and the tall, tall tale*. Bhaya Nair first discusses some really short (one line long) stories, before discussing the work of another scholar, Bauman, on tall stories. Bauman's stories are told by US coon (i.e. raccoon) hunters – an example is given below, after the activity. Note that both the short stories and the tall tales differ from the narratives of personal experience discussed in earlier sections in that, though told in conversation, they are fictions, or fabrications.

*   As you read Bhaya Nair's arguments, focus initially on why she regards the 'tiger' story as richer than the 'birds' one.

*   On Bauman's tall stories, consider what may be seen as the point of these stories – why they are not just lies, or bragging, or male stupidity.

*   Bhaya Nair ends the discussion by rehearsing a death-bed tall story told in the film *Fried Green Tomatoes at the Whistle Stop Café*. What in your own view might be the point of that story? And in what respects might the context of the 'frozen lake' story make it unlike typical tall tales?

Comment

This reading covers a number of topics, the central theme of which is the importance of in-group or insider cultural knowledge for a full grasp of the Labovian *point* of so many of the narratives we tell each other. Cultural knowledge is what prevents our stories seeming absurd or irrelevant.

*   Bhaya Nair argues that the common interpretation that the tiger ate the hunter can be explained by Grice's maxims, but that to understand why some people find the story amusing we need to appeal to cultural knowledge. In some cultures, brevity itself is regarded as witty; the story is also a type of ironic 'biter-bit' story; and it looks rather like a riddle, which we gain pleasure from solving. It is this culturally based inferencing that Bhaya Nair terms 'impliculture'. This cultural argument also suggests, of course, that not everyone will find the story amusing in this way.

- When she turns to Bauman's explanation of the tall story, Bhaya Nair suggests such stories need to be interpreted in terms of a particular cultural tradition. In tales that take this form, in this context, lying is socially sanctioned but the tales are more than lying – there is continuity with tales told by generations of hunters, the tales contribute to 'identity building' and are 'part of the fundamental ethos of sociability'.

- As for the fable told by Idgie to her dying friend in the film *Fried Green Tomatoes*, some may wonder whether the whole scenario is itself a tall story, on the grounds that telling any story when someone is dying may seem inappropriate. But then the fantastic and ritualistic aspect of prayers frequently resorted to in such circumstances might be cited as in some ways parallel. In any event we might suspect that death-bed tall stories are told for the benefit of the survivors, onlookers, witnesses, which in the case of *Fried Green Tomatoes* importantly comprise both the within-film teller, Idgie, and the film audience. They are the ones who need the consolation of the lake-shifting parable, something to shore up against their loss.

The 'frozen lake' story is most sharply atypical as a tall tale in that it is told to someone close to death. It is hard to think of a setting more unlike the norm of tall tale telling, which tends to be good ol' boys sitting around the campfire or bar after a good day's hunting, shooting the breeze, killing time, etc. Other contrasts include the fact that this is an all-female setting, intimate, interior, and the tale explicitly requested (rather than spontaneously delivered, as a bid for recognition and affiliation).

In light of Bhaya Nair and Bauman's observations about the palpable untruth of tall tales, we may be drawn to think that all narratives are tall tales and all tall tales are lies. But we can certainly distinguish the sheer fictional Indian rope-trickery of narrative lying ('moral lying', if you will, undertaken with no intent to deceive or aggrandise self at others' expense), from the petty, destructive, unimaginative falsehoods of immoral lies.

Although not explicit in the reading, Bhaya Nair's analysis suggests, I think, that the cultural-embeddedness of our narratives may prevent us from getting too lazy about our own culture, too passive: whenever stories challenge us (without defeating us, leaving us 'utterly baffled') as to their point or relevance, perhaps a kind of cognitive/cultural toning up or keeping fit goes on. One might add that Gricean conversational implicatures, found in all conversations regardless of culture, also contribute to our mental sharpness; and Bhaya Nair emphasises that these always play a role. But they are only part of the story, lacking cultural specificity. It is the cultural inferences we have to make in our telling and receiving of stories that for Bhaya Nair most enable the survival and evolution of our cultures.

A traditional 'coon hunting' story

The following story was recorded in Texas in 1973:

> This ol' boy, he had him a coon dog. He had him a little coon [hide-] stretcher, looked like a piece of wire, V-shaped. He'd bring it out of the house, he had that coon dog, and it'd go out in the woods, kill him a coon, bring it back to the house, and all that boy had to do was just skin that coon out, put on that stretcher and skin. He was doing that for about two or three years, and was plum proud of his dog, and everything, and was telling everybody in town how good that dog was.
>
> One day his mama told him to take the ironing board outside to fix it; there was something wrong with it. That dog seen that ironing board and that dog hadn't showed up yet.

(Bauman, 1986, p. 19)

This story may not make sense to you on first reading. It concerns a man who shows his dog a skin-stretching board. The dog goes off hunting and brings back a raccoon just the size of the board. One day, the man's mother puts her ironing board outside (much larger than a raccoon skin). The dog goes off and never returns. How you interpret the story will depend on cultural understandings about raccoons and raccoon hunting; the nature of this kind of story; and perhaps your own views on hunting.

With Bhaya Nair's reading we have palpably returned from the detail of Labovian formal analysis to recognising anew that narrative is a valued coping and enabling strategy for all humankind. Narratives are lamps as well as mirrors, not merely representations of one's self and identity but explanatory representations of the world – of what is the case, and how things are. Bhaya Nair suggests that stories may be seen as 'memes', passing on cultural ideas and understandings, and also that they are 'central to [our] being', helping to produce a unified sense of self. She reminds us, however, that our selves are as fragile and fabricated as the narratives we make and devour (as tender as hunter's meat, perhaps); and you can't hatch fledglings without breaking eggs.

2.6 Conclusion

In this chapter I have introduced a Labovian analysis of narratives of personal experience, highlighting how such conversational stories recurrently fit an implicit structure – with orientation, complicating action, and resolution as formally and semantically distinct core elements – over which evaluation material is laid so as to dramatise and intensify the story, underlining its point or tellability. We have seen that stories need not be new and that they may have a range of interactional functions, such as affirming shared values or solidarity (Norrick). We have also seen that any storytelling involves representing matters in one set of ways rather than another, with entities named one way and not another, and with some things commented on while others are passed over in silence. As a result, a telling can always be related to the teller's sense of self, identity and values (Schiffrin, Bock). But who is fit to judge those identity and value statements?, Bhaya Nair reminds us. If you are not a member of the particular culture from which a story emerges, you should be careful not to assume you fully grasp a story's resonances. Besides filling in a story's verbal gaps ('implicature'), we need to know its explanatory cultural background ('impliculture'), so culturally deep that it may get lost in translation.

In terms of the distinction made in Chapter 1 between textual and contextual approaches to the study of creativity in language, Labov's analysis is textual, looking at narrative structure, or the formal properties of stories. Bock draws on Labov, pointing to the complex structures of the stories she analyses, but she also takes a more contextual approach, looking at the perspectives of different narrators and how these are shaped by social and political contexts. Norrick and Schiffrin consider how stories are told and how they may be understood in particular family settings. Bhaya Nair extends the notion of context to take into account the broader relationship between narrative and culture.

I have suggested that storytelling is a core human activity. Narrative creativity is not the reserve of an elite cadre of inspired poets but something we all participate in, to a greater or lesser degree, in our everyday interactions. And I would add that we do so not – or not simply – because such linguistic creativity can be 'fun', an entertaining supplement to the core message, but rather because we have to, it being in our nature. Creative language use is deep at the core of our language uses and is not just an exceptional decoration; it is a means by which we adjust and adapt to changing circumstances, meet new challenges and needs, and make renewed sense of our lives.

READING A: Extracts from 'Twice-told tales: collaborative narration of familiar stories'

Neal R. Norrick

Narratives have a range of interactional functions. In these extracts, Norrick focuses on the role of family narratives in demonstrating group membership, or belonging, and conveying shared values.

Narration as ratification of group membership

Within the nuclear family [...] participation in co-narration [often] seems [...] concerned with demonstrating membership, i.e. with belonging in the family. Falk (1980) shows how couples display for others their joint participation in past events through co-narration in carefully orchestrated 'duets'. Cederborg and Aronsson, 1994, see disagreement about facts as accusation in family therapy sessions; but in my data, the disagreements disappear as family members allow each other to refresh their memories of details. Co-narration ratifies family membership and values not just *de jure* by birth, but de-facto by producing shared memories, feelings, and values. Children gain full family membership to the degree that they can contribute to family co-narration in appropriate ways. Grandparents, aunts and uncles, cousins, etc. may participate as family members in the retelling of some stories familiar to them, though they are excluded from others involving only the nuclear family. [...]

The first passage [below] illustrates a fairly common practice whereby group members relate recurrent shared past experiences in generalized form, without reference to any specific instance. Instead of pure past tense clauses in temporal order, as required by Labov's definition of narrative, these generalized collaborative exchanges thrive on verb phrases with *would* and *would be -ing*, along with *used to* forms. Explicit 1st person *we* pronouns frequently give way to 2nd person *you* with general reference. This passage provides a typical example in which participants recount a recurrent experience they had with a particular hairdresser [called Vance]. Annie and Jean are cousins in their late 20s or early 30s; Helen is Annie's mother and Jean's aunt. All three have lived in close proximity their whole lives, so that they may be said to form a loose family group. They are gathered before a late-afternoon Thanksgiving dinner in the living room of the house where Annie and Helen live.

Tipsy

ANNIE: And I always thought that her and Vance just were great
           [together]

JEAN: [Yeah.] Used to [get s–]

HELEN: [They were both] good.

ANNIE: Yeah. They were really good.

JEAN: You could go over there around the holidays and get <u>smashed</u> before you left [the place.]

HELEN: [Oh yeah.]

JEAN: We used to have the last appointment, right?
            Remember, the two of us would go?

ANNIE: Yeah, yeah.

JEAN: "Want some wine girls?"
            "Sure we'll have a glass of wine."
            You walk out of there you're half <u>tipsy</u>

ANNIE: You were under the <u>dryers</u>.

JEAN: Well sure. And he'd be pouring the wine and we were tipsy by the time we walked out of that place.

ANNIE: Then he moved all the way out at Rand Road.

JEAN: Near the town show, remember?

ANNIE: Yeah.

JEAN: [We went there.]

ANNIE: [We used to go there.] And then we went on to Union Road, when he was there.

JEAN: Yeah. Yeah. We followed him around.

Transcription conventions (adapted from Norrick):

She's out.	Full stop indicates falling tone.
Oh yeah?	Question mark shows rising tone.
nine, ten,	Comma indicates level, continuing intonation.
<u>damn</u>	Underlining shows heavy stress.
bu- but	A single dash indicates a cut-off.
[at all] [I just]	Aligned square brackets indicate simultaneous speech.
says 'Oh'	Quotation marks indicate speaker is quoting someone.
{sigh}	Braces enclose editorial comments and untranscribable elements.

Here again we find many of the same devices characterizing the exchange as a recollection of shared past experience. Jean initiates the co-telling with an ostensible request for confirmation, in the tag question 'We used to have the last appointment, right?' But she does not pause long for a reply, and receives none; so the question stands simply as a marker of shared background knowledge. Then, with 'Remember, the two of us would go?' Jean explicitly seeks testimony from Annie, who this time complies with 'Yeah, yeah'. Jean again questions Annie with 'remember?' later in the exchange, again receiving a positive 'yeah' in return. Jean's 'Well sure,' in response to Annie's 'You were under the <u>dry</u>ers,' and Annie's near repetition of Jean's 'We went there' as 'We used to go there,' are instances of checking details and coordinating accounts of the shared experience. All these markers of shared experience count as evidence of group membership.

Co-telling is quite prevalent, though Jean clearly remains the primary narrator. Helen confirms Jean's basic point about drinking at the hairdresser's at the outset, with 'Oh yeah'; and Annie not only confirms Jean's claims, but adds the salient detail about being 'under the dryers' as well. But Annie's co-telling veers off in the direction of telling what happened to Vance and his partner; this suggests another point about collaborative family tales, namely that disagreements during co-narration tend to arise especially about the point of the story. From Jean's perspective, the story focuses on the availability, consumption, and effects of alcohol at the hairdresser's; but Annie is far more concerned with Vance as a good hairdresser, and how the cousins followed him as he moved around. Jean comes around to this point of view in the end, agreeing with Annie and summarizing the story in line with her interpretation: 'Yeah. Yeah. We followed him around.' This final agreement about the point of the narration caps off an interaction already filled with signals of shared group identity and high rapport.

Narration to convey shared values

[...] Family members, as defined loosely or tightly by their social roles, may jockey for insider status in the course of an interaction. Of course, nuclear family members themselves sometimes tussle over the right to co-tell a story or to summarize its point; but the demonstration of membership goes beyond shared F-events for co-narration, to the demonstration of shared values. Even non-family members can gain a degree of acceptance by espousing values dear to the family; this is accomplished most expeditiously by constructing stories from one's own past which parallel those told in the family to which one seeks admission. Thus a person who cannot participate in co-telling a story familiar to group members can at least tell a story like it, which repeats its action and reiterates its values. This strategy becomes especially obvious in cases where daughters- or sons-in-law have entered a family by marriage, but so far share few F-events as a basis for co-narration. For such marginal family members who feel they are on temporary probation, displaying shared values is of special importance.

The following examples from a single setting demonstrate how family stories can serve to define characteristic family values vis-á-vis outsiders. In particular, the matriarch Lydia stands for frugality, which she learned from her mother and grandmother, namely the 'Grandma Imhof' described as 'the stingy one' by Lydia's husband, Frank. Although they laugh about

'F-events' are events shared by members of a family.

frugality and claim to have been embarrassed by the frugal habits of their parents, all the family members tacitly endorse it as a primary (family) virtue, as documented variously by my recorded material. Ned and Brandon, as sons of Lydia and Frank, have imbibed frugality, as it were; their respective spouses, Claire and Sherry, have to establish their in-group status through demonstrations of frugal behavior and, of course, appropriate stories. Sherry is particularly eager to confirm her family membership, since she has more recently married into the family, and comes from a background less obviously frugal than does Claire. The conversations take place at the home of Ned and Claire, where the others are visiting over the Thanksgiving weekend; in both, most of the participants remain seated at the dining room table, while Claire and Brandon move between the dining room and the adjacent kitchen.

Darned dish towels

FRANK: Grandma Imhof, she was the stingy one.

NED: Claire has <u>darned</u> dish towels.

FRANK: <u>Her</u> mother did it. Sure.

LYDIA: Well see I said if you grew up in a house where your mother [patched washcloths].

NED: [Remember darning, Sherry?]

SHERRY: I was going– "What are <u>darned</u> dish towels."

NED: Well. It's when you don't want to say <u>damn</u> dish towels. {General laughter} Don't you call that process darning?

LYDIA: But my mother just put them under the sewing machine and took two washcloths and made one. And <u>patched</u> the middle of a washcloth when it was worn out.

NED: Your mother didn't invent that huh huh huh.

LYDIA: And I said when you grow up like <u>that</u> it's hard to get with this world that throws things away.

CLAIRE: {arriving} Here are darned dish towels.

SHERRY: Huhhuh <u>darned</u> dish towels.

LYDIA: But were you ever embarrassed, Claire? When you invited <u>friends</u> to your house, did you ever have to be embarrassed? I was embarrassed when the girls from town came. {Laughter from Sherry, Brandon, and others}

NED: Our mother was embarrassed?

LYDIA: And saw <u>my</u> mother's patched washcloths. I tried to hide them really fast. {Sherry and Lydia in two-party conversation from here on}

SHERRY: We had a – my mom always had like a dish cloth that had holes
           in it? And I always still get holes in them before I throw them
           away. And he's like going, 'Don't you think we need a new dish
           towel?' And she always had an old <u>green</u> pad that she used to
           scrub the pans with. And we always called it that ratty green pad.
           And so in my mind it's <u>supposed</u> to be like really awful and ratty.
           Before you throw it away huhhahaha. And once a year I buy two
           new dish cloths whether I need them or not hehehe.

LYDIA: Khuh khuhhuh.

The whole family has gotten onto the topic of frugality – or stinginess, as
Frank insists on calling it – which suggests for Ned the example of darning
dish towels from his wife's family, and for Lydia her own mother's patching
washcloths. Then, in the midst of talk about darning dish towels, Lydia pieces
together her story about her mother's patched washcloths. Although Lydia
narrates through laughter and Ned's snide comments, her story elicits no real
co-telling, since it relates purely A-events; in particular, it focuses on Lydia's
own embarrassment and attempt to hide the offending washcloths when 'the
girls from town' came and saw them. Apparently not just thrift itself, but
suffering embarrassment for it from outsiders, assumes importance for Lydia.
Although Lydia declares her embarrassment about her mother's thrifty habits
in such a way as to elicit laughter from her listeners, it is clear from what she
has said before how she values frugality. It is also clear that 'the girls from
town' represent the rejected wasteful attitudes to which Lydia cannot get
accustomed.

'A-events' are
events known only
to the primary
storyteller.

It is most certainly clear to Sherry, who immediately seeks to paint herself
in Lydia's colors by constructing a parallel 'second story' [...]. Sherry's second
story corresponds to Lydia's original in multiple ways. First, it casts Sherry in
the same role as a daughter to a frugal mother. Sherry initially begins her
story with 'We had a –'; then she backtracks and self-corrects, placing
her mother up front with 'My mom always had ...' Then the story shows her
taking over her mother's thrifty habits – despite objections from her husband,
Lydia's son. Finally it lets her, like Lydia, express a sort of laughing
embarrassment, though she wisely eschews mention of a particular outsider
group like 'the girls from town.' Note especially the final, partially formulaic
statement that she buys new dish cloths 'whether I need them or not' – with
accompanying laughter, which Lydia echoes. This degree of congruency
between a second story and its original model [demonstrates] shared
attitudes. This is precisely what we expect in the sort of family story at
issue here.

Lydia's story about Sherry then leads into another 'frugal' story which
Sherry tells on herself, after prompting by husband Brandon. There follows
a truncated narrative which connects with our foregoing consideration
of collaboratively constructed narratives, and brings this investigation to
a close.

Rubber wallets

FRANK: We don't tear out coupons.

BRANDON: I think you've got to enjoy the process.

FRANK: We don't.

BRANDON: I don't,

FRANK: So:

BRANDON: She does. She's religious about it.

SHERRY: What, hon. {just tuning in to this conversation}

BRANDON: Coupons.

LYDIA: How I know she's the coupon lady. I've told the cute story about Elizabeth saying when her mom's ready to go out to the store, 'Got the coupons Mom?' I thought that was the cutest thing I'd ever heard.

BRANDON: Did you hear the one the other day? Tell the one about you in the grocery store Sher.

SHERRY: I was – I saw this new yogurt. That had only fifty calories. And you know they have the Yoplait that's a hundred and fifty, and the other is ninety, and Weightwatchers has a ninety calorie one – this one was fifty calories and I just looked at it and I went – Wow. And Elizabeth said, 'What. Did you see a really good price Mom?' Huh huh huh huh [huh huh huh huh.]

LYDIA: [Isn't that embarrassing] ha ha ha ha.

SHERRY: Huh heh heh. And I – I just started laughing and laughing. And I hugged her. And she was saying, 'Well, was it? Was it?' Said "No honey, I"

LYDIA: Maybe you'll have the joy of having your children tell you what I've had them say to me about my uh rubber wallets? And their scrounging cheap mother. I've been told that often. So I hope it happens to you too.

BRANDON: Rubber wallets?

LYDIA: Henry still today kids me about rubber wallets.

NED: I don't remember.

LYDIA: I wouldn't buy the boys little leather wallets when they were little. And he calls them rubber,

SHERRY: Hehheh.

LYDIA: Because he thinks his mother's such a terrible cheapskate.

BRANDON: Henry?

LYDIA:	Oh yes. He never lets me forget that. (h)Rubber (h)wallets huh huh huh huh.
NED:	Hehhehheh.
LYDIA:	And I know the exact little wallet he's talking about. I can <u>see</u> it as if it were yesterday.

Conclusion

Consideration of twice-told tales, of narrative events built around stories already familiar to the participants, offers a special perspective on conversational storytelling, because it emphasizes those aspects of narration beyond information, problem-solving, etc. In particular, we have seen that the retelling of familiar stories has three important functions, and all may co-exist in the same narrative event, though one function often dominates a whole narrative or a whole section of it. First, we retell stories to foster group rapport; second, we co-narrate familiar stories to ratify group membership; and third, we retell stories which reveal group values. Further, listeners unable to participate in the co-narration of group stories respond with parallel stories of their own which portray shared values.

We have seen that retelling can serve an informing function even when a story is known to the participants: both the primary teller and the others often gain insight into the events related through the dynamic give-and-take of co-narration. Retelling a particular story or type of story helps to coalesce group perspectives and values. Further, co-narration modulates rapport in multiple ways – first because it allows participants to re-live pleasant common experiences, second because it confirms the long-term bond they share, and third because the experience of collaborative narration itself redounds to feelings of belonging. The focus here, on narrative events in which the exchange of information counts for little, highlights the other functions that narration fulfils in group interaction.

References

CEDERBORG, A.-C. and ARONSSON, K. (1994) 'Conarration and voice in family therapy', *Text*, **14**, pp. 345–70.

FALK, J. (1980) 'The conversational duet', *Berkeley Linguistics Society*, **6**, pp. 507–14.

Source: NORRICK, N. R. (1997) ***Language in Society,*** **26(2), pp. 199–220.**

READING B: Telling truths: perspectives on a human rights violation

Mary Bock

The Truth and Reconciliation Commission recognised the value of narrative as a means towards fulfilling its mandated objective to write the South African national narrative of the preceding 30-odd years.[1] This task included uncovering factual details, as told by both perpetrators and victims,[2] about the gross human rights abuses that had taken place in the country during the years of the apartheid government; and promoting healing through inviting formerly voiceless people of the nation to tell their stories and receive public acknowledgement of their suffering. Aware that the hearing of multiple perspectives made it unlikely that they would be able to establish a single, uncontested version of events, the Commissioners describe themselves as working with 'four notions of truth': these are 'factual or forensic truth' that can be corroborated; 'personal or narrative truth', that is, the truth of individuals' experiences; 'social' or 'dialogue truth', to be reached through discussion and debate; and 'healing or restorative truth' that comes from acknowledgement of the pain of the teller (TRC Report, 1, pp. 110–14).

The narratives analysed in this article are about an incident that took place on 3 March 1986, when seven young activists were (ambushed and) shot by security policemen in Guguletu, a township on the outskirts of Cape Town. The story of the 'Guguletu Seven', as it came to be known, deeply shocking when it occurred, and dogged by unresolved questions about what really happened, was retold at both a Human Rights Violations (HRV) Hearing held by the TRC in November 1996 and an Amnesty Hearing in November 1997.[3] The narrators are a white journalist, Chris Bateman, who reported on the event for the *Cape Times* (4 March 1986) and later testified at the HRV hearing, and Thapelo Mbelo, a black former member of the special branch of the then South African Police (SAP), who was involved in the shootout and decided to apply to the TRC for amnesty.[4] Testifiers before the TRC were invited to speak in the language of their choice,[5] and Mbelo testified at the Amnesty hearing in his mother tongue, Setswana. However, he gave an account of his part in the event in English to the producer of a documentary film, *The Guguletu Seven*, made in 2000. This is the version that I analyse.

Approach to the analysis

Although both narrators are in agreement on core details of the central event, there are differences in their ways of telling it. Their stories are not opposing versions but rather counterpoints of an insider and an outsider perspective, both given at more than a ten-year remove from the actual event, and both versions raise questions about representation and truth-telling. In the analysis that follows, I ask the following questions of the texts: What are the recurring themes that suggest the main preoccupations of the narrators? What do their narratives tell us about their perspectives on the events they describe and about how they see themselves in relation to those events and to society? What characteristics, if any, do these narratives share? In what ways might they be seen to contribute to the search for truth and reconciliation?

In answering these questions, I have drawn principally on the work of Labov and Waletsky (1967), Labov (1972) and Gee (1991, 1997, 1999). These theorists focus on both structural and microlinguistic features of narrative, while emphasising that narrative should not be considered apart from the social and cultural contexts of its use. Labov's work is valuable particularly for his classification of the elements of narrative structure and his rich account of the syntactic markers of evaluation (1972). Gee's starting-point is that the structure of a narrative, which can be revealed by analysis of the text into lines, stanzas and parts, is an indication of the narrator's way of ordering and making sense of experience. Dividing the narrative in this way reveals the patterns of repetition and contrast which, he argues, indicate recurring themes and preoccupations of the narrator. He calls these patterns 'thematised echoes' (1997).

Textual analysis: (1) Chris Bateman's narrative

Chris Bateman's articles on the front page of the *Cape Times* of 4 March 1986 (see Figures 1 and 2 on pp. 95–6) broke the story of the killing of the seven Guguletu activists and uncovered discrepancies between the version given by the police and those of other witnesses.

Here, the TRC Commissioner asks Bateman, 'whether you would like to tell us your experience – what happened and what you can recall from the incident that happened 3rd of March 1986.' In the following extract Bateman describes what happened after he arrived at the scene of the event and failed to get information from the police officers present.

Transcription conventions:

The slight differences in the marking of each text are due to differences in the data. The first extract retains the original (TRC) transcriber's punctuation, which appears approximately to indicate pauses. Narrative clauses are numbered in sequence. Clauses that are asides to do with remembering, or identifying witnesses, are in square brackets. Clauses that are reported speech (in which Bateman cites others) are indented.

Stanza 1 (Arrival at the scene) (Orientation)

1   The police lifted the cordon
2   and we were kept back.
3   They lifted the cordon
4   and they withdrew.
5   The crowd was fairly hostile, but peaceful

6   and I looked around

7   and the most obvious place to find eyewitnesses seemed to be in the Dairy Belle hostel,

8   because it was overlooking the actual scene,

Stanza 2 (The first witness, Mazonke's, version of events) (Complicating action)

9   So I went in. [I was reminded when, in spite I was testifying now, that]

10   in fact, I did speak to the security guy first

11   who pointed me to where I subsequently found Bowers Mazonke

12   who isn't here today.

13   And he gave me a version of events, about a shoot-out between the police and a group of men.

Stanza 3 (The second witness, Mtuthu's, version) (Complicating action)

14   And then I went upstairs, [as I remember,]

15   and in one of the dormitories – [and it was a while back, you have to forgive me for perhaps being imprecise]. [I think] it was Cecil Mtuthu who I saw first

16   and he described the tail-end of the shoot-out,

17   in which opposite the dormitory we were in, under a gum tree, the police had walked up to a guy – to one of the people they had shot

18   and had in fact fired a bullet into him.

19   While he was prostrate on the ground.

Stanza 4 (Version of third witness, General Sibaca) (Complicating action)

20   Then there was a separate incident

21   [and as I remember], this was General Sibaca who told me this –

22   that there was a guy who either came out from the bushes or was near the bushes on the other side of the road – [as I remember]

23   confronted him, [again I was reminded about the kneeing and the belly and the kicking beforehand. I had in fact forgotten that detail.]

24   And police had walked up to him

25   And the policeman opposite them, sort of turned around

26   and looked for some kind of confirmation

27   which he got from a – [I imagine] senior officer. [This is General's relation of events to me]

28   and he turned back around

29   and then shot this guy at virtual point blank range.

Stanza 5 (Bateman warns of the seriousness of the allegations) (Evaluation)

30 I was struck by the similarity of the versions between Bowers
    Mazonke who spoke about the gum tree incident and Cecil Mtuthu
    and General Sibaca..

31 And I remember saying to them, [I spoke in Xhosa to them or
    Xhosa/Zulu. I can speak first language Zulu]

32   that this is quite a serious offence.

33   'You realise what you are saying?

34   What you are saying has great implications.'

35 and they were adamant

36   that in fact this is what has happened.

Stanza 6 (The police version) (Resolution)

37 So, I went back to the office,

38 subsequently found out

39   that the policemen who were involved
            in the shooting were available and at,

40 and because we were getting nothing from Pretoria of any precision or
    detail, Bishop Lavis station, [as I remember,]

41 we went to a police station – [it may well have been Bishop Lavis,]

42 where I in fact interviewed the policemen who were involved in the
    actual shoot-out

43 and they gave me their version of events.

Stanza 7 (Editor's decision to run the two stories) (Resolution)

44 The editor that night, at conference, questioned me quite closely.

45 It was Tony Heard

46 and decided that we would run with the stories.

47 And we ran [as I remember]

48 across the strap – the top of the front page was – man with hands in
    air shot – gunned down – words of that effect.

49 And then the body of the paper – the lead story was in fact the version
    given by the policemen involved in the story.

As the above and the following text show, analysis of the narrative elements
may reveal a more complex structure than that extrapolated by Labov from his
'danger of death' stories. Bateman's testimony contains the principal elements
of narrative, as described by Labov, with an orientation, the setting (stanza 1),
a complicating action, hearing the different witnesses' accounts (Stanzas 2, 3, 4)
and resolution, arriving at the decision to run the story (Stanzas 6 and 7).

Evaluation occurs throughout, and especially in Stanza 5, where Bateman assesses the situation. However, analysis of this text suggests two storylines which run concurrently. The overarching narrative is the narrator's search for a story, told in the part of the text that is not indented, in clauses that have 'I', 'we' or the designation of one of the other speakers as grammatical subject, and often represent speech acts. The core details of the incident are told in the indented sections, in the represented speech of the witnesses. These sections form, in effect, a series of mini-narratives, subordinated within the frame of the overarching story. Stanza 4 is a good example of such a mini-narrative, with its own abstract (line 20), orientation (22) and complicating action (23–27) which reaches a climax, rather than resolution, in lines 28 and 29.

It is likely that the speaker, aware that he is appearing in his professional capacity, would want to present himself as a reliable observer, and this is reflected in the fairly low-key markers of evaluation: 'the means used by the narrator to indicate the point of the narrative' (Labov, 1972, p. 366). I will analyse Stanza 5 to show how he uses external, embedded and internal evaluation and what meanings they point to.

In line 30 Bateman comments, from outside the narrative frame of events, on his response to the witnesses' accounts: 'I was struck by the similarity of the versions'. There is an example of embedded evaluation in lines 33–4, where Bateman cites himself telling his informants their stories had 'great implications'. Internal evaluation is indicated by vocabulary choices in the body of narrative, such as 'serious' (32) and 'adamant' (35). It is implicitly expressed in the intensifier *quite* in 'quite a serious offence' (32). *In fact* in line 36 (as in line 18) is also used emphatically. Through the emphases a contrast is implied, though not made explicit, between how the police might be expected to act in such a situation and what actually took place. Similar contrasts are implied in Stanzas 3 and 4 in the accounts of the police actions of shooting one wounded man and another who had given himself up.

Two threads run through the narrative, binding it and creating the thematic echoes that Gee speaks about. One thread is composed of the clauses and phrases alluding to the narrator's act of remembering (lines 9, 14, 15, 21, 22, 27, 31, 40, 41, 47). These form a meta-narrative which comments on the act of reconstructing the story. They remind the listener constantly of the immediate context: that Bateman is recalling the story more than ten years after the event and that he is striving for the accuracy appropriate to the formal nature of the hearing and his reputation as a journalist. The other thread is provided by the phrases in lines 13, 16, 21, 27 and 43 referring to the telling of the different versions, which occur like a refrain throughout the piece and reiterate a constant theme. This theme, the gathering of different versions, is given a marked twist in stanza 6, when he hears the significantly different police version.

Together these patterns – the layering of the narrative, evaluation and the thematised echoes – work to foreground the narrator's main concerns. These concerns are to represent in the overarching narrative the drama

Cape Times

FOUNDED 1876   TUESDAY, MARCH 4, 1986   40c (36c p

Man with hands in air shot — witness

By CHRIS BATEMAN

Witnesses to the tail-end of yesterday's shooting claimed that at least one suspected guerilla was shot and killed by police after attempting to give himself up.

They also claimed that another suspect lying wounded on the ground was "finished off " by the police squad.

The witnesses, all of whom willingly gave their names to the Cape Times, are residents at a dairy company boarding hostel which overlooks the street where the gunfight took place.

One witness said he was downstairs when he suddenly heard "explosions and gunfire". He had run to a window to see a man lying on the pavement across the road from him.

"One policeman just walked up to him and shot him in the head", he said.

A second boarder said that he had rushed outside to see people running. One man had his hands raised above his head when shots were fired and he collapsed, he said.

The witness claimed one shot hit the man in the head while others struck him in the legs.

A third witness said he saw police grab a man, take a pistol from the suspect's belt and then knee him in the stomach before punching him to the ground.

"A policeman some distance away said that they should shoot him. They then fired three shots into him with a rifle", he claimed.

The witness said a number of the suspects ran into the bush, firing back at the police with handguns. Police followed the suspects over a little rise and returned later carrying a plastic bag and a briefcase.

• A copy of the witnesses' allegations was telexed to police headquarters in Pretoria early last night and another copy handed to local police.

A police spokesman, Lieutenant Attle Laubscher, said last night that the police denied the allegations and rejected them "with the contempt they deserve".

• A 29-year-old resident of Montana who lives about 1 km from the bridge at the entrance to Guguletu said he heard "a very heavy explosion" about 7.30 am.

The man, who did not want to be identified, said he heard automatic-weapon fire about half a second before the explosion, "then a considerable amount of automatic rifle fire for 30 to 40 seconds".

"For the next five minutes or so there was sporadic firing which died away to single shots. About five to 10 minutes later police vehicles closed off the entrance to Guguletu.

"By the time I left for work there was a police Casspir and police at the bridge turning some people back."

Figure 1   The first version of Chris Bateman's story, as it appeared in the Cape Times (see overleaf too).

of the investigation, and indicate his and his editor's willingness to push the boundaries of the restrictive press legislation in order to uncover and publicise the conflicting stories. The accounts embedded in the witnesses' represented words highlight the nature of the events both by the repetition and the contrast with the version offered by the police.

(2) Thapelo Mbelo's narrative

While Chris Bateman appears to be making a relatively straightforward contribution to the overall aims of the TRC, Mbelo's position is more ambiguous. As a young, unemployed man, Mbelo was coopted into and trained by the Special Branch of the SAP. He and others in a similar position were used to combat resistance to the government, to infiltrate activist groups, to spy for the police and sometimes to foment unrest. He applied for amnesty before the TRC for his part in the Guguletu killings; and at the hearing he was faced by many opponents of the previous regime and the

7 die in battle with police

By CHRIS BATEMAN

Seven suspected urban guerillas were shot dead in a gunbattle with police in Guguletu early yesterday, seconds after being confronted by Peninsula Murder and Robbery Unit detectives on NY1.

Police inspect some of the weapons and ammunition recovered after the shootout in Guguletu yesterday. Permission had to be obtained from the police for this picture to be published.   Picture: Ivor Markham

Two policemen were slightly wounded, one after a hand-grenade was hurled at a police vehicle and another by wounded glass.

In what appeared to be a carefully planned police operation, the detectives confronted the suspects, about 7.20 am soon after they alighted from a stolen mini-bus.

Challenged by one detective who approached the group on foot with his sidearm drawn, one suspect suddenly produced a hand-grenade and threw it. It bounced off the front passenger door of the police car before exploding seconds later.

The suspects then fled in all directions and began firing with small arms and AK-47 assault rifles.

Explosion

The grenade thrower is believed to have been the first to die from a policeman's bullet.

Immediately after the grenade explosion, police special task force back-up vehicles drove up and a pitched gun-battle erupted lasting about five minutes, according to one source.

Sources said the stolen mini-bus drove back towards the group of suspects after the explosion in an apparent attempt to pick them up. However, police fire brought it to a standstill.

General Johan Coetsee, the Commissioner of Police, said yesterday that the ANC had planned an attack on a police vehicle in Cape Town and that "certain precautionary measures" had been taken.

According to one source the detectives who initiated the contact were "incredibly lucky" to escape with their lives.

The grenade which exploded had a 4.5 second delay, which enabled the police car to drive clear and the detective on foot to dive for cover, he said.

Splinters

The source said one of the guerillas had opened automatic fire on the detectives from behind a tree. However, one of the back-up force members had shot and killed him before the guerilla could find his target.

Another policeman in the back-up unit had an equally close shave. Bullets from a burst of AK-47 fire hit the magazine and muzzle of his rifle as he sat in his vehicle. Glass splinters flew into his eye.

Witnesses said some of the suspected guerillas fled over an open field towards thick bush, firing hand-guns over their shoulders at police.

At least one of these fugitives collapsed in the bushes, fatally wounded, they said.

Police followed the fugitives seconds later, disappearing over a small hill. They had returned several minutes afterwards carrying a plastic bag and a briefcase, the witnesses said.

By 10 am the entire battle area had been cordoned off by police and several Casspirs took up strategic positions.

Journalists were prevented from entering the area as police washed away blood from the road.

Senior policemen, including the Divisional Commissioner of the Western Cape, Brigadier Chris Swart, toured the scene.

Weapons confiscated by police are believed to include three AK-47 assault rifles, two hand-grenades. two Webley revolvers (.38 and .45) and a Tokarov pistol. A large quantity of AK-47 ammunition is also believed to have been recovered.

A pin which police claim was from the exploded grenade, was of South African manufacture.

Stoning

At 11.35 am, 15 minutes after police had left the area, about 75 youths – the remainder of a crowd of about 200 people who had been watching the police – gathered outside the hostel next to which the original incident had taken place. They began stoning a truck.

Minutes later a police car sped down NY1 towards the Guguletu police station, two policement firing several shots into the air from their service pistols. The youths fled, some shouting, "They are shooting at us, they are shooting at us."

The police car continued without stopping.

Figure 2   The second version of Chris Bateman's story, referred to by Bateman as the lead story, the version given by the police (see Stanza 7).

mothers of the slain activists. The extract below comes from an interview carried out for the documentary film *The Guguletu Seven*. Mbelo's narrative was told in a continuous chunk.

Transcription conventions:

As in extract 1, clauses are represented as numbered lines. Subordinate and other clauses that complete the main clause are included in the same line – e.g. 'then I recognised Jabu who was lying at the corner…'. Direct and indirect speech clauses are counted as part of the clause in which they are embedded because they do not contain mini-narratives as they do in extract 1. Because I have had access to the spoken version of this narrative, I have indicated pauses with slashes (/). Double slashes indicate noticeably longer pauses.

Part 1   (The shooting of man with his hands up)

Stanza 1 (The approach) (Orientation)

1   I went around the block /

2   that's a [course] in NY1 / [walking] with NY 111[6] / moving around the /

3   I think it's the Dairybelle hostel //

Stanza 2 (Gunshot heard) (Orientation)

4   and when I came back again in NY1 / so facing the bridge /

5   that's when we heard some gunshot going on /

6   and at that corner / I still remember two of this / one white guy went

7   I offloaded him at that corner /

8   and I went on /

Stanza 3 (Action begins) (Complicating action)

9   that's when I saw / someone running / and shooting with an AK

10 and that was Piet /

11 and more shots were heard from / very different directions /

12 and my car came to a stop /

13 I realised later it was hit

14 so / we just / got out

15 and / that // it was heavy shooting going on /

Stanza 4 (The man with his hands in the air) (Complicating action)

I have counted the noun phrase in 16 as a line because it foregrounds the 'topic' of the stanza.

16 and the / the man I shot //

17 he / he ca- / he came running out of the bush with his hands up/

18 he was talking in Xhosa that /

19 he can take us to where the others are

20 he had / he was holding his hands on top

21 and / told me in Xhosa that /

'don't shoot /

I will take you to where the others are' /

Stanza 5 (The shooting) (Complicating action)

22 and I relayed his message to all of the white guys who are there next to me

23 say /

'this man says there are other there' /

24 and the guy says

'skiet die donner' / (trans. Shoot the bastard)

25 and I shot at the man /

26 and this guy said to me

'Jy skiet kak' / you shoot shit /

27 and he put an R1 rifle on the guy's stomach /

28 he pulled the trigger /

29 and a round went out from the shoulder of the deceased //

Part 2   (Identifying the bodies) (Resolution)

Stanza 6 (Leaving the scene) (Orientation)

30 So from there on I remem- / I still remember /

31 then they said /

a helicopter was on standby /

32 I was taken to the helicopter //

Stanza 7 (Evaluation of event) (Evaluation/coda)

33 ah / I even ask myself today /

'was it futile /

was it really necessary to go and look
for those who got away?'

34 because / that was after the shooting now.

Stanza 8 (Request for identification) (Complicating action)

35 and then from there on / they came /

36 and we went to the / to all those people /

37 and they asked me

whether I recognised them //

Stanza 9 (Identifying the bodies) (Complicating action)

38 then I recognised Jabu / who was lying at the
    corner of the NY111 /

39 his head was facing NY NY1 /

40 and Piet was lying next to the fence / in NY1 /

41 Mandela was a bit next to the bushes there /

42 and the guy I shot was also there /

43 and they took us further in the bush

44 where / the other guys had some weapons and
    grenades next to them lying there /

Stanza 10 (Jabu and Piet) (Resolution)

45 and I only recognised about / only Jabu, er
    Mandela and Piet /

46 the rest I didn't recognise //

47 because Jabu and Piet were recognisable /

48 a Rastaman is / he / he stands tall

Mbelo's narrative falls into two parts, each containing its own narrative elements. In part 1, the orientation (Stanzas 1 and 2) describes the speaker's arrival at the scene. The complicating action is told in Stanzas 3, 4 and 5. Stanza 3 describes his perceptions of events immediately prior to the central event, Stanzas 4 and 5 the key moments of the appearance of the man running out of the bushes with his hands in the air, the orders to shoot him and the actual shooting. The climax comes in lines 28 and 29: 'he pulled the trigger and a round went out from the shoulder of the deceased'.

Part 2 describing the aftermath forms, in essence, a resolution to the narrative as a whole. It has its own narrative shape: In the orientation section, the narrator is taken to the helicopter (Stanza 6). External evaluation (in Stanza 7) interrupts the narrative of events. This stanza also acts as a coda, bringing the story up to the time of the telling – 'I even ask myself today'. Stanzas 8 and 9 represent the complicating action, the phases of the narrator's viewing and identification of the bodies. Stanza 10 is both resolution and evaluation, heightened particularly by the hesitations in 'a Rastaman is / he / he stands tall' (48).

One important difference between the two narratives is that whereas Bateman gives an outsider's perspective on the shooting, relying on witnesses to tell about the core event which he did not see, Mbelo was both an observer of and a participant in the events. His narrative and evaluation constitute an insider's perspective. Part of that insider's perspective is visual and temporal, as he takes the listener right into the scene and time of the action. Other grammatical features, such as the choice of the personal pronouns, tense and aspect, combine with the evaluative devices of repetition and contrast described by Labov, to convey the narrator's perspective on the scene and attitudes towards the actions and people involved.

Unlike Bateman's narrative, which is patterned on similarity with one significant difference, thematised echoes in Mbelo's story work mainly through contrast. The principal opposition is that between the black and white policemen that I have noted in (24) to (29). This opposition conveys a good deal of information, both about social relationships and responsibility. As a black, Mbelo would have been expected to obey, and not to give orders to, a white policeman. By quoting the words of the white man in Afrikaans, Mbelo appears to distance himself from, and at the same time to foreground, the crudeness of the expressions the other uses.[7] Although Mbelo openly admits agency in the clause 'I shot at the man', he represents himself as obeying orders. Responsibility for the death is laid at the door of the white policeman, whose active part in the shooting is recorded in lines (27) and (28). A long pause after the final terse line of the stanza emphasises this climactic moment in the narrative.

While the opposition is continued in Part 2, Stanzas 6 and 8, and emphasised by the pronoun subjects 'I' and 'they' – 'they' are in charge, taking Mbelo to the helicopter (32) so that he can identify the bodies – Mbelo's narrative moves back to his perceptions of the scene. Another vignette (Stanza 9) recreates the sight of the seven bodies lying in the road. The description is evaluative both in Labov's sense that it interrupts the narrative sequence, and in the poignancy evoked by Mbelo's use of the first names, Jabu, Piet and Mandela, and by the static, deathlike quality of the scene conveyed through the present progressive verbs, 'was facing', 'was lying'. His repetition of the names and the positive evaluation of the 'Rastaman' (Stanza 10) implies a sympathy for the activists' social practices and beliefs, which echoes his words in Stanza 7 of disquiet about the whole affair.

What makes Mbelo's narrative so interesting are the ambivalences. 'We' (5, 14) registers him as part of the group of policemen; yet he emphasises the social differences between himself and the white men, and he implies solidarity with the black activists. The time gap is important. In 1986 he might have been less ready to question his part in the operation. However, recalling the event later, he distances himself subtly through various features of the discourse, as the analysis shows.

Conclusion

I have drawn on the analytical approaches of Labov and Gee, to attempt a critical interpretation and comparison of two narratives. Combining their analytical tools has enabled me to show something of the two narrators' differences in perspective on the shooting of the Guguletu Seven as well as the shaping influences of the social and political contexts within which they both experienced and later retold their experience of the event. What becomes apparent from the analysis is that a similar approach may illuminate different aspects of different texts: the individual text and the analytical tools talk to each other in different ways. So patterning and evaluation in Chris Bateman's narrative highlight a journalist's search for a story and implicitly affirm his journalistic reliability. In Mbelo's narrative, they reveal a more personal stance, illustrating the position in 1986 of a black policeman in a racially divided country, and suggesting, ten years after the event, his conflicting feelings about the shooting and the responsibility for it.

The differences are partly accounted for by their individual narrative styles and the insider's as opposed to the outsider's perspective. But the immediate context of the TRC, the speakers' respective cultural backgrounds and the changed political context of 1996 are all important influences on the way they handle their narratives. Bateman does not have to apologise for his part in the event. His professional integrity is not under question by the TRC Commissioners. He can concentrate on telling the truth as he sees it. Mbelo, as a one-time member of the security forces and instrument of the apartheid government, is in a much more ambivalent position in the new political context. At his Amnesty Hearing, he had to face the mothers of the slain Guguletu activists. In an emotional interview after the hearing, some, though not all, of the mothers generously agreed to accept his apology. Although this narrative was told in an interview, the details are very much the same as he gave to the TRC. What is undeniable, however, is the sharpness of his evocation of the scene, which lends credibility to his version of the event.

Finally, these narratives illustrate a point, which the Commissioners were constantly aware of, about the multi-faceted nature of 'truth'. Bateman's narrative reports the accounts of three witnesses who have watched the same scene and observed and recalled different aspects of the event. As these narratives and those of other witnesses called to testify before the TRC show, one person's truth will differ in emphasis, selection, organisation and point of view from another's depending on his or her background, social role and aim in the telling of events. Seeking truth is a matter of sifting through and balancing these subtle differences. However, even if the South African story of those years is never finished, telling as much of it – or as many perspectives on it – as possible is important for the future of the nation. For as George Santayana has said: 'Those who cannot remember the past are condemned to repeat it'.[8]

Notes

1   The 1995 Promotion of National Unity and Reconciliation Act, Section 3, 1(a), requires the Commission to hear perspectives of both victims and perpetrators in order to 'establish as complete a picture as possible of the causes, nature and extent of the gross violations of human rights'.

2   The terms 'victim' and 'perpetrator' are problematic because they create positions or categories for those so described. Some victims preferred to call themselves 'survivors'. I have followed the TRC Report and retained the terms.

3   The conditions for amnesty were that applicants should make full disclosure of abuses committed by them and show that the abuses were committed with a political objective. Only three of the policemen involved in this incident applied for amnesty: Riaan Bellingan, Jimmy Mbane and Thapelo Mbelo.

4   The English interpretation of Mbelo's story as told to the TRC can be found on the TRC website.

5   South Africa now has 11 official languages.

6   When the black townships were built, the streets were identified by numbers. It appears to be largely forgotten now that NY stood for 'native yard'. The two words in square brackets in this line are puzzling but this was how the transcriber interpreted them.

7   Afrikaans was the language commonly used in the police force.

8   Desmond Tutu (1999, p. 32) quotes these words which are displayed over the entrance to the museum at the former concentration camp in Dachau.

References

GEE, J.P. (1991) 'A linguistic approach to narrative', *Journal of Narrative and Life History*, **1**, pp. 15–39.

GEE, J.P. (1997) 'Thematised echoes', *Journal of Narrative and Life History*, **7**(1–4), pp. 189–96.

GEE, J.P. (1999) *An Introduction to Discourse Analysis: Theory and Method*, London & New York, Routledge.

LABOV, W. (1972) *Language in the Inner City: Studies in the Black English Vernacular,* Philadelphia, University of Philadelphia Press.

LABOV, W. and WALETSKY, J. (1967) 'Narrative analysis: oral versions of personal experience', in J. HELM (ed.) *Essays on the Verbal and Visual Arts,* Proceedings of the 1966 Annual Spring Meeting of the American Ethnological Society, Seattle, Washington, University of Washington Press.

Lindy Wilson Productions (2000) *The Guguletu Seven*.

TUTU, D.M. (1999) *No Future without Forgiveness*, London, Rider.

Truth and Reconciliation Commission of South Africa Report, vols. 1 and 3 (1998), Cape Town, TRC Commission (distributed by Juta and Co Ltd).

TRC Transcripts available on www.doj.gov.za/trc

Source: commissioned for this volume.

READING C: Implicature and impliculture in the short, short story and the tall, tall tale

Rukmini Bhaya Nair

Implicature and impliculture

Grice's Theory of Conversational Implicature, which has had an indelible effect on all speech act and performative models, suggests that communication is at its most cooperative, that is, rationally efficient, when it conforms to the sub-maxims of Quality, Quantity, Relevance, and Manner. [...]

A successful narrative seems to be one where tellers' implicatures and listeners' inferences dovetail; or, to express it differently, narrative competence is best attested in cases where tellers and listeners culturally cooperate – are *able* to cooperate – in their evaluations [i.e. their understandings – Ed.]. This is not always possible in the absence of *specific cultural knowledge*, nor is it possible without recourse to *specific maxims such as the Maxims of Quality and Quantity*, as these appear to have a direct bearing on the manner in which narrative inferences are made, as I shall try to show below with reference to the genres of the short, short story and the tall, tall tale.

The original appeal of Grice's theory was that it showed how an apparently casual social activity like conversation, where 'meanings' were far from rigorously defined, was actually guided by norms of logical reasoning. The deductive apparatus used by conversationalists to retrieve implicatures from ordinary talk was little different from the 'rational' procedures used by philosophers to construe 'meanings' and construct 'theories of meaning'. Like philosophers, conversationalists too – despite their natural disadvantages! – made reference to notions like 'truth', 'economy of argument' and 'synthetic vs. analytic propositions' [roughly sentences that elaborate on, vs. sentences that reformulate, given information – Ed.], in order to make inferences; only the set of premises they relied on was rather large, including as it did contextual information. Grice's frequent references to contextual information, presumably not excluding culturally specific aspects of knowledge, as a resource for working out implicatures, make his work particularly attractive to those interested in pragmatic explanations of linguistic functioning.

Useful though the maxims are as overarching inferential norms, they must be supported, in the description of particular activities such as story-telling, or joke-recounting, or apologizing, or gossiping, by the rules of inferencing peculiar to those activities. [...] Cues to the structure of a story are derived from patterns of temporality [e.g. we expect events that happen later to be told later, and for order of telling to match up, normally, with order of occurrence – Ed.]. Causality and evaluation are typically associated with *narrative forms*, as distinct from *conversational conventions*, in any given culture. These patterns, it is suggested, are not fixed, like the six stable elements of earlier narrative grammar ([orientation], resolution, etc.), but allow for the fluid interplay of contextual and linguistic information in the creation of narrative meaning. To [turn], for example to the very short Bengali traditional story, which runs '*aekta bagh, aekta shikari, aekta bagh*' – 'A tiger, a hunter, a tiger.' In this particular story, the 'facts' to be explained are:

(a) that the proposition 'the tiger ate the hunter' is inferred by *all* competent hearers from this narrative sequence.

(b) that *some* competent hearers think this narrative amusing/ironic.

Now, Gricean theory can deal very well with the first of these facts. As the connections between the three [noun phrases] are not made explicit in the 'tiger story', we perceive in it a violation of Grice's Quantity Maxim, which enjoins conversationalists to be 'adequately informative'. Implicatures then follow by rule, via the following sort of reasoned steps:

(i)   The narrator has violated the maxim of quantity.

(ii)   From his violation + contextual knowledge (i.e. what I know about tigers and hunters, as well as the fact that the sequence is offered as a story), the narrator intends me to infer additional meanings not made explicit in his telling.

(iii) Since tigers eat people, and hunters are people, I can safely infer that the tiger ate the hunter.

However, it is not quite clear from Grice's steps how the second [effect] (b) [i.e. finding the story funny] is inferred, unless we know that in some cultures, excessive brevity is regarded as droll, the soul of wit, etc. The fashioning of this story in its truncated form may then be seen as exploiting this cultural norm. A typical story in many cultures is typically prolix, as it has not only to narrate the 'bare facts' but indicate through evaluative devices (asides, exclamations, intensifiers, etc.) the *significance* of those facts.

The 'tiger' story is slightly unusual in that it violates the maxim 'be adequately informative' in a way that runs counter to the usual run of narratives; it is *less* not *more* than adequately informative. But now imagine a culture where stories are standardly told through a staccato series of [noun phrases]. Consider, as an example from this hypothetical culture, story 2, quoted below:

A tree, a nest, two birds, three eggs, three fledglings, two birds again.

Here, it would be perfectly possible to infer the temporal → causal → informational → sequence of this narrative without finding it in the least funny or witty. If the 'tiger' story were recounted in this culture, it is reasonable to assume that it too would not be regarded as funny or witty, simply because it was in contravention of the Maxim of Quantity, as *we* interpret this maxim. In other words, we are now forced to ask: are the reasons for the 'tiger' story being regarded as 'funny' based on a violation of the quantity maxim alone? Or could it be that it is the culture-specific knowledge underlying this story – namely, that it is of the ironic 'biter-bit' variety – that contributes to the evaluative inference that it is funny? Part of my thesis in *Narrative Gravity* is that innumerable stories across cultures are fashioned as explanations for generalizations such as 'life is hard' or adages such as 'make hay while the sun shines'. Such general 'truths' are 'known' in particular societies, yet being general, they continually stand in need of *supporting evidence* from specific cultural ducts such as stories. [...]

The answer to the question 'why is the 'tiger' story funny, but not the equally laconic 'bird' story?' requires reference not only to Grice's Quantity Maxim, but also to the fact that we are trained to regard 'the biter being bitten', agent-as-victim, subject-as-object, and other such sets of reversals as ironic in many cultures. No such reversal [...] falls out from the second story, and so it might be inferred that it is less rich in [...] evaluation (Labov) [...].

Another cultural/pragmatic set of reasons which could influence a listener's positive evaluation of the 'tiger' story is connected not with its being a kind of saturnine revenge comedy, but with its generic specification. This sort of story as a genre seems to be quite close to a riddle in its advertised uninformativeness. So when we 'get' the point of the story, as when we 'get' a riddle, part of the pleasure is in our own cultural savvy. Cleverness pleases us, especially our own; conversely dullness frustrates, our own or anyone else's. Story 2, for example, is likely in the end to be evaluated as boring and pointless, except perhaps in a learning context, because it offers so little interpretive scope to the listener, so little scope for that always agile right hand of narrative inferencing. Despite its riddle-like structure, it does not live up to its promise, thus provoking the 'so what?' question which Labov suggests deals a death blow to any story. Story 1, on the other hand, also shaped like a riddle, justifies this generic resemblance to a riddle; it challenges the listener to display her cultural 'membershipping' by solving the puzzle in its sequencing [...] As contended earlier, much needs to be internalized about social values and beliefs (encoded, for instance, in idiom and adages), as well as about the structure of genres, before such a solution can be capably offered.

These arguments, deriving from the specific nature of cultural materials, are useful insofar as they enable a critique of some of the universal, and thus essentializing, assumptions of Gricean theory. They show that Grice's theory of conversational implicature may be deemed inadequate because it does not account for the *full* expansion of this sort of minimal narrative. It explains, at most, how the additional proposition 'the tiger ate the hunter' is computed, but not the additional non-propositional inference of irony which is what gives this story its evaluative 'point'. [...]

Cultural norms of interpretation – which I refer to as Impli*culture*, as distinct from Impli*cature* – thus seem not merely useful, but indispensable during the process of narrative inferencing. [...]

From the short, short story to the tall, tall tale

If we turn to the genre of the tall story now, a similar trend manifests itself. As Bauman (1986) in his examination of the tall stories of coon-hunting from the American Midwest has shown, any assessment of a tall claim within a subculture, such as that of the coon-hunters, depends on a thorough knowledge of the conversational display rituals of this group. An outsider may not, with equal confidence, be able to decide which facts are 'tall' and which are perfectly plausible. Specialized in-group knowledge thus becomes essential to inferencing in this genre of the tall story. In my view, Bauman's analysis of the 'coon' tall story is characterized, by the following features:

(a) *Moral* community 'issue[s] of truthfulness and lying' are addressed, via the 'tall' tale.

(b) The tall tale 'plays upon ... *another genre* of story which is ubiquitous among hound-dog men: narratives of personal experience about the special quality and hunting prowess of particular dogs. ... The more common story of personal experience, told straightforwardly as truth contextualizes the tall tale, it contributes to the latter's humorous effect by establishing a set of *generic expectations* that the tall tale can bend exaggeratedly out of shape. ... Thus *tall tales are lies*, insofar as what they report as having happened either did not happen or could not have happened' [italics mine – R.B.N.].

(c) Tall tales are often told in the third person, but when they are told in the *first person*, moving closer to generic narratives of personal experience, the teller is understood to be not simply a humorous liar but a *fabricator*, a 'con man'.

(d) The 'creative exaggeration' in the tall tale is an *'instrument for identity building*, for self-aggrandizement ... a means of enhancing one's own image ... a tendency towards 'stretching the truth' that has been widely reported in men's sociable encounters' [italics mine – R.B.N.].

(e) Tall tales are often marked by *formulaic iterative devices and a punchline*, which indicate the culmination of events.

(f) The 'expressive lying' in the coon-hunting tall tales place them in an American folk tradition 'in unbroken continuity with the generations of hunters, traders, and storytellers' making the tales a *'richly textured arena for the ethnographic investigation* of ... the negotiation of truthfulness and lying as action and evaluation in the conduct of social life' [italics mine – R.B.N.].

(g) In narratives of personal experience attempts at 'validation', stressing the plausibility of the narrative, are frequent, but in the tall tale these *validating moves could be subverted or discarded*, since here 'lying is overwhelmingly licensed as part of the fundamental ethos of sociability ... to call another man a liar in this context, then, is to threaten his "face", with some risk and no possible advantage to oneself; whereas, to give apparent acceptance to his accounts is to *store-up interactional credit* towards the unchallenged acceptance of one's own tales' [italics mine – R.B.N.].

In effect, Bauman pleads for a contextualized interpretation of the tall tale that sees it in relation to the cultural tradition within which it was generated. He stresses the interactional payoffs of this genre in an all-male, macho atmosphere where the tall tale becomes a variety of *performance*, and hence 'lying' gains social sanction.

Speaking of performativity the use of the tall tale at a pivotal moment in a recent popular film on the American Midwest, entitled *Fried Green Tomatoes* (John Avnet, 1992), illustrates well a point I have stressed before. The 'good' story, I have argued, is distinguished by the fact that it travels through social space, passing from person to person as a durable bundle of perlocutionary effects binding the community together. Thus a tall story embedded in the frame of another story functions very much like the prototypical cognitive structure designed to convert 'talk into text', that I've suggested narrative is. It works as a metaphor of survival.

To ask for a tall story in the face of imminent death constitutes an act of psychological self-preservation. *Fried Green Tomatoes* is a story told in flashback of the friendship between two feisty young women, Ruth and Idgie, who run a restaurant in remote Whistlestop, Alabama. During the course of the film, Ruth is stricken with cancer. An ominous clock ticks away in the dark interiors of the house, as the dying Ruth turns away a pastor and instead requests a story from Idgie – a tall story. Even the unconventional Idgie is embarrassed at the thought of delivering a tall story – virtually a lie, as Bauman points out – as a form of final absolution, but her love and grief overcome her inhibitions. And this is the story she tells:

> There was once a lake across from Ruth's house. One day a gaggle of geese alighted on it just as the wintry lake was freezing over. When the geese then flew across to the neighbouring state of Georgia, they carried the lake with them, frozen on their webbed feet. Now, Georgia has that lake.

As the tale ends, Ruth passes on peacefully. Fiction, the Paradox of the Indian Rope Trick asserts, thus reassures us, even as it lies or deludes. By making other worlds 'real' – excitingly and dramatically real – stories persuade us that all may not be lost. In this case, the tall story Idgie tells Ruth certainly mirrors the sociological theme of rivalry between the Southern states of Alabama and Georgia that is a constant leitmotif in the film, but it achieves

Meme was coined by Richard Dawkins by analogy with gene. It is designed to explain cultural evolution – how culture is passed on, and sometimes adapted, through time. A meme is a unit of cultural transmission: a specific idea, belief, or way of doing things. Examples would be tunes, catch-phrases, fashions, ways of making pots or building arches (Dawkins, 1976, p. 206) – or in Bhaya Nair's argument, stories.

more than this simple conversion of real life into reel life. [...] One could say that it transforms itself into a form of the Dennett/Dawkins meme – part of a cultural gene-pool. In keeping with the narrative paradigm of the Indian Rope Trick, it manages this by suggesting that dying and pain could themselves be illusions that can be substituted by other more entrancing illusions. Like the geese who fly off with a fictional lake as an icy shimmering attachment, the essential 'self' is freed in a narrative universe; it can wander eternally where it pleases, and thus defy the 'reality' of death.

One recalls here Virginia Woolf's phrase about the 'varied and wandering' nature of self. If the self is itself an illusion then a condemnation of tall stories, or indeed any form of fiction, seems pointless. The human species as a whole may be said to answer the dread Labovian question – What's the *point* of this story? – by making stories central to their being. That, at any rate, is Dennett's idea. We spend our lives unifying our frangible selves through the cognitive activity of story-telling because constructing the illusion of a self is what we are born to do. From this anti-foundationalist perspective, then, an individual self is 'really' just a *congeries* of story. My own further suggestion in this chapter has been that such a notion of the self as a centre of narrative gravity can be further connected to Dennett and Dawkins' other suggestion about humans as meme-generators. Since memes are culturally transmitted, narratives make ideal receptacles and/or formats for the transfer of durable memes, such as for instance, the riddle-like short stories and tall tales examined in this chapter.

References

AUSTIN, J.L. (1962) *How to Do Things with Words*, Oxford, Clarendon Press.

AVNET, J. (dir.) (1991) *Fried Green Tomatoes*, Universal Studios.

BAUMAN, R. (1986) *Story, Performance, and Event: Contextual Studies of Oral Narrative,* Cambridge, Cambridge University Press.

DAWKINS, R. (1976) *The Selfish Gene*, New York, Oxford University Press.

DENNETT, D. (1991) *Consciousness Explained*, Boston and New York, Little Brown.

GRICE, H.P. (1975) 'Logic and conversation', in P. COLE and J. MORGAN (eds) *Syntax and Semantics*, Volume 3, New York, Academic Press.

LABOV, W. (1972) *Language in the Inner City*, Philadelphia, University of Pennsylvania Press.

SEARLE, J.R. (1969) *Speech Acts*, Cambridge, Cambridge University Press.

SEARLE, J.R. (1979) *Expression and Meaning: Studies in the Theory of Speech Acts*, Cambridge, Cambridge University Press.

Source: an abridged extract from NAIR, R. B. (2002), *Narrative Gravity*, Chapter 5 'Rationality and relevance', Oxford, Oxford University Press.

Putting on the style

Susan McRae and Joan Swann

3.1 Introduction

In this chapter we turn to another aspect of language use that, like poetic language and conversational stories, can be seen to have rather literary associations: routine interactions between people are sometimes said to constitute everyday **performances**, in which people take on different interactional personae, representing certain versions of themselves to others. In talking together, speakers jointly negotiate (foreground or play down, challenge or seek to subvert) particular identities, or aspects of themselves. This may happen in narrative form as, in the stories they tell, narrators represent people and events in certain ways. The argument here however is broader: it is that all interaction between people can be seen as a type of performance.

The sociologist Erving Goffman is one of the best-known early exponents of this view of interaction as performance. Goffman (1959, p. 26) defines performance very broadly as: 'all the activity of a given participant on a given occasion which serves to influence in any way any of the other participants'. His model of interaction is termed *dramaturgical* (i.e. dramatic), incorporating theatrical terminology such as individuals playing a *part*, or putting on an *act* for an *audience*. He does not mean to suggest by this that performances are necessarily conscious or contrived (though they may be). His argument is that participants in an interaction need to know who (what kind of person) they are talking to and therefore look for signs in people's appearance and behaviour. Individuals in interactions necessarily *express* themselves and *impress* others in some way.

Chapter 1 discussed performance as one way of identifying artful language in spoken interaction – the idea that speakers often demonstrate 'a particular attention to and skills in the delivery of a message', and that this may be evaluated by an audience (Duranti, 1997). Goffman's conception is, however, rather wider, implying that speakers necessarily perform even when they, and their audience, show no evidence of attending to the interaction *as* performance. Goffman's ideas have been influential in the study of language in interaction, in which language may be seen as an interactional resource that is drawn on in the performance of speaker identities.

Goffman and everyday performance

Goffman points to research evidence that US college girls played down their intelligence in the presence of their boyfriends, which might be seen as a kind of performance. He continues:

> ... when we observe a young American middle-class girl playing dumb for the benefit of her boyfriend, we are ready to point to items of guile and contrivance in her behaviour. But like herself and her boyfriend, we accept as an unperformed fact that this performer *is* a young American middle-class girl. But surely here we neglect the greater part of the performance. It is commonplace to say that different social groupings express in different ways such attributes as age, sex, territory and class status, and that in each case these bare attributes are elaborated by means of a distinctive complex cultural configuration of proper ways of conducting oneself. To *be* a given kind of person, then, is not merely to possess the required attributes, but also to sustain the standards of conduct and appearance that one's social grouping attaches thereto. The unthinking ease with which performers consistently carry off such standard-maintaining routines does not deny that a performance has occurred, merely that the participants have been aware of it.

(Goffman, 1959, p. 81)

ACTIVITY 1   **Performance in interaction**

Allow
5–10 minutes

How do you respond to Goffman's ideas about everyday performance? How might these ideas apply to a couple of interactions you have recently taken part in?

To explore these ideas we focus on an aspect of language use that has been particularly well-studied within **sociolinguistics**: how speakers use certain varieties of English or, in bilingual contexts, English and other languages, to foreground different aspects of their identities. This is often discussed in terms of **speaking style**, where 'style' refers to the distinctive ways of speaking associated with particular speakers or particular contexts. In Section 3.2 we look at speakers' stylistic choices – the use of accent and dialect features, and of English itself in combination with other languages – in the routine performance of identities; and in Section 3.3 we turn to the strategic use of language varieties to shift between two or more identities; in Section 3.4 we examine varieties of English, and ways of using English, that have been associated with the performance of gender and sexuality. We also review some ideas about individual speakers' agency and creativity in the performance of identity.

Sociolinguistics

Sociolinguistics is the study of the relationship between language and society, or language and social life. Sociolinguistics highlights the communicative competence of speakers, the choices open to them and the ways in which they tailor language to different functions and interactional ends. Sociolinguistics stresses the variation inherent in a language, as speakers of different backgrounds use language not just for the communication of information but to express (and also create) an individual and/or group identity.

(Adapted from Swann et al. 2004)

3.2 English in style

'Asian Wall'

At lunch time in the spring of 1997, in an ethnically very heterogeneous junior high school in northern California, a crowd of Asian-American kids hangs out in a spot that is generally known in the school as 'Asian Wall'. Girls stand around in their high platform shoes, skinny bell-bottoms, and very small T-shirts, with hips cocked. As they toss their heads, their long sleek black hair (in some cases tinted brown) swishes across their waists, the slimness of which is emphasized by shiny belts. Some of them talk to, some lean on, quiet-demeanored boys with baggy jeans and baggy shirts, with hair long on the top and shaved at the bottom. Linda turns away from her group of friends with a characteristic tilted head toss, bringing her hair around her shoulders; and with an exaggerated high-rise intonation on the pronoun, she calls to a boy who's standing nearby, 'What are YOU?' Another girl, Adrienne, who happens to be walking by, answers on his behalf: 'He's Japanese-Filipino.' The boy smiles silently, and Linda turns back to her friends.

(Eckert and McConnell-Ginet, 1999, pp. 185–6)

Penelope Eckert and Sally McConnell-Ginet (1999) argue that the momentary event described above is one small move in the continuing construction of a range of identities. The exaggerated intonation on *you* is part of an Asian-American speaking style the researchers have observed in California schools. Along with certain ways of using language – calling out to a boy, speaking on his behalf – and clothing, hair and stance, a linguistic feature of this kind constitutes a communicative resource the young people may draw on, styling themselves and others in terms of gender, ethnicity, heterosexuality, life stage and social status.

Eckert and McConnell-Ginet's observation assumes that certain linguistic features – such as features of accent, dialect, or a particular language – acquire a complex of social meanings, based on their association with particular social groups and particular settings and activities. In urban, 'western' contexts, for instance, sociolinguistic studies of language variation and change have documented systematic differences in the speech of groups identified in terms of social class, gender, age, ethnicity. In the 'Asian Wall' case, Eckert and McConnell-Ginet note that the intonation pattern adopted by Linda is used mainly by Asian-American students and so becomes associated with an Asian-American identity; its use on this occasion calls up and foregrounds that identity, contributing to Linda's overall performance.

A C T I V I T Y 2   Messing with style (Reading A)

In Reading A, Penelope Eckert looks more closely at how speakers draw on combinations of linguistic features – in this case, grammatical and pronunciation features – to construct particular identities. She relates this to other ways of performing identities, principally clothing. The data Eckert discusses come mainly from her now classic study of linguistic variation amongst students in a US high school referred to as Belten High (Eckert, 1989; 2000). She focuses on the extent to which speakers orient to one of two class-based school groupings termed *jocks* and *burnouts*, and also how this interacts with gender. Eckert's study is ethnographic: she spent considerable time in her research context observing and talking to participants. She is able to draw on this knowledge to support her analysis of speakers' use of particular linguistic features.

For a brief explanation of ethnography, see Chapter 1.

Please now work through Reading A, identifying the main points that Eckert makes, and the evidence she provides to support her argument. Our comments follow.

Penelope Eckert sees speakers' stylistic choices as a process of 'bricolage', in which speakers draw on a mix of linguistic and other resources not just to recreate existing identities but to give these new twists. In her study of Belten High, the jock/burnout opposition she identifies is important, not because all students fall into one of these categories – there are in fact many 'in-betweens' – but because the categories are highly salient. Students tend to define themselves in relation to these categories. Gender is also an important aspect of students' identities; girls and boys both carry out and are associated with a different range of activities. Eckert identifies differences in the speaking styles of female and male jocks and burnouts but sees these not simply as reflecting group membership (such that people speak as they do because they are a male jock, female burned-out burnout, etc.). She argues that in speaking in a certain way, speakers are performing, and helping to construct a particular identity or set of identities. Language plays a part in this alongside clothing, etc.

Eckert's linguistic evidence is based on an analysis of speakers' use of grammatical features – in this case different forms of negation – and on speakers' pronunciation: how they pronounce particular sounds such as the vowels in words like *lunch, flesh* and *quite*. Within the community the pronunciation of these vowels is changing and individual speakers' styles will differ according to the frequency with which they use older and newer forms. Eckert argues that these overall speaking styles are socially meaningful – they convey something about the speaker.

Eckert identifies a relationship between category membership and gender, suggesting that:

- burnouts tend to use more non-standard forms of negation, a feature that is much rarer in the speech of jocks; jock girls are at the extreme end of the spectrum, using the lowest percentage of non-standard forms; on the other hand, burnout girls' use of non-standard forms is similar to that of burnout boys;

- there are however differences between jock boys: those who are primarily involved in student government use similar patterns of negation to jock girls but those who are primarily athletes use more non-standard forms;

- there are also differences between burnout girls: 'burned-out' burnouts use the highest percentage of non-standard forms of negation;

- differences are also reflected in pronunciation, with burnouts using more 'extreme' forms of new urban pronunciations than jocks, and jock girls being the most conservative speakers.

Eckert relates her interpretations to two opposing styles – 'suburban, preppy, institutional' vs 'urban and rebellious' – and suggests that speakers can draw on these to perform particular identities. For instance, amongst female burnouts, extreme use of non-standard forms of negation is associated with being a burned-out burnout, and more generally with a wild, urban style. In adopting these pronunciations, therefore, girls are both performing a burnout identity and reinforcing the meaning of the linguistic features themselves.

Like most sociolinguistic studies of language variation and change, Eckert focuses on speakers' use of certain dialect features: in this case, grammatical features and features of pronunciation. Different features (or, more accurately, different combinations of features) are associated with established and readily identifiable social groupings, such as social-class-based school groupings. We mentioned also, however, that speakers may use different forms of language to perform a wider range of social identities. In another US study, Mary Bucholtz (1996, 1999) looks at how speakers may construct a nerd identity. *Nerd* is found in many varieties of English as an insult term, referring to someone who is uninteresting, often socially inept, often studious (where this is viewed negatively) and sometimes obsessive about things others find boring. The *Oxford English Dictionary* locates earliest usages in 1950s' US English. The term is also used, knowingly and perhaps ironically, by people who self-identify as nerds. The Slashdot website, for instance (http://slashdot.org/ [accessed 9/6/2005]), offers 'News for nerds. Stuff that matters'.

In Bucholtz's study, young people who identified as nerds distanced themselves from other more popular groups in terms of coolness: cool people were those who, in various ways, were seen as 'knowledgeable of and participating in current trends in youth culture' (1996, p. 122). Nerds were not cool. Bucholtz cites one young woman who moved from a cool to a nerdy group of friends:

> Last year I was good friends with Kate but I never saw her on weekdays for some reason. I was sitting with this other group of people at lunch who were cool but they liked to talk about everyone who passed and make negative comments about everyone who passed and I just kind of sat there … At the end of the semester I said, 'What am I doing? Why am I not hanging out with [Kate]?' And so I moved in with [her group of friends]. … We're always the nerds. We like it. We're glad to be the nerds and the squares. We don't drink, we don't do drugs, we just get naturally high, we do insane, funny things. And we're smart. We get good grades.

(Cited in Bucholtz, 1996, p. 122)

The speech of Bucholtz's nerd informants could be characterised partly in terms of dialect features. In the case of sounds whose pronunciation was undergoing change, they used relatively conservative pronunciations. However, Bucholtz suggests they also created their own strategies to project a nerdy self, adopting a 'measured' style of speech that constructed them as 'untrendy' but also intelligent, as in the examples below.

An analysis of nerd interactions

One linguistic phenomenon that makes nerd speech distinctive is its measured quality, which lends weight to speakers' words, and the resistance to phonological processes characteristic of colloquial speech such as consonant cluster simplification and unstressed vowel production. I offer two examples, the first by a boy, Erich, and the second by a girl, Beth.

(1) 1   ERICH: U:h Hong Kong is a franchise too. Mr Lee's
     2   Greater Hong Kong. (sniff)

     3   MARY: Is it meant to be a funny book or is it [sort of a:]

     4   ERICH: [Yeah. I:t's]
     5   meant to be somewhat humor

     6   MARY: Yeah.

     7   ERICH: But (.) it's very good. It's very fun. Sumatran
     8   computer virus. (nasal laugh) Yeah. It's a
     9   compu- it's that a whole (.) long involved plot
     10   about this thing that's called [nɑmʃʊb]. Which is
     11   kind of like a computer program that will
     12   program your brai:n. (sniff) And uh

     13   MARY: Oka:y, (laugh)

     14   ERICH: it's it's very complicated. You have to really
     15   read the book to understand it.

(2) 1   BETH: I can't quite deal with it yet but
     2   it's (keeping [more and more])

     3   MARY: [What is it.] I've never heard of it.

     4   BETH: It's (.) it's this weird book. It takes plac:e in
     5   (.) [Den-]

     6   CHRISTINE: [Iceland] or something.

     7   BETH: Denmark.

     8   CHRISTINE: Denmark?

     9   BETH: Yeah.

     10   CHRISTINE: Oh. Oh, she's *from* Iceland.

     11   BETH: Yeah. She- she's from Greenland actually.

Note on transcription:

: = lengthened sound   [sort of]
                                    [yeah]   = overlapping speech

. = falling intonation   (.) = untimed pause

[nɑmʃʊb] – phonetically transcribed word, to show actual pronunciation

'Stops' are types of consonants, sometimes also termed 'plosives'; in English, /p/, /b/, /t/, /d/, /k/, /g/ are stops.

Both Erich and Beth use a measured speech style, slowing their rate of speech between certain words: in [lines 10–15] of Erich's transcript (*you have to really read the book to understand it*) and in line 1 of Beth's (*I can't quite deal with it*). This produces an effect of careful enunciation by inhibiting assimilation of final stops to adjacent initial stops. Erich also produces fully released final [t]s in *understand it* [line 15] and *somewhat humor* [line 5]. Erich's speech also shows some influence of spelling pronunciation in line 1 (*Mr Lee's Greater Hong Kong* [hɔŋ kɔŋg]). Likewise, Erich and Beth both resist reduction of unstressed vowels in [lines 8–9] of Erich's turn (*It's a* [ej] *computer*) and in Beth's line [11] (*Greenland actually* [grinlænd ækʃuwəlij]). The non-reduction of *-land* echoes Christine's use of this pronunciation of *Iceland* in line [10].

(Adapted from Bucholtz, 1996, pp. 125–6)

Eckert and Bucholtz discussed the use of English in monolingual contexts, where speaking style can be characterised in terms of speakers' overall use of particular linguistic features – in the examples represented above, grammatical and pronunciation features. Such styles are not static: they vary continually, allowing speakers to emphasise different aspects of their identity (e.g. appearing more or less jock-like, or nerd-like, on different occasions, or of course foregrounding entirely different aspects of their identities). Something similar may be observed in bilingual interactions, where languages have different associations or meanings. In this case, speakers may choose to use one language or another to represent different identities, or sometimes balance different identities by switching back and forth between languages, as in the example below, where three young men in Nairobi switch between Swahili and English (switches to English are in italics).

L. Mbona hawa *workers* wa East African Power and Lightning wakaenda *strike*, hata wengine nasikia washawekwa *cell*.
('*And why on earth did those East African Power and Lightning workers strike, even I've heard some have been already put in cells [in jail].*')

K. Ujue watu wengine ni *funny* sana. Wa-na-*claim* ati mishahara yao iko *low* sana. Tena wanasema eti hawapewi *housing allowance*.
('*You know, some people are very funny. They are claiming that their salaries are very low. They also say - eh - they are not given house allowances.*')

M. Mimi huwa nawafikiria lakini wao huwa na *reasonable salary*.
('*As for me, I used to think, but they have a reasonable salary.*')

K. Hujajua watu wengi *on this world* hawawezi kutoesheka. Anasema anataka hiki akipewa a–na–*demand* kingine.

('Don't you know yet that some people on this world [sic] can't be satisfied. He says he wants this and when he is given [it], he demands another [thing].')

L.   ... Kwani ni ngumu sana ku-*train* wengine? Si ni kupata *lessons* kidogo tu halafu waanze kazi?

('... Why is it difficult to train others? Isn't it just to get a few lessons and then they should start work?')

(Adapted from Myers-Scotton, 1993, pp. 118–19)

Carol Myers-Scotton argues that in this interaction there is no particular significance attached to individual switches between Swahili and English. The fact of switching, however, allows the young men simultaneously to signal different aspects of their identity: local solidarity (based on Swahili) and educatedness/upward social mobility (based on English).

3.3 Switching styles, switching identities

Switching styles in southern American English

[Pearl greets] two of her guests for a small Christmas Eve party ... She greets them in local standard [at her door] and then immediately switches to home style [in capitals].

[1]   Pearl: 1   it's so nice to see y'all

2   I'm so glad you could make it

3   please come in and find a seat

[The guests seat themselves and Pearl continues]

[2]   Pearl: 4   AIN'T THIS RAIN AWFUL?

5   I'M AWISHIN I COULD GO SOMEWHERE AND SEE ME SOME SUN

6   I AIN'T NEVER SEEN NOTHING TO BEAT ALL THIS RAIN

The only non-standard variant that we see in sequence [1] is the use of the plural form *Y'all*, but this is not a stigmatized form in southern English, because it is used across class boundaries in the South and is thus considered a component of local standard. In sequence [2], Pearl sits down with the same guests that she just greeted at the door. Now we see five separate examples of the more distinctively local variety, home style. First, Pearl uses the negative *ain't* to begin her conversation about the weather: AIN'T THIS RAIN AWFUL. Then *a* is prefixed before the verb *wishing*: I'M AWISHIN I COULD GO SOMEWHERE. In the same sentence, Pearl uses the personal dative *me*, as in AND SEE ME SOME SUN. [...] Finally, there is another occurrence of the negative form *ain't* in a negative sentence to end the exchange: I AIN'T NEVER SEEN NOTHING.

In sequence [1], Pearl greets her friends in local standard. When she goes to the door, even though she is greeting close friends, she is aware that the situation requires a relatively formal greeting. She wants to be seen as someone who is a 'hostess', someone who knows and understands her duties as hostess. Therefore, she uses local standard to establish this identity. However, in the same exchange, as her guests are seating themselves, it is also important for Pearl to re-affirm her identity as close friend and community member.

(Mishoe, 1998, p. 165)

The discussion in Section 3.2 centred on speakers' overall speaking styles, based on their use of a combination of linguistic features. It was also suggested, however, that particular linguistic features – from the selection of certain pronunciations to the selection of a language in bilingual contexts could be drawn on strategically in an interaction. Mishoe's study provides an illustration of this. Mishoe identifies two varieties of English in use in a small community in the southern states of the USA. These are: a local variety, which she terms 'home style', associated with informal talk in the home and local community; and a variety closer to US standard English, associated with more formal contexts (termed 'local standard'). Note that these are idealisations: individual speakers use a mix of linguistic variants in particular contexts. The argument is, however, that it is possible to make a general distinction between different styles; that these styles are meaningful; and that they may be drawn on to index a particular identity. A switch between styles therefore indexes a shift in identities, as in the interaction above. Individual switches like this may be related to the kinds of overall speaking style documented by sociolinguistic surveys such as Penelope Eckert's research, discussed in Section 3.2. In a discussion of what he terms 'dialect style', Nikolas Coupland comments:

Dialect style as persona management captures how individuals, within and across speaking situations, manipulate the conventionalised social meanings of dialect varieties – the individual through the social. But it is the same process of dialectal self-projection that explains the effect of dialect stratification when the speech of social groups is aggregated in sociolinguistic surveys. Individuals within what we conventionally recognise to be meaningful social categories enact dialect personas with sufficient uniformity for survey researchers to detect numerical patterns of stratification.

(Coupland, 2001, p. 198)

Switching between languages and varieties, conventionally termed **code-switching**, or sometimes **style-shifting** in monolingual contexts, constitutes routine interactional behaviour. It has been widely studied in English-speaking and other contexts (e.g. Auer, 1998; Heller, 1988; Myers-Scotton, 1998). In the remainder of this section we examine a type of switching that has come to be termed **language crossing** (Rampton, 1995/2004): the use of a variety of language associated with a social or language group that the speaker does not normally belong to. This is particularly relevant to our discussion of everyday performance as it has often been seen as a relatively artful type of performance, and also as an example of figurative language use.

ACTIVITY 3 Language crossing (Reading B)

Please now work through Reading B, 'Language crossing', by Ben Rampton. Note that, like Eckert's study, this is ethnographic: Rampton draws on a considerable amount of contextual knowledge to interpret the language patterns he observed amongst groups of young people living in the South Midlands in England. Rampton relates language use to **ethnicity**, and the development of new ethnicities. Some of the ideas discussed here are quite complex, but the points listed below should help structure your reading. Look out for the following:

- Crossing takes different forms, and has different meanings in different contexts – note the use of Panjabi within an episode of jocular abuse between friends in example 1, the use of Creole features to index resistance or non-compliance with a teacher in example 2, and the use of stylised Asian English as a 'put down' to a younger pupil in example 3.

- In crossing, people are not aspiring to the identity associated with their choice of language (i.e. a white Anglo speaker using Panjabi does not actually wish to be taken as Panjabi). Arguably, however, crossing does partly destabilise the fixity of inherited identities.

- Crossing can be seen as a form of figurative language – either metaphorical or ironic; it is figurative in the sense that speakers are not actually claiming the identity represented by the variety they select; in making this claim, Rampton draws on a distinction between 'situational' and 'metaphorical' code-switching associated with the sociolinguist John Gumperz.

- Rampton relates this to ideas about language developed by the Russian literary theorist and philosopher of language, Mikhail Bakhtin, and particularly to Bakhtin's notion of 'double voicing' (see below).

- Crossing may be cast as performance, in a way that extends this from a 'literary' to an 'everyday' sense.

> ## Bakhtin and 'double-voicing'
>
> Bakhtin's notion of 'double-voicing' ([1929] 1984), referred to by Rampton, is based on the idea that all language use involves speaking through the **voices** – utterances, along with their associated meanings – of others. Language is continually recycled and re-articulated, but words, phrases, etc. carry with them the 'taste' of other speakers and other contexts. 'Double-voicing' means that an utterance carries two sets of meanings or 'semantic intentions'. An example might be a narrator telling a story and quoting from another speaker in such a way that (e.g. by tone of voice) the narrator's viewpoint is evident behind that of the quoted speaker. Bakhtin distinguishes between 'uni-directional' and 'vari-directional' double-voicing. In the case of uni-directional double-voicing, although there are two voices, the semantic intentions are consistent; in the case of vari-directional double-voicing, the speaker introduces a new semantic intention directly opposed to the original one. An example of the latter might be political satire, or quoting someone ironically.
>
> Rampton relates this distinction to 'metaphorical' crossing, when a speaker takes on some of the meanings associated with a variety (as in the use of Creole in Reading B); and 'ironic' crossing, when speakers distance themselves from the variety they use (as in the case of stylised Asian English in Reading B).

The discussion in Reading B suggests that crossing may be seen as a relatively creative, artful activity: speakers orient towards other identities figuratively and temporarily, and Rampton himself sees this in terms of performance. Like other forms of linguistic creativity, crossing has certain local interactional functions (getting one's own back on a teacher, playfully insulting a friend, attributing 'diminished responsibility' to a younger pupil), but it may also be associated with longer-term reconfigurations of identities – as in Rampton's point about the emergence of 'new ethnicities'.

Sections 3.2 and 3.3 have suggested that particular languages and varieties constitute resources that may be drawn on by speakers in the everyday performance of interactional personae. The researchers we have cited also suggest that such local performances are related to (i.e. reflect but also bolster, renegotiate or perhaps challenge) established social categories, such as ethnicity, gender, jock and burnout identities, etc. Some of the most exciting ideas on identity and performance have been developed in relation to gender and sexuality, and it is to this topic that we turn in the next section.

3.4 Gender and sexuality: performativity and performance

Research into the relationship between language use and **gender** has traditionally focused on differences in the style of language used by female and male speakers. We mentioned in Section 3.2 that gender has been seen as an important factor in sociolinguistic studies of language variation and change: Penelope Eckert's study showed systematic but relatively complex patterns in the use of dialect features that could be related to gender and social-category membership. Another research tradition has focused on speakers' conversational styles or habitual ways of speaking. Research carried out in the 1970s and 1980s suggested that women and men adopted different interactional styles. Women's speech was often seen as more 'cooperative' and men's speech as more 'competitive'. Some features associated with women, however, (such as indirect speech, diminutives, certain intonational patterns) rendered their language relatively powerless. Such research is discussed in, for instance, Eckert and McConnell-Ginet (2003). Recent research has tended to focus less on such 'binary' distinctions between female and male speakers, acknowledging that there are differences between women and between men and, like Eckert, focusing on how gender may interact with other aspects of identity. Language may be seen as a reflection of social-category membership but, in line with other work discussed in this chapter, contemporary research on language and gender emphasises the way language is drawn on as a resource in the contextualised performance of gendered and other types of identity. A particularly interesting strand of research focuses on language, gender and **sexuality**.

> Eckert and McConnell-Ginet provide an introduction to language and gender. For examples of recent studies, see Coates (1998); Holmes and Meyerhoff (2003); Litosseliti and Sunderland (2002).

> The term 'transgendered' refers to people who, in various ways, cross between feminine and masculine identities and sexualities.

Language, gender and sexuality

Niko Besnier (2003) studied the language of transgendered male speakers in Tonga, focusing particularly on speakers' use of Tongan and English. The participants in Besnier's study were members of a group termed *fakaleitī* in Tongan (*faka-* means 'in the manner of' and *leitī* is a borrowing derived from the English word *lady*). The term *leitī* is sometimes used on its own. *Leitī* are typically felt to have a feminine comportment, to carry out work and engage in leisure pursuits associated with women, and to have sexual relations with 'straight' (non-*leitī*) men. Besnier argues that the language choices made by *leitī* have to do with the associations of English and Tongan in Tongan society.

English, in Tonga, is a language of prestige: 'linked to a colonial past, it dominates contexts of employment, education, modernity, transnationalism, contacts with the external world, and new forms of socio-economic hegemony such as entrepreneurship' (Besnier, 2003, p. 283). Those who have not had access to such privileges are more likely to use Tongan. But Tongan is also found as a language of resistance to English, and it is used in 'non-English' contexts such as oratory, ceremonialism and song and dance concerts. English also has undertones of (modern) femininity: it is associated with women's aspirations towards upward mobility and freedom from traditional constraints.

Leitī themselves orient towards English, even though they tend not to be socially privileged and often have limited proficiency in the language. Use of English, and code-switching into English represent femininity and worldliness, as well as a 'symbolic escape hatch out of social marginality':

> The claims embedded in their use of English and their code-switching serve as an idiom of resistance against the symbolic and material oppression that they experience as both transgendered persons and poor Tongans.
>
> (Besnier, 2003, p. 296)

The strategy is also risky, however: they may not be in a position to carry off an English-speaking identity and they may also find themselves alienated from the local context.

ACTIVITY 4   English and *leitī* identity in Tonga (Reading C)

As an illustration of Besnier's work, please work through Reading C, in which Besnier analyses examples of language use at a *leitū* beauty pageant. Identify the main points Besnier makes about the use of English in this context and its relationship to *leitī* identity. Our comments follow.

The 'Miss Galaxy' beauty pageant provides illustrations of the risks and potential rewards associated with the use of English. English allows *leitī* to lay claim to an 'extra-local' identity, to prestige, worldliness, modernity and femaleness – attributes which, ironically, they do not possess. An inability to sustain interaction in English exposes this artifice, and speakers are likely to be ridiculed. On the other hand one speaker, Lady Amyland, uses her limited English to turn the tables on a heckler and assert control over her own identity and the means through which she expresses it. Besnier sees Lady Amyland's brief utterance as expressing a complex set of social meanings, at least one of which (the 'insider' joke) would be available only to some participants.

Many studies of gender and sexuality have, like Besnier, foregrounded identities that are in some ways ambiguous and perhaps contested. Rusty Barrett (1999), for instance, studied the language use of African-American drag queens: in Barrett's study, men who self-identify as African-American and gay but, on stage, perform as white women, using hyper-feminine language and appearance. Although Barrett does not use the term, this could be seen as a form of crossing: the speaker's performed identity does not correspond to their self-categorised identity. Barrett shows how, in performance, drag queens sometimes code-switch between this form of stereotypical 'white women's' language, and other varieties to index, simultaneously, their identities as drag queens, African-Americans and gay men.

Similarly, Kira Hall (1995) studied the language practices of telephone sex workers: women (and one man in Hall's sample) who, through their use of language, create a fantasy persona for the sexual gratification of male callers. Hall found that these workers adopted a stereotypically feminine speaking style that bore many of the hallmarks of 'powerless' language identified in early research on language and gender. Such language became, however, a powerful commodity that could be sold at a high price, and the women themselves felt they were in a relatively powerful rather than powerless position. During each conversation they were constrained by the need to appeal to recognised stereotypes of femininity, but they created the fantasy and felt in control of the interaction. They also made a good living and enjoyed considerable autonomy in their working conditions (flexible hours, for example). The study therefore reveals a tension between speakers' creativity and constraint, power and powerlessness.

Barrett's and Hall's studies focus on the deliberate and self-conscious performance of identities, but gender and sexuality are also more routinely performed: Deborah Cameron (1997a, p. 62), for instance, studied the informal talk of male college students in the USA and found that, in their interaction, the young men engaged in gossip about 'gay' men (in fact, men who did not conform to mainstream norms of masculinity) to establish themselves, by contrast, as 'red-blooded heterosexual males: not women and not queers'.

Identity and performativity

Such studies, which emphasise the relative creativity of speakers in the performance of a range of gendered and sexual identities, have often been theorised in terms of **performativity**. Within linguistics, the term 'performativity' derives from speech act theory (particularly the work of J.L. Austin, 1962 and John Searle, 1969), a view of language as a form of action. Austin termed certain utterances performative in that they perform an action simply by virtue of being uttered (for instance, saying 'I promise to pay you' constitutes the act of promising). He came to realise, however, that all language performed an action (even a statement such as 'It's raining heavily' performs the act of stating). All language may, therefore, be regarded as performative. The concept has been extended and used, in relation to identity, by the feminist philosopher Judith Butler in her work on the enactment of gender. Butler (1990, p. 141) saw gender as being actively produced and continually 'created through sustained social performances'. Rather than being an attribute that people have, gender is something people *do*.

> Gender is the repeated stylization of the body, a set of repeated acts within a rigid regulatory frame that congeal over time to produce the appearance of substance, of a natural kind of being.

(Butler, 1990, p. 33)

Deborah Cameron, drawing on Butler's notion of performativity, argues that speech is part of the stylisation process:

> The 'performative' model sheds an interesting light on the phenomenon of gendered speech. Speech too is a 'repeated stylization of the body'; the 'masculine' or 'feminine' styles of talking identified by researchers might be thought of as the 'congealed' results of repeated acts of social actors who are striving to constitute themselves as 'proper' men and women. Whereas sociolinguistics traditionally assumes that people talk the way they do because of who they (already) are, the postmodernist approach suggests that people are who they are because of (among other things) the way they talk.

(Cameron, 1997a, p. 49)

This approach to identity is consistent not just with studies of gender and sexuality discussed in this section but also with studies of speaking style, language choice, code-switching and crossing discussed in earlier sections. In each case, identities may be seen as performed within specific interactions and, more fundamentally, brought into being as social categories through repeated performances. This view of identity allows speakers some measure of creativity (and personal agency) as performers and also assumes that identities may change (as they are performed differently or, perhaps, challenged or subverted). Identity, therefore, at the individual and also the social level is not a once-and-for-all attribute but something that is in a continuing state of becoming.

This does not, however, mean that people have unfettered creativity or agency. Butler herself refers to the existence of a 'rigid, regulatory frame', and there are a number of constraints on the performance of identity. Within any interaction certain identities will be perceived as 'normal' or expected, and speakers may only be able to challenge these at some cost. Furthermore, Cameron (1997b) suggests that playing with gender or other identity categories (e.g. by Barrett's drag artists or Hall's sex workers) depends upon existing norms of behaviour, which may actually be maintained by such performances. Cameron also points to the need to consider the institutional contexts and power relations within which gender (or other aspects of identity) are enacted.

A C T I V I T Y 5   Powerful speakers?

Allow
10–15 minutes

An illustration of Cameron's position can be seen in her critique of Hall's claim that sex workers' use of 'powerless' language paradoxically puts them in a powerful position: we reproduce this critique below. We suggest you consider and evaluate Cameron's argument in the light of your reading in this section.

A critique of Hall's sex workers study

Sex work can be seen as offering some women a relatively good economic deal, but this cannot be understood without reference to the gendered (also raced and classed) character of the economy more generally. The deal is only 'good' compared with other deals available to particular groups of women. Furthermore, women's value as sex workers is determined also by a specifically *sexual* economy in which the overall majority of customers are heterosexual men; women in this market may sometimes be the sellers, but they are always the goods. Whatever advantage individual women may derive from deploying a particular kind of language in telephone sex work, the system of meanings on which the marketability of that language depends does not advantage women collectively. By recycling the traditional conjunction of femininity, powerlessness and eroticism, the sex worker's linguistic performance actually reproduces the ideological supports which help to maintain women's collective subordination [...]. Nor does it alter the underlying material inequalities. Hall's sex workers are not downtrodden victims, but whatever power and agency they manage to acquire are contained within the system: they are not challenging the traffic in women, only the terms of their participation in that traffic.

(Cameron, 1997b, pp. 31–2)

Polari: language play and gay identity

Research discussed so far in this chapter has looked at the use of certain language varieties or speaking styles in the performance of identity. In the final reading, Reading D, we turn to a variety that may, in itself, be seen as a creative enterprise in that it was deliberately constructed and maintained as a secret language.

ACTIVITY 6   Polari (Reading D)

Reading D, by Paul Baker, discusses the development and use of Polari, a secret language variety employed by working-class gay speakers in Britain at a time when homosexuality was a criminal offence. Note that, because Polari was no longer in current use when Baker began his research, his data are not based on audio-recordings of naturally occurring talk, or on his own observations. The study relies on reports of men who had used Polari when they were younger, or on published sources such as word lists or media representations.

Please now work through Reading D, focusing particularly on the purposes for which Polari was used by different groups of speakers and in different contexts.

While the reading as a whole looks at Polari as a means of performing gay identity, Baker suggests that it could be used to different effect in different contexts. It could be drawn on to negotiate identity in risky situations, to express an alternative view of the world, to subvert powerful institutions, to maintain a certain type of 'camp' identity, as a form of parody, playfulness, or irony. Note that Baker sees some uses of Polari as a form of 'double-voicing', akin to the metaphorical and ironic use of language crossing discussed in Reading B.

Gay men's English

Baker points out the contextualised nature of the meanings attributed to language as well as their potential ambiguity (sometimes intentional ambiguity in the case of Polari). Ambiguity is a feature of many types of identity negotiation, and this can be valuable in situations where speakers are unsure about the type of person they are talking to. This is nicely exemplified by some data analysed by William Leap as part of a study of what he terms 'gay men's English'.

ACTIVITY 7   Dining out

Allow
5–10 minutes

The interaction below was overheard by Leap in a crowded bookstore-café in Dupont Circle, in what is sometimes termed Washington DC's 'gay ghetto'. Speaker A is enquiring about the availability of a table for a mixed-gender group, and speaker B is the café's maître d'hôtel. Neither speaker knows the other, and their conversation can be heard by others. Can you work out what is going on in the interaction? Compare your interpretation with Leap's below.

Leap's café data

1	A:	Table for five – how long do we wait?
2	B:	Table for five. [*Pauses, consults list*] About one hour.
3	A:	One hour. [*Consults with group*] Nope, can't do it.
4		That is too long.
5	B:	Try the Mocha House. They might not be too crowded
6		tonight.
7	A:	Yeah, OK, we can go there. But you people are more
8		fun.
9	B:	Well, I don't know about that. [*While he says this, moves head to side, drops voice level, gives trace of smile*]
10	A:	Yeah, you're right. [*Establishes direct eye contact
11		with maître d'*] Maybe the Mocha House is more fun,
12		but I still like your dessert drinks here.
13	B:	[*Not breaking eye contact*] Well, you'll just have to
14		come back and try us again sometime.

(Adapted from Leap, 1996, p. 2]

Note: this extract is transcribed from fieldnotes made by Leap at the time.

Leap draws on his inside knowledge of the local context to interpret this short sequence. He describes the opening of the conversation (lines 1–4) as typical of any similar café or restaurant encounter. However, although the two subsequent episodes (B's recommendation of an alternative restaurant in lines 5–6 and A's expression of preference for the present café in lines 7–8 and 11–12) may also seem gender neutral, Leap argues that they are full of 'connotative richness' in terms of the expression of gay identity. For instance, the Mocha House, although some distance from the present café, is still a popular meeting place for gay men. This would be known by speaker A if he were gay, and also familiar with the area. However, because the Mocha House also has a heterosexual clientele, speaker A need not read a gay-centred meaning into the utterance. In fact, there is no immediate evidence that A has interpreted the utterance as gay-centred. Nevertheless, he does remark that 'you people are more fun', an expression Leap argues is ambiguous. The underlying gay meaning is supported by B's statement, and his nonverbal behaviour. While A agrees that the Mocha House may be more fun, he cites another reason for wanting to eat in the present café – their dessert drinks (line 12). Leap interprets this as a less subtle orientation towards a gay focus ('dessert often provides a prelude to other activities'). He comments:

> This combination of verbal and nonverbal statements was much more forceful than any of the other statements in the text and provided the basis for the more elaborate and somewhat more gay-explicit version of 'please come again' that the *maître d'* used as his closing remark ...

(Leap, 1996, p. 4)

Leap's study provides a further example of the highly contextualised and subtle nature of the performance of identity. Furthermore, it has shown that identity may be signified by less obvious means than the use of specific linguistic features. Words and phrases that do not conventionally index gayness (or other aspects of identity) may nevertheless have this function when used between certain speakers, in certain ways, in certain contexts.

3.5 Conclusion

In this chapter we have considered how people may use language to 'style' themselves – to take on a particular persona or juggle between personae in interaction with others. The research we have discussed argues that language varieties (e.g. accents and dialects), and English itself in bilingual contexts, are meaningful: that varieties acquire meaning from their use by certain social groups, and may therefore be drawn on by speakers to indicate their association with such groups.

ACTIVITY 8   **Review**

Allow about
10 minutes

Chapter 1 established a distinction between approaches to the study of language that were relatively textual, focusing on the formal properties of language use; and approaches that were more contextualised – i.e. taking greater account of how language is used in context. How would you locate the readings in this chapter in terms of this distinction?

Comment

It seems to us that Penelope Eckert's research has a strong textual component, in that she focuses on the formal properties of speaking style: she identifies linguistic features (grammar, pronunciation), and looks at their distributional patterns – how they are distributed across social groups. However, she combines this with an ethnographic study, based on close contact with speakers, observation and interviews as well as recorded language data. This would give her a more contextualised understanding – i.e. she can see how the linguistic forms whose distributional patterns she documents may be used by particular speakers, in particular contexts, to particular effect.

Similarly, Paul Baker is interested in the forms Polari takes and how the terms in its lexicon derive from different linguistic processes (rhyming slang, reversals or back slang), but he also emphasises that Polari may be used in different ways — to maintain group identity, to subvert authority, to parody others — and that its meaning for its speakers is therefore highly context dependent.

Rampton's study of crossing and Besnier's study of code-switching between Tongan and English adopt an ethnographic methodology. They focus on the strategic use of language, or how speakers may adopt a particular language, or switch between languages to index a particular identity or shift in identity. Again, this is underpinned by a contextualised approach to the study of language use.

All these studies, like much contemporary work on language and identity, would see identity not simply as an attribute that affects the way we speak (so that someone speaks as they do because they are a jock or a burnout, etc.); but as something that is performed in context. The term 'persona', with its dramatic associations, is sometimes used to indicate that people take on, or foreground, certain aspects of their identity in interaction with others. The analogy may seem to work best for the performance of identities seen as figurative (metaphorical or ironic), or for performances that are more self-conscious and deliberate (Rampton, Besnier and Baker include examples of such relatively artful performances). But it is also extended to more everyday 'performance', where speakers routinely, through their use of language, take on, shift between, negotiate aspects of identity without consciously focusing on such interactional activity.

The notion of performance highlights speaker creativity, but as Cameron pointed out, the larger social context within which interactions take place and the power relations between participants necessarily affect what individual speakers may do. In claiming a particular identity speakers may of course seek to subvert power relations, but there is always a tension between speaker creativity and social, institutional and local (interactional) constraints.

READING A: Messing with style

Penelope Eckert

Our identities are not fixed things. Rather, our lives are a continuous development of a self, as we pursue desires and adapt to life stages and situations. A central part of our construction of selves is stylistic practice, in which we manage our external displays so as to provide others with a desired understanding of what we're like. This reading is about some ways in which we use language in stylistic practice.

Generally, as we refine and present selves to others, we try to do it subtly. We don't enunciate, 'Please think of me as a responsible businessman'. Rather, we put on a dark grey suit, white shirt and dark tie, carry a briefcase and avoid funny walks. When we use clothing, we're able to make statements without appearing to, as the clothing is taken as a reflection of what we are. Of course, not just anyone can wear these outfits successfully. A woman showing up in an outfit identical to those of the men around her may not be treated as responsible, and will likely find her gender and/or sexuality called into question. Many businesswomen, therefore, tweak the outfit – the suit will be red, the shirt will have frills, or the briefcase will be a big handbag – thus feminizing the style sufficiently to appear gender appropriate while claiming similarity to other business people.

This practice of appropriating existing resources to construct a style of one's own is fundamental to social life. Dick Hebdige (Hebdige, 1984) referred to this process as *bricolage*, whereby people recombine resources to create something new. When people do this, they have a sense of the existing styles, who wears them, who those people are and what the link is between their personae and their styles. They have a sense of the meanings of the elements that make up the styles (the color of the suit, the cut of the jeans, the logo on the tee-shirt). People have a sense of the social landscape, and of the distribution of stylistic elements across that landscape. Indeed, it is style that makes that landscape accessible, and people's stylistic moves place them in the landscape, and at the same time change that landscape if only a little.

I witnessed an excellent example of fashion bricolage while interviewing two teenage girls in 1985. These girls belonged to the dominant popular group in a high school, and like the others in the group, they regularly dressed in a clean-cut all-American style with designer jeans, polo shirts and pastel colors. At the same time, they had a certain admiration for the punks and new wavers, who appeared sophisticated and independent of high school norms. In contrast to the 'all American' look, the new wavers dressed primarily in black, and wore pegged pants (pants that narrow at the ankle). Wanting to make a move to signal their inclination towards that independence, yet finding black to be too strong a statement, the two girls pegged their blue jeans. Thus by attributing meanings to elements of a style, they were able to recombine elements to tweak their original style, thus tweaking their statement of what they themselves were like.

We do the same thing with language. While the basic features of our dialect are set in place by the environment in which we grow up, the actual deployment of those dialect features – as well as of many linguistic features that are not part of regional dialects – is left to individual agency. The things we say are of course central to who we are and who we become. But also, the ways we say those things are crucially important as well. Language offers up a wide range of resources that we can use and recombine to make moves very much like pegging one's designer blue jeans. Normally a very standard speaker, I can use nonstandard features for a particular effect. I can tell my class, when they complain about the difficulty of an assignment I've given them, 'I know it ain't easy'. This has a complex effect, suggesting familiarity, solidarity, and perhaps trivializing the difficulty. I can ask 'To whom am I speaking?' if I wish to intimidate. And I can ask 'To whom am I speakin'?' if I want to be comical. In these cases, I'm making momentary moves – moves that show stance in a particular situation. Stylistic practice, then, is a kind of performance (Goffman, 1959). A stylistic move can be momentary, showing stance in a particular situation, but also my 'self' can be seen as an accumulation of such moves – as the kinds of stances people come to expect me to take across situations. If I reduce -*ing* on occasion (as in *speakin'*), I signal something like informality in that particular situation. If I reduce it a lot of the time, the cumulative effect may be taken to indicate that I'm an informal person.

In a study of high school students in the Detroit suburban area, I was able to see how linguistic features, including current sound changes, serve as a stylistic resource in the construction of social class. But most important, class as such was not the focus of this stylistic work so much as the practices that articulate class with adolescent life. A girl who puts on her pink polo shirt in the morning is not saying to herself, 'I'm going to look nice and middle class today'. She might be saying, 'I'm going to look fresh, clean-cut and all-American today', or, more likely, 'I'm going to wow people with this shirt – it's just like the one that all the cool people wear, but nobody has this color'. And that fresh, clean-cut look, as well as the girl's friendship group, may be associated with a variety of things that define middle class adolescence.

Throughout much of the United States, particularly in schools with a predominantly white student population, two opposed social categories emerge around opposing orientations to the school institution. These categories differ in a variety of ways from region to region, but the underlying dynamics are the same – one category aligns with the school, the other in opposition to the school. In the northeastern part of the country, which includes the Detroit area, the common categories are called (and call themselves) *jocks* and *burnouts*. The jocks, named for their link to sports (although there are jocks who are not athletes), are students who locate their social lives in the school institution. They dominate extracurricular activities, and base their social networks on participation in these activities. They are the members and officers of the student council, the class officers, the cheerleaders and the football players. They are a hierarchical culture, competing for roles and constructing careers in the school's corporate culture. These careers, in turn, are closely linked to their college preparatory curriculum, as they all plan on attending university. The burnouts, on the other hand, find school activities both meaningless and infantilizing. Most of them follow a vocational curriculum, and are headed for the Detroit area workplace upon graduation. Strongly egalitarian, they see their friendships and their local base as enduring beyond high school, and they pursue their activities in their neighborhoods, and in the larger urban area. The jock–burnout opposition is based in deep class-based ideological differences, and is marked by considerable hostility – in some schools and at some times, violence erupts between members of the two categories.

Jock and burnout status is clearly related to students' class origins. But while as a whole the jocks come primarily from the upper half of the local socioeconomic hierarchy and the burnouts come primarily from the lower half, there are a number of jocks from working class families, and burnouts from middle class families.[1] And when we look at the linguistic patterns of the jocks and the burnouts, we find that they conform entirely to their social category – not to their class origins. Their language use corresponds to the place they are carving out for themselves in the high school, and together their linguistic choices constitute very clear jock and burnout styles. These styles are, in turn, middle and working class styles, but it is the complexity of the high school social order that gives these styles – and class – meaning.

The jocks and the burnouts together constitute just about half of the school population. But the centrality of the jock–burnout opposition in the school social order is evidenced in the fact that the remainder of the school student population refer to themselves as 'in-betweens', and commonly characterize themselves in terms of placement between the two poles – or the characteristics they share with the jocks on the one hand, and the burnouts on the other. Jocks and burnouts constitute the two extremes of common possibility in the school, and their stylistic behavior expresses this polarization.

The jocks and burnouts distinguish themselves in a variety of ways. The jocks' middle class and institutional orientation and the burnouts' working class, anti-institutional and pro-local orientation are in constant stylistic contrast. While the jocks make enthusiastic use of school facilities, for example, making their lockers into a home away from home, the burnouts refuse to eat the cafeteria food and don't use their lockers, spending their free time in school in the school courtyard. This courtyard has double symbolic value, since it is the school's smoking area, and smoking is a key burnout symbol. While the jocks organize dances in the school, the burnouts hang out in their neighborhoods or cruise into Detroit. The city represents a variety of things that burnouts value – it is the locus of their expected employment after high school, but more important, they view urban youth as more independent, tougher, more knowledgeable, more street-wise. Much of the symbolic practice of the jocks and the burnouts, therefore, expresses the opposition between an institutional and an urban orientation. The jocks wear designer jeans, polo shirts in pastel colors, school jackets and school sweaters, while the burnouts wear rock concert tee-shirts, Detroit jackets or jeans jackets over hooded sweatshirts, and dark colors, primarily black. (Note that the color symbolism described above in California is quite far-reaching.)

In the early eighties, when this research was in progress, bell-bottom jeans were on their way out and the new style was straight-legged jeans, even baggy jeans with pegged bottoms. As the jocks enthusiastically embraced the new styles, the burnouts hung onto the bell bottoms, both because of their association with 'freak' rebellion, and because the purchase of new fashions is what they see as an inappropriate statement of affluence. A quick quantitative survey of jean leg shapes shows the symbolic value of this shape. During lunch period, when students are free to wander around in one end of the building, the jocks and burnouts split up into their territories, and the in-betweens array themselves with, or between, the two territories. During lunch over a period of several days, I recorded the shape of each pair of jeans occupying three distinct areas in the school. I assigned numerical values to each jean width, representing a continuum of width and of trendiness: a value of 4 to the widest bells, 3 to the slightly more conservative flared jeans, 2 to straight legs and 1 to the most trendy pegged baggies. In the hall in front of the cafeteria, where the jocks gather after lunch, and where they set up tables to sell tickets to big events, the average jean leg width was 2.6. In the courtyard, where the burnouts go to eat fast food and smoke during lunch, the average width was 3.7. And in the hallway between these two areas, occupied mostly by in-betweens, the average jean leg width fell nicely in between at 3.

Like their clothing and activities, the jocks' linguistic style conforms with their institutional engagement and aspirations. Their grammar is overwhelmingly standard. The burnouts' anti-school stance, on the other hand, shows up clearly in their non-standard grammar. Thus, for example, it is not surprising that while the burnouts show a tendency to use patterns of nonstandard negation (e.g. *I didn't do nothing*), this pattern is rare in the speech of the jocks (see Figure 1). This little linguistic fact is not a reflection of what the jocks and burnouts 'know', since the burnouts do use a good deal of standard negation and there is no burnout who uses 100% non-standard negation. Thus while for some of the burnouts the use of non-standard negation might indeed come more easily, it is clear that in many cases it constitutes a stylistic choice. It is important to note the gender difference in Figure 1 as well – the jock girls' very limited use of nonstandard negation is a clear indication of their need to be 'squeaky-clean', while the burnout girls are under no such constraint, and their negation pattern is more like that of the burnout boys.

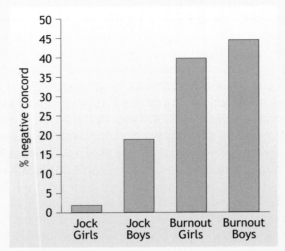

'Negative concord' refers here to the percentage use of non-standard patterns of negation.

Figure 1   % non-standard negation by gender and social category

If the jocks are the institutionally, career-oriented people, though, one might ask why the boys are using as much nonstandard negation as they are. Do all the jock boys use close to 20% negative concord? There are two primary ways in which boys become jocks. They can play on major varsity athletic teams, or they can participate in non-athletic student activities, particularly student government. Many of the jocks do both, but some only do one or the other.[2] As Figure 2 shows, it is the jock boys who are primarily athletes who use the preponderance of negative concord, while the jock boys who are not athletes – those who are primarily politicians – use the same squeaky clean grammar as the jock girls.

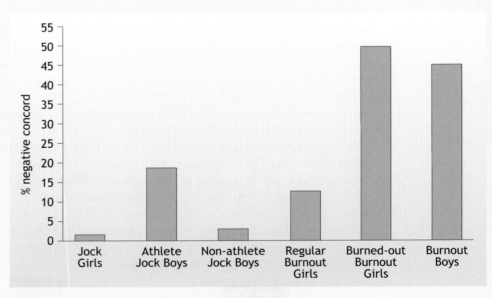

Figure 2   % non-standard negation by gender and subcategory

Meanwhile, there are two quite distinct groups of burnout girls. The vast majority of burnout girls, commonly referred to as the 'regular' burnouts, constitute a fairly large network, and their identities as burnouts are largely based on class ideology. While they get in trouble with the authorities because of their resistance to adult domination, they are not what one would call 'wild'. On the other hand, there is a smaller group of burnout girls who are considered – and who pride themselves in being – wild. These girls have been called 'burned-out burnouts', and refer to themselves as 'the biggest burnouts'. If the jock girls present a squeaky-clean style, the burned-out burnout girls present a wild urban style. As Figure 2 shows, the burned-out burnout girls are the biggest users of negative concord in the entire school, outdoing not only jocks and in-betweens, but the male burnouts as well. (This should give pause to anyone who claims that women's speech is more standard than men's. For a fuller discussion of this issue, see Eckert, 1990; Eckert and McConnell-Ginet, 1992.)

Non-standard grammar makes a huge statement. But vowels, while they may be more subtle, are also important resources in the construction of styles. The dialect of the Detroit area is characterized by long-term and continuing changes in the pronunciation of certain vowels (for discussion, see Eckert, 2000). There are some more recent pronunciations that show up only in the speech of younger people: the backing of /uh/ so that *lunch* sounds like *launch*, the backing of /e/ so that *flesh* sounds like *flush*, and the raising of the nucleus (the first part) of the diphthong /ay/ so that *quite* sounds like *quoit*. These three new changes are more common in the urban area than in the suburbs, and indeed appear to be spreading outwards into the suburban area. One might say that they contribute an 'urban' sound to speech. In keeping with their Detroit jackets and rock concert tee-shirts, both of which evidence a reaching out into the urban area, burnouts are the leaders in the adoption of these changes. Figure 3 shows the difference in the use of the backing of /e/ and /uh/ and the raising of the nucleus of /ay/ by gender and social category. The numbers shown are the percentage of use of extreme urban pronunciations for each vowel. The differences between jock and burnout pronunciations are not as stark as the differences in the use of negative concord. But they are statistically highly significant, and the cumulative effect across the vowels is quite striking. Also, while overall people raise the nucleus of /ay/ very little, the difference between the jocks' and burnouts' raising is significant both statistically and qualitatively, because the raising represented in this figure is extreme – with a nucleus pronounced as [o] or even [u]. As in the case of nonstandard negation, it is the jock girls who are the most conservative speakers, using more traditional pronunciations, and the burnout girls and boys both make the greatest use of the newer urban forms.

'Backing' and 'raising' refer to changes in the way sounds are articulated that result in shifts in pronunciation: backing means a sound is produced further back in the mouth, and raising that it is produced higher in the mouth.

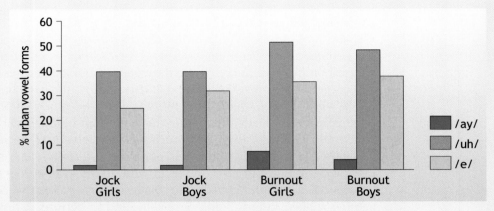

Figure 3　% urban forms of three vowels by gender and social category

If we put together all the differential features that jocks and burnouts employ – linguistic, sartorial, and other – we end up with two quite unmistakable styles. The one is suburban and school-oriented; the other is urban and rebellious. And while these styles appear to many as simply suburban and urban, they are quite tightly connected to class through a class-differentiated orientation in school. People often think of style as an add-on – as something people do for fun, for artifice, for pretense. But style is the means by which we put ourselves on the social table – by which we enter our identity work into the public arena, by which we make claims and by which we invite engagement.

Notes

1　For a detailed account of jock and burnout origins and ideologies, see Eckert, 1989.

2　Note that there are varsity athletes who are not jocks in this sense. Occasionally a burnout may play varsity sports, and some athletes are in-betweens.

References

ECKERT, P. (1990) 'The whole woman: sex and gender differences in variation', *Language Variation and Change*, **1**, pp. 245–67.

ECKERT, P. (2000) *Linguistic Variation as Social Practice*, Oxford, Blackwell.

ECKERT, P. and McCONNELL-GINET, S. (1992) 'Think practically and look locally: language and gender as community-based practice', *Annual Review of Anthropology*, **21**, pp. 461–90.

GOFFMAN, E. (1959) *The Presentation of Self in Everyday Life*, New York, Doubleday.

HEBDIGE, D. (1984) *Subculture: The Meaning of Style*, New York, Methuen.

Source: commissioned for this volume.

READING B: Language crossing

Ben Rampton

Ben Rampton's research on language crossing is based on an ethnographic study carried out in a neighbourhood in the South Midlands of England. Rampton studied the language of young people of Indian, Pakistani, African Caribbean and Anglo descent. He worked with a group of 23 eleven-to-thirteen-year-olds in 1984, and returned in 1987 to work with approximately 64 fourteen-to-sixteen-year-olds. He used radio microphones to record his informants' speech, along with observation, interviews and participants' commentaries on extracts from their interactions. Rampton identified about 68 examples of Panjabi crossing; 160 examples of what he terms 'stylised Asian English'; and more than 250 examples with a clear Creole influence. Crossing took place in interactions with adults, with peers, and in performance art.

Language crossing: a preliminary definition

The term 'language crossing' (or 'code-crossing') refers to the use of a language which isn't generally thought to 'belong' to the speaker. Language crossing involves a sense of movement across quite sharply felt social or ethnic boundaries, and it raises issues of legitimacy that participants need to reckon with in the course of their encounter. Language crossing was closely woven into everyday talk and social activity in the adolescent friendship groups I studied (Rampton, 2005; first edition 1995), but it occurred at moments when the constraints of ordinary social order were relaxed and normal social relations couldn't be taken for granted.

Example 1

Participants: Ray (13 years old, male, of Anglo/African-Caribbean descent; wearing radio-microphone), Ian (12 years old, male, Anglo descent), Hanif (12 years old, male, Bangladeshi descent), others.
   Setting: 1984. Coming out of lessons into the playground at break. Ian and Ray are best friends. Stevie Wonder is a singer whose song *I just called to say I love you* was very famous. Ray has a bad foot (see line 17).

See below for transciption conventions.

	RAY	IAN
	HANIF	( )
	IAN	((from afar)) RAY THE COOL RAY THE COOL
	HANIF	yeh Stevie Wonder YAAA ((laughs loudly))
5	RAY	[it's worser than that
	IAN	((singing)): [I just called to say
	HANIF	ha (let's) sing (him) a song
	IAN	I hate you
	HANIF	((loud laughs))
10	ANON	((coming up)) ( ) are you running for the school (.)
	RAY	huh
	ANON	are [you running for the school
	RAY	[no
	ANON	[I am
15	IAN	[he couldn't run for th- he couldn't [run for the school
	RAY	[SHUT UP
	RAY	I couldn- I don wan- [I can't run anyway
	HANIF	[right we're wasting our [time
	IAN	[I did
20	HANIF	[come on (we're) wasting our time
	IAN	[you come last ( )
	HANIF	[mumumu
	ANON	[I came second
	IAN	((singing)) I just called to say [I got] a big
25	RAY	[I hate you]
	IAN	[**lulla**]
		((Panjabi for 'willy'))
	HANIF AND OTHERS	((loud laughter))
	RAY	((continuing Ian's song)) so's Ian Hinks (1.5)
		((Ray laughs)) no you haven't you got a tiny one (.)
30		you've only got (a arse)

Transcription conventions:

[time [I did	overlapping speaking turns
(.)	pause of less than one second
(1.5)	approximate length of pause in seconds
wan-	break-off/unfinished word
CAPITALS	loud enunciation
((laughs))	'stage directions', or comments
( )	speech inaudible
(let's)	speech hard to discern, analyst's guess
bold	instance of crossing of central interest in discussion

Names have been altered.

In this extract, Ian directs some Panjabi abuse at his good friend Ray, and among other things, the formulaic use of song helps to ensure that it is understood as ritual and jocular, not personal and serious (cf. Labov, 1972; Goodwin and Goodwin, 1987). When he starts out in lines 6 and 8, he seems to be identifying himself with the first person expressed in the song, but when he repeats it in lines 24 and 26, it looks as though he's putting the words in Ray's mouth rather than claiming the 'I' for himself – certainly, Ray's retaliation in line 28 suggests that it's him that has been attributed the item in Panjabi, not Ian. Whatever, Ian comes off best in their brief exchange of ritual abuse: Ian's *lulla* upstages Ray's effort to pre-empt him in line 25; it is Ian who wins an enthusiastic response from third parties in line 27; and in lines 29 and 30, Ray evidently judges his own immediate retort (line 28) as itself rather weak.

The second example of crossing involves Creole.

Example 2

Participants: Asif (15, male, Pakistani descent, wearing a radio-microphone), Alan (15, male, Anglo descent), Ms Jameson (25 +, female, Anglo descent), and in the background, Mr Chambers (25 +, male, Anglo descent).

Setting: 1987. Asif and Alan are in detention for Ms Jameson, who was herself a little late for it. She is explaining why she didn't arrive on time, and now she wants to go and fetch her lunch.

```
1    MS J    I had to go and see the headmaster

     ASIF    why

     MS J    (        ) (.) none of your business

     ALAN    a- about us (        )

5    MS J    ((p)) no I'll be [back

     ASIF                     [((f)) hey how can you see the
             headmaster when he was in dinner (.)

     MS J    ((quietly)) that's precisely why I didn't see him

     ASIF    what (.)

10   MS J    I'll be back in a second with my lunch [( )

     ASIF                                           [((f)) NO ((loud tut))
             dat's sad man (.) (I'll b)
             I [had to miss my play right I've gotta go

     ALAN      [( with mine)

15           (2.5) ((Ms J must now have left the room))

     ASIF    ((Creole influenced)) **llunch** (.) you don't need no
             lunch [**not'n** grow anyway ((laughs))

     ALAN          [((laughs))

     ASIF    have you eat your lunch Alan
```

In this extract, lines 1–9 involve a verbal tussle in which Asif and Alan use questions to undermine the positions that Ms Jameson stakes out in what she says. Asif's question in line 2 treats the account she gives of her late arrival as inadequate; she rebuts his inquiry as illegitimate in line 3 but this is then undermined by Alan in line 4; and in lines 6–7, Ms Jameson is delayed in the departure she announced in line 5 by a question that upgrades the query over her initial excuse into an explicit challenge. All this time, she has been locked into the interaction by the boys' questions, but at line 10, she breaks out of this pattern, ignores Asif (line 9), again announces her departure and leaves without saying anything more. With Ms Jameson no longer attending to him, Asif launches into what Goffman calls 'afterburn' (1971, pp. 152–3) – dissident remarks about another person's unjust or offensive conduct produced just after they've left the scene – and in this display of resilience, Asif uses some Creole/Black English. Admittedly, it can sometimes be hard trying to distinguish Creole from the local multiracial vernacular, and Asif's pronunciation of *that* in *dat's sad man* is ambiguous. But in lines 16 and 17, he uses a characteristically Creole pronunciation of the vowel in *not* (cf. Wells, 1982, p. 576; Sebba, 1993, pp. 153–4), and the stretched [l] in his first *lunch* maybe connects with a black speech feature noted by Hewitt in south London (1986, p. 134).

The last example of crossing also relates to a breach of conduct, though here the putative offender is a younger pupil and the language used is a variety I've called stylised Asian English.

Example 3

Participants and setting: At the start of the school year, Mohan (15 years old, male, Indian descent, wearing radio-microphone), Jagdish (15 years old, male, Indian descent) and Sukhbir (15 years old, male, Indian descent) are in the bicycle sheds looking at bicycles at the start of the new academic year. Some new pupils run past them.

1	SUKHBIR	STOP RUNNING AROUND YOU GAYS (.)
2	SUKHBIR	[((laughs))
	MOHAN	((using a strong Indian accent for the words in bold:))
3		[**EH** (.) **THIS IS NOT MIDD(LE SCHOOL**) no more (1.0)
4		this is a respective (2.0)
5	ANON	(school)
6	MOHAN	school (.) yes (.) took the words out my mouth (4.5)

In this extract, Mohan is claiming that the norms of conduct appropriate to secondary pupils during breaktime have been broken. In line 1, Sukhbir uses his normal vernacular for what Goffman has termed a 'prime'. This occurs when someone has potentially offended another person, e.g. by flouting some social convention. The prime is designed to get the offender to make things better – perhaps by apologising or giving an explanation for their behaviour (Goffman, 1971, pp. 154ff., 109–14). In this case, no apology or other remediation is forthcoming. In line 3, Mohan's follow-up words seem merely to remind the (disappearing) pupils that old rules of conduct no longer apply, but the switch from his normal accent to stylised Asian English is significant. Stylised Asian English was stereotypically associated with limited linguistic and cultural competence (Rampton, 2005/1995a, chs 2.3, 3 and 6) and by implication the switch suggests the pupils are irresponsible or lacking in self-control.

Crossing: the definition elaborated

Two things seem to run through all of these examples (as well as many more). First, the speakers moved outside the language varieties they normally used and they briefly adopted codes which they didn't have full and easy access to. Other kids often commented on this code-crossing, and the fact that white and Panjabi youngsters generally avoided using Creole in the company of black peers, and that white and black peers hardly ever used stylised Asian English to address peers with Panjabi backgrounds, points to the constraints and sensitivities involved.

Second, these appropriations of someone else's language occurred in moments and activities when 'the world of daily life known in common with others and with others taken for granted' (Garfinkel, 1984, p. 35) was problematised or partially suspended. In Example 1, crossing occurred as a form of ritual abuse, which works by suspending normal considerations of truth and falsity (cf. Labov, 1972; Goodwin and Goodwin, 1987). In Examples 2 and 3, crossing occurred at moments when there was a heightened sense that decorum had been disrupted. And elsewhere it occurred in games and in the context of performance art, where there was an agreed relaxation of routine interaction's rules and constraints.

These points have important implications for our understanding of (a) ethnic processes and (b) the way social identities are negotiated in interactional code-switching.

Taking ethnicity first, crossing never actually claimed that the speaker was 'really' black or Asian – it didn't imply that the crosser could move unproblematically in and out of the friends' heritage language in any new kind of open biculturalism. The fact that crossing occurred in unusual, non-routine moments meant that, in the routine everyday world that adolescents treated as *normal*, the boundaries round ethnicity were relatively fixed. Even so, these boundaries weren't inviolable, and quite plainly, adolescents didn't submit reverentially to absolutist ideas about ethnicity being fixed at birth or during the early years of socialisation. Language crossing cannot be seen as a runaway deconstruction of ethnicity, emptying it of all meaning, but the significance of ethnicity wasn't left unquestioned, invisibly and incontrovertibly pervading common sense. Crossing was an established interactional practice that foregrounded inherited ethnicity itself, and in doing so, it at least partially destabilised it. As such, crossing warrants close attention in sociological discussion of the emergence of 'new ethnicities of the margins', multiracial ethnicities 'predicated on difference and diversity' (Hall, 1988).

Beyond that – second – the data on crossing points to the subtle ways in which youngsters *differed* in their alignment with *different* ethnic identities, and this becomes clear if we relate crossing to Gumperz's classic distinction between 'metaphorical' and 'situational' code-switching (Blom and Gumperz, 1972). Both types of code-switching introduce a different language variety into the ongoing interaction, but in situational code-switching, the switch to, say, more standard speech signals a shift in the situation – perhaps that the situation is becoming more formal. In contrast, metaphorical code-switching introduces a speech variety that is more incongruous and harder for the recipients to accept as language for continuing the interaction. Returning to the data in this paper, language crossing comes close to metaphorical code-switching by virtue of the fact that it generally violated taken-for-granted assumptions about everyday life and involved a combination of speaker and language variety that contravened normal expectations.

However, the 'metaphorical'/'situational' dichotomy is actually often a lot less clear than these definitions suggest. Studies of dead and 'sleeping' metaphor show that the distinction between the literal and the figurative, between the ordinary and the exceptional, is highly variable and often ambiguous (e.g. Leech, 1969; Lakoff and Johnson, 1980), and this is particularly relevant to the language crossing into Creole.

When youngsters switched into Creole, they often seemed to identify rather closely with the voice/accent they were using, and it sometimes seemed as though crossing looked towards the fusion of self and voice in a new identity capable of holding an uncontested place in everyday reality. A range of factors affected the extent to which crossers were able to project Creole as an authentic expression of their identity – who the speaker and recipients were, what their relationship was, the degree of their involvement with black culture, the particular occasion, the specific contours of the character being claimed, and so forth (see Hewitt, 1986, ch. 5; Rampton, 2005/1995a, chs 5, 8 and 9). In some exchanges, Creole only occurred in actions that were offered and taken as joking, while in others the same acts might be taken for real. But what was clear was that social reality, and the speaker's position within this, were the focus for some degree of interactional renegotiation. In fact, Creole crossing contrasted quite sharply with the use of stylised Asian English. From interviews and other evidence, it seemed that Asian English stood for a stage of historical transition that most adolescents felt they were leaving behind, and in one way or another Asian English consistently symbolised distance from the main currents of adolescent life. In line with this, stylised Asian English was often used as what Goffman calls a 'say-for' (1974, p. 535) – a voice not being claimed as part of the speaker's own identity but one that was relevant to the identity of the person being addressed or targeted (see Example 3).

This contrast can be systematised and elaborated with Bakhtin's notion of 'double-voicing'. Double-voicing describes the way that utterances can be affected by a plurality of competing languages, discourses and voices. With double-voicing, speakers use someone else's discourse (or language) for their own purposes, 'inserting a new semantic intention into a discourse which already has [...] an intention of its own. Such a discourse [...] must be seen as belonging to someone else. In one discourse, two semantic intentions appear, two voices' (Bakhtin, 1984, p. 189).

In fact, though, there are several kinds of double-voicing, and one of these is called *uni-directional*. With uni-directional double-voicing, speakers go along with the momentum of the second voice, though it generally retains an element of otherness which makes the appropriation conditional and introduces some reservation into the speaker's use of it. But at the same time, the boundary between the speaker and the voice they are adopting can diminish, to the extent that there is a 'fusion of voices'. When that happens, discourse ceases to be double-voiced, and instead becomes 'direct, unmediated discourse' (Bakhtin, 1984, p. 199). Double-voicing in Creole generally seemed to be uni-directional. Creole was much more extensively integrated into multiracial peer group recreation than either stylised Asian English or Panjabi, and it was used much more by members of other ethnic groups. Creole symbolised an excitement and an excellence in youth culture that many adolescents aspired to, and it was even referred to as 'future language'. For a great deal of the time, there was certainly some reservation in the way Creole was used by whites and Asians, but even so, crossers tended to use Creole to lend emphasis to evaluations that synchronised with the identities they maintained in their ordinary speech. In line with this, their Creole was often hard to disentangle from their local multiracial vernacular (Hewitt, 1986, pp. 148, 151) – in Bakhtin's terms, crossing in Creole came close to the point where uni-directional double-voicing shifted over into direct unmediated discourse (see example 2).

The opposite of uni-directional double-voicing is *vari-directional* double-voicing, in which the speaker 'again speaks in someone else's discourse, but introduces into that discourse a semantic intention directly opposed to the original one'. In vari-directional double-voicing, the two voices are much more clearly demarcated, and they are not only distant but also opposed (Bakhtin, 1984, p. 193). This often seemed to be the case with stylised Asian English.

Returning to the sociolinguistic research on code-switching, the 'uni-' vs 'vari-directional double-voicing' distinction points to different kinds of metaphorical code-switching, though it would be better now to use the term 'figurative code-switching' as a broad label to contrast with 'situational switching'. I shall use 'metaphorical' for a particular kind of 'figurative' language. According to Leech (1969), when people process metaphors, they work on the assumption that the figurative meaning is somehow complementary to the literal meaning, and this contrasts with 'irony', which works on the assumption that figurative and literal meaning are somehow in contrast/opposition. Shifting over to bilingual language use, the complementary nature of metaphor aligns it with uni-directional double-voicing, while the dimension of contrast in irony links into the vari-directional type. This can be summarised in the following scheme:

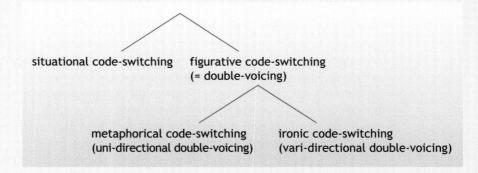

Crossing as performance

From the perspective of research on language crossing, it seems particularly important not to think of conversation as a genre distinct from stylisation and artful performance. As Bauman and Briggs stress, 'performances are not simply artful uses of language that stand apart both from day-to-day life and from larger questions of meaning' (1990, p. 60). Furthermore, crucially, performances allow the critical examination of language practices and the beliefs and values that underpin these: 'Performance [...] provides a frame that invites critical reflection on communicative processes' (ibid.).

All this seemed true in the performance of language crossing. First, crossing was often set off from ordinary talk with only the lightest change of 'key' (Goffman, 1974, ch. 3). It arose in spontaneous interaction in, for example, small-scale speech acts such as response cries, or in the vicinity of minor transgressions (see Examples 2 and 3 above). And second, in the analysis sketched out above, I have argued that crossing foregrounded ethnicity and that, at least partially, it constituted a challenge to dominant notions of ethnolinguistic identity and inheritance (for elaborations, see Hewitt, 1992; Rampton, 2005/1995a, ch. 12; 1995b).

References

BAKHTIN, M. ([1929] 1984) *Problems in Dostoevsky's Poetics*, Minneapolis, University of Minnesota Press.

BAUMAN, R. and BRIGGS, C. (1990) 'Poetics and performance as critical perspectives on language and social life', *Annual Review of Anthropology*, **19**, pp. 59–88.

BLOM, J. and GUMPERZ, J. (1972) 'Social meaning in linguistic structure: code-switching in Norway', in S. GUMPERZ, and D. HYMES, (eds) *Directions in Sociolinguistics*, Cambridge, Cambridge University Press.

GARFINKEL, H. ([1967] 1984) *Studies in Ethnomethodology*, Oxford, Oxford Polity Press.

GOFFMAN, E. (1971) *Relations in Public*, London, Allen Lane.

GOFFMAN, E. (1974) *Frame Analysis*, Harmondsworth, Penguin.

GOFFMAN, E. (1981) *Forms of Talk*, Oxford, Blackwell.

GOODWIN, M. and GOODWIN, C. (1987) 'Children's arguing', in S. PHILIPS, S. STEELE, and C. TANZ, (eds) *Language, Gender and Sex in Comparative Perspective*, Cambridge, Cambridge University Press.

HALL, S. (1988) 'New ethnicities', *ICA Documents*, **7**, pp. 27–31.

HEWITT, R. (1986) *White Talk Black Talk*, Cambridge, Cambridge University Press.

HEWITT, R. (1992) 'Language, youth and the destabilisation of ethnicity', in C. PALMGREN, K. LOVGREN, and G. BOLIN, (eds) *Ethnicity in Youth Culture*, Stockholm, Youth Culture at Stockholm University.

LABOV, W. (1972) *Language in the Inner City*, Oxford, Blackwell.

LAKOFF, G. and JOHNSON, M. (1980) *Metaphors We Live By*, Chicago, IL, Chicago University Press.

LEECH, G. (1969) *A Linguistic Guide to English Poetry*, London, Longman.

RAMPTON, B. (2005; first edition 1995a) *Crossing: Language and Ethnicity Among Adolescents*, Manchester, St Jerome Press; 1st ed. London, Longman.

RAMPTON, B. (1995b) 'Language crossing and the problematisation of ethnicity and socialisation', *Pragmatics*, **5/4**, pp. 485–514.

SEBBA, M. (1993) *London Jamaican: A Case Study in Language Interaction*, London, Longman.

WELLS, J. (1982) *Accents of English, 1–3*, Cambridge, Cambridge University Press.

Source: commissioned for this volume. (An earlier and more elaborated version appears in AUER, P. (1998)).

READING C: Extracts from 'Crossing genders, mixing languages'

Niko Besnier

In analysing the everyday language use of Tongan leitī, *Besnier found that they frequently switched between Tongan and English, even when their competence in English was limited and even when they referred to concepts that are highly specific to Tongan society and culture. He argues that the orientation to English and to the social and political associations of English in Tonga is 'part and parcel of* leitī *identity' (p. 286). One public context in which English figures prominently is the annual beauty pageant that* leitī *have staged since the early 1990s in some of the most prominent venues in the country.*

[Beauty pageants] are particularly interesting because, for many Tongans, they represent a context in which *fakaleitī* identity is most clearly elaborated. *Leitī* themselves and their non-*leitī* champions (principally members of a cadre of influential professional women *d'un certain âge*) see the pageant as a prime opportunity to present themselves in the best light and to seek control of their public image, and thus as a subtle but efficacious context for political affirmation. The Miss Galaxy beauty pageant is the most salient of these events, although it is only one of several comparable events held throughout the year. Like other important events in Tonga, the pageant has a high-ranking or otherwise prominent patron, who in recent years has been recruited from within the ranks of the royal family. Half of the jury of six or seven is composed of non-transgendered Tongan dignitaries (e.g. high-ranking army officers, intellectuals, and the winner of the mainstream

Miss Heilala pageant for 'real' women, which precedes the transgendered pageant), while the other half are 'distinguished' expatriates (i.e. temporary foreign residents of Tonga, such as businessmen, spouses of diplomats, and the occasional visiting anthropologist).

Sponsored by various businesses and organizations (e.g. hotels, hairdressing salons, rugby teams), contestants appear on stage in various costumes, ranging a gamut familiar from South Pacific pageants in general, which includes evening dress, *pule taha* 'island wear' (ankle-length skirt and matching short-sleeved top, worn with a tasseled fiber belt), and 'their own creations' (see Photograph 1). Each appearance is ostensibly designed to allow contestants to present themselves as attractive and feminine persons, following familiar patterns of beauty pageants around the world. The core of the pageant consists of several judged events, including an individual talent display, a brief interview (of the what-would-you-do-to-save-the-world? type), and catwalk parades. Interspersed are entertainment routines, which may include a hula performance by the emcee, a rock-and-roll standard sung by a local talent, a dance routine performed by all contestants to a popular Tahitian or disco tune, and a short classical and torch-song concert by non-transgendered performers.

What I designate 'extra-locality' pervades the entire atmosphere of the Miss Galaxy pageant. It is a feature of the pageant that organizers and contestants take great pains to elaborate, and that the audience expects of the show, although these expectations are always mitigated by the view that this extra-locality is fraudulent.

Photograph 1   The contestants at the end of the pageant posing around the newly elected Miss Galaxy 1997, the incumbent, and the emcee.

The most immediate and spectacular manifestation of extra-locality is the very name of the event. Both funny and poignant, 'Miss Galaxy' lays a claim on as ambitiously cosmopolitan an image as can be imagined, and plays on hyperbole in the same fashion as some of the camp aspects of the pageant (e.g. the more extravagant costumes and performances), creating humor while attempting to retain control of this humor. But extra-locality also saturates other aspects of the pageant. For example, one of the events requires contestants to appear in 'national' costume as representative of foreign 'countries' (e.g. Miss Rarotonga, Miss Switzerland, Miss South America). Similarly, at the organizing stage, candidates provide their age, vital statistics, occupation, and personal aspirations, which one of the organizers enters on bio-data sheets.[1] Clearly, what participants in the pageant aim for in this emulation of international pageant practices is the appearance of a glamor whose reference reaches beyond the confines of the local context. The extent to which participants are aware of the inspiration for these practices depends on their relative worldliness. While some *leitī* involved in the programming of the show have had the opportunity to watch televised international pageants, others must rely on second-hand reports of such events, what they can infer about them from watching the mainstream Miss Heilala pageant, and their imagination.

In addition to bearing the names of the countries they represent, Miss Galaxy contestants go by female-sounding stage names of their own choosing, and which they often use in everyday contexts. These stage names are often coinages that bear linguistic similarity to the person's original Tongan name (e.g. 'Suzie' from Sosefo), and are either English names (e.g. Priscilla Pressland) or exotic-sounding names with no connotation other than their generic foreignness (e.g. Aisa De Lorenzo, Aodushi Kiroshoto), but never Tongan names. The extra-local flavor also pervades the stage decorations (in 1997, flower arrangements and rather unfortunate bouquets of phallic-shaped multi colored balloons), the background music (for the opening, a medley of triumphalist classical themes such as the William Tell Overture), and the singing and dancing. When events are explicitly designed to add local color (e.g. a *tau'olunga* performance, a popular Tongan tune sung by one of the organizers), they are bracketed entertainment routines designed to fill the time while contestants are getting changed back-stage, and often look like strained token gestures. When a contestant does decide to perform a Tongan dance for a judged event, it is generally a spoof.

Perhaps the most powerful index of extra-locality is language use. Throughout the pageant, the dominant language is English. When contestants first present themselves, for instance, they do so in English:[2]

AISA: ((*walks up to the mike*)) Good evening ladies and gentlemen. My
         name is Aisa De Lorenzo, I'm eighteen years of age, and I
         represent, ((*pauses, raises arms triumphantly*)) BLUE PACIFIC
         TAXIS! ((*walks down catwalk*))

(1997, Sony, 2 1:07:36–1:08:20)

Each contestant will have memorized and rehearsed her lines prior to the pageant, and will take utmost care to pronounce them correctly and loudly. This does not prevent occasional slip-ups, which the audience will immediately ridicule boisterously. The important point is that, for most contestants, speaking English before a large and distinguished audience of elite Tongans (many of whom are bilingual) and foreigners represents a serious challenge: many *leitī*, particularly pageant contestants, speak minimal English, as poverty and marginality have barred them from opportunities to learn the language. A significant number have not traveled overseas, and those who have resided in industrial countries have not done so under privileged conditions.

By centralizing the English language and its associations, *leitī* position themselves on the side of prestige and worldliness, and in opposition to the use of Tongan and its localized connotations. But their sociolinguistic behavior, both in and out of the pageant, adds further complexity. Indeed, despite the obvious difficulties that *leitī* experience in speaking English during the pageant, many Tongans expect them to speak English more readily on a day-to-day basis than non-transgendered Tongan men, for a number of reasons. First, Tongans generally see *fakaleitī* as self-assured and brash creatures that know no shame (*ta'emā*).[3] While in actuality a significant percentage of *leitī* are self-effacing, the demeanor of other *leitī* underscores this stereotype. One illustration of this shamelessness is their very participation in a pageant that constitutes the prime locus of the formation and reinforcement of popular stereotypes of *fakaleitī*: contestants' behavior in the pageant can be moderately outrageous and is certainly viewed as exhibitionistic.

Second, stereotypes of *leitī* view them as oriented toward modernity, the West, transnationalism, and social change. Once again, the extent to which this stereotype reflects reality varies across individuals, but here as well it is certainly founded on undeniable (if partial) evidence. The uncompromisingly extra-local design of the pageant falls right in line with this expectation, both establishing and confirming the stereotypes held by audience members. Viewed in this light, the prominence of English in both public and private contexts is hardly surprising, since English is the language of extra-locality.

Finally, Tongans tend to view the use of English as having feminine undertones: as in many other societies in which a language of modernity competes with a code of traditionalism (e.g. Gal, 1979), the former is associated with women's aspirations for upward mobility and emancipation from the strictures of traditionalism [...]. When questioned on the matter, most Tongan men and women will state that women speak better English overall than men, and that this is due to the fact that girls study harder in school and that women are talkative 'by nature.' These familiar-sounding assertions bear witness to the fact that the gendering of language use is tacit and embodied in practice, rather than explicit and grounded in overt consciousness.

As a result of this gendering, men who speak 'too much' English do so at the risk of compromising their masculinity in the eyes of society at large. This concerns *fakaleitī*, who willingly go to great lengths to dislocate themselves from their masculine attributes. Interestingly, it also concerns overseas-born Tongans: their awkwardness in performing Tongan maleness, including speaking Tongan as a preferred language, frequently brands them as *fakaleitī*-like, regardless of whether they present any identifiable sign of effeminacy in their comportment. The use of English thus has many associations in addition to extra-locality: it potentially indexes deficient Tonganness, deficient masculinity, femininity, and transgendered identity, traits which may or may not overlap but which are all readily equated to one another. Thus failure to perform Tonganness can easily become a sign of imperfect masculinity and vice versa, unless it is mollified by convincing mitigating factors, such as elite status or wealth.[4]

Patterns of language use in the Miss Galaxy pageant, as well as the overall non-local ambience to which they contribute, are not without irony. As discussed earlier, most contestants live in relative poverty. In tune with their under-privileged status, many *leitī* speak English poorly. Sustaining the level of extra-locality expected of them is therefore difficult for many contestants, who switch to Tongan once they have delivered simple memorized lines. But English still remains dominant in the pageant: it is the language that the emcee uses to address the audience and, when he addresses the contestants, he does so first in English and then provides a Tongan translation, usually *sotto voce*. These communicative practices maintain English in the foreground, at the expense of Tongan.[5]

The difficulty contestants have in maintaining English as their working language during the pageant places them in an awkward position. For example, in the interview event contestants are given the choice of answering in English or Tongan, and most choose the latter. In 1997, one contestant chose English, and the audience initially reacted with a loud murmur of temporary admiration for her courage. However, it took little time for her to stumble, as she searched for an English word while waving her hand campily, while the audience, satisfied with the expected proof of the fraudulence of her claim to cosmopolitanism, began hooting and ridiculing, forcing her to abort her brave attempt:

EMCEE: What would you say about being a hairstylist, or – being – a working – what – what does it mean, like, to be working at Joy's Hair Styles? ((*sotto voce, summarizes the question in Tongan*)) *Ko e hā e me'a 'oku ke fai 'i he* hair salon?

MASHA: ((*takes cordless mike*)) Well thank you very much. ((*audience laughs, then shouts with admiration and encouragement*)) If you want your hair to be curled, ((*beckons with her hand*)) come over. ((*audience explodes in laughter and whooping, Masha laughs and then becomes serious and requests silence with the hand*)) Uh, I like it very much, and uh – I enjoy working there, with uhmm – ((*pauses, word-searches, waves her hand, audience explodes in laughter, drowning the remainder of the answer*)) blowers, ((*unable to finish, mouths*)) (thank you). ((*hands mike back and returns to her position*))

(1997, Sony, 4 0:02:45–0:03:55)

Photograph 2   Masha Entura searches for the English word she needs to answer her interview question.

Contestants thus are caught between a rock and a hard place: if they answer in English and make mistakes, they will be laughed at, and if they answer in Tongan, this very fact will be ridiculed as evidence that they are unable to carry through the artifice of extra-locality to its logical end. The ridicule that greets the choice of Tongan is congruent with many other aspects of mainstream Tongans' attitudes toward *fakaleitī*, both at the pageant and in day-to-day interactions. Mainstream Tongans indeed consider *fakaleitī* identity as essentially bogus: here are these men pretending to be women, and not just any women but cosmopolitan sophisticates, and yet they cannot even maintain their end of a simple conversation in English. At the pageant, it is not uncommon for drunken men or women to try to rip contestants' outfits and expose them as what they 'really' are, namely persons with male physiologies. Nothing generates greater hilarity than contestants losing their bra in the middle of a performance. In day-to-day interactions between *fakaleitī* and mainstream Tongans, the latter often express mock annoyance at the 'fraudulence' of *leitī* self-presentation and identity, while *leitī* argue back with 'proofs' that they are 'real women.'

However, like all ideological linkages that disadvantage some and benefit others, the linkages I have described are not immune to contestation on the part of those whom they marginalize. This was powerfully illustrated by a minor humorous incident in the 1997 pageant, when one of the contestants, the quick-witted 'Āmini or Lady Amyland, sponsored by Joey's Unisex Hair Salon, turned the tables on the audience during the interview event (and, perhaps, on society at large, even if only for a fleeting moment). Before she has a chance to answer the emcee's question, Lady Amyland is heckled by a drunken *leitī* in the audience, who urges her to answer her interview question in English (*faka-Pālangi*). The heckling draws some laughter, since everyone knows that Lady Amyland's English is poor and that she would make a fool of herself if she tried. But 'Āmini's repartee wins the prize:

EMCEE: Miss Joey's Unisex Hair Salon! What do you have to say to promote Joey's Unisex Hair Salon? *((lowers voice, translating into Tongan)) Ko e hā e me'a 'oku ke fai ke* promote *ai 'a e - ((rolls eyes, searches for Tongan word)) fakalakalaka ai 'a Joey's Unisex Hair Salon.*

'AHI: *((heckling from audience)) Faka-Pālangi, 'Āmini!*

AUDIENCE: *((laughter))*

'ĀMINI: Sorry excuse me, I'm a Tongan ( ) *((rest of answer drowned by deafening laughter, vigorous applause, cat-calls))*

(1997, Sony, 4 0:05:42—0:06:26, see Photograph 3)

'Āmini answers the heckler by reaffirming her Tongan identity and therefore her duty and privilege to answer the question in Tongan, an unexpected move which the audience (and any Tongan viewer of the video recording) found extremely humorous, because the claim is embedded in a context in which everything is done to foreground non-locality.[6] What Lady Amyland is doing here is part of a wider tacit project on the part of at least some contestants to take greater charge of the pageant and its effect on the audience. This project consists in stripping the audience (and society at large) of its privilege to ridicule contestants, and to take control of the boundary between humor and seriousness.

But the project goes further, and its meaning becomes clear when viewed in light of the previous analysis. Note that Lady Amyland asserts her claim to Tongan identity not in Tongan, but in English; the covert message is that one can assert one's Tonganness while controlling the tools with which one does so, and while using tools that are not part of the sanctioned repertoire. In addition, the preface of her repartee ('Sorry excuse me') is an inside joke which non-*leitī* audience members are unlikely to make sense of, a reference to another *leitī*'s awkward attempt, a few years earlier, to speak English to a prospective *Pālangi* date. The overall effect of Lady Amyland's repartee contests the power of dominant forces to dictate what counts as markers of locality and what does not; asserts that the claim to be part of the 'galaxy' does not necessarily deny one's local identity; and proclaims that being a *leitī* does [not] mean giving up one's place in Tongan society.[7]

Photograph 3   Lady Amyland savors the effect of her quick-minded repartee to a heckler.

Notes

1   Some of the information provided is fake or unrealistic, while other details are designed to be humorous. For example, contestants regularly claim 'high-status' feminine occupations such as 'nurse' and 'public relations' (*sic*) to add glamour to their profile, as well as 'future plans' to be 'computer operator', 'flying attendant' (*sic*), and 'to be a good wife'. The same practice of emulating international beauty contests is found in the pageants that transgendered persons stage in Jolo, Southern Philippines (Johnson, 1997) and in urban South Africa (Reid, 1999), both of which exhibit fascinating similarities to the Tongan material.

2   In the following discussion, I have not attempted to hide the identity of those concerned since my analysis is based on a public event. Extracts are identified by year of recording and video reference number.

3   A Tongan businessman told me that he had employed a *fakaleitī* to sell his products door-to-door precisely because *fakaleitī* worry little about shame, in addition to being gregarious and talkative. These traits are thus not necessarily seen as negative assets.

4   Many of the symbolic associations I describe here of course echo patterns found in many other societies. One is reminded of Willis's (1977) celebrated analysis of working-class masculinity among adolescents in English schools, Bourdieu's (1985) analysis of social class and 'refinement' in France, particularly as it relates to gender, and Ortner's (1991) study of social class and gender in New Jersey, among many other relevant examples.

5   English, as with other tokens of modernity and cosmopolitanism, also occupies a prominent role in many other public events in Tonga, including the Miss Heilala beauty pageant for 'real' women. However, in other events, these tokens are commonly on a par with Tongan and tokens of 'Tonganness'. In the Miss Heilala pageant, for example, the contestants' ability to perform tokens of Tonganness, including their linguistic skills, are scrutinized very closely. This scrutiny frequently places overseas-born contestants at a disadvantage, as discussed in Teilhet-Fisk (1996) and Besnier (2002).

6   The humor already began with the heckle itself, which is uttered in Tongan, despite the fact it urges the contestant to speak English, and which refers to the contestant by his everyday name, rather than her transgendered name.

7   I do not wish to imply that Lady Amyland's act of resistance was the result of a carefully engineered strategy on her part. For one thing, she was probably drunk, as many contestants are. However, we know from Scott (1985, 1990) that everyday acts of resistance need not be the outcome of calculated designs.

References

BESNIER, N. (2002) 'Transgenderism, locality, and the Miss Galaxy beauty pageant in Tonga', *American Ethnologist*, **29**, pp. 534–67.

BOURDIEU, P. (1985) *Distinction: A Social Critique of the Judgement of Taste*. translated by Richard Nice, Cambridge, MA, Harvard University Press.

GAL, S. (1979) *Language Shift: Social Determinants of Linguistic Change in Bilingual Austria*, New York, Academic Press.

JOHNSON, M. (1997) *Beauty and Power: Transgendering and Cultural Transformation in the Southern Philippines*, Oxford, Berg.

ORTNER, S.B. (1991) 'Reading America: preliminary notes on class and culture', in R.G. FOX (ed.) *Recapturing Anthropology: Writing in the Present*, Santa Fe, NM, School of American Research Press.

REID, G. (1999) 'Above the Skyline: Integrating African, Christian and Gay or Lesbian Identities in a South African Church Community', MA thesis, Department of Anthropology, University of the Witswatersrand.

SCOTT, J.C. (1985) *Weapons of the Weak: Everyday Forms of Peasant Resistance*, New Haven, CT, Yale University Press.

SCOTT, J.C. (1990) *Domination and the Art of Resistance: Hidden Transcripts*, New Haven, CT, Yale University Press.

TEILHET-FISK, J. (1996) 'The Miss Heilala beauty pagent: where beauty is more than skin deep', in C.B. COHEN, R. WILK and B. STOELTJE (eds) *Beauty Queens on the Global Stage: Gender, Contests, and Power*, London, Routledge.

WILLIS, P. (1977) *Learning to Labour: How Working Class Kids Get Working Class Jobs*, Westmead, England, Saxon House.

Source: BESNIER, N. (2003) in J. HOLMES and M. MEYERHOFF (eds) *The Handbook of Language and Gender*, pp. 289–301, Oxford, Blackwell.

READING D: Polari and gay identity

Paul Baker

Vada the trolling omee-palone with the bona lallies and the zhooshed riah! She's got a bijou lattie up the Kings Road but she spends all her dinarli on that bold piece of trade, the one ajax in the hob-nail batts. Ah well, your mother'll have to buy her own bevvy again ce soir.

Polari is a language variety spoken mainly by British working-class gay men and women in the first two thirds of the twentieth century. It had arisen from collisions between a number of other varieties that had been spoken in the eighteenth and nineteenth centuries by stigmatised or itinerant groups: beggars, prostitutes, seafarers, fairground and circus workers, travelling market traders and actors. It was closely related to an older form of language called Parlyaree, which had derived many of its words from Italian. Some Polari speakers added a smattering of idiomatic French to the language (e.g. *mais oui*), in order to suggest a hint of sophistication and worldliness.

Its home, if it could be said to have one, was London, where its lexicon was enriched by contact from Jewish communities and the docks of the East End as well as the music halls and theatres of the West End in the late nineteenth/early twentieth centuries. It also incorporated some rhyming slang and back slang words. For example, the Polari word *plates* meant *feet*, because it rhymed with the phrase *plates of meat*. The Polari word *ecaf* was just the word *face*, pronounced as if it was spelt backwards. During World War II, North American and Canadian GIs added American vernacular words to its expanding lexicon (*blowjob, cruise, naff*), while the drug subculture of the 1960s introduced a new set of terms (*blocked, randy comedown, doobies*). Therefore Polari consisted of a ragbag of vocabularies from a variety of groups. As a result, it tended to be subject to a great deal of synchronic and diachronic variation. There was another reason for this: its status as a secret language meant that new words had to be developed for the same concepts, as the older words were discovered by outsiders and rendered useless.

While it's possible to examine Polari from a number of perspectives, I want to mainly focus on its role in the construction or performance of identity. In the UK, homosexuality was illegal until 1967, so Polari served several functions. The language acted as a signifier for the gay subculture, allowing people to identify themselves to others who they didn't know very well but suspected might also be gay. Therefore people could negotiate a gay identity in risky contexts. But Polari could also be used among friends to talk about gay-related subjects in public spaces, such as on the train. Speaking in Polari was one way that people could construct a salient gay identity for themselves.

It's useful to think of Polari in terms of *anti-language* (Halliday, 1978). These were forms of language used by stigmatised or criminalised groups called anti-societies, which are used in order to create and maintain alternative social structures or realities based upon the values of the speakers. While some forms of language used by anti-societies can be more easily thought of as *jargon*, because they were simply used to disguise the user's speech and crimes, Polari was a form of language which achieved more than this. Importantly, it also expressed an alternative point of view about the world. For example, a Polari phrase like *bona lattie* translates into English as *nice house*. However, *bona lattie* means *nice house by the values of the gay subculture*. In addition, some Polari words were used to feminise members of the establishment, for example, the phrases *Betty Bracelets*, *Jennifer Justice*, *Lily Law* and *Hilda Handcuffs* all referred to the police. Such words subvert and question the hegemonic masculine identity of the average policeman, indicating one of the ways that Polari was used to mock and attack existing social systems. As well as reinterpreting existing concepts such as *bona lattie*, other Polari terms referred to concepts that were unfamiliar to mainstream culture – such as words for different types of gay people or sexual acts. Hearing Polari for the first time could also be the first hint to a gay person that a wider culture existed – one which was sufficiently established to have shared terms.

While initially used for protection, Polari also became a way for gay people to create and maintain a certain type of identity for themselves, based around the notion of camp performance. Polari is well-suited to fit within Harvey's descriptive framework for verbal camp (2000). This framework consists of four main strategies of camp: paradox, inversion, ludicrism and parody. These strategies are played out via surface features such as explicitness and covertness, grammatical gendered markers, double-entendre and use of French. In order to demonstrate how some of these strategies work, it's useful to examine an example from the Julian and Sandy sketches. Julian and Sandy were two camp characters in the BBC radio comedy series *Round the Horne* which ran in Britain from 1964–1969 on Sunday lunchtimes to a family audience. The characters were never explicitly referred to as homosexual but instead used a mixture of Polari, innuendo and euphemism to reveal their sexual identities and the gay content of their jokes – but only to those who were able to decode the clues.

SANDY:	Don't mention rugby to Jules! Ohh!
JULIAN:	Ha! Ha!
SANDY:	Ooh! Don't mention that to him.
JULIAN:	Ha! Ha!
SANDY:	Ooh! Here, no, here. He's sworn, he's sworn never to touch a pair of rugby shorts again. No listen, no listen ducky. After what happened.
JULIAN:	Oh! He swore he'd never tell.
SANDY:	Go on, tell Mr Horne about it, go on, tell him.
JULIAN:	No, no, no!
SANDY:	Go on, let yourself go.
JULIAN:	No!
SANDY:	Purge yourself! Purge, purge!
JULIAN:	Well. When I was younger I had a friend who was a WASP.
SANDY:	You mean that Jock.
JULIAN:	Yes, Jock, Jock. Oh, great butch omee he was.
SANDY:	Oh!
JULIAN:	Yes, bigger than that. Huge bulging lallies, and his eke! His eke! Eke like a great Greek god.
SANDY:	Greek god.
JULIAN:	Oh yes. We went to hairdressing school together. Anyroad up. He used to play rugger of a Saturday and he asked me to make up the number one week. Well everything went well to halfway through the match
MR HORNE:	What happened?
JULIAN:	Well I completely misunderstood the meaning of a forward pass. Shame.
SANDY:	No, but don't worry Jules, it's all eau under the pont now. That's your actual French.

(Extract from 'Bona Rags', BBC Radio *Round the Horne*, broadcast 17.03.1968)

The example above demonstrates parodies of (stereotyped) femininity via the use of exclamation and hyperbole, and aristocratic mannerisms via the use of French 'eau under the pont'. Ludicrism is demonstrated with double-entendres 'a forward pass' and 'sworn never to touch a pair of rugby shorts again', whereas paradox is achieved through the use of Polari to be covert about an explicit subject (same-sex attraction). Polari was often used in the Julian and Sandy sketches to allow them to eulogise about (or criticise) the physical qualities of other men – 'huge bulging lallies' – suggesting that it enabled the construction of two gay stereotypes: the predatory, lustful gay man and the bitchy queen. The use of innuendo relies on the listener having a sufficient understanding of its processes combined with existing knowledge about sexuality to correctly interpret the joke. Therefore younger listeners of the audience would have been protected from the more sexual content in the sketches.

'Grass in a garden? Oh, très passé!': Julian and Sandy give their verdict on Mr Horne's horticultural tastes in the sketch 'Bona Homes'

(Barry Took and Marty Feldman, *The Bona Book of Julian and Sandy,* 1976, London, Robson Books)

An examination of Polari's lexicon reveals some of the ways that it was most commonly used. Although about five hundred lexical items have been uncovered (Baker, 2002a, b), it is unlikely that many speakers would have known more than about twenty to fifty of these words and phrases, mainly taken from a core lexicon. About seventy per cent of the lexicon consists of nouns, of which the majority can be semantically classed into categories consisting of types of people, body parts, clothing and everyday objects. Verbs are mainly concerned with sexual acts, the act of looking at people, walking (often with the intention of seeking sexual contact), performance (in the theatrical sense) or ways of making oneself look attractive. Adjectives tend to be evaluative, depicting the speaker's emotional attitude towards a subject. Male and female pronouns are often used interchangeably (so *he* becomes *she*), while the depersonalising pronoun *it* was occasionally used to refer to a sexual partner. Only one preposition is known: *ajax*, most likely a truncation of *adjacent*, which suggests that the people being talked about were nearby.

Whether used in real life or in scripted comedy sketches, Polari constituted a situation-specific language resource that speakers could draw on, in addition to other types of identity construction (hairstyle, clothing, mode of walking, gaze, etc.). Many Polari speakers tended to be effeminate and working class as well as gay, so speaking Polari within the gay community tended to further delineate certain types of gay identity as opposed to others:

> I learned 'palari' [*sic*] when I was in the theatre, but it was a common language [...] It was common only among a certain class in the gay world. It was usually people like myself who were in the chorus, the common end of the structure, who used it.

('John', in Porter and Weeks, 1991, p. 138)

John's use of 'common' (three times in this short excerpt) is worth noting. Polari is seen as 'common' both in the sense of the frequency of its use, and in the sense of it being a signifier of social status.

For many Polari speakers their sexuality referenced a sense of internalised identity perhaps more than actual sexual behaviour. For example, in the Merchant Navy in the 1950s, working-class gay seafarers (who were employed as stewards or waiters) would often take a male 'husband' who would ostensibly identify as a married heterosexual man. The seafarers who identified as gay (or as 'queens' in 1950s parlance) would often wear women's clothing at drag parties or public performances and would also speak Polari as part of this identity. Men who had sex with men but didn't identify as gay did not normally use Polari. Nor did the middle-class gay seafarers who were officers (Baker and Stanley, 2003).

However, people who weren't effeminate or working class *would* speak Polari occasionally for various reasons – for example to parody those identities, to be uncharacteristically camp for humorous purposes or to distance themselves from an opinion that they held but felt that others may disapprove of. In Bakhtin's terms, this is a form of double-voicing in which speakers would insert 'a new semantic intention into a discourse which already has [...] an intention of its own' (Bakhtin [1929]1984, p. 189). For example, in some Julian and Sandy sketches, a middle-class, heterosexual character (Kenneth Horne – playing himself) sometimes uses a Polari word, causing the others to exclaim 'isn't he bold! I wonder where he picks it up?' Mr Horne's use of Polari is therefore ambiguous – suggesting that he may be gay, or may want the others to think he is or may be simply joking with them. Polari could therefore be used (particularly after 1970) in order to reference an old-fashioned, 'imagined' stereotype of an effeminate gay man, which explains its appearance in films made in the 1990s but set in earlier time periods such as *Velvet Goldmine* and *Love is the Devil*.

So was Polari an example of gender performance? Did people speak Polari *because* they were working class and effeminate, or was their class/ gender performed through their use of Polari? The answer is most likely both – consisting of a constantly reinforcing chain where language constructs identity which influences language which continues to construct identity and so on. What should be pointed out, though, is that such chains are not identical for each Polari speaker. Polari was used by a variety of different types of people in different ways and for different reasons. A middle-class gay man who spoke an occasional Polari word in an 'ironic' distancing way would be different from a working-class gay man who regularly conversed in Polari. Both uses of Polari are performative – but individual speakers' identities would also dictate how, when and why Polari would be used.

Polari could sometimes be used to insult, confuse and attack outsiders (or less knowledgeable members of the gay subculture):

> ... Polari has about it a particularly brittle, knife-edged feel. Nothing – in my chicken days – was more daunting than an encounter with some acid-tongued *bitch* whose tongue was so sharp that it was likely she would cut my throat with it. Those queans [*sic*], with the savage wit of the self-protective, could be truly alarming to those of us of a slower cast of mind.

(Burton, 1979, p. 23)

However, such displays of sharpness were likely to be fuelled by a range of motivations. As well as showing the wit of the speaker, they also acted as a form of verbal duelling (see Murray, 1979) for the entertainment of an audience (another take on the 'performative' use of language). They could be an indication of closeness between people: where there is a sense of shared identity and similarity, invective is sanctioned, either because it is understood to be a joke, and/or because it emphasises closeness – name-calling can occur and no real offence will be taken. They could also, however, be designed to wound, fuelled by dislike or envy. In some cases, interpretation would not be straightforward. Speakers could employ irony and humour with their Polari use to be intentionally ambiguous, for example by hinting that someone might be gay or by limiting the potential offence taken from an insult by framing it as a joke. Such ambiguity allowed speakers to shift their position at will and keep listeners guessing. Double entendres and suggestive euphemisms added to the deliberately opaque nature of the Polari utterance. When Kenneth Horne worried that audiences might see a secondary meaning in some of their conversations, Sandy replied that they didn't even see a first meaning, but they just laughed at anything that *might* be dirty.

Polari's link to comedy is therefore crucial – but ultimately one which limits its potential as a true language. It could be used as a way to mitigate appalling circumstances faced by homosexual men: arrests, entrapments, blackmail, hostility, etc. by rendering them comic. As a coping mechanism in the face of potential tragedy, Polari gives ironic distance from the real world, turning power structures upside down and viewing everything through a pair of camp-tinted spectacles where gossip and trivia are seen as more important than politics. However, in making a joke out of everything, it becomes difficult to express emotions such as real sorrow or anger in Polari. But such restrictions do not mean that a Polari-speaking identity is any less 'real'. The view that there is no 'one true me' is disputed by social constructionists (e.g. Burr, 1995) – Polari is therefore a useful tool in the performance of one identity or set of identities, characterised by its ambiguity: explicit yet secretive, protective yet aggressive, comedic yet useful in tragic situations. Rather than Polari being an external manifestation of a stable, fixed gay identity, it instead allowed speakers to construct a certain type (or types) of context-specific gay identity at will. Its role therefore reflects the sense of ambivalence that mainstream society feels towards homosexuality, and subsequently, the ambivalence that gay people have felt towards themselves in earlier times.

Lexicon of Polari terms

ajax	next to
aunt nelly fakes	earrings
batts	shoes
bevvy	drink
bijou	small and elegant
blocked	high on pills (drugs)
bold	shameless, confident, likely to be gay
bona	good
cod	bad
dinarli	money
doobies	pills (called Purple Hearts)
ecaf	face
eke	face
fake riah	hair
fantabulosa	wonderful
lallies	legs
lattie	home
naff	unfashionable, bad
nanti	none, nothing, don't
omee	man
omee-palone	gay man
plates	feet

Polari	to talk, gay 'language'
Polari lobes	ears
Polari pipes	telephone
randy comedown	desire for sex after a drug 'high'
riah	hair
she	he
sister	close friend
tbh	to be had (attractive or sexually available)
trade	sexual partner
trolling	walking
vada	look (at)
vogues	cigarettes
your mother	I
zhooshed	styled

References

BAKHTIN, M. ([1929] 1984) *Problems in Dostoevsky's Poetics,* Minneapolis, University of Minnesota Press.

BAKER, P. (2002a) *Polari: The Lost Language of Gay Men*, London, Routledge.

BAKER, P. (2002b) *Fantabulosa: A Dictionary of Polari and Gay Slang,* London, Continuum.

BAKER, P. and STANLEY, J. (2003) *Hello Sailor: The Hidden History of Gay Life at Sea*, London, Pearson.

BURR, V. (1995) *An Introduction to Social Constructionism*, London, Routledge.

BURTON, P. (1979) 'The gentle art of confounding naffs: some notes on Polari', *Gay News*, p. 23.

HALLIDAY, M.A.K. (1978) *Language as a Social Semiotic: The Social Interpretation of Language and Meaning,* London, Edward Arnold.

HARVEY, K. (2000) 'Describing camp talk: language/pragmatics/politics', *Language and Literature*, **9**(3), pp. 240–60.

JIVANI, A. (1997) *It's Not Unusual: A History of Lesbian and Gay Britain in the Twentieth Century*, London, Michael O'Mara Books.

MURRAY, S.O. (1979) 'The art of gay insulting', *Anthropological Linguistics*, **21**, pp. 211–23.

PORTER, K. and WEEKS, J. (eds) (1991) *Between the Acts: Lives of Homosexual Men 1885–1967*, London, Routledge.

Source: commissioned for this volume.

4 Child's play

Julia Gillen

4.1 Introduction

This chapter examines different approaches to children's creativity with language. Childhood is often presented as a period of life and a mode of being in which linguistic creativity occurs in some very interesting ways, and this chapter aims to provide a sense of the challenges children embrace, and even seek out, in order to become shapers of language. It is mainly concerned with children before puberty and focuses on oral rather than other channels of communication.

Considerable differences in emphasis have long existed within and across disciplinary approaches to children's language. This is largely because children's creative play with language is 'practice' in a dual sense – a social practice, and a rehearsal for adult life. As a **social practice** language play is an activity children engage in that is aways embedded in particular social and cultural contexts and which has certain meanings and values for speakers. In this sense, language play can be seen as worthy of investigation for its own sake. Also, given children's junior position in society, creative language play can at times be part of a rehearsal for practices they will participate in when older.

The disciplines in which children's language has been studied tend to stress one of these different aspects rather than the other. For instance, psychology, and its offspring **psycholinguistics** – the taking of a psychological approach to the study of language – pay some attention to children's creativity in language as part of a general aim of investigating how children become competent language users, with all that implies about not only linguistic understanding but also conceptual development.

Psycholinguistics

Psycholinguistics is the study of language and the mind, drawing on insights from psychology and linguistics. A major area of psycholinguistics is the study of children's language development.

Investigations that draw on folklore or **social anthropology**, in contrast, emphasise children's culture. Anthropologists may be concerned with children as learners, but childhood practices, including language practices, can also be studied in their own right. Folklorists too have been interested in **children's lore** – creative practices such as playground rhymes and games that are distinctively associated with childhood.

Social anthropology and folklore

Social anthropology is the branch of anthropology concerned with the study of culture and society. Social anthropologists tend to adopt ethnographic research methods, immersing themselves in the lives of particular cultural groups and seeking to gain an 'insider' perspective on their beliefs and practices. Language is seen as significant as an important means through which culture is manifested.

Folklore refers to the traditional cultural beliefs and practices of 'ordinary' people and to the study of these. This may include the study of 'children's lore'.

A classic study by the folklorists Iona and Peter Opie (1959) celebrated children's artful language play as a significant tradition, emphasising the 'part played by children in preserving certain rituals, customs and beliefs on behalf of the community as a whole' (Sealey 2000, p. 77). Rather than focusing upon the development of an individual's use of language, this perspective notes consistencies across time and place in children's practices:

> No matter how uncouth schoolchildren may outwardly appear, they remain tradition's warmest friends. ... they are respecters, even venerators of custom; and in their self-contained community their basic lore and language seems scarcely to alter from generation to generation.
>
> (Opie and Opie, 1959, p. 2)

It is therefore important to recognise that there are different views of childhood which may considerably influence ideas and conceptions about creativity in children's language. These are reflected in the studies discussed in the following sections.

4.2 Origins of creative speech

Playfulness starts in infancy, even before language is acquired. This section looks at connections between the capacities babies are born with, their propensity to interact with others and certain qualities of playfulness demonstrable in infancy. Children are born with a genetic predisposition not only to be able to learn language but to engage *actively*, to take the initiative as well as respond, within meaning-making practices. This has been demonstrated in research carried out by the psychologist Colwyn Trevarthen into what he termed, after Bateson (1975) **protoconversations** between infants and caregivers.

ACTIVITY 1   Protoconversations

Allow
15–20 minutes

In the box below, Trevarthen and Aitken (2001) discuss research evidence on 'protoconversations'. The sequence of photos overleaf shows an example of an interaction between an 11-week-old baby and his mother. On the basis of this information:

- What part do you think can a young baby play in interactions with a caregiver?

- Why do you think Trevarthen uses the term 'protoconversation' for these interactions?

The term 'infant' in developmental psychology is used to refer to babies under one year old.

'Protoconversations' in infancy

Details of the expression of the developing motives that drive the earliest communications of humans are summarised as follows. In the gentle, intimate, affectionate, and rhythmically regulated playful exchanges of protoconversation, 2-month-old infants look at the eyes and mouth of the person addressing them while listening to the voice. In measured and predictable cycles of response to regular time patterns in the adult's behaviour, the infant moves its face, which it cannot see or hear, and reacts with movements of face, hands or vocal system to modified patterns of adult vocal expression that it is incapable of mimicking, and that have not been available in that form *in utero*. The communicatively active hands of young infants may make expressive movements in rhythmic coordination with a person's speech ... and this can occur when the baby has been blind from birth, and thus never seen its hands or anyone else's hands ... Thus we may conclude that the infant has a coherent psychoneural organisation that specifies the timing and form of body movements. This organisation can react with appropriate dynamic changes to another person's dynamic expressions, matching their rhythms and accents. Evidently the responses of the infant are made expressive by internally generated motives and emotions that resemble those carried in the adult expressions. Infant and adult can, for a time, sympathise closely and apparently equally with one another's motive states, using similar melodic or prosodic forms of utterance and similar rhythms of gesture. This entails an absorption of the adult's motivations into an affectionate intuitive parenting mode that tends to mimic the infant and that releases in the adult a specialised, emotionally coordinated 'musicality' of voicing, with animated but sympathetic and joyful facial expressions and dance like postural, gestural movements that match vocal expressions, and affectionate and playful touching and moving of the infant's hands, face, or body ...

(Trevarthen and Aitken, 2001, p. 6)

🎞 *Picture story* GAMES WITH A TOPIC: 'COO' AND 'BOO'

Ethan, 11 weeks　　　(To take these pictures with just one camera, we placed a mirror next to Ethan.)

By around three months, babies can play face-to-face games that are often robust, vigorous and exciting affairs. They often take on a 'topic' for play - this can include jokes, as the two partners 'muck about' and watch each other's reactions. Two games are especial hits these days with Ethan and Julie - 'coo' and 'boo'. In 'coo', Ethan takes the initiative, and enjoys using the full force of his voice to create an impact on his mother. In 'boo', it is Julie who performs, while Ethan watches with anticipation and then enjoys sharing the climax with her.

1 Julie pays close attention as Ethan starts to coo.

2 His call is forceful and is directed right at Julie; she shows how impressed she is.

3 Ethan seems to feel the punch line is hilarious!

4 Now it is Julie's turn – Ethan watches his mother get ready – Ah...

5 ... Bb...

6 ... Boo!...

7 ... and Ethan is duly appreciative, joining in with Julie's laughter.

8 Ethan coos to Julie again...

9 ... and it is followed by raucous laughter.

10 Now Julie boos at Ethan – he's already finding it fun...

11 ... but is even more delighted as Julie laughs too.

Figure 4.1　The Social Baby (Murray and Andrews, pp. 66–7)

Comment

You may well have noted from the extract that a two-month-old baby, although immature in relation to adults in comparison with some species, is nevertheless capable of some quite remarkable feats. Despite her very immature capacities of visual perception, her brain is equipped so that she is disposed to look attentively at human faces. At the same time she listens to a voice – and indeed has already learned to recognise familiar voices in the womb. In rhythmic cycles of response, she can move her own face and hands and make sounds that are similar to those that an adult makes when engaged in such a dydadic (two-way) 'protoconversation'.

The term 'protoconversation' draws attention to the extraordinary phenomenon that well before the child can possibly engage in language, many features of a conversation are nevertheless present. When we engage in face-to-face conversation, there is a great deal of interaction going on outside the exchange of information. To be a competent and well-regarded conversationalist, one has to attend to the non-verbal elements of exchange, making use of eye contact that is regular and attuned without being constant staring. One has to indicate an appropriate level of attention through non-verbal communication and remain sensitive to the movements of another. Possibly the most essential element of conversations and protoconversations is sensitivity at turn-taking. In a conversation, the initiative may be held for a time by one person with the other responding, but there also need to be displays of initiative by the other participant. This joint attention and activity is illustrated in the photographs from *The Social Baby*.

Trevarthen and other researchers who have studied such infant–caregiver exchanges suggest firstly that the human baby is innately equipped to communicate, well before the onset of language; and secondly that this innate capacity consists of both the ability to respond and to take an initiating part. Trevarthen terms this 'purposeful intersubjectivity' – that is, that we are programmed, to use a common metaphor, to communicate effectively with others, to draw them into interactions so that we can better understand and engage with their own motives and needs. As Trevarthen and Aitken (2001, p. 3) summarise: 'This evidence of purposeful intersubjectivity, or an initial psychosocial state, must be fundamental for our understanding of human mental development ...'.

These findings about infants and early interactions are significant for an exploration of creativity in children's language for a number of reasons:

- Clearly, nobody can construct creative language without having learned to use language; and these investigations show that from the very beginning infants learn in an active way – that is they don't only respond and imitate, they have something of their own to contribute as well.

- Infants have a capacity to innovate, creatively embroidering a 'text' that someone else has offered as a resource; this is shown to be an innate human characteristic.

- The affective function of language use is clearly primary; playfulness is an intrinsic quality of human communication, even if some accounts have preferred to stress its information-transmission capacities.

- The phenomenon of protoconversations reveals the continuity of multimodal aspects of communicative practices from the earliest exchanges into what we more familiarly know as 'conversations'. Speakers' use of different communicative modes (language alongside a range of nonverbal systems) continues to be an important feature of all creative language use and interpretation.

- At a formal level, the interaction between baby and adult is also characterised by considerable repetition (in this case nonverbal), argued by Carter and others to be a marker of linguistic creativity.

This supports Cook's argument in Reading B of Chapter 1 that the 'bison' account of communication is inadequate.

Early storytelling

Organisation of talk, with considerable reliance on repetition and routine occurs at a number of language levels as the child develops into a language user. See for example, the pre-sleep monologues recorded by Nelson (1989), discussed by Levy (2003). These are extracts from two-year-old Emily's speech to herself while in bed, before sleep:

> my sleep
> Mommy came
> and Mommy get get up
> time go home
> ...
> yesterday my slept
> and say um
> and in Tanta house
> and Mommy woke my up
> and go time to go home
> ...

when when I sleeping Tanta house
Mommy came
wake my up
because time to go home (23;8)

23;8 means aged
23 months, 8 days.

The example shows, as suggested by Nelson's account, that the last
re-telling is more coherent than the first. Unlike the first, in the last unit the
setting is identified ('Tanta house') and temporal and causal relationships
between events are explicitly marked ('when I sleeping ... Mommy came'
and 'wake my up because time to go home). In Emily's attempt to 'make
sense of the world', she creates a more logically explicit account.

(Levy, 2003, p. 171)

Levy's interest here is in the development of coherence in children's discourse.
Emily's 'making sense of the world' was without an audience (were it not for
the presence of a linguist's tape recorder), yet is nonetheless I suggest both
creative and social in character. It is creative in that she is playing with different
ways of expressing something, overall for affective rather than informational
intent. She may find some comfort, perhaps some reinforcement of the sense
of identity that comes about through the recycling of memories into even
fragmentary narratives. Emily's text is social in the sense that Vygotsky,
(originally writing in the early 1930s) wrote: 'In the home environment ... the
process through which the child learns speech is social from start to finish.'
(Vygotsky, 1987, p. 90). Vygotsky argued that young children take note of
speech going on around them, participate and *internalise* cultural shapings of
language. Emily will have heard narratives, as people around her shape
understandings of the past, the present, significant people and features of her
environment in short accounts or narratives. Such narratives are creative in that
inevitably they involve selection in both content and style. In more mature
peoples' practices they may reasonably be linked both to lengthy works of
literary fiction and to the creativity evident in everyday language practices.
Bruner (1990) builds on Vygotsky's emphasis on the social and cultural
shapings of language practices to suggest that narratives about human events,
even as constructed by young children, are an important feature of the
construction of stability at individual and social levels. Through telling stories
that imply evaluations of diverse behaviours, we come to sufficiently share
a cultural and moral compass that facilitates the interpretation of narratives
whether literary or everyday. I shall look further at children's storytelling in
Section 4.4.

Emily's narrative is emergent of course, but as Levy has observed, she has
moved towards a way of recounting a sequence of events that in her society is
increasingly 'coherent' and 'logically explicit'. Such judgements are culture
specific. What counts as a coherent narrative will vary in different cultural
contexts (e.g. Hymes, 1996). You may have noticed the considerable amount of
repetition, of words and phrases, in Emily's story. She seems to be practising and

playing with different combinations of words. Dialogues and indeed monologues by children – as well as adults – can often contain word play, the root of 'everyday poetics'. I will now turn to this aspect of creative language use.

4.3 Word play and everyday poetics

This section looks at some examples of young children's word play that may be linked to creative processes in adult talk. The connections which can be made between literary language and everyday talk may be extended to young children's sound play even from the time of their earliest utterances. Studies of young children's sound play are often conducted with reference to how children develop knowledge about the phonology (i.e. the sound system) of their language. Here, I will focus on the creativity involved in such play. Phonologically, children show preferences for certain patterns in their early words. The most noticeable preference is for **reduplication**, the immediate repetition of the same syllable within a word, such as in the archetypal examples *dada* and *mama*. Lucy Barker, quoted by Peccei (1999, p. 105) heard [*roro*] for 'yoghurt', a common example of how children often display a preference for repetition, even if the particular way they simplify words varies individually.

Many parents and other people close to children have noticed a fondness for repetitive word play that, as Guy Cook argues in Reading B, Chapter 1, is actually characteristic of adults too, although generally in different settings. I was researching children's language in a nursery school when Charlie, aged 4' 8" (4 years, 8 months) stepped inside a toy telephone box and spoke into the receiver, in which there was a microphone linked to a tape recorder.

In the simple transcription that follows, the ends of lines indicate slight breaks; round brackets enclose uncertain transcription:

I'll ring you at half past two
and then poo
and you
at half past two
[two second pause]
now poo
[ten second pause, while C. looks around]
now poo
and voo
at half past two
(and then voo)
and poo
at half past –

At this point an adult came in the box as Charlie was dislodging the telephone rest, so he stopped.

Apart from phonological play, there are of course other aspects in which this text is playful and creative. Charlie has stepped into a fictional world, commonly entered into by young children – that of pretence. He pretends to be making a phone call and creates some features of the genre of telephone calling in actuality, though clearly engaging in playful activity rather than attempting a direct imitation of the practice. Charlie, like many other children in the nursery, often stepped either by himself or with others into the box and engaged in pretence talk. He clearly knew this was a toy phone and spoke in a rhythmic manner, not waiting for any exchanges. His talk displays the influence of cultural knowledge in the use of the common phrase in telephone discourse, *I'll ring you*, at the beginning. *At half past two* is a sensible enough continuation and sets up pleasing repetition of the single sound [uː]. Charlie goes on to play with repetition of the same sound, taking the opportunity in the non-public (non-linguistically supervised) venue of the phone box to bring in one of his favourite mildly taboo words. (*Poo* means 'excrement' in a children's register in the UK.)

Research on the linguistic creativity in young children's word play is rare in comparison with developmental studies focusing on their early word production, or the relationship between learning concepts and appropriate words. In Reading A, you will find extracts from a notable paper in this small field.

A C T I V I T Y 2   J's rhymes (Reading A)

In Reading A, Sharon Inkelas discusses a US study of a rhyming game played by a young child, J. As you work through the reading, note the distinction Inkelas makes between 'poetic rhyme' and 'word rhyme'. How does Inkelas account for J's changing use of English rhyming conventions? The reading contains some technical linguistic terms. Where these aren't explained in the text, they are glossed briefly in the margin.

Comment

Inkelas shows that J's first rhymes are 'poetic' – they follow the conventions of nursery rhymes and other children's rhymes J has been exposed to since infancy. J then begins to produce 'word rhymes'. These have different stress patterns from poetic rhymes, and are the kinds of forms adults produce when asked to rhyme words. Inkelas' study is developmental – she sees J's rhyming as going through two phases, the second more adult-like. In addition to the acquisition of rhyme, Inkelas' study provides evidence of children's developing understanding of the sound system of English. For Inkelas, J's rhymes suggest this occurs at an earlier age than claimed by other researchers.

J's acquisition of rhyme clearly reflects the kinds of language he hears around him at home. He is also unusual in having two phonologists for parents, who feed him particular words to rhyme. Different kinds of language play are likely to occur amongst children who grow up in different social and cultural contexts.

There is abundant evidence of different types of language play, amongst children of different ages, that may in some respects be considered poetic. I have included two further examples below, the first from a conversation between five-year-old girls.

ACTIVITY 3   **Being grandmother**

Allow
10–15 minutes

Look at the data below, a transcript of a recording made by Catherine Garvey, a researcher into young children's play and language. Two five-year-olds were playing while handling some toys, not looking at each other very much. What effects, that can be found in poetry and/or other literary forms, can you identify here?

M: And when Melanie and ... and you will be in here you have to be grand mother grand mother. Right?

F: (*distorted voice*): I'll have to be grand momma grand momma grand momma.

M: Grand mother grand mother grand mother.

F: Grand momma grand momma grand momma.

M: Grand mother grand mother grand mother.

F: Grand momma grand mother grand momma.

M: Momma.

F: Momma I ... my mommy momma. Mother humpf.

M: Hey.

F: Mother mear (*laugh*) mother smear.

M: (*laugh*).

F: I said mother smear mother near mother tear mother dear (*laugh*).

M: Peer.

F: Fear.

M: Pooper.

F: What?

M: Pooper. Now that's a ... that's a good name.

(Crystal, 1998, p. 168)

Comment

David Crystal, who has discussed this data in his book *Language Play* identifies:

- the use of nonsense words motivated by their sound;
- repetition again for pleasurable effect;
- modification of sounds within a word;
- use of alliteration;
- use of rhyme.

There is also considerable play with pitch movements but this is not shown on this transcript.

Note also the pleasure the children take in play, seen in their laughter; and the evaluation of play, 'that's a good name'.

In June Factor's dictionary, *Kidspeak* (2000), she gives examples of word play which have become part of children's discourse in Australia, within a powerful argument as to why we should take children's creative language seriously.

Kidspeak

Children play with language as joyfully and consistently as they play with objects. Verbal playfulness, the deliberate turning upside-down of everyday reality, appears to be a central feature of language development. It is through verbal play that children come to recognize, learn, repeat and invent language conventions.

Literary devices are employed for aesthetic effect: alliteration, assonance, onomatopoeia, metaphor and similar, repetition, substitution, nonsense syllables, intonation, rhyme, rhythm and pitch. *You're a poet and don't know it!*, the old cry of the playground, is an apt characterization of much of the colloquial language of the young.

The wit, humour, poetic devices and love of pun and absurdity which abound in Australian youngsters' colloquial speech underline the importance of non-referential uses of language to the species. *Sultanas* are dead flies, a *snot block* is a vanilla slice, a small brown marble a *poo*, one that is blue with white splotches a *galaxy*, a bra is an *over-shoulder boulder-holder*, menstrual pads are *surfboards*, and *nutcrackers* refers to a boy's tight bathing costume. The playful reconstruction of words for humorous effect leads to *penisbutter*, *vaginamite*, *bastardball* and *dwimp* ('a cross between a *dork* and a *wimp*'.) Rhyming slang, an inheritance from our early London settlers, lives on in the inner suburbs of Melbourne, where children *horse and cart* (fart), and *pickle and pork* (walk) across the *frog and toad* (road).

> Such verbal lore provides children with a stable, secure repertoire of language forms on which they may call at will. It is a means of experiment and imaginative invention which expands children's linguistic and cognitive horizons as it knits them ever more tightly into the culture of their community.
>
> (Factor, 2000, p. xxxii)

The next reading demonstrates how word play does not diminish as the nature of playful activities develop with maturity. It also makes the important point that playful talk does not only occur in the domains in which children are 'supposed' to engage in play.

ACTIVITY 4   Playful talk at school (Reading B)

Please work through Reading B, in which Rupert Wegerif discusses examples of creative, playful language used by British primary school children while they take part in classroom activities designed to encourage reasoning. Note:

- the different types of creativity that Wegerif sees pupils as engaging in;
- how linguistic creativity ('creativity type 1' in Wegerif's terms) may feed into a more educational type of creativity (termed 'creativity type 2').

Comment

Wegerif notes that linguistic creativity or language play is common in the classroom as in other contexts – it is hard to get children to discuss together without their being creative with language. In Wegerif's first example, children adopt different forms of word play alongside the task they are doing – word play is an accompaniment to the task in hand. However, Wegerif suggests that verbal creativity may also be more integral to the task children are engaged in, in which case it may form part of 'creativity type 2' – the kind of joint construction of meaning produced by children engaged in collaborative reasoning. In Wegerif's example 2, children play with language as they create text for a class newspaper. In example 3, children draw on metaphor to solve a reasoning problem. (You saw in Chapter 1, Reading C that metaphor is commonly used to explain ideas to others, in this case by teachers and doctors.)

As an educationist, Wegerif is concerned to develop children's reasoning. However, whereas reasoning in schools is traditionally associated with logic and the formation of critical judgements, Wegerif's data suggest that playful dialogue can be generative of new ideas. He points out that this sort of lively, associative thinking is present in adult interactions and indeed important and commercially valued in such spheres as marketing. He suggests that attention to the potentialities of creative language use leads to a different conception of reasoning: one that incorporates creativity and that has its roots at least in part in creative talk.

ACTIVITY 5   Language play in and out of school

Allow about 20 minutes

Compare the word play of J in Reading A with that of the children in Reading B. What similarities and differences do you note in the nature of the children's play, and its functions within interactions?

Comment

In both cases the word play occurs in the context of informal talk between people who know each other well: J is talking with his parents in a setting that has become something of a regular game between them. The children in Reading B are in a school setting yet are engaged in informal dialogue, in which their personal familiarity with one another is clearly important. In their word play both J and the children of Transcript 1 in Reading B exploit the potential of English phonology to playful effect, though part of the humour in Transcript 1 resides in the selection of incongruous words. The children of Reading B are also playful with language across different modes simultaneously, operating in both speech and writing. In addition, they are drawing on genres and practices distant from their current setting, yet with confidence and a creativity that extends into new domains.

Both these readings illustrate the *locally purposeful* nature of play. Previous chapters have emphasised the inherently human propensity for play; but in any single manifestation there are clearly ways in which being accustomed to the context has meant that each interactant appears reasonably confident that their purpose will be understood and responded to appropriately.

4.4 Make-believe: story and performance

Goldman (1998) provides a brief review of different perspectives on children's pretend play.

Guy Cook, in Chapter 1, Reading B, emphasizes children's preoccupations with fictional activity – their engagement with computer games, story and also their creation of imaginary worlds. Children's capacity for pretence, of various sorts, has been of interest to researchers across a range of disciplines. Much of the interest is developmental. Pretend play has been seen by psychologists as providing insights into children's cognitive development – their ability to imagine mental states they do not have, or understand other minds. It has also been related to children's language development (e.g. Fein, 1979). Within anthropology and other areas, it has been seen as a form of practice, in the sense of rehearsal, allowing children to practise certain activities and roles. Pretend play may also, however, be of interest in its own right, as an aspect of children's creative meaning-making.

Pretence may occur briefly and spontaneously in the course of ordinary everyday activities, as in the following example:

> Lindsey and I were gardening one day, potting new plants and transplanting those that had become root-bound. In the process, I selected a large clay pot that had been sitting neglected in a corner of the patio. I planned to use it for a large spider plant, and I asked Lindsey to hose it out. She had hardly begun her task, when she shoved the hose aside and stared intently into the depths of the pot.
>
> 'Hi', she said into the pot.
>
> I stopped my work and regarded her curiously. 'Who are you talking to?' 'Come and see, Mom!'
>
> At the bottom of the pot, in a puddle of water, was a small brown frog. Having a natural dislike for these creatures, I drew back.
>
> But Lindsey leaned in closer still and said, 'Hi, little fellow. Will you get my golden ball?' (October 27, 1986, 3;11)
>
> (Wolf and Heath, 1992, pp. 65–6; [Shelby Anne Wolf is Lindsey's mother])

Wolf and Heath document the ways in which, in Wolf's highly literary US household, episodes from children's literature were continually evoked by Lindsey and her sister in their own stories and dramas, but also in the course of more routine activities. Such play draws on diverse cultural resources in different contexts. Goldman (1998) notes that pretend play amongst the Huli, in Melanesia, draws on a storytelling genre associated with adult performances of myths, folktales and legends.

Pretence may also form part of more extended, creative episodes. I will give two examples in this section: a collaboratively constructed fictional narrative, and a dramatic performance.

The narrative on page 171 was constructed by two children, Emily (five years) and Jenny (eleven years), and collected by Suzanne Nance (unpublished). It is clearly a collaborative story. Its spontaneity is particularly evident at points where it is highly conversational in tone; however, like all narratives, it involves selection of material, and the chronological development of a sequence of events within a narrative structure, complete with conventional opening ('One day …') and closing ('The end').

Emily and Jenny's story

This activity took place in Emily's bedroom. Just before Emily's bedtime, the two girls often collaborated on creating a story together.

J: *Jenny and* [The girls are introducing themselves on the tape]

E: Emily. That's me.

J: *One day there was a little girl called Emily.*

E: Can't you just say, don't do the same. (This is said 'sotto voce')

J: *and um she had loads and loads of pets but her favourite pet was her unicorn. See Emily had a lot of strange pets. What other pets did you have Emily?*

E: Well I had a mammoth, a tiger, a cat, an owl, a dragon, a lizard, a monster and a sheep.

J: *But Emily's favourite pet was her unicorn – cos, what did you do with your unicorn?*

E: I – I – f – s – I said 'Fly unicorn, fly' so it flied right up to the moon.

J: *Wow, did you ride on it on the moon?*

E: Yeah. So I went on the moon

J: *so you*

E: (spoken louder) And I met a mouse and we had a tea party there.

J: *so Emily was sitting on the moon with her unicorn and some of her owls and then Emily said, "Oh look what I can see! It's a big... ... ..."*

E: It's a big... big... big... shooting star

J: *And it was so big it was going to crash on to the moon.*

E: So Emily... so Emily... so 'Fly unicorn, fly' and the owls went out of their [nests?] and parachuted theirselves on to the... on to the unicorn and they got back in time at their home.

J: *Meanwhile the moon crashed and went into a million pieces and Emily with her supersonic power got every single piece and got some of the unicorn's special glue and glued it all back together.*

E: So it shone again and it could go again but soon the sun came back and when the sun came back all the glue dried and... the moon crashed again 'cos all the glue dried.

J: *But Emily again with her supersonic power put it all back together by... er... licking it. The End.*

(Extract self-recorded around 2/4 July 2003)

Characters are clearly fictional and you may have immediately guessed some of the borrowed sources. Nance comments on the complex **intertextuality** evident in the story, as the children take on voices from myths, books, films and TV shows. She suggests that *Harry Potter* is probably the main source. Jenny refers to the unicorn as Emily's favourite pet. Others include a cat, a dragon and an owl – all of which feature in tales of magic. Jenny's reference to 'the unicorn's special glue' takes its theme from the special powers that the unicorn has in the Harry Potter books (unicorn horn, hair and blood, perhaps deliberately diluted by Jenny to 'glue'). Emily refers obliquely to *The Philosopher's Stone* and to *Alice in Wonderland* (meeting a mouse and having a tea-party). Emily loved Disney films and her call 'Fly unicorn, fly' echoes Wendy's call to Peter Pan, 'Fly Peter, fly.' Jenny has watched cartoons showing 'Super duper Sumos' – a possible source for her description of Emily's supersonic powers. All these sources were confirmed by the children's mother.

Intertextuality

'Intertextuality' was coined by Julia Kristeva, drawing on the work of the literary theorist Bakhtin to refer to the ways in which all utterances form part of a 'chain of speech communication' (Kristeva, 1986). All utterances or texts are inherently intertextual, made up of words and meanings from other texts. An obvious example is direct quotation from others, but intertextuality may also operate at a more abstract level, e.g. in the incorporation of particular genre conventions or ways of speaking about certain events. Intertextuality is a property of 'literary' as well as 'everyday' texts and may be exploited in e.g. parody or pastiche. The concept can be related to Bakhtin's notion of 'voices', which you met in Chapter 3.

(Adapted from Swann et al., 2004)

In their narrative Emily and Jenny evoke a fictional world that, in its complexity, can be linked with sophisticated fictions. These in turn often draw upon earlier stories, archetypal characters and myths. Our understanding of a fictional world newly encountered is likely to produce effects on us partly according to the extent with which pre-existing resonances occur. We don't want to hear exactly what we've heard before, but we will as we experience fiction (or any kind of text) make connections to our earlier experiences including those of other fictional creations.

It is clear from Jenny's supportive utterances that she is scaffolding Emily's learning, that is, facilitating her participation in this particular practice. Nance argues that this enables Emily to be 'a head taller than [her]self' (Vygotsky, 1967, p. 16), producing a satisfying story which she couldn't have managed on her own. Vygotsky suggested that the very activity of engaging in cooperative pretence play facilitates socialisation and helps children to learn how to take part in the cultural practices of the particular society in which they live.

Reading C, by Anthea Fraser Gupta, provides a further example of pretence, in this case **sociodramatic play**, in which two children engage collaboratively in a dramatic performance. As in Nance's study, the children are adept at weaving together various prior texts into a new creation.

Fraser Gupta's texts are mini-dramas, enactments, suitably modified (we presume) from events of everyday life. These data are particularly useful for exemplifying the suggestion made earlier that child's play is practice in a dual sense. In their use of code-switching between different languages, and the associated taking on of roles we see the sense in which play is rehearsal for future interactions and development of identity. But we also see here a practice, particular to childhood, of immersion into sociodramatic play.

A C T I V I T Y 6   Sociodramatic play in a multilingual society (Reading C)

The readings and examples in Chapter 3 illustrated how speakers drew on certain speaking styles (varieties of English or English alongside other languages) as resources in the performance of identities. Fraser Gupta illustrates something similar in Reading C, although in this case the children are more clearly 'in role', taking on the voices of different characters in dramatic performances. As you work through the reading note how, in this multilingual context, the children draw on language in their performance of the characters of a teacher and pupils in school.

Comment

As Fraser Gupta demonstrates, the children show considerable sensitivity to language. They select an appropriate language (English, Malay or Mandarin) for particular speakers and contexts, reflecting, as Fraser Gupta notes, the language patterns that are likely to obtain in the school they attend. Although she does not yet have a full command of standard English, Sunita, the older girl, also seems able to style-switch. She use standard forms in the role of teacher but switches to Singlish when the teacher expresses her anger towards a pupil. Language is therefore drawn on, highly effectively, to animate the characters in Sunita and Meera's dramas.

The data presented here suggest the importance of considering language use in multilingual environments. Sociodramatic play among monolingual children is a relatively well-researched area; there are many analyses which reveal children's sensitivity in the use of style-shifting. Andersen (1990), for example, worked with an ingenious research methodology whereby she and children manipulated puppets dressed in costume, talking 'in role'. Andersen's analyses demonstrate that even four-year-old children can play various roles in experimental settings, differentiating in systematic ways in the language they use to enact 'nurse' for example in comparison with 'patient' and 'doctor'. Fraser Gupta shows that such sensitivity can be demonstrated when different language codes are present in the environment. Even if unaware of the particular context of these extracts, you probably picked out some examples of usage of English appropriate to the school setting.

4.5 Children's lore

In the Introduction, I referred to the study of children's lore pioneered in Britain in the 1950s by Iona and Peter Opie. The Opies, and other researchers in the same tradition, have studied a range of children's rhymes, riddles and other language games in playgrounds and other contexts, and recorded the historical and geographical spread of children's lore. I mentioned that this research tradition documents and often celebrates children's cultural activity, seeing children as the preservers of tradition. However, children do not simply reproduce traditional language practices. There has also been a major focus of interest in how children adapt rhymes and riddles creatively, introducing contemporary resonances into traditional forms. Children's lore is characterised by striking forms of intertextuality, incorporating themes from several different sources.

The themes evident in children's lore also reflect shifting sets of values. As an example, consider the rhyme *My boyfriend gave me an apple*. This rhyme has been heard over several decades in many locations. It was recorded in Sydney, Australia in 1984 (Sydney Folklore Project, 2004) and in Lincoln, UK in 2000 (Firebird Trust, 2000):

> My boyfriend gave me an apple
> My boyfriend gave me a pear
> My boyfriend gave me a kiss on the lips
> And he threw me down the stairs.

In 1995 grandchildren of the folklorist traveller Wiggy Smith were recorded singing it on his CD, celebrating such children's rhymes as an element of their culture. The sleeve notes recognised that the rhyme was still current at the time in local playgrounds (Smith, 1995). Elizabeth Grugeon collected a modified version of this rhyme in the south-east of England in 1994, with the last verse as:

> I took him to the pictures
> To buy some bubble gum
> And when he wasn't looking
> I shoved some up his bum.

Grugeon (1999, p. 15) remarks that 'this rhyme is typical of the way taboo topics are used by young girls to subvert rhymes which originally put the girlfriend in a powerless position.' Rhymes offer opportunities for such modifications that in some ways seem to make them more relevant for new users. Modifications frequently feature at least mildly taboo inclusions and also serve to strengthen claims to pertinent aspects of identity. In this case, a satisfying twist has put the girls, who are the usual practitioners of clapping rhymes, into the triumphant position in the rhyme.

ACTIVITY 7   Exploring children's lore

Allow about
15 minutes

Because children's lore is so widespread, it is likely that adults will have experience of it either directly or indirectly. Can you recall any playground or street rhymes in English or other languages from your own childhood? Or have you observed more contemporary children's rhymes? Could any of these be traced back to earlier periods, do you think? Is there anything that marks out the versions that you know as belonging to a particular time or place – certain cultural references, for instance?

If you wish to look into the origins or distribution of these rhymes, there are many books available on children's lore, such as the unsurpassed classic works by Iona and Peter Opie. There are also an increasing number of serious sites on the internet which are repositories of information on nursery, playground and other children's rhymes.

Comment

Here are my own personal contributions, which may or may not be similar to your own. The fact of play in some sense may be universal but there will be cultural and linguistic variability.

I remember (growing up in Essex in the 1960s) singing as a clapping rhyme,

> I went to a Chinese restaurant
> To buy a loaf of bread
> They wrapped it up in a five pound note
> And this is what they said

As far as I recall the rhyme went into nonsense syllables (presumably to represent 'Chinese' in those relatively culturally ignorant times). It continued something like:

> Makaraka
> [line forgotten]
> Rom pom pooli
> Om pom poosh

Another version of this rhyme occurs several years later, in data collected by Grugeon in the late 1990s. (I have inserted line numbers for ease of reference.)

I went to the Chinese restaurant

[data collected in 1997 in Bedford, England]
Two girls played this as a combined clapping and miming routine.

1   I went to the Chinese restaurant
2   To buy a loaf of bread, bread, bread,
3   I wrapped it up in a five pound note
4   And this is what they said, said, said,
5   'My name is Elvis Presley
6   Girls are sexy
7   Sitting on the doorstep
8   Drinking Pepsi
9   Having a baby
10   Sitting in the navy
11   Boys to kiss, kiss [*hands to mouth and blow*]
12   Girls go woo' [*lift skirt to show knickers*].

(Grugeon, 2001, p. 111)

Grugeon notes that the Opies recorded almost exactly the same version (Grugeon, 2001, p. 111 – 'back seat' instead of 'doorstep') in Virginia Water, Surrey, in 1983 (Opie and Opie 1985, p. 467). Grugeon's five-year-old daughter had an earlier version of the rhyme in 1979. This did not include references to Elvis and Pepsi, but did include the refrain:

Elli, elli, chickali, chickali
Chinese chopsticks
Wily, willy whiskers
Pow, pow, pow.

which later became:

Rom pom pooli
Willa, willa whiskers
Injun chief say
How, how, how.

(Grugeon, 2001, pp. 111–2)

Turner et al. (1978) quote a version of the early section from Melbourne in 1966:

I went to a Chinese restaurant
To buy me a loaf of bread, pom, pom
He wrapped it up in a five pound note

And this is what he said: he said:
Oo ee oo ah ah
Ting tang walla walla bing bang.

(Turner, Factor and Lowenstein, 1978, p. 36)

I have heard Grugeon's lines 6–10 in exactly the same form, but embedded within a different rhyme, sung by my daughter and her friends in Lancashire in 2002.

The Opies and other researchers (e.g. Turner et al. 1978) demonstrate that some elements of children's rhymes have crossed extraordinary passages of time and space – countries and centuries. As an example, see Figure 4.2, in which the Opies trace a twentieth century rhyme back over 200 years. At the same time, elements of new popular culture references have always pervaded games and rhymes. The intertextuality of children's lore clearly means that this draws both on long traditions and elements of individual, additive creative modifications that will always remain anonymous. At any one time rhymes may have layered resonances while being experienced as fresh at the first point of contact. Indeed it is their flexibility and the possibility of introducing new elements that must keep them ever meaningful.

ACTIVITY 8   Contemporary lore in New Zealand (Reading D)

In Reading D, Janice Ackerley provides an example of a contemporary study of children's playground rhymes, focusing particularly on the range of intertextual references evident in these. As you work through the reading, note the formal properties of children's rhymes, the kinds of intertextual links made in the rhymes and the contemporary themes and issues addressed.

Comment

There is repetition in these rhymes, a strong sense of rhythm and simple end rhymes. All of these are likely to make the rhymes easy to remember and to chant or sing out loud. There are diverse intertextual references – children's nursery songs, TV programmes, popular brand names and the national anthem! The rhymes also incorporate a range of themes and issues, from a foot and mouth epidemic in Britain to cultural and national rivalries. They tend to be playful, sometimes parodying other songs and rhymes, playing with taboos and subverting cultural norms. For Ackerley, this provides evidence that children's lore is 'alive and well' and adapting to contemporary life.

Development of a playground rhyme

1725

Now he acts the *Grenadier*
Calling for *a Pot of Beer*
Where's his Money? He's forgot:
Get him gone, a Drunken Sot.

Lines from Henry Carey's ballad
'Namby Pamby' (1726 edn., E3–4).

1774

Whoes there
A Granidier
What dye want
A Pint of Beer.
Whoes there
A Granidier
What dye want
A Pint of Beer.

'Catch, The Soldier and the Ale House
Man' as noted down, with tune, by
Samuel Wesley when 8 years old
(British Museum, MS. Adds. 34998, f.34).

1780

Who comes here?
A Grenadier.
What do you want?
A Pot of Beer.
Where is your Money?
I've forgot.
Get you gone
You drunken Sot.

'Mother Goose's Melody' (1795 edn., p. 42).

c. 1907

Eenty, teenty tuppenny bun,
Pitching tatties doon the lum;
Who's there? John Blair.
What does he want? A bottle of beer.
Where's your money? I forgot.
Go downstairs, you drunken sot.

Collected from schoolchildren in Edinburgh.
Used for counting-out. Rymour Club,
'Miscellanea', vol. i, 1911, p.104.

c. 1910

Far are ye gaein'?
Across the gutter.
Fat for?
A pund o' butter.
Far's yer money?
In my pocket.
Far's yer pocket?
Clean forgot it!

Current among children in Forfar, c. 1910.
Jean C. Rodger, 'Lang Strang', 1948.

1916

Rat a tat tat, who is that?
Only Grandma's pussy-cat.
What do you want?
A pint of milk.
Where is your money?
In my pocket.
Where is your pocket?
I forgot it.
O you silly pussy-cat.

Used for skipping, 'London Street Games',
1916, p. 64.

Figure 4.2   Development of a playground rhyme (Opie and Opie [1959] 2001, pp. 10–11)

1939

A frog walked into a public house
And asked for a pint of beer.
Where's your money?
In my pocket.
Where's your pocket?
I forgot it.
Well, please walk out.

Used for counting-out in Swansea.

1943

Rat tat tat, who is that?
Only Mrs. Pussy Cat.
What do you want?
A pint of milk.
Where's your penny?
In my pocket.
Where's your pocket?
I forgot it.
Please walk out.

Used for counting-out in Alton.

1950

Mickey Mouse
In a public house
Drinking pints of beer.
Where's your money?
In my pocket.
Where's your pocket?
I forgot it.
Please walk out.

Used for counting-out in Alton.

1952

A monkey came to my shop
I asked him what he wanted.
A loaf, sir. A loaf, sir.
Where's your money?
In my pocket.
Where's your pocket?
I ain't got it.
Well, out you bunk.

'Skipping for two'. Girl, 12, Market Rasen.

1952

A pig walked into a public house
And asked for a drink of beer.
Where's your money, sir?
In my pocket, sir.
Where's your pocket, sir?
In my jacket, sir.
Where's your jacket, sir?
I forgot it, sir.
Please walk out.

Used for counting-out. Girl, 12, Cleethorpes.

1954

I had a little beer shop
A man walked in.
I asked him what he wanted.
A bottle of gin.
Where's your money?
In my pocket.
Where's your pocket?
I forgot it.
Please walk out.

Used for skipping in York City.

Ackerley's study is consistent with other research that emphasises the blend of continuity and adaptation in children's lore. Writing of Australian playgrounds, Factor (2004) comments:

> In these noisy, crowded, chaotic-looking spaces we can observe what I shall call the double helix of children's play: 'one strand representing the universal, ubiquitous features of child lore, the other the particular manifestations of children's play lives which result from particular circumstances' (Factor, 1988, xiv).
>
> (Factor, 2004, p. 143)

Children's rhymes and language games, then, show both a source of extraordinary continuity and many examples of creative innovation.

For Ackerley, as for similar researchers mentioned in this section, the interest is in children's rhymes as textual artefacts. Sometimes, as in the Opies' research, the times and places in which rhymes occurred are recorded, allowing researchers to document historical and geographical patterns and local adaptations. The social themes and issues addressed are of interest, but rather less so the local contexts of use – how particular children draw on these rhymes in certain contexts and to particular effects. This highly textual approach can be contrasted with more ethnographic studies of children's cultural practices, such as recent research on children's song carried out by Anne Haas Dyson (2003).

Dyson studied a group of six to seven-year-old children in a school in a socially and culturally diverse area of San Francisco. Dyson's observations ran over an eight-month period, and she observed and interacted with children in class (the daily language arts period), as well as in the playground and elsewhere. She was interested in children's creative use of song in these different contexts, and particularly in their playful appropriation and adaptation of material from a range of sources. These included children's lore in the traditional sense (e.g. playground rhymes) but also media and other genres: raps, R&B, hymns and folk songs. For Dyson these represent a 'landscape of voices' that allow children to assume various stances and roles. Singing a hymn, for instance, allowed two girls to evoke their roles as church members. A song from a (younger) children's television show enabled two boys to remember but also distance themselves from their time in pre-school and kindergarten. A rap, associated with teenagers, allowed children to take on an older voice, akin to dressing up and putting on lipstick. Dyson argues that:

Dyson's use of the term 'voices' – utterances and their associated meanings and values – derives from Bakhtin. See also Chapter 3, pp. 137–8.

> ... the children's socio-ideological landscape was partly enacted through musical voices. These voices provided children with whole utterances, utterance types or genres, and particular lyrics, and thus they became cultural stuff with which the children could construct their present lives, remember their pasts, and anticipate their futures. In so doing, they were at the very same time constructing themselves as members of varied social institutions, and, more broadly, of particular social and cultural spheres.
>
> (Dyson, 2003, p. 160)

Songs also served a number of (intertwining) social functions within interactions: they were a source of pleasure, they provided material for personal expression and performance, they were a context for play, and they allowed children to display knowledge and expertise. Because they were a means for children to act jointly, they could be used to express social affiliation or differentiation, as exemplified in the box below. While many of the children's songs were a form of popular culture, Dyson notes that they also provided resources that could be drawn on in official school contexts in various ways.

Using a song to mark friendship

Two close friends, Denise and Vanessa, are planning a girls' club with three other girls. Vanessa suggests a password for the club that only Denise will know. She then uses music to highlight her special relationship with Denise.

> Denise is giving directions for making the pages of the club book. Ariel, Nanette, and Elizabeth are attending and responding to Denise with their own suggestions. Vanessa starts singing a 'bouncy song' [...]:

Vanessa: Look at those girls ...
             OO – they look so fine
             Look at those girls ...
             OO – looking so fine
Denise is concentrating on the pages.
Vanessa: Come on, Denise. (to group) She's my best friend.
             She's hecka fun.
Denise: After you're done [with your page for the book], I'll sing with you.
And she did.

(Dyson, 2003, p. 164)

Like researchers of more traditional children's lore, Dyson is interested in children's appropriation of cultural resources, but she is concerned less with the form these take than with *how they are used* to particular effect in specific contexts. In terms of the distinction established in earlier chapters, this is a much more highly contextualised approach to the study of children's creativity with language.

4.6 Conclusion

Vygotsky remarked, 'Play is the natural means of a child's self-education, an exercise oriented toward the future' ([1935] 1993, p. 161). Through observing and analysing play, he suggested, one comes to see the development of a child's personality not so much as a 'passive unfolding of innate primary abilities' but rather that the 'process of emergence of character is not *unfolding* but *enculturation*'. In other words, through play the developing child actively learns to adopt cultural norms, and is shaped as a person in the process.

The data presented in this chapter suggests that passive 'unfolding' certainly does not characterise the lively exchanges depicted in *The Social Baby*. Research into 'protoconversations' has strengthened the argument that playfulness, in the sense of enjoyable exchange of affect, where informational content is absent or 'not the point', is a quality of the species. Furlow's (2001) overview of research from evolutionary neurobiology, neuroscience, behavioural ecology and other fields suggests that play, a behaviour restricted to more intelligent animals, actually increases children's potential for learning. He discusses work by the neuroscientist Siviy that shows how bouts of play increase the brain's activation of a specific protein associated with the stimulation and growth of nerve cells:

> 'Play just lights everything up,' [Siviy] says. He speculates that by allowing connections between brain areas that might not normally be connected, play may be enhancing creativity.
>
> (Furlow, 2001, p. 30)

I have argued that in considering creative language use it is useful to examine the early years, and even infancy. Research on child language is most often read and indeed conducted with a view to uncovering routes, or stages, to adult competence. In this chapter I have tried to demonstrate that the manifold varieties of everyday creativity in language, documented by researchers such as Carter (2004/Chapter 1, Reading A) and Cook (2000/Chapter 1, Reading B), have their roots in activities of the very young. One of the main aims of this chapter has been to probe children's linguistic creativity for its own sake, and also to illustrate something of the practices and relationships in which it flourishes.

Artistry in the English language is always related to a wealth of cultural resources, whether or not the breadth and depth of their origins is appreciated consciously. Enculturation is a notion that can perhaps bridge the two different perspectives on child's creativity that I have suggested dominate most previous views of the topic. From anthropology we have an emphasis on practices, children's lore and the sense of a continuing children's culture. From developmental psychology we have emphases on children's learning; at whatever level play is examined – for example nonverbal, phonological, discourse – it is chiefly regarded as rehearsal, as learning on the way to maturity. Child's play, as set within the perspective on artfulness developed in this book, can be viewed as above all an instance of enculturation: the active engagement with resources made available to the child in her or his society. Re-use, in new circumstances, leads to opportunities for transformations. The child as an individual, or indeed collaborator, brings imagination to weave a new text.

READING A: J's rhymes: a longitudinal case study of language play

Sharon Inkelas

Introduction

Linguists have long been aware that children's language play is a window not only into the creative nature of language acquisition but also into the degree to which the child has mastered, and can manipulate, the essential structures of his or her language (Ferguson and Macken, 1983). Despite this awareness, longitudinal studies of children's language play are rare. This paper documents an invented rhyming game developed at the age of two by J, a boy learning English. J played the game for over two years. His parents recorded many of his rhymes, providing a wealth of data into their structure. J's rhymes show that J was sensitive to two types of rhyming conventions in English. The first stage of his rhyming game follows the patterns of English poetic rhyme prevalent in the children's literature and nursery rhymes he was exposed to. The latter stages of his game instead follow the word-rhyme conventions used by adults when rhyming words out of a poetic context.

The existence of J's game highlights the sensitivity of children, even at a tender age, to the structural properties of spoken and literary language, and shows the importance of closely studying children's language play.

Some background on J

J invented his rhyming game at the age of two years, five months (2;5). At that time J already had a large vocabulary and fairly adult-like pronunciation. Typical of children of that age, he pronounced 'th' as [f] in words like *think* or *bath*, as [d] in words like *this*, and as [v] in words like *with*, but otherwise correctly pronounced all of the consonants and vowels of English. He also produced stress on the correct syllable of all words; as shown below, his rhyming patterns reveal that he controlled the difference between primary and secondary stress.

J played the game off and on for over two years, with the last documented instance of play occurring at 4;6. Initially all of the rhymes were volunteered; later his parents, both trained phonologists, began playing the game with him by feeding him words to 'rhyme'. J enjoyed this. Usually J knew and used the words he was rhyming, but sometimes his parents supplied words that were new to him. There was no difference in how he treated familiar and unfamiliar words. On thirteen occasions spaced over the two years during which J played this game, his parents wrote down the rhymes J produced, using phonetic transcription as needed. 220 rhymes were collected overall. This paper is based on those 220 productions.

The language game

Onset = consonant that precedes the vowel in a syllable.

J's rhyming game consisted of pronouncing a word (almost always correctly), followed immediately by a modified portion, which we may call the 'echo'. Echo modification involves two essential components: onset substitution, whereby 'b' or 'p' was inserted at the beginning of the echo (e.g. 'ant-bant'), and truncation, in which the echo copy of a long word was shortened.

The first phase: poetic rhyme

The first phase of J's game lasted for five months, from age 2;5 to 2;10. During this time 92 rhymes were transcribed.

Onset substitution

Throughout this phase of the game, J consistently supplied the echo with a beginning consonant different from that of the original, or 'source' word. In general the consonant was 'b'. However, as shown in the examples below, if the echo would have begun with 'b' anyway, J replaced it with 'p'. The result was that the echo always differed from the part of the source word that it corresponded to:

	Reduplicated form	Session no.
a.	ant-bant	1
	stem-bem	1
	plate-bate	1
	Ian-bian	2
	towel-bowel	2
b.	ball-pall	1
	bread-ped	1
	brave-prave	1
	bowl-powl	2
	blanket-planket	2

Onset differentiation is, of course, a typical characteristic of English rhyming conventions (see e.g. Stallworthy, 1983), to which J was amply exposed, via nursery rhymes and other rhyming children's literature, throughout his babyhood.

Over time, J expanded the set of consonants in the source that could trigger 'p' in the copy. Some five months into the period under study he revised the rules so that any voiced obstruent (consonants such as z, d, g, etc.) in the source would be replaced by 'p' if echo-initial. 'b' and 'p' remained the default echo-initial consonants until the very final stages of the game; in one final session, recorded at age 4;6, J was drawing on a much larger range of echo-initial consonants. Throughout the entire two years, however, J remained true to the principle that the echo and corresponding portion of the source could not begin with the same consonant. The requirement that onsets be different is of course highly reminisicent of English rhyming conventions, in which *ball-fall* would be considered a good rhyme and *ball-ball* a bad one.

Truncation

During both phases of J's game, long source words were truncated in a manner that was sensitive to the position of stress in the word. It is the conditions on truncation that distinguish the two major phases of J's game. During the first phase, J systematically cut the second, or 'echo' copy down to the rightmost syllable bearing any degree of stress: *alíve-bive, aórta-borta, Mìnnesóta-bota, Kàlamazóo-boo, ènginéer-beer, stègosáurus-baurus, ptèrodáctyl-bakyl.*

J made no distinction between primary (main) stress and secondary stress. To take one example, both *ènginéer* and *lúmberjàck* have stress on the first and third (last) syllables. They differ only in relative prominence, with the first stress being secondary in the case of *ènginéer* and primary in the case of *lúmberjàck*. In both words, the final syllable is the one to which J's echo is truncated: *ènginéer-beer, lúmberjàck-back*. When the rightmost stressed syllable is antepenultimate, the echo would be expected to be trisyllabic, e.g. *beautiful-peautiful*, a form produced at age 2;10. In the earliest stages of the game, J would condense trisyllabic echoes to two syllables: *Pamela-bama, Valerie-barry*, but by the end of the first phase he was producing trisyllabic echoes without a problem.

The second phase: word rhyme

In the second phase, starting at 3;2, J maintained essentially the same patterns of onset substitution, but abruptly changed his pattern of truncation: J now started truncating the echo to the portion beginning with the *primary* stress. For words in which a primary stress precedes a secondary stress, Patterns 1 and 2 thus produce different results, with Pattern 1 truncating to the portion beginning with the last syllable possessing any degree of stress (*hélicòpter-bopter,* not **hélicòpter-belicopter*), and Pattern 2 truncating to the portion beginning with the primary stressed syllable (*Álbuquèrque-balbuquerque*, not **Álbuquèrque-berque*). Once J shifted to Pattern 2, he applied it consistently, producing rhymes like *blúebèrry → blueberry-pueberry, Álbuquèrque → Albuquerque-balbuquerque* and *búllet tràin → bullet train-pullet train.*

'Obstruent' is a term sometimes used in the description and classification of speech sounds. It refers to sounds whose articulation involves the airflow being temporarily blocked or constricted in some way. In English most consonants are obstruents.

'Stress' refers to the prominence attached to certain syllables in a word or utterance ... In *alíve* the second syllable is stressed (marked with an acute accent); in *stègosáurus* the third syllable carries the main, or primary stress and the first syllable carries secondary stress (marked with a grave accent).

J's game as the acquisition of rhyme

The two phases of J's game correspond to two well-established, but distinct, traditions of rhyme in English: poetic rhyme (see e.g. Preminger and Brogan, 1993) and linguistic, or word, rhyme. Stallworthy (1983, p. 1410) defines poetic rhyme as matching 'the last stressed vowel and all speech sounds following that vowel'; refining this definition, Holtman (1996, p. 7) and Hanson (2003) characterise poetic rhyme as matching the portion of the line beginning with the last strong metrical position. According to Hanson (p. 9), 'It is in fact not final stressed syllables but rather the syllables which are in the final strong positions of the meter which normally define the beginning of the domain of end-rhyme in English [verse].' J was amply exposed to this kind of rhyme in children's literature, including lines such as the following:[1]

> 'Metre' (metrical) refers to regular patterning of stressed and unstressed syllables.

(a) Mountains and fountains / rain down on *me* /

    s   w   s   w /   s   w   s   w

    Buried in berries / What a jam jambo*ree*!

    s   w   s   w /   s   w   s <w>

(b) Good night stars Good night *air* /

    s w s <w> s w   s<w> /

    Good night noises every*where*

    s   w   s   w s w   s   <w>

(c) They left the house at half past *nine*

    w   s   w   s   w   s   w   s

    in two straight lines in rain or *shine*

    w s   w   s   w s   w   s

    The smallest one was Made*line*

    w   s w s   w   s w s

(d) Higgety-piggety, my fat *hen*

    s   w   s w   s   w s <w>

    She lays eggs for gentlemen

    s   w   s   w   s w s   <w>

> 'Foot' refers to a division of a line of verse containing a stressed syllable.

In all four sets of lines the rhyming sequence contains a proper subset of the syllables in the final word. In lines (a) and (b), each rhyming sequence (*me/-ree, air/-where*) constitutes the final stress foot of the word containing it. In line a), the final metrical foot corresponds to a primary lexical stress (*jàmborée*); in the last lines of (b), (c) and (d), the final metrical foot has secondary stress in the words containing it (*éverywhère, Mádelìne, géntlemèn*). This is exactly comparable to the truncation conventions in the first phase of J's game, in which the echo consists of the final metrical foot, regardless of whether it bears primary or secondary word stress, of the source word. For J in Pattern 1, *jàmborée* and *Mádelìne* would have have resulted in the monosyllabic rhymes *jamboree-bee* and *Madeline-bine*; in the lines above, they rhyme with the monosyllables *me* and *shine*, respectively. Even J's early compression of trisyllabic echoes to two syllables in words like *Valerie-barry* has precedent in English poetics, in which a medial unstressed syllable is often ignored for purposes of matching of lexical stressed and unstressed syllables to metrically strong and weak positions (see e.g. Hanson and Kiparsky, 1996).

Phase 2 of J's game, by contrast, reflects the behavior of adult English speakers when asked to rhyme words: outside of a poetic context (and the rhyming dictionaries geared toward poetic rhyme), primary word stress counts as the metrically strong position identifying the beginning of the rhyming sequence. Thus (according to J's mother's intuitions and confirmed by the Carnegie-Mellon University Pronouncing Dictionary) *háckbèrry* rhymes with *bláckbèrry* but not with *stráwbèrry*, despite the identity of the post-onset material ([ɛɹi]) in the final metrical foot of all three words.[2] *Mádelìne* rhymes with *Ádelìne*, but not with *Cárolìne* or *túrpentìne*. Similarly, *Àlabáma* rhymes with *pajáma*, and *Mìnnesóta* with *Dakóta*; like J in Pattern 2, adults rhyming words out of context tend to match main stressed syllables (and what follows), regardless of where in the word they fall.

Viewing J's game as reflecting his evolving understanding of rhyme explains a number of aspects of the game. First, it explains onset substitution. The literary rhyming conventions to which J was exposed require onsets to be different, as seen in the lines of verse cited above. Second, the rhyming hypothesis alone offers insight into why Pattern 1 precedes Pattern 2, rather than the reverse; J arguably had more exposure, through hearing books read aloud, to literary rhyme than to linguistic word rhyme at the time when he initially invented his game.

Conclusion

As has been noted many times before, children's language play provides an important window into the child's grammar at that point in acquisition. J's game highlights the important role that metrical feet, syllables, and syllable-internal structure play in children's language, a role recently argued for on the basis of unrelated data by Rose (2000); see also Echols and Newport, 1992; Fikkert, 1994; Gerken, 1994, 1996; among many others.

J's rhyming game also suggests that phonemic awareness – not to mention the ability to rhyme – occurs earlier than has standardly been assumed. The fact and nature of J's onset substitution clearly reveals awareness of segmentation, for which the ability to rhyme is a common test. Previous estimates of four years of age for the ability to rhyme (e.g. Menn and Stoel-Gammon, 1995, p. 351) may reflect the difficulty of communicating the rhyming task to a child in an experimental setting (see Lenel and Cantor, 1981); Menn and Stoel-Gammon (1995) make a similar point about segmentation tasks that have been used to assess phonemic awareness. The fortunate circumstance of volunteered rhymes allows phonemic awareness and rhyming abilities to be documented in very young children.

Notes

1   Line (a) is from Degen 1983; line (b) is from Brown 1947; line (c) is from Bemelmans 1963; line (d) is from Opie 1996.

2   The Carnegie Mellon University Pronouncing dictionary can be accessed at www.speech.cs.cmu.edu/cgi-bin/cmudict [accessed 15.7.05]. Users may search the dictionary for rhyming words via the RhymeZone website at www.rhymezone.com [accessed 15.7.05]. RhymeZone is operated by Lycos®, a registered trademark of Carnegie Mellon University.

References

BEMELMANS, L. (1963) *Madeline*, New York, Viking.

BROWN, M.W. (1947) *Good Night Moon*, New York, Harper.

DEGEN, B. (1983) *Jamberry*, New York, Harper and Row.

ECHOLS, C. and NEWPORT, E. (1992) 'The role of stress and position in determining first words', *Language Acquisition* **2**, pp. 189–200.

FERGUSON, C. and MACKEN, M. (1983) 'The role of play in phonological development', in K. NELSON (ed.) *Children's Language*, Hillsdale, NJ, Lawrence Erlbaum Associates.

FIKKERT, P. (1994) *On the Acquisition of Prosodic Structure*, Dordrecht, Holland Institute of Generative Linguistics.

GERKEN, L. (1994) 'A metrical template account of young children's weak syllable omissions from multisyllabic words', *Journal of Child Language*, **21**, pp. 565–84.

GERKEN, L. (1996) 'Prosodic structure in young children's language processing' *Language*, **72**, pp. 683–712.

HANSON, K. (2003) 'Formal variation in the rhymes of Tobert Pinsky's *The Inferno of Dante*', *Language and Literature*, **12**(4), pp. 309–337.

HANSON, K. and KIPARSKY, P. (1996) 'A parametric theory of poetic meter', *Language*, 72, pp. 287–335.

HOLTMAN, A. (1996) 'A generative theory of rhyme: an Optimality approach', *OTS Dissertation Series*, Utrecht, LEd.

LENEL, J.C. and CANTOR, J.H. (1981) 'Rhyme recognition and phonemic perception in young children', *Journal of Psycholinguistic Research*, **10**, pp. 57–67.

MENN, L. and STOEL-GAMMON, C. (1995) *The Handbook of Child Language*, Oxford, Blackwell.

OPIE, I. (ed.) (1996) *My Very First Mother Goose*, Cambridge, MA, Candlewick Press.

PREMINGER, A. and BROGAN, T.V.F. (eds) (1993) *The New Princeton Encyclopedia of Poetry and Poetics*, Princeton, Princeton University Press.

ROSE, Y. (2000) 'Headedness and prosodic licensing in the L1 acquisition of phonology', PhD thesis, McGill University.

STALLWORTHY, J. (1983) 'Versification', in A.W. ALLISON, H. BARROWS, C.R. BLAKE, A.J. CARR, A.M. EASTMAN and H.M. ENGLISH Jr. (eds) *The Norton Anthology of Poetry*, New York, W.W. Norton and Co.

Source: this paper is based on a longer study by the author, published in 2003 in *The Journal of Child Language*. Full acknowledgements can be found in that article. Here, the author particularly wishes to acknowledge Kristin Hanson for inspirational discussion of J's rhyming conventions, and, of course, J himself, for proving once again that toddlers make the best linguists.

READING B: Creativity and reason in classroom talk

Rupert Wegerif

It is actually very hard to get children to perform any kind of task at school without their being creative with language. In the following example three nine-year-old children, Sharon, Gail and Nick, were asked to work together around a piece of software called Bubble Dialogue. This software shows cartoon characters in a difficult situation and the users have to fill in the thought bubbles and speech bubbles of the characters. In this case the cartoon characters were called Jane and Robert. Jane knew that Robert had stolen some chocolates from the sweet shop. Now her money was missing and she thought Robert might have stolen that too. Sharon, Gail and Nick were asked to talk together about the issues and think about how the characters would feel. They did not really do that but they did produce some interesting word play. We join them as they construct together what they will type.

Transcript Extract 1: Funny money

SHARON: I think

GAIL: I think Robert stole the stuff

SHARON: That

NICK: That Robert stole my bunny

(Sharon and Gail laugh)

SHARON: My money

GAIL: Funny

NICK: It's not money, I said bunny

SHARON: It's his money

GAIL: I've said bunny

A few lines later they are typing in together the word 'chocolates' and Gail says: 'lovely, *yummy*, chocolates' echoing the earlier use of *money*, *bunny*, *funny*. She then continues in a different voice to indicate that she is quoting:

> life is in a box of chocolates

Nobody picks up this reference to the film *Forrest Gump*. Three lines later Gail tries another reference to a different context, singing:

> Choc-o-lets. Tasty. Cadbury's Quake

in the tune of an advertisement for Cadbury's Flake. This time Nick picks this up responding to use of 'Quake' with the word 'Quavers' which is a popular snack also advertised on TV. Sharon, who is typing this whole time, brings them back to the task, as she sees it, by saying 'Chocolates' and then beginning to spell it out: 'C, H, O, C'.

For now, the others join her in spelling out 'chocolate', but it is not long before the word-play breaks out again, 'chocolate' being turned by Sharon into 'choc, then it's late'.

Despite the teacher's best efforts, these children interpreted the task as more about typing words into the boxes than thinking about issues. This task-interpretation is a common one and probably reflects their educational history. What is interesting though, is that they cannot do this task straight; they rhyme and break into little songs, use silly voices and puns and generally play around with language. In this they are not exceptional. Ronald Carter (2004) argues that this creative 'poetic' use of language is so common in everyday talk amongst equals that it should be considered the norm.

On-task playful talk

I am not going to claim that rhyming *money*, *bunny*, *funny* and *yummy* is in itself something we should call 'reasoning'. However, it is creative in the sense in which we normally use the term 'creative'. Ronald Carter defines creativity in language as 'imaginative analogy', and this is very much what we see here. I will call this creativity type 1. More specialist definitions of the term creativity for use in education also often bring in the idea of 'resulting in a valued product' (e.g. NACCEE, 1999). I will call this creativity type 2. For creativity 1 to lead to creativity 2, shared ground rules are important. This is brought out in a transcript extract cited originally by Neil Mercer (1995, p. 101).

This example is from a session in which two ten-year-old-girls, Katie and Anne, were working on the production of their own class newspaper, using some desktop publishing software for schools called Front Page Extra. At the point the sequence begins, they have been engaged in the task for about an hour and a quarter and are trying to compose some text for their front page.

Transcript Extract 2: Fantabuloso

KATIE: Okay, so right then. What shall we write?

ANNE: We can have something like those autograph columns and things like that and items, messages

KATIE: Inside these covers (*pause 3+ secs*) Our fun-filled

ANNE: That's it!

KATIE: Something

ANNE: Something like that!

KATIE: Yeah

ANNE: Inside these fabulous fun-filled covers are – how can we have a fun-filled cover? Let me try

KATIE: Inside these (*pause 3+ secs*)

ANNE: You sound happy on this. Fantabuloso *(laughs)*

KATIE: inside these inside these fant, inside these fun-filled, no inside these covers these fantastic these brilliant

ANNE: Brilliant

KATIE: Is it brilliant?

ANNE: No

KATIE: No. Fantast fantabuloso shall we put that?

ANNE: Yeah (*inaudible*) fantabluloso.

KATIE: Fan – tab – u – lo – so

ANNE: Loso. Fantabuloso.

KATIE: Fantabuloso oso.

(Mercer, 1995, p. 101)

The importance of this example, and why I am returning to it again, is that here the children, Katie and Anne, apply word play to the task they have been given. Here creative word play moves over from just being a bit of fun to being useful in an educational context. Katie and Anne are taking their work seriously. They could almost be a couple of creative marketing executives trying to find a new name for a product. Products with very similar names – Fab, Fanta, Brillo, etc. – already exist and were presumably thought up through a similar kind of shared creative process. The difference between this and the 'money' transcript is that here the talk is oriented to finding the best possible solution to the problem set. Sharon, Gail and Nick do not link their verbal play to the task in hand, it is just a bit of fun, if anything it is subverting the task. Their play is creative in that it generates lots of new links and potential ideas – is life really like a box of chocolates? – but they do not build on any of them. Katie and Anne do build on each other's suggestions.

Their creative play becomes something I would like to call reasoning because they apply implicit shared criteria to select the preferred response. Katie asks 'Is it *brilliant?*' i.e does this word fit, and she agrees with Anna that it is not quite right. Both then converge on 'fantabuloso'.

Metaphors to solve a reasoning test problem

In several studies colleagues and I have been concerned to teach children to reason more effectively by carrying out problem-solving activities and exploring ideas through discussion. However, we also found that problems were solved not through explicit reasoning so much as through the generation of perspicuous representations that were based on physical metaphors. I will give a short example from the transcript data and then explain more what I mean.

Here is an extract from the group's talk after a series of lessons promoting the use of effective reasoning. (An analysis of the full transcript has been published in Wegerif and Mercer, 2000, so I will not repeat this here.)

In this task the children need to complete the pattern in the large shape by selecting one of the six alternatives offered below it.

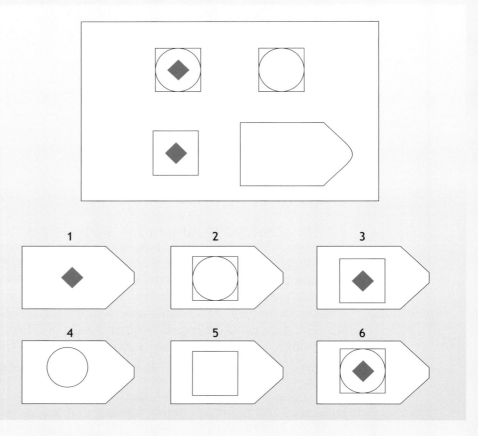

Figure 1   Pattern completion task

Transcript Extract 3: Taking the circle out

TRISHA: Look that's got a triangle, that's got a square, look that's got a
            square with a diamond with a circle in, that's got a square with a
            diamond in and that's got a square with a circle in so that's got to
            be a square

GEORGE: I don't understand this at all

TRISHA: Because look on that they've taken the circle out yes? So on that
            you are going to take the circle out because they have taken the
            circle out of that one

GEORGE: On this they have taken the circle out and on this they have taken
            the diamond out and on this they have put them both in, so it
            should be a blank square because look it goes circle square

SUSAN: It's got to be a blank square. Yeh it is.

Trisha's initial statement in this extract comes after a long discussion in which
different members of the group have tried out different alternatives and all
have paused for periods of several seconds staring at the problem with
concentrated expressions. Trisha appears to have understood the nature of
the problem but does not express it very clearly. George admits to being
baffled and Trisha responds by trying to generate an explanation that he will
understand. She does this by using the phrase 'taking the circle out'. This is a
physical metaphor for the relationship between parts of the pattern on the
page. George grasps this immediately and repeats it for himself. Susan also
now appears to understand the pattern. The relationship between the pictures
in the reasoning problem is not explicitly present in the picture, it cannot be
pointed at by Trisha, it can only be seen by George and Susan once it has
been made visible through a shared metaphor. This use of language to model
relationships and processes through the use of physical metaphors was often
found in the talk of children solving reasoning problems. Expressions such as
'getting fatter', 'that and that make that' or 'that turns around' or 'add that to
that and you get that' were common.

    The talk of Trisha and George contains explicit reasoning. But it is
interesting that, in order to see the problem together, they need to construct a
new shared metaphor. This act of creation links this talk to the talk of
transcript Extract 2: Fantabuloso. In one case there is creative exploration of
words for a newspaper headline, with the children settling on a word whose
form seems as important as the meanings it evokes; in the other case, creative
use is made of metaphor to understand a problem. In both cases the new
construction emerges out of an extended dialogue in which the participants
are struggling to create shared understanding and find a solution to a shared
problem.

Reflection

The first example given, that of Sharon, Gail and Nick, illustrates an almost random playful kind of word play as an end in itself with no obvious external motivation. In the second example, that of Anne and Katie, a similar kind of poetic resonance between words is put to use to help complete a written assignment. The final example, with George and Trisha, illustrates how the creative generation of a metaphor was essential to a group finding a shared solution to a reasoning test problem. The argument I wish to make through these examples is that verbal creativity (creativity type 1 as mentioned earlier) is an underlying and essential ingredient of the co-construction of meaning in dialogues (creativity type 2) and that this includes the case of explicit verbal reasoning.

As Janet Maybin (2003) argues, this kind of creative talk is an important part of schooling. It is very much what we see when children are solving problems together or constructing new shared understanding together. Close observation of actual reasoning frequently highlights the essential importance of creativity. Studies have shown that it is possible to teach ground rules of explicit reasoning in classrooms, to encourage more explicit challenges and reasoned justifications for example (e.g. Wegerif, Mercer and Dawes, 1999). Using the same principles it should therefore be possible to promote more creativity in dialogues through, for example, using open reflective questions with pauses that allow ideas to resonate a little before they are finally judged. This suggests that we need a new image of reason, not in terms of abstract logic, nor limited to explicit verbal reasoning, but instead an image of reason as a way of talking together that is essentially creative and that has its roots in playful talk as much as in critical talk.

References

CARTER, R. (2004) *Language and Creativity: The Art of Common Talk*, London/New York, Routledge.

MAYBIN, J. (2003) 'Voices, intertextuality and induction into schooling', in S. GOODMAN, T. LILLIS, J. MAYBIN and N. MERCER (eds) (2003) *Language, Literacy and Education: A Reader*, London, Trentham.

MERCER, N. (1995) *The Guided Construction of Knowledge: Talk Amongst Teachers and Learners*, Clevedon, Multilingual Matters.

NACCE (1999) *All Our Futures: Creativity, Culture and Education*: National Advisory Committee on Creative and Cultural Education, DfEE and DCMS.

VYGOTSKY, L. (1991) 'The genesis of higher mental functions', in P. LIGHT, S. SHELDON and B. WOODHEAD (eds) *Learning to Think*, London, Routledge.

WEGERIF, R. and MERCER, N. (1997) 'A dialogical framework for researching peer talk', in R. WEGERIF and P. SCRIMSHAW (eds) *Computers and Talk in the Primary Classroom,* Clevedon, Multilingual Matters.

WEGERIF, R., MERCER, N. and DAWES, L. (1999) 'From social interaction to individual reasoning: an empirical investigation of a possible socio-cultural model of cognitive development', *Learning and Instruction*, **9**(5), pp. 493–516.

WEGERIF, R. and MERCER. N. (2000) 'Language for thinking', in H. COWIE, D. AALSVOORT and N. MERCER (eds) *New Perspectives in Collaborative Learning*, Oxford, Elsevier.

WEGERIF, R. and DAWES, L. (2004) *Thinking and Learning with ICT: Raising Achievement in Primary Classrooms,* London, Routledge.

Source: shortened version of WEGERIF, R.B. (2005) 'Reason and creativity in classroom dialogues', *Language and Education,* 19(3).

READING C: Sociodramatic play in a multilingual society

Anthea Fraser Gupta

Introduction: bilingual children and code-switching

Children grow up bilingual if they live in families where two or more languages are regularly used. Some bilingual children are the children of mixed marriages: these children may be isolated from other similar bilinguals. But most bilingual children grow up in communities where others share their bilingualism: these children hear the adults in their community moving from one language to another, depending on the circumstances of discourse. All bilingual children need to learn when it is appropriate to use the languages they know. And in most bilingual communities there will be occasions where one language is appropriate, occasions when another is appropriate, and occasions when it is appropriate to mix the languages in the same utterance.

As an increasing volume of work is done on bilingual children, and especially as we begin to have more studies of children growing up in long-term bilingual societies, it is becoming apparent that children learn the skills of code-separation early and easily. It used to be said that bilingual children separated their codes by the age of two years. Reich (1986, p. 208) reports that most research suggested that the age at which the languages were separated was between three and five years. This age would now be considered far too late. Research on younger children suggests that codes are separated from the start (Genesee, 1989). Even style-switching within a language has been identified in children as young as a year (Ainsworth-Vaughn, 1990) and has often been clearly attested in children from three to five years old (e.g. Youssef, 1991; Gupta, 1994). Children make distinctions between people socially in all sorts of ways, and one of those ways is by

'Code' is often used as a general term for language or language variety (accent, dialect, register).

speaking differently to them. Code-selection is part of the earliest experience of a child.

Bilingual children do their best to use the languages that they know and that they believe their interlocutors to be able to use. This is seen very simply in the bilingual child's choice of code, which may be very sophisticated, showing a sensitivity to a range of social markers. They will, to the best of their ability, avoid words they know to be in the language their interlocutor does not know. They also sometimes talk about their language use. It has been suggested (there is a full discussion in Bialystock 2001, Chapter 5) that bilingual children have a higher level of metalinguistic awareness than monolingual children. This is a possibility, and it is certainly the case that we find it easier to identify the metalinguistic skills of bilingual children, because the differences between languages are large, socially important, and are labelled. In a situation when moving from one language to another is a central part of daily life, and something that is often talked about by adults, very young children (certainly by the age of three) can identify languages by name, and can talk about what they do: we can easily recognise this labelling as a demonstration of metalinguistic skill. But in the data I discuss here, the children do not overtly talk about language; rather their behaviour demonstrates their knowledge about language.

> 'Metalinguistic' awareness refers to knowledge about language.

Metalinguistic awareness can be manifested in sociodramatic play. This type of play is itself metalinguistic. When children role-play they adopt dramatic characters, and use dress, language, and gesture – the full repertoire of the actor – to enact imaginary scenes based on their own experience. Although the code-switching can be identified most dramatically in bilingual children, where codes are maximally differentiated, similar behaviour can be identified in the more subtle stylistic variation of monolingual children.

Sunitha and Meera: their community

In remarkable data collected by one of my former graduate students at the National University of Singapore, Radha Ravindran, two kindergarten children (aged four and six years) in play at home pretend to be at school. The recordings were made in Singapore in 1992.

These two girls are native speakers of Malayalam, a Dravidian language originating in India, which is very much a minority language in Singapore and is not supported in the school system (the context of the Indian community in Singapore is discussed by PuruShotam, 1998). Malayalam is being deliberately maintained in this family. Although all family members are fluent in English, Radha (the mother of one of the children) claims that the children spoke only a little English until they went to nursery school (age three), because of a family policy of maintenance of Malayalam. The children attended an English-medium kindergarten where the pupils were fairly evenly divided between 'Malays' and 'Chinese' (each girl was the only 'Indian' child in her class). This relatively equal distribution of Malay and Chinese children allowed the informal learning of Malay to be supported, as

> Note that Malayalam is not related to Malay, the Austronesian language originating in South-east Asia which is one of the official languages of Singapore.

Language in Singapore

Singapore is a city state of great linguistic and ethnic diversity. Because of its urbanisation, the different ethno-linguistic groups are in close contact. There has long been a complex system of lingua francas, and widespread learning of multiple languages. In recent years, the linguistic situation has become somewhat simpler, especially since education through the medium of English became the norm (from the mid-twentieth century, for more detail see Gupta, 1994). However, the majority of children still grow up bilingual, and monolinguals of any age are extremely rare. Since 1987 all education in Singapore has been through the medium of English, with children also studying a language officially congruent with their 'race' (formally allocated at birth based on paternal ancestry). Singapore has four official languages (English, Mandarin Chinese, Malay, and Tamil): the other language studied at school is nearly always required to be one of the remaining official languages. This 'second language' is often referred to in official literature as 'the mother tongue': this expression refers to the official language associated with the child's 'race', and not necessarily to the language(s) actually spoken from infancy. Children typically attend nursery school and kindergarten from the age of three, following a relatively formal syllabus, and primary school begins at age six (for full up-to-date information about Singapore's education system, see the *Ministry of Education* website).

well as the formal and informal learning of English, and, as we shall see, at least some formulaic learning of Mandarin.

English is important in Singapore as an official language. It is also one of the most common native languages of Singaporeans, and is in widespread use as an everyday language and as a lingua franca. I have analysed Singapore English as being 'diglossic' (using the definition of Ferguson 1959, for example, Gupta, 1994). In diglossia a language has two codes which are grammatically distinct, one of which (called the High or H code) is used in formal circumstances, and in education, and the other of which (called the Low or L code) is used in speaking with children, and in informal circumstances. In Singapore the H code is Standard English and the L code is a variety commonly known as Singlish (called 'Singapore Colloquial English' by me and by most other scholars). The diglossia of Singapore English is not perfect, mostly because Standard English can be used even in informal circumstances, but most Singaporeans do move between Standard English and Singlish depending on the context of use. The teachers in kindergartens can be expected to use Standard English in clearly pedagogic contexts, and are supposed to use it all the time. However, they are members of their own community, and are prone to use Singlish to children, and in moments of emotional engagement (Gupta 1994, pp.159ff).

Sunitha and Meera: their drama

The short extracts below (Texts A and B) reveal much about the sociolinguistic structure of Singapore that readers not familiar with Singapore or Malaysia will not immediately understand. The children use different codes to animate the characters in their dramatic performance, reflecting the language patterns of the classroom in a number of respects. Sunitha, when playing the role of teacher (throughout Text A, and Text B turns 6, 8), speaks only in English, in line with her own experience of her pre-primary education – she even makes an effort at using Standard English in the imitations of the teacher. When they pretend to be Malay girls in the class (in Text B, turns 1, 2, 3) they speak Malay. When they address the teacher, or play at teacher–child interaction, the imagined Malay children speak English (Text B, turns 5, 7, 9). At the end of the imagined school day they sing a 'goodbye song' in Mandarin (Text A, turns 19ff), which is part of the ritual of the kindergarten day in many Singaporean kindergartens. And the girls never speak Malayalam in this imagined school context.

Text A

[In this extract, Sunitha, age six, takes the role of the teacher, while the younger, Meera, age four, takes the role of a well-behaved pupil, but one who echoes everything the teacher says.]

Sunitha *[as teacher]*	Line up, everybody line up.	1
Meera *[chanting]*	Line up, line up. In a straight line.	2
Sunitha *[as teacher]*	Line up, line up. In a straight line.	3
Meera	Straight line. I straight.	4
Sunitha *[as teacher]*	Girls, where are your lines?	5
Meera	Girls, where are your lines?	6
Sunitha *[as teacher]*	Eh, why you rub the blackboard?	7
Meera	Girls, where are your lines?	8
Sunitha *[as teacher]*	Some of your friends haven't finished, you know.	9
	Why you go and rub the blackboard?	10
[pretends to punish the disobedient child]	Go and stand there, cannot go home. Stand there.	11
Meera	Put your legs like this.	12
	Stand there.	13
	Boys, where are your lines, and girls, where are your lines?	14

Sunitha [as teacher]	Boys stand here, girls, here.	15
Meera [as self?]	Ow, my neck pain.	16
Sunitha [as teacher]	OK. Sing your goodbye song	17
Meera	Goodbye to you, goodbye to you. Goodbye to teacher. Goodbye to friends.	18
[sings, in Mandarin]	Laoshi zaijian, , xiao pengyou wan-an *[teacher see-again little friend good-evening]* *[= 'Goodbye teacher, good evening little friends']*	19
Sunitha [sings]	Laoshi zaijian, xiao pengyou wan-an.	20
Meera [sings]	Laoshi zaijian, xiao pengyou wan-an.	21
Both [sings]	Laoshi zaijian, xiao pengyou wan-an.	22

(Radha Ravindran, unpublished data)

Sunitha is at an age where she is unlikely to have mastered Standard English, but where, based on my earlier research, she is likely to show the beginnings of differentiation between the H and L codes. Indeed, Text A shows that Sunitha in the role of teacher has a strong focus on H (Standard English). When she is acting as the teacher, Sunitha uses six of the grammatical features that I found useful as markers of Standard English:

A morpheme is considered the minimal unit of grammatical analysis, drawn on in the study of morphology or word structure. The word *lines* consists of two morphemes, *line* and *-s*, a plural marker; *finished* also consists of two morphemes, *finish* and *-ed*, a marker of the past participle.

- 4 plural morphemes: line*s* (5), friend*s* (9), boy*s*, girl*s* (15);
- one past participle morpheme: finish*ed* (9);
- and a perfective verb phrase: *have(n't) finished* (9).

These are compulsory in Standard English, but in Singlish, inflectional morphology is optional, and the base form of verbs and nouns can be used, without marking for tense, number or concord. Complex verb phrases of more than one word (as in the third example above) are also Standard English grammar. As teacher, Sunitha used only one of the forms that I found useful as markers of Singlish:

- a non-imperative verb without a subject: *cannot go* home (11).

(*continued overleaf*)

A pragmatic particle is a small word, usually at the end of a sentence, which indicates something about the attitude of the speaker to what they are saying. The pragmatic particles of Singlish have been borrowed from varieties of Chinese.

Strikingly, there are no pragmatic particles. Speakers of Singapore English are very aware of the pragmatic particles (*ah* and *lah* are the most common) as markers of Singlish. Sunitha doesn't use them, but she does use a Standard English discourse marker which means much the same as *lah* ('you know' in turn 9). Turn 9 is heavily Standard English: a Singlish translation could be something like 'Other people not finish lah' (as well as a number of other possibilities).

In Text A the younger sister, Meera, also uses 8 plural nouns, most of them repetitions of Sunitha's utterances. When she is pretending to be a pupil, she uses only one of the diagnostic features of Singlish:

*   BE-deletion: I straight (4)

Incidentally, the girls do both use other grammatical structures that identify them as speaking Singlish, but these are features which I did not find useful in my quantification of the codes:

*   uninflected verb form where Standard English would be inflected: *pain* (16). Note that in Singlish *pain* is a verb: the subject of the verb is *my neck* (as in 'my neck hurts' in Standard English). This seems to be an aside in Meera's own persona: the fact that it is in English might indicate that English is coming into increasing use as a domestic language for these children.
*   the use of *why*-interrogatives with subject-verb word order: *why you rub…* , *why you go and rub…* (7, 10).
*   In these extracts there are 4 *why*-interrogatives of the same structure, all of them functioning as rebukes from enacted teacher to enacted child. It is possible that Sunitha has not mastered the Standard English equivalent (something like 'Why did you clear the blackboard?'), but it is also possible that these interrogatives used as rebukes are simply more likely to be in Singlish than in Standard English, due to the raising of emotional level implied in a rebuke.

Text B

[In this extract, the girls take on the roles of good pupils, first talking among themselves in Malay (in the role of Malay girls), with many nouns of English origin reflecting cultural elements associated with education. They then approach the teacher, whose role is then adopted by the older girl. 'Noriana' is a name associated with a Malay girl.]

Sunitha [as pupil]	Noriana jahat. Bilang teacher.	1
	[*naughty tell*]	
	['*Noriana is being naughty. Let's tell the teacher*']	
Meera [as pupil]	[*not relevant to topic*]	
	Ini radio apa?	2
	[*This what*]	
	['*What radio is this?*']	
Sunitha [as pupil]	Noriana tak colour pencil. Kita bilang teacher eh.	3
	[*NEG We tell*]	
	['*Noriana hasn't got her colour pencils. We'll tell the teacher, shall we?*']	
[*pretending to address teacher*]	Teacher, Noriana don't have colour pencils.	4
Meera [*as pupil*] [*pretending to address teacher*]	Teacher, Noriana lost the colour pencil	5
Sunitha [*as teacher*]	Why you never bring anything to school ah?	6
Meera [*as pupil*]	Teacher, I and she share.	7
Sunitha [*as teacher*]	Why you never bring anything to school? Must have everything, you know.	8
Meera [*as pupil*]	She lost his colour pencil, she share with his sister, but she lost the colour pencil.	9

(Radha Ravindran, unpublished data)

Text B is more complex. At the beginning (turns 1–3) both girls are enacting Malay pupils, speaking in Malay with some inserted English nouns. Much of the Malay the girls hear from the Malay-speaking children in their class will include English loanwords in this way, with some of the words (such as *pencil,* with the Malay spelling *pensel*) being indigenised loanwords in Malay, and others (such as *teacher*) being English words often used in informal Malay mixed with English. In turns 6 and 8 Sunitha takes on the role of the teacher, while Meera maintains her role of the good pupil in which role she seems to use the past tense, *lost*, 3 times (5, 9): though this is a verb that may be more common in the past tense and the adjectival form ('It's lost') than in the present tense, and may be the only form Meera knows.

The Malay is simple, using vocabulary that is very much school-based. When Sunitha becomes the teacher (turn 6), she switches to English, the official language of the classroom. But this time she does not use a variety of English which is focused on Standard English (there are none of the Standard

English identifiers here). She uses two features that I argued characterised Singlish:

- one of the characteristic pragmatic particles: *ah* (6);
- a non-imperative verb without a subject: *must have* (8).

This teacher is very cross with the imagined Noriana, and apparently is expressing her anger in Singlish, in line with the patterned switching between Standard English and Singlish that kindergarten teachers in Singapore make (Gupta, 1994, pp. 159ff). Sunitha's use of Singlish is realistic, in that in pedagogical situations teachers sustain Standard English, while in disciplinary ones they are more likely to use Singlish. All of her utterances are well-formed Singlish, of a sort that could have been produced by adults. In both these extracts we see how the way in which discipline is maintained in a kindergarten is salient for children, and a focus of language learning (Gupta, 1994, pp. 159ff; Thompson, 2000, p.175).

These two girls were able to take the daily routines of the school day and embed them into dramas which incorporate the language shift that is part of their experience. They select Malay or English according to the character portrayed, add some routine Mandarin, and even vary their English in a realistic way. Their enactment shows that they have learned a great deal about how the languages of their repertoire function in the wider society, and they are able to exploit that knowledge in dramatic play, extending their imaginations and their social and linguistic skills.

References

AINSWORTH-VAUGHN, N. (1990) 'The acquisition of sociolinguistic norms: style-switching in very early directives', *Language Sciences*, **12**(1), pp. 22–38.

BIALYSTOCK, E. (2001) *Bilingualism in Development: Language, Literacy and Cognition*, Cambridge, Cambridge University Press.

FERGUSON, C. (1959) 'Diglossia', *Word* **15**, pp. 325–40. [Also reprinted. in LI, WEI (ed.) (2000). *The Bilingualism Reader*, London/New York, Routledge.]

GENESEE, F. (1989) 'Early bilingual development: one language or two?', *Journal of Child Language*, **16**, pp. 161–179. [Also reprinted in LI WEI (ed.) (2000) *The bilingualism reader*, London/New York, Routledge.]

GUPTA, A.F. (1994) *The Step-Tongue: Children's English in Singapore*, Clevedon, Multilingual Matters.

LEOW, B.G. (2001) *Census of Population 2000: Demographic Characteristics*, Singapore, Singapore Department of Statistics.

MINISTRY OF EDUCATION (Singapore) [online] www.moe.gov.sg/ [accessed 24.6.06]

PURUSHOTAM, N.S. (1998) *Negotiating language, constructing race: Disciplining Differences in Singapore*, Berlin/New York, Mouton de Gruyter.

REICH, P.A. (1986) *Language Development*, Englewood Cliffs, Prentice Hall.

THOMPSON, L. (2000) *Young bilingual learners in nursery school*, Clevedon, Multilingual Matters.

YOUSSEF, V. (1991) 'The acquisition of varilingual competence', *English World-wide*, **12**(1), pp. 87–102.

Source: commissioned for this volume.

READING D: Playground rhymes keep up with the times

Janice Ackerley

Iona and Peter Opie's research has shown us that children's nursery rhymes and playground rhymes have a firm grounding in history. Many of the rhymes currently heard in the New Zealand playground can be traced to origins in the United Kingdom, as far back as Elizabethan times. The skipping and clapping rhymes have origins in Black American culture.

As Course Director of the National Diploma of Children's Literature paper, 'Patterns of Language', I have the privilege of receiving and filing many examples of playground lore, collected by students of this course. Each year I receive hundreds of samples of playground rhymes and chants. On closer examination of these gems I have been interested to notice that a number of these rhymes have been adapted to fit in our world of hectic change. In a world of ever changing fashions in clothing, food, music, entertainment, technology and language, the rhymes of our playground have also been adapted to reflect the changing social trends and the consumerism that is part of today's society.

The rhymes of New Zealand school children deal frankly with social issues, including drugs, gangs and even the recent foot and mouth scare in the United Kingdom. There is a strong Maori–Pacific Island influence, and Aussie knocking is also featured. Our national anthem has many variations that reflect different aspects of our cultural identity. The influence of commercialism can be seen in the many rhymes including popular brand names and television programmes and movie stars.

One rhyme that was received from both ends of the country was a parody sung to the tune of *Row, Row, Row your Boat*:

> Roll, roll, roll your dope
> Scrunch it at the end,
> Spank it up
> And have a smoke

And pass it to your friend
Roll, roll, roll your dope
Scrunch it at the end,
Puff, puff
That's enough
Now pass it to your friend.

On the same theme and also parodied is the Maori song *Po kare kare ana*:

Po kare kare ana
I was smoking marijuana
I gave it to the teacher
She said, 'Come here!'
I said, 'No fear.
I'll be back next year
With a bottle of beer,
To rub in your hair.'

Gang warfare is featured in this rhyme sung to the theme of the television series *Beverley Hillbillies*:

There once was a man and his name was Tower.
He went down town to join Black Power.
There once was a man and his name was Bob.
He went down town to join Mongrel Mob.
Along came Tower with his 303
And he blew those boys right out of Beverley
(Hills – that is)

The recent foot and mouth scare in Britain brought forth this version of the nursery rhyme, *Mary had a Little Lamb*:

Mary had a little lamb,
Its feets were covered in blisters
Now its burning in the paddock
With all its brothers and sisters.

Playground rhymes with a specific New Zealand flavour can be seen to have a Maori–Pacific Island influence. The popular pastime of skipping has developed rhymes based on the Maori language:

Rahina, rahina, one, two, three,
Ratu, ratu, skip with me.
Rapa, rapa, turn around,
Rapere, rapere, touch the ground
Ramere, ramere, touch the sky
Rahoroi, the rope swings high
Ratapu, you're too slow,
End of the week, so out you go.

A rhyme touching on a more taboo subject of sexuality and body parts:

> I am the ghost of a place named Venus,
> Come near me and I'll bite your penis.
> I am the ghost of Hone Heke
> Come near me and I'll bite your teke.

Maori language is also included in parodies of traditional nursery rhymes:

> Twinkle, twinkle little star,
> Hemi had a paru car,
> Like a diamond in the sky,
> Hemi lives in a pig sty.
> Twinkle, twinkle little star,
> Hemi had a paru car
> (paru = dirty)

The coconut trees of the Pacific Islands are part of this counting out rhyme. In this ritual participants hold out a fist for the counter to tap as the rhyme is chanted. The person who receives the 'crack' is out, and the ritual continues:

> Co – co – nut, co – co – nut, co – co – nut.
> CRACK!

Mary, her lamb and her little 'bro' – a New Zealand slang term used by both Maori and Pakeha – feature in these variations:

> Mary had a little bro
> She took him to the fair.
> She saw a lamb that she loved so
> And swapped him then and there!

> Mary had a little lamb,
> She called it Little Bro
> One day she took it skiing
> And lost it in the snow.

Taunts against *pakeha*, and our sporting rivals, the Australians, are also prevalent in the playground:

> Catch a little pakeha,
> Put him in the pot,
> Mix him up with puha,
> And what have you got?
> Puha and pakeha stew

> God of Nations, in the scrum,
> Kick the Aussies, in the bum.
> If it hurts, serves them right.
> Blow them up with dynamite.

> I'm an Australian,
> Born and bred,
> Long in the legs,
> And thick in
> the head.

Variations of our national anthem abound, with some creative examples shown here:

> God of Nations, smell my feet,
> In the local pub we meet,
> Don't buy whisky, it's too dear,
> Buy our local DB beer.

> God of Nations, smell my feet,
> In the bonds of Shortland Street.
> Hear our voices, tweet, tweet, tweet.
> God defend our toilet seat.

> God of nations, in thy toes,
> In the bonds of panty hose!

Playground rhymes are not spared the effects of commercialism and media influence. Many of the trendy food brand names, such as McDonalds, Pepsi, Coke, Barbie and our own icons of Marmite and barbed wire fences are included in the folklore of New Zealand children. A 'step on a crack, marry a rat,' variation:

> Step on white,
> Marry Marmite,
> Good night.

As a challenge we find:

> Wanna fight? – Marmite
> If you wish. – Jellyfish
> Bring it on – Tampon

> Cows are in the meadow,
> Sheep are in the corn.
> Don't climb the barbed wire fence.
> You'll get your knickers torn!

An action rhyme involving precise hand movements features the ever favourite takeaway brands:

> McDonalds, McDonalds (make a big M with hands)
> Kentucky Fried Chicken (flap arms like a chicken)
> And a Pizza Hut (form a ^ with arms)

Popular drink brands form part of a partisan school chant:

> Pepsi Cola, Coca Cola, Lion Brown
> We're gonna hypnotise, paralyse and knock them down.
> With a F-I-G-H-T
> We're gonna score S-C-O-R-E
> We're gonna fight, we're gonna score
> We're gonna win 'em all
> Goooooooo _____ (name of school)

And also as playground taunts:

> Boys are spastic, made out of plastic.
> Girls are sexy, made out of Pepsi.

> Girls are sexy, made out of Pepsi.
> Boys are rotten, made out of cotton.

> Girls go to the gym, to get more slim.
> Boys go to rugby, to get more ugly.

Elastics, the girls' playground game, also features these traditional food favourites, including pavlova:

> Ice cream soda, pavlova
> Coca Cola, my friend out.
>
> Passion fruit and ice cream soda,
> Yum, yum, yum, it's pavlova.
>
> Fanta, Fanta, my friend Fanta.
> Is the nicest of them all
> My friend Fanta.

The television advertising has a feature in this parody of *Jingle Bells*:

> Jingle bells, jingle bells
> Santa Claus is dead.
> Teddy Bear, Teddy Bear,
> Shot him in the head.
> Barbie doll, Barbie doll,
> Tried to save his life.
> But a GI Joe from Mexico
> Stabbed her with a knife.

Television and movie stars, The Simpsons, Barney, Batman, Xena, Warrior Princess, Men in Black and the Spice Girls are included in recently collected rhymes:

> Bart versus Lisa,
> Who will win
> Their father's fat
> And their mother's thin.
> Their grandpa smells of whisky and gin.

A parody on the theme song of the beloved Barney, the purple dinosaur, shows no finer feelings for the sensitivities of the younger children:

> I hate you, you hate me,
> Let's get together and kill Barney.
> With a one punch, two punch, three punch, four
> No more purple dinosaur!

Batman and Robin have long been favourites [...]:

> Jingle Bells, Batman smells,
> Robin laid an egg.
> Oh what fun it is to see,
> The duo split today.
> HEY!

Our own super heroine, Xena the warrior princess, is featured in a hand clapping rhyme as a starter to the traditional game of paper, scissors, rock and stone:

> Xena (clap) Warrior (clap) Princess,
> Came here last year.
> Xena Warrior Princess
> Came here last year.
> Over, over, over.

(This is followed by the game paper, scissors, rock)

Hand clapping rhymes feature variations on the 'double this, double that' rhyme:

Double, double, men, men.	Double, double spice, spice.
Double, double, black, black.	Double, double, girls, girls.
Double men, Double black.	Double spice, double girls.
Double, double Men in Black.	Double, double Spice Girls.

When considering this selection of 'playground rhymes that change with the times', I also became aware of the many different categories of rhymes that have been collected by students of the Patterns of Language course over the last few years. Many of these rhymes have changed very little over the passage of time and those that were favourites of parents and grandparents are still around today. Some of the other categories of playground rhymes include parodies of songs and nursery rhymes, insults and taunts, counting-out rhymes, tongue twisters, chants, nonsense rhymes, skipping, clapping and elastics rhymes, politically incorrect sexist and sexy rhymes and rhymes that are simply just for fun.

Despite concerns that the technological revolution is responsible for taking the play out of our children's lives, these collections show that the rhymes of the New Zealand playground are still alive and well.

References and acknowledgements

OPIE, I. and OPIE, P. (1959) *The Lore and Language of Schoolchildren*, Oxford, Oxford University Press.

Christchurch College of Education. National Diploma of Children's Literature Folklore Collection. Collected by students of Patterns of Language CL713, 1994–2001.

Source: ACKERLEY, J. *Play and Folklore*, Issue 42, September 2002, pp. 4–8. This article was first published in New Zealand, in 'Talespinner' March 2002.

Making connections with new technologies

Sarah North

5.1 Introduction

This chapter examines the impact of communication technologies on the way we creatively deploy language resources. When a new communication technology first appears, it often stirs up controversy as to whether it will enrich or impoverish the language. Text messaging, for example, has received considerable media attention, and Activity 1 highlights some of the issues involved.

ACTIVITY 1   **Views on texting**

Allow about
10 minutes

The extract below comes from a newspaper article which highlights concerns about the impact of text messaging technology on society. What are your reactions to the issues it raises?

My smmr hols wr CWOT. B4, we usd 2go2 NY 2C my bro, his GF & thr 3 :-@ kds FTF. ILNY, it's a gr8 plc

Education experts warned yesterday of the potentially damaging effect on literacy of mobile phone text messaging after a pupil handed in an essay written in text shorthand.

The 13-year-old girl submitted the essay to a teacher in a state secondary school in the west of Scotland and explained that she found it 'easier than standard English'.

Her teacher, who asked not to be named, said: 'I could not believe what I was seeing. The page was riddled with hieroglyphics, many of which I simply could not translate.'

The Scottish Qualifications Authority has expressed concern about the problem in its report on last year's Standard Grade exams, and revealed that 'text messaging language was inappropriately used' in the English exam.

Judith Gillespie, of the Scottish Parent Teacher Council, said a decline in standards of grammar and written language was partly linked to the craze. 'There must be rigorous efforts from all quarters of the education system to stamp out the use of texting as a form of written language so far as English study is concerned.'

'There has been a trend in recent years to emphasise spoken English. Pupils think orally and write phonetically. You would be shocked at the numbers of senior secondary pupils who cannot distinguish between 'their' and 'there'. The problem is that there is a feeling in some schools that pupils' freedom of expression should not be inhibited.' […]

Translation: 'My summer holidays were a complete waste of time. Before, we used to go to New York to see my brother, his girlfriend and their three screaming kids face to face. I love New York, it's a great place.'

(Extract from an article by Auslan Cramb in *The Daily Telegraph*, 3 March, 2003)

Comment

My own reaction to media reports of this incident was rather sceptical. Would a secondary school student really have so little language awareness that she couldn't distinguish text messaging from essay style? I can't help suspecting that rather than dashing off a sloppy piece of writing, the student crafted her homework knowingly, perhaps to enliven a boring assignment, to wind up the teacher or even to experiment creatively with a new style. Whatever you may feel about English language standards in general, this article presents no hard evidence of harmful effects from text messaging. The spelling of *their* and *there* has long been a source of confusion for schoolchildren (and adults too for that matter), and exam candidates have always resorted to ingenious ways of abbreviating their answers when time starts to run out. Debates about freedom of expression versus standards of English raged long before text messaging was even dreamt of. So it seems that the article is blaming one particular technology for trends which may actually stem from a range of factors.

Over the centuries, humans have used various technological developments to help them communicate, ranging from clay tablets and quill pens to telephones and typewriters. The major development of recent years has been computer-mediated communication (**CMC**), which can be defined as 'communication [...] between human beings via the instrumentality of computers' (Herring, 1996, p. 1), using a variety of different digital technologies, such as email, newsgroups, online chat and instant messaging. Computer technology makes available an array of **multimodal** resources, which may involve not only written text, but other modes such as speech, music, and visual images. In this chapter, however, the focus is on text-based CMC – in particular, interactive communication in emails, text messaging, online chat and computer conferencing.

*The creative use of multimodality is explored later in this book and in the companion volume, **Goodman and O'Halloran (2006)**.*

Mode and medium

Discussion of CMC involves issues of mode and medium, terms which are used in different ways, sometimes interchangeably. In this chapter, I adopt the distinction drawn between them by Gunther Kress (2000). **Mode** relates to the means by which a message is represented, using for example the sounds of speech, the graphic system of writing or the gestures of sign language. **Medium**, on the other hand, relates to the means by which a message is transmitted. Speech, for example, could be transmitted through face-to-face conversation, a video-conferencing link or a telephone connection. Graphic symbols could be written in ink on paper, carved on stone, spray-painted on a wall or transmitted digitally via a computer.

A common stereotype represents computer users as isolated from society, spending long hours engrossed in surfing, chatting, gaming or hacking in the solitude of their own room. But no computer user is truly isolated, since the use of computer technology depends on the resources and opportunities provided by society. The way that individuals make use of any communication technology, whether ancient or modern, is affected by general features of the relationship between technology and society. In the first part of the chapter I will spend some time discussing the nature of this relationship, suggesting key issues that you will need to bear in mind later when considering how a communication technology might aid or impede creativity.

The remainder of the chapter will look at two aspects of creativity in CMC, one involving the introduction and spread of innovative ways of adapting to the new medium, and the other involving the artful deployment of existing language resources within the computer-mediated environment. Previous chapters have focussed more on artfulness, but in common use the term 'creativity' is often associated with novelty. By exploring the way that technology can stimulate novel uses of language, this chapter will also question whether novelty alone can be regarded as creative.

5.2 The impact of new technologies

Science and technology multiply around us. To an increasing extent they dictate the languages in which we speak and think. Either we use those languages, or we remain mute.

(Ballard, 1974, Introduction to *Crash*)

ACTIVITY 2   **Living with technology**

Allow about
10 minutes

It is often claimed that computer technology is revolutionising our lives. How far has computer technology affected the kinds of communication you yourself are involved in? What do you do now that you (or your parents) would have done differently before recent advances in computer technology?

Comment

The most striking changes in my own life have been at work, where a constant stream of email has displaced the handwritten memos that used to be part of the daily routine, and typewriters and stencil machines seem like antiques now that I can word-process a document, paste in downloaded graphics, and print multiple copies in a matter of minutes. Computer technology is also behind innovations in other aspects of my life, from the scanned photos or downloaded jokes emailed around family and friends, to the use of the internet to search a database or buy a train ticket. Not everything has changed, though. Like many other people, I still make outlines and drafts on paper, print out information rather than reading it online, and scribble comments in the margin, just as I have always done. Your own experiences may not be the same as mine, but you may have identified some areas where the use of computer technology has changed the way you communicate and others where it has had less effect.

One way of looking at the impact of new technologies is to consider their **affordances**. This term was first used by the psychologist Gibson (1986, p. 127) to refer to the possibilities that the environment offers to an animal. A tree, for example, affords perching to an eagle or resting in the shade to a lion. Affordances can be either negative or positive, and this will depend on the individual involved. For a human, water affords drinking and washing, but also drowning; for a fish, the affordances are quite different. As Gibson points out, an affordance may be present even though the observer fails to perceive it. For example, a baby may bang a spoon or chew a facecloth but a spoon still affords feeding and a facecloth still affords washing. Have you ever played one of those lateral thinking games where you have to think of as many uses as possible for a brick, or some such object? If so, what you were doing was listing the affordances of the object – the possibilities for action that it provides – however far-fetched some of those affordances might seem.

Affordances are properties of the environment, arising from its material characteristics. When we consider human actors, we need to take into account their **effectivities**, that is, 'the dynamic capabilities of that individual taken with reference to a set of action-relevant properties of the environment' (Zaff, 1995, p. 240). For example, a revolving door is designed to afford access to a building, but how far would it be accessible to a toddler, a wheelchair user or someone who had never seen one before? The use of any object, whether natural or produced by humans, depends not only on its affordances but also on the way these are perceived and interpreted by each individual. Although the nature of the object places some limits on how it may be used, it does not enforce uniform behaviour. In interacting with the environment, each of us brings to bear individual capabilities stemming from the experiences, resources and expectations provided by the culture in which we live. Technology is part of our environment, and the way we use it is affected by both its affordances and our own effectivities.

ACTIVITY 3   Who sets email style? (Reading A)

Reading A comes from an article by Naomi Baron which considers how language users adapt to new communication technologies by looking for guidance in the form of prescriptive rules, or by relying on their own coping strategies. In this extract, Naomi Baron examines how contemporary email usage has developed in the United States, and compares how the telegraph influenced language use in the nineteenth century.

Now read 'Who sets e-mail style? Prescriptivism, coping strategies, and democratizing communication access' by Naomi Baron. As you do, note examples of features of the technology (affordances), and characteristics of the users (effectivities), which may affect the use of email or other communication technologies.

Comment

Naomi Baron's article is quite detailed, and there are a range of possible responses to this activity.

Under features of the technology, I noted: ease of access, speed of transmission, degree of privacy, ability to delete the message, size of the display screen, time-out disconnection and possibility of transmission errors.

Under characteristics of users, I noted: education level, literacy level, familiarity with letter-writing, conceptual models of speech and writing, effects of English composition teaching, and affective factors such as excitement with the new technology.

The reading shows how, throughout history, people have found ways of adapting to new communication technologies, but suggests that this may sometimes create a tension between 'the excitement of linguistic freedom' and 'academically constructed standards for writing.' Naomi Baron's conclusion made me think back to the text message essay in Activity 1 ('My smmr hols wr CWOT'), where the media focus on academic standards contrasted with my own view of the essay as playful, creative even, in the way it exploited the language of text messaging.

'Spamming' means sending out large quantities of unsolicited material. The word comes from a British TV comedy sketch about a café where almost every dish included spam (a good example of the way internet users draw on popular culture to generate new words).

In some cases, it is possible to see a clear link between the affordances of the technology and the way it is used. For example, because computers typically have large display screens and QWERTY keyboards, they afford typing (and therefore longer messages) more easily than mobile phones. Because internet access is relatively cheap and there are no costs associated with distance or length of message, one of the things it affords is *spamming*. Although the transmission of unwanted advertising material may be a negative affordance for the receiver, it is obviously a positive affordance for the advertiser. Communication technologies certainly make things possible that used to be impossible or difficult. But how far do they revolutionise our lives?

Discussion about new technologies often swings from optimistic visions of a brave new world to gloomy predictions of decline and doom (Thurlow, 2003). Both these perspectives, however, share a similar view of technology itself as the driving force behind far-reaching changes in society or in individual behaviour. This position is known as **technological determinism**, which Chandler (1995) associates with a number of features, including:

- reductionism: the idea that complex issues can be simplified to a few basic factors;

- mechanism: the idea that social phenomena can be explained by regular rules of cause and effect;
- technological autonomy: the idea that technology exists independently of society.

The concept of technological determinism, however, is criticised by those who argue that technology is not an external force producing social consequences, but that society and technology are inextricably intertwined. Consider, for example, a simple tool like a torch. It can affect some aspects of your life by allowing you to see in the dark, but only as long as the battery lasts. To keep it functioning, you need a society organised in such a way that batteries can be produced and distributed, and without those systems, anyone who invented a torch would have little prospect of seeing it make much impact on society. Even when a particular artefact does become widespread, there is no guarantee that it will be used in the way its designers intended. Frisbees, for example, are said to originate from the pie plates produced by the Frisbie Baking Company, who certainly didn't anticipate that the undergraduates who ate their pies would then start skimming the plates through the air. So too, the internet itself was originally set up as a shared information space for government and academic institutions, with no thought of it developing into a means for millions of people to communicate through email, bulletin boards and chat. The impact of technology on society is clearly neither simple nor predictable.

The quotation from J.G. Ballard at the beginning of this section represents a deterministic viewpoint, with technology 'dictating' the way we speak and think. Naomi Baron's article, on the other hand, draws attention to the way that our use of technology is affected by sociocultural factors. Rather than the nature of the technology driving email style, she views it as reinforcing trends already existing in society towards a more informal style of writing. Other language scholars also tend to favour a sociocultural approach to new technologies. As Susan Herring argues:

> not all properties of [computer-mediated discourse] follow necessarily and directly from the properties of computer technology. Rather, social and cultural factors – carried over from communication in other media as well as internally generated in computer-mediated environments – contribute importantly to the constellation of properties that characterizes computer-mediated discourse.

(Herring, 2001, p. 625)

So far I have concentrated on the way that affordances and effectivities make things possible, but our use of technology is affected also by **constraints** which limit these possibilities (Norman, 1999). Some constraints are physical; for example, your ability to carry a suitcase will depend on how heavy it is. Within CMC, the computer keyboard presents a number of physical constraints which have implications for equality of access to computer technology. Since computers transmit information digitally, the symbols we use in writing have to be converted into a numeric code. The code first developed was ASCII (American Standard Code for Information Interchange), which allowed for 128 characters, of which half were reserved for letters (32 upper case and 32 lower case). Computer keyboards were originally designed for use with ASCII, making them ill adapted for languages that require more than 32 characters. Countries such as China and Japan use basically the same keyboards as in the west, but since their script cannot be matched directly to the keys, typing requires special software and more complicated input methods. Such constraints may have an effect on the nature of CMC; one research study, for example, found that in English, Japanese and Korean online environments, the way that participants adapted their writing practices to the new medium was influenced by the word-processing technology and the writing system (Fouser et al. 2000). Notice though that these influences involved not only the physical constraints of the technology, but also the cultural constraints of the script.

While physical constraints can be seen as the converse of affordances (both relate to the material environment), cultural constraints derive from shared cultural conventions; unlike physical constraints, they can, in theory, be violated. For example, English is written from left to right, but there is nothing to stop me from picking up my pen and writing in the other direction, as Arabic is written. The direction of handwriting is a cultural constraint. But cultural conventions may be built into the technology: my word-processing software, for example, forces me to type from left to right, even if I want to type in Arabic. In such cases, cultural constraints become materialised as physical constraints. The increasing global standardisation of electronic environments can be problematic for languages which are less dominant in these environments. As Koutsogiannis (2004, p. 175) points out in relation to Greek, 'the semiotic resources with which the new technology is equipped are alien to both the history and the culture of these societies'.

It would be a mistake, though, to focus only on the negative aspects of physical and cultural constraints. The English, Japanese and Korean participants in the study by Fouser et al. may have responded differently to the online environment, but none of them found it impossible to adapt their language to the medium. In fact, the constraints could themselves be seen as conducive to creativity, eliciting the skills needed to exploit the medium effectively.

Chat symbols in other languages

Since French and Spanish are written in Roman script, their chat symbols use some of the same effects as English. Notice, though, language-specific features such as X in French (where the words for *cross* and *believe* are homonyms) and X in Spanish (where it represents the /tʃ/ sound, influenced by the spelling of Catalan or Basque).

French

6né	ciné	*cinema*
bjr	bonjour	*hello*
savapa	ça va pas?	*is something wrong?*
X	crois, croit	*believe*

Spanish

TQM	te quiero mucho	*I love you*
sta noxe	esta noche	*tonight*
s3ado	estresado	*stressed out*
plas plas plas	[aplausos]	[clapping]

It is not so easy to abbreviate in languages like Chinese or Japanese that use a logographic script (characters). Japanese chat tends to make more use of the greater range of graphic symbols afforded by their word-processing software, allowing the creation of emoticons (smileys) which can be read vertically, rather than horizontally as in English. Similar symbols are widely understood in Japan through their use in the popular '*manga*' comic books.

Japanese emoticons

(@_@)	me ga mawaru	*I'm getting dizzy*
(>_<)	itai	*ouch*
(^λ^)	onegai	*please* (hands in front of face)
\(^o^)/	wa-i	*wow!* (arms in air)

(Images from http://club.pep.ne.jp/~hiroette/en/facemarks/ [accessed 6.6.2005])

Constraints and affordances together mark out the scope for creativity, not only in relation to computer-mediated communication, but with respect to any technology. As McCullough argues:

> ... the word affordance implies a finite budget of opportunities, and so it is complemented with the idea of 'constraint'. For a medium must also have limits. It is not too difficult to imagine that an unconstrained medium would have little identity. Presumably it would be unpleasant. Being able to do whatever one wants does not induce creativity so much as paralysis. But in reality, there is no ultimate medium. Constraints define specific formal possibilities and guide creativity into specific channels, much like banks define a river.
>
> In other words, constraint is a source of strength. [...] Only through the possibilities and limitations of structured substance does expression come into being – otherwise it remains only inspiration.

(McCullough, 1996, p. 199)

McCullough's argument suggests that creativity involves working with the medium, as a carpenter works with the grain of the wood. Working with a new medium may require adapting existing practices in order to exploit its affordances and constraints. The next section will move on to consider the ways in which people have adapted to the new medium of computer-mediated communication, and the extent to which this has involved creative use of language.

5.3 Adapting to change

ACTIVITY 4   The poetry of text

Allow about 15 minutes

While the text message school essay quoted in Activity 1 earned only media condemnation, the following poem by Hetty Hughes won first prize in a text message poetry competition run by the British newspaper *The Guardian*. What features do you think make it poetic? How far has the writer succeeded in working with the affordances and constraints of texting?

```
txtin iz messin,
mi headn' me englis,
try2rite essays,
they all come out txtis.
gran not plsed w/letters shes getn,
swears i wrote better
b4 comin2uni.
&she's african
```

(Keegan, *The Guardian*, 3 May, 2001)

Comment

Hetty Hughes' poem contains obviously poetic features such as assonance in the repeated /e/ and /ɪ/ sounds of the first two lines, a strongly rhythmic pattern, and internal half rhymes such as *messin/headn*, *letters/better*. It also represents dialect features often associated with British 'Creole' varieties, in the endings of *messin* and *getn* and the absence of the 'copular' verb (*is*) in *gran not plsed*, features which are heightened by contrast with the last line, where the grandmother's African background is conveyed in standard English. The last line is foregrounded not only by this stylistic variation but also by the disruption of the rhythmic pattern established in the rest of the poem. Rather than detracting from these effects, the use of text messaging could be seen to reinforce them. Text messaging itself tends to involve reduced endings and verb omission, and through this similarity with patois the language of the poem simultaneously evokes two overlapping styles, the written style of text messaging and the oral style of patois. The poem thus sets up an interplay between a series of opposites: writing/speaking in terms of mode, standard/patois in terms of dialect, and British/African in terms of origin.

In addition, we can see the poem itself as a hybrid form: part poem, part text message. In using text messaging, the writer had to operate within the constraints of the technology. Text messaging affords limited message length (usually restricted to 160 characters), and the size of the display unit also means that it can only be read one line at a time. But as suggested in the previous section, constraints are not necessarily negative. Poetry frequently operates within self-imposed constraints of form, and for the reader, the line-by-line presentation may make the experience more vivid. A text-message poem may perhaps stimulate the writer to creativity, and surprise the reader into seeing something fresh within a familiar form.

In merging text messaging with poetry, the poem provides an example of **interdiscursivity**, involving what Carter (2004, p. 183) describes as:

> a process in which a new discourse emerges to meet particular sociocultural goals and purposes; but the new hybrid discourse emerges by drawing, interdiscursively, on what already exists [...], further referring to, utilising and exploiting texts and discourses which are already socially and culturally in commerce.

Naomi Baron referred to a similar process in her discussion of the way novices develop coping strategies to deal with emails: as new technologies open up new ways of communicating, users explore their potential by drawing on and adapting the conventions familiar to them from other contexts.

Discourse, intertextuality, interdiscursivity

The concept of **intertextuality**, which you also encountered in Chapter 4, draws on Bakhtin's recognition that everything we say or write is influenced by all the other spoken and written texts we have assimilated in the past. Fairclough (1992, p. 102) comments that intertextuality relates to 'the productivity of texts, to how texts can transform prior texts and restructure existing conventions (genres, discourses) to generate new ones'. As this quotation suggests, intertextuality may involve both the way that a text incorporates other texts, for example by quoting or alluding to them, and the way in which it may draw upon different discourse conventions. The first aspect of intertextuality will be considered later in this chapter. In relation to the second aspect, Fairclough also introduced the term **interdiscursivity** to indicate the combination of discourse conventions that are drawn on in a text; he gave the example of a bank leaflet which mixes the discourses of advertising and financial regulation. An example from literature is the mixture of novel and recipe genres in Laura Esquivel's *Like Water for Chocolate.*

Discussions of interdiscursivity draw on a concept of **discourse** which is rather different from that introduced in Chapter 1, where discourse was defined simply as 'language use'. According to Swann et al. (2004, p. 83), we can recognise three broad meanings, with some slippage between them:

1   A stretch of language longer than a single sentence or utterance, such as a written paragraph or a spoken dialogue. [...]

2   A type of language used in a particular context, for example the language used by teachers and students in classrooms (classroom discourse) or the written language of medicine or law (medical or legal discourse).

3   In a more critical or abstract sense, a way of representing, understanding and being in the world. Discourse here refers not only to particular uses of language in context, as in (2) above, but also to the world views and ideologies ... which are implicit or explicit in such uses.

Interdiscursivity involves relationships between discourses in senses (2) and (3).

Several researchers have commented on the way that computer-mediated communication has blurred the distinction between speech and writing. Ferrara et al. (1991) suggest that 'interactive written discourse' is a hybrid discourse, involving a written text format together with speech-like features that derive from its interactional, real-time nature. Similarly, Collot and Belmore (1996) argue that 'electronic language' constitutes a new variety of language, with some features resembling spoken genres such as interviews, and others resembling written genres such as letters. David Crystal (2001, p. 239) suggests the term 'netspeak', describing it as 'a new medium of linguistic communication'. Regarding CMC as a new variety of language can be misleading, however, if it blinds us to the differences between the many different types of CMC. Email, bulletin boards, text messaging, online chat and so on, each have their own affordances and constraints, leading to differences in the way that users compose their messages. Naomi Baron's article gave an example of this in connection with message-length constraints on email and instant messaging.

While the technology places some limits on what can and cannot be done, it does not entirely determine the nature of the communication, leaving room for individual variation. If you look at your own email inbox, for example, you'll probably find considerable variation in the messages sent by different people. Brenda Danet (2001) suggests that individual variations of this sort may be related to 'style leakage', where writers drawing on their previous experiences transfer norms from familiar genres into a new and unfamiliar genre. In Naomi Baron's terms, we could identify 'style leakage' as a type of coping strategy.

The next reading considers how writers have adapted to the medium of IRC (Internet Relay Chat). IRC is one of several text-based technologies that allow users to join chatrooms (or channels) where they can communicate with other users synchronously (i.e. in real time). Web-based chat and instant messenger chat work in similar ways. Colour Figure 1 shows a screenshot of an online chatroom, illustrating some of its particular affordances and constraints. On the right you can see a list of the people currently in the chatroom, identified by their nicknames. The larger window contains a record of the dialogue between the participants; as each new line is added at the bottom, the text scrolls upwards, creating a dynamic display that can at times move very rapidly. The constantly scrolling text represents several different conversations occurring simultaneously, and if you are not used to online chat, the dialogue can at first seem confused and incoherent.

Below the main chat window is a line where you can type your own message; when you hit *Send*, your nickname and message appear as the next line on screen, visible to all the other participants. Instead of sending a message, you can also 'emote', that is, display what you are feeling or doing. From the list of emoticons, you can select a verb like 'hug', 'chuckle', or 'frown' which will then appear in the dialogue. In Colour Figure 1, for example, 'nz-fern' has chosen to 'wave', at line 4, rather than to speak.

ACTIVITY 5 Chatroom discourse (Reading B)

Please read 'Online discourse in a teen chatroom: new codes and new modes of coherence in a visual medium' by Patricia Greenfield and Kaveri Subrahmanyam. The authors argue that the language of chat is developing into a new **register** (a language variety that occurs in particular contexts). Based on the analysis of a sample of online chat, they examine the way that participants adapt to the demands of the medium by drawing on the resources of both oral and written English. They suggest that this type of adaptation involves creativity.

While you are reading, think in particular about (a) how these chatroom features relate to the affordances and constraints of chat technology, and (b) how far you think these features involve creative use of language.

Comment

Although Greenfield and Subrahmanyam do not talk specifically of affordances, they point out that chatroom users have developed strategies in response to features of chatroom technology, such as the speed of the interaction, the time lags involved, the number of participants, the lack of visual contact and the ability to scroll up and down. Greenfield and Subrahmanyam suggest that chatroom users have adapted to the technology in creative ways, by developing strategies such as distinctive nicknames and script, abbreviations, and slot and filler codes. This is the type of creativity that language users demonstrate whenever they produce novel techniques for dealing with novel situations. But once these forms have ceased to be novel, and are simply a routine part of the linguistic repertoire, are we still justified in regarding their use as creative?

The chatroom and text-messaging extracts illustrated so far have provided plenty of examples of novelty, particularly the language forms most often commented on in the media: acronyms such as *lol* (laughing out loud) and *cwot* (complete waste of time), and graphophonemic effects such as *NE1* (anyone) and *cooool*. The data from Greenfield and Subrahmanyam lend support to the view expressed by Susan Herring that such forms, 'rather than reflecting impoverished or simplified communication, demonstrate the ability of users to adapt the computer medium to their expressive needs' (Herring, 2001, p. 617). Similarly, Hutchby argues that:

> when people interact through, around and with technologies, it is necessary for them to find ways of managing the constraints on their possibilities for action that emerge from the affordances of given technological forms. This can be more or less problematic, depending on the characteristics of the technology and our level of familiarity with it. Sometimes, quite novel ways of accomplishing communicative actions arise at the interface of the actor's aims and the technology's affordances.

> (Hutchby, 2001, p. 30)

In discussing email, Naomi Baron (1998, p. 162) talks of 'a communicative modality in flux', and as long as norms are fluid, CMC in general will continue to show a high degree of variability, and therefore opportunities for linguistic creativity. However, as particular technologies become more familiar and routine, CMC may be expected to settle down in more predictable patterns. Susan Herring argues that with the spread of internet use, this process is already beginning, commenting that 'after barely more than 30 years of existence, CMC has become more of a practical necessity than an object of fascination and fetish' (Herring, 2004, p. 33).

The research by Greenfield and Subrahmanyam illustrates the way in which users of a new medium initially develop creative strategies to adapt to its affordances and constraints. Over time, some of these innovations are used more regularly, gradually becoming conventions of the newly emerging register. As CMC grows increasingly commonplace, it is likely to involve less linguistic innovation, and the forms discussed by Greenfield and Subrahmanyam will either die out or become routine. Yet novelty is not necessarily creative, and it is possible to use language artfully without necessarily inventing new linguistic forms. As I suggested in the introduction, we need to distinguish between the type of creativity involved in innovative adaptation to a new medium, and the more 'literary' type of creativity in which existing language resources are deployed artfully. While CMC encourages certain ways of adapting language forms creatively, it has also been associated with functions that may be seen to underlie other aspects of verbal art – in particular those associated with the presentation of identity.

5.4 Being online

One of the features of online chat is its apparent anonymity. Chatters normally use nicknames, remain invisible and communicate only through the keyboard. Although the development of webcams and voice chat may change this situation, it is generally the case that online chat displays few of the social cues by which we normally identify and categorise others. The issue of identity is therefore particularly salient in CMC.

Caution: Chatrooms exist only in virtual space, and the people chatting together may be physically located anywhere in the world. Online there is no way to be sure of anyone's personal characteristics, and some people exploit this anonymity by using chatrooms for pornography and abuse. The dangers are now widely recognised, and a number of internet sites provide advice about online safety, particularly for children.

However anonymous chatters feel, they may in fact reveal information about their identity through the language they use. In an English-medium chatroom, for example, particular vocabulary, grammar or spellings may indicate a variety of English which makes it possible to guess the participant's nationality. But there may be even subtler clues. For example, analysis by Paolillo (2001) suggested the use of different 'dialects' of chat within

Figure 5.1 'Innovations become routine' (www.blehert.com)

an IRC channel. Paolillo identified the frequency of interaction between the participants, who were mainly expatriate South Asians or their children, and found that certain features were associated with particular groups. For example, the use of 'z' spellings (as in *newz*) seemed to be associated with a hacker subculture. The use of 'u' and 'r' spellings (for *you* and *are*) was favoured by more peripheral participants, while Hindi code-switching was favoured by more central participants. However, participants in the *most* central group did not use much Hindi code-switching, and Paolillo suggests that their social position on the channel stemmed from other factors, such as being technically savvy and knowing the right music.

Goffman's work (see Chapter 3) has drawn attention to the way we perform the roles we fill, or aspire to fill. He notes the way we may unintentionally 'give off' clues to our identity through various aspects of our behaviour such as our clothes, bearing, gestures and language. On the other hand, we also dramatise ourselves, acting out each role by behaving in ways that are appropriate to it, while avoiding incongruities that would spoil the performance. 'The self ... is a dramatic effect arising diffusely from a scene that is presented' (Goffman, 1959, p. 223). Participants in CMC, as in other forms of communication, are involved in presenting themselves to an audience, and the linguistic choices that they make are part of the overall performance. Chatters who use abbreviations such as 'u' and 'r', for example, may be trying to present an appropriate 'wired' image in online chat (though Paolillo's research suggests that in some contexts these abbreviations may give off quite different information, identifying their users as relative outsiders). Online chat also seems to present opportunities for a more self-conscious dramatic performance in which participants use language to play out their chosen roles (Turkle, 1996).

ACTIVITY 6   **Chat-up lines**

Allow about 15 minutes

The extract below comes from data collected by Paolillo from the chatroom #india. Focusing on the interaction between 'Nagin' and 'Dr-pepper', what do you notice about the way they are presenting themselves? Is there anything artful about their use of language here?

Nagin and Dr-pepper

<Lamer-X> hi nagin

*Sahil waves to Nagin hi

<Dr-pepper> where r u ..nagin in dormz?

<Nagin> Lamerx Hey whats up?:)

<Nagin> Sahil :)

Notice the 'crying' emoticon   :-/ ***

<Lamer-X> nagin: nuttin just feeling old now that i've hit 22 today :-/ ***

<Nagin> Lamer Happy Birthday:) well I know how u feel I felt like that when i turned 21 back in may

<Lamer-X> nagin: heh

<Nagin> DrPepper kiya dhoond ra ha hai [*what are you looking for?*]

<Dr-pepper> ur phone number ... nagin

<Nagin> Dr Pepper u expect me to give it away just like that?

Ashiq is the nickname of one of the operators responsible for the channel, but it also means 'lover' in Hindi, often a tender, adoring lover.

<Dr-pepper> what should I do..to get it..nagin..any tests for this ashiq?

<Nagin> Dr Pep ashiq???? whoa I don't want any ashique

<Nagin> Dr Pep:)

<Dr-pepper> nagin..then what u want?

<Nagin> SYCLONE!!!!!!

<Dr-pepper> nagin..i fell in love with u..da first time I chatted with u

<Nagin> DrPep ooh yeah ... how sweet

<Dr-pepper> nagin ... it was love at first chat

<Nagin> DrPep haha

<Dr-pepper> nagin ... it seemz u have already lot of admirers

<Nagin> DrPep who me ... naaa ... I don't think so

<Dr-pepper> nagin ... tu kutte ayes? [*where are you?*]

<Nagin> DRPRP school

<Dr-pepper> nagin..so r u givin da number..dear?

(Paolillo, 2001, p. 189)

Comment

In this extract 'Dr-pepper' is trying to chat up 'Nagin' so that she will give him her phone number. This sort of interaction could also happen face to face, where it might show many of the same features. One of the main differences online, though, is that the participants can only project their identity by means of the symbols on the screen. Although 'Dr-pepper' and 'Nagin' appear to be a young man and woman, we know this through their words alone, which could of course be misleading. Both of them code-switch between English and Hindi/Punjabi, identifying themselves as western-oriented Indians, and they use features of chatroom language that Paolillo found associated with moderately central members of this online community.

In addition, there are aspects of artful self-dramatisation in the way the two flirt with each other, acting out the classic roles of ardent suitor and demure young girl. This performance is not created out of nothing: it is recognisable only because it echoes other exchanges in which the same roles are played out. Similar situations occur, for example, in the courtship scenes of Bollywood films, or in English folk songs such as *Oh no John no John no John no*. In this extract, both participants draw on existing cultural resources in performing their roles, using but at the same time parodying the language of courtship. 'Dr-pepper' himself refers to the cliché of 'love at first sight', playfully amending the phrase to 'love at first chat' to suit the online environment.

On the internet, participants typically have available a restricted range of resources for identity construction. In most forms of CMC, they can neither see nor hear each other, but communicate only by means of typewritten characters. Rather than impoverishing the dramatic possibilities, however, this absence of extralinguistic clues seems to encourage greater linguistic creativity. Carter (2004, p. 200) suggests that it may lead to heightened self-dramatism, with 'linguistic marking which is often creatively realised in schema-refreshing ways'. Even the nicknames that participants choose for themselves suggest an exuberant delight in playing with identity (Bechar-Israeli, 1995).

The disguised identities, the sense of self-dramatism, and the tendency to parody are reminiscent of the spirit of **carnival**, seen by Bakhtin as:

> a pageant without footlights and without a division into performers and spectators. In carnival everyone is an active participant, everyone communes in the carnival act ....The laws, prohibitions, and restrictions that determine the structure and order of the ordinary, that is noncarnival, life are suspended during carnival ... All *distance* between people is suspended, and a special carnival category goes into effect: *free and familiar contact among people.*

> (Bakhtin, 1984, pp. 122–3)

As in carnival, online chat often involves an element of profanation, which can be seen in the unrestrained use of taboo language, the frequent sexual references, and the occurrence of *flaming*. Bakhtin suggests that the licence of carnival overturns what is solemn and sacred, and in so doing, allows it to be renewed and reinvigorated. Online chat provides the opportunity for participants to try out new identities in an environment where many of the restraints on interaction no longer apply, and to play with language in a context where language is used mainly, if not entirely, for fun.

'Flaming' is the online use of insult to criticise or provoke.

5.5 The playful medium

A number of CMC researchers have drawn attention to the inherently playful nature of the medium (e.g. Daisley, 1994; Danet, 2001; Rouzie, 2001). Susan Herring suggests that this can be related to particular features of text-only CMC, including its early association with role-playing games, the lack of social accountability deriving from anonymity, and the lack of interactional norms in the early stages of a new medium. Above all, she suggests, 'Relaxed norms of coherence can be liberating, giving rise to increased opportunities for language play' (Herring, 1999, p. 9). Word play is also facilitated by the fact that because text remains visible on screen, participants can reflect on it more than is possible during face-to-face conversation. All these factors contribute to the way that cyberspace provides what has been called a 'playground of identity' (Vrooman, 2002, p. 52).

Nancy Baym (1995) suggests that humour has an important role in creating social meaning online, as participants build up a sense of solidarity through allusion to shared experiences. Even flaming can be seen to have a social function, with verbal duelling on screen evoking 'enthusiastic community participation and community identity' (Vrooman, 2002, p. 64). As Paul Baker comments in Chapter 3, Reading D, 'Where there is a sense of shared identity and similarity, invective is sanctioned, either because it is understood to be a joke, and/or because it emphasises the closeness between speaker and hearer'. Online humour occurs not only in the relatively frivolous context of online chat, but also in educational applications of CMC. In his account of the synchronous online discussion that took place within an American university course in computers and writing, Rouzie (2001) examines the use of 'serio-ludic discourse' in which work is interwoven with play. Relating this to Bakhtin's notion of carnival, he points to the way that students can, half-seriously, half-playfully, try out a variety of roles that may challenge prescribed norms. For example, in the following extract from a discussion on the role of technology, 'Mr. Mac' and 'Eric Loomis' can be seen 'ganging up' on 'Jim Davison', who surrenders the argument with a reference to walking the plank. The aggressive tone of the exchange is picked up in Mac's reference to a lynching, but the aggression is legitimised by framing it as 'just kidding'.

MR. MAC:	jim, come on, the destruction of society? can you get any less specific?
JIM DAVISON:	Mac: clarify [...]
ERIC LOOMIS:	Right on Mr. MAc. You tell Jim.
JIM DAVISON:	Tell me what?
ERIC LOOMIS:	Get a life Jim!
KYLE BRAUTIGAN:	Mac: I think Jim would say we're doing better because our technology is killing them and helping us.
MR MAC:	oh contrare, out tech isn't killing them our lack of it is, shall I continue
ERIC LOOMIS:	Right Mr MAc. You tell Jim Again!
JIM DAVISON:	I think they're gonna make me walk the plank. [...]
MR MAC:	i had a lynching in mind
MR MAC:	just kidding,jim

(Rouzie, 2001, pp. 262–3)

In reading this interaction, you may be reminded of Holmes and Marra's discussion of subversive humour (in section 1.5 of Chapter 1), which can be used not only to subvert authority but also to isolate an individual and expose their lack of conformity to group norms. In this case, Mac and Eric seem to be enforcing group solidarity by pressurising Jim to conform to what they hold to be a collective view. What is interesting is that 'Kyle Brautigan', who attempts to defuse the situation, does so in a far more serious tone, as if distancing himself from what is going on here.

Notice, though, how the humour of the interaction depends on the use of common cultural resources, drawing for example on idiomatic expressions such as 'get a life', the playfully mangled French of 'oh contrare', and the connotations associated with 'walking the plank' and 'lynching'. This aspect of the use of humour within CMC can be related to ideas about intertextuality. So, for example, the flirting dialogue between 'Nagin' and 'Dr-pepper' is constructed and interpreted against the background of many other written and spoken texts that involve flirting, while the ganging up against 'Jim' draws on other familiar scenes of verbal or even physical bullying. Intertextuality is evident also in the use of specific linguistic expressions. For example, the mention of *Superman* in the teen chatroom data (in Reading B, Figure 1, line 88) references the film and comic-book hero as well as Nietzsche's concept of 'Ubermensch', while the phrase 'love at first chat' in the #india data alludes to the many instances of 'love at first sight' in a variety of romantic texts. Although we cannot be sure how far writers and readers are conscious of specific references, our understanding of any text is shaped by our previous experiences of a multitude of other texts.

ACTIVITY 7   The creative use of intertextuality (Reading C)

Please read 'Discourses Я Us: Intertextuality as a creative strategy in Interactive Written Discourse (IWD)' by Angela Goddard. This article discusses her research with students on an online course where, as with Rouzie's research, the chatroom was open only to course participants. As you read, note the three areas where Angela Goddard identifies examples of the creative use of intertextuality, and think how they might relate to issues discussed previously in this chapter. How far do you agree with her interpretation of these intertextual references?

Comment

In her discussion of intertextuality, Angela Goddard points out the way that participants draw on their experience of other texts in three areas: using the language of physical location to locate themselves within the online environment; building on the visual aspects of the emerging text; creating a heightened sense of audience for the performance of identity.

At several points she relates these issues to particular features of the technology (that is, its affordances): for example, the uncertainty about physical location, the visual display of text, and the speed of interaction. She highlights issues raised earlier in the chapter about language play, identity construction, and self-dramatisation. Most of all, she focuses on the importance of common cultural references in building individual and group identity, and the way that intertextuality 'lays out known material and disrupts expectations by renegotiating it'. This, for her, is what lies at the heart of the students' creativity with the medium.

Analysing intertextuality involves interpreting the meanings that a particular reference may have for the conversational participants, but this raises questions about how far such meanings are accessible to an outsider. For example, Angela Goddard relates 'hi honey I'm home' to 1950s sitcoms and the films that draw on them, while for other readers the phrase may evoke Jack Nicholson in *The Shining* or the song *Honey, I'm home* by Shania Twain. Once you start looking for intertextual references, they seem to be everywhere, but it is hard to determine how far the producers and receivers of the text would have been conscious of them. You could argue, perhaps, that this simply demonstrates that intertextuality is fundamental to language use, whether or not we are aware of it. We seem to be predisposed to play with other texts, to borrow and rework them, and to value people who can do this most effectively. This predisposition may underlie literary creativity, but do we also expect a literary artist to know what he or she is doing, to be more than just an accidental poet?

5.6 Conclusion

In the heading to this chapter, I exploited the ambiguity of the expression 'making connections' to suggest three different aspects of CMC: the physical connections that afford computer-mediated communication, the social connections which participants create though interacting via computer technology, and the textual connections which seem to feature so prominently in online chat. All these seem significant in helping us to understand how participants in CMC exploit the possibilities of the medium, and in so doing, display the sort of verbal artistry that also underlies literary creativity.

Creativity operates within the affordances of the relevant technology, whether this is paper and pen or instant messaging. Most CMC researchers would argue, though, that our use of communication technology is shaped by the sociocultural context, and not simply determined by features of the technology itself. As communicators, we appear to be skilful in overcoming the constraints and exploiting the affordances of any particular medium. New technologies spur users to adapt their practices, both by drawing on existing strategies and developing new ones. Many of the characteristic features of CMC can be seen as creative adaptations to the medium, allowing users to manage interaction online, without a shared physical context. Within a new medium such as CMC, there is likely to be a period when norms are in flux, providing more than usual opportunity for individual variability and creativity. As time goes on, however, such innovation may decline, as what was once novel gradually becomes routine.

Creativity, however, does not depend on constant innovation. In this chapter, I have reviewed evidence suggesting that, underlying the novel features of CMC such as abbreviations and graphophonemic effects, the medium also fosters a playfulness that operates at deeper levels. This may derive in part from particular affordances, such as anonymity and looser coherence, but it also stems from the purposes that participants bring to CMC, and their interpretations of what is involved. For example, all communication involves the performance of identity, but the lack of extralinguistic and paralinguistic information seems to encourage exuberant self-dramatisation in the online environment. Humour is evident even when CMC is employed for serious purposes, and functions to build both individual and group identity. It draws in particular on intertextuality, with participants often showing a delight in the rapid exchange of shared cultural elements. These allusions both contribute to group solidarity and also allow for elements to be recombined in ways that can be surprising and revitalising – and it is this quality, perhaps, that most characterises examples of verbal art within CMC.

READING A: Extracts from 'Who sets e-mail style? Prescriptivism, coping strategies and democratizing communication access'

Naomi S. Baron

Can you divorce your spouse by e-mail? That question was handed to a court in the United Arab Emirates, when an American of Arab descent e-mailed his Saudi wife to break their marriage bonds. Islamic law holds that a man can divorce his wife

> simply by telling her 'I divorce you,' if certain conditions are met. [*The Gulf News*, which reported the story,] said the court would have to rule if the notification of divorce through the internet was valid under the Gulf Arab emirate's laws, or whether it should have been delivered verbally.

> (*BBC Online*, Friday, 5 May 2000)

What else should – or shouldn't – you do by e-mail? Send an apology? Your condolences? News to your former spouse of your remarriage? Our concern in this article is not with answers to these queries but with how we arrive at solutions. Are there identifiable principles upon which decisions are made or do usage patterns reflect social fiat? If the latter, who makes the rules, and on what basis? If there are rules (from whatever source), how do people learn about them? And are they followed? These issues assume special relevance when the number of people using a new technology suddenly expands, as in the case of e-mail.

Attitudes toward linguistic style – and resulting usage patterns – matter not because one style is 'right' and another 'wrong' but because heightened attention to stylistic concerns generally signals that significant social and/or linguistic change is afoot. [...]

Becoming a language user

How do language users of any medium – spoken or written, face-to-face or at a distance – attain proficiency and comfort in handling a given form of linguistic exchange? One method is to follow *externally generated prescriptions* for linguistic behavior. All societies have norms defining how people should interact with each other through language. Some of these norms are transmitted directly from one generation to the next, as when parents teach their offspring to say 'Please' or insist upon their children writing thank-you letters for birthday presents. In many communities, published usage and etiquette guides help novitiates develop new language practices as part of their quest for social betterment.

The other variable is *user-generated coping strategies*. In our encounters with language as young children, we must all figure out, largely on our own, how to make sense of puzzling messages and media. Toddlers cope with sounds they can't pronounce by reconfiguring adult words – 'spaghetti' may become 'pasketti' or 'fish' come out as 'fis'. Preschoolers coin words that logically might have existed – like 'gripsion' on analogy with 'traction' – and commonly treat writing as a form of drawing (Baron, 1992, pp. 94ff., pp. 202–5).

In the same vein, adults concoct individual or collective strategies for handling lexical issues or the challenges of written language. We invent names for new objects or situations we encounter, from 'pineapple' (literally, a fruit – an earlier meaning of the word 'apple' – that looks like a pine cone) to 'pregnant chad' (for some of the questionable Florida ballot punches in the 2000 American presidential race). In the realm of writing, from the early centuries of Christianity, authors and scribes made heavy use of abbreviations so as to reduce labor and expense.

The relative importance of prescriptivism versus individual coping strategies may shift from one linguistic medium to another, as well as between sociohistorical periods. [...]

Inventing the future

As a new technology for communicating at a distance, e-mail is once again challenging language users to work out stylistic conventions for approaching the medium. Our discussion here focuses on the effects of cost reduction and the concomitant surge in new usership on the question of who determines e-mail style.

As in the case of personal letter writing (and later, the telephone), falling prices and improvements in delivery systems have helped democratize e-mail, especially over the past decade. Howard Rheingold reminisces about how in 1985 he joined the early computer networking community known as the WELL (Whole Earth 'Lectronic Link), paying $3 an hour to access the system—resulting in a first monthly phone bill of over $100 (Rheingold, 2000, p. 25). Today, for around $20 a month, home computer users in the United States can literally access the 'whole earth' 24 hours a day (not only for sending e-mail but for multiple other internet uses) and at speeds that make modem transmission of the late 1980s and early 1990s pale. People with access to 'free' university or business connections reduce the cost to zero and often benefit from even faster transmission speeds.

As a medium for communicating at a distance, e-mail has experienced a meteoric rise. E-mail as a personal messaging system was invented a mere 30 years ago, and the publicly accessible internet infrastructure through which the preponderance of messages are sent is less than half that age (Hafner, 2001; Abbate, 1999). Yet by the end of 2001, more than 100 million American adults had internet access (Pew Research Center, 2001). Statistics collected at the end of 2000 indicate that of those with internet access, 49% sent e-mail messages on an average day (Pew Research Center, 2000).

How many e-mail messages do Americans send? It's hard to get precise figures, given that the internet is, by design, both decentralized and outside the purview of regulatory control. However, a few snapshot statistics give a sense of how ubiquitous electronic messaging has become. The International Data Corporation reports that 9.8 billion electronic messages are sent daily (presumably worldwide) (Hafner, 2001). A website at Clemson University (in South Carolina) indicates that by the end of the spring 2000 semester, students and employees at that university were downloading 2 million e-mail messages per school day. Given there were roughly 47,000 e-mail accounts on campus (as of September 2000), that averages out to almost 43 messages downloaded per person per day (dcit.clemson.edu/sig/email/statistic.htm).

Who is shaping the messaging style for this prolific medium? E-mail style guides began appearing in the business world in the mid 1980s (e.g. Shapiro and Anderson, 1985). The explosion in e-mail use in the 1990s brought forth a substantial number of books, articles and websites aimed at the wider public (e.g., Angell and Heslop, 1994; Flynn and Flynn, 1998; Hale and Scanlon, 1999; Lamb and Peek, 1995; Sherwood). But do people read them? [...] While I have no sales statistics on e-mail usage guides, such books don't appear to be topping the sales charts or going through many editions.

The social, educational, and fiscal circumstances surrounding e-mail at the turn of the new century are quite distinct from those facing earlier cohorts of new letter writers, telegraph users, and people making telephone calls. Those sending e-mail messages today are not using the medium for social mobility. They are educated, literate, and know how to write letters of the traditional sort. Most don't seem particularly concerned with understanding how the technology works (as long as their internet connections are functioning). Moreover, since the number of words in a message or the physical distance between sender and recipient doesn't affect cost (which is generally prepaid or free to the user anyway), those constructing e-mail messages are liberated from a number of considerations that were of paramount importance to earlier generations crafting language used at a distance.

If prescriptive guide books, educational issues, cognitive modeling, and cost considerations aren't shaping contemporary e-mail behavior, how are new users determining how to construct messages? Commonly, novices begin by using conventions familiar from traditional letter writing (or, in office contexts, memoranda). Like travelers adopting local customs, many users pick up conventions (e.g. regarding greetings or use of acronyms) from the e-mail they receive or, in the case of parents, from advice proffered by children.

Even the handbooks, articles, and websites that do exist offer little consistent help, should e-mail users seek guidance. While the advice extended in earlier letter writing guides was fairly homogeneous from one volume to the next, today's e-mail handbooks sometimes present starkly divergent views on how to formulate messages. For example, *Wired Style* breezily recommends writers to:

> Think blunt bursts and sentence fragments.... Spelling and punctuation are loose and playful. (No one reads e-mail with red pen in hand.)

> (Hale and Scanlon, 1999, p. 3)

while *The Elements of E-mail Style* is more conservative:

> By focusing on the 20 percent of English grammar, usage, and mechanics issues that cause 80 percent of the problems in writing e-mail, you can quickly and dramatically improve your e-mail messages.
>
> (Angell and Heslop, 1994, p. 4)

Contemporary e-mail etiquette often takes its cues as much from convenience as from prior social convention. Follow-up thank-you letters from job candidates were largely replaced by e-mail messages years ago. Condolence letters – which once had to be handwritten – now show up as e-mail or even e-cards (Cohen, 2000).

Underlying most decisions about how to formulate e-mail messages – formal or informal, sloppy or edited – are conceptual models individual users construct (generally unconsciously) of whether e-mail is more like speech or more like writing. That is, we must decide whether to employ conventions of informal speech (including assumptions that the message will be private and ephemeral, and that precision isn't overly important) or assumptions about more formal writing (that messages are durable and can end up in the hands of unknown others). Many computer users function with a mental model of e-mail as a private, speechlike medium of communication that disappears without a trace when 'deleted,' even when we rationally know better. However, there is also a good deal of variation across individual users (and usage contexts) in the extent to which we model e-mail as a spoken or a written medium (Baron, 1998, 2000; Crystal, 2001).

Beyond usage conventions, beyond etiquette, even beyond individual modeling strategies, the aspect of e-mail usage that may prove most linguistically interesting in the early twenty-first century is message length. In the initial days of e-mail, messages were short, typically confined to a single screen worth of text (Shapiro and Anderson, 1985, p. 23). Given the CRT (cathode ray tube) displays of the 1970s and early 1980s, this constraint meant few lines indeed.

As e-mail began pervading universities and then spreading to a larger general usership, e-mail length expanded. You could write at your leisure, compose with ease (given modern word processing features), and send off your message only when you were ready. Multipage e-mails became common.

Recently, however, three technological developments have begun to encourage shorter messages. The first, instant messaging, converts the monologue of writing into the dialogue of spoken give-and-take. Since the turns are shorter, so must our written messages be. The second development, hand-held devices for sending and receiving e-mail (such as Palm Pilots and cell phones), is best suited for short messages, given the lack of a real keyboard and the small screen for viewing what has been written. A third factor is the 'time out' program still included on many public-access computers and subscription dial-up services that disconnects users if there has been no internet activity for a set number of minutes. While some systems give the user warning, others simply terminate the connection. Shorter (and sloppier) e-mails that are shipped out within the allotted time are safer than more lengthy (and edited) messages. Abbreviations and elimination of words deemed superfluous render e-mail composition faster still.

The e-mail style now emerging is reminiscent of telegraphic language that appeared in the second half of the nineteenth century. While the driving force in composing telegrams was cost, the technology itself discouraged lengthy messages. Transmission bottlenecks were created at telegraph offices when swarms of reporters wanted to file stories, via the telegraph, at the same time. These communication log jams were eventually cleared by creation of the Associated Press (which made it possible to simultaneously file one story with hundreds of newspapers) as well as by a change in journalistic writing style from flowery to succinct (Blondheim, 1994; Hochfelder, 1999).

Did the technology impact language beyond the world of telegrams and news stories? Some have argued that mechanical limitations of the telegraph contributed to – or at least were supportive of – restructuring of American prose in the decades following the invention of the telegraph.

As early as 1848, the case was made that English prose style would become more concise as a result of cost constraints on sending telegrams. The argument, presented in an unsigned article in *The United States Magazine and Democratic Review*, went like this. Because the cost of sending telegrams is determined by the number of words in the message, 'the *desideratum* of the Telegraph ... is ... *How can the greatest amount of intelligence be communicated in the fewest words?*' The author proceeded to suggest that the 'terse, condensed, expressive' style of telegrams, 'sparing of expletives and utterly ignorant of synonyms,' would not be confined 'within the narrow precincts of the Telegraph office, or limited to the pen of the operator.' Why not? Because of the number of people whose own writing style would be influenced by the language they read daily in the newspaper, much of which had been sent over the telegraph wire:

> When a half column or more of every paper in the Union is filled with Telegraphic despatches [sic]; when these reports form a large part of the daily reading of thousands; when correspondence is hourly prepared and revised, throughout the whole extent of the United States, with a view to telegraphic transmission, is it too much to expect that this invention will have an influence upon American literature; and that that influence will be marked and permanent.

> ('Influence of the Telegraph,' 1848, pp. 411, 412)

[...] Over the past century and a half, English prose style has undergone a profound transformation. Compare the syntactically intricate and stylistically varied writings of, say, Thomas Babbington Macaulay with the far simpler, direct sentences of Ernest Hemingway (whose prose reflects his experience as a war correspondent, bound by the transmission strictures of the telegraph). Even so simple a measure as average sentence length reveals the shift. During the span of the nineteenth century, the average written English sentence was between 30 and 40 words long. By the 1980s, that number had shrunk to 20 words (Haussamen, 1994).

It's impossible to determine the extent to which the telegraph may have been responsible for this change. We know that many other forces were at work in America to bring about what has been called a 'democratic eloquence,' a 'plain, unadorned, declarative prose...', a prose leaner than anything traditional rhetoricians had favored except for the simplest of purposes' (Cmiel, 1990, p. 13). What we can say with certainty is that the telegraph – as a technology both prone to transmission error and costly to employ – reinforced reforming trends at work on American English both before and after 1844.

And what of e-mail? Is the use of e-mail – and its typical inattention to spelling, punctuation, and editing – affecting contemporary written American English?

In recent years, a number of literary critics have expressed concern over whether written English is becoming sloppier and losing some of its clarity and expressive power, at least in part due to the rise of electronic communication (e.g. Birkerts, 1994). However, another way to think about the problem is to ask whether English was already in the process of becoming less edited and less tightly argued than in decades past, with e-mail style reinforcing ongoing change rather than initiating it.

If we look carefully at the evolution of English composition instruction in America over the past 125 years, we find an increasing trend for pedagogy to encourage students to write informally, to focus on content rather than mechanics – to be, in short, more speechlike (Baron, 2000). Seen against this historical backdrop, we can conclude that e-mail style is, at a minimum, reinforcing ongoing trends in the evolution of English prose for writing to mimic informal speech.

While some composition and rhetoric professionals seem unconcerned about these trends, many teachers of writing are less sanguine. Moreover, besides stylistic considerations, there remains the issue of composition length. In the decade ahead, as we continue to increase the percentage of writing done online, contemporary e-mail patterns of ever-shorter messages may well influence our understanding of what constitutes 'good' writing when it does appear on the printed page.

In the early days of a new language technology, the excitement of linguistic freedom may outweigh concerns over whether the paths being defined create unintended consequences regarding precision and richness of linguistic expression. In the coming years, it will be interesting to see how the tension between individual coping strategies and academically constructed standards for writing online plays out.

References

ABBATE, J. (1999) *Inventing the Internet,* Cambridge, MA, MIT Press.

ANGELL, D. and HESLOP, B. (1994) *The Elements of E-mail Style*, Reading, MA, Addison-Wesley.

BARON, N.S. (1992) *Growing up with Language: How Children Learn to Talk*, Reading, MA., Addison-Wesley.

BARON, N.S. (1998) 'Letters by phone or speech by other means: The linguistics of email', *Language and Communication*, **18**, pp. 35–53.

BARON, N.S. (2000) *Alphabet to Email: How Written English Evolved and Where it's Heading*, London, Routledge.

BIRKERTS, S. (1994) *The Gutenberg Elegies: The Fate of Reading in an Electronic Age*, Boston, Faber and Faber.

BLONDHEIM, M. (1994) *News over the Wires: The Telegraph and the Flow of Information in America, 1844–1897*, Cambridge, MA, Harvard University Press.

CMIEL, K. (1990) *Democratic Eloquence: The Fight over Popular Speech in Nineteenth Century America*, New York, William Morrow.

COHEN, J. (2000) 'Sorry for your loss but not that sorry', *New York Times* 7 December: E1, E10.

CRYSTAL, D. (2001) *Language and the Internet*, Cambridge, Cambridge University Press.

FLYNN, N. and FLYNN, T. (1998) *Writing Effective E-mail*, Menlo Park, CA, Crisp.

HAFNER, K. (2001) 'The 30-year path of e-mail', *New York Times* 6 December, FL, F9.

HALE, C. and SCANLON, J. (1999) *Wired Style* (rev. ed.) New York, Broadway Books.

HAUSSAMEN, B. (1994) 'The future of the English sentence', *Visible Language*, **28**, pp. 4–25.

HOCHFELDER, D. (1999) 'Taming the lightning: American telegraphy as revolutionary technology, 1832–1860'. Unpublished doctoral dissertation, Department of History, Case Western Reserve University.

LAMB, L. and PEEK, J. (1995) *Using Email Effectively,* Sebastopol, CA, O'Reilly and Associates.

PEW RESEARCH CENTER (2000) *Pew Internet and American life project survey*, November–December. (www.pewinternet.org)

PEW RESEARCH CENTER (2001) *More Online, Doing More*. Pew Internet and American Life Project Internet Tracking Report, 18 February. (www.pewinternet.org)

RHEINGOLD, H. (2000) *The Virtual Community: Homesteading on the Electronic Frontier*, rev. edn, Cambridge, MA, MIT Press.

SHAPIRO, N.Z. and ANDERSON, R.H. (1985) *Toward an Ethics and Etiquette for Electronic Mail*, Santa Monica, CA, RAND.

SHERWOOD, K.D. [online] www.webfoot.com

Source: **BARON, N.S. (2002)** *The Information Society*, **18, pp. 403–13**.

READING B: Extracts from 'Online discourse in a teen chatroom: new codes and new modes of coherence in a visual medium'

Patricia Marks Greenfield and Kaveri Subrahmanyam

Processes of linguistic adaptation

Language users are creative and adaptive. When situational demands change, competent language users can readily change the form of their utterances. Thus, the same individual can convey the same intention (or illocution) using different locutionary (or linguistic) forms in a classroom versus a bar. Speech adaptations that occur in response to the social and communicative features of the setting are called registers; in contrast to dialects, which vary as a function of the user, registers vary as a function of setting and use (Hudson, 1980). Online chat is a new communicative environment (e.g. written medium, anonymity of conversation partners, multiple overlapping conversations, etc.) and we may expect it to elicit adaptations in participants' language use. In our analysis of chat, we will reveal some of the ways that users adapt to the demands of online chat by creating a register that utilizes the resources of oral and written English in creative ways. This is not surprising – younger people, who tend to frequent teen chatrooms, are generally at the vanguard of cultural innovations (e.g. Greenfield, 1999), and this has certainly been the case for the computer medium more generally (Greenfield, 1984).

To be functional as a means of communication, any register needs to be coherent to its users and allow them to construct a thread of connectivity between utterances produced by a single participant and, most important in the present context, construct threads of connectivity between utterances produced by multiple conversational partners. Establishing such coherence not only links utterances, but also links speakers (Tannen, 1987).

To adapt to text-based chatrooms, participants may need to create mechanisms of coherence or modify extant ones to establish and maintain conversational coherence. The need for coherence explains why users might construct strategies to adapt to the unique environment of chat. Our analysis of a chat transcript will support this argument with empirical data. [...]

Fig. 1 presents the entire chat session printout. It reveals the overall structure of conversation in a chatroom and the coherence that transpires, despite highly unfavorable conditions. In discussing elements of the chat conversation, we will insert lines from the printout into the body of the article. These examples will be given numbers in parenthesis, e.g., (1). Examples will also retain their line numbers so that they can be placed in the context of the total conversation shown in Fig. 1. Note that sometimes a contribution takes more than one line; this happens when the person hits enter before finishing the contribution. Dotted, solid, and dashed lines indicate the three main conversational threads going on in the room. [...]

Analysis

The main goal of our analysis was to delineate examples of strategies used to increase conversational coherence. We start by describing the main conversations occurring in the chatroom; then we describe the strategies that help chat users to approximate the speed of oral conversation, and finally present a taxonomy of strategies used by participants to achieve coherence.

Conversational threads in a teen chatroom

The term conversational threads refer to the different, but parallel conversations taking place simultaneously in the same digital space. In conventional face-to-face conversations, the conversational thread can easily be identified by simply following the turn-taking that occurs between participants. However, in most chatrooms, there are usually a number of participants in the conversation and their contributions do not necessarily follow in any logical sequential order as there are time lags based on system and server speeds. More important, because different subgroups of participants are simultaneously engaging in different conversations, different conversational threads are interpolated with each other. The Netspeak term *thread* is an apt metaphor for the way one must follow a conversation's twists and turns through other distinct conversations. Furthermore, each person can simultaneously participate in more than one conversational thread.

In many ways, chat resembles the complexity inherent in a cocktail party with multiple conversations in a small space, although the complexity of chat is greater than the multiple discrete conversations at a cocktail party. As in a cocktail party, one can 'eavesdrop' (in chat, visually, not aurally), and should avoid being distracted by conversations in which one is not involved. However, unlike a cocktail party, one can also participate simultaneously in more than one thread.

Our analysis of a sample session, based on an expert chatter's charting of the conversational threads and our own study of the printout, suggests that there are three main conversations with partially overlapping participants.

Figure 1 Diagram of conversational threads in an extended transcript from a teen chatroom. Conversation I is shown in dotted lines and Conversation 2 is shown in solid lines, and Conversation 3 is shown in dashed lines. Two lines to the same line indicates ambiguity about which thread that contribution belongs to.

1	MizRose76:	SHUT UP I DON'T NEED IT
2	MORN8SUN:	*no seriously ... the great one....this ass rang my bell talking about open the door*
3	Al commands:	YES YOU DO
4	SuddenReaction:	i do 14/m
5	You have just entered room	<<silver>>
6	Al commands:	DONT TRY TO DENY
7	Al commands:	(SHES IN DENIAL GUYS)
8	BLAKPower1413:	/89
9	Agreatonefeb74:	oh
10	MizRose76:	NO AM NOT
11	Mizprudel762:	press 14 if ya wanna chat 2 a 14/f/cali
12	MizRose76:	U R\
13	MORN8SUN:	*im like wrong bell...if he came again i would of cussed him out good and plenty*
14	MORN8SUN:	*one time i had too*
15	Al commands:	WHAT HAPPENED MORN?
16	BLAKPower1413:	14
17	Agreatonefeb74:	kewl
18	Al commands:	HAHAHH
19	Al commands:	I AM WHAT?
20	SwimteamBabe:	a/s/l
21	SuddenReaction:	who is f*** dany
22	Al commands:	THE GREATEST?
23	Al commands:	YA, I KNOW
24	MORN8SUN:	*fuckdany?*
25	MORN8SUN:	*lol*
26	MORN8SUN:	*what?*
27	MizRose76:	AL DID I GIVE U PERMISSION TO TALK TO NE ONE?
28	PinkBabyAngel542:	WHO BELIEVES SPEEDO'S (ON GUYS) AREN'T RIGHT
29	PinkBabyAngel542:	TYPE 3
30	Al commands:	WHAT!!!
31	PinkBabyAngel542:	3
32	DustinKnosAll:	3
33	SwimteamBabe:	3 any fine ladies want to chat press 69 or im me
34	BrentJyd:	
35	Al commands:	ARE YOU TRYING TO TALKBACK TO YOUR MASTER
36	Al commands:	??
37	Sportyman04:	hey
38	MORN8SUN:	*this ass came to myrang my bell talking about let me in*
39	PinkBabyAngel542:	ITS FRIGGING SCARY
40	MORN8SUN:	*im saying to myself*
41	MORN8SUN:	*fuck out of here*
42	MORN8SUN:	*lol*
43	MORN8SUN:	*what you think this is?*
44	Jesicaaaa:	14.f
45	SwimteamBabe:	tell me about it
46	Proffich:	guy in speedo I swim imm a guy its not a bad thing
47	MORN8SUN:	*i don't know him*

48	MORN8SUN:	*so why?*
49	PinkBabyAngel542:	sooo
50	Rollerbabe904590:	*Chat with me or im me press 420*
51	MORN8SUN:	*now this other fag came to my door with a rug*
52	LA Bluetue:	anyone wanna trade pics with a 15/m
53	MizRose76.	YEAH AM TALKING BACK TO U AND?
54	PinkBabyAngel542:	Gurl who swims with guys in speedo
55	MORN8SUN:	*I just looked through and went back to the comp*
56	MORN8SUN:	*im like no way*
57	MORN8SUN:	*hell no*
58	Sportyman04:	7777778888999999
59	SwimteamBabe:	you swim prffilch
60	MORN8SUN:	*and he just left*
61	Al commands:	YOU WILL GET WRATH OF SUPERGOD
62	MORN8SUN:	supergod?
63	Proffich:	of course
64	MORN8SUN:	*who is supergod?*
65	PinkBabyAngel542:	NASTY! 1T SHOWS OFF EVERYTHING!!!!!!
66	DustinKnosAll:	15/m/ga im me to chat or press 222
67	MAKERSCLUB701:	any girls in here wanna chat im me
68	Proffich:	its fun
69	Al commands:	THAT IS MY ALTEREGO
70	PinkBabyAngel542:	lol
71	MAKERSCLUB701:	17/m/fl :
72	MORN8SUN:	*you must have a lot of them?*
73	Al commands:	A N W Y A
74	MORN8SUN:	*huh?*
75	Swimteambabe:	and there'y too tight
76	Rollerbabe904590:	222
77	Al commands:	WHERE DID MY SLAVE GO TO?
78	Al commands:	I DONT
79	Al commands:	JUST A COUPLE
80	MORN8SUN:	*al...that's not how you spell master... ....!*
81	Sportyman04:	save me swimteambabe
82	Al commands:	YOU KNOW
83	DustinKnosAll:	Roller a/s/l
84	PinkBabyAngel542:	yup... even for grls at our school... show's off everything
85	SwimteamBabe:	very funny
86	MORN8SUN:	=)
87	Sportyman04:	i know
88	Alcommands:	MORN, MY NAME IS SUPERMAN
89	PinkBabyAngel542:	I'm telling ya... u dont wanna get T.H.O. in those
90	MORN8SUN:	*superman..*
91	Rollerbabe904590:	:)
92	Al commands:	CHECK MY PROFILE IF YOU DONT BELIEVE ME
93	MORN8SUN:	*ok*
94	Al commands:	THANX
95	MORN8SUN:	lol
96	MizRose76:	MORN DONT DO IT
97	MORN8SUN:	*why?*
98	MORN8SUN:	*what will happen to me?*
99	MizRose76:	BECUZ HES A FREAK
100	SwimteamBabe:	a/s/l

Conversation 1 (Fig. 1) is between MizRose76 and Al commands, with SuddenReaction coming in at one point and MORN8SUN joining in for an extended period at a later point. Conversation 2 (Fig. 1) is between MORN8SUN and Al commands, with a couple of ambiguous contributions from PinkBabyAngel542; however this conversation appears to decay when MORN8SUN enters the conversation between MizRose76 and Al commands. Conversation 3 (Fig. 1) takes place between PinkBabyAngel542, DustinKnosAll, SwimteamBabe, and Proffich.

As our analysis will make clear, it is important to note that some parts of the conversations are more ambiguous than others, and the coherence is less than perfect. For example, some utterances could be part of either of two conversations—for example, in line 39, where PinkBabyAngel's 'IT'S FRIGG1N SCARY' could be part of Conversation 2 or 3 (Fig. 1). [...]

Strategies that make chat approximate the speed of oral conversation

Conversation 1, like the other parts of the printout, confirms the presence of shorter, incomplete, grammatically simple, and often incorrect (grammar and typographical errors) sentences found in prior research on chat (Crystal, 2001; Werry, 1996). Clearly, not stopping to correct errors increases the speed of communication.

Participants adopt other strategies to increase the speed of an individual written utterance. For example, the speed of each conversational turn is increased by omitting periods and other punctuation. Pressing 'enter' is the default full stop in the chat register. Another technique that increases speed is the absence of changes of case, from upper to lower or back again. In our transcript, most of the participants communicate either all in uppercase (e.g. MizRose76, starting in line 1) or all lowercase letters (e.g. SuddenReaction, starting in line 4). Abbreviations, mostly unique to online chat, are another important feature of written language that constitute a chat-specific adaptation resulting in increased utterance speed (e.g. Fig. 1, line 25, 'lol' for 'laughing out loud').

Strategies for coherence

Our analysis suggests that in their quest for conversational coherence, participants use strategies adapted from face-to-face conversations and construct strategies specific to chat environments. Table 1 presents these different strategies organized by whether they are adapted from face-to-face conversation or are unique to chat environments. The latter group includes two subcategories: visual cues and conventionalized codes. For each strategy, we will also show how these strategies are used by interactants in chat conversations for role (establishing own identity or selecting one's conversation partners/addressee) or relevance functions. Together, these cues and codes contribute to coherence within (but not across) the various conversational threads.

Table 1

Taxonomy of strategies used by online chat participants to establish and maintain conversational coherence

Strategies adapted from face-to-face conversations

    Repetition

    Vocative cues

Strategies constructed for chat environments

    Visual cues

        Nickname format

        Distinctive script

        Visual record

    Conventionalized chat codes

        Request for numerals

        Standard graphic formats

        Slot-filler codes

Strategies adapted from face-to-face conversations

Repetition

One cue adapted from face-to-face conversation is repetition, which is used extensively in face-to-face encounters to establish coherence (Tannen, 1987). Repetition is also frequently used by chat participants to identify relevant utterances and is illustrated below in Example 1 from Conversation 1.

(1)

    35 Al commands: ARE YOU TRYING TO TALKBACK TO YOUR MASTER
    53 MizRose76: YEAH AM TALKING BACK TO U AND?
    61 Al commands: YOU WILL GET WRATH OF SUPERGOD

(Gaps in line numbers indicate intervening contributions that are not part of the conversational thread in question; these intervening turns can be seen in detail in Fig. 1.) We suggest that MizRose76's use of the words 'AM TALKING BACK TO U' in line 53 signals to Al commands that it is a relevant response to his earlier utterance in line 35. Al commands' response in line 61 makes it clear that he has understood line 53 as a response to his initiation in line 35. Although we present repetition as one possible cue, it is usually used in conjunction with other cues and we will point out the use of repetition when describing those cues. [...]

Another example of repetition occurs in Example 2, where PinkBabyAngel542 simultaneously creates relevance and attempts to identify potential conversational partners through a request for repetition (line 29), which is complied with in lines 31, 32, and 33.

(2)

> 28 PinkBabyAngel542: WHO BELIEVE'S SPEEDO'S (ON GUYS) AREN'T RIGHT
> 29 PinkBabyAngel542: TYPE 3
> 31 PinkBabyAngel542: 3
> 32 DustinKnosAll: 3
> 33 SwimteamBabe:3

This mode of recipient design is a very special adaptation to this medium and one that occurs often. Here PinkBabyAngel is merely trying to figure out who, among the group assembled in the chatroom, agrees with her and therefore might be compatible. Other members of the group must decide if they fit the desired category. This is a very common strategy and seems to be an adaptation to the disembodied nature of the social group.

Vocative cues

Another way is to select one's partner by using the vocative cue from conventional face-to-face conversation [...]. This is an example of importing a conversational strategy from oral discourse into this written medium. However, the nonsequentiality of chat makes the selection different from what conversational analysts describe for more traditional conversational media. In conversational analysis, the turn-taking system has a turn-allocation component that specifies how the next speaker is chosen (Sacks, Schegloff and Jefferson, 1974; Duranti, 1997). One mode of turn allocation is other-selection (current speaker selects next speaker). This is what the vocative does in chat. However, there is a difference. One is not necessarily selecting the next speaker in the chatroom. Instead, one is selecting the next speaker in a particular conversational thread; this person may or (more likely) may not be the next speaker.

Often participants clarify whom they are addressing, with whom they are initiating a conversation, or to whom they are responding by prefacing their contribution with the name of the addressee; one sees this in the following examples. In Example 3, MizRose76 signals that her intended addressee is Al commands by prefacing her utterance with 'Al.'

(3)

    27 MizRose76: AL DID I GIVE YOU PERMISSION TO TALK TO NE ONE?

Other examples of the vocative occur in Example 4, where MORN8 SUN also prefac[es] her utterance with 'AL,' and in Example 5, when Al commands starts his utterance with 'MORN.'

(4)

    80 MORN8SUN: al. .thats not how you spell master /

(5)

    88 Al commands: MORN, MY NAME IS SUPERMAN

On other occasions, one sees a modified vocative form where the name is affixed to the end of the statement as in [...] Example 6, line 15, when AL commands writes:

(6)

    15 Al commands: WHAT HAPPENED MORN?

Here Al commands has been responding to MizRose76 up to this point; so the use of Morn's name makes it clear that he/she is switching conversational partners. This example suggests that the vocative cue is more likely to be used under some conditions rather than others – for instance, when there might be increased ambiguity as to the identity of the addressee. [...]

Strategies constructed for chat environments

Visual cues

Among the strategies constructed for chat environments are various visual cues that play crucial role functions and help participants to establish their own identity and to select and identify their conversation partners. These visual cues or strategies capitalize on the visual nature of the online medium and are thus unique to chatrooms.

    Nickname format. The most basic visual cue is the distinctively visual format of the nicknames (or 'nicks'), which usually are a mixture of lower- and uppercase letters, numbers, and are frequently something catchy. Examples include MizRose7, MORN8SUN, and HOST PACK Jessi. Nicknames allow users to present only those aspects of their identity that they wish to reveal, such as their gender.

    Information about identity is relevant to role functions as in drawing the attention of a potential conversation partner (e.g., males looking to converse with females, look for female-sounding nicknames) and vice versa. Notice, for example, how some of the girls' names have a kind of sexualized and seductive quality; names like PinkBabyAngel could even be considered to be 'hypergender' signals (F. Steen, personal communication, 2002).

Nicknames continue to be important even after a partner has been selected as they stand out visually in the conversation thread (they stand out even in this document) and help participants keep track of what their conversation partners are saying. Here we see that the uniquely visual format of nicknames helps in drawing the attention of potential partners and intended addressees and subsequently helps participants follow the thread of a particular conversation, once they have an idea of who is participating.

Distinctive script. Another visual strategy is the use of a distinctive script by many of the participants. For instance, MizRose76 and Al commands use all capital letters to talk, while MORN8SUN uses lowercase italics. Colors (not visible in our black-and-white printout) further differentiate the participants. In the original printout, different participants use different colors for their contributions. For example, MizRose76 always writes in red, PinkBabyAngel52 always writes in pink, SwimTeamBabe writes in purple. Each of these colors is unique on the screen and makes identification of the writer easier for the other participants.

Importantly, an individual does not usually change either fonts or colors midway through a conversation. There is an implicit attempt to maintain continuity of identity in a situation where the usual markers of personal continuity, such as face, physical body, and voice, are absent. Such continuity is important for the role functions of identifying and selecting partners; it also helps participants know to look for the particular kind of text format being used by their conversation partners. Of course, others not participating in their conversation sometimes use the same format, and so presumably they have to ignore their contributions. There are fewer distinctive visual styles than there are participants in the chatroom; but, by reducing the possibilities, these styles still aid in the role functions of keeping track of identities and conversations.

Visual record of the conversation. A third visual strategy that users capitalize on is the visual record of the ongoing conversation. Participants can scroll up or scroll down the record on the screen when they do not understand the conversational thread or if they enter the room in the middle of a conversation and need to find out what the participants are talking about (Werry, 1996). The format of the visually distinctive nicknames and the particular fonts or colors used by participants not only aids in identifying and selecting partners; it also helps participants to keep track of the conversation and to more easily identify a relevant utterance. Clearly, knowing who has been in the conversation is a cue to potential relevance.

Conventionalized chat codes

Another group of strategies are a group of conventions or chat codes that have been constructed (and co-constructed) as specific adaptations to the chat situation.

Request for numerals. One code that is used for the role function of finding a conversational partner and initiating a conversation is the request for visually distinctive numerals, as in Example 9. Such strategies are necessary in order for users to select a conversational partner. Example 9 presents an offer (line 11) and an almost immediate acceptance from BLAKPower1413 (line 16). Presumably, the two then go to a private chatroom to converse with each other.

(9)

> 11 Mizprudel762: press 14 if ya wanna chat 2 a 14/f/cali
> 16 BLAKPower1413: 14

This is but one example where the use of numerals helps participants with the role function of selecting and identifying a respondent by requesting a sort of visual 'badge.' Note that the relevance function is achieved by repeating the requested numerals, so one can also see that the strategy of repetition is an intrinsic part of this chat-specific visual code. [...]

What is visually distinctive in these examples is the use of numbers amidst letters ensuring that the message stands out. The use of standard or conventionalized formats ensures that other users immediately understand the message and know how to respond, and the use of numbers makes it easy and quick to respond. Again, we see how users adapt to the temporal constraints and lack of face-to-face cues in chat environments by creating strategies that capitalize on the visual cues that are available and are rapid in a text-based environment. Using these strategies, participants are successful in identifying and selecting their conversational partners, the first step toward establishing and maintaining conversational coherence.

The use of visual imagery is not unique to chat conversations but is part of a larger trend involving the increased use of iconic modes of representation over written modes of representation for communication on the internet (Kress, 1998) and with computers more generally (Greenfield,. 1998; Greenfield et al., 1994a; Greenfield et al., 1994b). Importantly, visual imagery is not only incorporated into the conversation, it is also influencing the mode of written discourse that is used.

Standard graphic formats. Another chat code is the use of standard formats to initiate a conversation. Participants will frequently state their age, gender, and location in a set format so as to announce their presence in the room. In the following three examples, the numbers 14 and 17 are ages in years, f stands for female, and fl stands for the state of Florida. In other words, standard graphic formats incorporate abbreviations, mentioned earlier as an element in the chat register.

(12)

> 4 SuddenReaction: i do 14/m

(13)

> 44 Jesicaaaa: 14/f

(14)

> 71 MAKERSCLUB7O 1: 17/m/fl

These codes allow users to obtain information about the identity of a potential conversation partner, information that is readily available in face-to-face settings. Certainly, it is not a coincidence that age and sex are the most universal markers of social roles.

Thus, identification and selection functions often go together. For instance, in Example 9, Mizprude1762 in line 11 writes 'press 14 if ya wanna chat 2 a 14/f/cali.' Not only is she requesting numerals to identify a potential conversational partner, but she is also using the age/sex/location format to provide crucial identity information about herself.

Slot-filler codes. A variant of this type of code is the conversation opener, a/s/l (age/sex/location), which occurs in Examples 15 and 16. It represents the same graphic code, created for the chat environment, but in a slot-filler format. It is intended as the initiation element in an initiation-response pair, with the expected response to fill in the blanks regarding the participant's own characteristics, using the graphic format discussed above. This initiation-response pair is reminiscent of highly conventionalized adjacency pairs, such as greeting exchanges, in conversational analysis (Duranti, 1997; Schegloff and Sacks, 1973). We could think of it as a new type of adjacency pair created for this communicative environment—except that the two pair parts are rarely adjacent.

(15)

> 20 SwimteamBabe: a/s/l

(16)

> 100 SwimteamBabe: a/s/l

A well-used chat convention is that a/s/l stands for age, sex, and location. As noted above, it is often the first thing that participants spontaneously provide to the other chat participants. In this section, we see that it is also one of the first things they request of each other when meeting online for the first time. Note that a/s/l has the requisite brevity necessary to maintain the timing of oral conversation, but it uses abbreviations, a convention from the written medium. (Such initiations are not always successful, at least within the confines of our transcript, as in SwimteamBabe's initiations above.)

The distinctive visual appearance of the symbols again ensures that they stand out in the conversation. It is the opportunity for participants to present themselves and their identity to others and helps with selecting and identifying potential conversation partners. This is another example of how users have constructed a code to compensate for the anonymous nature of the medium – and helps them to quickly detect information that would otherwise be readily available in a face-to-face setting. [...]

The common thread through these examples is the use of a conventionalized format involving numerals and abbreviations within the chat environment. This format makes it easy for other users to create a relevant response and easy for the initiator to recognize the response as relevant.

Discussion

We have studied emergent conventions for constructing conversation in an online chatroom for teens. Chatrooms provide an interesting medium because they consist of multiple written conversations occurring at the same time. Because all conversations are sharing the same space, they become temporally distributed. Cues to coherence such as adjacent turns – available in conventional face-to-face or telephone conversations – are generally absent. We asked how participants are able to establish and maintain conversational coherence in the absence of cues, such as adjacent turns, and in the presence of multiple conversational threads among different subgroups of participants and how they solve central conversational functions, such as identifying the conversational partner and responses relevant to one's own utterances.

Our analysis suggests that chat participants are adapting to the online chat environment by using available cues and creating new strategies to recognize and select conversational partners (role functions) and to recognize and create relevant responses (relevance functions). The strategies that are used include ones familiar to us from face-to-face conversation – such as repetition and addressing intended conversational partners by name. Chat strategies also include unfamiliar ones created for the computer medium – such as requesting that potential addressees type in a particular set of numerals if they want to talk to a particular person or on a particular subject. Strategies also include creative amalgams, such as the slot-filler code. Although constructed in written form, the slot-filler code has the functional properties of adjacency pairs from oral conversation (Schegloff and Sacks, 1973), but without the formal property of adjacency. [...]

We suggest that the emerging language of chat can be thought of as a register created by language users to adapt to the communicative and social demands of this digital environment. Chat is incoherent only if one does not know the codified register. Some mechanisms used by participants to achieve coherence derive from oral communication, while others are inherently visual and derive from written communication. Together, these strategies constitute creative adaptations to achieve conversational coherence in the chat environment. They also allow participants to create brief utterances (Cherny, 1999; Davis and Brewer, 1997). In sum, it is through the creation of a codified register that chat participants have been able to achieve coherence in this new digital environment.

We submit that the first 'native speakers' of the chat register are children and adolescents. Indeed, if creating a chat register follows the pattern of creating other novel registers, such as Nicaraguan sign language

(Senghas, in press), adolescents could be particularly critical to its evolution. Because new technology has created a drastically altered communication environment, chat gives us an opportunity to see language evolution in unusually rapid action. The chat register continues to be under construction by users themselves, as they adapt to a unique environment that is a product of recent technological evolution.

References

CHERNY, L. (1999) *Conversation and Community: Chat in a Virtual World*, Chicago, IL, University of Chicago Press.

CRYSTAL, D. (2001) *Language and the Internet*, Cambridge, UK, Cambridge University Press.

DAVIS, B.H. and BREWER, J. (1997) *Electronic Discourse: Linguistic Individuals in Virtual Space*, Albany, NY, State University of New York Press.

DURANTI, A. (1997) *Linguistic Anthropology*, Cambridge, MA, Cambridge University Press.

GREENFIELD, P.M. (1984) *Mind and Media: The Effects of Television, Video Games, and Computers*, Cambridge, MA, Harvard University Press.

GREENFIELD, P.M. (1998) 'The cultural evolution of IQ', in U. NEISSER (ed.) *The Rising Curve: Long-term Gains in IQ and Related Measures*, Washington, DC, American Psychological Association.

GREENFIELD, P.M. (1999) 'Cultural change and human development', *New Directions in Child and Adolescent Development*, **83**, pp. 37–60.

GREENFIELD, P.M., CAMAIONI, L., ERCOLANI, P., WEISS, L., LAUBER, B. and PERUCCHINI, P. (1994a) 'Cognitive socialization by computer games in two cultures: Inductive discovery or mastery of an iconic code?', *Journal of Applied Developmental Psychology*, **15**, pp. 59–85.

GREENFIELD, P.M., deWINSTANLEY, P., KILPATRICK, H. and KAYE, D. (1994b) 'Action video games and informal education: Effects on strategies for dividing visual attention', *Journal of Applied Developmental Psychology*, **15**, pp. 105–23.

HUDSON, R.A. (1980). *Sociolinguistics*, Cambridge, Cambridge University Press.

KRESS, G. (1998) 'Visual and verbal modes of representation in electronically mediated communication: Potentials of new forms of text' in I. SNYDER (ed.) *Page to screen: Taking literacy into the electronic era*, London, Routledge.

SACKS, H., SCHEGLOFF, E.A. and JEFFERSON, G. (1974) 'A simplest systematics for the organization of turn-taking for conversation', *Language*, **50**, pp. 696–735.

SCHEGLOFF, E. and SACKS, H. (1973) 'Opening up closings', *Semiotica*, **8**, pp. 289–327.

SENGHAS, A. (in press) 'Intergenerational influence and ontogenetic development in the emergence of spatial grammar in Nicaraguan sign language', *Cognitive Development*.

TANNEN, D. (1987) 'Repetition in conversation: Toward a poetics of talk', *Language*, **63**, pp. 574–605.

WERRY, C.C. (1996) 'Linguistic and interactional features of Internet relay chat', in S.C. HERRING (ed.) *Computer-Mediated Communication: Linguistic, Social, and Cross-Cultural Perspectives*, Philadelphia, PA, John Benjamins.

Source: GREENFIELD, P.M. and SUBRAHMANYAM, K. (2003) *Applied Developmental Psychology* **24, pp. 713–38**.

READING C: Discourses Я Us: Intertextuality as a creative strategy in Interactive Written Discourse (IWD)

Angela Goddard

What is intertextuality?

'Intertextuality' as a concept in the study of language in use owes much to the broad tradition of Marxist sociopolitical analysis and in particular the work of Bakhtin ([1935]1981) and Kristeva (1974). Referring to the relationships established between texts as they are constantly produced and recycled, intertextuality is more than a simple exercise in tracing connections. Kristeva was concerned to stress the idea that every time an intertextual reference was created, it framed a new set of relationships and positions (Kristeva, 1986, p. 111).

The title of this article exemplifies Kristeva's concept of 'positionality'. At the most basic level, the title is an intertextual reference to a well-known toy megastore called *Toys Я Us*. That is as far as a 'banal' reading of intertextuality as a 'study of sources' would take us. But that is only the starting point in terms of the meaning of the reference. Why refer to a toy store, and why that particular store, in this reading? Perhaps I wanted to draw together discourses that are normally not connected – the serious and the playful, 'high' culture and popular culture – and suggest that they have more connection than we acknowledge. Perhaps I wanted to say that discourse analysts should focus on everyday uses of language in the wider culture, and get to grips with the real world. Perhaps I wanted to say something about discourses and identity: that discourses are all we have as a resource to construct 'reality' for us; that we create discourses, but discourses also create us.

What I have said above assumes a relationship between 'text' and 'discourse' where the use of texts builds into what Gee terms 'Discourses (with a big "D")' (Gee, 1999, p. 17). The latter are ways of talking, thinking and knowing that are embedded in cultures and articulated by speakers as cultural 'carriers' of meaning (Gee, 1999, p. 18). Speakers use cultural references to make meanings, with differing degrees of conscious awareness; and meaning is brokered as much by the listener or reader as the speaker or writer. So, while the 'Я Us' tag has a cultural meaning I can deploy, you may not accept the premise, although (depending on the culture you are from) you may still recognize the reference.

Whatever I was trying to do – and whatever you understood and accepted as the meaning of my title – the point is that intertextuality creates a new set of possible positions by taking established references and reformulating them. This idea – of the re-shaping of existing elements – formed the basis of Koestler's now famous definition of creativity:

> The creative act does not create something out of nothing, like the God of the Old Testament; it combines, reshuffles and relates already existing but hitherto separate ideas, facts, frames of perception, associative contexts. This act of cross-fertilization ... seems to be the essence of creativity.
>
> (Koestler, 1976, p. 645)

Although intertextuality has frequently been seen in those texts where producers have the time to develop elaborate conceits, such as literary texts and advertising (Cook, 1992; Goddard, 2002), the phenomenon has been less explored in texts that are composed on the hoof such as casual conversation and internet chat. However, as Carter (2004) shows, where researchers have taken the care to record and explore naturally occurring stretches of casual interaction, they are finding some highly patterned intertextual orchestrations.

Intertextuality and IWD

This article explores the phenomenon of intertextuality in 'chatroom' dialogues, focusing on the language use of undergraduate students who were largely unfamiliar with working online (see Goddard, 2003 and 2004). Chatroom discourse is a type of computer-mediated communication (CMC) which is often distinguished from other CMC genres by its synchronicity: that is, the need for interlocutors to be online simultaneously.

Although this type of computer-based discourse is commonly known as 'chat', the latter term is problematic within language study because it already labels a type of informal spoken language and can lead to a mistaken assumption that chatroom language is simply a version of speech. For this reason, Werry's (1996) suggested label – 'interactive written discourse' (IWD) is a useful reminder that when we 'chat' in chatrooms we are really writing to each other.

The most salient quality of IWD communication is its multimodality. It operates with constraints that in some ways are like those of spoken language: for example, it is composed in real time. On the other hand, IWD is written at the computer keyboard, using, in the main, conventional orthographic symbols, and with none of the visual cues that support face-to-face dialogue. Although IWD is interactive like speech, it is editable like writing, since participants can refashion their contributions before posting them up. In short, IWD offers new sets of communication conditions, and such new circumstances provide fertile ground for creative play and experimentation as users explore the parameters of their new medium. What follows is an account of some of the ways in which participants use intertextuality as a resource in that process of discovery.

Intertextuality and the architecture of elsewhere

Intertextuality demands, by its very nature, a known or shared text to be used for purposes of reference. In the IWD data collected, one type of material brought into play is language that indexes spatial location: for example, the deictics 'here' and 'there', and locative prepositions such as 'in' and 'out'. The IWD environment poses particularly tricky questions for participants about where interactions are occurring, disrupting our traditional notions of indexicality: although I am sitting at my own computer screen, if my writing appears on your screen, is that where 'I' am? Interestingly, we don't have the same sense of dislocation about our voices 'appearing' in other people's phone headsets. There is clearly something about the visual nature of writing that links it more generally with embodiment and identity. Certainly, seeing another participant's IWD output appearing on one's screen triggers a sense of an agency at work, but also a sense of rather ghostly magic because there is no visible hand 'there'. Notions of dis/embodiment form a recurring theme in CMC literature, where the kind of contradictions I have been describing are regularly noted. For example, Stone (1995) refers to CMC spaces as 'the architecture of elsewhere', a phrase which nicely summarises the way in which CMC texts can seem both tangibly present yet spatially elusive.

Such conundrums provide considerable linguistic mileage in the data for participants to play with ideas about location and visibility. One playful strategy is to use deictic terms, but to question their traditional parameters:

Author's note: The numbering of examples in this article is for ease of reference and does not reflect any ordering of items in the original chatlogs.

1.
Al>>there you are
Anne>>no, I'm not there, I'm here

2.
Ryan>> .   look im over here

Locations are also represented as physical scenes in the IWD data via use of 'in' by participants to describe having opened a chat page, and 'out' to describe the intention to close it. For example:

3.

Rebecca>>this room is getting very crowded – i'm begining to feel a bit clostraphobic in here

4.

Rebecca>>ryan, i am popping out for a minute to find out what we are supposed to be doing. don't go away!!!

With no more than verbal language as their building blocks, these users create spaces where there are none in reality. However, participants regularly go further than this, not just creating locations but particular kinds of locations. For example, the construction of the space as 'home' occurs regularly. Example 5 below is a lone occupant who posts what has been termed elsewhere a 'broadcast message' (Gillen and Goddard, 2003) acting as a call to others to join her; example 6 is from a participant who has re-entered the chatroom after having left to do a bulletin posting:

5.

Beatrice>>Anybody home????

6.

Rebecca>>hi honey i'm home!

The latter example marks a re-entry to a multi-party interaction, so is not a greeting to a particular individual. What it is, rather, is a playful characterisation of homecoming, based on American suburban 1950s TV sitcoms. Such sitcoms are frequently recycled, both in the form of 'classic' re-runs – *Bewitched, I Love Lucy* – and contemporary films with a retro theme – *Honey I Shrunk the Kids, Pleasantville*. Example 6 illustrates Bakhtin's ([1935]1981) concept of heteroglossia, or 'diverse voices'.

Heteroglossia is discussed in more detail in Chapter 9.

Bakhtin's account of heteroglossia in the novel focuses on the tensions between the voice of a character and that of the author, showing how one utterance supposedly from a character can be suffused with authorial intention, making the discourse a kind of double-voiced phenomenon.

If we apply the same framework to the IWD data, then we would say that Rebecca, an eighteen-year-old British female student, adopts the voice of a middle aged American man calling out to his stay-at-home wife. Although on one level there is fun simply stepping into 'character', Rebecca's use of intertextuality also allows her to take an authorial position on that character and, in the process, on the nature of the IWD world.

The 'home' of the suburban sitcoms named earlier is typically a piece of false consciousness, a fragile reality where the husband's expectations of ease and control quickly evaporate. So perhaps the IWD 'home' is no haven: rather than a cosy space, it just might be an unreliable simulation that could easily disappear. Rebecca's adoption of a particular kind of voice brings with it the original context of use, allowing us to see her authorship of the text and highlighting her own creative redeployment of intertextual material. Rather like the viewer of *trompe l'oeil* art, we can appreciate verbal intertextuality only if we are allowed to see the joins.

The same questioning of substantiality via the intertextual use of well known cultural material also occurs in references to the non-material world, as in this participant's broadcast opening:

7.

Glyn>>Hello spirits is their anyone out there?

Postings of the type '(is there) anyone/anybody (out) there?' are common as opening broadcasts by lone would-be chatters in both data sets. Such phrases carry an echoic quality for reasons that are difficult to pin down precisely, making them usefully plastic and adaptable. One intertextual link is of course the stereotypical séance routine 'is there anybody there?', which is being played on by Glyn in example 7. Other pieces of intertextuality could include *The X-Files* ('The truth is out there'), Pink Floyd's *Dark Side of the Moon* ('Hello ... is there anybody out there?'), both being explorations of alienation; and the old staple of UK English lessons up to the 1960s – the mystery poem, *The Traveller*, by Walter de la Mare (the opening line being '"Is there anybody there?" said the traveller, knocking on the moonlit door'). Regardless of whether we know the latter reference or not, its use by de la Mare might remind us that a version of the same phrase has come down through countless horror movies, as the hapless future victim steps into a darkened space and alerts the waiting psychopath to their presence.

What all these references share is an idea of contacting the unknown, the fear that that entails, and the menace that might be lurking in the darkness. In terms of characterising the IWD medium as experienced by these particular users, such a depiction is an understandable elaboration of a situation where group members had never met face to face (one of the data sets) or who, to start with, had only met once (a further data set); where most people were unfamiliar with working online and therefore didn't know the rules for interaction; and where participants were invisible.

Given that all sorts of dubious behaviour could be going on under cover of IWD-darkness, then, how reassuring to find a nicely antique English bobby watching out for trouble:

8.

Joanne>>hello hello hello

Author's note: The greeting 'hello hello hello' is stereotypically associated with British policemen ('bobbies') from a former time.

A data set from an intercultural project involving UK and Swedish students (see Goddard, 2003) provides some examples of intertextuality that offer a further elaboration of IWD spaces, this time with cultural references that relate to specific events and nationalities. For example, UK students used 'England calling', a phrase they attributed to the Eurovision song contest, the latter being prompted by memories of its most famous winners, the Swedish group, Abba; and the student below refers to a twentieth-century World War propaganda slogan:

9.

Gemma>>shshshshshsh you don't know who is listening, walls have ears remember

Gemma's warning to her UK friend is prompted by their discussion of 'foreignness', which had, up to this point, playfully considered whether their own surnames sounded foreign and concluded that the spelling of both their names would come into that category. Gemma is clearly worried that they will go too far and that their Swedish colleagues, for whom they are waiting, will log in and read the dialogue.

The 'walls have ears' slogan is an interesting text to see in use, for a number of different reasons. In the chatlog, there is clearly some confusion among the UK students between Sweden and Germany, which in itself perhaps accounts for the triggering of the old wartime phrase. But, like several of the other pieces of intertextuality discussed so far, it seems curiously archaic coming from a young speaker. However, I am looking at this from my own middle aged perspective, where for me, the phrase 'England calling' connotes English Armed Forces radio and even Lord Haw Haw, an English spy who broadcast pro-German propaganda radio bulletins beginning 'Germany calling', during World War II. Perhaps the call signs in Eurovision betray intertextually an interesting history of conflict and nationalism. Some would say that this is kept alive in Eurovision's blatantly biased voting patterns.

All the examples quoted so far endorse Voloshinov's idea that utterances exist in a complex network of intertextual relationships where any individual utterance is 'but one link in a continuous chain of speech performances' (Voloshinov, 1995, p. 115). Linguistic items bring their histories of usage with them, and speakers have to make their own new meanings from elements that are, as it were, already populated by others' voices. This idea stresses the larger social and political canvas that we all inhabit, seeing human speakers as creative re-fashioners of language rather than original inventors, and as participants in a historical conversation that is timeless: others after us will reconfigure our usages for their own needs and purposes.

Intertextuality as a speech-writing interface

The idea of a text that has both synchronicity and spatiality means that there are new intertextual relationships to be observed across modalities, as well as new forms of *intra*textuality as participants watch their discourse emerging as a visual co-production. This can, of course, be problematic: Gemma's concern that a Swedish colleague will enter the chatroom and be able to read her previous conversation about 'foreignness' reminds us that, in chatrooms, the writing is literally on the wall. On the other hand, that same visual quality seems to be an important facilitator to creative composition as each participant builds on others' contributions. For example, in 10, the play on twitch-bitch-witch certainly involves sound patterning, as does the use of /w/; but there is also a cumulative force in the frequent appearance of the letter sequences 'i-t-c-h' and 'w' within a short space of time (consecutive lines of play in a multi-party context suggests a fast response time). In 11, would 'chat/cat' have suggested itself had the word 'chat' not appeared as a visual item? In 12, Andrew's witty rejoinder plays on the absence of punctuation in Sorcha's comment; and Nathalie's recycling of 'high horse' suggests that she is calling it up as an image rather than as a saying. All these examples share qualities with supposedly 'literary' usages: sound patterning, puns, deliberate ambiguity and idiomatic language have been traditionally seen as part of the literary author's linguistic toolkit. Perhaps seeing a text evolve visually heightens participants' awareness of language patterns and encourages group artistry.

10.

(Andrew has been accused of 'twitching')

Glyn>>your name has been added to the list you will not see

another sunrise andrew

Ryan>>the blair twitch project

Alexandra>>So your a twitcher then Andy

Ryan>>smack my twitch up

RyanJ>>the wicked twitch of the west

RyanJ>>or wirral

11.

Ryan>>i like chat

Andrew>>its good isn't it

Ryan>>rather.

LucyN>>hi andrew

Ryan>>can we all be friends

Andrew>>Hi Lucy, I thought the chat had got your tongue,

excuse the pun

Ryan Schmidt>>nice

12.

DawnM>>Get off your high horse young man!!

Sorcha>>god andrew what have you started

Simon>>John wants to know how long people are going to be

here for

Natalie>>atleast the original high horse isn't here

Andrew>>I'm no god, but thanks for the compliment

In all the examples, there are rich intertextual references to culturally shared texts and voices. In 10, the media texts invoked all have a menacing theme, as if to perform Glyn's original threat; then Ryan's 'or wirral' executes a nice piece of comic bathos. In 11, the voices are genteel and proper, the pun playing on a quaint idiomatic usage consistent with polite society. In 12, Dawn's voice suggests a theatrical grande dame.

Intertextuality as a performance of identity

So far, intertextuality has been seen as a strategy which allows participants to explore the IWD medium by characterising it and by testing out its parameters. But intertextuality is also involved, of course, in constructions of identity.

Intertextuality is, by its very nature, attention-seeking. It lays out some known material and disrupts expectations by re-negotiating it. So, for example, creatively re-shaping greetings routines is rule-breaking behaviour that draws attention to itself. Equally, trying on different voices is a startling way to frame a new performance of oneself. Each new performance opens up new possibilities for positioning oneself and others. Rebecca's suburban husband (6), Glyn's tacky medium (7), Joanne's suspicious bobby (8), Gemma's watchful home-guard (9), Ryan's and Andrew's gentlemen (11), and Dawn's grande dame (12) are all customised for the occasion: they are creative responses to the local circumstances of the action.

What the examples of intertextuality in the IWD data all seem to share is a sense of their respective authors' knowing construction. Bakhtin's (1981) claim is that all utterances are dialogic because they presume an addressee. Utterances with strong intertextual references seem to go further than that. Foregrounding the constructed nature of one's own communication adds an aspect of performance to the mix, so that there is a heightened sense of audience. Where there are group orchestrations, such as example 10, it is easy to see how the group itself is its own audience, as each member finds a way to build a further intertextual reference from a previous contribution. The ability to react creatively and quickly to shared references also allows participants to become a cohesive group, even for the few seconds of the performance. Conversely, those who do not understand the references and cannot react accordingly will immediately be positioned as outsiders.

Multi-party interactions are understandably fertile ground for dramatic performances of intertextual dexterity. But there is also a performative aspect to some lone postings.

For example, in the following:

13.

Glyn>>I came, I saw, and nobody turned up

there is no one for Glyn to perform for. However, he still takes the trouble to construct an intertextual reference that ends with comic bathos. Caesar's grand conquest was thwarted because he was stood up. Glyn of course is commenting wryly on his own failure to find a fellow chatter, and his mock-heroic designation of himself is a neat way to sidestep the potentially face-threatening situation of *really* being a sad loner.

Goffman's (1981) interest in the social nature of discourse led him to deliberate on lone talk, and to conclude that we often address imaginary narratees in our ongoing identity-work. For example, someone tripping up a kerb will let out a 'response cry' (such as 'aargh!') after the event. This might seem to be drawing attention to the mishap, but Goffman points out that response cries typically mark the regaining of composure rather than its loss. Expostulating is therefore a way for us to construct ourselves as people who don't take paving stones lying down.

Similarly, Glyn's lone posting can be seen as drawing attention to his solitary status by mentioning it. And yet the fact that he can play intertextually, comically exaggerating his own dashed hopes, means that he is projecting an idea of himself as someone not fazed by adversity. As one participant said in written feedback collected via questionnaire: *Openings have to be bold and interesting to read*. Perhaps lone postings have to shout that little bit louder.

Conclusion

This account has offered some snapshots of student communities constructing a temporary world through computer-based discourse, and has focused on a particular communicative phenomenon: intertextuality. It must be remembered that IWD is not a fixed entity: one group's output is likely to vary considerably from the next. However, as far as these specific groups were concerned, intertextuality proved to be a creative strategy that enabled participants to fashion some interesting new positionalities from existing cultural resources. Although such resources are given, they are not fixed. As is shown by the data discussed in this article, each participant has the power to broker meanings afresh with every new usage:

> Communication ... must make use of the language, the texts, of others and because of that, those other voices provide both amplification and limitations of our own voices. A text which is appropriated for use in mediated action brings with it the conventionalizations of the social practices of its history of use. We say not only what we want to say but also what the text must inevitably say for us. At the same time, our use of texts in mediated actions changes those texts and in turn alters the discursive practices.

> (Scollon, 1998, p. 15)

Note: all IWD postings have been reproduced as originally written.

References

BAKHTIN, M. M. ([1935]1981) *The Dialogic Imagination: Four Essays* (trans. C. EMERSON and M. HOLQUIST), Austin, TX, University of Texas Press.

CARTER, R. (2004) *Language and Creativity*, London, Routledge.

COOK, G. (1992) *The Discourse of Advertising*, 2nd edn, London, Routledge.

GEE, J.G. (1999) *An Introduction to Discourse Analysis: Theory and Method*, London and New York, Routledge.

GILLEN, J. and GODDARD, A. (2003) 'Medium management for beginners: the discursive practices of undergraduate and mature novice users of internet relay chat, compared with those of young children using the telephone', in M. BONDI and S. STATI (eds) *Dialogue Analysis 2000, Selected Papers from the 8th IADA Conference, Bologna, Italy,* Niemeyer, TFC Bingen.

GODDARD, A. (2002) (2nd edn) *The Language of Advertising*, London, Routledge.

GODDARD, A. (2003) '"*Is there anybody out there?*": creative language play and literariness in internet relay chat' (IRC), in A. SCHORR, B. CAMPBELL and M. SCHENK (eds) *Communication Research and Media Science in Europe*, Berlin, Mouton De Gruyter.

GODDARD, A. (2004) '"*The Way To Write a Phone Call*": multimodality in novices' use and perceptions of interactive written discourse', in R. SCOLLON and P. LEVINE (eds) *Georgetown University Round Table on Languages and Linguistics: Discourse analysis and technology: Multimodal Discourse Analysis*, Washington, USA, Georgetown University Press.

GOFFMAN, E. (1981) *Forms of Talk*, Oxford, Blackwell.

KOESTLER, A. (1976) 'Association and Bisociation', in J.S. BRUNER, A. JOLLY and K. SYLVA (eds) *Play – Its Role in Development and Evolution*, London, Penguin.

KRISTEVA, J. (1974) *La Révolution du langage poétique*, Paris, Seuil.

SCOLLON, R. (1998) *Mediated Discourse as Social Interaction*, Harlow, Longman.

STONE, A.R. (1995) *The War of Desire and Technology at the Close of the Machine Age,* Cambridge, MA, MIT Press.

VOLOSHINOV, V.N. (1995) ' "Language, speech and utterance" and "verbal interaction" ' in S. DENTITH (ed.) *Bakhtinian Thought: A Reader*, London, Routledge.

WERRY, C.C. (1996) 'Linguistic and interactional features of Internet Relay Chat', in S. HERRING (ed.), *Computer-Mediated Communication: Linguistic, Social and Cross-Cultural Perspectives*, Amsterdam, John Benjamins.

Source: commissioned for this volume.

Writing the self

Janet Maybin

6.1 Introduction

The focus of this chapter is the relationship between language use, creativity and the self. We will be looking both at the kind of artful forms of text which were discussed in Chapter 1 and will also be extending the ideas about creative interactive performance in Chapter 3, applying these within the context of personal writing. I will treat **identity** not as a fixed set of attributes, but as a set of dispositions (some more open than others) which emerge through an interactive process between how one sees and expresses one's own position and meaning in the world, and how one is 'identified' by others. This process is both social and individual. Depending on their social background and experience, individuals are predisposed towards particular perceptions, actions and ways of reading the world and themselves, but they also exercise choice in expressing and presenting themselves in local activities and interactions, drawing on the resources available. I will use the term 'self' to refer to the more internal, subjective experience of identity.

In what ways do we perform or create particular kinds of identity through writing? How do different readers and audiences contribute to this identity? In this chapter I will focus on four **genres** of writing which seem particularly personal: diaries or journals, letter-writing, graffiti and web home pages. I will examine how these genres offer opportunities for creativity at the level of the text and will also look at how their interactional functions, and their embeddedness in social practices, shape this creative expression and its interpretation by different audiences. However solitary a diary or letter writer at their desk or computer may seem, or a graffiti writer with their spray can in a deserted city street at night, these acts of writing are addressed to specific audiences. Writers draw on the creative possibilities of shared generic conventions, and the texts they produce are interpreted, used and recontextualised in relation to broader social and cultural practices.

> ## Genre
>
> The term 'genre' is used in various connected ways within the field of language and literacy studies. Within this chapter, it has the following meanings:
>
> 1   Different types of literary texts, such as poetry, novels, plays. Sub-genres of these are defined according to their stylistic features and associated subject matter and audience. For instance the sub-genres of poetry involve lyric, epic, ballad and sonnet.
>
> 2   Groups of spoken or written texts with a similar social purpose and formal characteristics, e.g. diaries, advertisements, jokes. Bakhtin (1986) suggests that simple primary genres such as everyday conversation can be absorbed into more complex secondary genres such as novels.

6.2 Dear Diary

Goffman (1959) suggests that people have a 'front stage' style, a public persona designed to make a good impression on others, and also a more private 'back stage style' in places where they can relax their behaviour, reflect more openly and prepare their public 'front'.

The back-stage self

ACTIVITY 1   **Personal poetics**

Allow 20 minutes

If you have kept any kind of personal diary or journal, look at one or two pages and jot down any ways in which you feel this writing is contributing to your sense of yourself as a person. Note also any poetic uses of language, for example imagery, repetition or verbal play.

    Notice the ways in which the writer of the extract in the box below uses language poetically in the course of exploring personal feelings.

Journal extract

The following extract comes from the journal of a woman who lives in rural England. She has kept a journal since she was twelve years old. She says:

(death/loss)

(weirdness)

(widowed)

(fatherless)

> Friday 2nd January 2004
>
> A strange time, a time during which I have felt the tiredness that has always accompanied death/loss for me, & a disorientation and weirdness which seems to be about the loss being hard to locate within myself. I feel widowed "from a distance" — the "other parent" of my eldest children is dead. This leaves them fatherless, & yet they never had an involved father. There is still a gap. And it leaves me "co-parent-less", yet I never had an involved co-parent with him. So the loss is a floating loss, a difficult-to-anchor loss. S. is coming home tomorrow. The funeral is not until a week on Monday. The coming of this new year for me has been coloured by J's death — inevitably. We were to go to the field. To be outside, in the air, on the land, with fire and people. But I couldn't see my way to do that. I felt vulnerable, and didn't want to expose myself in that way.

Figure 6.1   Extract from a personal journal

Comment

The metaphoric description of the loss as 'floating', 'difficult to anchor' and 'difficult to locate', and the image of being widowed 'from a distance', seem to be part of this writer's struggle both to explore, and to find an accurate expression for, her current feelings. Her use of repeated structures and rhythms drew me in to a closer involvement with what she was saying: 'This leaves them fatherless, yet they never had an involved father ... And it leaves me co-parent-less, yet I never had an involved co-parent', 'The loss is a floating loss, a difficult-to-anchor loss'. This **parallelism** (the repetition of structural pattern, usually between phrases or clauses), which highlights the connection between present losses and past absences, helps to explain the floating, unanchored sense of loss of something that was never really there. When experiencing strong emotions, do we draw on poetic rhythm and imagery to try to express feelings which cannot be captured within more prosaic language?

Diaries recording and commenting on personal experience go back (in the English language) to the sixteenth century. Early diaries or journals may have grown out of the habit of keeping household accounts but as far back as the evocative entries in Samuel Pepys' famous seventeenth-century diary, they have also provided a private space for the writer's personal reflections. The growth of literacy, the increasing interest in travel and public affairs and the self-examination encouraged by Protestantism all contributed to the growth of diary keeping from this period onwards. Accounting to God for one's life's work was a common theme in the seventeenth and eighteenth-century diaries which survive and diarists also admonished themselves to become more virtuous. Colour Figure 3 shows the personal resolutions written by the English preacher John Wesley in his diary in 1738.

While diaries can provide a kind of backstage for the self, or a launching pad for an improved self, they have also been used by authors and poets for recording the raw material of immediate impressions later to be transformed into novels and poems. Dorothy Wordsworth wrote her Grasmere Journals partly to please her poet brother, who often used them as a source and would ask her to read out passages to revive his memory. A direct link can be drawn between Dorothy's journal description (15 April 1802) of quantities of daffodils growing among mossy stones by a lake which 'tossed and reeled and danced' and William's famous poem *Daffodils* (Darbishire, 1958, p. 142). In her journals Dorothy expresses her own romantic sensibility and love of nature and she also defines herself through her love for her brother. In another direct link between journal entry and poem, Sylvia Plath's diary entry while in hospital awaiting an appendix operation records that: 'A helpful inmate in a red bathrobe brings the flowers back, sweet-lipped as children. All night they've been breathing in the hall, dropping their pollens, daffodils, pink and red tulips, the hot purple and red-eyed anemones'. In her poem *Tulips*, this experience is reversioned and threaded with pain and foreboding:

The tulips are too red in the first place, they hurt me.
Even through the gift paper I could hear them breathe
Lightly, through their white swaddlings, like an awful baby.

(Sylvia Plath, cited in Mallon, 1984, p. 136)

At one level journal writing seems to be an intensely private activity, and the notion that diaries provide an intimate, uncensored record is exploited in the promise of revelations when the diary of a public figure is published, or humourously in popular fictional diaries like *The Secret Diary of Adrian Mole* and *Bridget Jones' Diary*. There is always, however, a sense of addressing someone else – an absent or imaginary friend, a neglectful lover, oneself, God or 'posterity'. Some diaries, such as those of travellers and politicians, may be written with publication in mind and the diaries of famous writers (e.g. Jonathan Swift, Sir Walter Scott, Lord Byron, Virginia Woolf) are often seen and valued as 'literature'. Not only may diaries be published, or provide the raw material for published work, but the diary form itself has been appropriated by novelists to produce imaginary diaries in the form of fiction, for example, *Journal of the Plague Year* (1722) by Daniel Defoe, *Dracula* (1897) by Bram Stoker, and *The Diary of a Nobody* (1863) by Grossmith.

Figure 6.2   The fictional diary of Adrian Mole (Townsend, 2002, front cover)

Weblogs

An increasingly popular medium for diary writing is the internet. Whereas the secrets of paper diaries can be closely guarded, weblogs or 'blogs' are potentially open to millions of readers, even though they often contain suprisingly intimate details of the writer's everyday life. Drawing on the affordances of the internet, blogs can include visual and other material, producing a kind of virtual scrapbook.

Blogs

A blog (a shortened version of 'web log') is a web page containing chunks of content ranging from the newest to the oldest, with the most recent posting at the top of the page. Authors may write entries about their everyday lives, world events, interesting material they have found on the web, or on specific expert topics. Since 1999, the public availability of weblog management tools has meant that virtually anyone with internet access can create their own blog. Because of the immediacy with which a blog can be updated, they can play an important part in the fast dissemination of news and information around the internet. For instance, during and after the 11 September 2001 attacks on the World Trade Center in New York, stories, photographs and movies posted on their blogs by people near to Ground Zero rivalled what was available in the mainstream media.

(Bausch et al., 2002)

What kind of potential do blogs offer for creative uses of language and identity work? I will focus on an example which became famous in early 2003. During the run-up to the American invasion of Iraq in November 2002, a young Iraqi writing under the pseudonym 'Salam Pax' began a weblog in English addressed to his friend 'Raed' who had currently moved away from home to study in Jordan and was proving an infrequent email correspondent. On his website *dear_raed*, Pax started keeping a personal log about life in Baghdad, which was also a letter to Raed. While many blogs are diary-like, Pax's is more of a hybrid cross between a diary and a series of letters. As he began making contact with other bloggers on the internet, he found that an increasing number of people from across the world were becoming interested in his site. Identifying himself as an Iraqi, Pax's postings began to be addressed to this wider audience of, as he termed them, 'non-Arablish speaking people'. Ranging over subjects such as his taste in music, criticisms of Saddam Hussein's regime and satirical responses to western news reports and propaganda, Pax's postings were read by an increasing number of web users daily as the American invasion grew nearer. There was considerable speculation about his identity – Was he a Ba'athist or CIA spy? Did he exist at all? – and incredulity that such a critical and irreverant commentator could survive within Saddam Hussein's regime. The 'Baghdad Blogger' was finally tracked down by a western journalist who discovered a young architect posting to his weblog from the office where he worked and from a computer in his bedroom. A series of extracts from Pax's weblog was published by a major British broadsheet newspaper, and later a selection of entries were collected together in a paperback book with announcements on the cover comparing Salam Pax to Ann Frank and Elvis Presley (Pax, 2003). During 2003 and 2004, Pax presented a number of video diaries on BBC's *Newsnight*, which included images of himself seated at his keyboard writing postings for his website, interspersed with video footage documenting life on the ground in Iraq.

ACTIVITY 2   The Baghdad blogger

Allow 30 minutes

The box overleaf contains brief extracts from postings in Salam Pax's blog. The first entry includes two imaginary dialogues he made up to convey what life was like in Baghdad. Taking into account the background information above as well, answer the following questions:

In what ways does Pax use language artfully, draw creatively on the socio-historical context and the affordances of the internet, to get his message across in these postings?

How might Pax's weblog be contributing to his identity?

Comment

As you saw in Chapter 5, computer-mediated communication seems to be particularly conducive to playfulness in language use. Pax uses word play to create social connection, both with 'Raed' through the palindrome 'dear_raed' and with his wider audience of western readers through the juxtaposition within his own name of the words for peace in Arabic and Latin, and the made-up word 'Arablish', an amalgam of 'Arabic' and 'English'. In the first posting on **28.9.02**, Pax's parody of programming language '[female_parental_unit]', '[evil_boss_unit]', helps to produce a deadpan absence of emotion in the face of enormous impending danger, conveying the surreal nature of life in pre-war Baghdad. The juxtaposition of banal everyday detail with the vast horror of the coming war runs through the entries on Pax's site. In the **12.10.02** entry the poetic parallelism of the phrases 'greed and power', 'me and you' and 'dead or injured' may not have been a conscious rhetorical device. But the description of the twenty-year-old soldiers with their fizzy drinks and chocolate under **20.03.03** is surely purposefully ironic in stressing the youth and ordinariness of the men who make up the Iraqui army.

Initially making creative use of a blog to get in touch with 'Raed' when he fails to answer his emails, Pax then responds to the increasing interest in his

Extracts from Pax's weblog

28.9.02

So what do you think is the most used word in our vocabulary these days? It is 'ba3deen' (for you non-Arablish-speaking people, it means 'later/afterwards'). Anything that has anything to do with a decision that will affect the future will be answered with 'BA3DEEN'.

Example 1

[salam]: Listen … I haven't been paid the last few months and you make me work like a slave. How about buying me a better monitor than the one I have? It flickers.

[evil_boss_unit]: We will think about it 'ba3deen'.

[salam]: What 'afterwards'? After I have lost my eyesight?

[evil_boss_unit]: No. Who cares about you these days. Wait till after it happens.

[salam]: Whaaa? I don't … ohhh, you mean *it*. I guess it's OK then, we'll see what happens afterwards.

Example 2

[salam]: Awww GOD! You still have those hideous curtains! You promised they will not stay!

[female_parental_unit]: Oh … I thought I'll keep them and change them afterwards.

[salam]: They are ugly and there's no excuse for not changing them … you know that!!

[female_parental_unit]: I said 'ba3deen' … and if it makes you feel any better they will probably be shredded by all the glass that will be flying thru them.

[salam]: Oh you mean *that* … OK, wait till 'ba3deen'.

12.10.02

What is truely ironic is that the Bush administration is using the same argument Saddam used to invade Kuwait for his invasion of Iraq. 'National security concerns' and 'helping the poor bastards over there to get rid of that evil government'. At least try to be original. I tell you it is all about greed and power – it always is. Me and you are only a future statistic. The question is in which column will we be listed, DEAD or INJURED.

14.02.03

… please always remember that I am no authority on anything. Quoting me like the journalist did there makes me a bit nervous: Salam says this, Salam says that. … Big media scares me. Trouble is never far away.

20.03.03

Today the Ba'ath party people started taking their places in the trenches and main squares and intersections, fully armed and freshly shaven. They looked too clean and well groomed to defend anything. And the most shocking thing was the number of kids. They couldn't be older than 20, sitting in trenches sipping Mirinda fizzy drinks and eating chocolate…

21.03.03

Please stop sending me emails asking if I were for real. Don't believe it? Then don't read it. I am not anybody's propoganda ploy – well except my own.

(Pax, 2003)

site with postings addressing a wider international audience. The anonymity of the web enables Pax to criticise both the Ba'athist regime and the western powers, for instance suggesting an ironic parallel between the Bush administration's invasion of Iraq and Saddam Hussein's 1991 invasion of Kuwait, in a context where voicing criticism in the real world would have been highly dangerous. This anonymity, however, raises questions for others about who Pax is and about whether he exists at all. As his fame grows, he expresses discomfort and fear about his safety, especially when people start quoting him as an authority. In addition to Pax's projection of himself as witty, courageous in his criticism of both Bush and Saddam Hussein and friendly to 'non-Arablish' people, the identity of 'The Baghdad Blogger' emerged through the responses of others and the appropriation of his writing into new generic forms. This appropriation also put a new kind of value on Pax's writing, elevating it from a personal log to a broadsheet newspaper and then a book.

Once finally located, Pax is given expert status through publication in a national broadsheet newspaper, projected as a kind of alternative cultural icon through his book and presented as a fledgling media personality in the video diary on *Newsnight*. The swiftness of these transformations is made possible by the globalised communication and media technologies at the turn of the twenty-first century which have produced the blog and facilitated the email dialogues in which Pax became involved. But, as we saw earlier, journal writing has always been in some sense **dialogic**, that is, responding to others and addressed to others, and journals have always had the potential to be readdressed to wider audiences.

The use of artful language and the dialogic construction of the self through writing (i.e. the shaping of self in the course of responding to others and anticipating their responses) will be discussed further in the following sections below, where we will also continue to explore the shifting boundaries and transformations between private and public texts.

6.3 The art of letter writing

In this section, I will focus on personal letter writing, which, it has been argued, is the most basic written genre and the root of other more complex generic forms. The art of letter writing has also long been a subject for instruction and amusement. Letter-writing manuals and collections of letters have been published in Britain since the sixteenth century.

Angel Day, a sixteenth-century rhetorician and writer, provided one of the first English letter-writing manuals for the new rising English middle classes. With the emphasis in this period on polite learning and classical rhetoric in writing, rather than on what we would now see as individual art and creativity, Day stressed the 'comelinesse' and social niceties of letter writing. An individual letter was expected to conform to the classical

Figure 6.3   Title page from Angel Day's 'The English Secretorie, 1586 (Altson, 1967)

rhetorical structure, and Day provided his own sample letters with the different sections marked. Examples included 'A conciliatory epistle of the third sort, wherein a gentlewoman is comforted on the death of her husband slain in the wars' and 'A sample petition in the nature of reconciliation from a son to his displeased father'. Interestingly, although *The English Secretorie* is ostensibly an instruction manual, behind a series of love letters later in the book a story of misunderstanding, jealousy, envy and reconciliation begins to emerge like a rudimentary trace of an epistolary novel. From the outset, it seems, letters could be used both for functional purposes and as a fictional form for pleasure and entertainment. Almost as soon as there were manuals telling people how to write letters, there were also collections of letters which were made to look authentic, but whose primary purpose was to entertain the reader – for example, Nicholas Breton's *A Poste with a Packet of Madde Letters* (1602), which included amusing fictional begging and railing letters, letters from misogynists trying to dissuade friends from marriage and letters from rustic wooers (Robertson, 1942).

With increasing mobility and migration in Europe, growing literacy and the development of the postal system, letter writing became more popular, first among the upper and middle classes and then more widely. As with journals, the initial focus on polite form was gradually replaced with more emphasis on the potential within personal correspondence for individual expression and intimate relationship. Altman (1982) argues that a set of paradoxes and contradictions make personal letter writing a particularly rich creative medium. She points out that letters have the capacity to overcome barriers of distance and space and can transform absence into presence. A letter can clarify, and it can also dissimulate. It is a reflection of the self and the self's relationships, often private and intimate, yet at the same time it reflects its intended audience, the 'drag of the face on the other side of the page', as Virginia Woolf puts it (Woolf, 1940, quoted in Jolly, 1997). A letter has a formal opening and closing, yet it can be elliptical and open-ended, referring implicitly to other letters within a chain of correspondence.

In the reading for Activity 3 below, Margaretta Jolly focuses on a point in British history when the practice of private letter writing reached a peak of popularity. She explores the possibilities for creativity within the everyday letters of ordinary people and argues that the ambiguity of the personal letter, as both communication and creation, produces a 'distinctive aesthetic of the everyday'.

ACTIVITY 3 War letters (Reading A)

Please read 'Sincerely yours: everyday letters and the art of written relationship' by Margaretta Jolly. Notice any ways in which the letter writers use rhythm or imagery artfully. Look out for their use of three-part lists of words or phrases (e.g. I came, I saw, I conquered), which are an important rhetorical device to move and convince the listener or reader (Wooffitt, 1996). In what ways are the letters an expression of identity?

Comment

The first letter writer, Rosewarne, uses metaphor ('my earthly mission fulfilled') and rhythmic parallel structures ('just eat and sleep, prosper and create', 'No man can do more, and no one calling himself a man could do less') to help construct his impending death as a glorious contribution to 'peace, justice and freedom' (a three-part list). He rhetorically aligns his mother's sacrifice with his own so that as he becomes a hero, she is constructed within the letter as a heroine. Through the subsequent publishing and reprinting of Rosewarne's letter, readdressed to the wider British public, Rosewarne and his mother become emblems of patriotic national identity. More generally, Jolly argues that soldiers' ongoing personal correspondence with family and friends helped them to preserve a part of their identity which could easily become lost, and provided an opportunity for men to express a 'less formulated domestic masculinity', gentle, affectionate and playful aspects of themselves which were not admissable within the context of war.

The second letter writer, Wandrey, draws on a range of metaphors and similes to try and convey the horror she is witnessing to her family in America: the corpse-like patients, tortured souls with 'calloused footsteps', their gratitude 'tears' at her heart; the place smells like 'rotten, rotten sewage'. Her letter is also rhetorically addressed to a higher audience, in the three repeated calls to God which echo through the letter (another three-part list), underlining the extremity of her situation. Through the force of her detailed imagery Wandrey comes across as compassionate, committed to her work and deeply shocked.

Jolly also shows how metaphor, parody and romantic comedy can be used in letters to entertain, to facilitate the exchange of confidences about sensitive topics such as courtship, sexual desire and pregacy, and to construct and maintain friendship across a class divide. Agnes Helme addresses her former teacher as 'Laughing Motorbyke' and hopes she won't have to 'garage' her laugh (in the quotation at the beginning of the Reading). On another occasion Helme parodies wartime officialese in starting a letter 'My dear instigator of laughs', and her 'pen flies' to transform a chance encounter into a romantic story in a letter for her friend. Humour among women is used here to overcome social barriers in a context where new sexual and class identities were emerging from the upheaval of the war.

ACTIVITY 4   Artful life writing

Allow 30 minutes

In what ways do the journals and letters discussed so far in this chapter draw on both everyday and more literary-like language? How far do you think that they provide different kinds of affordances for 'writing the self'?

Comment

In contemporary diaries and letters, the language style is often personal and informal, imitating, absorbing or reproducing everyday speech, as in Pax's imaginary dialogue and Helme's reporting of her encounter with the Canadian soldier. The examples in this chapter also illustrate creative uses of language often associated with literature: the use of imagery, evocative detail and rhetorical structures like three-part lists to increase emotional and persuasive impact, and parallellism to highlight contrast and nuance meaning. Diary and letter styles vary according to writer and historical epoch, connecting with different ways of viewing the self, different audiences and changing technological resources.

While I have argued that the shadow of possible future readers hangs over the journal writer's shoulder, one of the most striking differences in 'writing the self' through letters is their more intensely dialogic nature (which also emerges in Pax's hybrid blog). Letter writers may use language artfully to present personal experience and a particular kind of self, but that self is created in relation to a specific recipient, who then responds and confirms or in some way questions the presented identity. Letter writers also project the identity of their recipient – for instance, the mother as heroine in Rosewarne's letter and Valentine Morche as an 'instigator of laughs' in Helme's letter. Again, a recipient may respond to this projected identity, and so the negotiation of relationship and identity continues as letters go back and forth.

Like diaries, letters can become recontextualised within books which are treated as 'literature'. Although a piece of writing is partly defined as a particular genre from the inside through its structure and style, it also depends on social recognition and value as that genre, from the outside. We saw how Salaam Pax's hybrid blog mutated rapidly into a newspaper column, book and video diary, and Jolly points out the contrast between the immediate contemporary publication of Rosewarne's letter and the more problematic reception of Wandrey's writing. The letter genre also has the potential for artful use within fiction, first in early parodies of the letter-writing manuals and then in epistolary novels.

6.4 The writing on the wall

In this section, we turn to a very different kind of writing practice which also suggests interesting connections between writing, creativity and identity. We start by looking at the artfulness of graffiti, at the level of both text and interaction.

A C T I V I T Y   5   **Graffiti**

Allow 20 minutes

Identify any artful uses of language that strike you in the examples of graffiti below, such as repetition, puns, rhyme and rhythm.
In what ways is there a creative use of dialogic forms to produce humorous or ironic effects?

C o m m e n t

In Example a, the absurdity produced by morphological punning (a/lert) in the first line is developed further by two subsequent writers, who mimick a rational argument using the parallel pun 'a/loof'. This kind of 'dialogical creativity' emerges through the relationship between individual contributions.

(a)

be alert -
England needs lerts

WE HAVE TOO MANY LERTS
- BE ALOOF

don't be aloof, there's safety
in numbers - be alert

(b)

THE MEEK
SHALL INHERIT
THE EARTH

if that's alright
with you

(d)

Sheryl.C
For

Jason.L

4 ever
4 Always
4 years
4 Come
2 us
4 Part
2
Would break
my ♥

(c)

Buy a cottage in
Wales

COME HOME TO A REAL FIRE

Figure 6.4   Examples of graffiti

There is also a humorous relationship between different voices in Example b, where the response to the biblical saying based on St Matthew 5.5 enacts its message of meekness, and in Example c where the suggestion to buy a cottage in Wales at a time when English holiday homes were being burnt by Welsh nationalists is darkly ironic.

In Example d, with its use of the homophones '2'(to) and '4'(for), there is a rhythmic repetition of a pair of three-syllabled and then two pairs of two-syllabled lines, followed by a rhythmic break marking where the tone of the message changes with the longer 'would break my' and the iconically represented heart.

The long tradition of illegitimate, oppositional writing on public surfaces can be traced back to first-century Pompeii. Researchers have examined the playful aspects of graffiti in English, such as the ways in which puns and contradictory voices are used. They stress the importance of how graffiti is written in relation to its meaning and significance, and point out its inherently oppositional nature, either in specifically political terms or to the social establishment in general (Blume, 1985; Nwoye, 1993; Cook, 1996). Opposition is expressed through the illegitimacy of the graffiti act itself, through the content of the message and through stylistic features, for instance the use of non-standard spelling and punctuation which create a symbolic distance from authority. Sebba (2000) points out that some anti-standard practices have now become conventional practice within English-language graffiti, for instance, the spellings in 'KJ woz ere 97', the homophonic use of numbers in 'Jenny 4 CS 4'.

In addition to what might be called the traditional graffiti represented above, a new, rather more flamboyant form has been appearing on city landscapes since the 1970s. Both writing and art form, letters and names are spray-painted in a kind of decorative calligraphy which is often indecipherable to the uninitiated. In the United States, 'tagging', an embellished signature spray-painted on walls or vehicles, is said to have started in the summer of 1970 when a Manhattan youth sprayed his name and street number on ice-cream trucks in his neighbourhood. Spray-can graffiti has now developed into a distinctive subcultural practice, often associated in the United States with territorial marking by gangs with distinctive slogans, symbols and spelling conventions. A small number of studies have examined the significance this kind of graffiti writing holds for the writers themselves and its function for them in terms of claiming and expressing particular identities. For instance, Moje (2000, p. 651) describes how marginalised youth in Salt Lake City have appropriated gang writing styles, spelling rules and dress codes to 'claim a space, construct an identity and take on a social position in their worlds'. For these youth, who have not found value in mainstream culture, graffiti is 'a state of mind and a sign of respect'. In the Activity 6 reading below, Nancy Macdonald draws on her ethnographic study of young graffiti writers in London and New York to explain how graffiti writing plays a central role in the construction of a particular kind of young masculine identity. Coming from a background in sociology, she is interested in the way in which these young graffiti writers create and protect their own subcultural world.

ACTIVITY 6 The spray-can is mightier than the sword (Reading B)

Please read 'The spray-can is mightier than the sword' by Nancy Macdonald. In what ways is Macdonald suggesting that graffiti writing contributes to the construction of a masculine identity?

Comment

The illegality of graffiti, Macdonald suggests, is a central defining feature of the trials of courage and daring which establish these graffiti writers' respect, status and fame within their subculture. Macdonald argues that the elaboration of the struggle with authority, and the intense competition between the writers themselves, highlight a set of qualities which the youthful graffiti writers identify as 'manly' and 'masculine'. She suggests that some writers express sides of themselves in their graffiti which are not evident in the rest of their lives. These emerge particularly through the creative aspects of graffiti, including the materiality, shape and design of the script. Like a medieval manuscript, it communicates multimodally — through both the text and its decoration. The name, which is the basis of an art form where the look and sound of the letters are as important as the connotations of the word they spell, also expresses a desired identity for the writer. The placing of graffiti on fast-moving trains, or on buildings to stand out proud against the city landscape, brings this identity to life and gives it power and dominance within the urban environment.

Graffiti writers have their own criteria for judging the quality of particular tags or pieces and the effectiveness of their placing, but graffiti writing is often seen by mainstream society as a destructive rather than a creative act: it 'defaces' public places. The cleaning up of graffiti costs United States taxpayers billions of dollars a year (Walsh 1996). In her book about graffiti writers, Macdonald (2001) describes how some older writers make the transition into legality and respectability through taking on commercial graffiti work or putting up pieces in legal painting sites, eventually reaching a wider audience through exhibitions and coverage in specialist graffiti magazines and more general art magazines. While in the eyes of some members of their subculture these individuals might be seen to have 'sold out', they may gain respect and fame from a different kind of wider, international audience where graffiti is redefined as 'art' and they are seen as artists.

Bangalore, India (Kannada/English)

Auckland, New Zealand (English)

Milton Keynes, UK (English)

Oakland, USA (English)

Cape Town, South Africa (Khosa/English)

Figure 1
Clapping games around the world

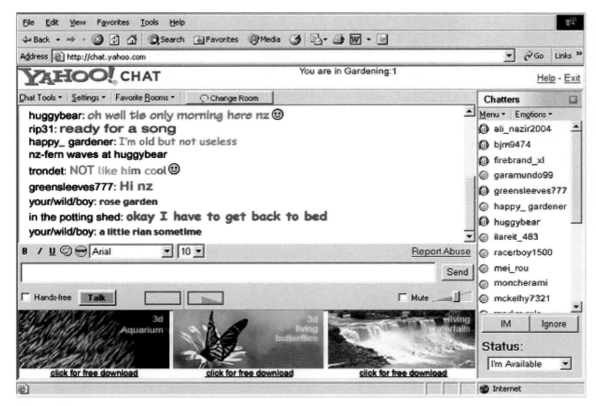

Figure 2

Screen shot of an online chatroom (http://chat.yahoo.com)

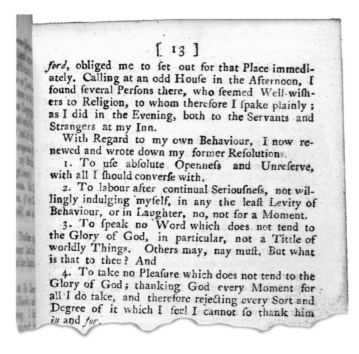

[13]

ford, obliged me to set out for that Place immediately. Calling at an odd House in the Afternoon, I found several Persons there, who seemed Well-wishers to Religion, to whom therefore I spake plainly; as I did in the Evening, both to the Servants and Strangers at my Inn.

With Regard to my own Behaviour, I now renewed and wrote down my former Resolutions.

1. To use absolute Openness and Unreserve, with all I should converse with.

2. To labour after continual Seriousness, not willingly indulging myself, in any the least Levity of Behaviour, or in Laughter, no, not for a Moment.

3. To speak no Word which does not tend to the Glory of God, in particular, not a Tittle of worldly Things. Others may, nay must. But what is that to thee? And

4. To take no Pleasure which does not tend to the Glory of God; thanking God every Moment for all I do take, and therefore rejecting every Sort and Degree of it which I feel I cannot so thank him *in* and *for.*

Figure 3

Extract from John Wesley's diary (British Library)

Figure 4
*The piecing of
one's name,*
artist: Sed
(photograph: KIRS)

Figure 5
Wildstyle,
artist: Sed
(photograph: KIRS)

Figure 6
Skore,
artist: Sed,
(photograph:
Frank Malt,
collection of steam,
London)

Figure 7
Revs and *Cost*
(Nancy Macdonald)

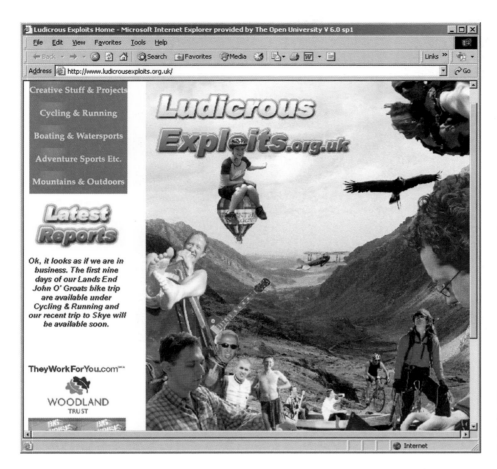

Figure 8
A personal homepage (Gary Nelmes)

Figure 9
Decorated envelope (Anita Wilson)

Figure 10
Signboard in the township
(Uta Papen)

Figure 11
Khowarib Campsite
(Uta Papen)

Figure 12
Victorian valentine
(Bridgeman Art Library)

Figure 13
Valentine (1860)
(Mary Evans Picture
Library)

Figure 14
The first Christmas
card (1843)
(Mary Evans Picture
Library)

Figure 15
Christmas card
(1880)
(Mary Evans Picture
Library)

6.5 Constructing the virtual self

One of the genres on the web most explicitly connected with constructing the self is the personal homepage. This is a website published or maintained by an individual, or group, which presents its author(s) to the world. It is different from a weblog in being primarily an 'all about me' collection of biographical details, interests, ideas, taste, beliefs and so on, rather than a journal with regular postings (although some homepages do include a diary). Homepages can be accessed through web directories or through web ring catalogues listing homepage owners who have joined together through common interest groups.

ACTIVITY 7   Homepages

Allow 15 minutes

The three examples below give a sense of the variety of homepages at the end of the twentieth century. It is also easy to find countless current examples on the internet. What opportunities do the three homepages described in the box below offer for self-presentation which are not available either in face-to-face encounters or written (on paper) accounts?

What's on a homepage?

In 1996, Jennifer Ringley, a twenty-year-old student, started a personal homepage which included poems, an online diary and the legendary 'JenniCam', which provided an uncensored nonstop-live video transmission from Ringley's house in California where she lives today (2001) with six cats, a dog and her boyfriend: 'I keep JenniCam alive not because I want to be watched, but because I simply don't mind being watched. It is more than a bit fascinating to me as an experiment, even (especially?) after five years. So feel free to watch, or not, as you so desire. I am not here to be loved or hated, I am here simply to be me.'

On the homepage of a professor of tele-learning, there are collections of her numerous lectures, publications, research projects and courses. The 57-year-old also gives information about her hobbies, her philosophy of life and her family.

The homepage of a 26-year-old German businessman who enjoys spending his free time on the internet and on music is written in German and English. There are numerous links on his page to websites for visually impaired and blind people, a group to which he himself belongs.

(Adapted from Doring, 2002, pp. 2–3)

It has been argued that representing oneself on a home page relieves some of the pressures of self-presentation in face-to-face interaction, in that there is more time to assemble a 'front' to present to the world, and much more personal control over how this is constructed. Writers can choose to be freed up from identification on the basis of age, gender, ethnicity or any other aspect of personal appearance. In addition to providing unfettered opportunities for self-presentation, homepages also offer new ways of creatively combining language with other semiotic features. These are explored more fully by Daniel Chandler in the next reading, where he analyses the use of different modes within the ongoing construction and reconstruction of homepages by their authors.

ACTIVITY 8   **Identities under construction (Reading C)**

Please read 'Identities under construction' by Daniel Chandler. What distinctive uses of language and other semiotic modes does Chandler see as involved with the presentation of the self on homepages? In what ways is identity expressed through these authorial practices?

Comment

Chandler suggests that verbal text can be combined with graphics, images, voices and music collected from around the web and real life, reassembled and recontextualised to present a flexible and changing self. Homepages appear to be the ultimate multimodal text in many ways. Texts and images are reframed by the author, who can highlight or 'reaccent' particular aspects of their meanings, in the context of their own uniquely assembled display. Chandler describes the typical practice of authoring as a kind of **bricolage** (i.e. a patchwork of items put together from whatever is available), whereby creativity and identity are expressed through the ways in which collected items are recombined and through hypertext links rather than through the construction of original text and images. He suggests that this re-use of existing materials undermines romantic notions of creativity which focus on individual originality. In many ways, Chandler is arguing, the semiotics of homepages suggest an emerging renegotiation and transformation of oppositions such as distance/ intimacy, private/public and self/other.

Eckert (in Chapter 3) also uses the concept of bricolage.

6.6 Conclusion

In this chapter I have explored the ways in which a number of genres provide opportunities for the expression and construction of the self. Texts do not, however, just reflect or bring into being certain attributes of the writer. Identity is also established through interactions with readers, emerging dialogically through the give and take of a chain of responses (most typically within letters). Writers can also be assigned new kinds of identity, in relation to the wider audiences involved when diaries, letters and graffiti are transformed into more publicly valued genres. Through their appropriation into more prestigious genres, or particular literary trends, texts can take on a life of their own beyond their original author's own life or original intentions.

The dialogic nature of texts is reflected within their different levels of verbal structure: the direct references to 'you' in Pax's weblog, the elliptical nature of letters within an ongoing correspondence, the addressing of diaries to the self or an imaginary friend, graffiti 'dialogues' and the intertextual references on an internet homepage. These dialogic features are linked with other creative uses of language (often associated with more literary texts) which are found in these everyday genres: decorative calligraphy, word play, imagery, irony, parody and rhetorical devices such as three-part lists. These features, as Jolly suggests, open up the potential for artfulness in ordinary communicative practices. At the level of the text, language provides a creative poetic resource to evoke thoughts, feelings and experience in striking ways. In addition, the act of writing itself reworks and re-presents personal experience and personal identity, not only to others, but also, through this dialogical lens, to the self.

These texts are all in some ways deeply personal, but they articulate the relationship between the private and the public in different ways. Diaries and personal correspondence are ostensibly private, but are sometimes readdressed and reproduced in more public genres. Graffiti and the web are ostensibly public, but offer particular opportunities for privacy and anonymity. Through recontextualisation (e.g. diaries and letters becoming part of a literature tradition), hybridisation (e.g. weblogs) and intertextuality (e.g. references and responsivity across letters, the bricolage construction of homepages), texts combine and are transformed into other kinds of texts, with new workings of the private/public relationship, new values and new possibilities for authorial identities.

READING A: Sincerely yours: everyday letters and the art of written relationship

Margaretta Jolly

> Dear Laughing Motorbyke,
>
> I hope you are having no trouble acquiring your petrel ration, because should you have to garage your laugh, you would hardly be the same person, at least to me.
>
> (Letter from Agnes Helme to her welding teacher Valentine Pearson – later Valentine Morche – in 1942, Jolly, 1997, p. 77)
>
> Letters for us stand for love, longing, light-heartedness and lyricism. Letters evoke passion, tenderness, amusement, sadness, rejoicing, surprise. And none of this possible without the Army Post Office.
>
> (Letter from Diana Hopkinson to her husband stationed in North Africa in 1941, Blythe, 1993, p. 17)

We delve into writing to charm and surprise absent friends. To lovers and families we may write more urgently to defy absence. Humbly dependent upon the post office for their audience, letters are probably the most common form of creative writing and historically the form least subject to monopoly by a particular sex or class (Altman, 1995, p. 101). But we still have few words to describe or understand the literary and cultural value of letters.

It is not that literary criticism has been silent about letter-writing. Classical Greek theorists discussed it as a branch of rhetoric, Renaissance scholars perfected the *ars epistolandi* and the seventeenth and eighteenth-century aristocracy devoted themselves to handbooks on the art. Recent years have seen a more theoretically informed epistolary criticism apply the insights of structuralism, feminism, dialogic theory and more, while of course, the tradition of popular guides to letter writing continues, now with the addition of email etiquette (Gilroy and Verhoeven, 2000). Yet critics even today have remained remarkably unadventurous in thinking beyond the conventionally 'literary' letters of public figures.

There are some good reasons for the scholarly hesitancy towards perceiving everyday letters as more than simply historical resources. How *do* we assess private, ephemeral genres not written for a public audience, especially those that involve some kind of interaction with others? And perhaps more fundamentally, how should we understand practical communication as an art form? Letters, provoked in the first instance by the wish to communicate across distance, flaunt the functionality of writing in a way that proves indigestible for much aesthetic theory. At the same time their subtle manoeuvring of relationships has been difficult for purely technical theories of literacy to appreciate.

In this article I will suggest that the ambiguity of the letter as both communication and creation is just what is aesthetically distinctive about the form, as correspondents, inspired by their small and particular audience, experiment with educating, persuading or informing each other. Moreover, I want to propose that letters are a test case for thinking about the creativity in everyday communication and indeed the way that *all* creative acts are relational, whether in the local contexts of friendship or enmity or the more general contexts of class and culture. The epistle is 'not a genre, but all genres, literature itself' Jacques Derrida declares (Derrida, 1980, p. 48). A simple indication of the writing relationship is the letter's address and closure, at once the most compact indication of the social context of the letter and yet also the place where invariably there is some reference to writing itself, such as apologising for not having replied sooner or awaiting a reply. This is why Louise Horowitz describes the form as paradoxically 'the ideal vehicle for communication of the passions allowing for the greatest *vraisemblance* [realism] (with "I" and "you" linked directly)' and also 'the intense consciousness of writing' (Horowitz, 1981, p. 6).

Far from being the passive vehicle of information, letters construct relationships and identities. On one level this is common sense: you adopt a polite tone when writing to the bank manager, a respectful one to your granny, a self-righteous vengefulness to your ex-lover. Less obvious is the persona you discover when maintaining a long-term correspondence without meeting in person, although lately people's experiences with email relationships have widely publicised this aspect of letter-writing. It is not necessary to say that letters are deliberate lies, although we might want to be suspicious of the assumption that they are the spontaneous outpourings of the true self. Rather, we need to see a subtle interchange between fantasy, writing and relationship. Janet Maybin's study of correspondences with prisoners on death row, for example, shows that letter-writing allows prisoners to create life-sustaining virtual families but also to develop a sense of inner self and self-esteem. Equally, their penfriends find altruistic intentions blown away in engrossing relationships that help them through traumas of their own (Maybin, 2000). Another example is Niko Besnier's analysis of the profuse correspondences of Nukulaelae migrants (living in other parts of the Tuvalu Islands such as Funaafuti). Their effusive news, advice, greeting, transaction, are cathartic because they are such concentrated communicative events, dependent upon limited delivery service, physical parting and longing, and the taboos that surround the expression of emotion in more quotidian exchange (Besnier, 1993). Again, Toby Ditz shows us that even the letters of American merchants in the eighteenth century were filled with a theatrical kind of 'honest' speaking that drew on and formed a 'discourse of occupational identity' (Ditz, 1999, p. 60).

Indeed, the idea that one would or should write intimate or informal letters itself only really developed in Europe in the seventeenth century as the result of new ideals of civilised conversation in the Enlightenment, while it was the emergence of a bourgeois culture of private life and romantic individuality that prompted its spread in the era of early industrial capitalism. In the nineteenth century the development of mass education and the advent of the penny post as well as a national postal system provided the conditions for letter writing as a working- as well as middle-class practice, entwined, of course, with the growth of migration and travel (Chartier, 1995). Today, email is democratising the notion of written relationship but is still restricted not only in terms of who has access to computers but in the conventions of memo-writing and office flirtation that dominate its style (Yates, 2000).

It is difficult, moreover, to separate the history of letter writing from the history of whose letters have survived, whether deliberately saved, published or accidentally preserved. Unsurprisingly, it has been the upper classes and professional writers whose letters have historically received most attention, a pattern still sustained by the biography industry. Nevertheless, as new forms of social and cultural history (especially women's and autobiography studies) have spot-lit the private and the marginal, increasing appreciation of everyday letters has been shown by archivists, editors and publishers – from correspondences between mothers and daughters (Payne, 1984), to the protests of American workers during the Depression (Markowitz and Rosner, 1987).

An adequate analysis of letters thus brings together many disciplinary perspectives, including historical, literary, psychological and sociological, while keeping one eye on how the letter got written, saved or reproduced in the first place. Let me demonstrate how this works with some ordinary people's letters from the Second World War.

Identities in conflict: correspondences from the Second World War

An airman's last letter

During the Second World War, the post was an omnipresent and highly emotional event. In Britain, 20 million letters and postcards were posted and delivered on average per day (Hay, 1946, p. 19). Christmas 1940, in the middle of the Blitz, saw 291 million letters sent, 9.5 million parcels, and 280 thousand greeting telegrams (Halstead, 1944, p. 36). The unprecedented geographical upheaval of the war, not just through the draft, but evacuation, war work, imprisonment and migration, catapulted ordinary people into writing. Indeed the wartime state and media recognised the power of letters by encouraging women to write to servicemen to keep up morale, and by publishing them as propaganda.

One such case was the last letter from an airman to his mother, published in *The Times* on 18 June 1940. A stock exchange clerk and only son of a widow, Vivian Rosewarne wrote the following before he was shot down on

Figure 1   Second World War poster
(Litoff and Smith, 1991, p. 120)

Figure 2   Writing from the trenches
(Tapert, 1984)

31 May [a complete version of the letter is included at the end of this reading]:

> Dearest Mother,
>
> Though I feel no premonition at all, events are moving rapidly and I have instructed that this letter be forwarded to you should I fail to return from one of the raids which we shall shortly be called upon to undertake. [...] I have always admired your amazing courage in the face of continual setbacks; in the way you have given me as good an education and background as anyone in the country; and always kept up appearances without ever losing faith in the future. My death would not mean that your struggle has been in vain. Far from it. It means that your sacrifice is as great as mine. Those who serve England must expect nothing from her; we debase ourselves if we regard our country as merely a place in which to eat and sleep.
>
> ('The Fight with Evil: "My Earthly Mission Is Fulfilled" ', 1940)

Drama inheres not just in its writer's anticipation of death but in the ironic survival of the letter itself. As personal communications that are also physical objects (especially when handwritten), all letters have the capacity to embody their sender in a uniquely literal, even fetishistic fashion. However, in the event of a letter received after the writer's death, this paradoxical combination of absence and presence hovers at tragic breaking point, since now absence is much more permanent than the letter-form can admit. The artistic paradigm that writing will transcend the writer is painfully literal here, and powerful for that reason.

Yet there is more we can say about the construction of this letter than its mediation between the living and the dead. Rosewarne's repeated call on his mother to accept and take pride in his death as sacrifice forms his core message. To do this, he has to justify not only his death but, far more difficult, her loss. He thus aligns her sacrifice with his, rhetorically drawing her into battle too as she who trained the warrior. 'Your sacrifice is as great as mine,' he argues, ingenuously, continuing (see full version in Appendix), 'Yet there is more work for you to do' as representative of the home front, and finally: 'You must not grieve for me, for if you really believe in religion and all that it entails that would be hypocrisy.' Here, he swells out of his immediate address to a euphoric vision of war as the essence of what it means to be human:

> Those who just eat and sleep, prosper and procreate, are no better than animals if all their lives they are at peace.

While he may believe this, the real issue is his unification of the interests of mothers and nations. The young officer's station commander was quoted as saying:

> This letter was perhaps the most amazing one I have ever read; simple and direct in its wording but splendid and uplifting in its outlook. [...] It was inevitable that I should read it – in fact he must have intended this, for it was left open in order that I might be certain that no prohibited information was disclosed.

> I sent the letter to the bereaved mother, and asked her whether I might publish it anonymously, as I feel its contents may bring comfort to other mothers, and that every one in our country may feel proud to read of the sentiments which support 'an average airman' in the execution of his present arduous duties. I have received the mother's permission, and I hope this letter may be read by the greatest possible number of our countrymen at home and abroad.

> ('The Fight with Evil: "My Earthly Mission Is Fulfilled" ', *The Times*, 1940)

While few wrote as deliberately as this, it is striking that most letters home from the front were also careful to avoid details of fear, killing, bad behaviour or anything that would compromise a patriotic, or indeed 'manly' image. This was not only the effect of military censorship, although clearly this was important. Just as much, it reflected the keeping up of morale and the need to preserve a sense of identity in new, strange contexts. However, many letters from men home show the heroic discourse of military identity wearing thin, in which a less formulated domestic masculinity slips through. Ronald Blythe's *Private Words: Letters and Diaries from the Second World War* contains several eloquent examples, from Private Ted Seckle's bewildered letters to a wife who had obviously left him and won't reply, to Louis Rose's longingly homesick confessions of missing his children (Blythe, 1993). In many ways, war letters expose the burden of the conventional gendered division of labour that sends men to war and keeps women disempoweringly 'protected'. In the next example, however, we see that the classic war correspondence between a waiting woman and a travelling man is displaced, in a letter from an American surgical nurse writing home from the concentration camp at Dachau.

Writing home the Holocaust

Allack, Germany, June 4, 1945

Dearest Family

I'm on night duty with a hundred corpse-like patients, wrecks of humanity [...] macerated skin drawn over their bones, eyes sunken in wide sockets, hair shaved off. Mostly Jewish, these tortured souls hardly resemble humans. Their bodies are riddled with diseases. Many have tuberculosis, typhus, enterocolitis, (constant diarrhoea) and huge bed sores.

Many cough all night long, as their lungs are in such terrible condition. They break out in great beads of perspiration. Then there is the room of those who are incontinent and irrational. It sounds like the construction crew for the Tower of Babel [...] Poles, Czechs, Russians, Slavs, Bulgarians, Dutch, Hungarians, Germans. What makes it so difficult is that I understand only a few words. Their gratitude tears at my heart when I do something to make them more comfortable or give them a little food or smile at them [...]

The odor from the lack of sanitation over the years makes the whole place smell like rotten, rotten sewage. We wear masks constantly although they don't keep out the stench. There are commodes in the middle of the room. Patients wear just pajama shirts as they can't get the bottoms down fast enough to use the commodes. God, where are you? Making rounds by flashlight is an eerie sensation. I'll hear calloused footsteps shuffling behind me and turn in time to see four semi-nude skeletons gliding toward the commodes. God, where were you?
You have to gently shake some of the patients to see if they are still alive. Their breathing is so shallow, pulse debatable. Many die in their sleep. I carry their bodies back to a storage room, they are very light, just the weight of their demineralized bones. Each time, I breathe a wee prayer for them. God, are you there?

[...] Our men sprayed the camp area to kill the insects that carried many of the diseases. We were told the SS guards who controlled the camp used to bring a small pan of food into the ward, and throw it on the floor. When the stronger patients scrambled for it, like starving beasts, they were lashed with a long whip. It's a corner of hell. Too shocked and tired to write anymore.

(Love, June 1994, pp. 225–6)

As with Rosewarne's letter, this is a strikingly rhetorical piece of writing, although June Wandrey's turn to older epistolary techniques of oratory and religious imagery is very differently motivated in attempting to convey the horror of Dachau. On one level this is an intensely personal description of her patients' suffering and a confession of inadequacy in being able to help or even understand, in which different languages and darkness become symbolic of a drastic separation of worlds. But alongside this she forces her readers to join her in another, more general and fundamental appeal to God. The repeated and increasingly direct demand for God's presence (the triple form of the question itself a classic trope), suggests there are two letters being written here, but in the more important address, a reply seems appallingly absent. In this way, although she presents herself as anything but detached from the scene around her, the letter is implicated in the failure of care that has led to this 'corner of hell'. Wandrey's mix of formal and informal registers suggests just how much she feels a duty to realise the experience for those ignorant or protected from it, even using the second person when describing having to shake the patients to see if they are alive. But for the same reason, the letter inevitably resounds against the debate over the representation and representability of the Holocaust. Some things are just too hard to write, even in a private letter.

It is apt, at this point, to consider the different ways that Rosewarne and Wandrey's letters were published. As we have seen, Rosewarne's letter received a great deal of circulation just after it was written, moving because it seems to evidence the greatest personal commitment to the 'just war'. However it was precisely its ordinary, private status that made the letter so immediately useful to the state, especially in what was being presented as 'the people's war', free from the imperialist propaganda of the First World War (Jolly, 1999). Consider that the *Times* reprinted the letter as a leaflet; *Times* readers wrote in suggesting it be read to boys in schools; broadcast; left on Church pews. The letter was displayed at the fund-raising 'Wings for Victory' rallies and Frank Salisbury painted the airman's posthumous portrait. Lord Wakefield wished he were not too old to make a similar sacrifice, praising the airman's mother as the letter's indirect author, in having 'given to the world a message of such rare power and beauty'. Eleanor Rathbone argued the sacrifice was not all in vain, and the editor of *The New World*, D.H. Barber, even renounced his pacifism on the strength of reading the letter. He attributes this to the letter's literary power: 'I ... cannot hold out any longer in face of the unstudied eloquence of your dead and anonymous contributor'.

In interpreting letters, we need therefore to think about how they can be 'readdressed' to a different public and what happens to their meaning when they are. Wandrey's letter, we may not be surprised to learn, was only published in 1989, as part of her memoir *Bedpan Commando: The Story of a Combat Nurse During World War II* (Wandrey, 1989). Full details of the Holocaust were not generally wanted decades after the war, even on the Allies' side. At the same time, the current market for Holocaust testimony is not straightforward either, reflecting difficult combinations of voyeurism and sympathy by those who had no part in the experience, and a culture of confession, trauma and scandal that permeates the publication of life writing as a whole. Additionally, as the inclusion of Wandrey's letter in Judy Barrett Litoff and David C. Smith's 1994 anthology *We're in This War, Too: World War II Letters from American Women in Uniform* (Litoff and Smith, 1994, pp. 204-6) implies, such publications reflect the rise of interest in women's lives and achievements. In many ways, as with the stories of Holocaust survivors, this has been a spur to uncovering previously hidden or undervalued histories. However, these agendas too can lose sight of the role of individual fantasies, literary constructions and mixed feelings that ultimately drive many personal letters and indeed, many memoirs (Jolly, 2004). Wandrey's letter could easily be subsumed in a heroic narrative of women at the front that, for example, underplays the importance of letters from civilian women at home. My final example turns to some of these to consider the poetry of a still more everyday kind of letter writing.

The laughing letters of women welders

In contrast to those of Vivian Rosewarne and June Wandrey, the correspondence of Agnes Helme and Valentine Morche did not have to mediate between home and front and so escaped some of the immediate pressures of self-shaping that this involved. Helme initially wrote to her old welding teacher Morche simply to thank her, having been sent to Sheffield to train with her when called up for welding work in 1942. But Morche's amusing replies provoked what became a lifelong correspondence, in which Helme wrote vividly about her experiences of working in a 'man's world', and most of all, about her romantic escapades. In contrast to Rosewarne's appeal to nationalist stabilities and Wandrey's self-conscious testifying, these unassuming letters between a working class trainee and a middle-class teacher reveal a story of new sexual and class identities emerging in the social shake-up of the war.

'My Dear Instigator of Laughs', Helme begins one letter in a parody of wartime officialese, having 'laughed until [she] cried' at the latest 'installment' of Morche's escapades with her refugee boyfriend. In another, she regales Morche with the tale of a journey to Scotland to visit her husband who was posted there. Due to travel problems, she ends up staying in a hotel on the way and 'what looked like a catastrophe ... really materialized into a beautiful adventure.' Asleep on the hotel settee, she is awoken 'with a very soft deep voice saying "Blondie – Blondie" '.

> I sat up quickly and found myself looking rather puzzled at the handsomest face, and the bluest eyes, I have ever seen.

(Jolly, 1997, p. 65)

The prince-like apparition turns out to be a Canadian soldier, who invites her to make up a party of four with him and another couple for the evening. She accepts, but it is perhaps significant that she decides to write at this point, as if to create her 'adventure' by invoking and writing to her projected conspirator. As she records that the Canadian, Eddie, admires how she scribbles away at her letter, the writing itself becomes part of the scenario she is describing; such that she flirts by writing as well as writing about flirting, synchronising narrative and event. This draws Morche too into the sexual tease as:

> Eddie has just come downstairs and pulled a wry face when he saw me still writing, he said, "Golly, it sure must be some letter, & some person to whom you are writing," I said, "How right you are – to both of them." ... if you could only hear the cracks he is making at this letter ... he just said if my pen was a horse he would back it, he has never seen a pen fly like mine does.

(Jolly, 1997, p. 66)

Displaying the hallmarks of epistolarity in exaggerating the letter's mediating and confidential qualities, Helme plays virtual relationships of both paper and flesh off against each other to construct a shared 'plot' between herself and her esteemed confidante.

Thus apparently simple writing pacts are transformed by a language of romance, jokes, puns, dialect, and ironic tale, displaying what Patricia Spacks has analysed as characteristic of the creative dimension of gossip: an 'aesthetic of self-containment, concentration on surface, valorising of story' (Spacks, 1986, p. 16). At the same time, the emphasis on pleasure and naughtiness is always double-edged, both denying and acknowledging the sexual struggles that women wage in peacetime as much as in war. In this sense, this forms an interesting parallel to the popular culture of rumour, joke and swearing that Paul Fussell has analysed in the world of male wartime service (Fussell, 1989, p. 35). For Fussell, these forms involve imaginative wit and a deep psychological need to make sense of the demeaning rules of much of military life as well as more obvious fears for survival. Civilian women like these letter-writers were neither restricted to camp-life nor, in their case, in danger of their lives. Yet the structures of the letters also reflect underlying controlling forces. Courtship, pregnancy, abortion, sexual harassment, sexual desire as well as the challenges of factory work 'among the men' all appear as fodder for what is ambiguously both entertainment and confession. In particular, Helme's later references to an unwanted pregnancy, constant ill health and frustrations at not being able to get on with welding, interweave her bubbly anecdotes with darker allusions to gin, 'little black pills' and 'little bits o' things' that she doesn't want to 'go any further'.

It is difficult to say whether Helme wrote with such style because she was relieved to find a confidante for taboo subjects, or whether she confided precisely because she enjoyed writing so much. But maybe this is a false opposition. Rather, the relationship that she struck with Morche, one in which she wished to impress and entertain, produced a particular version of self that teeters on bravado but is essentially comic and powerful.

For these women, writing was clearly a pleasure in itself. As Helme put it:

> I feel I could sit & write & write & better write, just as I loved to stand and talk to you, but although I have not told you all I should have liked, I really must make my Allenbury's Food, (builds bonny babies) and go to bed it is very very late.

(Jolly, 1997, p. 78)

Like 'standing and talking', letters for Helme are like conversation. But they are not simply transcriptions or extensions of speech. Helme is also exploring the distinctive pleasure of corresponding, which is generated as much by internal momentum – 'write & write & better write' – as by the wish to 'tell all'.

Conclusion

In this brief foray into some letters never intended for publication I have aimed to show some of the ways we can appreciate the art of everyday correspondence. In thinking about its potential to express and construct identities while mediating relationships, we see literacy as a social practice and, as the protean, ephemeral nature of letters reminds us, a historical one too. Our writing selves are particular to our projected reader, but also relative to time, place and the status of writing in our culture. Equally, letters help us to move beyond traditional literary models of the isolated genius, suggesting that all art finds its origin and end in relationships, however distant. As the literary form frankest about the wish to communicate, letters open up the mysteries of creative writing itself.

References

ALTMAN, J.G. (1995) 'Women's letters in the public sphere', in E. GOLDSMITH and D. GOODMAN (eds) *Going Public: Women and Publishing in Early Modern France*, Ithaca, NY, Cornell University Press.

BARTON, D. and HALL, N. (2000) *Letter Writing as a Social Practice*, Amsterdam, Philadelphia, John Benjamins.

BESNIER, N. (1993) 'Literacy and feelings: the encoding of affect in Nukulaelae letters', in B. STREET (ed.) *Cross-cultural approaches to literacy*, Cambridge Studies in Oral and Literate Culture, Cambridge, Cambridge University Press.

BLYTHE, R. (1993) *Private Words: Letters and Diaries from the Second World War*, London, Penguin, 2nd edn.

CHARTIER, R. (ed.) (1995) *Correspondence: The Uses of Letters from the Twelfth to the Nineteeth Centuries*, Cambridge, Polity.

DERRIDA, J. (1980) *The Post Card: from Socrates to Freud and Beyond*, trans. A. BASS, Chicago, University of Chicago Press.

DITZ, T. (1999) 'Formative ventures: eighteenth-century commercial letters and the articulation of experience', in R. EARLE (ed.) *Epistolary Selves: Letters and Letter-Writers, 1600–1945*, Aldershot, Ashgate.

'The Fight with Evil: "my earthly mission is fulfilled"', *The Times*, 18 June, 1940, p. 7.

FUSSELL, P. (1989) *Wartime: Understanding and Behavior in the Second World War*, New York, Oxford University Press.

GILROY, A. and VERHOEVEN, W.M. (2000) *Epistolary Histories: Letters, Fiction, Culture*, Charlottesville, University Press of Virginia.

HALSTEAD, I. (1944) *Post Haste: The Story of the Post Office in Peace and War*, London, Drummond.

HAY, I. (1946) *The Post Office Went to War*, London, HMSO.

HOROWITZ, L.K. (1981) 'The Correspondence of Madame de Sevigne: letters or belles letters?', *French Forum*, **6**, pp. 13–27.

JOLLY, M. (ed.) (1997) *Dear Laughing Motorbyke: Letters from Women Welders in the Second World War*, London, Scarlet Press.

JOLLY, M. (1999) 'Between Ourselves: letters as propaganda', in B. TAITHE and T. THORNTON (eds) *Propaganda: Political Rhetoric and Identity 1300–2000*, Phoenix Mill, Gloucs, UK, Sutton Publishing.

JOLLY, M. (2004) 'Myths of university: remembering the Second World War through letters and their editing', in A. VERNON (ed.) *Arms and the Self*, Kent, Ohio, Kent State University Press.

LITOFF, J.B. and SMITH, D.C. (eds) (1991) *Since You Went Away*, University of Kansas Press.

LITOFF, J.B. and SMITH, D.C. (eds) (1994) *We're in this War, Too: World War II letters from American Women in Uniform*, New York, Oxford University Press.

MARKOWITZ, G. and ROSNER, D. (eds) (1987) *'Slaves of the Depression': Workers' Letters about Life on the Job*, Ithaca, NY, Cornell University Press.

MAYBIN, J. (2000) 'Death Row Penfriends: some effects of letter writing on identity and relationships', in D. BARTON and N. HALL (eds) *Letter Writing as a Social Practice*, Amersterdam, Philadelphia., John Benjamins.

PAYNE, K. (ed.) (1984) *Between Ourselves: Letters between Mothers and Daughters 1750–1982*, London, Picador.

SPACKS, P.M. (1986, 2nd edn.) *Gossip*, Chicago, The University of Chicago Press.

TAPERT, A. (1984) *Despatches from the Heart*, London, Hamish Hamilton.

WANDREY, J. (1989) *Bedpan Commando: The Story of a Combat Nurse during World War II*, Elmore, OH, Elmore.

YATES, S. (2000) 'Computer-Mediated Communication: the future of the letter', in D. BARTON and N. HALL (eds) *Letter Writing as a Social Practice*, Amsterdam, Philadelphia, John Benjamins.

Appendix

Dearest Mother,

Though I feel no premonition at all, events are moving rapidly and I have instructed that this letter be forwarded to you should I fail to return from one of the raids which we shall shortly be called upon to undertake. You must hope on for a month, but at the end of that time you must accept the fact that I have handed my task over to the extremely capable hands of my comrades of the Royal Air Force, as so many splendid fellows have already done.

First, it will comfort you to know that my role in this war has been of the greatest importance. Our patrols far out over the North Sea have helped to keep the trades routes clear for convoys and supply ships, and on one occasion our information was instrumental in saving the lives of the men in a crippled lighthouse relief ship. Though it will be difficult for you, you will disappoint me if you do not at least try to accept the facts dispassionately, for I shall have done my duty to the utmost of my ability. No man can do more, and no one calling himself a man could do less. I have always admired your amazing courage in the face of continual setbacks; in the way you have given me as good an education and background as anyone in the country; and always kept up appearances without ever losing faith in the future. My death would not mean that your struggle has been in vain. Far from it. It means that your sacrifice is as great as mine. Those who serve England must expect nothing from her; we debase ourselves if we regard our country as merely a place in which to eat and sleep.

History resounds with illustrious names who have given all, yet their sacrifice has resulted in the British Empire, where there is a measure of peace, justice and freedom for all, and where a higher standard of civilization has evolved, and is still evolving, than anywhere else. But this is not only concerning our own land. Today we are faced with the greatest organized challenge to Christianity and civilization that the world has ever seen, and I count myself lucky and honoured to be the right age and fully trained to throw my full weight into the scale. For this I have to thank you. Yet there is more work for you to do. The home front will still have to stand united for years after the war is won. For all that can be said against it, I still maintain that this war is a very good thing; every individual is having the chance to give and dare all for his principle like the martyrs of old.

However long the time may be, one thing can never be altered – I shall have lived and died an Englishman. Nothing else matters one jot, nor can anything ever change it.

You must not grieve for me, for if you really believe in religion and all that it entails that would be hypocrisy. I have no fear of death; only a queer elation ... I would have it no other way. The universe is so vast and so ageless that the life of one man can only be justified by the measure of his sacrifice. We are sent into this world to acquire a personality and a character to take with us that can never be taken from us. Those who just eat and sleep, prosper and procreate, are no better than animals if all their lives they are at peace.

I firmly and absolutely believe that evil things are sent into the world to try us, they are sent deliberately by our Creator to test our metal because He knows what is good for us. The Bible is full of cases where the easy way out has been discarded for moral principles.

I count myself fortunate in that I have seen the whole country and known men of every calling. But with the final test of war I consider my character fully developed. Thus at my early age my earthly mission is already fulfilled and I am prepared to die with just one regret, and only one – that I could devote myself to making your declining years more happy by being with you; but you will live in peace and freedom and I shall have directly contributed to that, so here again my life will not have been in vain.

Your loving Son
Vivian

(Blythe, 1991, pp. 306–8)

Source: commissioned for this volume.

READING B: The spray-can is mightier than the sword: graffiti writing and the construction of masculine identity

Nancy Macdonald

Many of us probably do not go a day without seeing some form of street or subcultural graffiti. This is the type of graffiti that is generally written in spraypaint or marker pen, and positioned on the trains, walls and other public surfaces of our cities. While often highly visible, however, the meaning and significance of street graffiti tends to be private. Like urban wallpaper, it sits quietly in the background of our everyday lives – recognised, but rarely understood.

In this reading, I shall take a closer look at this form of graffiti and some of the reasons why it is written. As I found from my ethnographic research in London and New York, most illegal graffiti writers are young, in their teens/ early twenties, and for the most part, male. These young men explained to me the importance of graffiti for them and introduced me to a subcultural world with its own rules, rewards and social hierarchy. In this reading I shall explore the creative interplay between graffiti writing, youthful masculinity and the creation of identity. Some readers may be aware of the creative potential of graffiti as an 'art-form', but there is a much deeper level of creativity at play here in the multitude of ways in which young men use their graffiti as a resource to build their masculine identities.

Using graffiti to claim fame and 'make a name'

At its most basic level, graffiti is written to claim fame, respect and recognition, or as graffiti writers generally term it, to 'make a name'. There are two main graffiti forms that writers use, which both involve variations of the writer's adopted name: a simple and prolific inscription of the word, written rather like a signature – tagging – and a larger, more elaborate and stylistic rendering of this – piecing (see Colour Figure 4).

Taggers or 'bombers', as they are often known, are judged and respected for the 'quantity' of tags they have 'up'. The coverage of their work is also taken into account. To really taste rewards, a writer's tag should be seen in many different regions of the city or underground/subway system. Writers who manage this are labelled 'up' or 'all city', and may in this case, try to secure the coveted tile of 'King'. This is a prestigious award informally attributed to the writer that is considered to be 'all city' or, the most 'up' in a certain city or train line. Some writers will also try to make their own claim on this title either verbally, or visually by painting the symbol of a crown on top of their name.

While taggers use coverage and quantity as their tools to success, piecers use style. To carry good style, or produce work that 'burns', writers must

Figure 1   A Tag (Macdonald, 2001, p. 66)

Figure 2   Using a Crown to Claim the Title 'King'
(Macdonald, 2001, p. 79)

show proficient detailing techniques, competent letter formation and connections, and lastly, if the writer can manage it, an innovative lettering style. In the past, writers would push themselves to invent new styles, claiming these as their own through the use of a copyright symbol. Today the scope for innovation has declined and whilst originality is valued, it is not demanded. As the writer below testifies, a graffiti writer's personal style or imprint will usually lend graffiti's now established letter forms a unique flavour of their own:

> You build up a style, it's like your signature, a part of you, it's you saying something about yourself and putting it somewhere and other people see it and recognize it and click. (Prime)

What graffiti writers are doing here is competing for reputation and respect. They work hard to outdo each other, often moving through a phase of tagging before progressing onto piecing as a demonstration of their skill. They refer to their progress or journey through this subculture as a 'career'. As they climb to the higher levels of the subculture's hierarchy, and develop a reputation for themselves, the pace and energy of their activities often slows. The competitive demands made upon them begin to lessen, and they are more at liberty to live off the fame and reputation they have managed to develop. This 'retirement', as it is seen, generally comes at a time in life (late teens, early twenties) where new responsibilities and demands can kick in. These young men either no longer have the time to dedicate to their graffiti careers, or they start to receive respect and recognition in other parts of their life such as work. Until this time, however, the activities of a new or young graffiti hopeful are frenetic. As at the bottom rung of any career ladder, competition is fierce. There are a multitude of other hopefuls clamouring for position, and competing to reach the heady heights of their heroes. Graffiti at this stage requires complete focus and dedication.

Illegality, danger and the role of the police

It is not just their peers who graffiti writers are competing with when they write graffiti. Graffiti is illegal, and writers work hard to outwit the police and transport authorities. This illegality creates the risks and danger which are an intrinsic part of the 'buzz' of graffiti writing.

> If it was legal, there'd be no threat, graffiti would be a waste of time. I do graffiti for the excitement, it's like I get a big adrenalin rush out there. (Col)

A writer's artistic quest is also an important test of their bravery and resolve. As this writer explains it:

> It comes down to keeping grace under pressure. You know, you have trains burrowing down on you, cops chasing you, you have different gangs in there, you don't know what's going to happen and when you

finish and you come up . . . you're walking through some ghetto, which makes you feel kind of manly anyway, and you're thinking, 'Yeah I did it'. So there's a certain sense to the illegality. (Freedom)

Masculine validation does not just come from the physical or judicial risks. A significant feature of this subculture is the antagonistic relationship writers share with their enemy, the transport police. A graffiti writer evading the penetrating beam of police headlights and battling the authorities for control of the transport system, swiftly transforms himself from a graffiti writer into a war hero. Illegality and the militaristic relationship this has inspired between writers and the police works to pump a massive measure of added machismo into writers' actions.

The beauty of this subculture is it is a forum where everyone can achieve. Writers may be cunning rather than fast, brave rather than strong, and dedicated rather than talented. Constraints and barriers which might prevent a young man from achieving in the real world are removed. Writers choose a new name, and become a new person. In effect, they start a parallel life; one in which they have more control over the person they will become. Leaving behind the fixed and ascribed characteristics of their real-life personas, writers are judged within this subcultural world on their actions and achievements under their new name. As such, they can transcend the limits of race and class, and become what might seem impossible elsewhere – an underground celebrity, a masculine icon, or a respected war hero. Who you are in the 'real world' is largely irrelevant to who you can become in graffiti world, with one important exception. I found that few young women were accepted into this world, and those who were tended to be pushed to the sidelines by men who use it as a form of masculine 'safe house'.

Graffiti and the construction of identity

> What youths think about themselves, their environment and, maybe most importantly, what they want to be, is reflected in their tags, throw-ups, pieces, messages etc. They create identities for themselves. (Prime)

> (*Graphotism*, issue 3)

What's in a name?

The tag name a writer chooses is important as this can help them stand out in a crowd. As one of my informants, called Drax, pointed out:

> There's a lot of names like Sim, Sem, Cap, Kip, Cop, Ken, Cess, which are just quite irrelevant really, you have to work really hard to get those names noticed. (Drax)

Conversely, a 'good name' carries connotations and, as the writer below indicates, a great deal more impact:

> You just had to have a good name, good names usually made it. A lot of guys had bad names, it just didn't click. Like, Butch is a good name, wow Butch! (Dondi)

The name seems to work when it conjures up some form of desirable image:

> An example of a good name is 'ARGUE'. It looks fly [good] when written, sounds cool when spoken and conveys a combative attitude. On the other hand, 'ENEMA' (actual name) looks, sounds and conveys a shitty attitude. (Mark Surface)

> (*On The Go*)

If a name conveys an attitude, then it plays a very important role in the process of constructing an identity. Effectively, it stands 'as a communication to the world about how one is feeling about oneself and what it is about oneself one would like to advertise' (Feiner and Klein, 1982, p. 49). Consequently, writers need to think carefully about what they want to say about themselves. Acrid talks me through his intentions:

Nancy: So why did you choose your name?

Acrid: Do you know what Acrid means?

Nancy: Acrid, it's bitter.

Acrid: Yeah, that's me.

Nancy: How did you get that name?

Acrid: I liked the letters and I liked the meaning ... I just thought what word would suit me. (Acrid)

Drax explores this link between a writer's name and his search for identity below and explains the image he strove to create through his own choice:

Nancy: So the tag name's important, you choose that with care?

Drax: Yeah it is important, but there's some people who change their name every week because of problems with the police or they don't like the letters or they can't seem to find the right identity with it or whatever. . . . With mine, I was thinking, 'Yeah, yeah, this graffiti, I like it, I must get a tag', and I wanted something that sounded quite dynamic, you know, not one of those smooth names, Romeo or something, right. I suppose an X has got an element of that in it, one of those harsh sounding names. And then there's this Bond film, 'Moonraker', and there's a guy in it whose name's 'Drax', 'Drax Industries'. It just had this taking over the world kind of feel about it, this mad guy that was trying to take over everything.

The images writers choose to project through their choice of name are revealing. Most communicate notions of strength, power and control – 'Butch' is macho, strong and forceful. 'Acrid' denotes this strength through its associations with a bitter taste, the opposite to sweet; a shocking or disturbing experience. Likewise, 'Argue', as the writer explained, conveys this feeling through its combative undertones. Although 'Drax' as an isolated word has little meaning, the letter 'x', the sound of the word and its intertextual connotations impart a sense of power and dominance, a 'taking-over-the world kind of feel'.

Style as a statement

Given that the physical body is not a prominent feature in this subculture, what one wears and how one looks is not of great concern. Rather than clothe themselves, writers use their lettering styles to clothe their names: Often, the style is assertive:

> I don't believe it's possible for the aggressive vibes of graffiti not to show in any piece of art work produced by a writer. (Shock One)

> (*Graphotism*, issue 2)

Most of graffiti's lettering styles have a dynamic or robust appearance, giving writers' work a certain aggressive quality. 'Wildstyle' is probably the most provocative (see Colour Figure 5).

This script wraps the writer's name in a flurry of sharp peaks created by its angular, interlocking letters. From these, arrows project rather like guns or weapons that have been embedded to protect the name. Overall, the piece looks a bit like a powerful machine or an armoured tank, conveying a sense of confrontation and unstoppable motion. Buried in its imagery, the name/the self takes on these connotations. Take a look at Skore's style of work featured in Colour Figure 6.

In the quote below, Skore comments on the type of image his work appears to convey, an image which he suggests is unlike who he 'really is':

> I feel my graffiti has a very sharp steel feel to it, although I'm not a violent person at all. [...] Although I am a positive thinking person and anti violence, my pieces give the impression I'm a raving psychopath [...] The generally 'tooled up' nature of my work reflects this I guess. (Skore)

> (*The Real State*, issue 6)

Graffiti allows writers to project an alternative image of themselves, which does not have to be carried through into their everyday lives. While Hell's Angels or Skinheads have to live up to their image in the flesh and show that they 'deserve the uniform' (Brake, 1985), a bold aggressive graffiti writer can remain invisible and anonymous.

A question of location

Writers love seeing their written names around their environment. This enjoyment perhaps comes from seeing one's name as a representation of oneself; a self that is out there in the world, exposed, alone and, as this writer implies, irrepressibly independent:

Nancy: So what is it about that, the joy of seeing it again, just that it's there, it's permanent?

Zaki: Well, no, because you know that it might not last. Hmm, it's like if you do a drawing, you go away and you come back and it's there on a bit of paper, your drawing. But if you do graffiti, it's on a wall or a train or something, it's in a different element, it's on a medium that you've never seen before and it's out there in the world, sort of thing. I know it might sound stupid, but if you've done something inside, you've got on the light, it's inside in a familiar surrounding so it helps, but if it's outside, it's not natural ... it just stands out. It can be destroyed within hours and you're doing something that moves as well ... it moves around and then it gets killed.

In Zaki's animated narrative, the name or virtual self resembles a hunted animal, out there alone braving the rigours and hazards that it may encounter. It earns a boldness from this, as well as an apparent supremacy:

> Like you usually see letters on little things and to see a word that big moving along or even stationary on a wall, it's not what you'd normally see, it's out of its normal surroundings, it's blown up ... You see the colour or the outpouring of graffiti, it stands out amongst all that. (Zaki)

The names 'Revs' and 'Cost' in Colour Figure 7 impose themselves upon the unsuspecting environment, standing out and proud upon their conquered context. In this case, the hunted becomes the hunter. The speed and motion of the train surface, often used by writers to circulate their work, further magnifies this dominance. As this New York writer observes:

> That was the beautiful thing about it, that these pieces moved out of your sight and you couldn't arrest it, it arrested you for the few seconds that it was in the train station, for when it went by you, then it was gone. (Lee)

The name enjoys the same power as the machine it rides upon. It cannot be stopped. It lies beyond the control of those who see it passing. They can only watch as it thunders on to its next destination. Like the train, the name is literally and symbolically going places.

> Names help tame the powerful. Giving something a name or label offers the illusion of controlling or limiting it. The subway's powerful machines are tamed by placing one's name on them; the name celebrates victory and possession, like one's brand on a wild steer.
>
> (Feiner and Klein, 1982, p. 49)

'Shouting on the wall' – animating the graffiti identity

To an outsider, a wall covered in graffiti will probably look like a random mass of names, cluttered carelessly onto this urban canvas:

> The basic public walks down the road, sees a bit of spray paint and doesn't take a second look, just walks right past. For a graffiti artist, it's like living in another world. Every bit of writing on the wall means something and you take notice of it all. (Mear)

In actual fact, writers use their written names to engage in a complex form of symbolic exchange. This interaction enables writers to animate or bring the identity they have chosen to evoke to life. Knowing that this symbolic language is private to the sub-group, and often threatening to outsiders, adds to the pleasure.

Sign language

> When you watch the walls, the first thing you may notice is the way graffiti attracts graffiti. In its simplest sense, this is a way of saying hello. Just like friends who meet in the street and stop for a quick chat, 'You're letting them know you've seen them there, like instead of walking past the wall, "I know you've been here". (Acrid)

In a subculture fuelled by competition and divided by status, this greeting can also function as means of signalling one's respect. Positioning yourself up close to another writer's name indicates that they are worthy of your attention. You have granted them some importance by noticing them. The meaning changes rapidly, however, if this name is placed above rather than beside another's. This transforms a greeting into an unambiguous statement of superiority, a clear cut way of saying 'I'm better than you'.

Similarly, if you want to maintain good relations with your written neighbour, you should only greet them once. Crowding another writer's name with more than one of your own literally declares, 'I'm more than you'. A much larger name placed directly next to another's can relay a similar message. The greatest danger of proximity, however, lies in the possible contact your name might make with another's. If cramping a writer's space signals their insignificance, then encroaching on it to the point of touching or covering their name is an even greater insult. A writer should not make this contact 'unless you want to show a deliberate lack of respect for them. It's like you're showing, "Well I don't care about you, I'm just going to write the name on you"'. (Drax)

Figure 3   Saying Hello (Macdonald, 2001, p. 204)

Figure 4   I'm Better than You (Macdonald, 2001, p. 79)

Figure 5   You Mean Nothing (Macdonald, 2001, p. 79)

Figure 6   A Weapon of Assault (Macdonald, 2001, p. 79)

The greatest weapon available to writers, and the most extreme mark of disrespect, is the sprayed line.

A clear cut slash through another writer's name ignores all the rules which work to protect it and communicates the most extreme mark of disrespect. For Akit, whose name was once lined out:

Akit: It was the end of the world, you know. I was just like 'Oh my God, fuck, oh no!'

Nancy: By lining you, what are they saying?

Akit: 'You're shit, you're nothing.'

Retaliation, as this writer confirms, is the normal response to finding oneself crossed out:

If someone dogs [lines] me out, I just dog them out myself, see their tag, dog them out as well. (Rate)

Sometimes fights escalate into a 'cross out war', which can last for long periods and, like real conflict, extend to involve opposing groups or 'crews' of writers. These disputes may gradually fizzle out of their own accord, but in most cases a gesture of respect is used to signal a ceasefire. For example, a cross out war that raged for 18 months in London while I was conducting my research was eventually concluded when a writer dedicated one of his pieces to his sworn enemy. Like a handshake, he used this acknowledgement to call a truce.

Conclusion

I have illustrated some of the ways in which writers use their graffiti to 'make a name', and literally make themselves. Using a written word, they sculpt, shape and bring a whole new identity to life. Many writers choose a hard or 'macho' sounding name and then write this in a visually bold or aggressive style. This style can make them look like a 'raving psychopath', a 'violent person' or perhaps just bigger and bolder than they are in the mainstream world. This name is then situated outside, in locations which grant it a sense of fortitude, dominance and, depending on where it is placed, life. Positioned on a wall with other names, writers have the power to animate their personas and communicate; greeting, challenging, insulting, assaulting, attacking and fighting with other writers. Although these young men have a choice over what they can say about themselves with this identity, masculine narratives of strength, power and control appear to prevail. This written identity is clearly used as a masculine resource and an immensely powerful one at that. By picking up their spray cans and sticking with the wall, writers override the physical constraints which, as Willis (1990) recognises, might otherwise tarnish their masculine displays.

References

BRAKE, M. (1985) *Comparative Youth Cultures: The Sociology of Youth Cultures and Youth Sub-cultures in America, Britain and Canada*, London, Routledge and Kegan Paul.

FEINER, J. and KLEIN, S. (1982) 'Graffiti talks', *Social Policy* (US) **12**(3), pp. 47–53.

Graphotism, Wallington, Surrey, UK, Graphotism Urban Media, information available online at www.graphotism.com

On The Go, produced by Philly graffiti legend ESPO, no longer in production.

The Real State, produced in Sheffield by S. Budziszewski.

WILLIS, P. (1990) *Common Culture: Symbolic Work at Play in the Everyday Cultures of the Young*, Buckingham, Open University Press.

Source: commissioned for this volume. This article draws on research described in N. MACDONALD, (2001) *The Graffiti Subculture*, London, Palgrave.

READING C: Identities under construction

Daniel Chandler

What is a personal home page?

In this account of personal home pages I will describe some of the key
features of this genre and some of the functions that it seems to serve, in
particular in relation to authorial identity practices. I will be referring both to
my own online research and to pertinent observations by other researchers.
An example of a personal homepage is illustrated in Colour Figure 8.

Personal homepages can be regarded as those that are primarily about the
person who produced them. Such pages address the question, 'Who
am I?' (which, as the central question of adolescence, lends the genre a
particular – though not exclusive – potency for youthful authors). While the
fundamental technical difference between the medium of speech and that of
writing is that writing is *automatically recorded*, web pages introduce another
key feature: what is written on a web page (and stored on a web-server) is
automatically published on a global scale. Web pages that are 'personal' are
simultaneously public. It has been contended by media theorists such as
Joshua Meyrowitz (1985) that the adoption of new media seems to involve a
shifting or blurring of the boundaries of *public* and *private*. Without adopting a
stance of hard technological determinism, we may perceive such a shift in the
new genre of the personal homepage on the World Wide Web. The very name
'*home* page' is revealing in this context. John Seabrook comments that 'a home
in the real world is, among other things, a way of keeping the world out ... An
online home, on the other hand, is a little hole you drill in the wall of your real
home to let the world in' (Seabrook, 1995, 1997).

Asynchronous mass communication

Websites are frequently labelled as 'under construction'. However, the
construction involved is more than the construction of the sites: personal
homepages can also be seen as reflecting the construction of their makers'
identities. The Web is a medium with some marked differences from other
modes for the 'presentation of self in everyday life' (Goffman, 1969). It is 'one
of the first venues where individuals can construct portrayals of themselves
using information rather than consumer goods as their palette' (Erickson,
1996). The semiotic possibilities are unconstrained by material considerations –
though they remain constrained by the user's access to and competence in the
use of the relevant connotative stylistic and communicational codes (Chandler,
2001). Before the advent of the Web in 1993, 'one-to-many' communication as
a mode of self-presentation has been a tool of the privileged few. Web pages
offer the potential for mass communication in a medium which, despite far

from universal access, is incalculably more widely-accessible for self-presentation ('24/7') than conventional print publishing and the traditional mass media.

Like mass media texts and printed books, web pages are a form of *asynchronous* communication, unlike *synchronous* modes of communication such as the telephone, internet chatrooms and face-to-face interaction, which involve 'real-time' interaction. And yet it is interesting that critics often compare web pages (unfavourably) to face-to-face (and typically one-to-one) interaction. Steven Rubio complains: 'When you visit my homepage, you don't get to meet me, but only my presentation of myself' (Rubio, 1996; cf. Sandbothe, 1996). There is, however, nothing new about this feeling of textual autonomy in print (Chandler, 1995). 'Virtual selves' have existed ever since people have been publishing their writing. Plato noted this feature of the technology of books in the *Phaedrus* and *Seventh Letter*: people can encounter your ideas in the form of your 'textual self' (your article or book) without meeting you (a notion that alarmed Plato, since he privileged face-to-face dialogue). What is new about such virtual selves is that they have never before been available to so many people.

Comparisons of home pages with face-to-face interaction are misleading. Home pages offer readers none of the fleeting and situated particularity of face-to-face interactions, such as facial expressions, vocal cues, body language – posture, gestures and non-verbal mannerisms in general. The asynchronous nature of home page presentations of self makes them more comparable to textual forms (such as letters – and indeed more private forms such as diaries) than to speech interaction (such as face-to-face or telephone conversations). Also, unlike interpersonal communication, the potential mass audience of home pages makes them distinctively different from traditional forms of self-presentation, making them more comparable to mass media (such as published books, which for the purposes of self-presentation are available only to a privileged few). The personal home page is a *self-publishing* medium in both senses of the term: being able to produce web pages is like owning your own printing press, and what some might call 'self-advertisement' seems to be a key function. A male seventeen-year-old candidly admitted that in the case of his home page, 'the purpose of the site is to advertise me' (Chandler and Roberts-Young, 2000, p. 81).

Personal home pages may be more like texts on paper than face-to-face interaction but a comparison with paper-bound forms can be carried too far. Firstly, unlike printed media, web pages are *audio-visual* media (although, at least at present, web pages tend to feature *text* more than conventional audio-visual media have done – much as any new medium seems initially to imitate earlier forms). More fundamentally, however, web pages are at least potentially much more *dynamic* than print – although not all home page authors exploit these possibilities. An oft-mentioned feature of this is that they can be linked to each other in complex ways using *hypertext*, in contrast to what some have seen as the linear nature of print. But perhaps most dramatically personal home pages have none of the *fixity* of print (I came across one British home page entitled 'He changes his web pages more often than his underpants'!). An eight-year-old homepage author reported that she 'kept adding things when I think of them'. The Web is a medium ideally adapted to the dynamic purposes of identity maintenance. Home pages can be continually revised, making them closer in this sense to the provisional, informal and personal status of notes and drafts rather than to the formal and public status of published text. The weblog may be updated more regularly (Jung 2003), but whereas blogs involve revision by accretion, personal home pages are potentially more radically revisionist (obscuring their own evolution).

Bricolage

While personal home pages make public the personal, they also make personal the public, since home page authors engage in *bricolage* (Lévi-Strauss, 1974, p. 21), adopting and adapting borrowed material from the public domain of the Web in the process of fashioning personal and public identities. Graphics, sounds, text and the code used to generate a particular format are often copied or adapted from other people's pages. Indeed, the virtual and digital nature of the Web as a medium supports the re-use in *bricolage* of existing materials since the model may be abstracted limitlessly while remaining untouched in the site where the *bricoleur* found it.

Bricolage involves more than simply the appropriation of materials: it also involves the construction of the *bricoleur*'s identity (Lévi-Strauss ibid.; Jenkins, 1992). The values of the *bricoleur* are reflected in the assumptions underlying specific inclusions, allusions, omissions, adaptations and arrangements. Eclectic borrowing may sometimes seem to generate a postmodern mixture of styles rather than a distinctively 'personal' style, but individuality may nevertheless 'leak' through the ways authors conform with or diverge from dominant stylistic conventions (Miller, 1995; Miller and Arnold, 2001, p. 77).

This brief account may seem to suggest that *bricolage* is a rational, conscious and deliberate practice. But it is seldom like this. Indeed, *bricolage* lends itself to what may be experienced by the *bricoleur* as 'discovery'. One teenage author reported that she got her ideas 'by playing around with pictures, etc.' (Chandler and Roberts-Young, 2000, p. 84). This is very much a 'dialogue with materials'. Especially in a virtual medium one may reselect and rearrange elements until a pattern emerges which seems to satisfy the contraints of the task and the current purposes of the user. Indeed, no version of the resulting text need be regarded as final – completion may be endlessly deferred in the medium in which everything is always 'under construction'. Nor should *bricolage* be regarded as a practice of unconstrained individual creativity. The notion of the author's re-use of existing materials should indeed go some way to undermine romantic notions of creativity and originality. The *bricoleur*'s strategies (see box below) are constrained not only by pragmatic considerations such as suitability-to-purpose and readiness-to-hand but by the experience and competence of the individual in selecting and using 'appropriate' materials. While the social shaping of such practices may not often be visible to the user, subcultures generate conventions about materials and uses which are deemed appropriate for their members. The habitual use of certain signifying practices is indeed a mark of membership of particular subcultural groups. When an academic friend showed me his web pages for the first time some years ago he drew my attention to the pinkish-purple background and asked me what significance I attached to this. I confessed that it signified nothing in particular to me, and he then announced that it signified his gay identity (to which the *content* of the pages did not allude at all).

The Bricoleur's Web Kit

Types of activity

- *Inclusion*. What different ideas and topics are included?
- *Allusion*. What ideas and topics are being referred to?
- *Omission*. What's left unsaid or is noticeable by its absence?
- *Adaptation*. How are materials and ideas added to or altered?
- *Arrangement*. How is everything organized on the page?

Types of content

- personal statistics and biographical details;
- interests, likes and dislikes;
- ideas, values, beliefs and causes;
- friends, acquaintances and personal icons (e.g. celebrities).

Types of structure

- written text;
- graphics — whether still or moving — and other artwork;
- sound and/or video (e.g. associated webcams);
- short screenfuls to long scrolls of text;
- single page or many interconnected pages;
- separate windows or frames;
- an access counter (i.e. number of people who've visited);
- a guestbook;
- links for other pages (e.g. a 'cool links' section);
- an email button or chat button.

(Adapted from my own list by Thurlow et al., 2004, p. 194)

The building blocks of web page identity

The *content* of personal home pages can be recognised as drawing on a palette of conventional paradigmatic elements, most notably: personal statistics or biographical details; interests, likes and dislikes; ideas, values, beliefs and causes; and friends, acquaintances and personal 'icons'. Creating a personal home page can be seen as building a virtual identity insofar as it flags topics, stances and people regarded by the author as significant (as well as what may sometimes either be 'notable by its absence' or 'go without saying'). Sherry Turkle notes that in a home page, 'One's identity emerges from whom one knows, one's associations and connections' (Turkle, 1996a, p. 258). There's a well-known web aphorism: 'show me your links and I'll tell you who you are'. Where such links are to the pages of friends or to those who share one's interests this can be seen as involving the construction of a kind of 'virtual community' by homepage authors (Rheingold, 1995).

Although home pages authors choose what to reveal about themselves in the formal *content* of their pages, the *form* in which they do so may involve both intentional and unintentional disclosures (as well as sometimes leading to misinterpretation). In an online interview I conducted (19/9/96), Iain, a British home page author, wrote: 'The way I code my page is very reflective of the way I work and live – sort of ordered and trying to keep structure to it. Some pages I have seen obviously reflect arty-type personalities. I look at mine and think yep, this says science-type person.' The *process* of composition is not visible to the reader, of course, but in a study by other researchers, Angela (30) noted her acute awareness of issues of impact: 'I made an outline of what I wanted to convey on the site and the possible content... Then I thought about the connotations associated with each piece ... I was meticulous, I'm an accountant, you know' (Schau and Gilly, 2003, p. 395). On the most mundane level, a self-authored page may show that the author used a standard authoring package or wrote the code directly. Spelling, punctuation and grammatical idiosyncrasies tend to glare at the literate reader in beautifully-displayed and illuminated text on the screen.

Constructing identities

At least as much as in writing on paper (Chandler, 1995, Chapter 4), constructing a personal home page can be seen as shaping not only the materials but also (in part through manipulating the various materials) one's thoughts and feelings. In an online interview, home page author Tristan commented regarding his pages: 'It helps to define who I am. Before I start to look at/write about something then I'm often not sure what my feelings are, but after having done so, I can at least have more of an idea'. Another home page author, David, told me that 'despite being a private person, I decided to publish what I wrote on my Home Page. I was the intended audience, as strange as it sounds. Somehow, publishing my feelings helped validate them for myself' (email 27/2/98). While this may be a familiar function for writing with conventional media, the Web makes this process very public indeed. Where home pages perform such functions for their authors, the Web seems to be leading to what might formerly have been private writing (such as in a personal diary) being laid before the eyes of the world. Some home page authors are extraordinarily frank and revealing about themselves compared to what might ordinarily expect in face-to-face interaction with strangers. However, we should not exaggerate the post-modernity of such a phenomenon. As long ago as 1580, as another experimental genre and identity tool (the personal essay) was being forged, Montaigne had remarked wrily that 'many things that I would not confess to any one in particular, I deliver to the publick; and send my best friends to a bookseller's shop, there to inform themselves concerning my most secret thoughts' (Montaigne, 1580, Bk. III, 9, in Cotton's translation).

Some critics have expressed an anxiety that web pages may lead people to manipulate their public identities more than has been possible with traditional media. Howard Rheingold has argued that 'the authenticity of relationships [and identities] is always in question in cyberspace, because of the masking and distancing of the medium, in a way that it is not in question in real life' (Rheingold n.d.). Clearly, different media and modes of communication facilitate and inhibit different patterns of behaviour. We do not present ourselves in any kind of writing in the same way as we do in face-to-face interaction. Even related online genres such as the personal home page and the weblog offer different affordances and constraints for self-presentation: for instance, blogs do not erase earlier standpoints as personal home pages do— a feature that led one commentator to claim that weblogs enable 'a more "truthful" presentation of self' (Jung, 2003, p. 5).

For some, personal home pages may offer a 'rehearsal' area. In his online interview with me Iain wrote: 'You can get things right and project a different "you" to the world – sort of, "Hey, this is who I am!"'... I think the important thing is you can only show the bits of you want and hide the bad bits you would get rid of if you could' (19/9/96). A British home page author denied this in his own case: 'Mine is confessional. Try to show warts and all' (David, email 27/2/98). I have encountered a number of examples of the use of unconnected web pages (often on different websites) to present oneself in different ways, notably amongst home page authors who are gay but not 'out'. Not having to reveal some facets of oneself has particular advantages for those from marginalised groups. James, a gay British internet user, told me in an online interview that having a home page meant that he was out in cyberspace long before being out in daily life, and found it useful to say to people, 'Oh, didn't you know?', feeling able to treat the issue as old news. Similarly, for Rob in London, his web page provided 'a very easy way for me to come out. I could say, "check out my website" and knew they'd come across the gay part. More importantly, they could find out in my own positive terms and think about it before reacting' (email 1/6/97). Home pages evidently enable some people 'to present the selves that may not otherwise be displayed in "real life"' (Cheung, 2000, p. 50).

Adopting a notion from Sherry Turkle (1996a, p;. 260; 1996c, p. 173), I would suggest that home pages are objects which enable their authors to think about their identity. They can be seen as one of Foucault's 'technologies of the self' which allow us to reflect on and transform the way we think of and present ourselves. Some people clearly feel 'more themselves' on the internet than they do in RL. We may acknowledge this phenomenological perspective even if we question the unitary notion of the self to which it alludes. Some people feel better able to articulate their thoughts, feelings and personalities in writing than in face-to-face interaction (Chandler, 1995, p. 46).

RL = real life

Many of the criticisms of presence on the internet seem to have advanced little beyond Plato's fears about the technology of writing. Critics who suggest that someone's online persona may not represent what the author is 'really' like could be seen as phonocentric, privileging, in the romantic tradition, spoken, face-to-face interaction as somehow more 'real'. Without surrendering to the excesses of postmodernist rhetoric or hard technological determinism, we may acknowledge that for some authors at least, personal home pages offer a sense of empowerment that could help us both to question romantic assumptions about 'authenticity' and to reassess the sociality of writing.

References

CHANDLER, D. (1992) 'The phenomenology of writing by hand', *Intelligent Tutoring Media*, **3**(2/3), pp. 65–74.

CHANDLER, D. (1993) 'Writing strategies and writing tools', *English Today*, **9**(2), pp. 32–8.

CHANDLER, D. (1994) 'Who needs suspended inscription?', *Computers and Composition*, **11**, pp. 191–201.

CHANDLER, D. (1995) *The Act of Writing: A Media Theory Approach*, Aberystwyth: University of Wales, Aberystwyth.

CHANDLER, D. (1996) 'Shaping and being shaped: engaging with media', *Computer-Mediated Communication Magazine* (February), http://www.december.com/cmc/mag/1996/feb/chandler.html

CHANDLER, D. and ROBERTS-YOUNG, D. (2000) 'The construction of identity in the personal homepages of adolescents in Wales', *Welsh Journal of Education*, **9**(1), pp. 78–90.

CHANDLER, D. (2001) *Semiotics: The Basics*, London, Routledge.

CHEUNG, C. (2000) 'A home on the web: presentations of self in personal homepages', in D. GAUNTLETT (ed.) *Web Studies: Rewiring Media Studies for the Digital Age*, London, Arnold.

ERICKSON, T. (1996) *The World Wide Web as Social Hypertext*, [online] http://www.pliant.org/personal/Tom_Erickson/SocialHypertext.html (accessed 3.5.05)

GOFFMAN, E. (1969) *The Presentation of Self in Everyday Life*, Harmondsworth, Penguin.

JENKINS, H. (1992) *Textual Poachers: Television Fans and Participatory Culture*, London, Routledge.

JUNG, E. (2003) 'Weblogs: a new phenomenon?', [online] http://onoffonoff.org/imma/ct/Weblogs-CT_EdwardJung.pdf (accessed 3.5.05)

LÉVI-STRAUSS, C. (1974) *The Savage Mind*, London, Weidenfeld & Nicolson.

MEYROWITZ, J. (1985). *No Sense of Place: The Impact of Electronic Media on Social Behavior*, New York, Oxford University Press.

MILLER, H. (1995) 'The presentation of self in electronic life: Goffman on the internet', paper presented at *Embodied Knowledge and Virtual Space* conference, Goldsmiths' College, University of London, June, 1995 [online] http://ess.ntu.ac.uk/miller/cyberpsych/goffman.htm (accessed 3.5.05)

MILLER, H. and ARNOLD, J. (2001) 'Self in web home pages: gender, identity and power in cyberspace', in G. RIVA and C. GALIMBERTI (eds) *Towards Cyberpsychology: Mind, Cognitions and Society in the Internet Age*, Amsterdam, IOS Press.

RHEINGOLD, H. (n.d.) 'Multi-user dungeons and alternate identities', *The Virtual Community: Homesteading on the Electronic Frontier*, New York, HarperCollins (Chapter 5), available online at http://www.well.com/user/hlr/vcbook/vcbook5.html (accessed 3.5.05)

RHEINGOLD, H. (1995) *The Virtual Community: Finding Connection in a Computerized World*, London, Minerva.

RUBIO, S. (February 1996) 'Home page', *Bad Subjects,* **24**, [online] http://eserver.org/bs/24/rubio.html (accessed 3.5.05)

SANDBOTHE, M. (March 1996) 'Interactivity, hypertextuality, transversality', printed version in *Hermes: Journal of Linguistics,* **24**, February 2000, available at http://www.sandbothe.net/267.0.html (accessed 3.5.05)

SCHAU, H.J. and GILLY, M.C. (2003) 'We are what we post? Self-presentation in personal web space', *Journal of Consumer Research,* **30**(3), pp. 385–404.

SEABROOK, J. (1997) *Deeper: A Two-year Odyssey in Cyberspace*, London, Faber.

THURLOW, C., LENGEL, L. and TOMIC, A. (2004) *Computer Mediated Communication: Social Interaction and the Internet*, London, Sage Publications.

TURKLE, S. (1996a) *Life on the Screen: Identity in the Age of the Internet*, London, Weidenfeld & Nicolson.

TURKLE, S. (1996b) 'Virtuality and its discontents: searching for community in cyberspace', *The American Prospect,* **24** (Winter 1996), pp. 50–7, available at http://www.prospect.org/print-friendly/print/V7/24/turkle-s.html (accessed 3.5.05)

TURKLE, S. (1996c) 'Parallel lives: working on identity in virtual space', in GRODIN and LINDLOF (eds) *Constructing the Self in a Mediated World,* Thousand Oaks, CA, Sage Publications, www.sagepub.co.uk.

Source: commissioned for this volume.

Author's note

The author reserves the right to publish online versions of this paper. This is an abridged and updated version of 'Personal home pages and the construction of identities on the Web', available at the time of writing at: http://www.aber.ac.uk/media/Documents/short/webident.html
Note that some of the online documents listed are no longer available.

7 Literacies, collaboration and context

Uta Papen and Karin Tusting

7.1 Introduction

Previous chapters have explored creativity and artfulness in English language, spoken and written, at the level of the text, and in the context of everyday interaction and the negotiation of identity. In this chapter we will move outwards from texts and specific interactions and address the creativity and artfulness inherent in people's everyday practices of producing and interacting with texts, that is, their **literacy practices** – the ways people use and interact with texts in particular contexts, and the meanings that these hold for them.

The chapter begins with a general reflection on the creativity involved in people's everyday literacy practices, and then draws out some of the characteristics of this creativity: the collaborative nature of many creative literacy practices; the impact of the particular contexts these practices are situated within, each with their own opportunities and constraints; and the way people respond creatively to changing discourses and sociocultural conditions in the literacy practices they engage in.

We will be arguing that creativity in written language is dependent on and emergent from the creative literacy practices through which texts are constructed, and that there is also creativity in the ways texts are read and used. Such practices are shaped by people drawing actively on the possibilities offered by the particular social situations in which they are embedded, in order to achieve their own goals and purposes.

Literacy is seen as part of people's social practice (which was defined in Chapter 4).

7.2 Creativity in everyday literacy practices

We start by asking you to consider some examples of people using and constructing written language in their everyday lives, taken from *Local Literacies*, a study of the everyday literacy practices of people in one area of the town of Lancaster, in the north-west of England (Barton and Hamilton, 1998).

ACTIVITY 1 Literacies in everyday life

Allow about 15 minutes

Read the examples below. For each of them, think about whether or not you would consider them to be 'creative', and why (or why not).

Writing your autobiography

Harry reads authentic war stories throughout his life, after serving in the Second World War as a young man. He talks about and exchanges these books with friends. In later life, he writes letters to magazines, trying to trace old comrades. He takes great care over the tone of the letters, writing them out several times until he is happy with them. Eventually, he starts up a regular correspondence with one old shipmate. He goes to a veterans' association meeting and afterwards writes a short story for the veterans' magazine. He writes it by hand, and a friend over the road types it out and sends it off. Eventually, he starts to work on writing his own story, again writing it out by hand. He will ask his son to type it up for him, and at the same time to 'flower it up a bit'.

Local newsletter

Shirley is a key figure in her local neighbourhood, liaising between residents and the local Housing Action Project. She has been involved in many local campaigning activities: editing the newsletter at the nursery school; fundraising and being press officer for the local dyslexia association; setting up a neighbourhood watch scheme. She is editor of the local residents' association newsletter. This involves writing out editorials by hand and giving them to one of the paid workers in the Housing Action Project, who types them out, pastes them up and duplicates them.

The Allotment Association

The annual general meeting (AGM) of the local Allotment Association is full of texts and activities around texts. It follows an established set of rules, with a set sequence of events: secretary's reports, treasurer's reports, any other business. All the officers who speak make reference to handwritten notes. Questions raised from the floor sometimes refer to records such as rule books. This is a regular, repeated event, with a standard, agreed format.

When the council tried to sell off the allotments land to a local developer, the association organised to resist this threat. This involved drawing on and constructing a range of reading and writing activities: holding weekly meetings to discuss strategy; starting a letter-writing campaign by distributing a newsletter to 1,400 local people encouraging them to write to the council in protest; displaying protest posters. A resident who had been involved in a car-parking campaign was invited onto the action committee; local radio stations and newspapers were contacted. In order to achieve this, people had to learn new practices and draw on new sources of knowledge.

Break-in literacy

Joanna's house is broken into just after she has moved in. She has to make an inventory of what was stolen, make a police report, and fill in insurance forms. She must assemble receipts and financial details, and work out how all of this can best be presented to make her case. Without knowing how to do this in advance, she has to make it up as she goes along.

(Adapted from *Local Literacies*, Barton and Hamilton 1998)

Comment

Harry's writing of his autobiography is typical of the sorts of things we often think about as 'creative' writing. It emerges from a combination of his memories of a particularly significant time in his life and the reading he has been doing around similar topics. Slowly, he starts to write about these memories, first in letters, then in a short story. Eventually, he starts on a fully fledged book of his own, which represents his personal experience in a creative way.

The other three examples may not appear to be 'traditionally' creative activities. They are not individuals working to produce works of art or literature. However, they are all examples of people actively drawing on and reconstituting available resources to construct original texts and to achieve their purposes in the world.

We may not necessarily see local newsletters as being 'artful' in the way a piece of literature is considered to be. Nonetheless, the process of putting together the newsletter involves drawing together a variety of elements from different sources, reshaping them for a particular purpose, and thereby crafting something new. Barton and Hamilton (1998, pp. 108–9) analyse the text of a year's worth of newsletter editorials that Shirley has written. They demonstrate how she constructs a particular version of what is going on in the local area, in which the residents are addressed as a coherent community with shared interests. This is a creative construction of a harmonious world very different from that which emerges from other local texts, such as the minutes of residents' association meetings, in which it is people's conflicting agendas that come to the fore.

The Allotment Association's literacy practices show various types of creativity. Each AGM is a unique interaction, created jointly by a group of people, each of whom brings their own concerns. However, the particular meeting practices and the texts (minutes, reports, accounts) which are produced from the meeting follow a well-established pattern which varies little from year to year. When there is a sudden crisis, the members of the association are forced to find new and creative ways of responding to it.

This involves drawing on their existing resources (such as the knowledge of a trainee solicitor who is also an allotment holder) in a new way, producing different sorts of texts in pursuit of a particular purpose. They think of a wide variety of new ways of producing and using texts to achieve their principal goal of survival.

Finally, Joanna is involved in what we might think of as a very mundane everyday literacy activity. Filling in forms and collecting supporting paperwork is normally seen as a fairly routine administrative task. But Joanna is doing this in a completely new situation which she has never encountered before, and at a time when emotions may be running high. She has to work out what is meant by making inventories, making reports, and filling in forms. She has to make decisions about how much of her personal life she wants to reveal in the information that goes into these documents. Within relatively constrained circumstances, she uses her creativity to work out her own ways of going about this unwelcome literacy task. Later, her knowledge becomes a resource in the local community which other people going through similar experiences can draw on and reshape in their own circumstances.

ACTIVITY 2   Your own creative literacy practices

Allow about
30 minutes

Make a list of the activities you have engaged in with written texts in the past day or two. These might include writing letters, keeping track of appointments in a diary, reading and writing emails, reading the newspaper, planning a holiday, doing a project management flowchart. Try and think as broadly as you can and include all of the activities you can think of which involved written texts – you may be surprised how many there are!
Now look back over the list.

- Which of these literacy practices would you classify as being 'creative', and in what way?
- Are there any common features of these 'creative' literacy practices?
- Are there any which you would say had *no* element of creativity?

We will ask you to refer back to your list later in the chapter.

It is very hard to find an example of a literacy practice that is entirely 'uncreative'. Indeed, there is an argument that all meaning-making processes have a creative element. We will start from the premise that 'creativity' refers to 'making something which is new, which did not exist before the creative act', or 'making something which is original, which is unlike things that have been made before'. Our perspective is that all meaning making involves bringing together existing cultural resources for a particular purpose in a particular setting. While the meaning-making resources which are drawn on in this process have come from people's previous experiences and may be culturally typical, this combination of particularities is always unique, and without the human effort which has gone into the construction of the sign, it would not exist. From this perspective, all communication is creative in both of the senses above ('something new' and 'something original'), even where the text (spoken or written) is an exact copy of one that has been used many times before and even where the text itself does not appear particularly artful.

To examine a text and to try to categorise it as being 'more' or 'less' creative is therefore to overlook the creativity inherent in all meaning making. We ask what this perspective can add to our understanding of the characteristics of creativity in our particular sphere of interest: that is, written language, and how it is produced and interpreted in social life. Instead of examining texts to see if one can 'find' creativity in them, we examine the everyday literacy practices through which people in a range of different settings produce and interact with texts, and draw out the creativity inherent in those practices.

See Chapter 3 for a definition of ethnography.

Most of the readings and research on which this chapter will draw come from people who have studied literacy from an ethnographic perspective. Barton and Hamilton, Camitta, Merchant, Papen, Wilson, Ahearn and the other researchers whose work we will be presenting here studied texts (and their creative aspects) not in isolation, but in the context of the social and cultural practices they were part of. They spent considerable time immersing themselves – as much as this was possible – in the social and cultural worlds of their subjects. They relied on participant observation and prolonged interaction with the people they worked with to try to understand what they thought about the texts they produced and used. Moreover, they took into account the broader social and political context within which creativity in writing is located. In the rest of this chapter, we are going to draw out some of the principal characteristics of such a perspective: what becomes visible when you examine writing through looking at practices as well as texts, and what this implies about creativity in writing.

7.3 Collaboration in creative literacy practices

The traditional image of the lone artist in his attic is challenged by Carter (2004) and Williams (1983), who draw out the historical development of this view, relating it to the shift away from collaborative artistic work of the Middle Ages and towards the western focus on the individual 'genius' from the Renaissance and Romantic eras. In contrast, Carter's own work emphasises the ubiquity of collaborative verbal creativity in much ordinary everyday spoken interaction. This is true not only of spoken interaction, but also of reading and writing. By focusing on people's literacy practices, rather than just on the texts which they produce, it becomes clear that in many cases, creative texts are often produced as a result of interactive collaboration.

Collaboration in everyday literacies

The examples from Barton and Hamilton (1998) in the text box above highlight the importance of collaboration in creative literacy practices. Even Harry's work on his autobiography – the most 'traditionally' creative example cited – involves collaboration and interaction throughout. He talks about and exchanges war stories with friends; he writes to magazines to try to trace old colleagues. It is at a meeting of the veterans' association that he first talks about writing a short story; he collaborates with a friend 'over the road' in the physical production of the story, and with the magazine in its publication. While the writing of his autobiography by hand is done alone, all of these conversations and interactions contribute to its production. And he then collaborates with his son, both on its physical production and on developing its style ('flowering it up a bit').

Shirley's newsletter editorials, although written by a single individual, emerge from the series of meetings and informal interactions that she engages in day to day in her role as liaison person. They are written in an informal dialogic style, addressing the reader directly. The example reproduced in Barton and Hamilton (1998, p. 110) begins 'Hi Everyone!! Yes, it's me again!!' They include direct appeals to the reader ('Please, please send in items for the Newsletter'), and references back to events which members of the community have been involved in ('Can I thank everyone who came to the meeting ... it was great to see the return of some very familiar faces'). Barton and Hamilton point out that elements such as these in the text of the newsletter are shaped by the discursive conventions of oral meetings, a context of interaction which Shirley engages in often and with which she is very familiar. She is drawing on the practices learned in these collaborative interactions to create something new in writing.

The literacy practices of the Allotment Association are obviously collaborative, in a variety of different ways. The meeting is constructed jointly by a group of people talking together. They draw on texts which represent other meetings and thereby the history of the association, bringing in a chronological element of dialogue with previous AGMs. In the crisis with the council, the same group of people reaches outwards to incorporate new individuals and groups into their goals and purposes. They use texts in creative ways to achieve this, particularly by using the newsletter to encourage hundreds of local people to join them textually in their struggle to keep the land, in the letter-writing campaign, and by starting a press campaign to involve local print and broadcast media and thereby make sure their voices were heard more widely. These were new practices for most of those involved, which were invented by coming together in weekly meetings and talking about strategies. This included talking with people who had been involved in similar campaigns previously and drawing on their knowledge to create a new set of literacy strategies appropriate to their own purposes.

In order for Joanna to be able to fulfil the requirements of the texts, she has to collate information and complete forms related to the break-in. She needs to talk to police and insurance company representatives, as well as perhaps drawing on the advice of friends and family, activities that may be invisible in the completed documentation but which shape the way she approaches it and the form it finally takes. She is engaging in collaborative activity and drawing on the social resources around her in order to be able to create what is, for her, a new type of text.

These are all examples of particular individuals engaging in creative collaboration around writing and text production. We now move on to consider the place of collaborative creative writing in the setting of one particular community: that of a 1980s' American high school.

ACTIVITY 3

'Vernacular writing: varieties of literacy among Philadelphia high school students' (Reading A)

The study recounted here was a three-year project in which Miriam Camitta spent time with a group of high-school students in the United States, documenting and analysing the different forms of writing that adolescents were engaging in, and what this meant within their lives and their culture. Before reading, think about the following questions:

- What sorts of different literacy practices do you think she might have found? Think about your own school years. What kinds of literacy practices did you and your schoolmates engage in? What about the literacy practices of your own children or any young people you know?

- To what extent might you expect adolescents' writing practices to be creative?

- What role do you think collaboration might play in their writing?

Now please read the selection from Camitta's work in Reading A.

Comment

Camitta's research revealed a wide range of literacy practices that the adolescents she worked with engaged in. While some of them (such as Shelly, writing poems and journals alone at home) fit the 'solitary writer' paradigm, most of the writing practices described involve other people in key roles – whether as readers, as audience, as co-composers or as editors. Even in the examples of private writing, most of this writing is about explaining and exploring personal relationships, and is therefore situated within what Camitta calls a 'web' of social activities and relationships. Where other people are involved, they take an active role in the text-production process at all stages. And this involves not just reading and responding to the texts, but editing, scribing, helping with decisions, circulating, and archiving.

The adolescents in Camitta's study are not only producing creative texts, but also creating and developing new sorts of collaborative writing practices. One could even argue that the performance of their texts is creating a new practice, a hybrid of the practices of rehearsal, performance and editing, which itself feeds back into the writing process. For the most part, the writing practices Camitta has identified are not school practices. They are the result of the students' own engagement with written texts and they are self-learned rather than taught in the classroom. In fact, many of these writing and performance practices are very different from the traditional 'plan, draft, rewrite, share' model of writing that the standard language arts curriculum of the time was advocating, and part of Camitta's goal in doing this research was to explore whether classroom teaching could be developed to be more in line with adolescents' everyday practices.

ACTIVITY 4   Collaboration in vernacular writing

Allow about
20 minutes

Camitta's work shows clearly how writing, performance and collaboration were intertwined in the creative process in the practices of the adolescents she worked with.

- To what extent do you think Camitta's observations about collaboration in creative literacy practices are generalisable, and to what extent do you think these practices were connected with the particular features of a tight-knit highly networked US high school in the early 1980s?

Think back to the literacy practices of young people today that you thought about before reading the article.

- In what ways are they similar or different to the activities Camitta describes? Do they still write poems, keep diaries and pass around notes under the table, while pretending to listen to their teachers? Or would they rather use their mobile phones?

- What about your own literacy practices as an adolescent – were they similar to or different from the ones Camitta identifies?

Think about the different settings in which you engage or have engaged, in writing, in different forms.

- How many of these involve collaboration, and to what extent?

- How does collaboration shape the form and content of the texts that are eventually produced?

- Has there been a time in your life when more (or less) of your writing involved collaboration?

7.4 The influence of context

The significance of collaboration and interaction in creative literacy practices demonstrated above is just one aspect of the influence of context on the creative practices which emerge. In this section we will consider in a more general sense how the *context* of reading and writing shapes creative practices.

Any given context is associated with a particular set of possibilities. Some of these have been considered in Chapter 5, in relation to the affordances and constraints of technologies. We have seen in Reading A the way the teenagers drew on the cultural resources available to them, reshaping and reconstructing existing texts and genres in new ways. The examples of 'patchwork' and 'mosaic' texts show teenagers drawing on the intertextual resources available, appropriating existing phrases from popular songs and re-combining them to create a new product. They combine the discourse conventions of poetry, journal and letter writing to make a new hybrid product. They take advantage of the material affordances open to them, such as the school copier, to produce and distribute their texts.

In addition to its possibilities, any given context also has associated limitations. In Camitta's study, the adolescents are constrained in time and space by the requirements of the school day. They have to be in particular classrooms at particular times, and their activities while they are in class are supposed to be tightly controlled. Nevertheless, they manage to make creative use of the possibilities available to them within these constraints: writing between class periods, at lunchtimes, and before and after school, and taking advantage of opportunities such as 'private writing time' in class which they reshape to become time for their own writing.

The possibilities associated with a setting do not *determine* what is created within any given context; but they do shape what is possible. In the examples from *Local Literacies* above, Harry was constrained from writing his own story for many years by his perceived lack of education. Through the other writing activities he engages in, he opens up new possibilities for himself and becomes aware of his own potential as a writer. He draws on the resources of his social context both to produce the text in the appropriate material form by having other people type it up for him, and to develop its stylistic form by asking his 'more educated' son to 'flower it up'. The Allotment Association are constrained in their struggle against the Council by their lack of knowledge and lack of numbers. The committee creatively draws on the trainee solicitor's legal knowledge and the local residents' campaigning experience, and thereby develops new literacy practices of resistance and struggle which enable its survival. Joanna is constrained by her lack of previous relevant experience, but draws on the possibilities of other knowledgeable people both in her social circle and in her official capacity, and on the particular affordances of the forms she has to fill in, to work out her own ways of negotiating the insurance requirements.

In this section we will consider the influence of the possibilities and constraints of particular contexts on literacy practices, first looking at how creative literacy practices emerge from situations characterised by social constraints, and then at the impact of the affordances of new information technologies.

Creative literacies in situations of social constraint

ACTIVITY 5   Creativity and constraint

Allow 15 minutes

Think about your own creative literacy practices, as you have identified them in the earlier activities in this chapter. How are these shaped by the affordances and constraints of your own circumstances?

We will shortly be looking at a reading about the literacy practices engaged in by people in prison.

- What sorts of literacy practices do you think these might be?

- What might be the purposes and goals of prisoners engaging in them?

- What sorts of texts would you expect to emerge from this combination of affordances and constraints?

ACTIVITY 6   A strategy for survival (Reading B)

Now read 'Creativity in language as a strategy for survival' by Anita Wilson.

Some of the most innovative practices described by Wilson are to do with enabling forms of collaboration and communication which the prison setting is designed to prevent: from shouting out of windows to stamping an improvised code out on the floor. What does this tell us about the claims made in the previous section about the importance of collaboration?

Wilson suggests that creativity can emerge from situations of powerlessness and that anguish and struggle can inspire creativity. Can you think of examples of this from your own (or other people's) life?

Comment

Wilson describes a broad range of creative uses of language (oral, written and visual) in the prison setting. Without doubt, these prison literacies are the products of inventive minds with a specific ability to make do with what is available (matchsticks, toilet bowls, etc.). They are also striking examples of how those who live in particularly confined settings develop the ability and talent to imagine using objects and materials in ways that are completely different from their intended function.

The key theme in Wilson's reading is the role of literacy and creativity in relation to maintaining an individual identity in the face of the prison institution and prison life. The driving motivation for the creative uses of literacy here is the desire and need to maintain a sense of self as agent and not just as subject to other people's desires and rules. The prison is one of the classic examples the French cultural philosopher Foucault (1980) used to explain the power of discourses (and the institutions behind them) over the individual. He distinguished between self as subject – to someone else – and self as agent. This distinction allows us to expose the ways we as individuals are constituted by the powerful societal discourses that work to confine our individual selves and the way we act and think (see Foucault, 1980). However, in his later works, Foucault (1985) elaborates on the 'productive' aspects of power and he uses the concept of 'techniques of the self' to illustrate the willingness and ability of the individual to maintain a 'self' that is self-directed rather than governed by others. Such techniques are situated in the realm of the everyday, so they can include things such as sticking posters onto walls or writing poems on pieces of paper. Wilson's cases are examples of such attempts to maintain a sense of self in the face of a prison world whose overarching power works toward constraining and 'reforming' (and perhaps even destroying) individual selves. She shows how the struggles that result from such contexts can be a trigger for creativity.

Maintaining an identity in prison, as Wilson shows, is also part of a struggle to create and maintain a cultural space (what she calls, following Bhabha, the 'third space') in situations where the individual is effectively being wiped off the social landscape.

The affordances and constraints of new technologies

The discussion above focused on the influence of particular sets of constraints on literacy practices. We will now turn to an example of the possibilities opened up by new sets of affordances.

The introduction of computer technologies has introduced a broad range of new media to our semiotic landscape. Kress (1998) has worked extensively on reading and writing in the technology driven environment of our modern societies, and uses the idea of affordances and constraints to examine the role of different media in the production of texts. New technologies, he argues, present particular new sets of affordances and constraints which people use creatively in practice, for instance, in the way people use text messages, emails and the possibilities offered by hypertext.

As you saw in Chapter 5, the constraints of particular forms also generate creative new literacy practices. For instance, text messagers use a variety of non-standard linguistic forms, such as contractions, abbreviations, phonetic spelling and emoticons, to convey meaning within the very limited possibilities of a 160-character message. While public views on texting are highly divided, with some scholars publicly denouncing texting as 'poor penmanship' and 'bleak, bald, sad shorthand' (Sunderland, *The Guardian* 11.11.02), many others have seen the creativity that marks this new practice. Referring to SMS communication in Germany, Androutsopolous and Schmidt (2002, p. 49) refer to the 'creative language use, drawing on and playfully combining a wide range of linguistic resources' that is characteristic of the writers of text messages. In a study of mobile phone communication in Hong Kong, Bodomo and Lee (2002) claim that new forms of language and literacy emerge from the introduction of new communicative tools and media, identifying distinctive jargons and 'technobabbles' associated with online communications, as well as new digital literacies.

Kress (2003, p. 36) uses the two concepts of 'transformation' and 'transduction' to explain why in his view creativity is an inherent feature of contemporary communication. Transformation refers to the way the producer of a text can alter and adapt the forms of signs within a mode in relation to their needs and interests, such as in the lexical inventiveness associated with texting. Transduction refers to the moves of 'semiotic material' across modes, where meaning that was originally configured in one (or several) modes is moved across to a different one. This happens for example when the young people in Reading A 'perform' a story, a poem or a rap song, which they originally produced in the written mode and then shifted to the oral. Another example is when teenagers use chatrooms to meet up and converse with 'virtual friends'.

In a study of the online literacy practices of a group of secondary school girls in England, Merchant (2001) found that these girls used chatrooms extensively and that they had 'real' and 'virtual' friends, both of whom they communicated and chatted with in similar ways. However, 'online' chatting requires transduction: what is commonly performed through oral means is moved to the written mode when taking place in online chatrooms.

Merchant's paper explores a number of issues that support our own position on creativity in everyday life literacy. He shows the creativity that can be found in texts and practices, by examining both the new forms of texts generated by the girls (such as for instance their informal, conversational style, and their 'creative approach to spelling'), as well as the new forms of social interaction they develop in the course of using chatrooms. The girls explore visual and textual modes in their use of the internet, chatrooms and emails creatively, combining emoticons and specifically created abbreviations with picture files and websites that they exchange as part of their virtual conversations.

Their online literacy activities are described as an example of the new communicative practices that are currently developing. The driving force behind these changes, in his view, are the girls themselves. He talks about them as the 'innovators in language use' who 'experiment' with what the new medium has to offer and 'create' new forms of writing (p. 296). (See also Reading B in Chapter 5.) In his conclusion, Merchant speaks about the girls' internet practices as 'a new and fast form of written conversation' (p. 303) and he brings in the question of power. Traditional views of language try to regulate and even to dismiss these new forms of writing. However, using Bourdieu's (1984) concept of **linguistic capital**, Merchant argues that through their experimentation with the new medium the girls in his study acquire important skills that could be very valuable on the job market and may become capital in a new communicative and social order. A comparison between Merchant's findings and Camitta's study (Reading A) shows how teenagers' literacy practices have changed dramatically. While the students in Camitta's study did not yet rely on any electronic technology for their production of texts, for the teenagers in Merchant's study, the computer has become an everyday tool of writing and social interaction.

Another example of the possibilities offered by new technologies is the internet encyclopedia 'Wikipedia' (http://en.wikipedia.org), a collaborative encyclopedia which can be updated and changed by anyone accessing the pages. This produces an up-to-date, dynamic and constantly changing representation in which everybody's knowledge counts, a new sort of encyclopedia in which the authority of any entry can be contested and emerges from a process of dialogue and debate. The possibilities of new technologies therefore challenge conventional notions of creativity in several ways. Wikipedia shows their potential to 'democratise' authorship, expanding the possibilities which have historically been restricted to only those forms of creativity privileged by the publishing system; on the internet, everybody can be a published author. They also fundamentally challenge our understanding of what 'literacy' is and what makes literacy creative. Writing, as Kress (2003, p. 36) argues, has become 'part of the whole landscape of the many modes available for representation'. Thus, written language is only one of many other modes available to the creative writer.

The recent drastic changes in our literacy practices confirm a view of language and of literacy as constantly shifting and changing social and cultural practices. Again, this has important implications for how we think about creativity. If language is believed to be a relatively stable system, creativity at the level of the system can only be rare and something special, requiring an exceptional talent. However, if we think about language as a system 'in use' or 'in flow', a system that is constantly created and re-created, changed and adapted, then creativity even at this level turns into a normal event – 'the everyday process of semiotic work as meaning making' (Kress, 2003, p. 40).

7.5 Creativity in the context of social and cultural change

So far we have focused on the way creativity emerges from the constraints and possibilities of the immediate situation, such as within a constraining institution like the prison or the school, or in the possibilities drawn on by a group of people or an individual with regards to their own reading and writing. In this section, we emphasise the need to situate creativity in its broader political and economic contexts. Creative literacies, in the realm of everyday life, are embedded in social and cultural practices which, in turn, are situated in broader structures: institutional, political, economic. These structures and their associated social practices (including their language practices) are not stable or inert, but in a state of constant movement and change. Therefore, we need to adopt a diachronic or historical perspective when studying literacy and creativity.

ACTIVITY 7

Local literacy practices in Namibia: creativity and constraint (Reading C)

Please read Reading C by Uta Papen, 'Local literacy practices in Namibia: creativity and constraint'.

Have a look at the examples of creativity that Papen describes. What is the role of the social, economic and political context in making creativity possible or in restricting it?

What is the role of language in Papen's examples of creativity?

Creativity and learning – taking hold of new literacies

Changing socioeconomic conditions are often accompanied by changes in the linguistic and semiotic means that are available to a community. This can result in the opening-up of new communicative possibilities, or in the suppression and gradual disappearance of more 'traditional' practices. Such changes in the communicative repertoire may be the result of policies imposed from above, or they may arrive in the wake of broader processes of political and cultural imperialism. Colonialism's impact on local languages and local literacy practices is a good case in point. Reading C shows that in today's world, the influence of the global economy, the movements of capital and people and the discovery of new consumer markets have profound effects on our linguistic landscape.

Individuals and communities who live through times of rapid social and economic change often find themselves in situations where they need to adapt quickly to new linguistic contexts, learn new languages and engage with new forms of texts. Such processes of learning frequently involve creativity: creativity in the exploration of available resources (including resources that could accelerate the process of learning) as well as creativity that stems from the combination of new and old practices and text types, resulting in the creation of new hybrid genres and the recontextualisation of words and phrases into new discursive contexts. The examples in Reading C illustrate such processes. The tour guides from Face-to-Face Tours for example relied on 'literacy mediators' to help them deal with an unfamiliar text type (their flyer). Mr Kashango relied on snippets of his own knowledge of English words and phrases, which he recombined in an unusual fashion, creating a sign that bears witness to his linguistic apprenticeship. These examples demonstrate how people take hold of new communicative practices and create their own strategies to acquire the languages and literacy practices they need. In many cases, these are not the result of structured processes of teaching and learning in language classes or vocational courses, but happen through processes of informal learning, which require the exploratory and creative minds of individuals and communities who take up new language and literacy practices.

In his book *Illegal Alphabets and Adult Biliteracy*, Kalmar (2001) has documented how a group of illegal immigrants from Mexico who came to Cobden, a small town in Illinois, in the search for work, devised a strategy to help each other learn the English language. Living in a situation of economic scarcity, legal insecurity and isolation, these Mexicans created an alphabet that allowed them to write English 'the way it sounds' (p. 37). Their alphabet follows Spanish phonetic rules, but still allows the reader to arrive at a pronunciation that is recognisable for a native speaker of English. Figure 1 provides an example of the word lists that members of the group who were involved in the creation of the alphabet and the production of the 'Cobden' dictionaries collated over a process of several months.

The Mexicans of Cobden created their phonetic alphabet in response to a particular linguistic constraint. The main problem they faced was that the English spelling system did not work for them. Spanish orthography is based on the principal of one letter representing one sound. This is not the case with the English language. The driving force behind the creation of the hybrid alphabet was to find a way to write English so that the Mexican reader could pronounce English words the way they sound. A second related problem was that while many of the immigrants used dictionaries, these were of limited use to them, as they did not include any pronunciation guides.

Although far from being their only problem, their inability to speak English was perceived by the immigrants as a factor that exacerbated many of the social, legal and economic issues they faced. This is one of the merits of Kalmar's account: he situates the linguistic invention that he describes in the complex context of the Mexican immigrants' lives and is careful not to detach their attempts at learning English from their situation as illegal immigrants and low-paid contractual workers. In doing so, Kalmar supports our argument about the situated nature of creative literacy practices.

In Alfonso's own Handwriting

guare yu duen
que hace usted (= what are you doing)

town	taun	pueblo
right	ruit	derecho
left	LEFX	izquierdo
south	SAUTF	al sur
north	nourt	al norte
east	ist	al este
west	uest	al oeste
to call	tu cou	llamar
to telephone	tu telefon	telefonear
to look up	tu luk up	buscar
sick	sick	enfermo
broken	broken	quebrado
to transport	tu trensport	transportar
to hurry up	tu urrillop	darse prisa
guilty	guiolty	culpable
truth	chtrud	verdad
lie	lai	mentira
language	lenguech	idioma
trip	truip	viaje
to buy	tu bai	comprar
to reach	tu ruich	alcanzar
to cost	tu cost	costar
to desire	tu disiar	desear
right	ruat	derecho, correcto
right away	ruat avey	en seguida
away	avey	ausente, fuera

Figure 7.1   A Cobden word list (Kalmar, 2001, p. 55)

The situation of the Mexican immigrants in Illinois and the community-based tourism workers in Namibia shows how creativity emerges out of situations of broader social, political and economic constraint, where what is possible and what is achieved are restricted by available financial means, by difficulties in accessing dominant literacy practices, by social relationships of power and dominance and by institutional contexts. However, merely to say that a context is restricted may in a sense be misleading. It may precisely be the context of restriction out of which an imaginative response can emerge. In Reading B, Wilson made the same argument with regards to prison literacies that she discussed. With regards to literacy and creativity more specifically, the examples discussed here and in Reading C show what people do with literacy, or with new literacies, rather than what literacy does to them (cf. Barton, 1994). The Mexican immigrants used their own Spanish language and literacy skills and their understanding of phonetics creatively to devise for themselves an innovative way of learning English pronunciation. The graffiti artists in Katutura, signwriters such as Mr Kashango and tour guides like Simon and his friends all take hold of new literacies for their own particular purposes and in doing so they make use of the skills and resources they possess. In other words, the emphasis is on how people 'seize hold' of new literacies (Kulick and Stroud, 1993, p. 55).

Have a look at the box below. You will find more examples of creativity in writing and creative uses of new literacy practices, this time from a detailed ethnographic study of literacy practices in Nepal carried out by the anthropologist Laura Ahearn (1999). These examples once again illustrate the role of social and cultural change in the creation of new literacy practices.

Invitations to love

Sarita, I'm helpless, and I have to make friends of a notebook and pen in order to place this helplessness before you. Love is the sort of thing that anyone can feel – even a great man of the world like Hitler loved Eva, they say. And Napoleon, who with bravery conquered the 'world', united it, and took it forward, was astounded when he saw one particular widow. Certainly, history's pages are coloured with accounts of such individuals who love each other ... in which case, Sarita, I'll let you know by a 'short cut' what I want to say: Love is the agreement of two souls. The 'main' meaning of loving is 'life success'. I'm offering you an invitation to love.

(Ahearn, 1999, p. 199)

This is a letter, written in 1992 by a young man called Bir Bahadur to Sarita, the woman who was later to become his wife. The words in quotation marks were written in English. The rest of the letter is translated from Nepali. The above letter is just one of more than 200 love letters which Ahearn collected over several years of fieldwork in Junigau, a rural community in Nepal. Beginning in the 1980s, Junigau, a community of about 1,250 people belonging to a Tibeto-Burman ethnic group, witnessed rapid social and economic change. Greater access to education, in particular for women, which became possible with the opening of the village's first high school in 1983, had a significant impact on gender relations and marriage practices in Junigau. Young people increasingly began to resist arranged marriages and to choose their own partners. It is in the context of these changes that Ahearn describes what we would call the 'creative agency' of young people taking up love-letter writing. Not only do these young people create 'a new epistolary genre' in their community (Ahearn, 1999, p. 199), they also invent a new form of prolonged courtship, previously unknown in Junigau: courtship by way of writing.

The young Nepalis in Junigau draw on a variety of sources of inspiration when writing their letters: commonly known romantic tropes, but also booklets that offer guidance on how to write a good love letter (another new genre that emerged as a result of cultural change). They write in a mixture of the local Nepali dialect and standard Nepali, interspersed with English words and sometimes with phrases in Hindi and Sanskrit. In their letters, young people express feelings and ideas for which there are no other acceptable cultural channels in Junigau, such as strong expressions of romantic love. Their letters contain the projected and desired identities of a generation of young Nepalis who are searching for their own place in a society that is undergoing rapid social and cultural transformation. This can for example be seen in the new ideas about personhood and individual agency which they express in their letters. These are radically different from the traditional Nepali belief in fate as the main determinant of one's life.

> Some people say that if it's their lot in life, (whatever it is) they'll do it. But it seems to me that it's up to each person's own wishes ... Even without my telling you this, you would be knowledgeable about it.

> (Extract from a letter by young woman to her lover, Ahearn, 2001, p. 152)

> ... May our love reach a place where we can in our lives overthrow any difficulties that arrive and obtain success ...

> (Bir Bahadur, in Ahearn, 2001, p. 151)

It is, in particular, ideas and phrases related to development, to 'success' and to individual agency that appear frequently in love letters and that are often written out in English.

These letters are, without doubt, creative responses to a novel social situation. The writers of these love letters are trend-setters in a world that changes at a rapid pace. They create new epistolary styles and new languages, and in doing so, they put their own mark on the ongoing process of social and cultural change that their village has experienced since the 1980s.

In Ahearn's examples, creativity can be seen both in the texts (in this case the new genre of love letters) and in the new social practices (courtship by way of writing) that they are part of. Both Ahearn's and Papen's (Reading C) examples also demonstrate the writers' engagement with new discourses and new identities, a point to which we will now turn.

As indicated earlier, changing socioeconomic conditions are usually accompanied by changes in the cultural environment as well as in the networks of social and institutional relationships people are part of. This may lead to major transformations not only in people's ways of speaking and writing, but also in their way of seeing the world and themselves. Such changes are particularly salient for our understanding of creativity in relation to discourse and identity.

Let us briefly explain what we mean by 'discourses' here. Expanding on Definition 3 of 'discourse' in Section 5.3 of Chapter 5, we use the term here to refer to values, ideologies, forms of knowledge, identities and beliefs and the way they are communicated using language and other semiotic means that are associated with a particular institution, with a particular group of people or a subset of the community (Foucault, 1980; Fairclough, 2003; Gee, 1999). If we want to understand creativity in everyday uses of reading and writing, we have to pay attention to such discourses. Researchers in the New Literacy Studies (see Rockhill, 1993; Kell, 1996, 1999; Papen, forthcoming) have argued that as a social and cultural practice, literacy or written language is always embedded in particular social contexts and in the discourses that dominate in these contexts. It is our argument that creativity lies not only in the 'taking up' of new literacy practices, but also in the appropriation of the new discourses these contain. In the process of becoming familiar with new text types (e.g. a promotional flyer), the guides from Face-to-Face Tours acquainted themselves with the dominant discourses of tourism. In doing so, they adapted to and adopted new identities: they portrayed their community and themselves in ways that appealed to the tourist gaze.

These examples from Namibia and Nepal reveal the role of broader global influences of Western capitalist culture and its accompanying language practices and discourses. In Ahearn's examples, the letters are mainly written in Nepali, but their authors use English words and phrases to express ideas, such as the values of individual fulfilment and 'progress', that are new within Nepali communities. These show the process of identification with new discourses. But the influence goes both ways; it is not just that social and cultural change have caused creativity within literacy practices, literacy and writing are also causal factors in the process of social change. It was the availability of literacy that allowed women to start writing letters; it was the learning of English and the exposure to all sorts of new texts (magazines, films, school textbooks) that brought young people into contact with rich sources of ideas, identities and personalities, which in their letters they combine to fashion selves and others (themselves and their lovers) in ways that stem from their own desires.

7.6 Conclusion

This chapter has taken a broad approach to what creativity in written language means. By starting from a focus on practices around reading and writing, rather than starting with texts, we have been able to construct a particular set of understandings about creativity in written language. We have demonstrated the importance of collaboration and interaction in what has sometimes been seen as an individual enterprise. We have looked at the importance of the possibilities and constraints of particular contexts and technologies in shaping the forms of creativity which arise, and we have shown how creativity in written language can emerge in situations of constraint and confinement and can change in response to broader sociocultural forces and changing discourses.

This could imply an understanding of creativity as essentially emerging from the social context, and indeed we have challenged decontextualised and individualistic ideas about creativity throughout. However, in every section we have also seen how people are working with the resources available to them, to try to achieve their own goals and purposes.

The term 'goals' here should be understood in its broadest sense. These goals may relate to play, personal satisfaction, social communication, economic needs or identity work. There is a very powerful goal motivating the creativity in everyday literacy practices in prisons: 'keeping one's mind'. This is reminiscent of the creativity demonstrated by the Allotment Association in the first set of examples, when their survival was under threat. In the adolescent cultures studied by Camitta, concerns about social relationships are absolutely central, and creative literacy practices are part of creating and maintaining relationships and aligning oneself with specific cultural groups.

Creativity in written language is neither a decontextualised, individual activity, nor is it entirely shaped by the context within which it is situated. We are arguing that creativity in literacy is emergent not from an individual mind, nor from the social context, but from a relationship between the two: an active agent, creatively constructing texts and practices in pursuit of their own enterprises, by drawing on and combining elements available to them from all the aspects – interactional, contextual and sociocultural – of the settings in which they are working to achieve their goals.

READING A: Extracts from 'Vernacular writing: varieties of literacy among Philadelphia high school students'

Miriam Camitta

> It makes you feel good knowing you have a friend who will accept your writing. It makes you feel good to feel that safe.
>
> (Conversation, eighteen-year-old female)

> LET ME BE ME
> Let Me Be Me
> Let Me Dream til I can fulfill Dreams.
> Let Me follow Dreams, so that I May see where they May lead me,
> Let Me write til my hands are to fall,
> Let me spread all the Joy
> Which I have received,
> Let Me be Me, For there's
> No One Like Me.
>
> (Poem, seventeen-year-old female)

The two teenage writers, whose oral and written commentary about writing are quoted above, consider writing to be at the heart of their quests for meaning and identity. At eighteen, each had, for several years, kept diaries, maintained intensive correspondence with friends and relations, and composed poetry. Each believe that writing is central to transacting social relationships, to making meaning out of their lives, and that the act of writing signals that the truth is being told about them. Although much of what they wrote was private, an important component of their writing was its social aspect – its place in the web of activities that structured their intimate relationships.

Both of these writers were participants in a three-year study that I conducted of the writing of adolescents living in Philadelphia, a large urban centre in the north-eastern section of the United States. For each, as for many of the others with whom I worked, writing was a familiar, everyday activity. Used in a number of conventional ways, writing offered them options for expression as did dance, instrumental music, drawing and song.

This kind of writing is vernacular, that which is closely associated with culture which is neither elite nor institutional, which is traditional and indigenous to the diverse cultural processes of communities as distinguished from the uniform, inflexible standards of institutions. As such, the texts represented in this study are not essays, the officially designated discourse genre of academia, but rather are those that adolescents choose to write within the framework of adolescent culture and social organisation, those that have come to be called 'unofficial'. Taken as a whole, they are the discourse of social life.

Although the scope of the study did not encompass writing as it is practised as a consequence of the educational curriculum, the study was initiated at City High School (a fictional name for a public high school in a north-eastern city of the United States) because it was there, in my capacity of teacher, that I was able to locate individuals who would participate in the work.

The students with whom I worked lived in the greater Philadelphia area, and attended the one of four sites of City High School which shall be referred to as colony 'A'. They were white, black, hispanic, male and female. They ranged in age from fourteen to eighteen. The actual participants in the study were my students; however, they were able to tell me a great deal about the writing practices of their friends and relations whose texts were included in their 'writing collections'.

The setting for vernacular writing

My study of adolescent writing looked at writing in three kinds of settings: in the environs of the school proper, before and after the official school day, and during non-assigned student time; in my classroom; and in the homes of several of the participants. However, through interviews with the adolescents who participated in my study, and through reading the contents of written artifacts, it became clear to me that almost any time or place can be an opportunity for writing. Adolescents write when they are alone, with friends, amongst their classmates, and in large groups of strangers. The scenes of adolescent vernacular writing are the school classroom, when they are supposed to be following the lesson; the hallways and entranceways of the school building; the bus or subway stop; bus or subway; the bedroom, in the middle of the night; the attic, during the day or early evening when the rest of their family is around the house; the basement, with friends, where they rehearse raps, graduation speeches and routines for talent shows.

The activities of about 170 students at colony A of City High School were observed both in and outside of classes. During non-assigned school time, students could be found clustered about in small groups, seated around the many long cafeteria-style tables in the hall, in the vestibules or landings, propped on the old, deep window sills at either end of the hallways, or sprawled over the four, large marble steps leading up to the front door. These spaces were the settings for conversation, 'hanging out', and also for writing: inscribing slam books, autograph and year books; composing group and individual letters, flyers announcing school-related events and out-of-school social events; copying chain letters; composing raps and practising them; writing in journals and notebooks; sharing writing; composing flyers announcing 'jams', school dances and bake sales; and reading letters and notes from other students. I was sometimes drawn into these writing activities as a consultant, although most often, I was a casual observer.

Much of the writing that adolescents do is a form of social activity. For example, some types of writing that took place during free time, such as letter-writing, students told me, were meant to be exchanged during class, or in-between class periods. Some students used lockers as places to exchange letters. One student used a classroom desk that she shared with another student who had the same teacher at a different time period as a place to drop off letters that she had composed either during free time, at home, or in class.

Another form of writing, adapted specifically to the classroom, or any context where oral conversation is difficult, or proscribed, is the 'dialogue note', so-called because it is comprised of short queries or statements requiring an answer. The dialogue note, a 'quick communication fix', as one individual described it, is passed between two individuals, who take turns writing and answering, as can be seen below:

trouble —
Are you going to the fair or theater tomorrow with [teacher's name]?

Love, Reds

Reds,
   I said I was, but ...
Trouble,
   But what ...
I don't want to go to Jersey that late
Just go with [teacher's name]

Love, Trouble[1]

Several adolescents who participated in the study had dialogue notes in their writing collections that had been written on a bus, when the correspondents were prevented from conversing orally because they were not seated next to one another. One individual showed me a dialogue note, written on a bus, that had been passed to a young man who interested her and her friend, becoming a sort of letter of introduction.

The third setting in which I was able to study adolescent writing was in the homes of those students who agreed to work with me more intensively, about ten in all. These individuals were essentially my key informants, who not only shared their extensive writing collections with me, but devoted many hours to interviews and conversations about their lives, adolescent life in general, and about writing as they experienced it and as they believed others did. Although I was able to discuss writing with many students at colony A, only these ten became regular informants, and only five of those were key. Through these students, I became privy to letters, diaries, poetry, and their large collections of writing. While many of these texts were composed in other settings, they were archived at home in larger collections of writing, and among personal possessions and memorabilia.

Conducting fieldwork in respondents' homes seemed to elicit detailed descriptions of how they lived on a daily basis, the kinds of relationships they had with their friends and relations, their complaints and their problems. Topics we discussed, when I did not direct the conversation, mainly were about the relationships respondents had with friends, relations, and lovers.

Many of the texts that I read in the setting of my students' homes paralleled the intimate and personal content of the conversations we were having. Letters, diaries, journals and poems were filled with the uncensored expression of feelings and details about their experiences. Often, the conversation amplified the content of the texts, or texts were used to exemplify a topic of conversation. For example, Shelly, in discussing the conflicted but intense relationships she had with her best friend and her boyfriend, showed me letters and poems she had written which touched upon various aspects of the conflict. At times we discussed her dissatisfaction with her appearance. Then she brought out photographs of herself taken at a time when she liked the way she looked, and showed me current journal entries which consisted of lists of foods and their calorific values that she had consumed on the day of the entry, a description of her exercise regime, and letters to friends in which she was critical about her appearance. [...]

Writing roles/literate behaviour

The individuals who contributed most intensively to my research – my key informants – were essentially writers or authors. They practised writing routinely and regularly. However, many students at City High School, although not exactly authors, were conversant with a variety of written genres and could assume a number of roles in a writing event. It is thus possible to argue that adolescents form a literate community within which various forms of literacy are practised. In addition to being authors, they were the editors and the critical audience for those who were authors; the publishers and the consumers of adolescent literature; the readers of poetry and the recipients of notes. They acted as consultants and as ghost writers. They were experts of a sort, familiar with the forms of taste and style, but not regular producers of texts.

Individuals acting in extra-authorial roles collaborated with authors in the production of texts. They read and responded to the written form. They helped writers with lexical and metrical choices, as well as with content decisions. They often collaborated in the editing stage of the composing process. They were the scribes, working either in manuscript, typescript, dot matrix, or photocopy. Their role in the literate community was to participate in the reproduction and transmission of written texts. These individuals often disseminated copies of written texts among other adolescents. They were motivated by taste, that is, they sought to reproduce and disseminate texts that appealed to them, that were interesting or amusing.

Finally, being part of the literate adolescent community meant being a reader/editor of adolescent literature, those who determined which texts were circulated and which were not. Often self-appointed, reader/editors gained standing as arbiters of taste if the texts reproduced met with widespread enthusiastic reception.

Sylvia, a fan of Vicki's poetry, typed and reproduced Vicki's poem on the office copier, then distributed it among several students who were known by her to be poetry aficionados. Lonnie's raps circulated among rap enthusiasts, promoted by his collaborator, Anthony. Nikia acted as rap adviser and consultant to Lonnie, although she herself did not compose raps. Monique, Theresa and Jan circulated their books of poems among friends, who borrowed them for up to a week at a time. John's biting letters that satirised a teacher and a student enjoyed a wide circulation among City High School students. They were so popular that several students came forward and claimed authorship.

In addition to direct and indirect involvement with writing and the production, publication and dissemination of written texts, adolescents collected, archived and artifacted writing and written texts. Adolescents collected their own texts and those of other adolescents. They also collected texts from magazines, newspapers, greeting cards, textbooks and anthologies, and from other sources as well. These collections were archived, with no regard for provenance or authorship, in books, folders, envelopes, boxes and drawers. Certain texts were artifacts, such as greeting cards and books; others were artifacted, that is, made into books or greeting cards, appended to greeting cards, or transformed into plaques. These collections were very important to adolescents, counted among their most important possessions. Christa willed her collection to Monique, her best friend. When Janet assembled her collection of current writing, she asked her best friend to keep it 'safe' for her. Vicki's self-made book of original poetry circulated among her friends and admirers of her writing.

Vernacular writing process

As suggested by the findings of the literacy project, aspects of cultural process attributed to folk or vernacular culture, such as performance and collaboration, are central to the processes of vernacular writing, where the text is the vehicle for accomplishing culture. Bauman and Bruner have each suggested that performance necessarily entails collaboration by involving the audience directly or indirectly in the construction of the text (Bauman, 1987; Bruner, 1986). The act of sharing a text with a reader or listener is a kind of performance that makes writing a collaborative venture between author and an audience composed of readers or listeners. The response of this audience to the text often inspires the author to change the text, which then reflects both the contributions of the audience as well as the author.

Performance may occur during drafting, as it does in the construction of personal letters. Partially, or wholly composed letters are frequently read aloud to an audience of at least one listener, or given to a reader, who offers advice about rhetorical strategies that is often considered crucial to the effect of the letter upon its intended receiver.

Letter-writing among students at City High School is frequently a collaborative activity, often involving a sharing event that functions as performance. Several of these students read drafts of letters aloud to friends prior to sending them, at which time they receive advice about phrasing, tone and content. Shelly and her friends confer over the composition of 'Dear John' letters, offering advice in the form of comments such as 'No, don't say it like that', or 'Don't write that', because 'it sounds like you want him back'. Christa, whose main mode of communicating with her estranged father is through letter-writing, plans and revises her letters with exacting care, often soliciting advice on wording, spelling and diction. For Christa, each letter is seen as a way to improve their communication, through accurate portrayal of her feelings. [...]

Rap is original verse, composed in rhymed couplets. Although it is intended to be orally performed to the beat of popular music, it is often composed in writing. Adolescent 'rappers' and erstwhile 'rappers' often carry notebooks in which are inscribed their own raps, and in which they record the raps of other amateurs and professionals. A major component of rap composition is the 'rehearsal' performance, in which the rapper tries out his rap orally in front of a small audience of friends.

At rap rehearsals at City High School during free time, students often solicited and received advice from a small audience of editors and 'consultants'. The rap consultant and editor listens to the rapper perform the rap orally, then offers advice about metrical construction and performance, diction, and rhyming. Sometimes, the editor or consultant reads the rap and 'corrects' it, that is, substitutes words that don't sound right, because they aren't in the particular slang vocabulary of the moment, or because they don't rhyme or conform to the meter.

In this way, raps are revised as a result of the feedback rappers receive in these rehearsal/performances. Rap consultants or experts who are often a part of the rehearsal/performance audience, and act as editors of rap texts, enter into collaborative composition with rap composers. [...]

The performance of a rap or of a letter is a collaborative venture, engaging audience and author in a critical dialogue. Through that dialogue, the experience of the individual is brought into focus with that of the group, through the interplay between author and audience which reshapes experience for each via the text. Thus, a text is subject not only to the conventional rhetorical strategies that reflect the collectivity of cultural expression, but is often collectively shaped during its actual composition.

This collaboration between author and audience that takes place during the creation of a text points to the role that writing has *vis-à-vis* culture. Sharing texts is an event that is the locus of the experience of the individual author with that of the audience. Sharing or performing texts brings the experience of the individual into focus with the group. The performance of the text and the response of the reader/listener/audience to the text of individual experience has the effect of reshaping experience for both the author and the audience.

Vernacular texts

The vernacular writing of adolescents constitutes a non-canonical literature marked by both its play with the conventions of folk as well as formal literature. The style, structure, and content of this literature frequently result in innovations to the traditional genres. It is a body of literature composed of cultural material that is appropriated and reassembled in vernacular and often creolised formats.

Two vernacular formats are the result of 'patchwork' and 'mosaic', composing techniques employed by adolescent writers which date to the middle ages (Bakhtin, 1986). In the case of both patchwork and mosaic, texts are constructed through the appropriation of words and phrases from oral tradition, popular culture or literary texts. The mosaic technique is differentiated from patchwork in that mosaic texts are constructed entirely from materials appropriated from various cultural sources, while patchwork texts are original to the author with occasional insertions of appropriated material.

> Mosaic
> Help! I need somebody! Help! Not just anybody! Help! I need somebody now. Lady love never smiles so lend your love to me a while, do with me what you will, break the spell and take your fill. On and on we rode the storm the flame's back and the fire's gone, on this empty bed is a night alone, I realized that long ago. Is anybody out there? Is anybody there'? does anybody wonder? Does anybody care?[2]

> Patchwork
> 'Dad's obstacle course'
> Why do you confuse me so?
> So many questions unanswered, untold
> Should I stay or should I go?
> Which way is up?
> (I think you went down.)
> Where's the door 'gotta get out of here.[3]

In each of these examples, borrowed lyrics, phrases and words refer to their sources implicitly, combining in a way that is both original to the writer and derivative of others. Patchwork and mosaic are examples of vernacular authoring techniques by which culture is reorganised by the individual through the appropriation of its materials.[4]

Another composing technique that resulted in the creation of vernacular formats is merging two or more genres or embedding one genre into another. An example of the former is the poem/letter, in which the poem is framed by the letter format, and poetic diction substitutes for conversational prose narrative. An example of the latter is the embedding of a poem, popular song lyrics or a rap into a letter. [...]

Conclusion

In conversations with adolescents about their writing, and through reading their texts, I came to understand better the ways in which writing figures in adolescent social life – as a part of conversation, a mode of self-disclosure, a personal statement and monument to the individual. I saw that personal and creative writing is a motion towards intimacy, and that its exchange weaves the strands of friendship and understanding.

For adolescents, writing, thinking, talking and feeling are interconnected activities, multiple channels and levels of discourse upon a topic. Talking with me about their personal lives when we were supposed to be talking about writing was not a divergence from the task, but in fact, exemplified the way that writing was connected to the rest of their lives.

Adolescents express their inner life through writing, believing that in the act of writing they are telling the truth about themselves. Writing invents and authenticates the individual through the process of discovery, inscribing the experience of the individual in time, and becoming a souvenir of that experience.

The vernacular writing of adolescents is cultural dialogue, a discourse that shifts back and forth among ideas and texts, fashioning experience discursively. For Edward Bruner, culture, or society, is constituted by the public performance (through texts) of the individual apprehension of experience (1986). The text, according to Bruner, stands in a dialogic relationship to the individual and society: it is constructed by the individual, who, through the public performance of the text, constructs society, which, in turn, influences the construction of the text on the individual level. [...]

References

BAKHTIN, M.M. (1986) The *Dialogic Imagination: Four Essays*, in M. HOLQUIST (ed.), trans. C. EMERSON and M. HOLQUIST, Austin, University of Texas Press (first published 1981).

BARTHES, R. (1977) *Image, Music, Text*, trans. S. HEATH, New York, Hill and Wang.

BAUMAN, R. (1987) *Text, Story and Event*, Cambridge, Cambridge University Press.

BRUNER, E.M. (1986) 'Experience and its expressions', in V.W. TURNER and E.M. BRUNER (eds) *The Anthropology of Experience*, Chicago, Ill, University of Illinois Press.

FOUCAULT, M. (1977) *Language, Counter-Memory and Practice: Selected Essays and Interviews*, trans. D.F. BOUCHARD, New York, Cornell University Press.

Notes

1   Classroom correspondence, from writing collection, 1984.

2   Student's writing collection, 1982.

3   Student's writing collection, 1982.

4   For a discussion of the disappearance or death of the author, see Foucault (1977) 'What is an author', pp. 113–38, and Barthes (1977) 'The death of the author', pp. 142–8.

Source: CAMITTA, M. in B. STREET (ed.) *Cross-Cultural Approaches to Literacy*, Cambridge, Cambridge University Press, pp. 228–46.

READING B: 'Auld Frankie Vaughan was swingin' his grin up by the Drummy while Clint Easterhoose was slinging his thing on the silver screen. Acid drops in the rain of the summer of blood. So cool it was fuckin' freezin' man!' – Creativity in language as a strategy for survival

Anita Wilson

Introduction

Traditionally, when we think of creativity, we envisage something that occurs in enjoyable and spontaneous ways, in environments that are safe and supportive. We talk about the 'creative process' and of supporting 'the creative arts'. We use 'creative writing' classes as a form of self-expression and we often applaud, commend, or position someone as 'being creative'. But I want to suggest that we take a different approach and instead ask the question 'Can creativity occur under duress or in the face of adversity, and if so what form might it take?' The answer might be both 'yes' and 'surprisingly prolific'. If we take a broad culturally diverse stance we gain an opportunity to explore the notion that creativity can emerge from a position of powerlessness and can utilise anguish and struggle for its inspiration. This does not mean that distressing circumstances necessarily produce depressing art. American blues music, for example, emerged from the pain of slavery, great works of Western art have been produced by artists on the edge of sanity and writers driven by despair and depression contribute greatly to the English poetry tradition. So to look more closely at sites of struggle, at specific environments, and the language and creative processes embedded within them might prove a fruitful area of investigation. That is my intention for this reading. Even so, it might come as something of a surprise to the reader that within an environment as suppressed and controlled as a prison, opportunities for creativity are substantial, prolific and diverse.

Background

To a reader with little or no understanding or knowledge of prison life, incarceration and creativity might appear as conflicting and irreconcilable terms and concepts. Yet from my perspective as a prison ethnographer I see creativity and ingenuity manifested in prison in a variety of astounding and innovative ways. Unlike the outside world, however, while instances of creativity occur as much for creativity's sake, the vast majority of innovation in the prison setting is used not for play, humour or dalliance, but in order to 'keep your mind' as a prisoner once told me and to encourage a sense of mental agility in a world designed to reduce everything and everyone to conformity and orthodoxy.

I want to begin with his quote, sent to me some ten years ago at the start of my ethnographic research when I was beginning to recognise the ways in which prisoners sought to keep a sense of social and personal identity in an institutional world. I have used the quote many times as his language encapsulates far better than mine the overarching need to be creative in the prison setting.

Brief disturbances of polluted waters

It is a silent battle – not with a recognised enemy – it is a battle with our minds. To win we have to pamper our minds, cater for them, bribe them, keep them occupied or lose them. If we lose our minds, we lose ourselves and the battle. It is a battle I will not and cannot lose.

(Personal correspondence, 29 April, 1994)

Not only does the writer's language come within our parameters of creativity, it also illustrates the fact that creativity – including that which uses language as its medium – is not a luxury but a required strategy employed in order to remain sane as a human being. So we can now refine the question and ask 'In what ways are prisoners creative?' In truth, the process is an organic one, influenced by many factors such as time, environment, culture or human state of mind. And it is also important to recognise that ethically speaking there are substantial areas of creativity within prisons that I cannot or do not want to bring into the public domain. The creative ways in which people in prison occupy their time or communicate with each other and with their outside worlds need to be understood within the context in which they occur and many of the complexities of prison life cannot be appropriately contextualised within this reading. However, as an ethnographer who has shared and/or observed many day-to-day instances of prisoner creativity – language and non-language oriented – there are aspects of the creative process that prisoners and I are prepared to reveal here. While the emphasis of this volume is on creativity in language, it is important to remember that that creativity (and language) are themselves situated and contextualised by the environments, spaces, times, and cultures in which they finds themselves. So I am going to begin by giving a giving a few brief general comments about creativity in terms of space and materiality before going on to look more closely at creativity and language within the spaces that prisoners manage to carve out.

Prisoners' creativity – spatial and material

In terms of spatial creativity, I have noted elsewhere that at the broadest level prisoners create a culturally appropriate third space in which to live out – rather than exist within – their incarcerated lives. For more detail I refer the reader to 'Researching in the third space' (Wilson, 2003) and encapsulate the concept with the following explanation:

> All those who spend time in prisons remain aware both of the outside worlds they have left behind and the perceived threat of Prisonisation with which they are faced. Rather than forget the former or be drawn into the latter, I maintain – and prisoners validate – that acquired knowledge of both 'Prison' and 'Outside' allows them to create a culturally-specific environment – a 'third space' – in which to live out their everyday lives.

> (Wilson, 1999, p. 20)

Within this space and in line with the culturally-appropriate rules through which such a space is organised, prisoners are inventive and imaginative at many levels. Creativity in material terms takes many forms and appears to transcend both time and space. In Victorian prisons, for example, Mayhew and Binny (1862) noted that female prisoners fashioned 'letter bags' out of scraps in which to keep their correspondence. Mack (1989, p. 161) noted that prisoners in the USA made hats from underwear to protect their hair from lice. In the escape from Whitemoor prison (1995), it was noted that 'of the vast array of items used in the escape, only a very limited number are considered to have been "imported": the majority had been manufactured or adapted on site' (Woodcock, 1994, p. 19). During my long-term field observations, prisoners have shared with me that they fashion nooses from bedsheets, hone blades from plastic utensils and make picture frames, tobacco tins and jewellery boxes from matchsticks. They use toothpaste to stick their posters on the wall and carve objects from bars of soap. Some use their toilet bowls in which to make illicit alcohol! Even within these few examples of material creativity, language-related activities and practices emerge. The possession of 'letter bags' implies that language is both written and read. Picture frames suggest that prisoners have an awareness of the 'language of images' (Mitchell, 1980) as an appropriate means of communication and sticking up posters with toothpaste brings together pre-existent material practices (using posters for decoration) and culturally specific creativity (sticking them up with toothpaste!). It has become apparent to me that literacy and language-related activities and practices take a central role in the day-to-day lives of people in prison and hence they are also placed at the center of the third space model (Wilson, 2000). It follows on, then, that creativity will also be focused around language and it is to creativity both around and within written and spoken texts that I now want to turn.

Creativity around language

[looking for people to participate in a specific piece of research involving a number of young men in one prison, two prisoners] [...] say that the guy next door -'midget' – would also be quite happy to do it – they ask him by calling through the wall via the electric cable fixing which links the two cells – the answer comes back via the toilet bowl and it is answered from my side through the air vent at the top of the wall which is accessed by climbing onto the toilet seat.

(Research observation, 1997)

One of the main purposes of engaging with oral or written language is to communicate and in a world where communication is severely restricted, and in order to keep one's mind through the medium of social interaction, people in prison find ingenious ways to maintain channels of oral communication. Shouting out of windows between cells and across prison yards seems to be universal and activities noted by Sharansky (1988) below – including a toilet bowl episode – are reflected in many scenarios I have witnessed or which have been recounted to me.

[...] there was intense intercell communication. The toilets were the most effective means but it took a lot of work to remove the water... we also used the radiators. You would press your mug against the heating pipe and speak into it; to listen you'd turn your mug upside down.

(Sharansky, 1988)

It is also significant that 'pressing your mug against the heating pipe' bears a strong resemblance to childhood practices around tin cans and pieces of string!

Prisoners are no less creative around the material transmission and transference of written texts across hostile space. In South Africa, for example, political prisoners on Robben Island used tennis balls to relay messages to each other, slitting the ball and inserting a written note before hitting over the intervening walls. In St Petersburg prison, written texts are transformed into paper darts and directed onto the public streets below. In France, the Revolutionist Kropotkin noted that:

[...] on one occasion, a petty lawyer, detained in the prison, wished to send to me a note... quite a number of men took the liveliest interest in the transmission of that message, which had to pass through I don't know how many hands before it reached me.

(Kropotkin, 1988, p. 465)

From personal experience, prisoners tell me that they transmit written messages by the practice of 'swinging a line' which requires attaching the text to a piece of string (or unraveled prison blanket), 'swinging' it to the cell next door or lowering it to the cell below.

Modes of communication can also be synthesised, again illustrated so clearly by Kropotkin and supported by current prisoners who tell me of similar practices where literacy and numeracy, the written, the spoken and the heard are meshed together in a creative and successful way.

> From all sides I heard knocks with the foot on the floor … conversation was soon established and usually conducted in the abridged alphabet; that is, the alphabet being divided into six rows of five letters, each letter marked by its row and its place in the row.

> (Kropotkin, 1988, p. 359)

In yet another variation, texts can transcend the spoken or the written and move into virtual spaces where they become what I have referred to as 'mental' literacy (Wilson, 1999). This occurs primarily in the lives of those prisoners housed in punishment cells where they are often denied access to resources such as pen and paper. They resort to retaining language 'in their heads'. The creative process however continues and people tell me that they mentally critique their own poetry, making virtual changes, rehearsing the language until such times as they may (or may not) be able to write it down. Some prisoners also tell me that 'in your head' is not only the most creative but also the safest place to store texts that hold special significance because 'no-one can steal them from you'.

From a visual perspective, prisoners take written texts and bring them within what Mitchell (1980) refers to as the 'language of images' and what I have termed 'visual literacy' (Wilson, 2000), decorating their cells with posters, cards, letters and photographs in order to create a montage that depicts their personal rather than their prison identity. While the practice is almost universal, prisoners maintain a sense of individuality by putting their own personal imprint on each display (see Wilson, 2003, p. 305 for an example).

It follows that for a group of people who identify creativity as an essential strategy to 'keep one's mind', that they would apply it equally successfully within as well as around written and spoken texts. It is in such instances that aspects of personal and cultural circumstance become particularly significant as people strive to retain a sense of individual rather than institutional identity and to which I now turn.

Creativity within language

> I think it's really the digger code you're after, you know the secret one that wouldn't really be a secret if I told you now would it!

> (Personal correspondence, 7 July 1997)

Creative communication does not stop at 'shouting out of cell windows' or 'using the toilet as a telephone'. Prisoners who may be in most need of 'keeping their mind' resort to even more complex strategies. As noted from the quote above, the 'digger code' – spoken or shouted between the cells in the punishment block – remains a secret shared only by those who have experienced extreme deprivation, and regimes in many parts of the world force prisoners to devise equivalent culturally specific codes in order to talk to each other about court cases, current political situations or to offer moral support. At its simplest, the code relies on systems of syllabic juxtaposition or embellishment. At its most complex, these systems are inter-changed frequently in order to ensure that they remain outside the comprehension of wider audiences.

At a more general level, especially among young prisoners, words that are meaningful one week may have lost their currency by the next. Being referred to as 'safe' – a term used to define someone who can be trusted – may be superseded by the term 'sound' for example or some other phrase entirely. To be currently and creatively 'au fait' with the accepted terms is a pre-requisite of third space membership. At the time of writing this piece, 'off road' is the current term for being in prison while 'on road' refers to when a person is back out 'on the streets'. Even this is too general an observation as each term may or may not be used in the future, dependent upon the cultural background – in prison and geographical terms – of the person who uses it.

When thinking about creativity, it is important not only to link language use to the culture of the environment in which it takes place but also to the language associated with a person's cultural heritage to which they continue to refer as they strive to retain a sense of personal self within the institution.

Creativity and culture

'Auld Frankie Vaughan was swingin' his grin up by the Drummy while Clint Easterhoose was slinging his thing on the silver screen. Acid drops in the rain of the summer of blood. So cool it was fuckin' freezin' man!' (This is to depict the year 1969 from a Glesca point of view. The Easterhouse street gang amnesty made all the news and lasted until Frankie Vaughan went home to Hollywood the following week).

(Personal correspondence, circa 1999)

Language in the third space draws on both outside and inside cultures for its inspiration and from the first day that I met the author of the piece above and his fellow prisoners I was struck by the fact that although they were physically disconnected from their cultural roots, the content of their language, the play with words and the specific culturally defined humour continued to bind them to the sociocultural landscape from which they originated. The piece above, written in prison as a means of 'keeping my mind', holds strongly to its linguistic roots, reflecting a sharp Glasgow wit and the ability to merge written and spoken linguistic genres. Its energy and vibrant imagery acted as a antidote to the blandness and numbingly predictable regime of prison life. In other systems, Scottish prisoners intent on holding to their language have creatively embedded 'Scottishness' into English jail graffiti such as 'toorin' their system' and 'AC fae Dundee' and have told me their letters have been held back for censure because they have written in what has been termed 'Scottish dialect'. This affirmation seeps into visual representation. I have noted the visual affirmation of cultural links in poetry given to me by Zeki in which illustration reflects his Turkish heritage (Wilson, 2003, p. 302). To keep the Celtic connection I share an additional example below on how this plays out in terms of the creative decoration of envelopes [see Colour Figure 9].

On the other side of the world, young African-American prisoners use equally creative language to write and perform hip-hop poetry which resonates with both their 'out of prison' and 'inside prison' experiences while in the UK young Black men in prison incorporate rap into their nightly conversations as they shout to each other through the bars of their windows after lights out. At its most extreme, prison poetry is used creatively as a foil for prison experience. 'Toasting' – an American phenomenon of performance poetry found in the county jails undertaken by one prisoner to an audience of others – uses derogatory language and often describes the foulest of imaginary predicaments in order to dilute the conditions in which the performer and the listeners find themselves (Jackson, 1974). In third space terms it draws on both 'inside' and 'outside', coming up with poetry such as 'The convict's prayer' based on the 23rd Psalm including the lines:

> The warden is my shepherd, I shall always want
> He maketh me to lie down behind the green door
> He leadeth me beside the wagon of salty water
> He kills my soul …
> I fear all evil for he is with me
> His pistol and solitary discomfort me
>
> (Jackson, 1974, p. 69)

This use of the poetic form illustrates one aspect of what I have come to understand as prisoners' preferred form of creative language – their love of and use of poetry. Engagement with poetry takes many forms. Some prisoners prefer to read citing 'love poetry', Edgar Allen Poe and Tennyson as favourites. Others take up the work of other prison poets and read their work, often embedding it within their personal correspondence. For the majority of prisoners, however, writing poetry is considered an acceptable and valued activity. It often takes surprisingly uncreative forms, holding to conventional rhyme, meter and stanza and frequently reflects conventional topics such as love, death, romance and epic. This conformity is off-set however by the creative use of language. This might be as detailed as a change from *s* to *z* as in 'The kidz theze dayz' – a private poem that was shared with me after a long process of negotiation – which also takes a creative stance on form (aided by the centering function on the computer!):

> They're only nine yearz old and they're smoking dope
> by the time they reach ten they're hooked on coke
> approaching eleven they've already done bird
> but the problem iz we think they're scared
> scared of what and scared of who because
> they're not scared of me and they're not scared
> of you they colour the wallz with aerosol sprayz
> but that's what they're like.
> THE KIDZ THEZE DAYZ
> (RC)
> (Ramon, C.)

It might be embedded within the language itself such as in 'Beyond the bounds of boundary' – a poem that falls within the mental literacy framework – and which is expanded further by the creative use of punctuation and form:

> O'yes! I see it all now
> Lazie-rays rounding out
>   From my brow
> In ever expanding circular patterns
> Turning to the rhythm of
>   The matter in the heavens
> (T. C. Campbell)

It might take on a visual quality where the impact of the words are equalled by the impact of the image itself as in the illustration opposite of 'Remember If ... .' The reader needs to be aware that this was a creative collaboration where the wishes of the author – as a strategy for keeping his mind – were followed by myself insofar as the poem and the idea of the swallow image were his and the access to the computer was mine.

From the discussion above, it can be seen that prisoners' engagement with poetry and indeed with creative processes around spoken and written language goes far beyond what we might conventionally construe as 'creative'. I want to end with some concluding remarks about how this discussion on creativity in prisons can be taken forward.

Remember if....
If one night on a gently sloping hill of grass
You should lay dreaming
As the turmoil of the world
And time rolls past
To find you in the morning
With dew on your hair
And the scent of flowers in the air....
If you should be still and at peace
With yourself and all else
And time is without pressure
If you saw the moon fade
With the dawning of the sun
As they dance with heavenly leisure....
If in your thoughts of loving kindness
I should tumble through your mind
Even, as a shy nervous shadow
Perhaps you may care to follow
That fading track of memory
That's all that's left of me
For you're living now in the tomorrows
Of when you and I were free....
If you should see where I'm going
And once more live the part
Before it fades away   From the Book of Passing Thoughts
I will be honoured
What more can I say ....   By Tommy Campbell
And if I should disturb you
From your slumber
As you recall the fate of me
Do not despair
But stop and ponder
For though I'm chained in solitary
My mind is free to wander....
Small consolation you may say
Yet small as it may well be
It's as good as wings to me
So smile and look yonder
And should you see me fade away
With the dawning of the sun
As your consciousness awakes
And the new day has begun....
Remember I was with you
And we danced across the heavens
With the wind in the wings of our minds
Fluttering softly back through time
Pray...
Don't lock my memory.....
Away....

Figure 1   'Remember if' (T. C. Campbell)

Concluding remarks

It would seem that creativity in language is not a simple concept. We need to look at all aspects of language, written, spoken, and visual for example. It requires investigation and discussion from a variety of angles including creativity around as well as within language. We need to think about it as being influenced and situated within a variety of salient contexts such as time, environment, culture and space. Creativity – certainly in the context I have described – goes beyond our traditional frameworks of creativity as a positive, recreational, voluntary or peripheral notion.

It also transpires that creativity cannot be constrained within any particular domain but exists in the domain of the everyday as well as the academic or the artistic. Finally, if we take the time and have the commitment, it can be found in the most unlikely places, being used by an unlikely group of people for the purpose of 'keeping their mind'.

References

JACKSON, B. (1974) *Get your Ass in the Water and Swim like Me*, Cambridge Mass, Harvard University Press.

KROPOTKIN, P. (1988) *Memoirs of a Revolutionist*, New York, Dover Publications.

MACK, N. (1989) 'The social nature of words: voices, dialogues, quarrels', *The Writing Instructor*, **8**, Summer.

MAYHEW, H. and BINNY, J. (1862, 1971) *The Criminal Prisons of London and Scenes of Prison Life*, London, Frank Cass & Co. Ltd.

MITCHELL, W.J.T. (1980) *The Language of Images*, Chicago, University of Chicago Press.

SHARANSKY, N. (1988) *Fear No Evil*, New York, Random House.

WILSON, A. (1999) 'Reading a library: writing a book – the significance of literacies for the prison community'. PhD (unpublished, Lancaster University).

WILSON, A. (2003) 'Researching in the third space – locating, claiming and valuing the research domain', in S. GOODMAN, T. LILLIS, J. MAYBIN and N. MERCER (eds) *Language, Literacy and Education: A Reader*, London, Trentham.

WOODCOCK, SIR JOHN (1994) *The Escape from Whitemoor Prison on Friday 9th September 1994 – The Woodcock Enquiry*, London, HMSO.

Source: commissioned for this volume.

READING C: Local literacy practices in Namibia: creativity and constraint

Uta Papen

Introduction

Katutura Face-to-Face, written in large letters on their advertising flyer, is the name of a small tour guiding business that takes tourists to the township of Windhoek, the capital of Namibia. Over the past 15 years, Namibia has seen its tourism industry growing steadily. In recent years a growing number of community-based tourism enterprises, run by black and coloured Namibians, have entered the tourism market. Face-to-Face Tours are such a community-based tourism enterprise (CBTE). When I asked the guides from Face-to-Face Tours how they had come up with the name for their business, they readily admitted that theirs was not a new idea: Simon, the founder of the group, had known of a similar tour guiding business in Soweto and had simply copied their slogan.

So is this creativity? Perhaps not. After all, copying someone else's invention hardly qualifies as a creative act. And yet, if we think about marketing for example, it heavily relies on copying and reappropriating what others have already done. Using language creatively, indeed, often means reinventing or reappropriating older forms. Seen from this angle, what Simon and his colleagues have done is an act of creative imagination, discovering the potential in a phrase that they found somewhere else and adapting it to their own purposes.

The reasons I consider Simon's adaptation of his competitors' slogan to be a creative act will become clearer once I have said more about the context of tourism in Namibia. Community-based groups such as Simon and his friends often start with no experience of tourism at all, they have little access to training and they lack the capital that would allow them to invest in elaborate marketing campaigns. What they achieve develops out of situations of constraint with limited resources available.

In this brief paper, I examine creativity in such situations of constraint and scarcity. More particularly, I discuss creativity in the context of changing socio-economic conditions as they affect individuals and communities. In doing so, I will look at specific social, cultural and institutional environments and the forms of language and literacy emerging from them. Creativity, in these environments, is driven by particular needs, for example the need to make money, to learn a new language or to acquire the skills of a job for which one had little prior training.

The examples I discuss over the following pages are part of a larger ethnographic research project on literacy in Namibia, carried out in 1999 and 2000.[1]

Namibia: a land of opportunities?

Namibia, situated north of South Africa and south of Angola, is a country of vast opportunities. This, at least, is how the country presents itself to foreign investors and to the growing numbers of visiting tourists. Once a German colony and later governed by South Africa, the country achieved its independence late, in 1990. Since the South African regime implemented apartheid in Namibia in much the same way as it did on its own territory, the country shares a lot with its southern neighbour.

The legacies of apartheid are still visible today. In Windhoek, the capital, tourists can now visit Katutura, the former township for black citizens. Even today Katutura remains an entirely black neighbourhood, set apart from the modern city centre of Windhoek and its middle-class suburbs.

But Katutura is not the derelict place that you might imagine. Its inhabitants are neither desperate nor subdued. A lot is happening these days in Katutura. With the help of government loans, people build new houses or renovate their old homes. They set up their own businesses and make a living as food vendors, hair dressers and dress makers, car mechanics or tour guides.

Katutura is an ideal place to explore the 'literacy environment', that is, the forms of literacy which we find in the public environment of towns and villages. There is a lot of creativity in some of these public literacies. The following section illustrates how people in the township use literacy in creative ways.

Advertising: promotional literacy practices in Katutura

Advertising is a truly global phenomenon. Throughout the world, urban spaces have turned into landscapes of buying and selling which rely on a variety of linguistic and visual practices to attract the viewer's eye to an ever growing number of services and products. Advertising has always been a playing field of creativity, and with the increasing saturation of global markets, the need for ever more inventive publicity strategies has become a matter of survival for producers all over the world. The so-called developing world and its many small-scale producers and informal markets are no exception to this.

Driving through the main streets of Katutura, the visitor cannot fail to notice the huge advertising spaces of multinational companies and big chain stores. But as soon as one leaves the central commercial area of Katutura and enters the realm of the township's informal economy, the bright colours of the adverts begin to fade and there are no more neon signs or iron plates. Instead, everywhere, on houses, shacks and stalls are self-made boards and handwritten inscriptions. Signs, made of wood, cardboard or other cheap materials, direct the visitor to a shebeen (a local bar) or a cuca shop (a small grocery shop).

These signs are part of the marketing campaigns of Katutura's business men and women. Most of the signboards in Katutura are made by the traders themselves. As you can see from Colour Figure 10, people make do with what is available to them. Creativity here has a material aspect.

There is much creativity in what the signboards say. Looking again at Colour Figure 10, we can see the text's adaptation of different genres and phrases, resulting in an eclectic mix of styles. I did not have the chance to talk to Mr Kashango, so I can only guess at what he meant to say on his signboard. 'Just find me here any time…' is a friendly, informal way of addressing his clients, township dwellers like himself. It nevertheless conveys an important piece of information: his business is open 24 hours a day seven days of the week. You can ask Mr Kashango for help at seven in the morning, when your radio doesn't work, or in the middle of your Saturday dance night, when your tape recorder breaks down.

Another creative strategy is the use of the owner's nickname on the signboard. 'Alles' in German means 'everything'. Although English nowadays dominates Namibia's linguistic landscape, German is still widely used, in particular in Windhoek and other cities. It is possible then that Mr Kashango's nickname is indeed 'Alles'. Does this also mean that he can repair 'alles' – everything? Adding the nickname creates a sense of familiarity and closeness with potential customers. Mr Kashango is likely not to be the only person in his part of the township who repairs radios and TV sets, so has to make himself known to his customers. Trying to create a sense of closeness and familiarity by using informal language and nicknames could be seen as part of this strategy.

Yet, the text of the signboard ends with a strikingly formal sentence, in which Mr Kashango thanks the readers of his signboard. 'Thank you for your cooperation' is a common phrase that Mr Kashango may have come across in some official text and which in his eyes may have seemed a suitable addition to his notice. The result of his adaptation is a bricolage of genres and registers that could be dismissed as the effect of Mr Kashango's poor knowledge of the 'language of advertising', but which may in fact be the result of some careful thinking and creative appropriation of a new language (English) Mr Kashango is unlikely to have been highly familiar with.

The graffiti example [opposite, Figure 1] illustrates similar moments of appropriation and recontextualisation. Recontextualisation takes place when genres and discourses that originate in one particular social practice are brought to use in a different social context (see Fairclough 2003). In the above example, Mr Kashango has adapted a phrase that we would expect to be part of the communicative practices of bureaucratic institutions. Figure 1 shows further examples of recontextualisation. Once again, I can only speculate about the writer's intention. What strikes me in the text is the use of 'CO^2' and 'V.I.P.', both abbreviations that the writer must have picked up in some other context. CO^2 could have been found in a school textbook; V.I.P. on the radio, on TV or in a magazine. Magazines of the type of *OK* or *Hello*

Figure 1   Graffiti (Uta Papen)

are well known in Namibia. They are produced in South Africa, but sold widely in the country. In both instances, the phrase has been moved to a different context and appropriated for a different purpose.

The two examples discussed above illustrate the role of different languages and language varieties with regards to creativity in literacy. Before Namibia became independent, Afrikaans was the dominant language of the country. Under South African occupation, black and coloured Namibians were prevented from learning much English in school, as the regime promoted the teaching of Afrikaans and provided instruction in the mother tongues. At independence, English was made the official language and henceforth became the language of all government communication. Today English is also the language of business and of tourism and in Katutura, which houses people from many different language groups, it serves as an important language of interethnic communication. Many people in Katutura do not have the time or the means to attend English language classes, although such classes are offered by the government as part of a major adult basic education programme (see Papen, 2005). But as Figure 1 and Colour Figure 10 have shown, this does not mean that they do not make use of the new language. They do so in many creative ways. Driving through the township, you will hardly find any signs, notices or graffiti written in local languages.

Literacy, creativity and tourism: learning the languages (and literacies) of tourism

Simon, Anna and Elisabeth, the guides from Face-to-Face Tours, are young school leavers, who grew up in the township. When Simon, the founder of the group, had finished secondary school, he worked as a taxi-driver, taking tourists from the airport to their hotels in Windhoek's city centre. His clients often asked him where he came from and wanted to know about the township. It was then that he had the idea to set up a tour guiding business.

The three friends set up Face-to-Face Tours in spring 1999. Since then, they have offered guided tours through the township to groups of 2–6 visitors. They show their clients the markets of the township, its bars and shops and the places where the struggle for independence and against apartheid took place. The tour also includes a visit to a recycling project, one of the new initiatives that have sprung up in Katutura in recent years. At present, Face-to-Face Tours are the only company that takes tourists to the township. Other tour agencies offer 'city tours', but these are limited to the city centre and the oldest neighbourhoods of the town, where the first German settlers lived. Some of the 'city tours' drive their buses through the main street of Katutura, but they usually do not stop in the township.

When Simon and the others first started the tours, they had little idea of where to take the tourists and what they might want to see. In fact, as Simon told me in one of our conversations, they did not even know what tourism was. It took quite a lot of creative thinking for them to imagine what a foreign visitor might like to see. For Simon and the others, who grew up in Katutura, the township was a boring place, which had little to offer and nothing to be fascinated about. But once they had been on their first tours, they soon began to gain an understanding of the main discourses that shape the tourists' ideas of the township as a place of 'real' African life and a symbol of resistance against apartheid and South African occupation. In their flyer [see Figure 2], they skilfully address these discourses of otherness and authenticity. While it highlights the township's past, its political history and its unique cultural setting, the leaflet also responds to the tourists' desire to see the 'real' Namibia, that is, to get a glimpse of contemporary life in a black township.

But what do tourism discourses such as the ones Face-to-Face Tours use in their flyer have to do with creativity? Tourism discourses are essential if we want to understand tourism texts (flyers, brochures, signboards, websites and others) and the 'design work' (Gee, 2000, p. 185) – creative work – that goes into their production. Tourism discourses are the representations of a place (and/or a group of people) created for tourists (Lindknud, 1998). Such discourses respond to what Urry (2002) has called the 'tourist gaze': how tourists look at a place, what they want to see and do, but also what they do not like to see and therefore will turn their eyes away from. Groups such as

Face-to-Face Tours respond to the tourist gaze by *creating* particular place-myths: ideas about a place that appeal to the foreign guests' dreams and imaginations (Lash and Urry, 1994, p. 265).

EXPERIENCE KATUTURA face to face

The tour you've been looking for. The only tour which opens vast historical Kautura – diverse in culture and lifestyles – the first colonial suburb of Namibia. No mass tour package. Trained indigenous tour guides help you create an exclusive adventure of living Katutura, allowing you to combine sightseeing with selective focus on wild life, bird-watching or historical/cultural points of interest.

City Tours

Tintenpalast. The seat of the Namibian legislative assembly, known as the "Tintenpalast" or Ink Palace, dates back to the German colonial era.

Craft Centre. An interesting array of traditional Namibian arts and crafts; plus a coffee shop with flair.

Game Tours **Daan Viljoen Game Park** lies about 24 kilometres west of Windhoek, set in the hills of the Khomas Hochland. Various species of antelope, as well as zebra, baboon and ostrich can be viewed. Bird life is prolific: about 200 species are represented. Hiking trails: 1.5-kilometre and a semi-circular route of 9 kilometres.

Desert Tours **Spitzkoppe**. Popularly known as the Matterhorn of Namibia, the Spitzkoppe rises 1829 metres above the Namib plain and is the site of a number of rock paintings. This day-tour also takes you to the fascinating Namib Desert and to the coastal town of **Swakopmund**, centre of art nouveau culture at the turn of the century.

Katutura Tours **Penduka**. Goreangab Dam offers an interesting variety of activities and experiences, such as hiking trails, music and drama presented by local Penduka women, and diverse cultures at home in the traditional village.

Shifidi Homestead. Observe typical Katutura lifestyles of urban blacks. Meet Hilde Shifidi, whose father, Immanuel Shifidi, was brutally murdered while addressing a political rally soon after he was released from Robben Island. At the homestead: history of Immanuel Shifidi, traditional meals and beverages on request, traditional music and dancing.

Katutura face-to-face Tours
Guided tours for individuals and groups; transfers from International Airport to town.

Phone & fax   061-265 446
P.O. Box 22389
Windhoek, NAMIBIA

Figure 2   'Experience Katutura face to face'

Apart from a short basic training in tourism, offered by a Namibian organisation, Simon and his friends had had no professional training in tourism or tour guiding. In that situation, the best they could do was to identify and explore the sources available to them. They went back to their old school books to refresh their knowledge of the township's past. They went around the township to look for places of interest and to talk to people who remembered the apartheid past and the forced move into Katutura. For further inspiration they relied on their clients.

The guides from Face-to-Face Tours also relied on literacy and discourse mediators to help them access and understand new literacies and new forms of knowledge. When they first set up their business, Face-to-Face Tours asked a friend, who works as a journalist, to help them with the design and the production of their flyer. While I worked as a researcher with them, they approached me for help with writing the text for a new promotional flyer. They asked me, because they knew I would be able to draw on both my experience as a tourist myself and my English writing skills.

The above are examples of creativity that can be found in the search for and the use of resources that allow people to take hold of new economic opportunities. What I am interested in here is not primarily the creativity of any text itself, but the imaginative ways that lead to their production and use. A crucial point to make about such creative literacy practices is that they emerge out of particular socio-economic contexts. In a positive sense, people like Simon and his friends are opportunists. Being inventive about the kind of resources they could access and seizing opportunities (even such unexpected ones as the appearance of a foreign researcher who was interested in their own reading and writing practices) is a sign of creative thinking that while recognizing the constraints of any given situation is able to identify the opportunities, or the affordances, to borrow Kress' (2003) term, inherent in any communicative context.

Where there are no computers or digital cameras: creativity and multimodality

The Khowarib camp [see Colour Figure 11] is another community-based tourism enterprise that was set up in recent years. It is located near the main road which leads through the central parts of Namibia towards the Kaokoveld in the north-west. Khowarib is an ideal stopping point on the way to the north, and as the signboard indicates, the people of the Khowarib community have more to offer to the tourists than just a place to put up their tent. However, like other CBTEs, Khowarib has no easy position in the dense Namibian tourism market. The mainstay of the Namibian tourism industry is safari and wildlife tourism. The structures of the tourism market reflect the inequalities inherited from the colonial and apartheid eras: by and large the sector is in the hands of private – white – businesses, hotels, lodges, guest farms and tour agencies. These have close contacts with travel agencies in the sender countries and can rely on a regular stream of visitors. There are limited opportunities for newcomers such as Khowarib or Face-to-Face Tours, who face the competition of these more established providers. Furthermore, many of the CBTEs are located in relatively remote areas, away from the well-known sites and the established tourist routes. As a result, CBTEs have to make particular efforts to attract tourists to their services.

A closer examination of the text and its accompanying drawing shows the semiotic work that went into the design of the signboard and that is necessary in order to turn local places into tourist attractions. The Khowarib campsite offers 'natural showers' (built of mostly local materials) because its owners know that the tourists who are on their way to the wilderness of the Kaokoveld are likely to have come to Namibia for its flora and fauna and its unspoilt natural environment. These tourists regard themselves not only as nature lovers but also as conservationists who are keen to support the local economy. Yet, although they want 'natural' showers, after a day of travelling through the dusty Namibian countryside, the typical European or North American tourist is unlikely to stop at a campsite that does not provide the modern luxury of running water!

The motifs chosen for the drawing on the right side of the signboard are stereotypical representations of African village huts. Visitors will recognise these symbolic representations and the fact that they look hand-drawn rather than commercially produced is likely to add to their appeal. Such hand-drawn images represent what Jewitt and Oyama (2001) call a sensory modality, which is assessed by its viewers not in terms of its reality value, but its assumed authenticity, responding to the tourists' search for an 'authentic' experience of African life. In the case of this signboard, text and image reinforce each other's message. Creativity here is located in the choice of words and motifs as well as in the combination of textual and visual elements. The creative thinking that went into the production of Khowarib's sign is an example of the kind of creativity Kress (2003) refers to when he talks about 'the everyday process of semiotic work' (p.40), which requires the sign-producer (and this counts for any form and materiality of sign) to be aware of and to exploit the meaning potentials of the different resources available to them.

Conclusion

Camitta (1993), Wilson (2000) and other researchers suggest that vernacular writing is often driven by moments of rebellion and resistance to dominant forms of literacy, and dominant forms of living and being, as they are sanctioned by schools and society. In the cases I have looked at here, creativity was not driven by resistance to dominant practice, but by the desire and need to take hold of new languages and new writing practices, including the dominant writing practices of powerful elites.

Creativity, in these cases, is manifest in people's efforts to take hold of new ideas and their verbal and written manifestations. This is never a process of mere repetition, but always entails adaptation and change. This is certainly evident in the way local tourism workers and CBTEs not only exploit, but 'create' a niche for themselves in the Namibian tourism market. They do so by selectively highlighting the strategic advantages they have. In the case of Face-to-Face Tours this is their status as 'indigenous' (black) guides, who can take tourists to places where a white guide would never be able to get to. For the Khowarib camp, it is its unique location in a beautiful part of the country that appeals to the Western tourists' longing to rebuild their ties with nature and their interest in 'primitive' forms of life. It is these advantages that the two CBTEs creatively explore in their leaflets and signboards.

To end, I want to highlight two points that emerge from the examples of creativity in Namibia that I presented here. The first point is the situated nature of creativity. My examples suggest that creativity is always contextual and that what is found to be creative in one context may look rather conventional and unimaginative in another. It follows from this that what is creative about a particular text cannot simply be 'read off' or identified by studying the text alone, but requires extensive knowledge of the context and conditions out of which a particular text emerged and within which it is read.

My second and final point is that creativity does not only take place in exceptional circumstances, the idealised long-prepared moment of creative activity. Not only is creativity an everyday life process, it often happens in situations which at first glance do not appear to be conducive to creative activity at all. In situations of rapid socio-economic and cultural change, as in the examples I discussed here, creativity becomes a virtue, if not a necessity, in the struggle to adapt to and benefit from the changing environment.

References

BARTON, D. and HAMILTON, M. (2000) 'Literacy Practices', in D. BARTON, M. HAMILTON and R. IVANIC (eds) *Situated Literacies*, London, Routledge.

CAMITTA, M. (1993) 'Vernacular writing: varieties of literacy among Philadelphia high school students', in B. STREET (ed.) *Cross-Cultural Approaches to Literacy*, Cambridge, Cambridge University Press.

FAIRCLOUGH, N. (2003) *Analysing Discourse. Textual Analysis for Social Research*, London, Routledge.

GEE, J.P. (2000) 'The New Literacy Studies: from "socially situated" to the work of the social', in D. BARTON, M. HAMILTON and R. IVANIC (eds.) *Situated Literacies*, London, Routledge.

JEWITT, C. and OYAMA, R. (2001) 'Visual meaning: a social semiotic approach', in T. VAN LEEUWEN and C. JEWITT (eds) *Handbook of Visual Analysis*, London, Sage.

KRESS, G. (2003) *Literacy in the New Media Age*, London and New York, Routledge.

LASH, S. and URRY, J. (1994) *Economies of Signs and Space*, London, Sage.

LINDKNUD, C. (1998) 'When opposite worldviews attract: a case of tourism and local development in Southern France', in S. ABRAM and J. WALDREN (eds) *Anthropological Perspectives on Local Development. Knowledge and Sentiments in Conflict*, London and New York, Routledge.

PAPEN, U. (2005) 'Reading the bible and shopping on credit: literacy practices and literacy learning in a township of Windhoek, Namibia', in A. ROGERS (ed.) *Urban Literacies*, Hamburg, UIE.

URRY, J. (2002) *The Tourist Gaze: Leisure and Travel in Contemporary Societies*, 2nd edn, London, Sage.

WILSON, A. (2000) 'There is no escape from third-space theory: borderland discourse and the "in-between" literacies of prisons', in D. BARTON, M. HAMILTON and R. IVANIC (eds) *Situated Literacies*, London, Routledge.

Notes

1   This research was supported by a King's College London Association (KCLA) research studentship and by the University of London's Central Research Fund. I thank both institutions for their support.

Source: commissioned for this volume.

8

The 19th-century communication revolution

David Vincent

8.1 Introduction

This chapter provides an historical perspective on literacy and creativity in nineteenth-century Britain, a century of enormous technological and social change and a particularly significant time for literacy. It was during this period that Britain, in common with neighbouring countries in north-west Europe, became for the first time a primarily literate society. Most of the population learned to read and write and the opportunities for practising their new skills expanded dramatically. As listeners and occasionally as readers, the labouring poor had been engaged with print since at least the Reformation, if only in the form of the Bible and Common Prayer Book. What makes the nineteenth century so fascinating is that not only did so many more readers gain access to so much more imaginative literature, but that the newly literate also began to find means of self-expression through the written word. As they did so, we can begin to examine the interaction between creativity and the economic, social and political struggles of men and women experiencing unprecedented changes in the home and the workplace.

The process of change from an oral to a literate society was multilayered and the turning points were rarely as decisive as official accounts suggest. Resources for creativity ranged from traditional oral activities and popular vernacular texts to new opportunities for written communication and the increasingly available works of English literature. In this chapter I shall focus on the literacy practices of the newly literate mass of the British population, treating reading and writing as closely interconnected and examining the expanding opportunities for obtaining and reading creative texts as well as for writing them. I shall look at the dynamics of everyday creativity along two axes of change.

First, there is the interaction between the individual reader and writer and broader political, social and economic forces. In promoting mass literacy the government was responding to the pressures created by the Industrial Revolution, and in turn the use of literacy was conditioned by demography and urbanisation, by the technology of the production and distribution of print, by the transport and market systems, and by the domestic and cultural practices of the labouring poor.

Second, there is the interaction between dimensions of creativity. The shift of emphasis between oral and written forms of communication cannot be associated with a unilinear growth of opportunity for imaginative discourse. In part it was a matter of movement between different categories of social and individual communication. In part it was a matter of children negotiating the pressures of conformity and self-expression in an increasingly schooled society. In part it was a matter of the newly literate exploring the affordances of contemporary technologies and the possibilities of creativity in forms of reading ranging from simple chapbooks to full-length novels, and in forms of writing ranging from short, misspelt postcards to published prose and poetry.

In order to understand creative literacy practices in the nineteenth century, we need to start by examining what was actually involved in the process of becoming literate at this point in British history. This chapter therefore begins with literacy itself (section 8.2). It asks questions about what the term meant in this era, and about the place of agency and creativity in the process of acquiring the capacity to read and write. It invites you to consider what it was like to encounter marks on a page or a blackboard for the first time, and how the process of instilling these skills affected how they could be put into practice in later life.

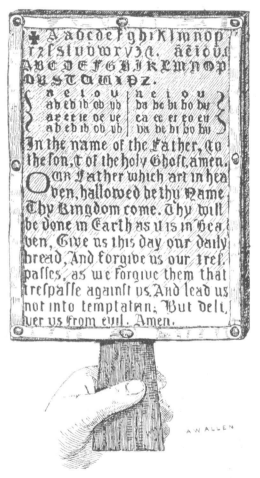

HORN-BOOK IN THE BRITISH MUSEUM.

Figure 8.1   A horn-book, 1750. Horn-books were made of a piece of paper fastened onto a wooden paddle and protected with a thin transparent layer of cow's horn. They were still being used to teach reading at the beginning of the 19th century. (Mary Evans picture library)

Section 8.3 looks at how new forms of popular reading responded to the complex communication strategies of the newly literate. It lays particular emphasis on the hybrid, makeshift nature of engagements with print, and on the growth of a new reading public. Section 8.4 examines the most characteristic forms of everyday writing in the era, the penny post, valentines, Christmas cards and holiday postcards. These presented the barely literate with genre-specific possibilities for employing the skills of penmanship laboriously acquired in their childhood.

Figure 8.2 Chapbooks. Developing out of the earlier ballad literature, 18th and 19th century chapbooks were small publications containing folk stories, poems, songs, religious tracts and other short texts. They were sold by 'chapmen' (pedlars)

Section 8.5 takes as an example of literary creativity the genre of working-class autobiography which serves both as an important category of evidence of everyday engagements with reading and writing and as a significant example of sustained creative endeavour in the period.

The chapter uses as evidence both quantitative and literary material. Creativity cannot be counted, but officials of the period laid great store by their newly discovered capacity to compute communication skills, and it is necessary to engage critically both with the figures and with the assumptions which they embody. The texts range from literary ephemera such as postcards and valentines to autobiographies. However fragmentary the artefacts, they all had their own conventions of composition and construction. However inexperienced the writers, they all had to engage with the traditions of their genre and the expectations of their readers.

8.2 Learning the art of literacy

The finest poet to emerge from the ranks of the English labouring poor in the nineteenth century was John Clare. He was born in 1793 in the village of Helpston in Northamptonshire. This small community had both a tradition of literacy and a demand for learning. Clare's forebears were farm labourers who had doubled up as parish clerks, recording the business of the church and keeping its registers. Although it was still two decades before the state took an interest in elementary schooling, Clare had no difficulty in finding opportunities to learn his letters. He was first sent to Mrs Bullimore's dame school in the village where he learned his ABCs. After two years he moved to the makeshift schoolroom run by Mr Seaton in the vestry of the parish church of the neighbouring village of Glenton. After a time he was transferred to a third school with a scholarly but poor teacher named James Merrishaw.

Nonetheless, it was a makeshift education. Attendance took second place to the demands of the family economy. As the seasons turned, Clare and the other village children were taken from the classroom to the fields to work alongside their parents. In winter there was more time for letters, but also more hardship. Mr Seaton's school was a two-mile walk along dark lanes to an unheated and dimly lit classroom. The teachers came and went with almost as much frequency as their pupils. There was no certainty in the process except that one day, in Clare's case when he was twelve, the absences from formal instruction would become permanent.

Elementary education in this era was not so much absent as disorderly. There was already sufficient demand from the rural as well as the urban labouring poor to attract a host of men and women into the educational marketplace as teachers. But they had no qualifications and little security of status or income. Like their pupils they moved between the classroom and manual labour as circumstances dictated. Some were incompetent and cruel; some inadequate and kindly; and some were possessed of a natural gift for teaching that surmounted every material obstacle. Clare was moved by the contrast between the learning and the indigence of his final schoolmaster James Merrishaw:

> Either to sing or plan or write or read
> In each his powerful genius would succeed
> Now he where all this ellegance was shown
> 'Lies mouldring in the grave without a stone.'

(Robinson and Powell, 1989, p. 58)

For the parents there was no certainty of provision, merely the opportunity in all but the remotest communities to purchase a service. Then from 1833 the state intervened with the dual ambition of extending and standardising the teaching of literacy. It began cautiously by subsidising the voluntary church educational societies, before finally requiring every community to have a school in 1870, and every child to attend it in 1880. The target of reform was as much the unqualified teacher as the uneducated child. A relentless battle was waged against those moving directly from the ranks of the labouring poor to teaching in the classroom. Even so, parental preference for the more accommodating regime of the unsupervised teacher was so strong that it was only in the last quarter of the nineteenth century that the state succeeded in imposing monopoly control. Efforts to instate an official programme of mass literacy were everywhere compromised by the persisting role of working people as purchasers or suppliers of instruction. The parents in the communities of the labouring poor were not passive players in the

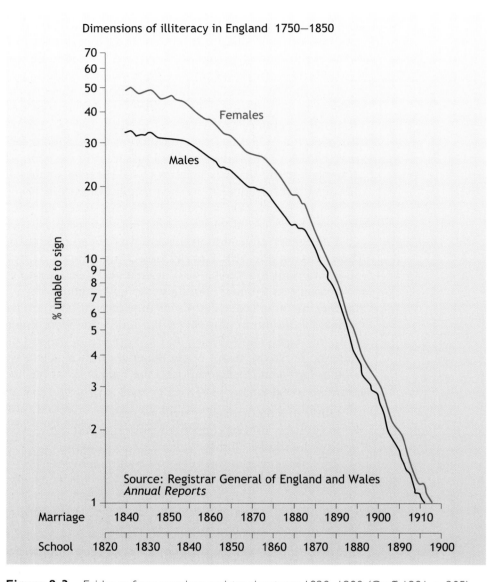

Figure 8.3 Evidence from marriage register signatures 1820–1900 (Graff, 1981, p. 205)

drama of mass literacy; until the state finally closed down the private market in elementary education, families had been active consumers, choosing what kind of schooling should be purchased and how it should be used.

ACTIVITY 1   Literacy statistics

Allow 20 minutes

Statistics provide one point of departure for thinking about agency and capacity in this arena. Look at Figures 8.3, 8.4 and 8.5, which display literacy data derived from signatures on marriage registers. From 1837 onwards these constituted the first official measure of communications skills. In Figure 8.3, the

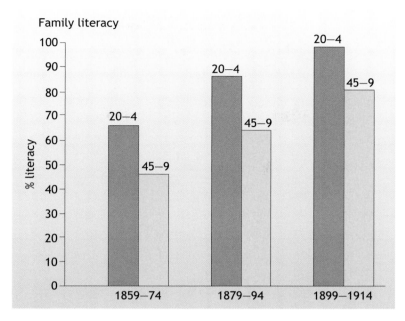

Figure 8.4   Literacy by generation 1859–1914 (Vincent, 1989, p. 27)

percentage unable to sign is given by date of marriage and there is a second date line indicating the time when the bride and groom will have been at school (around fifteen years before their wedding). In Figure 8.4, the literacy levels of the 20–24 age group are compared with those of the 45–9 age group at three points in the nineteenth century. Figure 8.5 displays the patterns of literacy of all the parties in the ceremony – bride, groom and two witnesses from the records of 10,542 weddings between 1839 and 1914. It shows that, taking the period as a whole, all four of the signators were able to write their names at only 54.8 per cent of weddings. The more detailed breakdown of figures for the fifteen year intervals show how the various combinations of signators' ability to sign changed during the period.

- What evidence do the graphs provide for the effectiveness of state education in promoting literacy in nineteenth-century Britain?

- How did the communication skills of different age groups vary in the transition to mass literacy?

- How different are the trajectories of change revealed by the literacy networks from those of individual brides or grooms?

Literacy networks – skilled labourers

Groom	Bride	First witness	Second witness	All period Number	%	1839–1854 Number	%	1859–1874 Number	%	1879–1894 Number	%	1899–1914 Number	%
L	L	L	L	2,644	54.8	358	27.7	449	37.8	734	65.1	1,103	90.6
L	L	L	X	213	4.4	65	5.0	85	7.1	50	4.4	13	1.1
L	L	X	L	171	3.5	29	2.2	45	3.8	52	4.6	45	3.7
L	L	X	X	61	1.3	19	1.5	25	2.1	16	1.4	1	0.1
X	X	X	X	314	6.5	179	13.8	109	9.2	22	2.0	4	0.3
X	X	X	L	78	1.6	40	3.1	26	2.2	12	1.1	0	0
X	X	L	X	173	3.6	98	7.6	55	4.6	18	1.6	2	0.2
X	X	L	L	131	2.7	60	4.6	49	4.1	18	1.6	4	0.3
L	X	L	L	328	6.8	131	10.1	93	7.8	83	7.4	21	1.7
L	X	L	X	228	4.7	114	8.8	79	6.6	31	2.8	4	0.3
L	X	X	L	70	1.5	27	2.1	32	2.7	10	0.9	1	0.1
L	X	X	X	138	2.9	80	6.2	39	3.3	18	1.6	1	0.1
X	L	L	L	138	2.9	40	3.1	40	3.4	45	4.0	13	1.1
X	L	L	X	55	1.1	19	1.5	29	2.4	5	0.4	2	0.2
X	L	X	L	36	0.7	10	0.8	16	1.3	7	0.6	3	0.2
X	L	X	X	49	1.0	25	1.9	18	1.5	6	0.5	0	0
				4,827	100.0	1,294	100.0	1,189	99.9	1,127	100.0	1,217	100.0

Figure 8.5 Literacy networks (Vincent, 1989, Appendix B) [L = literate, X = non-literate]

Comment

These statistics provide some very basic information about the growth of literacy skills in nineteenth-century Britain. Nineteenth-century commentators tended to use them to justify expenditure on schooling, but the chronology of change in the statistics throws attention on the role of the parents who sent their children to school in the era before compulsion, or taught them at home. Allowing for the gap between schooling (over by ten or eleven at the latest) and marriage (usually in the mid-twenties), we have to go to the mid-1890s to discover a cohort whose literacy was entirely the product of public funding and control. By then, the struggle for mass nominal literacy was almost over. The state was still too weak to impose its authority or raise sufficient taxes until some combination of parental and voluntary action had created a widespread acceptance of the need for the skills of reading and writing.

Commentators tended to focus on the individual brides and grooms as they completed the registers with a signature or a cross. They paid less attention to the attainments of different cohorts of the population who lived and worked alongside each other. At a time when the possession of these communication skills was expanding rapidly, the young tended to be more literate than the old and were often called upon to read or write on their behalf (the same is true, in a more compressed form, with contemporary computer literacy). Whilst the marrying cohort was universally literate by the First World War, illiterates amongst older cohorts were still a reality in the inter-war period.

Commentators also ignored the attributes of the basic social groups which came together at a wedding. In the makeshift world of the labouring poor, the key capacities for physical and cultural survival were as much shared as personal attributes. If we take as a group bride, groom and the two witnesses (who were usually family members) at the ceremony we can gain an insight into the basic communication units in which people lived. In this way the statistics can show us that literacy was distributed more widely at an earlier period than the returns for individual brides and grooms suggest, and conversely that illiteracy was more widely distributed and lingered longer.

The statistics probably indicate a basic reading ability, and some familiarity with the task of inscribing words, but they tell us nothing about how well people could read or write, still less how often they did so. If we want to understand how the child and the adult used these skills and how they related to other modes of communication, we need to move beyond the statistics. We should begin with the official curriculum. The long-term attack on the parent's freedom to operate in the marketplace had its counterpart in an attempt to curtail the child's creativity in the lessons. In the early classrooms of the subsidised and inspected church schools, the first encounter with literacy took the form of rote-learning the alphabet followed by tables of syllables. Put in front of you the opening page of William Markham's *An Introduction to Spelling and Reading English* (Figure 8.6) which was continually in print from 1728 until 1885. Chant the scraps of syllables over and over again, until reading becomes a strange, abstract process, dissociated from your competence in speech. Then engage with what was considered progress in reading, the encounter not with meaning but with complexity. The fragments of words were followed by long tables of monosyllabic words succeeded by words of two, three and up to seven syllables. The peak of achievement was the tongue twisters listed in Figure 8.7, which is taken from a widely used mid-century classroom textbook. The only concession to context was a focus on hard words in the Bible – how many of Markham's 'Scripture Proper Names of One, Two, Three and Four Syllables' (Figure 8.8) can you manage with fluency? This was a method of learning to read as old as printing itself. What changed was the context in which it was used. Where once the child and its untrained teacher was free to move around between whatever scraps of print and writing were available, now the rigid, cost-effective organisation of the new pedagogy imposed a systematic, enclosed progression through the primers. The pupil's encounter with the written word commenced with the deconstruction of its oral communication skills, and proceeded by means of an application not of its imagination but rather of its capacity to synthesise what were regarded as the component elements of language. Writing meant copying. It was a form of manual skill, designed only to equip adults for simple correspondence or at most routine clerical tasks.

Eaſy Syllables of Two Letters.

a	e	i	o	u		a	e	i	o	u
ab	eb	ib	ob	ub		ap	ep	ip	op	up
ac	ec	ic	oc	uc		ar	er	ir	or	ur
ad	ed	id	od	ud		as	es	is	os	us
af	ef	if	of	uf		at	et	it	ot	ut
ag	eg	ig	og	ug		au	eu	—	ou	—
ah	eh	—	oh	—		aw	ew	—	ow	—
ak	ek	ik	ok	uk		ax	ex	ix	ox	ux
al	el	il	ol	ul		ay	—	—	oy	—
am	em	im	om	um		az	ez	iz	oz	uz
an	en	in	on	un						

Figure 8.6   Spelling table (Markham, 1738)

WORDS OF SEVEN SYLLABLES

an-ti-tri-ni-ta′-ri-an
cir-cum-am-bu-la-ti-on
cir-cum-na-vi-ga-ti-on
dis-con-ti-nu-a-ti-on
de-te-ri-o-ra-ti-on
di-ver-si-fi-ca-ti-on

ex-com-mu-ni-ca′-ti-on
ex-em-pli-fi-ca-ti-on
i-den-ti-fi-ca-ti-on
im-ma-te-ri-a-li-ty
im-pe-ne-tra-bi-li-ty
in-di-vi-si-bi-li-ty

la-ti-tu-di-na′-ri-an
mal-ad-mi-nis-tra-ti-on
mis-re-pre-sen-ta-ti-on
na-tu-ra-li-za-ti-on
ple-ni-po-ten-ti-a-ry
pre-de-ter-mi-na-ti-on
ra-ti-o-ci-na-ti-on

re-con-ci-li-a′-ti-on
re-ex-a-mi-na-ti-on
su-per-an-nu-a-ti-on
su-per-er-o-ga-ti-on
tran-sub-stan-ti-a-ti-on
va-le-tu-di-na-ri-an
vo-la-ti-li-za-ti-on

Figure 8.7   Spelling table (Innes, 1835)

Scripture Proper Names of One, Two, Three and Four Syllables

N.B. A 1. signifies the Accent is on the first Syllable; A 2. on the Second; A 3. on the Third.

A¹ Ain

Bell	John	Uz	A-haz
Buz	Jude	Zin	Al-van
Cain	Kish	Ziph	Am-mon
Cham	Kore	Zug	A-mos
Cush	Luke	Zuph	Am-ram
Dan	Luz	Zur	A-nak
Eve	Mafh	**A2**	An-nas
Gad	Medes	Aa-ron	Ar-gob
Gath	Nun	Ab-ba	Ar-non
Gog	Og	Ab-da	A-saph
Greece	Paul	A-bel	Ash-dod
Ham	Phut	Ab-ner	A-shur
Heth	Ram	A-chan	A-tid
Hur	Reu	Ach-bor	A-vith
Jah	Rome	A-chifh	A-bra-ham
James	Saul	A-dam	A-bi-gail
Job	Shem	A-gag	A-ma-lek
	Shur	A-gur	Ab-sa-lom
	Ur	A-hab	An-ti-och

A2	B1	
Ab-di-ah	Ba-al	Ca-leb
A-bag-tha	Ba-bel	Car-mi
A-bi-el	Ba-rak	Ce-phas
A-bi-ram	Ba-ruch	Che-rub
A-bi-shag	Be-red	Cof-bi
A-hi-tup	Beth-jah	Cu-fhi
A-ho-lah	Bil-hah	Clau-di-us
Am-mi-el	Bo-az	Cle-o-phas
A-sa-hel	Boz-rah	**C2**
A-ta-rah	Ba-by-lon	Ca-fhu-him
Az-ma-veth	Bar-na-bas	Cen-chre-a
A-za-bah	Bar-fa-bas	Co-ni-ah
A-bed-ne-go	Bdel-li-um	Cho-ra-zin
A-bi-me-lech	Ben-ja-min	Ca-per-na-um
A-bi-na-dab	Beth-le-hem	Cen-tu-ri-on
A-cel-da-ma	**B2**	Ci-li-ci-a
A-dul-la-mite	Ba-a-nah	Cor-ne-li-us
A-hi-to-phel	Ba-dai-ah	Cy-re-ni-us
A-mi-na-dab	Ba-rab-bas	**D1**
A-pol-ly-on	Bar-jo-na	Da-than
A3	Bel-fhaz-zar	Da-vid
A-bi-e-zer	Beth-ho-ron	De-mas
A-bi-le-ne	Beth-a-ba-ra	Dib-lath
A-ba-zi-ah	Be-thu-li-a	Di-nah
A-ma-ri-ah	**B3**	Do-eg
A-na-ni-as	Ba-al-ze-phon	Dor-cas
A-ri-stag-chus	Ba-ra-chi-as	Do-chan
Ar-tax-erx-es	Bar-ti-me-as	Da-ma-ris
A-th-li-ah	Bo-a-ner-gea	Da-ni-el
A-tha-i-ah	**C1**	De-bo-rah
A-za-ri-ah	Cal-cor	De-li-lah
		Di-dy-mus

Figure 8.8   Spelling table (Markham, 1738)

Within the inspected classroom, the second half of the nineteenth century witnessed a reluctant concession to the creative minds of the children who were now incarcerated for an increasing length of time. Change was a product partly of professional self-reflection as the inspectors and the staff of the training colleges deliberated upon the processes and outcomes of the new system. And it was partly a consequence of the need to strike a kind of bargain with the families of the labouring poor. The state was still too uncertain of its powers and resources to impose education on an unwilling population. The acceptance of regulation required some recognition of the aspirations of parents and the inclinations of their children. Alongside the rigours of the syllabic method, 'look and say' was introduced in the middle decades of the century. Pupils were permitted to encounter whole sentences early in their course of study, and to use guesswork as well as mechanical assembly to work out the meaning of what they were reading. At the same time, the anthologies of prose and poetry that had been suppressed in the early official curriculum now began to find their way back into the classroom.

The child whose curiosity survived the gruelling early engagement with the alphabet could now begin to explore carefully selected examples of contemporary and historical literature.

There was also a small relaxation in the teaching of writing. In 1871, what was termed 'composition' entered the curriculum. In practice this meant writing short letters and very simple stories but at least pupils were being permitted to arrange words in a different order to those dictated to them. Only a small minority of elementary schoolchildren scaled the Parnassian heights of this curriculum. In 1882, just after attendance became compulsory, less than 2 per cent of the pupils were entered for Standard VI where composition took place and encounters were made with 'a passage from one of Shakespeare's historical plays, or from some other standard author, or from a history of England'. For this fortunate few, the absolute opposition between organised education and the development of the imagination was beginning to break down.

For most of the labouring poor, therefore, the impact of mass literacy was registered not in the classroom but in the slowly evolving interplay between a complex set of cultural resources that embraced the spoken and the written. The child grew up amidst a range of communication skills in its family and in the surrounding neighbourhood. The adults with whom it lived and worked were not divided into opposing camps of literate and illiterate but displayed instead a wide-ranging body of capacities which they applied to a wide range of artefacts. They were taught in the schools to dismiss what was termed the 'oral culture'. Since at least the Reformation, the communities of the labouring poor had engaged at some level with the printed word; the enclosed, undefiled oral tradition was an invention of nineteenth-century antiquarians. Most households of the labouring poor possessed some religious literature and even in the remoter rural communities it was possible to supplement the Bible or Prayer Book with the wares of the chapmen who walked from village to village selling penny stories, almanacs and fortune tellers. Equally, the new generation of schoolchildren was everywhere faced with the lineaments of older forms of storing and communicating knowledge and imagination. As the young John Clare began to venture into the world of print in his own right, he wrote an account of his development as a poet in the form of an autobiographical letter to his friend and publisher John Taylor, who also published John Keats. A particular influence in the growth of his creative skills was his father, who linked the narrow literary tradition of the community with its broader oral tradition:

> my father could read a little in a bible or testament and was very fond of the supersti[ti]ous tales that are hawked about a sheet for a penny, such as old Nixons Prophecies, Mother Bunches Fairey Tales, and Mother Shiptons Legacy etc etc he was likewise fond of Ballads and I have heard him make a boast of it over his horn of ale with his merry companions at the Blue bell public house which was next door that he could sing or recite above a hundred

(Robinson and Powell, 1996, p. 2)

Clare's own development as a poet rested on the twin foundations of the Blue bell public house and the labours of Mrs Bullimore, Mr Seaton and James Merrishaw.

THE FAMOUS MOTHER SHIPTON.

Figure 8.9   Mother Shipton (1488–1561) was a Yorkshire prophet who wrote her predictions in verse. These were first handed down by oral means, and from the mid-17th century, printed copies, often with later embellishments, circulated widely. (Mary Evans picture library)

8.3 Popular reading practices: from broadsides to Dickens

The long tradition of singing and narrating in the families of the labouring poor made the growth of mass reading an evolutionary rather than a revolutionary process. Writing, the second of the two skills taught in the new elementary schools, presented a greater challenge to inherited modes of communication. The schooled children were for the most part not expected to use writing as a form of self-expression, still less as a mode of creative endeavour. The signature inscribed in the marriage register might be the only use ever made of the skill of making letters. Almost all craftsmen were educated by the beginning of the nineteenth century, and some applied their literacy (and their numeracy) in the course of their business. With the coming of the railways and the growth of the post office, a new breed of literate manual worker was created, and increasingly factory owners needed their employees to be able to read the notices over the machines. Most employers, however, valued elementary education more for the moral discipline they assumed it engendered than for the specific communication skills it produced, and for the majority of workers in most nineteenth-century occupations there would be little need or opportunity to apply the lessons from the schoolrooms directly in the workplace.

The first flood of popular literature produced in response to the rapid expansion of urban communities and the increasing communication skills of their inhabitants were essentially hybrid in form. Figures 8.10 and 8.11 overleaf show examples of the most popular genre in the second quarter of the nineteenth century, the broadsides produced in response to notorious crimes and executions. These were sold for a penny in astonishing numbers, with seven-figure circulations claimed for some of the more successful publications – by far the largest production run of any manufactured object of the era, in any category of consumption. At this stage they were produced by hand-operated iron-frame presses. The discovery of the scale of demand for popular literature eventually encouraged the most ambitious publishers to invest in expensive steam presses.

The broadsides (transcribed in a larger font in the Appendix on pages 387–391) introduce us to two dimensions of creativity in popular reading: firstly, the interplay between the conventions of a genre and the particularity of a narrative, which in these cases were based on real events; secondly the level and form of active response that the purchased material required or provoked in the consumer.

Just Published—thewhole Partculars of a most

CRUEL MURDER,

Committed by Charles Young, a Grazier, upon the Body of his Sweetheart Mary Ann Walmsley.

Shewing, how under pretence of Marriage, the Villain Seduced her, and how she became Pregnant by him ; after which he gave her a deleterious drug, which threw her into a deep sleep, when the Monster stabbed her to the heart with a knife, and threw her Body into a Lake, which was wonderfully discovered by a Shepherd's dog. Also, the Committal of the Murderer.

Mary Anne Wansley.

A shepherd driving forth his flock,
 to feed by dawn of day,
By chance he came unto the lake
 Where th' murder'd damsel lay.

And while upon its banks he stood
 His dog with sudden spring,
Div'd into the chrystal flood,
 and out her corpse did bring.

A Very interesting and amiable female, the daughter of a highly respectable individual in the West Riding of Yorkshire, and who is steward to a nobleman, became attached, owing to repeated solicitations, to a young grazier, whose family connexions were co-equal with her own. Their walks, in the evening, were frequent, and the attachment on the part of Mary Ann's lover, apparently increased at each succeeding interview.

About a fortnight since, they were seen together, for the last time, by some villagers crossing a stile, which leads to a lonely spot in that neighbourhood. Her ruin having been previously effected, she paid him her last visit with a determination of putting his honour to the test, as her destruction otherwise would be complete. He appeared, with his usual duplicity, to hold out the most sincere promises of marriage, which he pledged himself, most solemnly to fulfill. They had strayed to a considerable distance when they seated themselves on a green shady bank, at the back of which was a pond of considerable depth, and here the traitorous wretch put his diabolical plan into execution. Wine, it is supposed, from a flasket, was proffered to her to quench her thirst, into which the villain had infused a deleterious drug, for the purpose of throwing her into a deep sleep in order that he

might dispatch her. In a few minutes she sunk back asleep, when the villain plunged a knife into her breast, and she expired upon the spot. He endeavoured to conceal the two-fold murder by plunging her body into the adjoining pond ; but " murder will out" in nine cases out of ten, and the following circumstance proves that an all-seeing Providence directs the most miraculous means of bringing such miscreants as the one before us to the bar of retributive justice.

A few mornings after the perpetration of this horrid deed, a shepherd was passing over the field with his dog and crook, when his attention was suddenly drawn to the pond by the moanings of his faithful companion, who dived into the water, and, in a few minutes brought to the margin of the bank the lifeless body of the unfortunate Mary Ann. A rigid enquiry immediately took place, and the result was, the instant apprehension of the supposed murderer, who was examined and finally committed to prison upon the capital charge, where his reflections ought to be of the most agonizing description, and at the ensuing Assizes he will doubtless forfeit his worthless life as a partial atonement for the heinous offence he has committed against the laws of God and man.

The following letter, which she evidently intended for her base seducer and murderer, was found, amongst others, in one of he private drawers :—

Dear Charles,
 Unless you perform your often repeated promise of marriage, I shall become a mother under the most wretched circumstances, My loving and affectionate parents are at this moment totally unconscious of the disgrace which I am hourly advancing upon them and myself.   Do, for God's sake, meet me this evening at the usual spot, and may that meeting prove the sincerity of your intentions, and our future mutual happiness.   Oh, do not—do not deceive
 Your loving, though desponding,
        MARY ANN.

J. Catnach, Printer, 2, Monmouth-court
 7 Dials.

MELANCHOLY VERSES.

O, all ye maidens fair, beware
 Of this my wretched fate ;
Nor e'er be led in treach'rous snare,
 Or you'll repent too late.

For man's deceptive, you all know,
 Till once his end he gains ;
Then leaves you, sad disgrace to show,
 For all his amorous pains.

A maiden, chaste, I once was deem'd
 By all---the village pride ;
For virtue none was more esteem'd,
 It was my constant guide.

The villain plunges a knife into her breast.

Till faithless Charles entwin'd my arms,
 And vow'd he'd constant be ;
'Twas then I lost a virgin's charms,---
 And thus he's ruin'd me.

But who would e'er suppose a fiend,
 Could to your bosom creep ;
Then from you suddenly be wean'd
 To plunge you in the deep

A murder, base, lurk'd in his breast,
 As you've the story read ;
But whilst my soul does calmly rest,
 To dungeons he'll be led.

Figure 8.10   19th-century broadsides (James, 1976, p. 248)

A Horrible MURDER,
A Father Cutting his Child's Head off!

A MOST horrid Murder was committed on Thursday night at Whitechapel, by a Father, upon his Child, an Infant about four months old. The man whose name is Sheen, resides at No. 1, Christopher-Alley, Lambeth-street, near the Police Office, and obtained his living by selling wood about the streets. It appears that on several occasions when he had returned home intoxicated, and quarrelled with his wife, he had threatened to murder the child, by cutting its head off, but it is most singular that there appears to exist no cause which could induce the wretch to commit such a diabolical act. It was his only child, and from enquiries that have been made it does not seem that he entertained any jealousy respecting his wife. About seven o'clock last evening he returned home intoxicated, and said to his wife that he would cut the child's head off. She did not pay the slightest attention to his threat, and about an hour afterwards he sent her out to procure some tea, in her absence he cut the child's head from the body, he then threw the body under the bed, and placed the head on the table, where it was found by the Mother on entering the room. Sheen has absconded, but Dalton, an Officer of Lambeth-street, is in search of him. Sheen is about 30 years of age, and his wife is about the same age.

It appears that immediately after he committed the murder, he went to the residence of his father and brother, in White's-yard, Rosemary-lane, and told them that he had been playing at skittles, had quarrelled with an Irishman, and had stabbed him in the back with a knife, which he then produced. He was afraid, he said, of being apprehended for the outrage, and therefore begged them to assist him with the means of making his escape. Neither father nor brother had any money to give him, but the father took him to a Mr. Pugh, a carpenter, in Carnaby-market, who had known the family when they resided in Radnorshire and he advanced Sheen, 18 shillings, and also lent him a coat as he declared he had left his own in the skittle ground, whereas he left it in the room, after he had committed the murder, and where it was found covered with blood, Mr Pugh, declared, if he had for a moment suspected he had committed so foul a crime, he would have seized him, and brought him to justice.

It appears that the murderer and his wife had cohabited together for some time before their marriage, that having burthened the parish with several children, the parish Officers caused him to be apprehended, and he had his choice either to give security for the maintainence of the children or to marry the woman, and as is usual in such cases to receive a reward from the parish of 5l sheen accepted the 5l, and only 12 weeks ago they were married.

tThe mother of the unfortunate child said that on Thursday evening, when sheen, came home he was intoxicated, and requested her to make him some tea; that she went out for the ingredients, and left him in the room lying on the bed where the child was also lying asleep. she was gone about a quarter of an hour, when on her return, and opening the room door, her feelings of horror can be more easily conceived than described, when she beheld the head of her child on the table, with its eyes fixed towards the door, and the body on the bed. sheen had, on several occasions, declared he would murder the child, since the birth of the infant he hated it so much that he frequently struck it on its mother's knee. Last Sunday week he struck it such a violent blow, that the lump is now visible on its head. The Jury returned a verdict of Wilful Murder against the Father, who has not yet been taken.

A Copy of Verses.

YE tender loving mothers all,
    Who love your offspring dear,
Fast from your eyes the tears will fall,
    When this sad tale you hear.
A frightful and a horrid deed,
    I quickly shall unfold,
This most appalling fact to read,
    Will make your blood run cold.
The murders' name is William Sheen,
    O horrible to write,
The wicked wretch did often swear
    He'd take his infants life.
On Thursday night he bade his wife
    To go and buy some tea,
That he, the monster might complete
    The horrid tragedy.
His wife had scarcely left the room
    when he did grasp the babe,
So sweetly smil'd the harmless child,
    Mercy it seem'd to crave;
His deadly knife the monster drew,
    And hacked off its head,
And then the bleeding body threw
    All underneath the bed.
The mother shortly did return
    And grief her heart did wring,
On the table stood her baby's head,
    Its lips still quivering.
The floor with blood was dyed red,
    Most frightful for to see,
And the cruel father gone and fled,
    But taken he soon will be.
The wretched mother shriek'd and cried,
    In agony and distress,
No language surely could describe
    The sorrows of her breast.
Inhuman man, thy infan'ts blood,
    Loud to the LORD doth cry,
Vengeance will recompense the deed,
    From it thou can'st not fly.
Cards and Bills Printed very Cheap by J. Catnach, 2, Monmouth-court, F Dials.

Figure 8.11   19th-century broadsides (James, 1976, p. 251)

ACTIVITY 2   **Broadsides**

Allow 30 minutes

Please examine Figure 8.10 'Cruel murder, committed by Charles Young ...' and Figure 8.11 'A horrible murder, a father cutting his child's head off!' (See also Appendix pp. 387–391)

- What different modes of communication are being used in the broadsides and how do these cater for the diverse literacy skills and oral traditions of their audience?

- In what ways do the broadsides mix sensationalist images with moral messages?

Comment

The term 'multimedia', which is a commonplace in our electronic culture, can legitimately be applied to the characteristic products of the first era of mass popular literature in which different visual and print forms are brought together in cheap, standardised products. The broadsides belonged to the era when the market comprised literate, illiterate and all the intervening levels of partial literacy. Unlike the simple binary measures of the Registrar General terms, they mirror an immense range of attainments in this era of transition. Those who could not read at all could enjoy the lurid woodcuts. These were sometimes produced for the particular broadside but more often recycled from the stock on the printer's shelves. Or they could listen to the verses, which would be sung by the street-sellers to a popular tune of the moment, and could be committed to memory. It was not even necessary to part with a penny to gain some entertainment from the genre. Those who had gained a little education could use the aural or visual clues as a guide to making out the formulaic but gripping texts. In many respects these were more effective teaching primers than those produced specifically for the classrooms (Figures 8.6–8.8). As with subsequent popular melodramatic forms they appear to invite the reader into a violent world of bloodshed and retribution. There are obvious parallels between the treatment of crime in the broadsides and in modern tabloid newspapers. Equally, you might compare this hybrid literary and oral form with the presentation of sensation on television or film. The broadsides and the Sunday newspapers which began to appear in the 1840s provoked consternation amongst moralising observers, but they can also be seen as evoking an intense but ethically disciplined response from the readers. The startling events, complete with the child's severed, bleeding head looking out from the page, could not fail to attract the attention of the passing purchaser. But if you read through the texts, you will find a constant evocation of a domestic morality, with the narratives and the verses upholding the process of trial and punishment, and reflecting the language of the Bible with which the newly literate would be familiar.

The most explosive literary phenomenon of the era was that of Charles Dickens. His first story was published four months after the passing of the 1833 Education Act and his sudden death occurred whilst the 1870 Act was going through parliament. Through his capacity to generate what would now be termed a multimedia industry, he created what was widely viewed as a new 'reading public'. Alongside the brilliant exploitation of the format of cheap serial publication, his characters and narratives were translated, with or without his permission, into plays, songs, prints, plagiarised versions (often by the broadsheet publishers) and a host of three-dimensional objects such as mass-produced busts of leading characters. It was impossible to define the boundaries of this reading public which embraced those who read every line of the novels and those who never read a word Dickens wrote but felt themselves familiar with his literary creations and followed their adventures. This reading public reached its most characteristic form when it just listened at public readings that Dickens performed to mass audiences in the last thirteen years of his career (Vincent, forthcoming). Look at the advertisement (Figure 8.12) Dickens placed in his two-penny periodical *Household Words* (1850–59), through which he commented on the cultural transformations of his era. His itinerary is a tribute both to his national celebrity and to the power of steam: both his personal mobility and the scale of his popular success depended on the railway network which was built in two bursts of activity in the late 1830s and late 1840s. It is in this sense that his era can be termed a communications revolution, in the same way as can the coming of electronic forms of information technology a century and a half later.

MR. CHARLES DICKENS'S

READINGS

Mr. CHARLES DICKENS will read at SHREWSBURY on the 12th of August; at CHESTER on the 13th; at LIVERPOOL on the 18th, 19th, 20th and 21st; at DUBLIN on the 23rd, 24th, 25th and 26th; at Belfast on the 27th and 28th; at CORK on the 30th and 31st of August.

Figure 8.12   Dickens' advertisement in *Household Words*

Poor readers found it easy to encounter print, but difficult to control their patterns of consumption. With new fiction priced in the 1830s at a guinea and a half for a three-volume novel – a month's wage for a labourer – the newly literate depended on chance discoveries, loans, or purchases from second-hand bookstalls for their encounters with what they regarded as serious literature. This meant that for much of the nineteenth century, the newly literate tended to engage with the creative output of a generation or

Crudely printed and illustrated, the 8-page Victorian 'Penny dreadfuls' provided affordable melodramatic reading matter for the rapidly expanding urban working classes.

more behind their own times. The publishing trade responded unevenly to the opportunities presented by the growth of a mass market. Above the level of the resourceful and commercially unprincipled publishers of broadsheets, "penny dreadfuls", and from mid-century, popular Sunday newspapers, the more respectable firms brought down the prices of new literature only to a price affordable by the lower reaches of the middle classes. The only intersection of mass production and canonical literature was in the field of cheap reprints. By the end of the nineteenth century, the penny which at the beginning of the century could purchase a broadsheet or a twenty-page chapbook would now buy complete texts of Shakespeare or Dickens.

As a mass reading public became visible, middle-class commentators began to worry about it. The state hoped that an increasingly capital intensive market would exercise sufficient discipline on how the newly literate would use their skills. However, there could be no guarantee that this would happen, nor could outsiders be certain that they had a comprehensive view of what was being bought and how it was being consumed. From the middle decades of the nineteenth century there has been a continuing debate about whether the growth of mass literacy created a single reading public.

ACTIVITY 3   The unknown public (Reading A)

Please read the extracts from 'The Unknown Public' (Reading A). This unsigned contribution to Charles Dickens' *Household Words* was written by his protégé, Wilkie Collins. Collins, who was later to invent the modern genre of the literary thriller, has here found 'a mystery which the sharpest man among us may not find it easy to solve'.

Notice how Collins frames his account as an adventure into unfamiliar territory. Why was Collins interested in the reading habits of the 'unknown public' and what conclusions did he draw from his investigation?

Comment

Explorations of 'unknown' England were characteristic of this period. They exploited the middle-class fears about the rapidly urbanising society in which ever larger numbers of the labouring poor lived adjacent to but hidden from their more educated superiors. The form combined the model of the official inquiry into a social problem, which began with the 1832 Poor Law Report, and the genre of voyages of exploration which stretched back into the eighteenth century. They often appeared as serious journalism, most famously in Henry Mayhew's *London Labour and the London Poor* of 1861 which began as a series of articles in *The Morning Chronicle*. Wilkie Collins was the first to address the issue of popular reading and in anticipation of his subsequent career as a novelist, he made a particular feature of penetrating a secret world with its 'mysterious publications'. It was a pioneering and influential article. Later, when Q.D. Leavis published her *Fiction and the Reading Public* (which invented the discipline of literary sociology in 1932), she used Collins' announcement of a new literary continent for her epigraph.

Household Words, as its masthead indicated, was a two-penny periodical which enjoyed a circulation of around 100,000. Like the novels of its editor, it appeared to be reaching deep into the popular market, but the bulk of its purchasers were in fact from the lower middle class. The readership for Collins' article did not overlap with the readership he was describing. Like so many contemporary observers, Collins was deeply impressed by the sheer numbers of both readers and reading matter. His estimate of a 'reading public of three millions which lies right out of the pale of literary civilisation' is as good a guess as could be made then or since. Scale of demand was being met by scale of production, as his witness vividly stated: 'Why Lord bless your soul, just take 'em up and look for yourself, and say if they ain't good pennorths! Look what a lot of print in every one of 'em! My eye! What a lot of print for the money.' The account of multiple literary genres dominated by fiction was repeated by all subsequent enquirers into nineteenth-century reading. Collins' central conclusion, that 'the Unknown Public is, in a literary sense, hardly beginning, as yet, to learn to read', was a challenge both to his own readers and to subsequent scholars of popular literature. The modern study of the full range of popular reading practices commences with Richard Hoggart's *The Uses of Literacy* in 1958 (see also Altick, 1957 and James, 1974).

8.4 The Penny Post: valentines, Christmas greetings, and holiday postcards

Unlike elementary schools elsewhere in western Europe, where writing was taught some years after reading, the tradition in England was for the skills to be learned alongside each other. The state thus had an interest in promoting not only the appropriate consumption of literature, but also the constructive use of the pen. Here the issue of creativity was at once narrower and more complex. Only a minority of the newly literate could find the opportunity to write, and fewer still to publish, fiction and poetry. For the mass of the population, the principal arena for self-expression on paper lay in correspondence. Here the interactions between form and variation, and between pro-forma and personalisation, took on an oblique form.

In 1840, the Whig government had made a bold attempt to transform the engagement of the labouring poor with the practice of writing. It needed to create an incentive for parents to send their children to what was still a voluntary system of subsidised education. More broadly it was concerned that the rapid process of urbanisation and industrialisation was undermining the working-class family. Some means had to be found of maintaining its cohesion and disciplinary functions in spite of the physical dispersal of its members and a partial solution was cheap correspondence. The early nineteenth-century post office had charged the recipient, not the sender, of a letter on the basis of the distance over which it had been conveyed up to a maximum of 6*d*. This made the rare and unforeseeable occurrence of a delivery a threatening event for a labouring household, which would rarely have such a sum to spare. The result was summarised by Douglas Jerrold:

> The postman rarely knocks at the doors of the very poor, and when, perchance, he stands at the threshold of the indigent, it is too often to demand a sacrifice. The letter that he proffers must, perhaps, be purchased at the price of a dinner: at any cost, however, the letter must be purchased; for it comes from one who, it may be, has been silent for years; a far off son, a married daughter. To thousands a letter is a forbidden luxury: an enjoyment, not to be sought by those who daily struggle with the dearest necessities, and who, once severed from a long distant home, are mute because they cannot fee the post, and will not, must not, lay the tax on others wretched as themselves.

(Jerrold, 1878, p. 254)

The solution advanced by a group of reformers led by the social reformer Rowland Hill was to reverse the process of payment and remove the factor of distance from communication. A letter would now cost the flat rate of a penny, with the payment signified by the new device of an adhesive postage stamp. The key to the success of the reform was scale: the task of transporting the increased volume of correspondence would be solved by the steam engine. The fledgling railway companies in the 1830s were eager to gain lucrative postal contracts. The unknown factor was whether the mass of the population would begin to respond to the incentive to write. The results were unexpectedly poor. Instead of a predicted sixfold increase in correspondence, postal flows merely doubled. The old system had been inefficient but profitable. The Penny Post reduced revenues by 75 per cent, losing the government nearly £1.2m in revenue, many times more than it was directly investing in schooling. Furthermore, it was evident that such increase as there had been was largely driven by the middle classes, eagerly seizing on the opportunity to conduct their personal and business affairs at less cost. Charles Dickens was particularly disappointed. He had seen the reform as a means of creating a writing public as extensive and as active as the reading public he had called into being. Instead, the Penny Post had revealed how little progress had been made, in spite of all the schools and writing manuals. The occasional letter which was attempted served only to highlight the deficiencies of the working class's grasp of the basics of written communication. Dickens cited at length from a letter written home by an emigrant shepherd, exactly the kind of family contact the reform had been designed to promote. It was, he wrote:

> a lesson and a censure on that want of national means of education from which at least one-third of the adult population of England suffer, and of which the writer is an especial victim and example: – 'Deer mother and father ad sisters i root thes few lines hooping to find you All well for I arr in gudd halth my self and I wood root befor onley i wos very un setled and now i have root I houp you will rite back as soon as you can and send how you all arr and likewise our frends and I am hired my self for a sheeprd 12 munts for 19 pound and my keep too for it was to soun for our work when I arrive in the country it is a plesent and helthay cuntry and most peple dows well in it as liks onley it is a grait country for durnkerds...'

> (Dickens, 1850a, p. 562)

In the short term, it was not so much the possibility of letter writing as the mass production of sentiment that drew the newly educated into the postal system.

ACTIVITY 4   The Penny Post (Reading B)

Please read 'The Penny Post' by David Vincent (Reading B) which examines the history of the valentine and the postcard in popular culture, and look at the examples of valentine cards in Colour Figures 12 and 13.

In what ways did printed valentines and other cards extend, or limit, the opportunities for the creative expression of sentiments?

Comment

The cheap, mass-produced card was a quintessential product of the first era of mass communication. It raises in a particularly acute form the question of how far increases in education and technology were facilitating or constraining feeling and imagination. In response to the growth in the use of the mails and technical changes in the printing industry, entrepreneurs created a new market for pre-printed expressions of sentiment that excused the sender from the task of composition. At one level they appear to represent the founding case of mass production standardising feeling since, like the broadsides, they combine text and illustration but with minimal attempt at specifying person or emotion. Consider the formulaic text embedded in a lace and flower design (Colour Figure 12), and a stylised soldier wooing his girl (Colour Figure 13). They are the template for all the greeting cards of the modern era. They raise the more general issue of how users can generate meaning out of a mass-produced cultural object. The stark polarity between the potentiality of the personal interaction and the banality of the object paradoxically makes the valentine the most creative of all forms of popular printed communication. Those who found it so difficult to 'grapple with a pen', and those who rarely received correspondence of any kind, could deploy the ready-made text to encode meanings which are irrecoverable by the modern reader.

It is interesting that Dickens did not think for a moment that the valentine represented the death of feeling. On the contrary, he was entranced by the communication of an eruption of amorous feelings through the post office. He peeped through the windows of St Martins Le Grand Post Office in London:

> Thus the sacrifices to the fame of St Valentine – consisting of hearts, darts, Cupid peeping out of paper-roses, Hymen embowered in hot-pressed embossing, swains in very blue coats and nymphs in very opaque muslin, coarse caricatures and tender verses – caused an augmentation to the revenue of this anniversary equal to about 70,000 missives ... The entire correspondence of the three kingdoms is augmented on each St Valentines day to the extent of about 400,000 letters ... As to the rooms, revealed through gratings in the wall, traversed by the ascending and descending-room, and walked in by the visitors afterwards, – those enormous chambers each with its hundreds of sorters busy over their hundreds and thousands of letters – those dispatching places of a business that has the look of being eternal and never to be disposed of or cleared away – those silent receptacles of countless millions of passionate words, for ever pouring through them like a Niagara of language and leaving not a drop behind – what description could present them?

> (Dickens, 1850b, pp. 8–9)

The Christmas card was the invention of the age. It precisely fulfilled the hopes of the postal reformers, serving to both dramatise domestic virtue and connect dispersed members of the family network. Unlike the valentine, it only required the skill of signing a name, which any school would teach. Unlike the valentine, the bulk of the cards display a didactic message. Whilst sender and recipient at Christmas invested less meaning in the communication than on February 14, the cards themselves carried more. Colour Figure 14 shows the first modern Christmas card in circulation in Britain, designed by J.C. Horsley in 1843 with a colour version sent out by Henry Cole in 1846. As Colour Figures 14 and 15 suggest, they celebrated not Christianity itself, but the sanctity of the family and a vision of support and dependency in the home.

Mass participation in the process of writing had to wait until the end of the century. By this time, almost all brides and grooms could manage to sign their name on a marriage register. The key innovation was the picture postcard, a product of technical advances in colour reproduction, changes in postal regulations, and the growth of seaside holidays. Because of their role as a photographic record of a vanishing world they have since been collected for their unwritten side. Historians have yet to turn them over and recognise their function as the first vehicles for popular written self-expression. These were likely to be the only forms of literary communication in which some writers ever engaged. The cramped space on one half of the card was the ideal space for the newly literate to try out their skills. Unlike the formal letter, whose rules of layout and conventions of address had now become a topic of examination in the elementary school curriculum, the postcard had few overt disciplines. Yet it was still a literary artefact with its own tacit rules and expectations. It contained its essential elements in endless permutations that worked with and against its narrow form. Experience and sentiment were distilled into tightly constructed, often abbreviated sentences, and re-imagined by the distant recipient.

8.5 'This brief sketch of my lowly career': working-class autobiography

The genre of working-class autobiography constituted the most sustained form of prose writing by the newly literate in the nineteenth century. Full-length novel writing remained largely the preserve of the better educated, as did more extended non-fiction works of science or philosophy. Research has located about a thousand texts written by men and sometimes women born during the nineteenth century. Their authors lived in varying conditions. In their ranks are to be found beggars, thieves and labourers, and also the relatively prosperous amongst the working class, such as skilled artisans. Unlike their twentieth-century counterparts, few could aspire to upward social mobility through education and self-improvement. For the most part they were required to support themselves through manual labour, but at some point, usually but not exclusively towards the end of their lives, they felt compelled to construct a portrait of their self-development.

Such texts cannot be read as 'typical' of the working class as a whole but neither can their relevance be confined to a narrow occupational or intellectual elite. Their authors engaged with broad currents of social, economic and political change, and in doing so they organised their narratives in ways which reflected wider currents of understanding about the formation of character in the period. For this chapter, two short extracts from autobiographies have been selected which have a multiple resonance for the issues of literacy and creativity. They are a product of a growing sense by working people that they could make their own lives, outside the narrative of religious destiny and in spite of the social, economic and political forces with which they had to contend. Even those that seem closest to oral reminiscence are complex compositions, with the writers working within and against a set of literary conventions. They are our main source of knowledge about the limits and possibilities of working men (and occasionally women) making the transition into print.

ACTIVITY 5   Working-class autobiographies (Readings C and D)

Please read the extracts from John Clare's *Sketches in the Life of John Clare Written by Himself and Addressed to his Friend John Taylor ESQR March 1821* (Reading C) and *A brief Autobiographical Memoir* by J.A. Leatherland (Reading D).

A sub-genre grew up of autobiographical introductions to poetry collections. John Clare was early into the field, composing his *Sketches* when he was still only twenty-four years old. John Taylor, to which it was addressed, was not just his friend but also his publisher, and Clare's account was part of his strategy of entering the world of London letters. J.A. Leatherland, in common with most autobiographers, set down his 'Autobiographical Memoir' towards the end of his life, as a means of explaining his career as a factory worker, radical politician and local poet.

In what ways do these extracts illustrate the mixture of oral and literate creative influences on Clare and Leatherland's reading and writing?

The journey from copying out letters to composing and publishing structured texts was long and difficult. Its destination raised in a transparent form major issues surrounding the dramatic expansion in the use of literacy in this period. The more sustained achievements in prose and poetry draw attention to the ways in which writing did not displace but rather overlaid non-literate traditions of self-expression. They demonstrate how traditions and conventions in different forms of communication informed the creative process, both constraining and constructing the representation of an individual's life and feelings.

The transition from bare literacy to formal publication was frequently assisted by an intermediate structure such as a church, trade union or political group. Participating in the organisation of a chapel or a union branch gave lessons both in personal self-confidence and in the business of managing pen and paper. However much he may have come to have regret the passion of its politics, J.A. Leatherland's period as the secretary of the Kettering Chartist Association will have taught him how to write various categories of prose as he mastered the demands of minutes, agendas, correspondence with other branches, manifestos, placards and political journalism. The growth of local newspapers from mid-century also provided part-time or even full-time opportunities for those whose horizons otherwise remained confined to manual labour, as Leatherland was to discover. The fact that these environments were largely a male preserve may help to explain why only about one in ten of the extant working-class autobiographies in this period were written by women.

The acquisition of some kind of proficiency as a writer assisted the task of writing a memoir, but there remained crucial questions of purpose, truth and structure. In the hands of the least experienced autobiographers the task could look disarmingly simple. Anthony Errington, a Northumberland waggonway-wright, dealt with the question of intention in a single sentence. 'The reason of my wrighting the particulars of my life and Transactions are to inform my family and the world' (Errington, 1823, p. 26). Another early autobiographer, Benjamin Shaw, wrote with home-made spelling in a home-made book with home-made pen and ink, and fashioned his own defence of the reliability of his enterprise:

> in the following pages, I have put down a few [...] notes kept by me, for my own use, mostly of the latest dates, mentioned, &c – I have not attempted to deceive any that may read this account, by falsehoods or by selecting those circumstances that might make the most favourable appearance – but I have simply attempted to state facts, whether hounourable or shameful – as I consider truth the most valueable ingredient in any History or Biographycal account.

(Shaw, 1826, p. 1)

At one level, many of the writers could claim that they were just extending into printed form the broad tradition of oral reminiscence which in all communities had supplied every child with much of what it knew about its world. As in his poetry, so in his autobiography, John Clare was conscious that he was reworking rather than reinventing an indigenous mode of expression: 'There is a pleasure in recalling ones past years to recollection; in this I believe and I think every bosoms agrees and returns a ready echo of approbation and I think a double gratification is witness'd as we turn a repetition of our early days by writing them down on paper' (Clare, 1821, p. 1).

But however unsophisticated their approach, these writers had to negotiate as complex issues of literary creativity as the more distinguished intellectual autobiographers of the period such as John Henry Newman or John Stuart Mill. Every account of a life dealt with the limitless range of recollected events and experiences by deploying a narrative strategy derived from an oral or literary discourse. The genre was fed by two streams, the spoken tradition of family reminiscence and the religious tradition of spiritual self-examination. The former gave the writer the sense of an audience, whether or not the text would ever be published. The latter supplied the account with a ready-made trajectory where the subject progresses through a sequence of transgression, conversion and redemption. Benjamin Shaw began in the first tradition, supplying potted biographies of his relatives, and then tried the second. He had experienced a standard Baptist conversion in his late twenties. After a period of religious crisis,

> god was Mercifull, & spoke Peace to my Soul, & now I found that Peace with god which Passeth all understanding, & rejoiced all the day long, & saw every thing in a new light, I wondered that I never saw them before, my heart was Chainged, & my life was Chainged of course.

(Shaw, 1826, pp. 39–40)

Shaw's faith never left him completely and traces of the standard spiritual progression can be detected in the subsequent narrative, including a number of providential escapes from death. Now, however, there was a competing structure. He had taught himself to write at the age of twenty in order to correspond with a literate sweetheart. In a period of convalescence following an industrial injury he embraced the pursuit of knowledge. He became a classic case of the literate mentality, fascinated with printed learning in all its aspects, and with the organising power of writing. His memoir was not only structured by his search for books but fully indexed, as were the collections of aphorisms and medical cures he made in separate notebooks.

In the readings for Activity 5, it is possible to trace both the spiritual and the self-improving narrative traditions. Leatherland (1862, p. 1) presents himself as moral lesson, showing his readers 'the blessed results of virtuous actions, and warning them to shun the breakers upon which others have been wrecked'. But, like Shaw and the bulk of the working-class autobiographers of the period, his strategy of selection and interpretation is centred on the pursuit of knowledge under difficulties. In common with most texts, there is only limited reference to his occupational experiences, less about his domestic life and none at all about his sexual history. Instead there is detailed discussion about relations with readers and non-readers, about what he read and how he struggled to get his own writing read by others. This drama had meaning for every other self-taught reader who had sought to obtain and make sense of the growing volume of the printed word in their lifetimes. It was also a narrative that communicated to middle-class readers of the texts, who were by turns worried and comforted by the fierce appetite for literature that the schools and the technological changes of the period had aroused. In this most extensive form of working-class creativity in the nineteenth century, reading in this sense became writing.

What is striking in the accounts of the creative identities of Clare and Leatherland is the absence of boundaries either as to time or to imaginative form. Clare portrayed himself in verse as the inheritor of an ancient, collective tradition of song:

> The only tune he knows still whistling oer
> & humming scraps his father sung before
> As 'wantley dragon' or the 'magic rose'
> The whole of music which his village knows
> Which wild remembrance in each little town
> From mouth to mouth thro ages handles down

(Deacon, 1983, p. 10)

More recent scholarship has established that this wild remembrance was in turn infused with print, having incorporated texts and tropes from the chapbooks that had been circulating almost since the invention of print. The children listened to these songs, and to the stories told to them on winters' evenings that might be drawn from either oral or printed forms. Whilst Leatherland was saving up pennies to buy fairy stories his mother was reading to him 'Bunyan, Addison, Watts, Cowper, and others of our standard authors, noted for their simplicity'. Just as their schooling was a matter of inconsistent attendance and incomplete learning, so their lives as readers were hand-to-mouth existences, with no final control over what could be read or how it could be connected together. As writers of poetry and of autobiography they faced a constant struggle to get into print, and to give adequate expression to their complex and fragmented literary resources.

In his study of the Parisian poor, Daniel Roche insisted that the consumption of print, just as its production, was an active and unpredictable process:

> Like writing, reading is an act of mediation susceptible to infinite modulations, and nothing in notarial records tells us how to distinguish between fluent reading which presupposes the regular handling of books, the irregular, infrequent deciphering of print often linked with pictures, or reading aloud, shared among several people, which may have been an act of friendship, even love, or sociability.

(Roche, 1987, p. 215)

This was the case in every sector of society, but it was particularly apparent amongst those who experienced the coming of mass literacy. The defining characteristics of the age were abundance and the absence of control. The combined impact of state intervention, technological advance, economic growth and the development of a new literary market offered the labouring poor unprecedented possibilities of reading and writing. But whether as children intermittently attending lessons in which literacy was made an increasingly artificial skill, or as adults striving to impose links between oral and written modes of communication, nothing came easy. At a basic level, creativity was forced upon the new readers and writers as they sought ever-more ingenious ways of gaining access to books or finding their own ways into print. Those who sought to engage in literary creativity in its modern sense, as published writers of poetry and prose, struggled both to earn a living and to make sense of cultural traditions that embraced fairy tales and folk songs and the flowering of the novel form in the nineteenth century. Their autobiographies bear witness to the possibilities of the first phase of modern mass communication, and to the immense difficulties faced by those most determined to exploit them.

8.6 Conclusion

It is possible to argue that the contemporary preoccupation with revolutions in mass communication needs to be tempered by a realisation that the internet is not the first nor even the most significant transformation in the ways in which individuals and societies have deployed tools and technologies to connect with each other and to enrich their creativity. The engagement with this historical example both disciplines and enriches our understanding of the current dilemmas. It emphasises the extent to which we must embed our enquiries in the specific material and cultural circumstances of the era. Learning to read in an early nineteenth-century classroom was in its substance and implications utterly unlike the contemporary British child's encounter with school literacy and the classroom computer, despite the sometimes alarming parallels between the inspected curriculum of the mid-nineteenth century and the national curriculum of the early twenty-first. The pedagogy, the availability of texts in the home and the market, the nature of other non-literate modes of expression and imagination, the impact of material deprivation on the process of learning to write and the implications of becoming literate for an occupational future, were all particular to the period. At the same time we can see how the questions we now ask about how systems for communication structure the ways in which we invent ourselves and develop our imaginations are not confined to the impact of modern information technology. In each case there are the complex journeys between bare competence and sophisticated command, between scarce and unrestricted access, between passive possession and active use of skills, between the intervention of the person and the standardisation of the product, between old and contemporary mechanisms for generating, transmitting and storing ideas and information. And in each case creativity has a double resonance: the determination with which individuals and groups improvise their resources for communication, and the ingenuity with which they seize the opportunities to extend and give form to their ideas and imagination.

Appendix: Broadsides

(transcribed from pp. 373–4)

Just Published – the whole Particulars of a most **CRUEL MURDER**, **Committed by Charles Young, a Grazier, upon the Body of his Sweetheart Mary Ann Walmsley**.

Showing, how under pretence of Marriage, the Villain Seduced her, and how she became Pregnant by him; after which he gave her a deleterious drug, which threw her into a deep sleep, when the Monster stabbed her to the heart with a knife, and threw her Body into a Lake, which was wonderfully discovered by a Shepherd's dog. Also the Committal of the Murderer.

A shepherd driving forth his flock,
To feed by dawn of day,
By chance he came unto the lake
Where th' murder'd damsel lay.

And while upon its banks he stood
His dog with sudden spring,
Div'd into the chrystal flood,
And out her corpse did bring.

A Very interesting and amiable female, the daughter of a highly respectable individual in the West Riding of Yorkshire, and who is steward to a nobleman, became attached, owing to repeated solicitations, to a young grazier, whose family connexions were co-equal with her own. Their walks, in the evening, were frequent, and the attachment on the part of Mary Ann's lover, apparently increased at each succeeding interview.

About a fortnight since, they were seen together, for the last time, by some villagers crossing a stile, which leads to a lonely spot in that neighbourhood. Her ruin having been previously effected, she paid him her last visit with a determination of putting his honour to the test, as her destruction otherwise would be complete. He appeared, with his usual duplicity, to hold out the most sincere promises of marriage, which he pledged himself, most solemnly to fulfil. They had strayed to a considerable distance when they seated themselves on a green shady bank, at the back of which was a pond of considerable depth, and here the traitorous wretch put his diabolical plan into execution. Wine, it is supposed, from a flasket, was proffered to her to quench her thirst, into which the villain had infused a deleterious drug, for the purpose of throwing her into a deep sleep in order that he might dispatch her. In a few minutes she sunk back asleep, when the villain plunged a knife into her breast, and she expired upon the spot. He endeavoured to conceal the two-fold murder by plunging her body into the adjoining pond; but 'murder will out' in nine cases out of ten, and the following circumstance proves that an all-seeing Providence directs the most miraculous means of bringing such miscreants as the one before us to the bar of retributive justice.

A few mornings after the perpetration of this horrid deed, a shepherd was passing over the field with his dog and crook, when his attention was suddenly drawn to the pond by the moanings of his faithful companion, who dived into the water, and, in a few minutes brought to the margin of the bank the lifeless body of the unfortunate Mary Ann. A rigid enquiry immediately took place, and the result was, the instant apprehension of the supposed murderer, who was examined and finally committed to prison upon the capital charge, where his reflections ought to be of the most agonizing description, and at the ensuing Assizes he will doubtless forfeit his worthless life as a partial atonement for the heinous offence he has committed against the laws of God and man.

The following letter, which she evidently intended for her base seducer and murderer, was found, amongst others, in one of her private drawers:

Dear Charles,

Unless you perform your often repeated promise of marriage, I shall become a mother under the most wretched circumstances. My loving and affectionate parents are at this moment totally unconscious of the disgrace which I am hourly advancing upon them and myself. Do, for God's sake, meet me this evening at the usual spot, and may that meeting prove the sincerity of your intentions, and our future mutual happiness. Oh do not – do not deceive.

Your loving, though desponding,

MARY ANN

J. Catnach, Printer, 2, Monmouth-court 7 Dials.

Melancholy verses

O, all ye maidens fair, beware
Of this my wretched fate;
Nor e'er be led in treach'rous snare,
Or you'll repent too late.

For man's deceptive, you all know,
Till once his end he gains;
Then leaves you, sad disgrace to show,
For all his amorous pains.

A maiden, chaste, I once was deem'd
By all – the village pride;
For virtue none was more esteem'd,
It was my constant guide.

Till faithless Charles entwin'd my arms,
And vow'd he'd constant be;
'Twas then I lost a virgin's charms,
And thus he's ruin'd me.

But who would e'er suppose a fiend,
Could to your bosom creep:
Then from you suddenly be wean'd
To plunge you in the deep.

A murder, base, lurk'd in his breast,
As youv'e the story read;
But whilst my soul does calmly rest,
To dungeons he'll be led.

[Illustration Caption:] The villain plunges a knife into her breast.

A Horrible MURDER A Father Cutting his Child's Head off!

A Most horrid Murder was committed on Thursday night at Whitechapel, by a Father, upon his Child, an Infant about four months old. The man whose name is Sheen, resides at No. 1, Christopher Alley, Lambeth-street, near the Police Office, and obtained his living by selling wood about the streets. It appears that on several occasions when he had returned home intoxicated, and quarrelled with his wife, he had threatened to murder the child, by cutting its head off, but it is most singular that there appears to exist no cause which could induce the wretch to commit such a diabolical act. It was his only child, and from enquiries that have been made it does not seem that he entertained any jealousy respecting his wife. About seven o'clock last evening he returned home intoxicated, and said to his wife that he would cut the child's head off. She did not pay the slightest attention to his threat, and about an hour afterwards he sent her out to procure some tea; in her absence he cut the child's head from the body, he then threw the body under the bed, and placed the head on the table, where it was found by the Mother on entering the room. Sheen had absconded, but Dulton, an Officer of Lambeth-street, is in search of him. Sheen is about 30 years of age, and his wife is about the same age.

It appears that immediately after he committed the murder, he went to the residence of his father and brother, in White's-yard, Rosemary-lane, and told them that he had been playing at skittles, had quarrelled with an Irishman, and had stabbed him in the back with a knife, which he then produced. He was afraid, he said of being apprehended for the outrage, and therefore begged them to assist him with the means of making his escape. Neither father nor brother had any money to give him, but the father took him to a Mr Pugh, a carpenter, in Carnaby-market, who had known the family when they resided in Radnorshire and he advanced Sheen, 18 shillings, and also lent him a coat as he declared he had left his own in the skittle ground, whereas he left it in the room, after he had committed the murder, and where it was found covered with blood. Mr Pugh declared, if he had for a moment suspected he had committed so foul a crime, he would have seized him, and brought him to justice.

It appears that the murderer and his wife had cohabited together for some time before their marriage, that having burthened the parish with several children, the parish Officers caused him to be apprehended, and he had his choice either to give security for the maintenance of the children or to marry the woman, and as is usual in such cases to receive a reward from the parish of 5l Sheen accepted the '5l' and only 12 weeks ago they were married.

The mother of the unfortunate child said that on Thursday evening, when Sheen came home he was intoxicated, and requested her to make him some tea; that she went out for the ingredients, and left him in the room lying on the bed where the child was also lying asleep. she was gone about a quarter of an hour, when on her return, and opening the room door, her feelings of horror can be more easily conceived than described, when she beheld the head of her child on the table, with its eyes fixed towards the door, and the body on the bed. Sheen had, on several occasions, declared he would murder the child. Since the birth of the infant he hated it so much that he had frequently struck it on its mother knee. Last Sunday week he struck it such a violent blow, that the lump is now visible on its head. The Jury returned a verdict of Wilful Murder against the Father, who has not yet been taken.

A Copy of Verses

YE tender loving mothers all,
Who love your offspring dear,
Fast from your eyes the tears will fall,
When this sad tale you hear.
A frightful and a horrid deed,
I quickly shall unfold,
This most appalling fact to read,
Will make your blood run cold.

The murdrers' name is William Sheen,
O horrible to write,
The wicked wretch did often swear
He'd take his infants life.
On Thursday night he bade his wife
To go and buy some tea,
That he, the monster might complete
The horrid tragedy.

His wife had scarcely left the room
when he did grasp the babe,
So sweetly smil'd the harmless child,
Mercy it seem'd to crave.
His deadly knife the monster drew,
And hacked off its head,
And then the bleeding body threw
All underneath the bed.

The mother shortly did return
And grief her heart did wring,
On the table stood her baby's head,
Its lips still quivering.
The floor with blood was dyed red,
Most frightful for to see,
And the cruel father gone and fled,
But taken he soon will be.

The wretched mother shriek'd and cried,
In agony and distress.
No language surely could describe
The sorrows of her breast.
Inhuman man, thy infants blood,
Loud to the LORD doth cry;
Vengeance will recompense
the dead,
From it thou can'st not fly;

Cards and Bills Printed very Cheap by J. Catnach, 2 Monmouth-court, 7 Dials

READING A: Extracts from 'The Unknown Public'

Wilkie Collins

HOUSEHOLD WORDS.
A WEEKLY JOURNAL.

CONDUCTED BY CHARLES DICKENS.

N⁰· 439]   SATURDAY, AUGUST 21, 1858.   { Price 2d.
                                                                         { STAMPED 3d.

THE UNKNOWN PUBLIC

Do the subscribers to this journal, the customers at the eminent publishing-houses, the members of book clubs and circulating libraries and the purchasers and borrowers of newspapers and reviews, compose alto-

the speculative daring of one man could open a shop, and the human appetites and necessities of his fellow mortals could keep it from shutting up again, there, as it appeared to me, the unbound picture quarto instantly entered, set itself up obtrusively in the window, and insisted on being looked at by

Do the subscribers to this journal, the customers at the eminent publishing-houses, the members of book-clubs and circulating libraries, and the purchasers and borrowers of newspapers and reviews, compose altogether the great bulk of the reading public of England? There was a time when, if anybody had put this question to me, I, for one, should certainly have answered, Yes.

I know better now, I know that the public just now mentioned, viewed as an audience for literature, is nothing more than a minority.

This discovery (which I venture to consider equally new and surprising) dawned upon me gradually. I made my first approaches towards it, in walking about London, more especially in the second and third rate neighbourhoods. At such times, whenever I passed a small stationer's or small tobacconist's-shop, I became conscious, mechanically as it were, of certain publications which invariably occupied the windows. These publications all appeared to be of the same small quarto size; they seemed to consist merely of a few unbound pages; each one of them had a picture on the upper half of the front leaf, and a quantity of small print on the under. I noticed just as much as this, for some time, and no more. None of the gentlemen who are so good as to guide my taste in literary matters, had ever directed my attention towards these mysterious publications. My favourite Review is, as I firmly believe, at this very day unconscious of their existence. My enterprising librarian who forces all sorts of books on my attention that I don't want to read, because he has bought whole editions of them at a great bargain, has never yet tried me with the limp unbound picture quarto of the small shops. Day after day, and week after week the mysterious publications haunted my walks, go where I might; and, still, I was too inconceivably careless to stop and notice them in detail. I left London and travelled about England. The neglected publications followed me. There they were in every town, large or small. I saw them in fruit-shops, in oyster-shops, in lollypop-shops. Villages even – picturesque, strong-smelling villages – were not free from them. Wherever the speculative daring of one man could open a shop, and the human appetites and necessities of his fellow mortals could keep it from shutting up again, there, as it appeared to me, the unbound picture quarto instantly entered, set itself up obtrusively in the window, and insisted on being looked at by everybody. 'Buy me, borrow me, start at me, steal me – do anything. O inattentive stranger, except contemptuously pass me by!'

Under this sort of compulsion, it was not long before I began to stop at shop-windows and look attentively at these all-pervading specimens of what was to me a new species of literary production. I made acquaintance with one of them among the deserts of West Cornwall, with another in a populous thoroughfare of Whitechapel, with a third in a dreary little lost town at the north of Scotland. I went into a lovely county of South Wales; the modest railway had not penetrated to it, but the audacious picture quarto had found it out. Who could resist this perpetual, this inevitable, this magnificently unlimited appeal to notice and patronage? From looking in at the windows of the shop, I got on to entering the shops themselves, to buying specimens of this locust flight of small publications, to making strict examination of them from the first page to the last, and finally to instituting inquiries about them in all sort of well-informed quarters. The result – the astonishing result – has been the discovery of an Unknown Public; a public to be counted by millions; the mysterious, the unfathomable, the universal public of the penny-novel Journals.*

I have five of these journals now before me, represented by one sample copy, bought hap-hazard, of each. There are many more; but these five represent the successful and well-established members of the literary family. The eldest of them is a stout lad of fifteen years standing. The youngest is an infant of three months old. All five are sold at the same price of one penny; all five are published regularly once a week; all five contain about the same quantity of matter. The weekly circulation of the most successful of the five, is now publicly advertised (and, as I am informed, without exaggeration) at half a Million. Taking the other four as attaining altogether to a circulation of another half million (which is probably much under the right estimate) we have a sale of a Million weekly for five penny journals. Reckoning only three readers to each copy sold, the result is *a public of three millions* – a public unknown to the literary world; unknown, as disciples, to the whole body of professed critics; unknown, as customers, at the great libraries and the great publishing-houses; unknown, as an audience, to the distinguished English writers of our own time. A reading public of three millions which lies right

---

* It may be as well to explain that I use this awkward compound word in order to mark the distinction between a penny journal and a penny newspaper. The 'journal' is what I am now writing about. The 'newspaper' is an entirely different subject, with which this article has no connection.

out of the pale of literary civilisation, is a phenomenon worth examining – a mystery which the sharpest man among us may not find it easy to solve.

In the first place, who are the three million – the Unknown Public – as I have ventured to call them? The known reading public – the minority already referred to – are easily discovered and classified. There is the religious public, with booksellers and literature of its own, which includes reviews and newspapers as well as books. There is the public which reads for information, and devotes itself to Histories, Biographies, Essays, Treatises, Voyages and Travels. There is the public which reads for amusement, and patronises the Circulating Libraries and the railway book-stalls. There is lastly, the public which reads nothing but newspapers. We all know where to lay our hands on the people who represent these various classes. We see the books they like on their tables. We meet them out at dinner, and hear them talk of their favourite authors. We know, if we are at all conversant with literary matters, even the very districts of London in which certain classes of people live who are to be depended upon beforehand as the picked readers for certain kinds of books. But what do we know of the enormous outlawed majority – of the lost literary tribes – of the prodigious, the overwhelming three millions? Absolutely nothing.

I, myself – and I say it to my sorrow – have a very large circle of acquaintance. Ever since I undertook the interesting task of exploring the Unknown Public, I have been trying to discover among my dear friends and my bitter enemies, both alike on my visiting list, a subscriber to a penny novel-journal – and I have never yet succeeded in the attempt. I have heard theories started as to the probable existence of penny novel-journals in kitchen dressers, in the back parlours of Easy Shaving Shops, in the greasy seclusion of the boxes at the small Chop Houses. But I have never yet met with any man, woman, or child who could answer the inquiry, 'Do you subscribe to a penny journal?' plainly in the affirmative, and who could produce the periodical in question. I have learnt, years ago, to despair of ever meeting with a single woman, after a certain age, who has not had an offer of marriage. I have given up, long since, all idea of ever discovering a man who has himself seen a ghost, as distinguished from that other inevitable man who has had a bosom friend who has unquestionably seen one. These are two among many other aspirations of a wasted life which I have definitely given up. I have now to add one more to the number of my vanished illusions.

In the absence, therefore, of any positive information on the subject, it is only possible to pursue the investigation which occupies these pages by accepting such negative evidence as may help us to guess with more or less accuracy, at the social position, the habits, the tastes, and the average intelligence of the Unknown Public. Arguing carefully by inference, we may hope, in this matter, to arrive, by a circuitous road, at something like a safe, if not a satisfactory, conclusion.

To begin with, it may be fairly assumed – seeing that the staple commodity of each one of the five journals before me, is composed of

Stories – that the Unknown Public reads for its amusement more than for its information.

Judging by my own experience, I should be inclined to add that the Unknown Public looks to quantity rather than quality in spending its penny a week on literature. In buying my five specimen copies, at five different shops, I purposely approached the individual behind the counter, on each occasion, in the character of a member of the Unknown Public – say, Number Three Million and One – who wished to be guided in laying out a penny entirely by the recommendation of the shopkeeper himself. I expected, by this course of proceeding, to hear a little popular criticism, and to get at what the conditions of success might be, in a branch of literature which was quite new to me. No such result, however, occurred in any case. The dialogue between buyer and seller always took some such practical turn as this:

Number Three Million and One "I want to take in one of the penny journals. Which do you recommend?"

Enterprising Publisher: "Some likes one, and some likes another. They're all good pennorths. Seen this one?"

"Yes".

"Seen that one?"

"No".

"Look what a pennorth!"

"Yes – but about the stories in this one? Are they as good, now, as the stories in that one?"

"Well, you see, some likes one, and some likes another. Sometimes I sells more of one and sometimes I sells more of another. Take 'em all the year round, and there ain't a pin, as I knows of, to choose between 'em. There's just about as much in one as there is in another. All good pennorths. Why, Lord bless your soul, just take 'em up and look for yourself, and say if they ain't good pennorths! Look what a lot of print in every one of 'em. My eye! What a lot of print for the money!"

I never got any farther than this, try as I might. [...]

Having, inferentially, arrived at the two conclusions that the Unknown Public reads for amusement, and that it looks to quantity in its reading, rather than to quality, I might have found it difficult to proceed further towards the making of new discoveries, but for the existence of a very remarkable aid to inquiry, which is common to all the penny novel-journals alike. The peculiar facilities to which I now refer, are presented in the Answers to Correspondents. The page containing these is, beyond all comparison, the most interesting page in the penny journals. There is no earthly subject that it is possible to discuss, no private affair that it is possible to conceive, which the amazing Unknown Public will not confide to the Editor in the form of a question, and which the still more amazing editor will not set himself seriously and resolutely to answer. Hidden under cover of initials, or Christian names, or conventional signatures, such as Subscriber, Constant Reader, and so forth, the editor's correspondents seem, many of them, to judge by the published answers to their questions, utterly impervious to the sense of ridicule or shame. Young girls beset by perplexities which are usually supposed to be reserved for a mother's or an elder sister's ear only, consult the editor. Married women, who have committed little frailties consult the editor. Male jilts in deadly fear of actions for breach of promise of marriage, consult the editor. Ladies whose complexions are on the wane, and who wish to know the best artificial means of restoring them, consult the editor. Gentlemen who want to dye their hair, and get rid of their corns, consult the editor. Inconceivably dense ignorance, inconceivably petty malice, and inconceivably complacent vanity, all consult the editor, and all, wonderful to relate, get serious answers from him. No mortal position is too difficult for this wonderful man; there is no change of character as general referee, which he is not prepared to assume on the instant. Now he is a father, now a mother, now a schoolmaster, now a confessor, now a doctor, now a lawyer, now a young lady's confidante, now a young gentleman's bosom friend, now a lecturer on morals, and now an authority in cookery. [...]

Here are ten editorial sentiments on things in general, which are pronounced at the express request of correspondents, and which are therefore likely to be of use in assisting us to form an estimate of the intellectual condition of the Unknown Public:

1   All months are lucky to marry in, when your union is hallowed by love.

2   When you had a sad trick of blushing on being introduced to a young lady, and when you want to correct the habit, summon to your aid a manly confidence.

3   If you want to write neatly, do not bestow too much ink on occasional strokes.

4   You should not shake hands with a lady on your first introduction to her.

5   You can sell ointment without a patent.

6   A widow should at once and most decidedly discourage the lightest attentions on the part of a married man.

7   A rash and thoughtless girl will scarcely make a steady thoughtful wife.

8   We do not object to a moderate quantity of crinoline.

9   A sensible and honourable man never flirts himself, and ever despises flirts of the other sex.

10 A collier will not better his condition by going to Prussia.

At the risk of being wearisome, I must once more repeat that these selections from the Answers to Correspondents, incredibly absurd as they may appear, are presented exactly as I find them. Nothing is exaggerated for the sake of a joke; nothing is invented, or misquoted, to serve the purpose of any pet theory of my own. The sample produced of the three million penny readers is left to speak for itself; to give some idea of the social and intellectual materials of which a portion, at least, of the Unknown Public may fairly be presumed to be composed. Having so far disposed of this first part of the matter in hand, the second part follows naturally enough of its own accord. We have all of us formed some opinion by this time on the subject of the Public itself; the next thing to do is to find out what that Public reads.

I have already said that the staple commodity of the journals appears to be formed of stories. The five specimen copies of the five separate weekly publications now before me, contain, altogether, ten serious stories, one reprint of a famous novel (to be here-after referred to), and seven short tales, each of which begins and ends in one number. The remaining pages are filled up with miscellaneous contributions, in literature and art, drawn from every conceivable source. Pickings from Punch and Plato; wood-engravings, representing notorious people and views of famous places, which strongly suggest that the original blocks have seen better days in other periodicals; modern and ancient anecdotes; short memoirs; scraps of poetry; choice morsels of general information; household receipts, riddles, and extracts from moral writers; all appear in the most orderly manner, arranged under separate heads, and cut up neatly into short paragraphs. However, the prominent feature in each journal is the serial story, which is placed, in every case, as the first article, and which is illustrated by the only wood-engraving that appears to have been expressly cut for the purpose. To the serial story, therefore, we may fairly devote our chief attention because it is clearly regarded as the chief attraction of these very singular publications.

Two of my specimen-copies contain, respectively, the first chapters of new stories. In the case of the other three, I found the stories in various stages of progress. The first thing that struck me, after reading the separate weekly portions of all five, was their extraordinary sameness. Each portion purported to be written (and no doubt was written) by a different author, and yet all five might have been produced by the same man. Each part of each successive story, settled down in turn, as I read it, to the same dead level of the smoothest and flattest conventionality. A combination of fierce melodrama and meek domestic sentiment; short dialogues and paragraphs on the French pattern, with moral English reflections of the sort that occur on the top lines of children's copy-books; incidents and characters taken from the old exhausted mines of the circulating library, and presented as complacently and confidently as if they were original ideas; descriptions and reflections for the beginning of the number, and a 'strong situation,' dragged in by the neck and shoulders, for the end – formed the common literary source from which the five authors drew their weekly supply; all collecting it by the same means; all carrying it in the same quantities; all pouring it out before the attentive public in the same way. After reading my samples of these stories, I understood why it was that the fictions of the regularly-established writers for the penny journals are never republished. [...]

And this sort of writing appeals to a monster audience of at least three millions! The former proprietor of one of these penny journals commissioned a thoroughly competent person to translate The Count of Monte Christo, for his periodical. He knew that there was hardly a language in the civilised world into which that consummate specimen of the rare and difficult art of story-telling had not been translated. In France, in England, in America, in Russia, in Germany, in Italy, in Spain, Alexandre Dumas had held hundreds of thousands of readers breathless. The proprietor of the penny journal naturally thought that he could so as much with the Unknown Public. Strange to say, the result of this apparently certain experiment was a failure. The circulation of the journal in question, seriously decreased from the time when the first of living story-tellers became a contributor to it! The same experiment was tried with the Mysteries of Paris and the Wandering Jew, only to produce the same result. Another penny journal gave Dumas a commission to write a new story, expressly for translation in its columns. The speculation was tried, and once again the inscrutable Unknown Public held back the hand of welcome from the spoilt child of a whole world of novel-readers.

How is this to be accounted for? Does a rigid moral sense permeate the Unknown Public from one end of it to the other, and did the productions of the French novelists shock that sense from the very outset? The page containing the Answers to Correspondents would be enough in itself to dispose of this theory. But there are other and better means of arriving at the truth, which render any further reference to the correspondents' page unnecessary. Some time since, an eminent novelist (the only living English author, with a literary position, who has, as yet, written for the Unknown Public) produced his new novel in a penny journal. No shadow of a moral objection has ever been urged by any readers against the works published by the author of It Is Never Too Late To Mend; but even he, unless I have been greatly misinformed, failed to make the impression that had been anticipated on the impenetrable Three Millions. The great success of his novel was not obtained in its original serial form, but in its republished form, when it appealed from the Unknown to the Known Public. Clearly, the moral obstacle was not the obstacle which militated against the success of Alexandre Dumas and Eugène Sue.

What was it, then? Plainly this, as I believe. The Unknown Public is, in a literary sense, hardly beginning, as yet, to learn to read. The members of it are evidently in the mass, from no fault of theirs, still ignorant of almost everything which is generally known and understood among readers whom circumstances have placed, socially and intellectually, in the rank above them. The mere references in Monte Christo, The Mysteries of Paris, and White Lies (the scene of this last English fiction having been laid on French ground), to foreign names, titles, manners and customs, puzzled the Unknown Public on the threshold. Look back at the answers to correspondents, and then say, out of fifty subscribers to a penny journal, how many are likely to know, for example, that Mademoiselle means Miss? Besides the difficulty in appealing to the penny audience caused at the beginning by such simple obstacles as this, there was the great additional difficulty, in the case of all three of the fictions just mentioned, of accustoming untried readers to the delicacies and subtleties of literary art. An immense public has been discovered: the next thing to be done is, in a literary sense, to teach that public how to read.

An attempt, to the credit of one of the penny journals, is already being made. I have mentioned, in one place, a reprint of a novel, and later, a remarkable exception to the drearily common-place character of the rest of the stories. In both these cases I refer to one and the same fiction – to the Kenilworth of Sir Walter Scott, which is now being reprinted as a serial attraction in a penny journal. Here is the great master of modern fiction appealing, at this time of day, to a new public, and (amazing anomaly!) marching in company with writers who have the rudiments of their craft still to learn! To my mind, one result seems certain. If Kenilworth be appreciated by the Unknown Public, then the very best men among living English writers will one of these days be called on, as a matter of necessity, to make their appearance in the pages of the penny journals.

Meanwhile, it is perhaps hardly too much to say, that the future of English fiction may rest with this Unknown Public, which is now waiting to be taught the difference between a good book and a bad. It is probably a question of time only. The largest audience for periodical literature, in this age of periodicals, must obey the universal law of progress, and must, sooner or later, learn to discriminate. When that period comes, the readers who rank by millions, will be the readers who give the widest reputations, who return the richest rewards, and who will, therefore, command the service of the best writers of their time. A great, an unparalleled prospect awaits, perhaps, the coming generation of English novelists. To the penny journals of the present time belongs the credit of having discovered a new public. When that public shall discover its need of a great writer, the great writer will have such an audience as has never yet been known.

Source: COLLINS, W. (1858) *Household Words*, 439, 21 August, pp. 217–22.

READING B: Extracts from 'The Penny Post'

David Vincent

By [the 1880s] the postal flow was reaching a rate of fifty letters a head and there was some evidence that correspondence was beginning to play a larger part in the family life of the labouring poor. The most striking examples of the use of the post in creating or sustaining relationships were to be found not in everyday letter writing but rather in specialised forms of communication relating to particular events and ceremonies. Of these the earliest and until the last quarter of the nineteenth century the most important, was the sending of valentines.

The observance of 14 February underwent a metamorphosis during the eighteenth century which was later to befall many other customs. What had begun as an exchange of gifts, with many local variations of obscure origin was gradually transformed into an exchange of tokens and letters which in turn began to be replaced by printed messages from the end of the century (Cremer, 1971). As the gifts were translated into writing and then into print so profits accrued to both the Post Office and commercial publishers. And as the price of both postage and the valentines came down, so larger sections of the population entered the market. By 1835 the Secretary of the Post Office was recording 'that on or about St Valentine's Day there is a most extraordinary influx of many thousand letters' (Staff, 1969), and with the coming of the Penny Post, which amongst much else relieved loved ones of the necessity of paying for the compliments they received, the practice boomed. Rowland Hill calculated that 400,000 valentines were sent in 1841 (Hill, 1841), and by 1850 the flow had passed half a million, 'gorging the general as well as the local posts with love epistles' (Fraser's Magazine, February 1850). In London alone the extra mail on 14 February rose from 430,000 in 1863 to one and a half million in 1871 (Postmaster General, 1863).

'Cupid's Manufactory', as Dickens called it, which at its peak employed as many as 3,000 women, catered for all tastes, and, most important, for all levels of income and literacy. The quality of the poetry and spelling of the penny cards issued by firms such as the great broadside publisher James Catnach suggested that they were composed, bought and read by those with only a limited command of written English (Smith, 1857). For those who retained some literary ambition of their own, 'Valentine Writers' were on sale, providing specimen verses and replies which could be adapted to the particular romance. Given that most courtship took place within walking distance of the couple's home, it is possible that hand-made and hand-delivered valentines flourished well before penny postage. We find, for instance, the young weaver Samuel Bamford exchanging home-produced 'love billets' with his sweetheart at the end of the 1790s (Bamford, 1893). The arrival of the printed card tended to stereotype and ultimately to vulgarise the expression of affection, but at the same time it increased both the number of those able to engage in this form of communication and the distance over which contact might be made. The Post Office's calculation that 'those sent from London to the country were more than twice as numerous as those sent from the country to London' (Postmaster General, 1866) suggests that valentines were being used by migrants to sustain affairs with girls left behind in their home villages.

The decline of the valentine was as rapid as its rise, but less easy to explain. By the time Flora Thompson was growing up in the early 1880s, the 'daintily printed and lace bedecked valentines' had been superseded by 'crude coloured prints on flimsy paper representing hideous forms and faces intended to be more or less applicable to the recipient' (Thompson, 1982, p.486), and these in turn had disappeared by 1914. Whether the vulgarisation of the form was a symptom or a cause of its fall from fashion remains unclear; however, it was quickly replaced by a more generalised and eventually more prolific expression of sentiment, the Christmas card.

The first modern card appeared in 1843, designed by Henry Cole, Rowland Hill's chief assistant in the introduction of the Penny Post. Early versions were patterned closely on the valentine, and it was not until the 1860s that the genre began to achieve an identity of its own. The development of cheap colour printing enabled firms to publish increasing numbers of attractive cards at prices from a penny upwards. The consequent growth in seasonal mail first became apparent at Christmas 1877, when the Postmaster General reported that an extra four and a half million letters had passed through the Inland Branch (Postmaster General, 1878). Within two years the London Post Office was dealing with a rush of nine million items and the public was being asked to relieve pressure by posting early (Postmaster General, 1880). As with the valentines, the new custom appears to have embraced the entire social spectrum. At the top end of the market were expensive novelties and picturesque depictions of the children of the poor; at the bottom were millions of mass-produced cards produced by firms such as Raphael Tuck and offered for sale not only in stationers but tobacconists and toy shops (Buday, 1964). From the beginning, secular themes predominated. The exchange of cards celebrated less the Nativity and more family and friendship.

The third major innovation of the period was the picture postcard. The halfpenny postcard had been an immediate success on its introduction in 1870, but until 1894 customers were forced to use official pre-paid cards (Alliston, 1899). The removal of this restriction, followed by the relaxation of regulations over the size of the card in 1899, led the way to the inclusion of photographic views. By the year ending March 1901, over 350 million cards were being delivered in England and Wales, about fifty for each household (Postmaster General, 1901). In 1902 permission was given to write the message on the same side as the address, leaving the reverse for the picture alone, and the subsequent craze for sending and collecting postcards was only brought to an end by the outbreak of war (Staff, 1966).

All classes of society could participate. The rich could display their life-style by the size of their cards and the proof they gave of the distance which had been travelled; the poor could celebrate their growing opportunities to visit the seaside. At last Rowland Hill's original hope that mobility would promote correspondence was being realised on a mass scale. However, the writers were travelling in search of pleasure rather than work. The enlarged use of the post was a consequence of an increasing standard of living, cheaper transport and a shorter working week. To a certain extent it was also a consequence of the rise in literacy rates, which had passed 90 per cent by the time the picture postcard came into being. But as with the valentine and the Christmas card, the essence of the success of this genre was the minimal demand it made on the skills of both correspondent and recipient. There was little that could be written and little that needed to be read on one half of one side of a card.

A final indication of the dynamics of correspondence in this period may be gained by setting the postal rates in the context of European development as a whole. ... half a century after the introduction of the Penny Post, the United Kingdom had much the heaviest flow of mail. The rest of Europe, indeed the rest of the world save the United States, which was to gain the lead in the 1890s, struggled in our wake. This in itself was a cause of much national pride. 'If asked for a true index of the degree of civilisation attained in a given country', wrote Henniker Heaton at Queen Victoria's Golden Jubilee, 'I should suggest the number of letters forwarded and received by its inhabitants' (Heaton, 1897). As early as 1858 the Postmaster General had drawn attention to the fact that as many letters were being delivered in Manchester alone as in the whole of Russia, and the subsequent work of the Universal Postal Union confirmed Britain's success (Postmaster General, 1858).

The one index of progress to demonstrate any consistent relationship with the postal service is the other major form of inland communication in the nineteenth century, the railway. In one sense the connection is obvious. The railway and postal systems were created alongside each other throughout Europe, and from the beginning were dependent on each other's development. Without the introduction of a rapid and reliable means of transport, the postal reformers could not have realised their ambitions and conversely the fledgling railway companies derived immense benefit from the revenue generated by carrying mail. Rowland Hill in fact attributed part of the fall in profits following the introduction of the Penny Post to the exploitation by the railway companies of their position as monopoly carriers on important routes. (Hill, 1841). He was, however, successful in persuading the Brighton Railway Company, of which he became chairman, to carry letters free of charge, on the grounds that 'residence in Brighton, and therefore custom to the railway, would be increased by every addition to postal facilities between that town and the metropolis' (Hill and Hill, 1880).

By 1890 most countries had completed their rail networks, and those with a small population scattered over a wide area, such as Norway or Finland, had achieved per capita distances as high as the United Kingdom. Just as the post represented the employment rather than merely the possession of literacy, so its mirror image was to be found in the business rather than the existence of the railway.

The financial interdependence of the two forms of communication only partly explains their affinity. Of greater importance were the common features in the pattern of demand for each service. Like the post, the early growth of the railway was largely dependent on middle-class patronage. And whereas the needs of business and businessmen generated much of the custom, there was from the beginning an unexpectedly high volume of recreational use by those with the time and money to exploit the new opportunities (O'Brien, 1983). Working-class people by contrast continued to walk to work, or in search of work, and confined their recreational activity to the vicinity of the home. The penny a mile 'Parliamentary Train' was introduced only four years after the Penny Post, but for the labouring poor a railway journey remained an even more special occurrence than the receipt of a letter. The most immediate impact of the railway on this section of the community, as was the case with the Post Office, was in the provision not of a new service but of a new form of employment. It took a long time for the working class to begin to make large-scale use of the new means of transport, and with the exception of a limited amount of commuting to work in the biggest cities, the journeys were made not by individuals but by families. Communication was for pleasure. It was both a consequence and a celebration of a marginal increase in prosperity. Literally and symbolically the railway and the post came together at the seaside. The working-class family left home on the excursion train and returned through the picture postcard.

References

ALLISTON, N. (1899) 'Pictorial post cards', *Chambers Journal*, October.

BAMFORD, S. (1893) *Early Days*, London.

BUDAY, G. (1964) *The History of the Christmas Card*, London.

CREMER, W.H. (1971) *St Valentine's Day and Valentines*, London.

Fraser's Magazine (1850), 'The Post Office', February, XLI, 227, London.

HEATON, H. (1897) 'Postal and telegraphic progress under Queen Victoria', *The Fortnightly Review*, CCCLXXVI (June).

HILL, R. (1841) 'Results of the new postage arrangements', *Quarterly Journal of the Statistical Society of London*, July.

HILL, R. and HILL, G.B. (1880) *The Life of Sir Rowland Hill and the History of the Penny Postage*, London.

O'BRIEN, P. (1983) 'Transport and economic development in Europe, 1789–1914', in P. O'BRIEN (ed.) *Railways and the Economic Development of Western Europe, 1830–1914*, London.

POSTMASTER GENERAL (1858) *Fourth Annual Report of the Postmaster General on the Post Office*, London.

POSTMASTER GENERAL (1863) *Ninth Annual Report of the Postmaster General on the Post Office*, London.

POSTMASTER GENERAL (1866) *Twelfth Annual Report of the Postmaster General on the Post Office*, London.

POSTMASTER GENERAL (1871) *Seventeenth Annual Report of the Postmaster General on the Post Office*, London.

POSTMASTER GENERAL (1880) *Twenty-fourth Annual Report of the Postmaster General on the Post Office*, London.

POSTMASTER GENERAL (1880) *Twenty-sixth Annual Report of the Postmaster General on the Post Office*, London.

POSTMASTER GENERAL (1886) *Forty-seventh Annual Report of the Registrar General*, London.

SMITH, C.M. (1857) 'The Press of the Seven Dials', in *The Little World of London*, London.

STAFF, F. (1966) *The Picture Postcard and its Origins*, London.

STAFF, F. (1969) *'The Valentine' and its Origins*, London.

THOMPSON, F. (1982 edn) *Lark Rise to Candleford*, Harmondsworth.

Source: VINCENT, D. (1989) *Family, Literacy and Popular Culture England 1750–1914*, Chapter 2, Cambridge, Cambridge University Press.

READING C: Extracts from 'Sketches in the life of John Clare'

John Clare

There is a pleasure in recalling ones past years to recollection; in this I believe every bosoms agrees and returns a ready echo of approbation and I think a double gratifycation is witness'd as we turn to a repetition of our early days by writing them down on paper   on this head my own approbation must shelter its vanity while thus employ'd, by consisting self-satisfaction a sufficient apology. But I am carless of praise and fearless of censure in the business, my only wish being to give a friend pleasure in its perusal for whom and by whose request it is written and as I have little doubt of being able to accomplish that matter those who (strangers to the writer) that it displeases need not be startled at the disappointment.

I was born July 13, 1793 at Helpstone, a gloomy village in Northamptonshire, on the brink of the Lincolnshire fens. [...] Both my parents was illiterate to the last degree   my mother knew not a single letter and superstition went so far with her that she beleved the higher parts of lear[n]ing was the blackest arts of witchcraft and that no other means coud attain them   my father coud read a little in a bible or testament and was very fond of the supersti[ti]ous tales that are hawked about a sheet for a penny, such as old Nixons Prophesies, Mother Bunches Fairey Tales, and Mother Shiptons Legacy etc etc   he was likewise fond of Ballads and I have heard him make a boast of it over his horn of ale with his merry companions at the Blue bell public house which was next door that he coud sing or recite above a hundred   he had a tolerable good voice and was often calld upon to sing at thos convivials of bacchanalian merry makings [...] As my parents had the good fate to have but a small family, I being the eldest of 4, two of whom dyed in their Infancy my mothers hopfull ambition ran high of being able to make me a good scholar, as she said she expirenced enough in her own case to avoid bringing up her childern in ignorance, but god help her, her hopful and tender kindness was often crossd with difficultys; for there was often enough to do to keep cart upon wheels, as the saying is, without incurring an extra expence of putting me to school, though she never lost the opportunity when she was able to send me, nor woud my father interfere till downright nessesity from poverty forced him to check her kind intentions; for he was a tender father to his children, and I have every reason to turn to their memorys with the warmest feelings of gratitude and satisfaction, and if doing well to their childern be an addition to rightousness I am certain god cannot forget to bless them with a portion of felicity in the other world, when souls are called to judgment and receive the reward due to their actions commited below. In cases of extreeme poverty my father took me to labour with him and made me a light flail for threshing, learing me betimes the hardship which adam and Eve inflicted on their children by their inexperienced misdeeds, incuring the perpetual curse from god of labouring for a livelihood, which the teeming earth is said to have produced of itself before, but use is second nature, at least it learns us patience   I resignd myself willingly to the hardest toils and tho one of the weakest was stubborn[n] and stomachful and never flinched from the roughest labour   by that means I always secured the favour of my masters and escaped the ignominy that brands the name of idleness   my character was always 'weak but willing'. I believe I was not older than 10 when my father took me to seek the scanty rewards of industry   Winter was generally my season of imprisonment in the dusty barn   Spring and Summer my assistance was wanted elswere in tending sheep or horses in the fields or scaring birds from the grain or weeding it, which was a delightfull employment, as the old womens memorys never faild of tales to smoothen our labour, for as every day came new Jiants, Hobgobblins, and faireys was ready to pass it away   as to my schooling, I think never a year passd me till I was 11 or 12 but 3 months or more at the worst of times was luckily spared for my improvement, first with an old woman in the village and latterly with a master at a distance from it   here soon as I began to learn to write, the readiness of the Boys always practising urgd and prompted my ambition to make the best use of my absence from school, as well as at it, and my master was always supprisd to find me improved every fresh visit, instead of having lost what I had learned before for which to my benefit he never faild to give me tokens of encouragement   never a leisure hour pass'd me with out making use of it   every winter night our once unlettered hut was wonderfully changd in its appearance to a school room   the old table, which old as it was doubtless never was honourd with higher employment all its days then the convenience of bearing at meal times the luxury of a barley loaf or dish of

potatoes, was now coverd with the rude begg[in]ings of scientifical
requ[i]sitions, pens, ink, and paper one hour, jobbling the pen at sheep hooks
and tarbottles, and another trying on a slate a knotty question in Numeration,
or Pounds, Shillings, and Pence, at which times my parents triumphant
anxiety was pleasingly experiencd, for my mother woud often stop her wheel
or look off from her work to urge with a smile of the warmest rapture in my
fathers face her prophesy of my success, saying 'shed be bound, I shoud one
day be able to reward them with my pen, for the trouble they had taken in
giveing me schooling', and I have to return hearty thanks to a kind
providence in brining her prophesy to pass and giving me the pleasure of
being able to stay the storm of poverty and smoothen their latter days; and as
a recompense for the rough beginnings of life bid their tottering steps decline
in peaceful tranquility to their long home, the grave. Here my highest
ambition was gratifyd for my greatest wish was to let my parents see a
printed copy of my poems   that pleasure I have witness'd and they have
moreover livd to see with astonishment and joy their humble offspring
noticed by thousands of friends and among them names of the greatest
distinction, the flower and honour of his native country   surely it is a
thrilling pleasure to hear a crippled father seated in his easy arm chair
comparing the past with the present, saying 'Boy who coud have thought,
when we was threshing together some years back, thou woudst be
thus noticed and be enabled to make us all thus happy.' About this time,
which my fathers bursts of feeling alludes too, I began to wean off from
my companions and sholl about the woods and fields on Sundays
alone   conjectures filld the village about my future destinations on the
stage of life, some fanc[y]ing it symptoms of lunacy and that my mothers
prophecys would be verified to her sorrow and that my reading of books
(they woud jeeringly say) was for no other improvment then quallyfiing an
idiot for a workhouse, for at this time my taste and passion for reading began
to be furious and I never sholld out on a Sabbath day but some scrap or
other was pocketed for my amusement   I deeply regret usefull books was out
of my reach, for as I was always shy and reserved I never woud own to my
more learned neighbours that I was fond of books, otherwise then the bible
and prayer Book, the prophetical parts of the former, with the fine Hebrew
Poem of Job, and the prayers and simple translation of the Psalms   in the
latter was such favourite readings with me that I could recite abundance of
passages by heart   I am sorry to find the knowledge of other books shoud
diminish the delight ones childhood experiences in our first perusal of those
divine writings. I must digress to say that I think the manner of learing
childern in village schools very erronious, that is soon as they learn their
letters to task them with lessons from the bible and testament and keeping
them dinging at them, without any change, till they leave it   A dull boy
never turns with pleasures to his school days when he has often been beat 4
times for bad readings in 5 verses of Scripture, no more then a Man in
renewd prosperity to the time when he was a debtor in a Jail   Other books

as they grow up become a novelty and their task book at school, the Bible, looses its relish   the painful task of learning wearied the memory   irksome inconvenience never prompts reccolection   the bible is laid by on its peaceful shelf and by 9 Cottages out of 10 never disturb'd or turnd too further then the minutes referance for reciting the text on a Sunday, a task which most christians nowadays think a sufficient duty at least in the lower orders I cannot speak with assurance only where expirience informs me   so much for village schools

About now all my stock of learning was gleaned from the Six-penny Romances of 'Cinderella', 'Little Red Riding hood', 'Jack and the bean Stalk', 'Zig Zag', 'Prince Cherry', etc etc etc and great was the pleasure, pain, or supprise increased by allowing them authenticity, for I firmly believed every page I read and considered I possesd in these the chief learning and literature of the country   But as it is common in villages to pass judgment on a lover of books as a sure indication of laziness, I was drove to the narrow nessesity of stinted oppertunitys to hid in woods and dingles of thorns in the fields on Sundays to read these things, which every sixpence thro the indefatigable savings of a penny and halfpenny when collected was willingly thrown away for them, as oppertunity offered when hawkers offerd them for sale at the door   to read such things on sundays was not right   while nessesity is a good apology for iniquity and ignorance is more so I knew no better and it may be said that ignorance is one of the sweetest hopes that a poor man carries to the grave [...]

I have often absented my self the whole Sunday at this time nor coud the chiming bells draw me from my hiding place to go to church, tho at night I was sure to pay for my abscence from it by a strong snubbing   I at length got an higher notion of learning by going to school and every leisure minute was employ'd in drawing squares and triangles upon the dusty walls of the barn   this was also my practice in learning to write   I also devourd for these purposes every morsel of brown or blue paper (it matterd not which) that my mother had her tea and sugar lapt in from the shop   but this was in cases of poverty when I coud not muster three farthings for a sheet of writing paper   the saying of 'a little learning is a dangerous thing' is not far from fact   after I left school for good (nearly as wise as I went save reading and writing) I felt an itching after every thing.

Source: ROBINSON, E. and POWELL, D. (eds) (1996) *John Clare by Himself,* **Ashington, Mid Northumberland Arts Group.**

READING D: Extracts from 'Autobiographical memoir'

J.A. Leatherland

It is with no self-complacent feelings that I sit down to pen this brief sketch of my lowly career. On the contrary, I review my past life with deep humility, and can only bring myself to the task of recording its history in the hope that it may prove instructive, as the experience of every human being must, if faithfully narrated. Providence has not seen fit to allow to any person the chance of living over again; but the history of those who have traversed a similar path – who have been elated by similar joys, and depressed by similar sorrows as their neighbours; who have substantially felt the same emotions, experienced the same griefs and cares, and committed the same errors as common humanity – in a measure serves the purpose to the young and inexperienced; showing them the blessed results of virtuous actions, and warning them to shun the breakers upon which others have been wrecked.

Auto-biography is also of service, as showing the varying force of circumstances upon different orders of mind – while one individual succumbs to them and sinks beneath their pressure, another with heroic vigour rises above them, and bends them to his will, or snaps asunder the bands, as Sampson the green withes that bound his sinewy limbs. It also reveals, as no other record can, the secret springs of action – the hidden, latent motives which spring up in the heart, and lead to conduct often enigmatical to the keenest and most diligent observer. But I must check my pen. I am not about to write an essay upon Auto-biography, but to furnish the reader with my own, which I will endeavour to do succintly and truthfully, begging his utmost candour in the perusal.

I was born at Kettering, on the 11th day of May, 1812 – a dark day in the annals of England, noted for the assassination of the Hon. Spencer Percival, then Premier of England, and M.P. for Northampton. My father was a carpenter, but I remember little of him, for before I had completed my sixth year, he died, and I was left, with a younger sister, to the care of a widowed mother, who although in deep poverty, did her best to bring us up in comfort and respectability.

From almost infancy I was sent to a dame school, of which that pourtrayed by Shenstone is a model; but I do not remember learning the alphabet, or being puzzled by the awful hornbook. My mother also (blessed be her memory), taught me as only a mother can, and impressed upon my childhood those maxims of christian morals which are more valuable than an inheritance. She had a literary taste, and often used to please me with the rehearsal of those sweet little artless poems, which are the gems of our language. She moreover, read to me from Bunyan, Addison, Watts, Cowper, and others of our standard authors, noted for their simplicity, so that I early imbibed an æsthetic taste; and though circumstances denied me a classical education, I was enabled to drink at the 'well of English undefiled.'

I was, as I have said, from my childhood, passionately fond of books, and whenever I had a spare coin, off I used to run to the bookseller's shop for the tale of 'Mother Hubbard,' 'Goody Twoshoes,' 'Little Red Riding Hood,' and such-like lore. One day I bought a penny book, and being too impatient to wait until I got home, I began to peruse it in the street, and whilst so engaged, a puff of wind, to my no little vexation, blew it out of my hand into the kennel. Whilst I was weeping over its soiled pages, a gentleman passed me, and after enquiring what was the matter, gave me a sixpenny piece, telling me to dry up my tears and buy a better. Instantly my childish heart bounded with joy. I seized the proffered money, and ran to Mr Dash's – whose windows were dearer to me than the pastry-cook's – and purchased a copy of a topographical work, called 'Thirty-two Remarkable Places of Old England,' with which I was amused for years. *The* book of my boyhood was, however, the 'Pilgrim's Progress,' a beautiful edition of which was given me by a paternal uncle. I used to read it from morning to night, and could not but believe the pilgrimage to be a real one, and often wished my mother to set out, with me and my sister, upon the journey. She endeavoured to explain that it set forth the pilgrimage through this world to a better; but I could not understand how it could be, and longed to visit the House Beautiful, and even to brave the lions, and the grim fangs of Apollyon. This book it was that early awakened my imaginative powers. A dream which my mother related to me about this time also strangely impressed me. It was in the year 1817, after two bad harvests. There was a great scarcity, and she told me how she dreamed that she saw Famine come into the house, a gaunt monster, holding up his lean, bony fingers, and staring with wolfish eyes! – how he tried to snatch the bread off the table; and how he howled, and howled until she awoke! The impression the relation of this dream made upon me I have never lost, and the reader will find that allusion is made to it in the Poem entitled 'Poverty' at page 150 of this Volume. I was also much struck with many parts of the Bible. My favorite chapters were the xv. of the i. Ep. of Corinthians; the xi. of Hebrews; Ezekial's vision; and most of the Apocalypse. These I used to read over and over again, but could not go on with the dry ceremonies of the Israelites recorded in Leviticus, or what appeared to me to be the barbarous slaughter of the Canaanites and Philistines; and to this day I have not read these portions of scripture consecutively. I also used to think the Epistles dry reading, but these are now my favourite parts of the Book of Inspiration. [...]

In 1824, I was sent to learn the shoemaking craft, to which probably I should have been destined had not employment fallen off; but as trade was bad, I left it, and was placed in the loom under my father-in-law, where I continued until the spring of 1829, when I was apprenticed to Ribbon Weaving for five years. [...]

One of the most sorrowful of scenes witnessed under the sun, is that of a sickly youth, worn down with rain and disease, wearily wending his way to a factory on a cold and dark winter's morning. This, many, many times, has been my lot; for, from my earliest days, I was a weakly boy, and suffered acutely from *calculi* in the bladder and kidneys. I have often felt in the morning as though I must have lain down on the factory steps and died; but a long day's work was before me, with the cruel taunts and jeers of my shopmates if I complained. I was, up to thirty-eight years of age, frequently afflicted with these torturing paroxysms; but strange to say, since a dangerous illness, which seized me in the autumn of 1850, I have scarcely had a symptom of this complaint. [...]

I served my apprenticeship until twenty-one years old, and continued working for my master for about three years afterwards. I then left the ribbon factory and learned to weave velvet. Here I worked in a room with seven others – young men of quite different habits to my former shopmates. Gilbert's Map of the World hung at one end of the room, and entomological specimens adorned the window-sills. Here, instead of teasing and tormenting one another, all were affable and courteous, and each ardently bent on acquiring knowledge. It was like escaping from captivity to liberty –from Pandemonium to Paradise! Everyone seemed so kindly disposed and so intelligent, that it was a pleasure to be among them; and I cannot help here mentioning the fact, that of those seven individuals, the six who survive, have with one exception, made their way in the world, and have attained a superior position to that of artisans.

I now devoted more time to literary pursuits, and passed my days very pleasantly with my intelligent shopmates. We clubbed together, and bought 'Harris's Hermes,' from which we gained some knowledge of the principles, elements, and philosophy of language generally, and of the English tongue in particular. We also formed the nucleus of a Mutual Instruction Society; arranged classes, and delivered lectures; and thus we both disseminated and received instruction. I have often blushed at my youthful complaisance and vanity in so early attempting to act the part of a professor; but whilst endeavouring to teach others, I was of necessity obliged to study the subjects myself, and in this way my crude and humble attempts became an important means of self-cultivation. As I never possessed in the slightest degree the power of extempore speaking, I was obliged to commit to paper the whole of my performances, which were therefore a kind of essays on the subjects I took in hand, and the writing of these trained me somewhat in the art of composition.

Some years before I made my *debût* as a lecturer, I had won some local celebrity as a versifier. I was passionately fond of poetry, being led to its study by accidentally meeting with Milton's minor poems, when about fourteen years of age. Though so young, I was instantly charmed with 'Comus,' and read it so much, that I could repeat it nearly all by heart. I still think it one of the most beautiful poems in the language, and deem it a pity it is not more generally appreciated. [...]

I found velvet-weaving a highly suitable occupation for the exercise of thought and meditation – much more so than my former employment. In the ribbon loom, the worker has to manage a number of pieces at once, every one of which requires his care and attention; but in velvet weaving, the work is more under his command, and there is only one piece of work to superintend, and with good silk and use, the work becomes little more than mechanical, and. affords scarcely any interruption to mental exercises. There is also far less noise attending the manufacture; and, owing to stopping every third time the shuttle is thrown across, to cut out the wire, the muscles are not kept in such constant motion. Some weavers of plain silk, place books before them to read whilst at work. I never could manage this with any good result: I think the secret of doing things well, is to do only one thing at a time. My plan therefore was to read at leisure intervals, and to ruminate on such reading whilst engaged in manual occupation. If in the course of my thoughts, anything struck me particularly, I made a note of it in a memorandum book, which I kept by the side of my loom for the purpose. [...]

My reading at this time was desultory. I perused almost everything that came in my way. I was very fond of 'Plutarch's Lives,' Gibbon's and Robertson's Histories, the 'Spectator,' Dr Johnson's writings, and Boswell's inimitable portrait of him; and I studied all the British Poets that fell in my way, from Chaucer to Byron. Periodical literature also engaged my attention. 'Tait' I read and enjoyed for years – especially the articles contributed by De Quincy – and I was not a little proud on a poem of my own being admitted into its pages. From 'Chambers's Journal,' I gleaned much useful information, and it was a great treat when any stray numbers of 'Blackwood,' 'Fraser,' or the 'Quarterly Review' came in my way. One of the latter, containing a capital account of Sir James Macintosh, as well as other brilliant articles, was a prize I once found on the counter of a grocer, and which I rescued from the ignominious fate of being torn up into butter papers. This I eagerly read, and afterwards studied for some years. 'Blackwood' I more than once saved from a similar fate, perusing their contents again and again, enjoying a rich intellectual repast. [...]

In 1838, some gentlemen of Kettering offered prizes for the two best essays on the Best Means of Improving the Condition of the Working Classes. I tried my hand, and was fortunate enough to obtain the first prize, the adjudicators stating as the ground of their award, that they considered the one written by me the most practical treatise. The second was obtained by a fellow-workman, and has since been printed. This success cheered and encouraged me, and I determined to persevere in my literary studies. Another circumstance stimulated me still farther. The late Earl Fitzwilliam, happening to hear something about the essays, did us the honour to request the loan of them for perusal. They were forwarded, and after a time returned, with a very complimentary letter, and the following Christmas his Lordship kindly sent me a generous token of his approval. This was highly encouraging. But the paper was a crude performance and it contains several things to which I could not now subscribe. Its tone was too political – too revolutionary – and I have alluded to it, as affording an introduction to a period of my life that I look back upon with regret and remorse. [...]

The Reform agitation had stirred society to its very depths, and caused political subjects to be freely canvassed among the people. As the trading classes had obtained the suffrage for themselves, it was but natural that working men should wish to possess it as well, and think themselves wronged by being excluded from voting for members of parliament. I was one of those who thought so, and I joined a society, which though at first it did not pledge itself to anything definite, afterwards became nothing less than a thorough-going Chartist Association – and a very notorious one it was. The Charter, and the Charter alone, was held to be the great panacea for the cure of every evil – social, moral, religious, and political. This flame was fanned by itinerant demagogues, who went about seeking whom they might devour – men who certainly possed [sic] the power of extemporizing with a vengeance, but who, making a market of the passions and feelings of the people, cared about the real interests of the nation, not one straw.

This society chose me its secretary; and as its leading men were my seniors – many of them persons whom I had long regarded with esteem, and had looked up to for teaching and guidance, my own minister being one of them – I thought I could not do wrong in accepting office. Indeed I esteemed it an honor; and as my own intentions were honest, I gave others credit for honesty as well, and entered upon the duties without a thought or a dread of coming evil. I soon, however, found that I could not go to the extreme lengths of many of the fraternity, neither could I tolerate the chiefs whom they seemed so much to admire. [...] I saw that it is easy to destroy, but difficult to construct, and harder still to establish. I was also disgusted with the conduct of many, who, arrogating to themselves the name of 'Liberals' were the most illiberal of any. I saw that it was not liberty they wanted, so much as political power.

Source: LEATHERLAND, J.A. (1862) *Essays and Poems, With a Brief Autobiographical Memoir*, London. W. Tweedie.

9 Locating creativity in texts and practices

Janet Maybin

9.1 Introduction

The chapters of this book have offered a broad sweep of different approaches to studying everyday creativity and artistry in the English language. In the first part of the book we moved from considering the poetics of casual talk and the patterned structures of conversational narrative to analysing language styling and performance and then on to creativity in children's talk. Discussion in later chapters ranged from the uses of new communication technology and the creation of identity in particular written genres to a discussion of the creative dimensions of literacy practices and a historical case study of creative literacy in rapidly changing nineteenth-century England. Within the various chapters we have offered different ways of conceptualising what counts as creativity and artistry in language, and illustrated a variety of approaches to how it can be analysed. These have ranged from approaches focusing on language at the level of text, to those setting language creativity within the context of broader sociological and historical processes.

All of the chapters contribute, in various ways, to the underlying argument of the book: that the seeds of artistic and literary uses of English, which are developed in literature and high verbal art, are all to be found in everyday uses of the language. There is linguistic creativity in talk and everyday writing, and creativity in language also emerges from interactions between people and in relation to the potential resources and constraints of particular contexts.

In this chapter, I shall develop this argument further by looking more closely at some of the theory about language and communication which underpins the material in the preceding chapters. Throughout the book we have placed a particular emphasis on social dimensions of language and I shall focus on two different sources of ideas which have been highly influential in studies of language and social life: the Russian language philosopher Mikhail Bakhtin's theory of the multi-voiced and dialogic nature of language, and the ideas of the North American sociologist Erving Goffman about the artful presentation of the self in everyday life. I will also look at how the North American linguistic anthropologist Deborah Tannen draws on Bakhtin's work in her argument about the creativity of everyday uses of reported speech. My aim is to link these readings with earlier parts of the book, and also to follow up and develop some of the ideas contained in them more fully. First, in Section 9.2 below, I want to examine how we might begin to draw together an overall framework for looking at creativity in everyday language, from the various approaches taken across the book.

9.2 A framework for analysing language creativity

There is a delicate balance between documenting and analysing the more vernacular kinds of language creativity which we have been presenting, and sliding into the position that all meaning making is creative and so, therefore, are all uses of language. Our own starting point for looking at creativity was Jakobson's notion of the poetic function of language, where there is a 'focus on the message for its own sake' (quoted in Chapter 1, p. 10). Jakobson saw the poetic function as always potentially there, in any communication, surfacing when there is a particular highlighting of sounds, rhythm, grammar or meaning so that some aspect of language itself is foregrounded and catches the audience's attention. Speakers, in fact, seem to be unconsciously drawn towards poetic uses of language; Jakobson (1960) suggests that choosing to say 'Joan and Margery' rather than 'Margery and Joan', or 'the horrible Harry' rather than 'the dreadful Harry' reflects people's natural propensity to poetic patterns of rhythm and sound. Similarly, as we saw in Chapter 6, ordinary personal letters and diary entries include poetic repetition and imagery. While in everyday talk and writing the poetic function may be a minor element in comparison with, for example, the information content of the message or the persuasive nature of an argument, in poetry it becomes the dominant function. In a poem, language is crafted together as a self-contained whole and the verbal form is itself the focus.

We have taken up Jakobson's point that the poetic function of language, while particularly dominant in poetry, is also found in other less formal kinds of verbal art. This is shown especially clearly in the discussion of morphological inventiveness, puns and metaphors in Chapter 1, narrative structures in talk in Chapter 2 and children's linguistic inventiveness in Chapter 4, where we focus on the form of the text. These chapters also develop Jakobson's point that the poetic function of a communicative act, realised through highlighting particular aspects of the linguistic system, is always combined with the other functions of language. Puns and metaphors can be used to bond or exclude, as can storytelling which is also 'directly connected to our making and remaking of our identity and our relationships' (p. 54 of this volume). We have suggested that creativity extends beyond the linguistic artistry in the text on which Jakobson focuses, to include a speaker or writer's particular attention to performance, to ways of getting a message across and to interacting with others.

Jakobson's poetics, which is tied to the formal properties of language as an abstract system of sounds, grammar and meaning, exemplifies what Carter (2004) calls the inherency model of language and creativity. Once we started to look at performances of identity and artful uses of language within social interaction, we needed to develop a somewhat broader concept of creativity in language than one focused on text alone. While still acknowledging the importance of formal creativity, many of the chapters also draw on what Carter identified as a second approach to understanding creativity in language: the sociocultural model. Within this model, creativity in language is seen as determined, to a greater or lesser extent, by social, cultural and historical factors. Chapter 3 develops the notion of oral language use as part of artful performance in relation to 'styling the self'; Chapter 4 looks at children's language creativity in the context of social practice; Chapter 5 examines communication and creativity on the internet; and Chapter 6 discusses the relationship between creativity and identity in written genres. In each case, there is attention to the manner in which a communicative activity is carried out, and the creative use of the potential resources of particular communicative contexts and generic processes. These potential resources are partly shaped by the technologies available, by the affordances, constraints and effectivities discussed in Chapter 5 and also by institutional, cultural and historical factors, which are explored at greater length through the ethnographic accounts in Chapter 7 and the historical account in Chapter 8.

Our second model, the sociocultural model, informs a variety of approaches, ranging from research combining textual with some kind of social analysis to research based on the premise that creativity in language is always a social construction. Most chapters have included some attention to the 'self-referential' creative formal features of talk and text – for instance the choice of one language or speaking style rather than another, word play on the internet, the parallelism in diaries and letters, poetics in prison writing. Generally, however, Chapters 3–8 gradually broaden out in the later chapters to what might be termed more sociocultural approaches (including historical analyses). There is thus an incremental building-up of layers of analysis through the book: from looking at how language creativity is realised through manipulating aspects of the linguistic system in specific stretches of talk or written texts, to examining how it also emerges in the course of interactions between people, to examining its relationship to particular institutional and cultural contexts and particular moments in history.

This gradual broadening-out involves a shift from locating creativity within a specific 'artefact', as it were (a piece of transcribed talk or a written text), to looking at language creativity as a *moment within a dynamic process* which may not make sense without a knowledge of what comes before and after, and of contextualising factors. Within everyday social practice, what counts as creative may be contested as life moves on; today's creative chat-room usage may be tomorrow's accepted internet convention, the teenage creative uses of language for styling as Jocks or Burnouts may later be looked back on by older individuals as simple conforming to a subcultural convention. Even within the course of a single interaction, a speaker's purpose in using language creatively may be overturned and subverted by another speaker. Specific extracts of text, such as a conversational narrative, or a written letter, can be seen as a momentary crystallisation of meaning within dynamic social processes which are often masked within more formal textual analysis. To address creativity within these more dynamic, contextualised processes, researchers have drawn on theory from anthropology and history, as well as from linguistics.

The third, most recent, model that Carter identifies has only surfaced occasionally in the book. This is the 'cognitive model', which assumes universal human mental propensities for creativity in language and its cognitive effects. The model comes originally from a tradition of experimental research in psychology. A number of linguists have become interested in the cognitive implications of poetic or artful uses of language. Chapter 1 included Lynne Cameron's reading about metaphor as a fundamental property of the human mind and Guy Cook's argument about the schema-refreshing and evolutionary benefits of language play. Michael Toolan suggests in Chapter 2 that narrative is central to 'mind, intelligence and self-understanding' and may be 'the key species-distinctive thing we do, the chief means by which we adapt and change, over the course of our own life time and as a species across the millennia' (p. 72). In Chapter 4, Julia Gillen refers to the argument that play, including language play, increases children's potential for learning (p. 182). The ways in which theories of cognition help to account for the effects of linguistic creativity in literary texts are explored in our companion volume *The Art of English: Literary Creativity* (Goodman and O'Halloran [eds] 2006). In this first volume, we have focused more centrally on exploring the textual and social dimensions of creativity in everyday talk and literacy.

Table 1 opposite illustrates, in general terms, the movement through the book from the more textually focused analyses at the beginning, to broader sociocultural and sociohistorical analyses at the end, bearing in mind that textual creativity continues to feature throughout the book. There is often an overlap between analytic approaches, for instance narrative analysis often includes a story's social functions as well as its structure, and interactional analysis sometimes broadens into ethnographic analysis. 'Discourse' in analysis type number 6 is used to refer to ways of representing, understanding and being in the world which encode particular world views and ideologies (see discussions of the term 'discourse' in Chapters 5 and 7). It could be argued that critical discourse analysis and historical analysis are equally 'broad', along different dimensions.

Analysis type	Examples	
1 Linguistic analysis, word and sentence level	Different forms of poetic language, e.g. word play, metaphor, children's phonological play.	TEXTUAL
2 Linguistic analysis beyond the level of the sentence	Labovian narrative analysis; joke format.	
3 Multimodal analysis	The contribution of other modes as well as verbal texts, and the relationships between modes, to creative effects, e.g. the importance of letter shape in graffiti, the use of design features in online creativity.	
4 Interactional analysis	Social function, e.g. word play or narrative including/excluding others; stylistic choices indexing identity; broadening to 5 below.	
5 Ethnographic analysis	How creative language practices are embedded within and emerge from social practice in particular contexts, e.g. creative literacy in prison.	
6 Critical discourse analysis	Analysing creativity in relation to discourses, e.g. creatively engaging with a new discourse of tourism in Namibia.	
7 Historical analysis	Relationship of creative literacy practices to social, economic and political change, e.g. shaping stories in response to changing historical circumstances, hybrid oral/literacy mix in broadsheets.	CONTEXTUALISED

Table 1   Approaches to researching language creativity

A C T I V I T Y 1   **Locating creativity**

Allow about
45 minutes

Think back over previous chapters and readings in this book, and identify three readings that have particularly interested you. Bearing in mind that researchers may draw on more than one approach, which of the analytic approaches in Table 1 above do you think they each draw on in their work?

Comment

You may have found that most authors of readings use complementary analytic procedures which appear in different parts of Table 1. Some readings provide a strong focus on textual analysis, for example Sharon Inkelas' study of a two-year-old's play with rhyme in Chapter 4 (which she also links to developmental issues) or Mary Bock's application of Labovian narrative analysis to stories about the 'Guguletu Seven' in Chapter 2. Bock also links her analysis to questions of identity construction in narrative, in relation to historical change in South Africa (approach 7). She considers the shaping influence of the political and social context, both of the original experience and of its retelling in the narratives. While textual analysis is important in Penelope Eckert's discussion of teenagers' pronunciation of particular vowels for self-styling and Ben Rampton's analysis of code-switching in Chapter 3, these researchers also use ethnographic analysis in order to demonstrate the creative effects of specific pronunciations and Rampton focuses on telling interactions between particular individuals. In Chapter 6, Greenfield and Subrahmanyam analyse textual creativity in online chat, and also relate this to chatters' interactive strategies. Besnier in Chapter 3, Macdonald in Chapter 6 and Wilson, Camitta and Papen in Chapter 7 provide more ethnographically orientated accounts, which also include some multimodal textual analysis. In his reading in Chapter 8, Vincent shows how the creative design and use of mass-produced greetings cards only became possible as the result of economic and technological changes at the end of the nineteenth century and the other two readings in Chapter 8 also show, from a contemporary nineteenth-century viewpoint, how possibilities for creative literacy practices are patterned historically.

In many ways this book has been about exploring and expanding the sociocultural model of language and creativity, while also paying close attention to textual artistry. The next section addresses a body of theory about how language creativity works which has had a seminal influence both on the study of literature and on contemporary language studies, particularly within sociocultural approaches.

9.3 Heteroglossia, dialogicality and creativity

Working in the 1920s on a philosophy of language which he wanted to ground within the communicative activities of everyday life, the Russian literary scholar Mikhail Bakhtin developed a 'sociohistorical' theory of language in opposition to two dominant inherency models of language in the early twentieth century and also in opposition to the prevailing ideological approach within Russian Marxism. First, Bakhtin criticised the strong distinction between literary and practical language drawn by the formalists (the influential group of Russian literary critics which originally included Jakobson). The Formalists saw literary language as uniquely different from ordinary everyday language because of its use of specific devices which focused attention on language itself. In contrast, Bakhtin argued that language use in literature was not special and different, but that literature was just one set of genres out of the wide range of different speech genres within social life.

Second, Bakhtin criticised the conceptualisation of linguistics in terms of an abstract theoretical model. He argued that, in practice, the meaning and significance of language comes, more crucially, from the myriad connotations of words which accumulate through their use in particular contexts, and through their associations with particular speaker intentions. Bakhtin's is a much more social and ideological conception of how language works than the traditional linguistic model. The heart of language, for Bakhtin, is not an abstract symbolic system, but a constant struggle between the 'centripetal' forces which produce 'standard language' and a 'literary canon', and the 'centrifugal' forces which are expressed through different dialects, diverse speaking styles, and the kinds of language crossing, intertextuality and hybrid genres discussed in previous chapters. For Bakhtin, this struggle between opposing forces is what keeps language alive, enabling shared meaning and also providing scope for creativity and change.

Finally, Bakhtin argued against the prevailing early twentieth-century Marxist conception of literature as simply an ideological reflection of the authors' economic and social position. He was more interested in incorporating the formal properties of language, and its evaluative functions, within an overall social theory of language (literary and everyday), which he called a 'translinguistics'. Bakhtin's emphasis on the social origins and workings of language creativity places him within the broad category of approaches which we have termed 'sociocultural'. His writing is sometimes rather convoluted and I shall provide explanatory notes on the different sections of the extracts from his work in Activity 2. The box below contains brief explanations of four Bakhtinian concepts which are explored further in the reading: heteroglossia, dialogicality, speech genres and evaluation.

The definition of 'evaluation' draws also on the work of Bakhtin's close colleague, Volosinov. (Some critics have suggested that work attributed to Volosinov was actually written by Bakhtin).

Bakhtinian concepts

Bakhtin sees the language we use as **heteroglossic** or 'many-voiced' (literally, 'many-tongued'), made up of voices and texts associated with different contexts and different social groups. When we use a word or phrase, an important part of its meaning comes from its contextual and social connotations, and it also carries a taste of previous speakers' intentions. Where it is possible to discern both the speaker's own voice and a voice they are reproducing from somewhere else, Bakhtin refers to the utterance as 'double-voiced' (see Chapter 3). The connotations of other voices are exploited in intertextual references (see Chapters 4 and 5).

Dialogicality refers to the way in which all uses of language face both backwards and forwards. Utterances both respond in some sense to previous utterances, and also anticipate their own response. For

Bakhtin, all written works, including literature, are also always in some sense a response, and at the same time addressed towards an implied audience (notice the way in which his own work is itself a response to prevailing theories). This intrinsic responsive and addressive impulse, which forms the very basis of communication, affects the form and meaning of all levels of language use and can, itself, stimulate creativity (see the discussions of letter writing and Pax's blog in Chapter 6).

Bakhtin sees all language as patterned into **speech genres** (which include both spoken and written forms). Speech genres are the relatively stable patterns in composition, style, themes and points of view in uses of language which emerge in different spheres of human activity (Bakhtin, 1986). They range from everyday chat and informal written notes to political speeches, courtroom discourse, newspapers and all kinds of literary genres. Speech genres are defined both from the inside, through language form, and from the outside, through social recognition and value. They are learned at the same time as language itself but are more flexible than grammar. Over time, simple primary genres are absorbed into more complex secondary genres and genres diversify and hybridise (see Chapters 5 and 6).

All language use is **evaluative**, because it always emerges from a speaker or writer's situated perspective within a particular material world. Only aspects of the social environment which have social meaning and value are codified within semiotic systems and so evaluation moulds referential meaning right from the start and determines what is referred to in the first place (Volosinov, 1973). Words carry particular evaluative **accents** from their previous use, and speakers may **reaccent** other people's reported words, to give them a different evaluative meaning. While the Bakhtinian concept of evaluation includes the speaker's stance and purpose, like Labov's description of the 'evaluative' function of a narrative (see Chapters 2 and 9), it also makes more fundamental claims about the nature of language itself.

You may like to refer to this box as you are working on the reading from Bakhtin, and also look back to where these concepts are used in previous chapters, in order to check your understanding.

ACTIVITY 2   **Heteroglossia (Reading A)**

In Reading A, which includes several extracts from his long essay 'Discourse in the novel', Bakhtin explores his conception of the heteroglossic or 'many-tongued' nature of language. Please read the first paragraph, in which Bakhtin introduces his argument that the study of verbal art must overcome the split between formal approaches to theorising language (abstract linguistics and formalist stylistics) and the equally abstract Marxist ideological approach. Instead, he wants to build a broader based language theory that encompasses all genres and recognises the sociohistorical forces which shape them.

Read each of the remaining sections (a)–(d) in conjunction with each of the following four sub-activities. (The Comment which follows on page 422 covers all these sub-activities.)

Activity 2(a)   The struggle between centripetal and centrifugal forces

This is Bakhtin's argument against the 'unitary' notion of language as a fixed linguistic system, which he believes abstracts language from the ongoing struggle between unification and diversity which characterises its lived reality. Standard, correct language and esteemed literary styles are not out there waiting to be identified but are 'posited', and have to be constantly defended against the pull of centrifugal forces. Notice that Bakhtin stresses the potentially positive and negative aspects of both centripetal and centrifugal tendencies, and their evaluative ideological components.

What centripetal forces are you aware of, in your current language experience (for example the pull of a dominant or standard version of a language, the influence of canonical literature)? In what ways are these forces intersected with opposing, centrifugal tendencies?

Activity 2(b)   Genres and 'social languages'

Although Bakhtin starts with the term 'literary language', he is discussing the way in which *all* language is stratified into different genres. Genres (the relatively stable patterns of composition style, themes and points of view in different social activities) and social languages (connected with different social groups, e.g. professions, age groups and other discourse communities) are both key dimensions of heterglossia.

Do you accept Bakhtin's argument that words always have a 'taste' of previous contexts and intentions and that there are no neutral words or forms? Can you identify examples, either within the book or from your own experience, where speakers or writers make creative use of the 'taste of words'?

Activity 2(c)   The dialogic nature of verbal representation

For Bakhtin, there is no simple straight symbolic equivalence between a word and what it represents, because meaning always emerges partly through the intrinsic dialogicality of language use (see Box above).

Bakhtin sees an object (i.e. what a word represents) as already saturated with the meanings which have been attributed to or associated with it in the past, so a fresh reference to the object travels through the atmosphere created by these dialogic threads, perhaps echoing some previous references or challenging others. In this way, there is a dialogic relationship between a new word referring to and conceptualising an object, and other previous references and conceptualisations in the past. The impossibility of a singular, unimpeded meaning is not seen by Bakhtin as a negative state of affairs. On the contrary, it is this atmosphere of alien words and value judgements which cluster around the object, through which the word passes like a light ray, which 'makes the facet of the image sparkle'. How might these ideas apply to a particular example? For instance, if I talk about a rose, how might this reference 'brush up against' previous references to roses?

Activity 2(d)   Reported voices

This section focuses on an important aspect of heteroglossia and a ubiquitous feature of everyday talk: the reporting of other people's words. Bakhtin stresses that the meaning of a reported voice, however accurately repeated, is always changed because it is being used in a new context, in line with the reporting speaker's intentions. It is therefore 'dialogized', or brought into a dialogue with the current speaker who, through the way in which they report it, expresses varying degrees of agreement or disagreement, approval or disapproval.

Look out for examples of reported speech in everyday talk, and notice the ways in which the reporting speaker is signalling their own position in relation to the words they are reporting.

Comment

An example of the interplay of centripetal and centrifugal forces (see 2a above) is the establishment of a new slang or way of writing which purposefully subverts and departs from the standard form. This, however, gradually becomes established with its own conventions, which then exert a new set of centripetal pressures on speakers and writers. While some of these may be pulled by centrifugal forces to break away again with new forms of language usage, their language will always be also shaped by the centripetal forces of standardisation. Bakhtin suggests that if centripetal forces become too strong, language ossifies and stagnates, and if the centrifugal forces overwhelm, it fragments and communication becomes impossible.

Bakhtin's view of language suggests that creativity does not just involve manipulation of the linguistic system, but also an attention to the myriad social connotations of particular words and forms and the tastes of particular contexts and genres which they bring with them (2b above). It way be easier to see how some words will 'taste' of their past uses than others. Interestingly, however, work in corpus linguistics reveals the nuances of meaning attached to quite ordinary words or phrases, across corpora of large amounts of spoken or written text. For instance, Bill Louw (1993) collected together the uses of the phrase 'days are' from across a large corpus of different kinds of texts to demonstrate its generally negative connotations, which are exploited in

Philip Larkin's poem *Days*, which opens 'What are days for?/Days are where we live./They come, they wake us/Time and time over.' The negative associations of such a seemingly innocuous phrase as 'Days are ...' would not have emerged in a formal textual analysis or been immediately intuitively obvious, yet these connotations contribute in an important way to the mournful, ironic tone of the poem.

There are numerous examples across the chapters of this book where there is creative play with the connotations which words bring with them from other speakers and contexts: Al Capone' (ch. 1); Creole or 'stylised Asian English' voices and the meanings which this language crossing invokes (ch. 3); children reproducing teacher and pupil voices (exploiting the associations of different languages) in imaginary play (ch. 4); creative references to different voices and texts in chatroom talk (ch. 5) In all these examples, speakers and writers are creatively exploiting the heteroglossic nature of language.

Bakhtin suggests that these associations are invoked in a dialogical manner (2c above). When I talk about a 'rose', for instance, there could be a kind of dialogue between how I am using the word and how it has been used in the past to invoke, beauty, purity, English gardens or Englishness. My usage might echo one or more of these connotations, or perhaps provide an ironical contrast. Think of William Blake's poem which begins: 'O Rose, thou are sick!/The invisible worm.....'. The dark violence of the worm's destruction emerges, dialogically, in contrast to the associations of a rose with beauty, purity, and so on. Bakhtin would see Blake's use of the term 'rose' 'brushing up against' connotations from its previous uses in the past. At a more mundane level, remember the small scruffy pigeon in Chapter 1, Activity 1, which was described first as 'a thug among pigeons' and then by further speakers as 'Al Capigeon' and 'The godfeather'. These separate descriptions are immediately brushing up against each other, building up the humorous comparisons cumulatively and collaboratively, each utterance gaining significance from its relationship to the others, as well as to the pigeon. As Joan Swann points out, 'The godfeather' would probably not have been said without 'Al Capigeon'.

Reproducing other people's voices is a particularly rich way of making intertextual links – for example to a gangster film, street talk or classroom dialogue. Sometimes voices are explicitly quoted, as is discussed in the last section of the Bakhtin reading, or they may be taken on more fully and reproduced as if they were the speaker's own, for instance when a child repeats something their parent has said, or we reproduce an argument heard from a friend which particularly impressed us. Between the two poles of explicit reporting and complete appropriation, Bakhtin (1984) suggests there are a number of hybrid forms, where speakers signal a more subtle double-voicing through tone of voice, accent or some other aspect of styling. For instance the internet chatter in Goddard's research who announced

'Hi honey I'm home!' was not explicitly quoting another voice, but was still invoking and playing with its associations in films and sitcoms. The Anglo- and African Carribean boys who muttered Panjabi words under their breath in Rampton's research seemed to be taking on a different language in talk to themselves, but were in fact signalling their 'street credibility' to others overhearing them. In uni-directional double-voicing like this last example speakers align themselves with a voice, while still signalling, perhaps through their tone of voice, that it is 'taken on'. In contrast, in vari-directional double voicing, a speaker indicates some opposition to the voice they are reproducing, for instance in parody or irony. Sometimes the direction is not quite clear, especially if oral cues are not available, for instance in the 'Hi honey I'm home!' example.

Uni-directional and vari-directional styling are, for Bakhtin, routine within everyday communication, as are explicit reporting and the full appropriation of another voice. We turn now to focus more closely on explicit reporting, which Bakhtin discussed in the last section of his article. Even where we are ostensibly merely reproducing what someone else has said, there is considerable potential for creativity, as we shall explore in the next section below.

9.4 Reported dialogue in talk

> They come bustin' through the door,
> Blood is everywhere,
> It's on the walls, on the floor, everywhere
> (sobbing) 'It's okay Billy, we're gonna make it'
> (normal voice) 'What the hell's wrong with you'

(From the beginning of a story told by a trainee doctor who's just come home from his work in the emergency room of a hospital, Tannen, 1989)

JULIE	I swore at my mum the other day because she started, she hit me
KIRSTY	What did you do?
JULIE	I swore at my mum, I says 'I'm packing my cases and I don't care what you say' and she goes 'Ooh?' and *(I go)* 'Yea!'. I'm really cheeky to my mother.

(From a conversation between two ten-year-old girls about whether it's wrong for children to swear, Maybin, 2006)

In Chapter 2 on narrative, Michael Toolan points out how the use of reported voices in conversational stories is important as 'embedded evaluation'. You may have noticed that reported speech occurs especially at the climax of the 'complicating action', when it's most important for the narrator to have the full attention of their audience. For instance, Alison voices her thoughts at the moment of the car accident 'I remember thinking then "we're gonna turn over we <u>gonna</u> turn over there's just no way that we're gonna come through this ...'''. And in Reading A by Neal Norrick, Jean gives the punch line of her anecdote about the hospitable hairdresser in the form of a brief verbal exchange: '"Want some wine, girls"/ "Sure we'll have a glass of wine". "You walk out of there you're half tipsy"'. In oral stories, reported speech (or reported thought) creates a sense of immediacy, of actually being there, which grabs and holds the listeners' attention. It also, as Toolan points out, helps to convey the significance of the related events for the narrator and for the point of the story. Alison's thoughts at the moment of impact underline just how lucky she was to escape with her life, and Jean conveys what was unusual and memorable about the hairdresser through a snatch of conversation.

Recreated dialogue is also fairly ubiquitous in oral performance and oral language more generally. Children's playground rhymes include reported talk, for instance, 'I went to a Chinese Restaurant/To buy a loaf of bread, /I wrapped it up in a five pound note / And this is what they said, /'Eenie meanie makaraka/ Om pom poosh' (Chapter 4). Think also of how the 'nerd' in Bucholz's research (Chapter 3), like Alison, represents her internal reasoning process as a dialogue with herself: 'At the end of the semester I said "What am I doing? Why am I not hanging out with Kate?"'.

At this point you may well be asking yourself what is creative or artistic about these non-narrative examples. Aren't they just a straight reporting of what someone has said or thought? In Reading B below, Deborah Tannen uses Bakhtin's ideas about reported speech to argue that its use in everyday talk is always essentially creative. Tannen's larger argument is that the seeds of literary forms of reported dialogue, repetition and imagery are all found in conversation, where they are important because they create involvement – involvement of the self in the conversation, involvement with the topic being spoken about, and interactional involvement with another speaker. This involvement produces an aesthetic experience of coherence, both in terms of self and meaning, an emotional response of connectedness (sharing the same world of discourse) and intellectual and emotional insight. While patterns of repetition of sounds, words and phrases draw conversationalists into a kind of rhythmic ensemble, imagery and reported speech provide evocative detail which sparks the listener's imagination so that they contribute to the shared sense-making from their own experience. Details create images, images create scenes and scenes spark emotions, making possible both understanding and involvement (Tannen, 1989). Thus, the listener conjures up a whole accident scene from Alison's inner thought, and the partying atmosphere at the hairdresser's from a single invitation to have some wine.

Tannen's argument about the centrality of involvement to communication has a definite cognitive dimension in her consideration of the internal mental effects of repetition, imagery and dialogue. But she is rather more concerned with the emotional aspect of aesthetic effects than Cook or Carter, whose work you studied earlier in the book. Tannen is also very interested in how these strategies work at the level of ordinary conversation, in their linguistic realisation in talk and their interactional and sociocultural effects. The reading below comes from a chapter by Tannen on reported speech in her book *Talking Voices*. She takes the ideas presented in the Bakhtin reading as her starting point – that our talk is always full of other people's voices, that those voices bring a myriad of contextual connotations with them and that we re-use and frame the voices in line with our own current intentions.

ACTIVITY 3   Oh talking voice that is so sweet (Reading B)

Please read the extract from 'Oh talking voice that is so sweet' by Deborah Tannen (Reading B). Do you agree with Tannen that 'uttering dialogue in conversation is as much a creative act as is the creation of dialogue in fiction and drama'? As you read, think about examples from your own experience to add to the ones which Tannen provides.

Comment

For Tannen, a brief snatch of reported speech has the creative power to invoke whole events, experiences and thought processes, together with the connotations of particular experiences and scenes which are imaginatively interpreted by the listener. She shows how the reported words themselves are essentially created by the reporting speaker. Reported dialogue is reconstructed (and in some cases constructed) in order to illustrate the essence of a point the speaker wants to convey. Thus, different kinds of reconstructed dialogue (or thought) are used to recreate the shame of being chastised in front of friends, to demonstrate personal skills in classroom management or baseball and to evoke a shared experience of childrearing. The speaker is creative in reporting a voice which will resonate in a particular way within the reporting context, and in devising the actual 'reported' words. Tannen also discusses elsewhere how this reframing can quite subtly change the meaning of the original speech. Thus, for instance, people may complain that the meaning of their words was changed because a vital word was omitted, or that what they said was reported 'out of context'. Because of the way in which the current speaker's intentions always lie behind and colour the representation of reported speech, it is always 'double-voiced' discourse (Bakhtin 1984), reflecting the intentions of both the reported and reporting speakers.

ACTIVITY 4   Reported speech and evaluation

Allow about
10 minutes

As a follow-up to Tannen's foregrounding of reported dialogue as creative art, look back at the two quotations at the beginning of this section (p. 424). How might the reported speech be contributing to the evaluative function (i.e. the point the narrator is trying to get across) in a) the doctor's story and b) the girl's anecdote? In what ways is the reported speech 'double-voiced'?

Comment

In both cases, the reported voices are urgent and shocking, increasing the impact of the scenes they evoke, thus strengthening the points of the stories. Snatches of dialogue convey the sense of crisis and chaos in the hospital emergency room and the flavour of the altercation between the mother and daughter. Evaluation is also conveyed through the double-voicing. In the first example, we hear the voice of the narrator behind the characters' dialogue, conveying just how challenging the young doctor's work in the emergency room is. In the second example, Julie recreates the angry exchange with her mother in a way which emphasises her own righteous assertiveness, while also helping her to explore the question of whether it is ever right for children to swear. Julie's 'I'm packing my cases and I don't care what you say' sounds like a phrase she has picked up from other conversations she has heard. We don't know whether she actually said this at the time, but it is important in her reporting of the event because it 'tastes' of scenes of family break-up and serves to catch Kirsty's attention and underline just how serious the row was.

9.5 Performance and face-work

Many of the uses of reported speech cited by Tannen in her reading, and in the anecdotes above, are examples of the performance of identity. Through our representation of our own and other people's voices, we present ourselves as particular kinds of people (canny teachers, anxious mothers, incredulous tourists, over-worked doctors, feisty daughters), and convey our perspective on the people and world around us. These identities, however, are not set in stone. In Chapter 3 (p. 103), we saw how, within everyday interactions, 'speakers jointly negotiate (foreground or play down, challenge or seek to subvert) particular identities, or aspects of themselves'.

The ideas of Erving Goffman about language as social action, where people present aspects of themselves in strategic performances and where social roles and rituals are played out in local interactions, have been a key influence on studies of talk. In this book, Goffman's work has underpinned part of the sociocultural model of language creativity, providing a theoretical resource for researchers who are interested in how creative language behaviour emerges out of social interaction. This section reviews two influential ideas from Goffman's work: first what he calls 'face-work', and secondly his conception of social life as a stage and social interaction as dramatic performance.

Actors in a social encounter, according to Goffman, take up a particular position and act out a 'line', 'a pattern of verbal and non-verbal acts' through which they express their view of the situation and their evaluation of the participants, especially themselves (Goffman, 1969). Through this 'line' actors claim a **face**, an image of themselves related to positive social attributes;

for example, they present themselves as knowledgeable, brave, clever, kind, competent and so on. Some encounters may sustain the actor's taken for granted face, others establish a face that is better than they expected and still others challenge their self-image ('she put on a brave face') or may result in a 'loss of face'.

People experience strong feelings connected to their 'face', and can be creative in the kinds of avoidance and corrective processes they bring into play in order to defend this aspect of self-image. You may remember the example from Goffman in Chapter 3 of young American middle-class girls playing dumb for their boyfriends. In conforming to a social expectation, these girls are protecting their boyfriends' face by signalling his intellectual superiority and also protecting their own face by avoiding the label of unattractive over-cleverness. Similarly, the student who publicises the fact she is receiving a phone call in the example below is presenting herself as popular and sought after, enhancing a positive face. A contemporary equivalent might be a young person's frequent and ostentatious use of their mobile phone, or a chatter's complaint, during a computer-mediated conversation, that they are having to deal with so many simultaneous conversations.

Manipulating 'given-off' impressions

[W]hen an individual appears in the presence of others, there will usually be some reason for him to mobilize his activity so that it will convey an impression to others which it is in his interests to convey. Since a girl's dormitory mates will glean evidence of her popularity from the calls she receives on the phone, we can suspect that some girls will arrange for calls to be made, and Willard Waller's finding can be anticipated:

'It has been reported by many observers that a girl who is called to the telephone in the dormitories will often allow herself to be called several times, in order to give all the other girls ample opportunity to hear her paged'.

(Goffman, 1969, pp. 15–16)

To prevent threats to their own face, people may avoid situations where these are likely to occur. They may keep off certain topics, present a diffident or self-belittling front, or hedge claims about themselves. In order to protect others they show respect and politeness, use discretion to avoid contradicting the positive claims being made, or use indirectness and ambiguity. Joking, and explaining and neutralising a potentially offensive act, also help to maintain the face of others, and keep an encounter and a relationship running smoothly. When someone threatens the face of another in a way which can't be avoided or overlooked, the offender may try immediately to repair the situation, or they may be *challenged* to do so by other participants. Repairs may involve claiming that the offender was only joking, or that extenuating circumstances forced them to act in this way. Someone who loses face themselves through a social gaffe, or showing up their incompetence, may again offer a joke against themselves 'I was so sure this would be simple!', or claim extenuating circumstances 'I've had to do all this on my own', or take on the incapacity as part of themselves 'I can't read train timetables to save my life'.

This *offering* to correct the loss of face has to be then *accepted*, and finally a sign of *gratitude* offered by the forgiven person, in order to re-establish the expressive order. This ritual dance of challenge, offering, acceptance and thanks may itself be challenged when an offender refuses to repair their threat and the interaction may deteriorate into bluster, retaliation, and finally withdrawal in huff, effrontery or outrage. The violent feelings of anguish and anger accompanying such a scene are, Goffman argues, as integral a part of the ritual exchange as the words spoken (like Tannen, he clearly acknowledges the emotional dimension of communication). In most cases, participants work hard and inventively to avoid any serious loss of face, accompanied as it is by such strong emotions.

ACTIVITY 5   On face-work (Reading C)

Please read Reading C, which is a short extract from Erving Goffman's essay 'On face-work'. Does your own experience bear out his analysis?

Comment

For Goffman, the self is both a kind of player in a ritual game, and also the image which emerges through the interaction. He describes the complex verbal footwork (e. g. 'innuendo', 'well-paced pauses') and interactional strategies in which speakers may engage. It is particularly striking how intensely interactional the face-work described by Goffman is: it appears that the loss of face in others can be just as discomforting as in oneself. Some social situations are particularly risky in terms of potential face threats, for instance if they involve the breaking of normal social taboos.

ACTIVITY 6   Saving face

Allow about
15 minutes

How is a face-threat being managed in the two extracts below from health-care interactions? In what ways might the management of face be particularly important in these encounters?

(a)   A patient is undergoing mammography

PATIENT: There's not very much to put on there *(compression* begins) You're going to squash what I have left! (laughter)

(Ragan, 2000, p. 274)

(b)   The patient has just had a pelvic examination

PROVIDER: All done. That's it.

PATIENT: Gee that was fun (laughter)

PROVIDER: (overlapping laughter) Oh you wanna do it again?

PATIENT: (laughter)

PROVIDER: okay so I'll run all this stuff to the lab.

(Ragan, 2000, p. 277)

Comment

The patient's self-deprecating use of humour in the first example and the humorous exchange in the second example help to mitigate the face-threatening nature of intrusive and potentially painful procedures carried out by strangers on normally private areas of the body. The joking helps to create a rapport between patient and health-care professional, diverts attention from physiological distress, reduces anxiety and 'rekeys' an embarrassing situation overshadowed by the potentially devastating medical results into one which is 'not so bad'. Joking and laughing are also a way of the patient signalling that they are coping, and thus putting on a 'good face' in uncomfortable circumstances. Patient and practitioner often collaborate to frame examinations as non-threatening, as in the interaction in example b above (Ragan, 2000).

In addition to the use of humour, there have been examples of other creative face-saving devices in previous chapters. In Chapter 3 Ben Rampton gives an example of what Goffman terms 'afterburn': 'dissident remarks about another person's unjust or offensive conduct produced just after they've left the scene' (p. 134). In this way, Asif displayed resilience to his friends without having to direct a face-threatening act explicitly at his teacher (or run the risk of losing face himself through her response). And in Chapter 5, Nagin and Dr Pepper's playful performance of a chatting-up routine leaves open the face-saving option that they are 'just joking around', while still preparing the ground for a more serious relationship. Sarah North suggests that the lack of extralinguistic and paralinguistic information seems to 'encourage exuberant self-dramatisation in the online environment' (p. 230).

Goffman's concept of face was taken up and developed by the linguists Penelope Brown and Stephen Levinson (1987), who suggested that protecting one's own and others' face involved both positive politeness (appreciating and approving someone's self-image) and negative politeness (avoiding intruding or imposing on another). Positive and negative politeness strategies may be reflected in particular language uses, for instance, indirectness in requests and euphemisms for intimate personal matters. Different cultures may vary in their emphasis on either of these aspects of face: for instance, British people have a reputation for emphasising the importance of negative politeness. Cultural practices of politeness may be codified in social etiquette manuals, and indeed influenced the early English letter-writing manuals discussed in Chapter 6. Parodies and transgressions of politeness provided popular raw material for English playwrights in the 'Comedy of Manners' tradition (e.g. Sheridan, Wilde). In contemporary hip hop, rudeness is ritualised within the verbal duelling and rap contests referred to by Guy Cook in Chapter 1 ('Your momma drink pee/your father eat shit'). In these ritual contests, prowess is proved through quick creative repartee.

Through their use of language, then, Goffman sees people as managing their own and other people's face in order to present themselves in as positive light as possible. In the course of everyday activities, people present themselves in particular ways to achieve specific effects, and we are constantly monitoring and evaluating our own and other people's performances, in order to pursue our personal goals. He suggested that people give direct verbal information (honest or dishonest) about who they are, and they also, consciously or unconsciously, 'give off' information. These are, Goffman suggests, two different kinds of sign activity, and each has the potential to inform or delude. '**Giving expression**' and '**giving off expression**' can both involve language creativity. In Chapter 2, where Alison tells the story about the car crash, she gives direct expression to her fear at the time as part of the narrative evaluation: 'I've never been so scared in my life'. However, Toolan also suggests that Alison 'does a lot of verbal work, to tell herself and her audience ... that she is female, heterosexual, middle-class but not "posh" (posh people don't say *pegged it*), 'ordinary', vulnerable, more lucky than unlucky (as we might all like to be), ordinary enough to be scared, terrified, in a car crash – but spirited enough to be able to be light-hearted about it afterwards' (p. 63 of this volume). Alison may not have said these things directly (there is often a hazy boundary between giving and giving off expressions), but listeners infer them from the way in which she speaks and tells the story, and doubtless also from her physical appearance and nonverbal behaviour. Clearly, people 'give off' many more impressions about themselves than they 'give' in a more direct way.

The giving off of a particular impression may involve the manipulation of a communicative event as in the box on page 428, or it can involve a range of different choices in terms of language and style. For instance, in Reading B in Chapter 2, Mary Bock notes that the ex-policeman Mbelo chose to explain his involvement in the murder of the Guguletu Seven to the South African Truth and Reconciliation Commission mainly in Tswana, rather than in English or Afrikaans. In this way he expressed solidarity with the families of the dead black activists. In Chapter 3, Niko Besnier explains how the Tongan *leiti* use English to give off an aura of worldliness, modernity and femaleness. And Penelope Eckert discusses how choices in grammar and pronunciation, together with dress styles, are a kind of performance, and that, over time, the repetition and accumulation of these performances (which give off the expression of Jockness or Burnoutness) become an intrinsic part of who a person is. For Eckert, the expressions we give and give off are part of the ongoing construction of identity.

In Chapter 6 Daniel Chandler discusses how people give off information about themselves through the design of their personal web pages. Of course, this information has to be picked up and interpreted in order to be effective: Chandler remarks that he initially failed to grasp the significance of the pinkish purplish background in a friend's web page. Usually, Goffman suggests, respondents are particularly sensitive to 'given off' information, because they use it to check on the validity of what is conveyed more explicitly and directly controlled by the actor. He argues that we are constantly involved in online impression management, continually checking and rechecking the impression we are making on others through the cues they provide and also processing and checking our own impressions of them, continually probing beneath the different layers of appearance presented.

So far, we have focused on Goffman's ideas about interactive language creativity at a very local level, among a small number of individuals. Goffman also saw interactive creativity as happening on a larger scale, within workplaces and institutions. In the next reading (Activity 7), Goffman develops his metaphor of social life as a series of performances on different kinds of stages. In public life, he sees people as often acting in 'teams' that put on 'shows' for particular audiences. The staff of a hotel, or the doctors and nurses in a hospital, produce a kind of collaborative performance for their guests or patients. These performances, Goffman suggests, require some kind of 'back stage' area, where professional masks are dropped and the front stage show is prepared.

ACTIVITY 7   **Frontstage or backstage? (Reading D)**

Please read the short extract (Reading D) from 'Regions and region behaviour', a chapter from Erving Goffman's *The Presentation of Self in Everyday Life*. How far do you agree with Goffman's account of the differences between 'front region' and 'back region' (i.e. frontstage and backstage) behaviour? Notice how the broadcasters exploit these differences. Can you think of any examples from earlier chapters, or from your own experience, where speakers manipulate the boundaries between front and backstage behaviour creatively?

Comment

You may have noticed differences between people's 'frontstage' and 'backstage' behaviour from your own everyday experience. Switching between them sometimes requires a carefully contrived performance. For instance, a hostess may put on a bright carefree manner for guests arriving a few minutes after she has had a blazing family argument, or a business director racked with personal doubt may adopt a confident and purposeful manner at the annual shareholder's meeting. When I was growing up, men often indulged in 'backstage behaviour' in the bars of Public Houses (so I was told), while women and mixed groups were directed into the 'lounge bar'. And a group of young women cracking dirty jokes about men and doing their hair and makeup together in the cloakroom at the local disco did feel somewhat like the preparation for a team performance. Different regions for behaviour are acknowledged in expressions like 'behind closed doors', 'off the record', or 'letting their hair down'. Goffman points out that backstages also involve performance, and that any situation will contain elements of both regions.

The differences between front and backstage behaviour and the possibility of transposing them is a creative resource for humour. The broadcasting professionals' jokes about backstage suddenly being transformed into frontstage behaviour reflect misadventures frequently exploited in comedies, where characters' backstage behaviour becomes inappropriately revealed. In addition to transposing behaviour and regions, humour can be created through the infiltration of one region by another. In his reading in Chapter 3, Niko Besnier explains how differences between the Tongan beauty contestants' on and off stage personas are creatively exploited in the jokes and banter at the Miss Galaxy pageant, and how these differences were creatively reconfigured by Lady Amyland.

Anthropologists would suggest that we ritually mark and celebrate the disruptions in boundaries between front- and backstage behaviour and between politeness and rudeness (for instance in carnival-like behaviour), in order to release emotions which would otherwise undermine an inevitably leaky social structure.

9.6 Conclusion

In this final chapter of the book I started by reviewing some of the different approaches to identifying, analysing and conceptualising language creativity, which are presented across the different chapters and readings. While these range from more textually focused analyses to ethnographic and historical studies, we have placed a particular emphasis on socially orientated approaches and explanations. In examining the various kinds of creativity in everyday talk and literacies, we found we had to move beyond Jakobson's definition of the poetic function of language as a focus on the message for its own sake, which is founded in the formalist conception of literary language as linguistically distinct from other genres. In order to start to understand the nature of creativity in 'ordinary' language, we also needed to consider the interactive features and functions of talk and literacy, and the creative potential of different environments and points in history.

As a way of filling out and developing this social approach, I have focused on ideas from the work of two influential theorists, Bakhtin and Goffman. Their writings are drawn on, explicitly and implicitly, at various points across the book. Bakhtin developed what has been called a sociohistorical theory of language, within which meanings of words are seen to derive from the ways in which they invoke different social languages and genres and different cultural movements and ideologies. Bakhtin offers a socially and ideologically sensitive way of looking at the artful use of the complex connotations of words and phrases, and at the ways in which intertextual referencing can be a source for creativity. Bakhtin's insistence on the dialogical nature of all language use suggests that a range of different levels of dialogic links are involved in utterances. These links themselves can be artfully used to express particular nuances and evaluative perspectives. For instance, Bakhtin stresses that reporting the speech of others, a ubiquitous way of invoking personal experience, is always managed creatively to convey a particular evaluative viewpoint. This idea is developed more fully within the reading by Deborah Tannen.

While Bakhtin provides a basis for looking at creativity in historically and socially constituted discourse, Goffman develops a detailed account of the dramatic and performative aspects of everyday encounters, grounding creative uses of verbal and body language within the social interactive order and in relation to the goals and agendas of individual actors. As a 'ritually delicate object', the speaker has to creatively manage subtle and complex interactive routines in order to sustain context-sensitive presentations of the self, and to protect their own face and the faces of others.

One of the consequences of tracing how the seeds of artistic and literary uses of English are to be found in everyday uses of the language has been the need to draw on work from a number of different approaches in order to examine linguistic, interactional, ethnographic and sociohistorical analyses of creativity in talk and literacy. This has enabled us to explore a range of different dimensions of artistry and creativity in everyday uses of English, and to suggest a number of different ways towards understanding its nature and meaning.

READING A: Extracts from 'Discourse in the novel'

Mikhail Bakhtin

The principal idea of this essay is that the study of verbal art can and must overcome the divorce between an abstract 'formal' approach and an equally abstract 'ideological' approach. Form and content in discourse are one, once we understand that verbal discourse is a social phenomenon – social throughout its entire range and in each and every of its factors, from the sound image to the furthest reaches of abstract meaning. [...]

(a) The struggle between centripetal and centrifugal forces

Unitary language constitutes the theoretical expression of the historical processes of linguistic unification and centralization, an expression of the centripetal forces of language. A unitary language is not something given (*dan*) but is always in essence posited (*zadan*) – and at every moment of its linguistic life it is opposed to the realities of heteroglossia. But at the same time it makes its real presence felt as a force for overcoming this heteroglossia, imposing specific limits to it, guaranteeing a certain maximum of mutual understanding and crystallizing into a real, although still relative, unity – the unity of the reigning conversational (everyday) and literary language, 'correct language.'

A common unitary language is a system of linguistic norms. But these norms do not constitute an abstract imperative; they are rather the generative forces of linguistic life, forces that struggle to overcome the heteroglossia of language, forces that unite and centralize verbal-ideological thought, creating within a heteroglot national language the firm, stable linguistic nucleus of an officially recognized literary language, or else defending an already formed language from the pressure of growing heteroglossia.

What we have in mind here is not an abstract linguistic minimum of a common language, in the sense of a system of elementary forms (linguistic symbols) guaranteeing a *minimum* level of comprehension in practical communication. We are taking language not as a system of abstract grammatical categories, but rather language conceived as ideologically saturated, language as a world view, even as a concrete opinion, insuring a *maximum* of mutual understanding in all spheres of ideological life. Thus a unitary language gives expression to forces working toward concrete verbal and ideological unification and centralization, which develop in vital connection with the processes of socio-political and cultural centralization. [...]

But the centripetal forces of the life of language, embodied in a 'unitary language,' operate in the midst of heteroglossia. At any given moment of its evolution, language is stratified not only into linguistic dialects in the strict sense of the word (according to formal linguistic markers, especially phonetic), but also – and for us this is the essential point – into languages that are socio-ideological: languages of social groups, 'professional' and 'generic' languages, languages of generations and so forth. From this point of view, literary language itself is only one of these heteroglot languages – and in its turn is also stratified into languages (generic, period-bound and others). And this stratification and heteroglossia, once realized, is not only a static invariant of linguistic life, but also what insures its dynamics: stratification and heteroglossia widen and deepen as long as language is alive and developing. Alongside the centripetal forces, the centrifugal forces of language carry on their uninterrupted work; alongside verbal-ideological centralization and unification, the uninterrupted processes of decentralization and disunification go forward.

Every concrete utterance of a speaking subject serves as a point where centrifugal as well as centripetal forces are brought to bear. The processes of centralization and decentralization, of unification and disunification, intersect in the utterance; the utterance not only answers the requirements of its own language as an individualized embodiment of a speech act, but it answers the requirements of heteroglossia as well; it is in fact an active participant in such speech diversity. And this active participation of every utterance in living heteroglossia determines the linguistic profile and style of the utterance to no less a degree than its inclusion in any normative-centralizing system of a unitary language. [...]

(b)   The stratification of language into genres and 'social languages'

Literary language – both spoken and written – although it is unitary not only in its shared, abstract, linguistic markers but also in its forms for conceptualizing these abstract markers, is itself stratified and heteroglot in its aspect as an expressive system, that is, in the forms that carry its meanings.

This stratification is accomplished first of all by the specific organisms called *genres*. Certain features of language (lexicological, semantic, syntactic) will knit together with the intentional aim, and with the overall accentual system inherent in one or another genre: oratorical, publicistic, newspaper and journalistic genres, the genres of low literature (penny dreadfuls, for instance) or, finally, the various genres of high literature. Certain features of language take on the specific flavor of a given genre: they knit together with specific points of view, specific approaches, forms of thinking, nuances and accents characteristic of the given genre.

In addition, there is interwoven with this generic stratification of language a *professional* stratification of language, in the broad sense of the term 'professional': the language of the lawyer, the doctor, the businessman, the politician, the public education teacher and so forth, and these sometimes coincide with, and sometimes depart from, the stratification into genres. It goes without saying that these languages differ from each other not only in their vocabularies; they involve specific forms for manifesting intentions, forms for making conceptualization and evaluation concrete. And even the very language of the writer (the poet or novelist) can be taken as a professional jargon on a par with professional jargons. [...]

But the situation is far from exhausted by the generic and professional stratification of the common literary language. Although at its very core literary language is frequently socially homogeneous, as the oral and written language of a dominant social group, there is nevertheless always present, even here, a certain degree of social differentiation, a social stratification, that in other eras can become extremely acute. [...] All socially significant world views have the capacity to exploit the intentional possibilities of language through the medium of their specific concrete instancing. Various tendencies (artistic and otherwise), circles, journals, particular newspapers, even particular significant artistic works and individual persons are all capable of stratifying language, in proportion to their social significance; they are capable of attracting its words and forms into their orbit by means of their own characteristic intentions and accents, and in so doing to a certain extent alienating these words and forms from other tendencies, parties, artistic works and persons.

Every socially significant verbal performance has the ability — sometimes for a long period of time and for a wide circle of persons — to infect with its own intention certain aspects of language that had been affected by its semantic and expressive impulse, imposing on them specific semantic nuances and specific axiological overtones; thus, it can create slogan-words, curse-words, praise-words and so forth.

In any given historical moment of verbal-ideological life, each generation at each social level has its own language; moreover, every age group has as a matter of fact its own language, its own vocabulary, its own particular accentual system that, in their turn, vary depending on social level, academic institution (the language of the cadet, the high school student, the trade school student are all different languages) and other stratifying factors. All this is brought about by socially typifying languages, no matter how narrow the social circle in which they are spoken. It is even possible to have a family jargon define the societal limits of a language, as, for instance, the jargon of the Irtenevs in Tolstoy, with its special vocabulary and unique accentual system.

And finally, at any given moment, languages of various epochs and periods of socio-ideological life cohabit with one another. Even languages of the day exist: one could say that today's and yesterday's socio-ideological and political 'day' do not, in a certain sense, share the same language; every day represents another socio-ideological semantic 'state of affairs,' another vocabulary, another accentual system, with its own slogans, its own ways of assigning blame and praise. [...]

Thus at any given moment of its historical existence, language is heteroglot from top to bottom: it represents the co-existence of socio-ideological contradictions between the present and the past, between differing epochs of the past, between different socio-ideological groups in the present, between tendencies, schools, circles and so forth, all given a bodily form. These 'languages' of heteroglossia intersect each other in a variety of ways, forming new socially typifying 'languages'. [...]

As a result of the work done by all these stratifying forces in language, there are no 'neutral' words and forms – words and forms that can belong to 'no one'; language has been completely taken over, shot through with intentions and accents. For any individual consciousness living in it, language is not an abstract system of normative forms but rather a concrete heteroglot conception of the world. All words have the 'taste' of a profession, a genre, a tendency, a party, a particular work, a particular person, a generation, an age group, the day and hour. Each word tastes of the context and contexts in which it has lived its socially charged life; all words and forms are populated by intentions. Contextual overtones (generic, tendentious, individualistic) are inevitable in the word.

As a living, socio-ideological concrete thing, as heteroglot opinion, language, for the individual consciousness, lies on the borderline between oneself and the other. The word in language is half someone else's. It becomes 'one's own' only when the speaker populates it with his own intention, his own accent, when he appropriates the word, adapting it to his own semantic and expressive intention. Prior to this moment of appropriation, the word does not exist in a neutral and impersonal language (it is not, after all, out of a dictionary that the speaker gets his words!), but rather it exists in other people's mouths, in other people's contexts, serving other people's intentions: it is from there that one must take the word, and make it one's own. And not all words for just anyone submit equally easily to this appropriation, to this seizure and transformation into private property: many words stubbornly resist, others remain alien, sound foreign in the mouth of the one who appropriated them and who now speaks them; they cannot be assimilated into his context and fall out of it; it is as if they put themselves in quotation marks against the will of the speaker. Language is not a neutral medium that passes freely and easily into the private property of the speaker's intentions; it is populated – overpopulated – with the intentions of others. Expropriating it, forcing it to submit to one's own intentions and accents, is a difficult and complicated process. [...]

(c) The dialogic nature of verbal representation

The living utterance, having taken meaning and shape at a particular historical moment in a socially specific environment, can not fail to brush up against thousands of living dialogic threads, woven by socio-ideological consciousness around the given object of an utterance; it cannot fail to become an active participant in social dialogue. After all, the utterance arises out of this dialogue as a continuation of it and as a rejoinder to it – it does not approach the object from the sidelines.

The way in which the word conceptualizes its object is a complex act – all objects, open to dispute and overlain as they are with qualifications, are from one side highlighted while from the other side dimmed by heteroglot social opinion, by an alien word about them. And into this complex play of light and shadow the word enters – it becomes saturated with this play, and must determine within it the boundaries of its own semantic and stylistic contours. The way in which the word conceives its object is complicated by a dialogic interaction within the object between various aspects of its socio-verbal intelligibility. And an artistic representation, an 'image' of the object, may be penetrated by this dialogic play of verbal intentions that meet and are interwoven in it; such an image need not stifle these forces, but on the contrary may activate and organize them. If we imagine the *intention* of such a word, that is, its *directionality toward the object*, in the form of a ray of light, then the living and unrepeatable play of colors and light on the facets of the image that it constructs can be explained as the spectral dispersion of the ray-word, not within the object itself [...], but rather as its spectral dispersion in an atmosphere filled with the alien words, value judgments and accents through which the ray passes on its way toward the object; the social atmosphere of the word, the atmosphere that surrounds the object, makes the facets of the image sparkle.

The word, breaking through to its own meaning and its own expression across an environment full of alien words and variously evaluating accents, harmonizing with some of the elements in this environment and striking a dissonance with others, is able, in this dialogized process, to shape its own stylistic profile and tone. [...]

Language – like the living concrete environment in which the consciousness of the verbal artist lives – is never unitary. It is unitary only as an abstract grammatical system of normative forms, taken in isolation from the concrete, ideological conceptualizations that fill it, and in isolation from the uninterrupted process of historical becoming that is a characteristic of all living language. Actual social life and historical becoming create within an abstractly unitary national language a multitude of concrete worlds, a multitude of bounded verbal-ideological and social belief systems; within these various systems (identical in the abstract) are elements of language filled with various semantic and axiological content and each with its own different sound.

(d) Reported voices

The transmission and assessment of the speech of others, the discourse of another, is one of the most widespread and fundamental topics of human speech. In all areas of life and ideological activity, our speech is filled to overflowing with other people's words, which are transmitted with highly varied degrees of accuracy and impartiality. The more intensive, differentiated and highly developed the social life of a speaking collective, the greater is the importance attaching, among other possible subjects of talk, to another's word, another's utterance, since an other's word will be the subject of passionate communication, an object of interpretation, discussion, evaluation, rebuttal, support, further development and so on. [...]

The topic of a speaking person has enormous importance in everyday life. In real life we hear speech about speakers and their discourse at every step. We can go so far as to say that in real life people talk most of all about what others talk about – they transmit, recall, weigh and pass judgment on other people's words, opinions, assertions, information; people are upset by others' words, or agree with them, contest them, refer to them and so forth. Were we to eavesdrop on snatches of raw dialogue in the street, in a crowd, in lines, in a foyer and so forth, we would hear how often the words 'he says,' 'people say,' 'he said ...' are repeated, and in the conversational hurly-burly of people in a crowd, everything often fuses into one big 'he says ... you say ... I say ...'. Reflect how enormous is the weight of 'everyone says' and 'it is said' in public opinion, public rumor, gossip, slander and so forth. One must also consider the psychological importance in our lives of what others say about us, and the importance, for us, of understanding and interpreting these words of others ('living hermeneutics').

The importance of this motif is in no way diminished in the higher and better-organized areas of everyday communication. Every conversation is full of transmissions and interpretations of other people's words. At every step one meets a 'quotation' or a 'reference' to something that a particular person said, a reference to 'people say' or 'everyone says,' to the words of the person one is talking with, or to one's own previous words, to a newspaper, an official decree, a document, a book and so forth. The majority of our information and opinions is usually not communicated in direct form as our own, but with reference to some indefinite and general source: 'I heard,' 'It's generally held that ...' 'It is thought that ...' and so forth. Take one of the most widespread occurrences in our everyday life, conversations about some official meeting: they are all constructed on the transmission, interpretation and evaluation of various kinds of verbal performance, resolutions, the rejected and accepted corrections that are made to them and so forth. Thus talk goes on about speaking people and their words everywhere – this motif returns again and again; it either accompanies the development of the other topics in everyday life, or directly governs speech as its leading theme.

Further examples of the significance of the topic of the speaking person in everyday life would be superfluous. We need only keep our ears open to the speech sounding everywhere around us to reach such a conclusion: in the everyday speech of any person living in society, no less than half (on the average) of all the words uttered by him will be someone else's words (consciously someone else's), transmitted with varying degrees of precision and impartiality (or more precisely, partiality). [...]

The following must be kept in mind: that the speech of another, once enclosed in a context, is – no matter how accurately transmitted – always subject to certain semantic changes. The context embracing another's word is responsible for its dialogizing background, whose influence can be very great. Given the appropriate methods for framing, one may bring about fundamental changes even in another's utterance accurately quoted. Any sly and ill-disposed polemicist knows very well which dialogizing backdrop he should bring to bear on the accurately quoted words of his opponent, in order to distort their sense. By manipulating the effects of context, it is very easy to emphasize the brute materiality of another's words, and to stimulate dialogic reactions associated with such 'brute materiality'; thus it is, for instance, very easy to make even the most serious utterance comical. Another's discourse, when introduced into a speech context, enters the speech that frames it not in a mechanical bond but in a chemical union (on the semantic and emotionally expressive level); the degree of dialogized influence, one on the other, can be enormous. For this reason we cannot, when studying the various forms for transmitting another's speech, treat any of these forms in isolation from the means for its contextualized (dialogizing) framing – the one is indissolubly linked with the other. The formulation of another's speech as well as its framing (and the context can begin preparing for the introduction of another's speech far back in the text) both express the unitary act of dialogic interaction with that speech, a relation determining the entire nature of its transmission and all the changes in meaning and accent that take place in it during transmission. [...]

Source: BAKHTIN, M., adapted from 'Discourse in the novel' in *The Dialogic Imagination*, University of Texas Press, 1981.

READING B: Extracts from 'Oh talking voice that is so sweet': constructing dialogue in conversation

Deborah Tannen

Reported speech and dialogue

For Voloshinov/Bakhtin, dialogue is crucial: not dialogue *per se*, that is the exchange of turns that is of central concern to conversation analysts, but the polyphonic nature of all utterance, of every word. This polyphony derives from the multiple resonances of the people, contexts, and genres with which the utterance or word has been associated. As Bakhtin ([1952–3]1986, p. 91) puts it, 'Each utterance is filled with the echoes and reverberations of other utterances to which it is related by the communality of the sphere of speech communication.' [...]

   Not only is every utterance dialogic, but also hearing and understanding are dialogic acts because they require active interpretation not passive reception. In exploring dialogue in this sense, Voloshinov ([1929]1986) devotes extensive analysis to reported speech. He introduces this focus as follows:

> The productive study of dialogue presupposes, however, a more profound investigation of the forms used in reported speech, since these forms reflect basic and constant tendencies in the active reception of other speakers' speech, and it is this reception, after all, that is fundamental also for dialogue.
>
> (p. 117)

[...] In his extended discussion of reported speech, Voloshinov criticizes 'earlier investigators' for 'divorcing the reported speech from the reporting context':

> That explains why their treatment of these forms is so static and inert (a characterization applicable to the whole field of syntactic study in general). Meanwhile, the true object of inquiry ought to be precisely the dynamic interrelationship of these two factors, the speech being reported (the other person's speech) and the speech doing the reporting (the author's speech). After all, the two actually do exist, function, and take shape only in their interrelation, and not on their own, the one apart from the other. The reported speech and the reporting context are but the terms of a dynamic interrelationship.
>
> (p. 119)

Furthermore, Bakhtin ([1975]1981, p. 340) observes:

> that the speech of another, once enclosed in a context, is – no matter how accurately transmitted – always subject to certain semantic changes. The context embracing another's word is responsible for its dialogizing background, whose influence can be very great. Given the appropriate methods for framing, one may bring about fundamental changes even in another's utterance accurately quoted. [...]

My concern in this chapter incorporates Voloshinov's notion that the reported speech and the reporting context are dynamically interrelated as well as Bakhtin's that the meaning of the reported speech itself can be – indeed, I would say, is inevitably – transformed by the reporting context. Moreover, I wish to call attention to the dynamic relationship between the reported speech and the *reported* context. I am claiming that the term 'reported speech' is grossly misleading in suggesting that one can speak another's words and have them remain primarily the other's words.

My reasons for claiming that one cannot, in any meaningful sense, 'report' speech are as follows. First, much of what appears in discourse as dialogue, or 'reported speech,' was never uttered by anyone else in any form. Second, if dialogue is used to represent utterances that were spoken by someone else, when an utterance is repeated by a current speaker, it exists primarily, if not only, as an element of the reporting context, although its meaning resonates with association with its reported context, in keeping with Bakhtin's sense of polyphony. In the deepest sense, the words have ceased to be those of the speaker to whom they are attributed, having been appropriated by the speaker who is repeating them. ... In short, I wish to question the conventional American literal conception of 'reported speech' and claim instead that uttering dialogue in conversation is as much a creative act as is the creation of dialogue in fiction and drama. [...]

Reported speech is constructed dialogue

To support this claim, I present in this section brief examples taken from narratives recorded by participants in casual conversation with their families and friends. Each example is accompanied by brief discussion demonstrating that the dialogue animated in the narrative was not actually spoken by the person to whom it is attributed. In other words, it is not reported speech but constructed dialogue. The following examples, in the order in which they appear, illustrate dialogue representing what wasn't said, dialogue as instantiation, summarizing dialogue, choral dialogue, dialogue as inner speech, the inner speech of others, dialogue constructed by a listener, dialogue fading from indirect to direct, dialogue including vague referents, and dialogue cast in the persona of a nonhuman speaker.

Dialogue representing what wasn't said

(1) comes from a conversation in which a young woman tells her friend that when she was a little girl, her father frequently embarrassed her by berating her in front of her peers for not having responded to his orders quickly and efficiently. She represents, in the form of dialogue, what she did not say to her father:

> (1) You can't say, 'Well Daddy I didn't HEAR you.'

This is a clear example of dialogue constructed rather than reported as the speaker states explicitly that the line of dialogue was not spoken.

Dialogue as instantiation

Specific dialogue is often constructed to illustrate an utterance type that is represented as occurring repeatedly. Several examples follow.

(2) is from a conversation that took place among several women who work together, while they were having lunch in a restaurant. In this excerpt, Daisy animates a line of dialogue in order to illustrate the shared maternal experience of ceasing to accompany their children in play activities when it is no longer required.

(2) DAISY The minute the kids get old enough to do these things
              themselves,

     MARY   [that's when
            ['You do it yourself.'

     DAISY Yeah that's when I start to say ...

→   'Well ... I don't think I'll go in the water this time.

→   Why don't you kids go on the ferris wheel.

→   I'll wave to you.'

It is clear from the general time frame established, 'The minute the kids get old enough' ('the minute' is, of course, meant figuratively, not literally), that the dialogue (indicated in the example by quotation marks and arrows at the left) is offered as an instantiation of a general phenomenon. This becomes even clearer when the context suggested by the dialogue changes before our eyes from 'go in the water' to 'go on the ferris wheel.' Although rhythmically one blends into the other in a single coherent flow of discourse, the scene changes as the general point of the story is instantiated in two different scenes: from going swimming to going on a ferris wheel.

(3) is taken from a young man's account of having been punished as a boy. As background to the story about a specific instance of punishment, he establishes that his mother set his father up as the one to fear:

(3) whenever something happened,

→   then 'Oh wait until your father comes.'

As in the previous example, although this may well be the gist of what the mother said, there is no reason to believe that these are precisely the words she always spoke every time. Another level on which this dialogue could not have been spoken as it is represented here is that of language: The teller of this story is a native of a Spanish-speaking country, so anything his mother said to him when he was a boy was said in Spanish.

Finally, a teacher recounts what he says to a new class when he appears before them as a substitute teacher:

(4) I have very strict rules,
     a:nd ... one of the first things I tell them
     after I tell them my name,

→   is ... 'When you follow my rules,

→   you'll be happy,

→   when you do not follow my rules,

→   you will be-

→   Pain and consequences.

→   You will be very UNhappy.'

Once more, it is highly unlikely that these precise words were uttered each time the teacher entered a new class – especially considering the abrupt cutting off of breath following 'be' and preceding the highly stylized interjected phrase, 'pain and consequences.' But the sense of what the teacher presents himself as saying to each class is better captured by a particular instance of speech than it would be by a general summary representing the gist of what he always says (for example, 'I tell them that they will be happy if they follow my rules but they will be unhappy if they don't').

Summarizing dialogue

(5) shows a line of dialogue that is explicitly identified as representing the gist rather than the wording of what was said in a single discourse. The speaker says she was part of a group having dinner at a Philippine restaurant when one of the members of her dinner party loudly criticized the restaurant, within earshot of the staff:

(5)   and this man is essentially saying
→   'We shouldn't be here
→   because Imelda Marcos owns this restaurant.'

By using the present tense ('this man is essentially saying') as well as the first person pronoun ('We shouldn't be here') and proximal deixis ('We shouldn't be here because Imelda Marcos owns this restaurant.'), the speaker casts her summary of the man's argument in dialogue. But she characterizes it as a summary, what he 'essentially' said rather than what he specifically said.

Choral dialogue

The next example comes from a narrative that was told by a woman (who happened to be me) about an experience in the Athens airport: A Greek woman tried to go directly to the front of a line in which Americans (including the speaker) had been waiting for a number of hours. The Americans objected to her behavior and resisted her justifications for breaking into the line until she said that she had small children with her.

(6)   And then all the Americans said
→   'Oh in that case, go ahead.'

In this example, the dialogue is attributed to more than one speaker: 'all the Americans.' This is impossible, unless one imagines the line of Americans speaking in unison like a Greek chorus, which is unlikely (despite the Hellenic setting of the story), and, as I can attest, not the case. Rather, the line of dialogue is offered as an instantiation of what many people said.

Similar examples are frequent in the narratives collected. Just one more will be given. In (7) a woman is telling about having seen two mothers on a subway train with their children:

(7)   and the mothers were telling the kids,

→   'Hold on to that, you know, to that post there.'

Since they are not likely to have spoken in unison, the wording supplied instantiates rather than represents what the *two* mothers said.

Dialogue as inner speech

People often report their own thoughts as dialogue. (8) is taken from a narrative about riding the New York subway. The speaker describes a strange man who entered the car and:

(8)   started mumbling about ... perverts,

→   ... and I thought 'Oh God,

→   if I am going to get-

→   someone's slightly psychotic attitude on perverts

→   I really don't feel like riding this train.'

It is unlikely that these words actually represent the words the speaker spoke to himself at the time, if he spoke to himself in words at all, especially since the phrase 'slightly psychotic attitude' seems stylized for performance effect.

The inner speech of others

If it is questionable that dialogue in a narrative accurately reproduces what a speaker thought at a time past, it is unquestionable that when a speaker reports what someone else thought, the words thus animated in dialogue do not correspond to words actually thought by the other person. [...]

(9) presents the thoughts of another person as dialogue, but introduces them not so much as what he actually thought but as what he must have been thinking, judging from his behavior and facial expression. In a story about a baseball game, the teller increases the impact of his greatest remembered pitch by describing the batter:

(9)   And he- you could just see him just draw back like

→   'Man, I'm going to knock this thing to Kingdom Come.'

By dramatizing the confidence of the batter, the speaker intensifies the dramatic tension that will be resolved when he triumphs over the batter by pitching his deceptive 'knuckleball.'

The word 'like' is frequently used to introduce dialogue that, in a sense, is just what it says: not what the person actually said but rather what the person appeared to have felt like. Thus in (10) a woman tells of an incident in which her fifteen-year-old sister was riding a bicycle with a basketball stuffed under her shirt, giving her the appearance of being pregnant. She fell off the bike when she was almost hit by a bus. The narrator says,

(10)   And the bus driver was like 'Oh my Go::d!'

The speaker is not suggesting that the bus driver literally said 'Oh my God,' but that his reaction was such that he must have been thinking something like that. Although the speaker cannot know what the bus driver felt (she wasn't even there), she can use the resource of presenting what he felt like in order to make her story dramatically, effective.

(11) is taken from a story about a tourist's experience in Japan. The teller was one of a group being led by a Japanese guide when:

(11)   And um they didn't tell us,

       first of all

       that we were going into the bath

       so we were standing in the room,

       and they said 'Okay, take your clothes off.'

→   We're like 'What?!'

       and um

       [listener: It's prison]

       they gave us these kimono

       and we put the kimono on,

       they brought us to this other room

       and they said, 'Okay, take the kimono off.'

→   And we're like 'What are you talking about?'

Lines attributed to the speaker(s) who gave orders to disrobe are introduced by the word 'said,' whereas the reactions of the speaker and other members of his group (represented in a single voice) are introduced with a form of be + like. There is no suggestion, however, that the speaker and his friends actually said, 'What?' and 'What are you talking about?' but simply that they felt in a way that would be reflected in such utterances. It is likely that they did not actually say anything but just complied with the directions they were given. Casting their thoughts as dialogue allows a dramatization based on the state of their understanding of events at the time, rather than the clarity of hindsight.

Dialogue constructed by a listener

In the conversational narratives I have examined, a listener often supplies a line of dialogue animated in the role of a character in someone else's story.

In (2), the listener, Mary, constructed an utterance in the role of Daisy (or any parent) addressing her children:

	DAISY	The minute the kids get old enough to do these things themselves,
→	MARY	[that's when
		['You do it yourself.'

The 'you' in Mary's utterance refers not to the conversationalists present but to the children in Daisy's discourse who want to do something adventuresome. In this active form of listenership, the listener's construction of dialogue appropriate to someone else's narrative demonstrates how thoroughly the listener appreciates the perspective of the speaker. When a listener utters a line of dialogue for a story she isn't telling, that dialogue certainly cannot be considered 'reported.'

Even more extreme is (12), in which a listener supplies a line of dialogue that is intentionally absurd, This excerpt follows an amusing story told by Lois about how her brother cast a fishing rod and accidentally sunk a lure in their father's face. Lois describes her father arriving at the hospital holding the lure in his face. Joe, a listener, offers a line of dialogue spoken by a hypothetical nurse that satirizes the absurdity of the situation:

(12)	LOIS	So he had the thing.
		he's walkin' around ...
→	JOE	'Excuse me, Sir, you've got a lure on your face.'

Encouraged by general laughter, Joe goes on to construct an equally absurd response by Lois's father:

→	JOE	'Ah ... lure again?
		[laughter]
→		Boy ... gets stuck there every week.'
		[laughter]

Joe uses Lois's story as material for elaboration; by constructing dialogue, he creates a dramatic scene even more absurd than the one Lois described.

Fadeout, fadein

In (13), an excerpt from a narrative told by a woman about her experience with a dentist, an indirect quotation fades into a direct one:

(13)	It was like he was telling everybody
→	To 'have your wisdom teeth taken out.'
	And I didn't see any point
	as long as they weren't bothering me.

'Telling everybody to' is the grammatical means of introducing an indirect quotation, but it is followed instead by a direct quotation: 'have your wisdom teeth taken out.' The speaker might recall what the dentist said to her, but she can't know the precise words in which he spoke to 'everybody.' Finally, she concludes as if the reported line had been spoken to her ('I didn't see any point as long as they weren't bothering me').

(14) is taken from the same story as (7), about the mothers in the subway car:

(14) And uh finally the mother opened up the stroller
→   you know and uh told the kid to 'SIT THERE.'

As in (13), the mother's speech is introduced with the word 'to,' suggesting that indirect discourse is to follow. But by assuming the voice quality of a mother giving instructions to her child, the speaker ends by animating rather than reporting the dialogue.

Vague referents

(15) comes from the same discourse as (1), in which a young woman tells how her father embarrassed her by giving her peremptory orders in front of her peers. In (15), the use of vague referents makes it clear that the dialogue was never actually spoken as reported:

(15) He was sending me out to get tools or whatever
→   [imitating father] 'Go get this
→   and it looks like this and the other'

If her father had uttered precisely these words, not even he could have expected her to locate what he wanted.

Nonhuman speaker

The preceding examples come from conversational narratives. However, discourse need not be narrative to exploit the expressive potential of constructed dialogue. The final example comes from conversation taped at a dinner party. A guest notices the host's cat sitting on the window sill and addresses a question to the cat: 'What do you see out there, kitty?' The host answers for the cat:

(16) She says,
→   'I see a beautiful world just waiting for me.'

The host animates the cat's response in a high-pitched, childlike voice. By animating dialogue, the two speakers create a spontaneous mini-drama with the cat as central character. The constructed dialogue becomes a resource for a fleeting but finely coordinated verbal *pas de deux* performed by a pair of speakers. [...]

Conclusion

I have argued [...] that the term 'reported speech' is a misnomer, an abstraction with no basis in the reality of interaction. When speakers cast the words of others in dialogue, they are not reporting so much as constructing dialogue. Constructing dialogue creates involvement by both its rhythmic, sonorous effect and its internally evaluative effect. Dialogue is not a general report; it is particular, and the particular enables listeners (or readers) to create their understanding by drawing on their own history of associations. By giving voice to characters, dialogue makes story into drama and listeners into an interpreting audience to the drama. This active participation in sensemaking contributes to the creation of involvement. Thus understanding in discourse is in part emotional.

[...] The constructing of dialogue for framing as reported speech reflects the dual nature of language, like all human behavior, as repetitive and novel, fixed and free, transforming rather than transmitting what comes its way. Moreover, and perhaps paradoxically, it is a supremely social act: by appropriating each others' utterances, speakers are bound together in a community of words.

Constructing dialogue, moreover, is an example of the poetic in everyday conversation, in the terms of Friedrich (1986), it is a figure that fires the individual imagination. The creation of voices occasions the imagination of alternative, distant, and others' worlds by linking them to the sounds and scenes of one's own familiar world.

References

BAKHTIN, M.M. ([1975]1981) *The Dialogic Imagination*, Austin, The University of Texas Press.

BAKHTIN, M.M. ([1952–3]1986) 'The problem of speech genres', in C. EMERSON and M. HOLQUIST, trans. V.W. McGEE (ed.) *Speech Genres and Other Late Essays*, Austin, The University of Texas Press.

FRIEDRICH, P. (1986) *The Language Parallax: Linguistic Relativism and Poetic Indeterminacy*, Austin, Texas, University of Texas Press.

Source: TANNEN, D. (1989) *Talking Voices*, Cambridge, Cambridge University Press.

READING C: Extracts from 'On face-work'

Erving Goffman

Cooperation in face-work

When a face has been threatened, face-work must be done, but whether this is initiated and primarily carried through by the person whose face is threatened, or by the offender, or by a mere witness, is often of secondary importance. Lack of effort on the part of one person induces compensative effort from others; a contribution by one person relieves the others of the task. In fact, there are many minor incidents in which the offender and the offended simultaneously attempt to initiate an apology. Resolution of the situation to everyone's apparent satisfaction is the first requirement; correct apportionment of blame is typically a secondary consideration. Hence terms such as tact and *savoir-faire* fail to distinguish whether it is the person's own face that his diplomacy saves or the face of the others. Similarly, terms such as *gaffe* and *faux pas* fail to specify whether it is the actor's own face he has threatened or the face of other participants. And it is understandable that if one person finds he is powerless to save his own face, the others seem especially bound to protect him. For example, in polite society, a handshake that perhaps should not have been extended becomes one that cannot be declined. [...]

Since each participant in an undertaking is concerned, albeit for differing reasons, with saving his own face and the face of the others, then tacit cooperation will naturally arise so that the participants together can attain their shared but differently motivated objectives.

One common type of tacit cooperation in face-saving is the tact exerted in regard to face-work itself. The person not only defends his own face and protects the face of the others, but also acts so as to make it possible and even easy for the others to employ face-work for themselves and him. He helps them to help themselves and him. Social etiquette, for example, warns men against asking for New Year's Eve dates too early in the season, lest the girl find it difficult to provide a gentle excuse for refusing. This second-order tact can be further illustrated by the widespread practice of negative-attribute etiquette. The person who has an unapparent negatively valued attribute often finds it expedient to begin an encounter with an unobtrusive admission of his failing, especially with persons who are uninformed about him. The others are thus warned in advance against making disparaging remarks about his kind of person and are saved from the contradiction of acting in a friendly fashion to a person toward whom they are unwittingly being hostile. This strategy also prevents the others from automatically making assumptions about him which place him in a false position and saves him from painful forbearance or embarrassing remonstrances.

Tact in regard to face-work often relies for its operation on a tacit agreement to do business through the language of hint – the language of innuendo, ambiguities, well-paced pauses, carefully worded jokes, and so on. The rule regarding this unofficial kind of communication is that the sender ought not to act as if he had officially conveyed the message he has hinted at, while the recipients have the right and the obligation to act as if they have not officially received the message contained in the hint. Hinted communication, then, is deniable communication; it need not be faced up to. It provides a means by which the person can be warned that his current line or the current situation is leading to loss of face, without this warning itself becoming an incident.

Another form of tacit cooperation, and one that seems to be much used in many societies, is reciprocal self-denial. Often the person does not have a clear idea of what would be a just or acceptable apportionment of judgments during the occasion, and so he voluntarily deprives or depreciates himself while indulging and complimenting the others, in both cases carrying the judgments safely past what is likely to be just. The favourable judgments about himself he allows to come from the others; the unfavourable judgments of himself are his own contributions. This 'after you, Alphonse' technique works, of course, because in depriving himself he can reliably anticipate that the others will compliment or indulge him. Whatever allocation of favors is eventually established, all participants are first given a chance to show that they are not bound or constrained by their own desires and expectations, that they have a properly modest view of themselves, and that they can be counted upon to support the ritual code. Negative bargaining, through which each participant tries to make the terms of trade more favourable to the other side, is another instance; as a form of exchange perhaps it is more widespread than the economist's kind.

A person's performance of face-work, extended by his tacit agreement to help others perform theirs, represents his willingness to abide by the ground rules of social interaction. Here is the hallmark of his socialization as an interactant. If he and the others were not socialized in this way, interaction in most societies and most situations would be a much more hazardous thing for feelings and faces. The person would find it impractical to be oriented to symbolically conveyed appraisals of social worth, or to be possessed of feelings – that is, it would be impractical for him to be a ritually delicate object. [...] If the person were not a ritually delicate object, occasions of talk could not be organized in the way they usually are. It is no wonder that trouble is caused by a person who cannot be relied upon to play the face-saving game.

Source: GOFFMAN, E. (1967) *Interaction Ritual*, Penguin.

READING D: Extracts from 'Regions and region behaviour'

Erving Goffman

Given a particular performance as a point of reference, it will sometimes be convenient to use the term 'front region' to refer to the place where the performance is given. [...] The performance of an individual in a front region may be seen as an effort to give the appearance that his activity in the region maintains and embodies certain standards. These standards seem to fall into two broad groupings. One grouping has to do with the way in which the performer treats the audience while engaged in talk with them or in gestural interchanges that are a substitute for talk. These standards are sometimes referred to as matters of politeness. The other group of standards has to do with the way in which the performer comports himself while in visual or aural range of the audience but not necessarily engaged in talk with them. I shall use the term 'decorum' to refer to this second group of standards, although some excuses and some qualifications will have to be added to justify the usage. [...]

It may be noted that the part of personal front I have called 'manner' will be important in regard to politeness and that the part called 'appearance' will be important in regard to decorum. It may also be noted that while decorous behaviour may take the form of showing respect for the region and setting one finds oneself in, this show of respect may, of course, be motivated by a desire to impress the audience favourably, or avoid sanctions, etc. Finally, it should be noted that the requirements of decorum are more pervasive ecologically than are the requirements of politeness. An audience can subject an entire front region to a continuous inspection as regards decorum, but while the audience is so engaged, none or only a few of the performers may be obliged to talk to the audience and hence to demonstrate politeness. Performers can stop giving expressions but cannot stop giving them off. [...]

When one's activity occurs in the presence of other persons, some aspects of the activity are expressively accentuated and other aspects, which might discredit the fostered impression, are suppressed. It is clear that accentuated facts make their appearance in what I have called a front region; it should be just as clear that there may be another region – a 'back region' or 'backstage' – where the suppressed facts make an appearance.

A back region or backstage may be defined as a place, relative to a given performance, where the impression fostered by the performance is knowingly contradicted as a matter of course. There are, of course, many characteristic functions of such places. It is here that the capacity of a performance to express something beyond itself may be painstakingly fabricated; it is here that illusions and impressions are openly constructed. Here stage props and items of personal front can be stored in a kind of compact collapsing of whole repertoires of actions and characters. Here grades of ceremonial equipment, such as different types of liquor or clothes, can be hidden so that the audience will not be able to see the treatment accorded them in comparison with the treatment that could have been accorded them. Here devices such as the telephone are sequestered so that they can be used 'privately'. Here costumes and other parts of personal front may be adjusted and scrutinized for flaws. Here the team can run through its performance, checking for offending expressions when no audience is present to be affronted by them; here poor members of the team, who are expressively inept, can be schooled or dropped from the performance. Here the performer can relax; he can drop his front, forgo speaking his lines, and step out of character. [...]

Very commonly the back region of a performance is located at one end of the place where the performance is presented, being cut off from it by a partition and guarded passageway. By having the front and back regions adjacent in this way, a performer out in front can receive backstage assistance while the performance is in progress and can interrupt his performance momentarily for brief periods of relaxation. In general, of course, the back region will be the place where the performer can reliably expect that no member of the audience will intrude.

Since the vital secrets of a show are visible backstage and since performers behave out of character while there, it is natural to expect that the passage from the front region to the back region will be kept closed to members of the audience or that the entire back region will be kept hidden from them. This is a widely practised technique of impression management, and requires further discussion. [...]

[Goffman gives the example of Shetland Hotel, from his sociological fieldwork in Scotland.] In the kitchen where the staff ate and spent their day an informal, egalitarian crofters' culture prevailed, while in front of guests staff took up a hierarchy of different roles and spoke and behaved much more formally. The doors leading into the kitchen were a constant sore spot in the organisation of work; the maids who were ferrying the food wanted to keep them open, and had little to lose from guests glimpsing life in the kitchen. The managers, however, wanted to keep the doors closed, so that their middle class persona with the guests would not be discredited by a disclosure of their kitchen behaviour.

Another interesting example of backstage difficulties is found in radio and television broadcasting work. In these situations, the back region tends to be defined as all places where the camera is not focused at the moment or all places out of range of 'live' microphones. Thus an announcer may hold the sponsor's product up at arm's length in front of the camera while he holds his nose with his other hand, his face being out of the picture, as a way of joking with his team-mates. Professionals, of course, tell many exemplary tales of how persons who thought they were backstage were in fact on the air and how this backstage conduct discredited the definition of the situation being maintained on the air. For technical reasons, then, the walls that broadcasters have to hide behind can be very treacherous, tending to fall at the flick of a switch or a turn of the camera. Broadcasting artists must live with this staging contingency.

[...] Throughout Western society there tends to be one informal or backstage language of behaviour, and another language of behaviour for occasions when a performance is being presented. The backstage language consists of reciprocal first-naming, cooperative decision-making, profanity, open sexual remarks, elaborate griping, smoking, rough informal dress, 'sloppy' sitting and standing posture, use of dialect or sub-standard speech, mumbling and shouting, playful aggressivity and 'kidding', inconsiderateness for the other in minor but potentially symbolic acts, minor physical self-involvements such as humming, whistling, chewing, nibbling, belching, and flatulence. The frontstage behaviour language can be taken as the absence (and in some sense the opposite) of this. In general, then, backstage conduct is one which allows minor acts which might easily be taken as symbolic of intimacy and disrespect for others present and for the region, while front region conduct is one which disallows such potentially offensive behaviour. It may be noted here that backstage behaviour has what psychologists might call a 'regressive' character. The question, of course, is whether a backstage gives individuals an opportunity to regress or whether regression, in the clinical sense, is backstage conduct invoked on inappropriate occasions for motives that are not socially approved.

By invoking a backstage style, individuals can transform any region into a backstage. Thus we find that in many social establishments the performers will appropriate a section of the front region and by acting there in a familiar fashion symbolically cut it off from the rest of the region. For instance, in some restaurants in America, especially those called 'one-arm joints', the staff will hold court in the booth farthest from the door or closest to the kitchen, and there conduct themselves, at least in some respect, as if they were backstage. Similarly, on un-crowded evening airline flights, after their initial duties have been performed, stewardesses may settle down in the rearmost seat, change from regulation pumps into loafers, light up a cigarette, and there create a muted circle of non-service relaxation, even at times extending this to include the one or two closest passengers.

More important, one ought not to expect that concrete situations will provide pure examples of informal conduct or formal conduct, although there is usually a tendency to move the definition of the situation in one of these two directions. We will not find these pure cases because team-mates in regard to one show will be to some degree performers and audience for another show, and performers and audience for one show will to some extend, however slight, be team-mates with respect of another show. Thus in a concrete situation we may expect a predominance of one style or the other, with some feelings of guilt or doubt concerning the actual combination or balance that is achieved between the two styles.

Source: GOFFMAN, E. (1959) *The Presentation of Self in Everyday Life*, **Penguin.**

References

AHEARN, L. (1999) 'True traces: love letters and social transformation in Nepal', in D. BARTON and N. HALL (eds) *Letter Writing as a Social Practice*, Amsterdam, John Benjamins.

AHEARN, L. (2001) *Invitations to Love: Literacy, Love Letters and Social Change in Nepal*, Ann Arbor, University of Michigan Press.

ALTICK, R.D. (1957) *The English Common Reader: A Social History of the Mass Reading Public 1800–1900*, Chicago, Chicago University Press.

ALTMAN, J. (1982) *Epistolarity: Approaches to a Form*, Columbus, Ohio State University Press.

ALTSON, R.C. (1967) *English Linguistics 1500–1800 (A Collection of Facsimile Reprints)* No. 29, Menston, England, The Scholar Press Ltd.

AMRITAVALLI, R. and UPENDRAN, S. (1990) 'The humorous bilingual: the possible significance of jokes in "Indian" and English. Paper presented at the National Seminar on Perspectives on Indian English. Central Institute for English and Foreign Languages, Hyderabad.

ANDERSEN, E.S. (1990) *Speaking with Style: The Sociolinguistic Skills of Children*, London, Routledge.

ANDROUTSOPOULOS, J. and SCHMIDT, G. (2002) 'SMS-Kommunikation: Ethnografische Gattungsanalyse am Beispiel einer Kleingruppe', *Zeitschrift fuer Angewandte Linguistik*, **36**, pp. 49–81.

AUDEN, W.H. (1976) *Collected Poems*, ed. E. Mendelson, London, Faber and Faber.

AUER, P. (ed.) (1998) *Code-Switching in Conversation: Language, Interaction and Identity*, London and New York, Routledge.

AUSTIN, J.L. (1962) *How to Do Things with Words*, Cambridge, MA, Harvard University Press.

BAKER, P. (2002) *Polari – The Lost Language Of Gay Men*, London, Routledge.

BAKHTIN, M. ([1935]1981) *The Dialogic Imagination*, Austin, University of Texas Press.

BAKHTIN, M. ([1929]1984) *Problems of Dostoevsky's poetics*, ed. and trans. C. EMERSON, Manchester, Manchester University Press.

BAKHTIN, M. (1984) *Problems of Dostoevsky's Poetics*, Minneapolis, University of Minnesota Press.

BAKHTIN, M. ([1953]1986) *Speech Genres and Other Late Essays*, in C. EMERSON and MICHAEL HOLQUIST (eds) Austin, University of Texas Press.

BALLARD, J.G. (1974) *Crash!*, Paris, Calmann-Lévy.

BARON, N.S. (1998) 'Letters by phone or speech by other means: the linguistics of email', *Language and Communication*, **18**, pp. 133–70.

BARRETT, R. (1999) 'Indexing polyphonous identity in the speech of African American drag queens', in M. BUCHOLTZ, A.C. LAING and L.A. SUTTON (eds) *Reinventing Identities: The Gendered Self in Discourse*, New York, Oxford University Press.

BARTON, D. (1994) *Literacy: An Introduction to the Ecology of Written Language*, Oxford, Blackwell.

BARTON, D. and HAMILTON, M. (1998) *Local Literacies: Reading and Writing in One Community*, London and New York, Routledge.

BATESON, M.C. (1975) 'Mother-infant exchanges: the epigenesis of conversational interaction' in D. AARONSON and R.W. RIEBER (eds) *Developmental Psycholinguistics and Communication Disorders: annals of the New York Academy of Sciences*, vol. 263, New York, New York Academy of Sciences.

BAUMAN, R. (1986) *Story, Performance, and Event: Contextual Studies of Oral Narrative*, Cambridge, Cambridge University Press.

BAUSCH, P., HAUGHEY, M. and HOURIHAN, M. (2002) *We Blog: Publishing Online with Weblogs*, Indianapolis, IN, Wiley.

BAZERMAN, C. (1999) 'Letters and the social grounding of differentiated genres', in D. BARTON and N. HALL (eds) *Letter Writing as Social Practice*, Amsterdam, John Benjamins.

BAYM, N. K. (1995) 'The performance of humor in computer-mediated communication', *Journal of Computer-Mediated Communication*, **1**.

BECHAR-ISRAELI, H. (1995) 'From <Bonehead> to <cLoNeHeAd>: nicknames, play and identity on Internet Relay Chat', *Journal of Computer-Mediated Communication*, **1**.

BESNIER, N. (2003) 'Crossing genders, mixing languages: the linguistic construction of transgenderism in Tonga', in J. HOLMES and M. MEYERHOFF (eds) *The Handbook of Language and Gender*, Oxford, Blackwell Publishing.

BLUME, R. (1985) 'Graffiti', in T. VAN DIJK (ed.) *Discourse and Literature*, Amsterdam, Benjamins.

BLYTHE, R. (1991) *The Penguin Book of Diaries*, London, Penguin.

BLYTHE, R. (1993) *Private Worlds: Letters and Diaries from the Second World War*, London, Penguin.

BODOMO, A. and LEE. C. (2002) 'Changing forms of language and literacy: technobabble and mobile phone communication', *Literacy and Numeracy Studies*, **12**(1), pp. 23–45.

BOURDIEU, P. (1984) *Distinction: A Social Critique of the Judgment of Taste*, London, Routledge and Kegan Paul.

BOXER, F. and CORTES-CONDE, F. (1997) 'From bonding to biting: conversational joking and identity display', *Journal of Pragmatics*, **27**, pp. 275–94.

BROWN, P. and LEVINSON, S. (1987) *Politeness: Some Universals in Language Usage*, Cambridge, Cambridge University Press.

BRUNER, J. (1991) 'The narrative construction of reality', in *Critical Inquiry*, **18**(1), pp. 1–21.

BUCHOLTZ, M. (1996) 'Geek the girl: language, femininity and female nerds', in N. WARNER, J. AHLERS, L. BILMES, M. OLIVER, S. WERTHEIM and M. CHEN (eds) *Gender and Belief Systems: Proceedings of the Fourth Berkeley Women and Language Conference*, April 19–21, Berkeley, CA, Berkeley Women and Language Group.

BUCHOLTZ, M. (1999) ' "Why be normal?": language and identity practices in a community of nerd girls', *Language in Society*, **28**, pp. 203–224.

BUTLER, J. (1990) *Gender Trouble: Feminism and the Subversion of Identity*, London, Routledge.

CAMERON, D. (1997a) 'Performing gender identity: Young men's talk and the construction of heterosexual masculinity', in S. JOHNSON and U. MEINHOF (eds) *Language and Masculinity*, Oxford, Blackwell.

CAMERON, D. (1997b) 'Theoretical debates in feminist linguistics: questions of sex and gender', in R. WODAK (ed.) *Gender and Discourse*, London, Sage Publications, www.sagepub.co.uk

CARTER, R. (1999) 'Common language: corpus, creativity and cognition', *Language and Literature,* **8**(3), pp. 195–216.

CARTER, R. (2004) *Language and Creativity: The Art of Common Talk*, London, Routledge.

CHANDLER, D. (1995) *Technological or Media Determinism*, [online] www.aber.ac.uk/media/tecdet (accessed 14.10.2005)

CHANDLER, D. (1997) 'Writing oneself in Cyberspace' [online] http://www.aber.ac.uk/media/Documents/short/homepgid.html (accessed 1.08.03)

CHOMSKY, N. (1965) *Aspects of the Theory of Syntax*, Cambridge, MA, MIT Press.

COATES, J. (ed.) (1998) *Language and Gender: a reader*, Oxford, Blackwell Publishers.

COATES, J. (2002) *Men Talk: Stories in the Making of Masculinities*, Oxford, Blackwell.

COLLINS, W. (1858) 'The Unknown Public', *Household Words*, **1**(1), 30 March, pp. 8–9.

COLLOT, M. and BELMORE, N. (1996) 'Electronic language: a new variety of English', in S. HERRING (ed.) *Computer-Mediated Communication: Linguistic, Social and Cross-Cultural Perspectives*, Amsterdam, Benjamins, pp. 13–28.

COOK, G. (1994) *Discourse and Literature: The Interplay of Form and Mind*, Oxford, Oxford University Press.

COOK, G. (1996) 'Language play in English', in J. MAYBIN and N. MERCER (eds) *Using English: From Conversation to Canon*, London, Routledge.

COOK, G. (2000) *Language Play, Language Learning*, Oxford, Oxford University Press.

COUPLAND, N. (2001) 'Language, situation and the relational self: theorizing dialect style in sociolinguistics', in P. ECKERT and J. RICKFORD (eds) *Style and Sociolinguistic Variation*, Cambridge, Cambridge University Press.

CRAMB, A. (2003) 'Girl writes English essay in phone text shorthand', *The Daily Telegraph*.

CRYSTAL, D. (1998) *Language Play*, Harmondsworth, Penguin.

CRYSTAL, D. (2001) *Language and the Internet*, Cambridge, Cambridge University Press.

DAISLEY, M. (1994) 'The game of literacy: the meaning of play in computer-mediated communication', *Computers and Composition*, **2**, pp. 107–19.

DAMASIO, A. (2000) *The Feeling of What Happens*, New York, Harvest Books.

DANET, B. (2001) *Cyberpl@y: Communicating Online*, Oxford, Berg.

DARBISHIRE H. (ed.) (1958) *Journals of Dorothy Wordsworth*, London, Oxford University Press.

DAVIS, J. and MITCHELL, C. 'You are my Sunshine'. Copyright 1940 and 1977 by Peer International Corporation.

DEACON. G. (1983) *John Clare and the Folk Tradition*, London, Sinclair Browne.

DENNETT, D. (1991) *Consciousness Explained*, Boston, Little Brown.

DICKENS, C. (1850a) 'Easy spelling and hard reading', *Household Words*, **4**(27), 24 August, p. 562.

DICKENS, C. (1850b) 'Valentine's day at the post office', *Household Words*, **4**(27), 24 August, p. 8–9.

DICKENS, C. (1851) 'The birth and parentage of letters', *Household Words*, **4**(79), 27 September, p. 79.

DORING, N. (2002) 'Personal home pages on the web: a review of research', *JCMC*, **7**(3).

DURANTI, A. (1997) *Linguistic Anthropology*, Cambridge, Cambridge University Press.

DYSON, A.H. (2003) 'The stolen lipstick of overheard song: composing voices in child song, verse and written text', in M. NYSTRAND and J. DUFFY (eds) *Towards a Rhetoric of Everyday Life: New Directions in Research on Writing, Text and Discourse*, Wisconsin, University of Wisconsin Press.

EAGLETON, T. (1983/1996) *Literary Theory: An Introduction*, Oxford, Blackwell.

ECKERT, P. (1989) *Jocks and Burnouts: Social Categories and Identity in the High School*, New York, Teachers College Press.

ECKERT, P. (2000) *Language Variation as Social Practice*, Oxford, Blackwell.

ECKERT, P. and McCONNELL-GINET, S. (1999) 'New generalizations and explanations in language and gender research', *Language in Society*, **28**, pp. 185–201.

ECKERT, P. and McCONNELL-GINET, S. (2003) *Language and Gender*, Cambridge, Cambridge University Press.

ERRINGTON, A. (1778–1825) 'The reason of my wrighting', in P.E.H. HAIR (ed.) (1988) *Coals on Rails, Or The Reason of my Wrighting*, Liverpool, Liverpool University Press.

FACTOR, J. (1988) *Captain Cook Chased a Chook: Children's Folklore in Australia*, Ringwood, Penguin.

FACTOR, J. (2000) *Kidspeak: A Dictionary of Children's Words, Expressions and Games*, Victoria, Melbourne University Press.

FACTOR, J. (2004) 'Tree stumps, manhole covers and rubbish tins: the invisible play-lines of a primary school playground', *Childhood*, **11**(2), pp. 142–54.

FAIRCLOUGH, N. (1992) *Discourse and Social Change*, Cambridge, Polity Press/Blackwell Publishers.

FAIRCLOUGH, N. (2003) *Analyzing Discourse: Textual Analysis for Social Research*, London and New York, Routledge.

FEIN, G.G. (1979) 'Echoes from the nursery: Piaget, Vygotsky and the relation between language and play', *New Directions in Child Development*, **6**, pp. 1–14.

FERRARA, K., BRUNNER, H. and WHITTEMORE, G. (1991) 'Interactive written discourse as an emergent register', *Written Communication*, **8**, pp. 8–34.

FIREBIRD TRUST (2000) [online] www.firebirdtrust.sagenet.co.uk/clap/clap.html (accessed 19/01/05).

FOLK MUSIC INDEX [last updated 2001] http://folkindex.mse.jhu.edu/B16.htm#Buiabo (accessed 28/10/03).

FOUCAULT, M. (1980) *Power/Knowledge, Selected Interviews and Other Writings 1972–1977*, New York, Pantheon.

FOUCAULT, M. (1985) *The Use of Pleasure*, vol. 2, trans. H. Hurley, Harmondsworth, Penguin.

FOUSER, R.J., INOUE, N. and LEE, C. (2000) 'The pragmatics of orality in English, Japanese and Korean computer-mediated communication', in L. PEMBERTON and S. SHURVILLE (eds) *Words on the Web: Computer-Mediated Communication*, Exeter, Intellect, pp. 52–62.

FURLOW, B. (2001) 'Play's the thing', *New Scientist*, **9** (June), pp. 28–31.

INNES, H. (1835) *The British Child's Spelling Book*, 3rd edition, London, John Limbird.

GEE, J.P. (1999) *An Introduction to Discourse Analysis: Theory and Method*, London/New York, Routledge.

GIBBS, R.W. (1992) 'What do idioms really mean?', *Journal of Memory and Language,* **31**, pp. 485–506.

GIBBS, R.W. (1999) 'Taking metaphor out of our heads and putting it into the cultural world', in GIBBS, R.W. and STEEN, G.J. (eds) (1999) *Metaphor in Cognitive Linguistics*, Amsterdam/Philadelphia, John Benjamins.

GIBBS, R.W. and STEEN, G.J. (eds) (1999) *Metaphor in Cognitive Linguistics*, Amsterdam/Philadelphia, John Benjamins.

GIBBS, R.W., Jr (1994) *The Poetics of Mind: Figurative Thought, Language and Understanding*, Cambridge, Cambridge University Press.

GIBSON, J.J. (1986) *The Ecological Approach to Visual Perception*, Hillsdale, NJ, Lawrence Erlbaum.

GOFFMAN, E. (1959) *The Presentation of Self in Everyday Life*, New York, Doubleday Anchor.

GOFFMAN, E. (1969[1959]) *The Presentation of Self in Everyday Life*, London, Penguin.

GOFFMAN, E. (1972) *Interactional Ritual: Essays on Face-to-Face Behaviour*, London, Penguin.

GOFFMAN, E. (1981) *Forms of Talk*, Philadelphia, University of Pennsylvania Press.

GOLDMAN, L.R. (1998) *Child's Play: Myth, Mimesis and Make-believe*, Oxford/New York, Berg.

GOODMAN, S. and O'HALLORAN, K. (eds) (2006) *The art of English: literary creativity*, Basingstoke, Palgrave Macmillan in association with The Open University.

GRAFF, H.J. (1981) *Literacy and Social Development in the West: A Reader*, Cambridge, Cambridge University Press.

GRICE, H.P. (1975) 'Logic and conversation', in P. COLE and J. MORGAN (eds) *Syntax and Semantics, 3: Speech Acts*, New York: Academic Press.

GRUGEON, E. (1999) 'The state of play: children's oral culture, literacy and learning', *Reading*, **33**(1), pp. 13–6.

GRUGEON, E. (2001) ' "We like singing the Spice Girl songs ... and we like Tig and Stuck in the Mud": girls' traditional games on two playgrounds', in J.C. BISHOP and M. CURTIS (eds) *Play Today in the Primary School Playground*, Buckingham, Open University Press.

GUPTA, A.F. (1994) *The Step-Tongue: Children's English in Singapore*, Clevedon/Philadelphia, Multilingual Matters.

HALL, K. (1995) 'Lip service on the fantasy lines' in K. HALL and M. BUCHOLTZ (eds) *Gender Articulated: Language and the Socially Constructed Self*, New York, Routledge.

HALL, S. (1992) 'The Question of Cultural Identity,' in S. HALL, D. HELD and T. McGREW (eds) *Modernity and Its Futures*, Cambridge, The Open University.

HARRÉ, R. (1998) *The Singular Self: An Introduction to the Psychology of Personhood*, London, Sage Publications, www.sagepub.co.uk.

HARRIS, R. (1998) *Introduction to Integrational Linguistics*, Oxford, Pergamon.

HELLER, M. (ed.) (1988) *Codeswitching: Anthropological and Sociolinguistic Perspectives*, Berlin, Mouton de Gruyter.

HERRING, S. (1996) *Computer-Mediated Communication: Linguistic, Social and Cross-Cultural Perspectives*, Amsterdam, John Benjamins.

HERRING, S. (1999) 'Interactional coherence in CMC', in *Proceedings of the 32nd Hawaii International Conference on System Sciences*.

HERRING, S.C. (2001) 'Computer-mediated discourse', in D. TANNEN, D. SCHIFFRIN and H. HAMILTON (eds) *The Handbook of Discourse Analysis*, Oxford, Blackwell, pp. 612–34.

HERRING, S.C. (2004) 'Slouching toward the ordinary: current trends in computer-mediated communication', *New Media & Society*, **6**, pp. 26–36.

HODGE, R. and KRESS, G. (1988) *Social Semiotics*, Ithaca, Cornell University Press.

HOGGART, R. (1958) *The Uses of Literacy*, Harmondsworth, Penguin Books in association with Chatto and Windus.

HOLMES, J. (2000) 'Politeness, power and provocation: how humour functions in the workplace', *Discourse Studies* **2**(2), pp. 159–85.

HOLMES, J. and HAY, J. (1997) 'Humour as an ethnic boundary marker in New Zealand interaction', *Journal of Intercultural Studies*, **18**(2), pp. 127–151.

HOLMES, J. and MARRA, M. (2002a) 'Over the edge? Subversive humor between colleagues and friends', *International Journal of Humor*, **15**, pp. 65–87.

HOLMES, J. and MARRA, M. (2002b) 'Having a laugh at work: how humour contributes to workplace culture', *Journal of Pragmatics*, **34**, pp. 1683–1710.

HOLMES, J. and MEYERHOFF, M. (eds) (2003) *The Handbook of Language and Gender*, Oxford, Blackwell Publishing.

HUTCHBY, I. (2001) *Conversation and Technology*, Cambridge, Polity Press/ Blackwell Publishers Ltd.

HYMES, D. (1962) 'The ethnography of speaking', in T. GLADWIN and W. STURTEVANT (eds) *Anthropology and Human Behavior*, Washington DC, Anthropological Society of Washington.

HYMES, D. (1981) *In Vain I Tried To Tell You. Essays in Native American Ethno-poetics*, Philadelphia, University of Pennsylvania Press.

HYMES, D. (1996) *Ethnography, Linguistics, Narrative Inequality, Towards an Understanding of Voice*, London, Taylor and Francis.

HYMES, D. (2003) *Now I know only so far. Essays in Ethnopoetics*, Lincoln, University of Nebraska Press.

INNES, H. (1835) *The British Child's Spelling Book*, 3rd edn, London, John Limbird.

JAKOBSON, J. (1960) 'Closing statement: linguistics and poetics', in T.A. SEBEOK (ed.) *Style in Language*, MIT Press.

JAMES, L. (1974) *Fiction for the Working Man*, Harmondsworth, Penguin.

JEFFRIES, L. (2001) 'Schema affirmation and white asparagus: cultural multilingualism among readers of texts', *Language and Literature*, **10**(4), pp. 325–43.

JERROLD, D. (1878) 'The postman', in K. MEADOWS *Heads of the People*, London, Willoughby & Co.

JOHNSON, A. (1997) *The Hidden Writer: Diaries and the Creative Life*, New York, Doubleday.

JOLLY, M (1997) 'Everyday Letters and Literary Form: Correspondence from the Second World War', unpublished MPhil, University of Sussex.

KALMAR, T.M. (2001) *Illegal Alphabets and Adult Biliteracy: Latino Migrants Crossing the Linguistic Border*, Hillsdale, NJ, Lawrence Erlbaum Associates.

KEEGAN, V. (2001) 'Hitting the jackpot', *The Guardian*.

KELL, C. (1996) 'Literacy practices in an informal settlement in the Cape Peninsula', in M. PRINSLOO and M. BREIER (eds) *The Social Uses of Literacy*, Cape Town and Amsterdam, Sached Publishers and John Benjamins Publishers.

KELL, C. (1999) 'Teaching letter writing: the recontextualisation of letter-writing practices in literacy classes for unschooled adults in South Africa', in D. BARTON and N. HALL (eds) *Letter Writing as a Social Practice*, Amsterdam, John Benjamins.

KOUTSOGIANNIS, D. (2004) 'Critical technoliteracy and "weak" languages', in I. SNYDER and C. BEAVIS (eds) *Doing Literacy Online: Teaching, Learning, and Playing in an Electronic World*, Cresskill, NJ, Hampton Press, pp. 163–84.

KRESS, G. (1998) 'Visual and verbal modes of representation in electronically mediated communication: the potentials of new forms of text', in I. SNYDER (ed.) *Page to Screen: Taking Literacy into the Electronic Era*, New York, Routledge.

KRESS, G. (2000) 'Multimodality', in B. COPE and M. KALANTZIS (eds) *Multiliteracies: Literacy Learning and the Design of Social Futures* London, Routledge, pp. 182–202.

KRESS, G. (2003) *Literacy in the New Media Age*, London and New York, Routledge.

KRESS, G. and VAN LEEUWEN, T. (2001) *Multimodal Discourse: The Modes and Media of Contemporary Communication*, London, Arnold.

KULICK, D. and STROUD, C. (1993) 'Conceptions and uses of literacy in a Papua New Guinean village', in B. STREET (ed.) *Cross-Cultural Approaches to Literacy*, Cambridge, Cambridge University Press.

LABOV, W. (1972) *Language in the Inner City*, Philadelphia, University of Pennsylvania Press.

LABOV, W. and WALETZKY, J. (1967) 'Narrative analysis: oral versions of personal experience', in J. HELMS (ed.) *Essays on the Verbal and Visual Arts*, Seattle, University of Washington Press.

LAKOFF, G. and JOHNSON, M. (1980) *Metaphors We Live By*, Chicago and London, University of Chicago Press.

LAKOFF, G. and TURNER, M. (1989) *More than Cool Reason: A Field Guide to the Poetic Metaphor*, Chicago and London, University of Chicago Press.

LEAP, W.L. (1996) *Word's Out: Gay Men's English*, Minneapolis, University of Minnesota Press.

LEATHERLAND, J.A. (1862) *Essays and poems with a brief autobiographical memoir*, London, W. Tweedie.

LEITH, D. (1997, 2nd edition) A Social History of English, London/New York, Routledge.

LEMKE, J.L. (1989) 'Social semiotics: A new model for literacy education', in D. BLOOME (ed.) *Classrooms and Literacy*, Norwood, NJ, Ablex Publishing.

LEVY, E.T. (2003) 'The roots of coherence in discourse', *Human Development*, **46**(4), pp. 169–88.

LITOSSELITI, L. and SUNDERLAND, J. (eds) (2002) *Gender Identity and Discourse Analysis*, Amsterdam, John Benjamins.

LOUW, B. (1993) 'Irony in the text or insincerity in the writer: the diagnostic potential of semantic prosodies', in M. BAKER, G. FRANCIS and E. TOGNINI-BONELLI (eds) *Text and Technology: In Honour of John Sinclair*, Philadelphia, John Benjamins.

MACDONALD, N. (2001) *The Graffiti Subculture: Youth, Masculinity and Identity in London and New York*, London, Palgrave.

MALCOLM, I.G. and SHARIFIAN, F. (2002) 'Aspects of Aboriginal English oral discourse: an application of cultural schema theory', *Discourse Studies*, **4**(2), pp. 169–81.

MALLON, T. (1894) *A Book of One's Own: People and Their Diaries*, New York, Ticknor and Fields.

MARKHAM, W. (1738) *An Introduction to Spelling and Reading English*, 5th edition, London.

MAYBIN, J. (2006) *Children's Voices: Talk, Knowledge and Identity*, Basingstoke, Palgrave.

McCULLOUGH, M. (1996) *Abstracting Craft: the Practiced Digital Hand*, Cambridge, MA, MIT Press.

MERCHANT, G. (2001) 'Teenagers in cyberspace – an investigation of language use and language change in internet chatrooms', *Journal of Research in Reading*, **24**(3), pp. 293–306.

MISCHLER, E.G. (1999) *Craft Artists' Narratives of Identity*, Harvard, Harvard University Press.

MISHOE, M. (1998) 'Styleswitching in southern English', in C. MYERS-SCOTTON (ed.) *Codes and Consequences: choosing linguistic varieties*, Oxford/New York, Oxford University Press.

MOJE, E. (2000) ' "To be part of the story": the literacy practices of gangsta adolescents', *Teachers College Record*, **102**(3), pp. 651–90.

MURRAY, L. and ANDREWS, L. (2000) *The Social Baby*, Richmond, Surrey, UK, CP Publishing.

MYERS-SCOTTON, C. (1993) *Social Motivations for Codeswitching: evidence from Africa*, Oxford, Clarendon.

MYERS-SCOTTON, C. (ed.) (1998) *Codes and Consequences: Choosing Linguistic Varieties*, Oxford/New York, Oxford University Press.

NAIR, R. B. (2002) *Narrative Gravity: Conversation, Cognition, Culture*, Delhi, Oxford University Press.

NELSON, K. (1973) 'Structure and strategy in learning to talk', *Monographs of the Society for Research in Child Development*, **38** [serial no. 149], pp. 1–137.

NEW LONDON GROUP, THE (1996) 'A pedagogy of literacies: designing social futures', *Harvard Educational Review*, **66**, pp. 60–92.

NORMAN, D.A. (1999) 'Affordance, conventions, and design', *Interactions*, **6**, pp. 38–43.

NORRICK, N.R. (1997) 'Twice-told tales: collaborative narration of familiar stories', *Language in Society*, **26**(2), pp. 199–220.

NORRICK, N.R. (2000/2001) 'Poetics and conversation', *Connotations*, **10**(2–3), pp. 43–267.

NORRICK, N.R. (2001) 'Issues in conversational joking', *Journal of Pragmatics*, **35**, pp. 1333–1359.

NWOYE, O.G. (1993) 'Social issues on walls: graffiti in university lavatories', *Discourse and Society*, **4**(4), pp. 419–42.

OPIE, I. and OPIE, P. (1959) *The Lore and Language of Schoolchildren*, London, Clarendon Press (Oxford University Press, 1967).

OPIE, I. and OPIE, P. (1985) *The Singing Game*, Oxford, Oxford University Press.

PAOLILLO, J.C. (2001) 'Language variation on Internet Relay Chat: A social network approach', *Journal of Sociolinguistics*, **5**, pp. 180–213.

PAPEN, U. (forthcoming) 'Reading the bible and shopping on credit: literacy practices and literacy learning in a township of Windhoek, Namibia', in A. ROGERS (ed.) *Urban Literacies*, Hamburg, UIE.

PAX, S. (2003) *The Baghdad Blog*, London, Atlantic Books/The Guardian.

PECCEI STILWELL, J. (1999) *Child Language*, 2nd edn, London, Routledge.

POLANYI, L. (1985) *Telling the American Story: From the Structure of Linguistic Texts to the Grammar of a Culture*, Norwood, NJ, Ablex.

PONSONBY, A. (1923) *A Review of English Diaries from the Sixteenth to the Twentieth Century with an Introduction on Diary Writing*, London, Methuen.

RAGAN, S.L. (2000) 'Sociable talk in women's healthcare contexts: two forms of non-medical talk', in J. COUPLAND (ed.) *Small Talk*, London, Routledge.

RAMPTON, B. (1995) *Crossing: Language and Ethnicity among Adolescents*, London, Longman.

RAMPTON, B. (2005, 2nd edn) *Crossing: Language and Ethnicity among Adolescents*, Manchester, St. Jerome Press.

ROBERTSON, J. (1942) *The Art of Letter Writing: An Essay on the Handbooks Published in England during the Sixteenth and Seventeenth centuries*, London, Hodder and Stoughton.

ROBINSON, E. and POWELL, D. (eds) (1989) *The Early Poems of John Clare 1804–1822*, vol. 1, Oxford, Clarendon Press.

ROBINSON, E. and POWELL, D. (eds) (1996) 'Sketches in the Life of John Clare Written by Himself and Addressed to his friend John Taylor Esqr March 1821', *John Clare by Himself*, Ashington, Mid Northumberland Arts Group.

ROCHE, D. (1987) *The People of Paris: An Essay in Popular Culture in the 18th Century*, Leamington Spa, Berg Publishers.

ROCKHILL, K. (1993) 'Gender, language and the politics of literacy', in B. STREET (ed.) *Cross-Cultural Approaches to Literacy*, Cambridge, Cambridge University Press.

ROUZIE, A. (2001) 'Conversation and carrying-on: play, conflict, and serio-ludic discourse in synchronous computer conferencing', *College Composition and Communication*, **53**, pp. 251–99.

SCHANK, R. (1995) *Tell me a Story: Narrative and Intelligence*, Evanston, Northwestern University Press.

SCHIFFRIN, D. (1996) 'Narrative as self-portrait: sociolinguistic constructions of identity', *Language in Society* **25**, pp. 167–203.

SEALEY, A. (2000) *Childly Language: Children, Language and the Social World*, Harlow, Pearson Education.

SEARLE, J.R. (1969) *Speech Acts: An Essay in the Philosophy of Language*, Cambridge, Cambridge University Press.

SEBBA, M. (2000) 'Spelling rebellion' in J.K. ANDROUTSOPOULOS and A. GEORGAKOPOLOU, A. (eds) *Discourse Constructions of Youth Identities*, 2003, viii, pp. 151–172, Amsterdam/Philadelphia, John Benjamins.

SEMINO, E. (1997) *Language and World Creation in Poems and Other Text, Harlow*, Addison Wesley Longman.

SHAW, B. (1826) 'Benjamin Shaw's family records', in A.G. CROSBY (ed.) *The family records of Benjamin Shaw, Mechanic of Dent, Dolphinholme and Preston, 1772–1841*, Stroud, Alan Sutton Publishing.

SHORT, M (1996) *Exploring the Language of Poems, Plays and Prose*, London, Longman.

SMITH, W. (1995) *Band of Gold* CD, [online] www.mustrad.org.uk/articles/smith.htm (accessed 27.6.05) (*Wiggy Smith and other Smith Family members Band of Gold, MT CD 307*) http://folkindex.mse.jhu.edu/B16.htm#Buiabo

STEVENSON, R.L. (1882) 'A gossip on romance', *Longman's Magazine*, **1**(1).

STREET, B. (2000) 'Literacy events and literacy practices: theory and practice in the New Literacy Studies', in M. MARTIN-JONES and K. JONES *Multilingual Literacies: Reading and Writing Different Worlds*, Amsterdam and Philadelphia, John Benjamins.

SWANN, J., DEUMERT, A., LILLIS, T. and MESTHRIE, R. (2004) *A Dictionary of Sociolinguistics*, Edinburgh, Edinburgh University Press.

SYDNEY FOLKLORE PROJECT (2004) [online] http://warrenfahey.com/sydney-project.html (accessed 27.6.05)

TANNEN, D. (1989) *Talking Voices: Repetition, Dialogue and Imagery in Conversational Discourse*, Cambridge, Cambridge University Press.

THURLOW, C. (2003) 'Generation Txt? The sociolinguistics of young people's text-messaging', *Discourse Analysis Online* [online] www.shu.ac.uk/daol/index.html (accessed 3.11.05).

TOOLAN, M. (1996) *Total speech: An Integrational Linguistic Approach to Language*, Chapel Hill, Duke University Press.

TREVARTHEN, C. and AITKEN, K.J. (2001) 'Infant intersubjectivity: research, theory and clinical applications', *Journal of Child Psychology and Psychiatry*, **42**(1), pp. 3–48.

TURKLE, S. (1996) *Life on the Screen: Identity in the Age of the Internet*, London, Weidenfeld & Nicolson.

TURNER, I. (1978) 'The Play Rhymes of Australian Children: an interpretive essay', in I. TURNER, J. FACTOR and W. LOWENSTEIN *Cinderella Dressed in Yella*, 2nd edn Richmond, Australia, Heinemann.

TURNER, I., FACTOR, J. and LOWENSTEIN, W. (1978) *Cinderella Dressed in Yella*, 2nd edn, Richmond, Australia, Heinemann.

VINCENT, D. (1989) *Literacy and Popular Culture in England 1750–1914*, Cambridge, Cambridge University Press.

VINCENT, D. (forthcoming) 'Victorians reading Dickens', in J. BOWEN and R.L. PATTEN (eds) (forthcoming) *The Palgrave Guide to Charles Dickens*, London and New York, Palgrave.

VOLOSINOV, V.N. ([1929]1973) *Marxism and the Philosophy of Language*, trans. L. MATEJKA and I.R. TITUNIK, Cambridge, MA, Harvard University Press.

VROOMAN, S.S. (2002) 'The art of invective: performing identity in cyberspace', *New Media & Society*, **4**, pp. 51–70.

VYGOTSKY, L.S. (1967) 'Play and its role in the mental development of the child', *Soviet Psychology*, **5**, pp. 6–18.

VYGOTSKY, L.S. (1987) 'Thinking and Speech', in R. RIEBER and A. CARTON (eds) *The Collected Works of L.S. Vygotsky*, vol. I, *Problems of General Psychology*, including the volume 'Thinking and speech' trans. N. Minick. New York, Plenum Press.

VYGOTSKY, L.S. (1993) 'Introduction: fundamental problems of defectology', in R. RIEBER and A.S. CARTON *The Collected Works of L.S. Vygotsky*, vol. 2, *The Fundamentals of Defectology (Abnormal Psychology and Learning Disabilities)*, New York, Plenum Press.

WALSH, M. (1996) *Graffito*, Berkeley, North Atlantic Books.

WIDDOWSON, H.G. (2002) 'Verbal art and social practice: a reply to Weber', *Language and Literature,* **11**(2), pp. 161–67.

WILLIAMS, R. (1983) *Keywords: A Vocabulary of Culture and Society*, 2nd edn, London, Fontana Press.

WOLF, S.A. and HEATH, S.B. (1992) *The Braid of Literature: Children's Worlds of Reading*, Cambridge, MA, Harvard University Press.

WOLFSON, N. (1982) CHP, *The Conversational Historical Present in American English Narrative*, Cinnarminson, NJ, Foris Publications.

WOOFFITT, R. (1996) 'Rhetoric in English' in J. MAYBIN and N. MERCER (eds) *Using English: From Conversation to Canon*, London, Routledge.

ZAFF, B. (1995) 'Designing with affordances in mind', in J. FLACH et al. (eds), *Global Perspectives on the Ecology of Human-Machine Systems*, Hillsdale, NJ, Lawrence Erlbaum Associates Inc.

Acknowledgements

Grateful acknowledgement is made to the following sources for permission to reproduce material in this book.

Text

Page 18: Merwin W.S. and Masson, J. Moussaieff, trans. *Sanskrit Love Poetry*, New York, Columbia University Press, 1977, reprinted as *The Peacock's Egg*, San Francisco, North Point Press, 1981; *pages 29–36:* reprinted by permission of Sage Publications Ltd from Ronald Carter, 'Common language: corpus, creativity and cognition', *Language and Literature*, vol. 8, no. 3, © 1999 Sage Publications; *pages 41–42:* Morgan, M. (2002) *Language, Discourse and Power in African American Culture*, p. 112, Cambridge University Press; *page 42:* reprinted by arrangement with the Estate of Martin Luther King Jr., c/o Writers House as agent for the proprietor New York, NY and by kind permission of IPM/The King Estate, Copyright 1963 Martin Luther King Jr., copyright renewed 1991 Coretta Scott King; *page 44:* Copyright © 1965 by Warner Bros. Inc., copyright renewed 1993 by Special Rider Music, all rights reserved, international copyright secured, reprinted by permission; *pages 77–83:* Norrick, N. R. (1997) 'Twice-told tales: Collaborative narration of familiar stories', *Language in Society*, Cambridge University Press; *pages 85–87:* Truth and Reconciliation Commission, www.doj.gov.za; *pages 89 and 90:* reprinted with permission of Independent News & Media SA (pty) Ltd; *pages 97–102:* Nair, R.B., 'Implicature, Explicature and Impliculture in the Short, Short Story and Tall, Tall Tale', *Narrative Gravity: Conversation, Cognition, Culture*, pp. 229–237, Routledge, Taylor and Francis Books Ltd; *pages 124–130:* extracts from Eckert, P. and McConnell-Ginet, S. (1995) 'Constructing meaning, Constructing Selves', Kira Hall and Mary Bucholtz (eds) *Gender Articulated: Language and the Socially Constructed Self*, Routledge, by kind permission of Taylor and Francis Group LLC; *pages 140–148:* Besnier, N. (2003) 'Crossing Genders, Mixing Languages: The Linguistic Construction of Transgenderism in Tonga', Holmes, J. and Meyerhoff, M. (eds) *The Handbook of Language and Gender*, pp. 289–301, Blackwell Publishing Ltd; *page 151:* Took, B. and Feldman, M. (1968) Extracts from 'Bona Rags' as broadcast on *Round the Horne*, by kind permission of Lynden Took; *pages 178–179:* Opie, I. and Opie, P. (1959) *The Lore and Language of School Children*, pp. 10–11, Oxford University Press; *pages 183–188:* edited version of Sharon Inkelas 'J's rhymes: a longitudinal case study of language play', *Journal of Child Language* 30, pp. 557–581, 2003, © Cambridge University Press; *pages 189–194:* Wegerif, R. (2005) 'Reason and creativity in classroom dialogues', *Language and Education*, Multilingual Matters; *pages 203–208:* Janice Ackerley; *page 209:* Cramb, A. (2003) 'Girl writes essay in phone text shorthand', *The Daily Telegraph* © Telegraph Group Limited; *page 217:* Copyright © Hetty Hughes; *pages 231–236:* Baron, N.S. (2002) 'Who sets e-mail style? Prescriptivism, coping strategies, and democratizing Communication Access',

The Information Society, vol. 18, Taylor and Francis Books Ltd;
pages 238–250: Marks Greenfield, P. and Subrahmanyam, K. (2003) 'Online discourse in a teen chatroom: new code and new modes of coherence in a visual medium', *Applied Developmental Psychology*, Elsevier Science Ltd;
page 265: extract from 'Tulips' by Sylvia Plath, Edwards Fuglewicz;
pages 282–284 and 291–292: John and Doreen Moyles; *pages 285–286:* from *We're in this War Too: World War II Letters from American Women in Uniform*, edited by Judy Barrett Litoff and David C. Smith, Copyright © 1994 by Judy Barrett Litoff and David C. Smith, used by permission of Oxford University Press, Inc.; *page 327:* Kalmar, T.M. (2001) *The Cobden Glossaries, Illegal Alphabets and Adult Biliteracy: Latino Migrants Crossing the Linguistic Border*, Lawrence Erlbaum Associates Inc.; *pages 332–339:* Camitta, M. (1993) *Vernacular Writing: Varieties of Literacy among Philadelphia High School Students, Cross-cultural Approaches to Literacy*, Cambridge University Press; *page 346:* Copyright © Professor Bruce Jackson, reproduced by permission; *pages 404–407:* Clare, J. (1996). *Sketches in the Life of John Clare*, Robinson, E. and Powell, D. (eds), *John Clare by Himself*, Carcanet Press Limited; *pages 399–403:* Vincent, D. (1989) Extracts from *Literacy and Popular Culture: England 1750–1914*, 'Family', pp. 32–49, Cambridge University Press; *page 423:* from 'Days' by Philip Larkin, *Collected Poems* by Philip Larkin, Faber and Faber Ltd and The Society of Authors as the Literary Representative of the Estate of Philip Larkin; *pages 435–441:* from *The Dialogic Imagination: Four Essays* by M. M. Bakhtin, edited by Michael Holquist, translated by Caryl Emerson and Michael Holquist, Copyright © 1981 by permission of the University of Texas Press; *pages 441–450:* Tannen, D. (1989) 'Oh talking voice that is so sweet: construction dialogue in conversation', *Talking Voices*, pp. 98–133, © Cambridge University Press, reproduced with permission; *pages 451–452: Interaction Ritual* by Erving Goffman, Penguin Books 1971, 1972 and the Erving Goffman Estate, Copyright © Erving Goffman 1967; *pages 453–455: The Presentation of Self in Everyday Life* by Erving Goffman, Allen Lane, The Penguin Press, 1969 and the Erving Goffman Estate, Copyright © Erving Goffman, 1959.

Illustrations

Page 152: Took, B. and Feldman, M. (1976) *The Bona Book of Julian and Sandy*, pp. 45–46, by kind permission of Lynden Took; *page 160:* photographs and text from: *The Social Baby*, pp. 66–67, Clive Dorman and The Children's Project; *page 223:* Copyright © 2004 Dean & Pam Blehert; *page 265:* Front cover of *The Secret Diary of Adrian Mole Aged 13 ¾* by Sue Townsend, Penguin Books, 2002, Copyright © Sue Townsend 1982; *page 283:* Tarpet, A. *Despatches from the Heart* (1984) Copyright © Hamish Hamilton; *pages 294 and 301:* Nancy Macdonald; *page 361:* Mary Evans Picture Library; *page 371:* Mary Evans Picture Library.

Colour illustrations

(In the *Colour Figures* section between pages 276 and 277)

Figure 1 (top right): Janice Ackerley; *(middle left)* Courtesy of Michael Britton; *Figures 4 and 5:* KIRS; *Figure 6:* Frank Malt; *Figure 8:* Courtesy of Gary Nelmes; *Figure 12:* Victorian valentine Card, English School (19th century) / © Cheltenham Art Gallery & Museums, Gloucestershire, UK / Bridgeman Art Library; *Figures 13, 14 and 15:* Mary Evans Picture Library.

Tables

Page 192: Wegerif and Dawes, *Thinking and Learning with ICT: Raising Achievement in Primary Classrooms*, p. 38, Taylor and Francis Books Ltd; *page 364:* 'Annual percentages of males and females unable to sign at marriage, England and Wales, 1839–1912' (source: Registrar General of England and Wales Annual Reports); Crown copyright material is reproduced under Class Licence Number C01W0000065 with the permission of the Controller of HMSO and the Queen's Printer for Scotland; *pages 365 and 366:* Vincent, D. (1989) *Literacy and Popular Culture*, Cambridge University Press.

Every effort has been made to contact copyright holders. If any have been inadvertently overlooked the publishers will be pleased to make the necessary arrangements at the first opportunity.

Physical Management in Neurological Rehabilitation

WATER DAMAGE NOTED.

SC 12/06

Dedicated to the residents and staff at
the Royal Hospital for Neuro-disability, Putney
and to my father, Peter,
who cherished textbooks.

For Elsevier

Publishing Director and Senior Commissioning Editor: Mary Law and Heidi Allen
Project Development Manager: Dinah Thom
Project Manager: Derek Robertson
Designer: Judith Wright